B.C. 46599

LIBRARY OF
CONGRESS
SURPLUS
DUPLICATE
NOT FOR RESALE

THE HOLLYWOOD CULTURE WAR

THE HOLLYWOOD CULTURE WAR

What You Don't Know CAN Hurt You!

Michael Vincent Boyer

Copyright © 2008 by Michael Vincent Boyer.

Library of Congress Control Number: 2008904727
ISBN: Hardcover   978-1-4363-4586-6
           Softcover   978-1-4363-4585-9

All rights reserved. No part of this book may be reproduced or transmitted in any form or by any means, electronic or mechanical, including photocopying, recording, or by any information storage and retrieval system, without permission in writing from the copyright owner.

This book was printed in the United States of America.

To order additional copies of this book, contact:
Xlibris Corporation
1-888-795-4274
www.Xlibris.com
Orders@Xlibris.com
50416

CONTENTS

Preface 13

Introduction 15

1) **The War Escalates** 19
    - Hollywood Takes Revenge 23

2) **How The War Began** 30
    - The Quiet Conspiracy And The Gang Of Four 34
    - Soul Selling And Closing The Deal 39

3) **The War Heats Up: Hollywood And Washington** 46
    - Bob Dole Exposes "Slime Warner" 48
    - The Appropriations "Bill": Values For Votes 52

4) **"Hollywood Bill"** 56
    - The Cautionary Tale: A Close Encounter Of The First Kind 56
    - Stage Left: Clinton Enters The Culture War 62
    - Birds Of A Feather Stick Together 67
    - School Shootings Make Good Fundraisers 69
    - Hollywood Bill's Honey Money List 70
    - Clinton's Meltdown Path To 9/11 84

5) **The Hollywood Media Defense** 97
    - To The Freshman Class Of 2012 97
    - The Clinton's Hollywood Media Defense Team 99
    - Unresolved Crimes 103
    - A Time For Closure 124
    - Hollywood Bill And Hillary's Traveling Crime Show 128

6) **The Rise And Fall Of The Obama Nation** 131
    - David Geffen 137

- Jesse Jackson 139
- George Soros 143
- The Audacity Of A Child's Hope 150
- Obama's New Age Christian Reformation:
  Evangelical Left Vs. Evangelical Right 157
- The Hollywood Bible 164
- Dreams From My Hollywood Fantasies:
  Daydreams And Fables 166
- The Rulers Of The Darkness Of This World 171

7) **The Ratings Fiasco** **176**
- The Crossover Deception:
  The Movie House To Your House 183
- Who Exactly Is Rating The Movies? 186
- Sample MPAA Ratings Including "Rating Reason" 192
- Christian Movies Will Be Rated Accordingly 195
- How Filmmakers Cheat For Ratings 199

8) **The End Of Television** **201**
- The Mystery Phone Call 205

9) **The Big Lie And Value Manipulation** **215**
- Why Walt Disney Rolls Over In His Grave 219
- Desentivity Training 221
- Strangulation Manipulation 225
- Aversion To Perversion 230

10) **Springtime For Stalin: Roots Of Hollywood Radicalism
(Or, Why Jane Loves Hanoi And Clooney Hates McCarthy)** **236**
- Welcome To The Party 240
- The Seeds Take Root 245
- Reagan Rising 252
- Showtime In Washington 253
- The Blacklist Myth 257
- Hollywood Holds A Grudge 264
- As For McCarthy 266

11) **Jane Fonda: The Enemy Within** **272**
- Apololgies, Denials, And Lost Causes 273
- Treason, Sedition, And Lies 278
- Jane Fonda Is A Gnostic, Not A Christian 288

12) Oliver Stone: Natural Born Killer? **297**
- Oliver Stone: The Drug Addict 300
- Oliver Stone: Death By Film... 305
- NBK Death Toll . . . And Counting 313
- The Oliver Stone Effect... 314
- The Belushi Factor 316

13) Stepping Up To The Plate: The MPAA's Mandate For Drug Testing..... **320**
- Special Thanks To Fatty Arbuckle.................................... 320
- Sports And Drug Testing: A Page From The Playbook 322
- Hollywood's Turn: Who Should Be Tested? 332
- What About Non-studio Employees? 342
- Press Release: "Smoking-bad; Drugs-okay!" 345

14) Intermission **348**

15) Dawn Of The New Age: The Long Arm Of Mephistopheles **354**
- Crowley's Hollywood Congregation 361

16) Celebrity Gods **366**
- "The Secret" And "The Promise" Oprah Vs. Jesus........... 374
- Scientology, The Devil And The Deep Blue Sea.............. 378
- Hollywood's Scientology Celebrities 383

17) Mind Benders And Gender Benders **387**
- Going Dark.. 391

**18) Hollywood's Road To Perdition: The Twenty Year Battle
To Destroy The Culture (1948-1968)** **397**
- Post Scripts And Post Mortems 427
- Profanity Insanity: The Unsung Villain And
  The Death Of Comedy 441

19) Warning! Hip-hop And Rap Music Can Kill You **446**
- The Hip-hop "Rap Sheet" 449
- Straight To The Source 454
- Old School Versus New School.. 458
- Enter The Messenger: The Truth Behind Hip-hop 465
- Holy Hip-hop, Gangsta Gospel And Christian Rap 469
- Unintended Consequences: Don Imus Shakes
  Up Hip-hop Nation 471

- Good News! Hip-hop Is Dying—finally! 480
  - Hip-hop Hollywood, Sports And Killing Dogs 480

20) The Velvet Mafia: Fact Or Fiction 483
  - David Geffen And Hollywood's Heterophobia 491
  - Geffens's Dark Legacy 496

21) The Incredible Shrinking Box Office 500
  - Blame It On Jack 503
  - Condescending Contempt 505
  - Lessons From Greco-Roman Entertainment 511

22) Riding With The Devil (Christians & Jews Need Not Apply) 516
  - The ABCs Of Hollywood Judeo-Christian Bashing 522
A. The Confrontational Attack 522
  - A Small Sampling (1980 To Present) 539
  - Slicing, Dicing And Splattering The Faithful 540
B. The Sophisticated Attack 541
  - Decoding Da Vinci's Fiction 545
  - Mr. And Mrs. Dan Brown's Private Agenda 549
  - Enter The Hollywood Demons: The Ron Howard You Never Knew 552
  - Christian Collusion 554
  - Twist Of Faith? 559
C. The Back Door Attack: Harry Potter And J. K. Rowling 562
  - Glossary Of Occult Terminology 567
  - The Amazing Adventures And Allure Of Harry Potter 572
  - I Anticipate A Deeply Religious Experience 576
  - J.K. Rowling: Gothic Punk Rocker From Hell 579
  - More Back Door Attacks From Hollywood 589

23) J.K. Rowling's New World Disorder 594
  - Rowling's Defenders 596
  - The Church Of Scotland Defense 602
  - Comparisons To Tolkein And Lewis 606
  - Potterethics 607
  - Rowling's Detractors 609
  - Dire Warnings 613
  - We Know Harry, But Who Is Tony Blair? 615
  - Rowling's Final Solution: The Ultimate Death 619

24) Fighting Back Against Hollywood: Television A La Carte **621**
- The Breast Seen 'Round The World 624
- Television Is Now "A Public Health Crisis" 628
- A Litany Of Lies 630
- Unintended Consequences: New Opportunities 634

25) A Grassroots Victory **640**

26) The Entertainment Resource Guide: Winning The Culture War **645**

Appendix **649-674**

Acknowledgements **675**

Endnotes **677**

Index **711**

Notable Quotables **729**

CULTURE (kul-cher), noun—the concepts, habits, skills, arts, instruments, institutions, etc. of a given people in a given period; civilization.

WAR (wor), noun—Open conflict between countries or between factions within the same country. Any active hostility or contention; conflict; strife.

A great civilization is not conquered from without until it has destroyed itself from within.
—Will Durant
1885-1981

PREFACE

Time would eventually reveal the parallel universe of the movie industry I had come to co-exist in apart from the reality of American life "between the coasts" as the entertainment industry refers to "the rest of America." For twenty years I scouted and coordinated locations for over 200 feature films, television movies, episodic TV, mini-series, music videos and documentaries.

After spending twelve-hour days, week after week, month after month, I began to piece together the strands of a long dark thread over the years that formed the common cord of a collective mind-set and worldview held closely by Hollywood. As these filmmakers opened up during our long morning to night journeys in search of the perfect movie location, they always felt strongly compelled to share their passionate and personal visions of the new world their mad movies promised to deliver. It wasn't about entertainment or even compelling storytelling. Making movies by the new generation of Hollywood was all about *power*—the power to change the way you and I think—and not for the better.

After a million miles on the speedometer, I discovered Hollywood was on a mission of "value manipulation" to reorganize the "common people" of the heartland into a New Age Hollywood nation where ideas, speech, and even thoughts are dictated by a handful of entertainment conglomerate temples. Main Street would become a subsidiary of two other streets on both coasts—Hollywood Boulevard and Madison Avenue. To a large extent, Main Street is well past the halfway mark as slaves to the Hollywood culture.

This book describes how the Hollywood Culture War began, the people involved, where the battle stands today, and how you can take action to prevent the future colonization of your state, your community, and your home by an industry run-amuck and violently intent on destroying your life, simply for "entertainment value."

Take a stand. Set yourself free and declare your independence from Hollywood!

INTRODUCTION

There is a war raging in America, an open and armed conflict. A battle not fought with forged weapons, but a war based on words and images. The battleground is the marketplace of ideas; the definition of values, morality, right and wrong, good and bad; a battle for the very heart, mind, soul, and spirit of the individual in particular and the nation as a whole. It is a Culture War.

While being fought on many fronts, the focus of the war is centered around the so-called entertainment industry whose products include feature films, television movies and programming, DVDs, video games, the internet, and music. The content has mutated into increasingly coarse, gratuitous, vulgar, and grotesque imagery unlike anything that has ever assaulted the human senses, and much worse, the creators and distributors of contemporary entertainment are pushing a perverse private agenda that reflects the innermost thoughts of their cluttered, uncultured minds. These private agendas, in the form of "entertainment," are transmitted to the big screen at local theaters and to the small screen in family living rooms.

On the other side of the war is a large cross-section of Americans that cuts across political persuasions, religious affiliation, educational, economic boundaries, race, ethnicity, and all ages of men and women, boys and girls. This growing group of Americans are fed up with being spoon-fed a corrosive worldview by an entertainment industry that attacks the very values Americans embrace and hold close to their hearts, values sacred to the healthy growth of mind and body, the values that bind together individuals, families, communities, and the nation as a whole, and that are necessary for the prosperous functioning of a cohesive society.

"Hollywood has completely lost touch with the American people,"[1] Ben Stein noted recently. Stein should know. As an economist, political commentator, and former presidential advisor, Stein is also a member of the Screen Actors Guild (SAG). Radio talk show host Mike Gallagher added, "Hollywood typically rejects heartland values .... They can make successful movies, they just don't want to."[2] This is a bad time to invest in Hollywood. Even Wall Street is having second thoughts.

One of the hallmarks of a profitable theatrical entertainment industry is the weekend box office tally, an indicator of new movie success and the longevity of previously released films. In June 2005 Hollywood experienced the longest downturn in straight weekend box office returns ever recorded; eighteen straight losing weekends in a row. "That's the longest streak ever," wrote Patty Ruhle of *USA Today*.[3] When ticket sales made a slight rebound in 2006, it was barely more than one percent and still less than ticket sales in 1998. More significant is that during those eight years between 1998 and 2006 the U.S. population gained more than twenty million people, reaching a record 300 million. As a percentage of the population, attendance at theaters has actually been dropping for the ten years prior to 2008. Furthermore, ticket sales in 2005 dropped by almost 130 million individual admissions from 2004.[4] And ticket sales for 2004 were already down significantly from 2003.[5]

According to Dan Ramer, editor of dvdfile.com, "Part of that may be due to more people purchasing DVD players, . . . but clearly a contributing factor is also the product, the films themselves."[6] A March 2006 survey by the Movie Advisory Board asked, "Why Not Go to a Theater?" The number one reason given by respondents? "Movies are not very good and do not meet expectations."[7] And, the *Wall Street Journal* reported on August 17, 2007, that financiers on Wall Street were re-thinking their investments in Hollywood due in part to "lackluster results." In January 2008, the Digital Entertainment Group reported that sales and rentals of DVDs fell for the first time in the ten year history of the format.

Consider the title of a *Newsweek* article by veteran movie critic David Ansen, "Is Anybody Making Movies We'll Actually Watch in 50 Years?"[8] As the end of the 20th century neared, an Associated Press poll titled "The 25 Greatest Movies of the Century" was compiled by AP movie reviewers. Of the twenty-five movies listed, only two were released after 1968, the year Jack Valenti, president of the Motion Picture Association of America (MPAA), forced the now infamous Movie Ratings Scheme on the American movie audience. As a result, the American culture has slid consistently into what the late Steve Allen termed "a moral sewer."

Most readers of *The Hollywood Culture War* will learn for the first time about the "Quiet Conspiracy" by the "Gang of Four" to destroy the Golden Era of filmmaking, which Valenti made official on November 1, 1968. More ominously, Valenti's actions have negatively affected almost every aspect of the culture, far beyond the entertainment industry and into almost every aspect of American life. Valenti unleashed a dark side of the increasingly influential entertainment industry that has determined to dictate what course the nation will take in all matters of the culture, both here and abroad. *Radical Son* author David Horowitz noted, "During the '60s we unleashed some demons into the culture that needed to be called back."[9]

THE HOLLYWOOD CULTURE WAR

You will learn, and most likely be shocked, by the who, what, where, when, and why of these events that have occurred and discover the origin, strategy, and escalating nature of the ongoing struggle that lies at the heart of the Culture War spreading throughout America and around the world. In the end, you will learn how to protect yourself from the rampant Hollywood agenda of manipulating your values, your sacred beliefs, your personality, and even the manipulation of the way you think about yourself and those close to you.

It's time to enlist and join in the Culture War against Hollywood—before it's too late.

CHAPTER 1

THE WAR ESCALATES

> *If you say the heart and soul of this country is found in Hollywood, I'm afraid you're not a candidate of conservative values.*
> —President George W. Bush
> 2004 Acceptance Speech

Hollywood, and everything it stands for, hates you and everything you stand for; with a few notable exceptions. Very few. At the same time, Hollywood loves you; loves your money, as any good free-enterprise industry should. The only problem is that Hollywood used to give *you* what you wanted to watch. Now Hollywood gives you what *they* want you to watch. *Not* an example of good free enterprise. But ultimately, free enterprise has always fallen on the shoulders of the consumer. Enter *caveat emptor*: let the buyer beware.

This is the heart of the Culture War that America has plunged into and is waging against an entrenched entertainment industry that is fiercely intent on changing the way you think. Call it what it is: value manipulation.

A perfect example is writer/director Kevin Smith who boasted, "I always like to think of it like, I've got 'em sitting there—whip a little message at them, whip a little moral at them, whip a little of what *my* view of the world is, because that's what every good filmmaker does. And *we'll* lead the world to the twenty-first century and I'll make a profit on their backs."

Screenwriter Paul Schrader was discussing the trend in many movies over the last twenty years that displayed a contemptuous audience attitude, which he referred to as "nose-thumbing movies . . . . The message they say is, 'We don't care if you like us and we don't like you.'" Furthermore, Schrader noted, "People have this mistaken notion that the Hollywood system has principles, morals, and values . . . . It doesn't."

Consider the "cradle to grave" marketing strategy as announced by CBS chief Les Moonves at the occasion of the once-famous network's merger with Sumner Redstone's Viacom. "We'll get them from the time they're two until the time they're eighty."[1]

Children are being specifically targeted. Veteran entertainment columnist Timothy Gray, writing for the industry rag *Variety*, shouted, "To hell with the little nippers. I want adult entertainment and I want it now." He added, "Tykes don't want to be protected . . . and it's not clear they need to be protected."[2]

And the elderly, or anybody over forty-nine, are being equally targeted—for extermination. After Disney-owned ABC finally cancelled the low-performing social/sexual agenda evening sitcom *Ellen*, the program's creator and writer, Tim Doyle, angrily declared, "There's a group of older people who will never accept it. But there's a lot of empty cemeteries, and when they're filled, the world will be a lot more tolerant."[3]

The malicious and predatory nature of these comments, along with a marked increase and intensity in violent, sexual, anti-social, and profane movies, television programs, video games, and music, helped to ignite the Culture War in the late 1980s and early 1990s. While the term "Culture War" had been used frequently throughout the late 1980s regarding educational, social, and political issues, the first time the term was attached to the entertainment industry can be traced to a lecture in November 1990. The title of the lecture was "Popular Culture and the War Against Standards," by Michael Medved, co-host of PBS's *Sneak Previews* with Jeffrey Lyons.[4] The lecture would later form the genesis of Medved's influential best-seller *Hollywood vs. America* in 1992, referring to the "Culture War." (The term "Value War" was an early variation and was first used by media consultant Larry Poland in his 1988 book *The Last Temptation of Hollywood*. Also, in 1992 Pat Buchanan's keynote speech at the Republican National Convention was dubbed the "Culture War" speech.)

The year before, in 1991, the national audience was showing their frustration at the box office when motion picture attendance plunged to its lowest levels since 1976. By 1992, motion picture attendance dropped to its lowest level ever as a percentage of the American population.[5] The growth in individual, community, and national outrage toward Hollywood was accompanied by an explosion of media and entertainment watchdog organizations; well organized, highly resourceful, and able to attract membership and supporters in the millions.

As mainstream America battled back against Hollywood, the industry became more recalcitrant, condescending, odious, and political. During the 2004 presidential election, Democratic presidential candidate Senator John Kerry appeared at a high-profile Radio City Music Hall fundraiser with Whoopi Goldberg, John Cougar Mellencamp, and other Hollywood personalities.

It was a night of big mistakes that proved the curse of aligning politically with Hollywood celebrities. First, Goldberg described Republican candidate and sitting

President George W. Bush in terms too vulgar for network news, but not for the internet where millions read Whoopi's deep-seated and tawdry comments. Finally, as the fundraiser came to a close, Senator Kerry told the audience that the Hollywood celebrities on stage with him represented a cross-section of America when he should have said they represented a cross-section of a small sliver of Los Angeles. Kerry's star-struck embrace of the contentious Hollywood community and his short-sighted remarks at Radio City Music Hall may very well have cost him the election.

On September 2, 2004, President Bush gave his acceptance speech for the Republican nomination for re-election as president of the United States. For the first time in the history of American political conventions, Hollywood was specifically singled out as a de-facto enemy of American values when Bush said, "If you say the heart and soul of America is found in Hollywood, I'm afraid you're not a candidate of conservative values."[6]

The statement drew an uproar of applause from the delegation gathered at Madison Square Garden. The one exception was spotted by the network cameras that zoomed in on a disheveled, unshaven, sweat-hog wearing a baseball cap and a sarcastic grin by the name of Michael Moore. Moore's film *Fahrenheit 9/11* was an overzealous attempt by the ambush filmmaker to turn swing voters away from President Bush using wide-eyed conspiracy theories spliced together with stock footage and foreboding music. To Moore, his movie was the ultimate use of film as political weapon.

Senator John McCain of Arizona was more direct in his keen recognition of Hollywood and Moore as cunning liars and practitioners of mass deception. "Our choice wasn't between a status quo and the bloodshed of war. It was between war and a great threat. Don't let anyone tell you otherwise. Not our critics abroad. Not our political opponents. And certainly not a disingenuous filmmaker who would have us believe that Saddam's Iraq was an oasis of peace when in fact it was a place of incredible cruelty."[7] McCain's speech drew thunderous applause as the lumpy filmmaker chortled with a smug sense of accomplishment that, at the very least, his efforts were singled out for derision.

Certainly Moore's film did nothing but help President Bush, who won re-election on November 7, 2004. In early 2005, a billboard appeared high above Sunset Boulevard and next door to the Kodak Theater where the haughty Hollywood elite would be walking down the red carpet to attend the 2005 Academy Awards. The billboard shouted out in large block letters, "THANK YOU HOLLYWOOD!" On one side of the sign President Bush was seen, larger than life, smiling from the podium. On the other side, a montage of the bellicose celebrities whose loud mouths and lifestyles swung the swing vote to Bush: Whoopi Goldberg, Chevy Chase, Martin Sheen, Barbara Streisand, Sean Penn, and Michael Moore.

Advice to future political candidates: Never invite Whoopi Goldberg to help raise funds.

David Bossie, president of Citizens United erected the billboard and commented that "Having an America-hater like Mr. Moore lecture Americans on how to vote was a gift." Bossie noted that political campaigns may never be the same after 2004. "Political discourse will never again be solely between the candidates for office and their political constituents, but will be fought through filmmakers, pundits, and internet bloggers."[8]

The re-election of George W. Bush as president in 2004 drew extensive coverage in exit polls and interviews, which questioned why voters picked Bush over Senator Kerry. One of the keynote speakers was former Democratic Senator Zell Miller of Georgia who noted after the election that the Bush victory "is about the soul of the nation." The longtime senator and former governor added that "this was the most important election of our lifetime."[9]

Also taking a retrospective view of the election, Rev. Franklin Graham noted that "we have lost our moral compass and a lot of it has to do with the entertainment industry."[10] Independent filmmaker Evan Maloney made the direct point that "Hollywood has to realize they're not a political party, they're a business."[11] The reason Hollywood is attempting to push its twisted far-left political agenda is because "The Hollywood elite has contempt for basic American values," according to former Speaker of the House Newt Gingrich.[12]

Immediately after the election, the Pew Research Center conducted an exit poll to question the choices made by the electorate. The National Election Poll found that a majority of voters said their choice for president was motivated by a concern for moral values more than any other issue.[13]

Newsweek columnist Jonathan Alter tried to call "values" voters a myth, and a "funny thing" that happened on "the way back to Pleasantville." A week after the election, columnist Linda Feldman wrote, "For social conservatives, the chance to turn back a cultural revolution that arguably began with the invention of the birth control pill—which in turn launched the sexual revolution—has been a long time coming."[14]

Gary Bauer, head of the American Values organization argued that Bush's victory could be defined as a culturally conservative growing coalition, stating that its broadening membership "includes people who listen to James Dobson on *Focus on the Family* and also includes the guy sitting in his living room with his Budweiser who is just damned tired of seeing his middle-American values trashed by the cultural elites."[15]

In one statement issued after the election, James Dobson noted that "Hollywood has inflicted great damage to children and families."[16] Dobson's observations echoed a similar view by former Secretary of Education William Bennett who called the entertainment industry an increasingly dominant and destructive force on America's social landscape. Stated more bluntly by radio talk show host Dr. Michael Savage, "We voted to stop the sewer line running from Hollywood into our homes."[17]

While the war in Iraq and terrorism has redirected much of the nation's attention, the Culture War continues unabated in America. Pew Research conducted another poll in May 2007 asking what were the toughest challenges facing parents. Cultural factors topped the list with four in ten Americans (38%) listing their top concerns as the impact of television, the movies, drugs, alcohol, and peer pressure.

President Bush should also thank Janet Jackson for his second term re-election to the presidency. Earlier in 2004, Jackson was performing at a massive freak show produced by MTV, also known as the Super Bowl halftime show, in which she flashed "the breast seen 'round the world." Millions of parents had, fortunately, already spirited their children out of the living room after angry crotch-grabbing hip-hoppers had strutted across the make-shift stage. The rest were left dumfounded as to how they were going to explain this "wardrobe malfunction" to their kids.

The exit polls conducted by the Pew Research Center already confirmed what many Americans had been venting for decades. As writer Linda Feldman reported, "For several years, surveys have shown a large majority are worried about declining morals. Their voices were heard, for example, in the outcry over decency on the airwaves sparked by [the] Super Bowl halftime show."[18]

The former singer, unable to carry a tune any longer, had resorted to predatory sexual exhibitionism at the last televised venue intended for family viewing. This could put Janet Jackson in a special category of "broadcast predator" in a league of equal or greater danger than allegations against big brother Michael Jackson. The broadcasters and the football commissioner should have known better.

The Democrats were slow to acknowledge the importance of "the moral question" in presidential elections. But by 2006, former Clinton advisor Paul Begala admitted that "You can't ignore those social and cultural values."[19] The "Rajin' Cajun" James Carville agreed.

In 2006 popular commentator and author Bill O'Reilly sharpened the definition of the Culture War in his best-selling book *Culture Warrior*. "The far left smear machine is already cranked up over traditionalists who believe the country is noble—America is a noble nation, we can make mistakes, but basically at the heart of our system is a nobility that makes the world a better place—and secular progressives, who believe America is a deeply flawed nation that needs a fundamental overhaul."

HOLLYWOOD TAKES REVENGE

There is a bigger side show that takes place in Hollywood every spring known as the Academy Awards. The awards are voted by Hollywood insiders and granted to their fellow Hollywood insiders. This ego-boosting and ego-breaking event is preceded for many months by other award ceremonies such as guild awards and press association awards.

The 2007 Academy Awards would return to the lackluster selection of Hollywood's personal favorites, with a few notable selections that even "the rest of America" might approve of. The main attraction this time would be the Oscar host, or hostess, depending on which gender she was bending at the time. The audience of industry insiders would chuckle and snicker at Ellen DeGeneres' social/sexual/political double-entendres and heterophobic jabs.

The only other notable distraction during the 2007 Academy Awards was the Oscar given to Al Gore for his New Age factual-fiction film called *An Inconvenient Truth*, in which manipulated science touted the end of the world due to "global warming." Shortly after, Scott Pelli compared "global warming deniers" to "Holocaust Deniers." A Napa Valley resort replaced the *Gideon's Bible* with Al Gore's book. By July 2007, researcher James Taylor of the Heartland Institute had declared almost 100% of Al Gore's movie as false. Economist Walter Williams echoed the sentiments of many when he declared "global warming" as the "new Communism."

But it was the 2006 Academy Awards and the previous award ceremonies of the Golden Globes that would demonstrate Hollywood's eagerness to take revenge on President Bush's promotion of conservative values over Hollywood values. The less-than-stellar line-up of movies Hollywood was pushing on the American and worldwide audience were among the most perverse and subversive films ever rolled out by the "entertainment" industry.

It became very obvious in early 2006 that Hollywood was escalating the Culture War by promoting their collective, warped worldview as the payback response to President Bush's speech at the Republican National Convention and the billboards that loomed high over Sunset Boulevard the year before. Nobody in the mainstream media would make that connection, then or now—at least not publicly.

During the 2006 orgy of award ceremonies of movies offered up by Hollywood, many industry insiders, observers, and entertainment press noted the wide array of small-budget movies that were gaining the attention of cinematic critics and worldwide industry film distributors. These "little movies" certainly were not getting the attention of middle-America until the sponsors of the Golden Globe Awards, the star-struck and left-leaning Hollywood Foreign Press Association (HFPA), began announcing candidates for the 2006 awards. The winners are often an "astral-projection" forecast of future Oscar nominees and winners. That these foreign press writers set the tone for what is "hot" in Hollywood filmmaking is testament to their nickname in certain quarters as HETPA (Hollywood Euro-Trash Press Association).

Among the carnival side show films receiving the attention of the Golden Globe ceremonies was *Transamerica*. The movie was not about the San Francisco financial giant and its landmark pyramid skyscraper. This twisted low-budget feature follows the life of a man who becomes a woman and in the process discovers that he/she/it has a son from a previous relationship when he/she/it was still just a man. The filmmakers take a deeper stab at the faith-based community when the "character" is also revealed to be a born-again Christian.

The gender-bender sex obsession of Hollywood continued with *Breakfast on Pluto* about the "adventures" of a transvestite during the 1970s. The film, like *Transamerica*, received nominations for a Golden Globe award. *Capote* was another low-budget release based on the life of Truman Capote during the period when the homosexual* author was conducting research on the slaughter of a Kansas farm family by two drifters in the 1950s. Capote developed a psycho-sexual fascination with one of the killers and reportedly wept when the killer was executed by hanging.

Among the perverse sex themes Hollywood rolled out at the 2005-2006 festivals and award ceremonies, there were also the usual "blame America first" and anti-democracy-themed movies such as *Syriana*, starring George Clooney as a disaffected CIA agent who feels betrayed by his government. The film paints an emerging sympathy for terrorism as Clooney's character discovers that "big-bad-oil" is responsible for the world's problems. There was no mention in the ending credits that Clooney was driven to the set every day by oil-based petroleum.

Clooney was also the star and producer of *Good Night, and Good Luck*, another tired portrayal of Hollywood's love affair with the unending hatred of Senator Joseph McCarthy. The Senator is portrayed as completely uninformed, wrong on all matters of national security, obsessed, crazed, and poised to destroy America when the all-knowing gallant press, led by Edward R. Murrow (Dan Rather's mentor), comes to the rescue. The film is largely contrived, purposely leaving out basic historical facts and ignoring the truth that McCarthy actually "got a lot of the answers right" according to Arthur Herman, author of one of the definitive biographies *Joseph McCarthy: Re-examining the Life and Legacy of America's Most Hated Senator.*

But the most bizarre film to debut during the 2006 Golden Globes was *Paradise Now*, a sympathetic portrait and not too subtle glorification of suicide bombers in

---

* *The word "homosexual" will be used in this book with the same definition that has been applied for over 26 centuries, since ancient Greece, to describe individuals or action "of or characterized by sexual desire for those of the same sex."*[20] *The word "gay" will only be used in the context referring to statements by individuals or organizations that use this word. "Gay" was hijacked of its original meaning in a publicity stunt perpetuated by Allen Ginsberg in 1971. The word-of-mouth campaign originally stated "homosexuals are 'gay' and heterosexuals are 'sad'." Only the first half remained in the popular lexicon. The use of "homosexual" in this book is never applied in a derogatory manner.*

the Mideast, focusing on the "sacrifices" they make, and the unwavering support of their families. The Hollywood Euro-Trash Press Association "honored" the film by voting it a Golden Globe award for Best Documentary. That's right; best documentary for the hard working, self-sacrificing suicide bombers exactly like the suicide bombers who slammed two commercial airlines into the World Trade Center, one airline into the Pentagon, and a fourth into the fields outside Shanksville, Pennsylvania, although the last flight, United 93, was actually the first counter-attack in the war on terror since the passengers bravely overtook the terrorists.

This is the mind-set of Hollywood *and* the Euro-Trash entertainment press, the fifty-something slump-shouldered hippies with tuxedos and ponytails who fondly remember Mick Jagger's "Sympathy for the Devil." And the lunacy didn't stop there.

Even Steven Spielberg's *Munich,* released at the same time, seems to equate Israel's attempt to track down and kill the murderers of their 1972 Olympic weight lifting team as no different than the "hard-working" terrorists themselves. The entire film bogged down in moral ambiguity and, like the aforementioned movies, proved to be a major money loser and flopped at the box office, proving that Hollywood is on a high-priority mission to change your outlook on the world, even if the industry has to take a profit hit.

The entertainment industry's social/sexual/political agenda was best epitomized during the same festival award season by Hollywood's "darling" among the pack, *Brokeback Mountain*, a movie about homosexual cowboys, or as *USA Today* reporter Scott Bowles described the film, as "two cowboys who struggle with their love for each other."[21] Hollywood promoted the film as a "gay cowboy romance" and later simply as a "cowboy romance" in a typical attempt to trick potential moviegoers into thinking that a good old-fashioned western has resurfaced at the local multi-plex. *Brokeback Mountain* was seen by fewer people in three months than the audience for ABC's *Dancing with the Stars* in one week.[22]

This feeble attempt to break the mold of the American cowboy by activist director Ang Lee became the stalwart in-your-face response to the George Bush GOP presidential acceptance speech of 2004. More evidence of this could be found in the numerous "spoof posters" showing up on the internet and in college dorm rooms with the photos of President Bush and Vice-President Cheney superimposed over the faces of *Brokeback* actors Heath Ledger and Jake Gyllenhaal from the theater poster. The Gay and Lesbian Alliance Against Defamation (GLAAD) was so excited about *Brokeback* that it established a special "resource guide" with articles and information on support groups for homosexual cowboys and farmers.[23]

What excited the depravity factor among the Hollywood creative community more than anything else were the very explicit scenes of two "cowboys" having sex with each other. This effectively put the movie in the category of "gay porn" even though critics were vainly trying to equate it as the *Guess Who's Coming to Dinner* of the twenty-first century.[24]

Not only was *Brokeback* a favorite at the Golden Globes, it became the sweetheart contender at the 2006 Academy Awards receiving eight nominations. As a reminder, the American audience has no say in the vote for Oscar-winning films. "Select" members of the movie industry make their choices for who will receive the much-worshipped little statue with the art-deco face. Hollywood's heavy hype campaign during Oscar season is a clear indication of the mind-set and personal worldview of the filmmakers in today's Hollywood.

Brokeback is the best example of Hollywood's virulent campaign of value manipulation, discussed in Technicolor detail in Chapter 9, The Big Lie and Value Manipulation. The "Cowboy Love Story," as it was also promoted to the mass audience, fit in perfectly with *Variety* magazine's Timothy Gray condemning children to hell and broadcasting his crusade of "I want adult entertainment and I want it now."[25] Gray, the veteran columnist for *Variety*, is also a vocal admirer of the porn business in Hollywood as evidenced by his many glowing reviews for the pornography industry in Tinseltown.

Actor Terrance Howard, also nominated for another money loser, *Hustle and Flow*,[26] was quick to carry Hollywood's water and fight for the industry's side in the Culture War when he bloviated loudly about *Brokeback*, shouting, "Sometimes you have to say 'To hell with audience reaction. We could be at the start of a cultural revolution.'"[27] In other words, "Culture War."

Oprah Winfrey came to the rescue by endorsing *Brokeback* only four weeks after she was bamboozled for endorsing fraud artist James Frey's best-selling "memoir" *A Million Little Pieces*, which was filled with half-truths and outright lies. And joining Winfrey in the heterophobic euphoria for promoting Brokeback Mountain was the perpetual pervert of the airwaves, Howard Stern, who pumped up the movie on his radio show. Only Hollywood producers would embrace this endorsement of the mentally disturbed "shock jock" who once commented on the Columbine High School massacre with outrage; not at the killing of innocent students, but outrage that the two student killers didn't have sex with their victims before shooting them.[28]

Brokeback Mountain certainly didn't help the sagging viewership of the once-popular Awards ceremony on television. "Without a blockbuster, without a *Lord of the Rings* installment, audiences stay away from the worldwide telecast of the Oscars, . . . but the obvious problem is they also stay away from the movies themselves," reported television movie correspondent Bill McCuddy.[29]

Every year producers of the Academy Awards claim that the ceremony is broadcast to "one billion viewers worldwide." Just because it is "broadcast" to one billion viewers, there is no indication that everybody is "tuning in." The truth behind the Hollywood lie is that the 2006 Oscar telecast was actually watched by 38 million viewers, the third straight year of lost viewership and the lowest since 1997.[30] The 2008 Oscars had been dubbed the "Bucket of Blood" awards and, as a result, the ratings were the lowest in televised history.

As for *Brokeback Mountain*, the eight Academy nominations resulted in only three actual awards. The voting members of the Academy executed a counter-revolt as the result of many large metropolitan newspapers insisting that *Brokeback Mountain* would be a shoe-in and, therefore, "gay rights" would be advanced in America. Not that Hollywood didn't agree with them; Hollywood just doesn't like anybody second-guessing them.

Wrapping up the state of morally bankrupt films at the 2006 Oscars, Hollywood defended the social/sexual/political movies by perpetuating "The Big Lie" first foisted on the public by Irving Thalberg of MGM in the late 1920s. Reflecting on the 2006 Academy Awards, distribution executive Jeff Goldstein of Warner Brothers surmised that "It's natural that the best movies are going to reflect what's going on in people's lives."[31] Did Goldstein forget that this wasn't "The People's Choice Awards?"

Perhaps the most bizarre attack on President Bush came in the form of an assassination—on film—from UK broadcaster Channel 4 (More 4). Directed by Gabriel Range, *Death of a President* debuted at the September 2006 Toronto Film Festival and was quickly picked up for distribution in the U.S. by New Market Films, with the help of the William Morris Agency.

The British producers created a new category called "fictional documentary" in which they leaped into the future to depict an assassin shooting President Bush to death in October 2007. The rest of the film is treated as a "retrospective assassination" in which people reflect on where they were at the time of the president's "death" and how it has affected America. It is clear that the movie was a fantasy of the producer's wishful thinking in a largely secular and anti-Bush England. John Beyer of the UK television pressure group MediaWatch said the film was "irresponsible" and could even trigger a real assassination attempt, adding that "There's a bit of feeling against President Bush and this may well put ideas into people's heads."[32]

Producer Peter Dale has picked up Hollywoodspeak by declaring, "It's an extraordinarily gripping and powerful piece of work."[33] Of course, Hollywoodspeak is good old fashioned "double speak" as Orwell termed it, and Dale couldn't help but add, "I hope that people will see that the intention behind it is good."[34] And what "good intent" did Dale have in mind? The film bombed.

Surely Oliver Stone had "good" intent when he made *Natural Born Killers*, a horrific blood-splattered film that Stone claimed was an exposé of the press frenzy in covering a murder spree by two crazed killers in 1994. Of course, after a six-year-long wrongful death trial, and more than twenty dead bodies (and counting), Stone's attorney said that was not his "intent."

THE HOLLYWOOD CULTURE WAR

Commenting on *Death of a President*, a White House spokesman had no comment because "it does not dignify a response."[35]

That low-key "no comment" was in stark contrast to former president Bill Clinton's desperate response during the same week in reacting to a largely factual account of Clinton's repeated failure to capture or kill Osama bin Laden as depicted in the ABC-TV movie *Path to 9/11* based in part on the 9/11 Commission Report headed by Senator Thomas Kean, who also served as the film's technical advisor. Clinton and over a dozen former cabinet members, hacks, and the current Democratic leadership in Congress demanded extreme editing and ultimately would settle for nothing less than the movie being pulled, which it was not. The furious Democratic party resorted to last minute e-mails across America pleading with people not to watch the film.

Actor Sean Penn had a particular axe to grind in September with President Bush in Toronto as the B-grade actor was attending the film festival in a vain attempt to promote his poor remake of *All the King's Men*. Penn, a real-life airhead much like his dope-smoking character in *Fast Times at Ridgemont High*, referred to President Bush as Beelzebub, the Hebrew Old Testament reference to the devil. Penn was one of the actors pictured on the "Thank you, Hollywood" billboard that loomed over Sunset Boulevard for so long that he almost blew a gasket. Penn failed to mention that he was once married to Beelzebub, the self-proclaimed Kabbalah occult worshiper named Madonna. *All the King's Men* turned out to be one of the biggest money losers in Penn's career.

September was also "pile-on" time for washed-up musicians who cranked out one-hit singles bashing Bush. Among those venting their hatred of Bush through song were Bruce Springsteen, Neil Young, Greenday, the Dixie Chicks, and even Burt Bacharach who has decided to sell auto insurance while singing off-key, unable to keep his head erect long enough to maintain a final screeching note. (This is more an offense to the insurance industry than to Burt Bacharach.)

Added to all these woes, were Bush's continued efforts in September 2006 and throughout 2007 to battle Congress for the right to wiretap terrorist phone calls. And in a seemingly surreal empathy toward captured terrorists by Congress, the President was forced to confront the Senate over Section 3 of the Geneva Convention, which forbids such *inhumane treatment* as, in the view of Arthur Sulzberger's *New York Times*, the playing of the Red Hot Chili Peppers' music to enemy combatants sitting in cold rooms.

Granted, that is inhumane treatment to anybody except their limited fan base, but it worked, providing American intelligence officers with some of the most valuable intelligence to date. And the federal courts finally gave President Bush "official" authorization to wiretap terrorist phone calls in July 2007. How hard was that?

The best advice for radical filmmakers and musicians in the field of informed political discourse and debate is to adopt the title of radio talk show host Laura Ingraham's best-selling book: *Shut Up and Sing*.

CHAPTER 2

How the War Began:
THE "QUIET CONSPIRACY" AND THE "GANG OF FOUR"

> *We kept it very quiet at the time.*
> —Director Mike Nichols

The declaration of a Culture War from the entertainment industry was announced officially on November 1, 1968, by the new MPAA president Jack Valenti only two years after being "anointed" to the position by the major motion picture studios. The declaration of a war came in the form of an "abolition" as Valenti set out to "free the screen" from the slavery of the MPAA's own Production Code, a basic guiding code of content followed by the major studios for almost forty years. (The Production Code has been frequently termed the Hays Code after MPAA's first president Will Hays.)

Valenti's "Reconstruction" was a program he dubbed "The Voluntary Ratings System," which would forever divide the American family and moviegoing audience into age-restricted groups. The underlying effect, and perhaps the true intent, was to enable "dark," "cutting-edge," and "rogue" filmmakers to produce largely "adult" films with the legitimate Seal of Approval from the MPAA.

Most major theater owners would not allow a film to be shown without the MPAA seal. The National Association of Theater Owners (NATO) was privately persuaded early on by Valenti to take part in the "Emancipation Proclamation," though some theater owners feared the drastic move would spell a prescription for disaster and their worst fears would, indeed, come true.

While the Production Code of 1930 was never perfect, it was constructed like a Constitution—open for amendments. But to abolish it was revolutionary and enormously misguided. In fact, the Production Code ushered in the "Golden

Era" of filmmaking offering classic entertainment and challenging content open and accessible to people of all ages with a unique feature known as "dual understanding" that allowed moviemakers to tackle controversial subject matter with the implied content that adults understood at its deeper meaning and that children understood at a surface level (see Appendix III). As author Gregory Black described the Production Code, "While the audience knew full well what was going on, it would be left up to their imagination to conjure up the details."[1]

One of the best examples of the "dual understanding" strategy by a director working under the Code was Robert Mulligan's screen adaptation of the classic *To Kill a Mockingbird* in 1962. The widely popular and award-winning film tackled a series of heated and controversial issues including racism, rape, murder, mental illness, and even the insinuation of incestuous rape. To examine how Mulligan was able to accomplish this is discussed in detail in Chapter 14, INTERMISSION, in which an adult reflects on what he remembered in watching the movie as a five-year-old child as opposed to what his parents gleaned from the same movie as they sat together in the theater.

Valenti's alternative was not only less than perfect, it was a ploy conceived in secrecy, deception, and the apparent intent to install the "forbidden fruit" agenda that filmmakers continue to use today to change and warp the value system of the audience. The debauched columnist for the industry rag *Variety*, Timothy Gray, wrote that "nothing is as enticing as forbidden entertainment."[2]

Children grow up now wondering why some movies and television shows are off limits to them but perfectly okay for their parents. With ratings appearing on television in 1997, at Valenti's guidance, the family has been thrown into a moral quagmire of trying to decide what is "safe" and what is "dangerous" to watch, not only for their children, but also for themselves as adults—if they plan on being good role models.

Columnist Ellen Goodman of the *Boston Globe* best summarized the whole Ratings Scheme as a "lame solution" when she wrote that "The rites of passage to adulthood are now defined by card-carrying access to alcohol, tobacco, and big-screen mayhem. What message does that send about what it means to come of age?"[3]

The result of Valenti's Ratings Scheme would prove to be a total disaster of escalating monolithic proportions, which has continued to plague the culture as a whole to this day and worsens with every passing year.[4] Because the dark side of Hollywood filmmaking was unleashed by Valenti's rewriting the rules, the influence has spread to television programming, DVDs, downloadable content to computers, iPods, cell phones, and further deteriorated the music industry. Even literature, publishing, magazines, fashion, lifestyles, politics, social policy, education, workforce philosophies, and family structure have taken on a detrimental value system that Hollywood promotes 24/7.

Not only was Valenti's change a disaster, its effects were immediately catastrophic at the box office. In 1965, weekly movie attendance averaged 44 million viewers. In 1969, the year after Valenti established the Ratings Scheme, weekly attendance dropped to only 17.5 million, a mass exodus of more than sixty percent of the American movie-going audience.[5] Many moviegoers simply never returned to the theater after 1968's orgy of X-rated and R-rated films flooded the box office. To this day, weekly movie attendance has never returned to the 44 million weekly tickets of the pre-Ratings Scheme era, also known as the Golden Era. And considering the U.S. population has gained an extra 100 million people since 1968, the box office failure is far greater as a percentage of the U.S. population.

Examining the period of Valenti's reclusive maneuvers between 1966 and 1968 shows an unusual sense of urgency and timing in his rush to destroy the Production Code, which was administered by the MPAA, and replace it with a scheme of his own making. Only now, more than forty years later, are we learning the sequence of secret events surrounding the entertainment industry's first major salvo against the American culture.

Much of the information has been gleaned by the key players themselves, especially Valenti who died only three years into retirement in 2007 after thirty-eight years promoting and defending unremitting debauchery in American society. In his own words on the official MPAA website and in op-ed pieces and interviews, Valenti recalled the period with the same old story encapsulated in a few paragraphs or a simple two-column newspaper article. But what he volunteered says much about the West Coast mindset of a man paid one million dollars a year to carry the movie industry's dirty water.

According to Valenti, his sense of urgency to destroy the Production Code and open Pandora's Box was his first priority. His words and tone also reveal insight into Valenti's condescending, arrogant, and jaded vision of his own personal worldview. Valenti would ascribe the urgent need for change to "a time of rebellion among the young, of abandonment of social restraints." This clamorous and chaotic "riots in the streets" reasoning demanded his "immediate action."[6]

Venting even further on the MPAA website, "From my first day of my own succession [his words] to the MPAA president's office, I had sniffed the Production Code constructed by the Hays Office." What Valenti "sniffed" was an "odious smell" that he felt was constraining filmmakers during this time of "rebellion" in America and "torment in our society" and "I determined to junk it at the first opportune moment."[7] That last line is one to remember as Valenti would soon be faced with having to make a decision about film content for which he "claimed" or rather "determined" there was no "fixable" or "amiable" solution—except for his own.

Right up to the moment Valenti slipped into a coma in 2007, his venom toward the Production Code seemed almost obsessive, as if to validate his campaign to install moral relativism into the entertainment industry and ultimately the entire culture. Valenti's demonizing of his predecessors at the MPAA only served his own self-deception to falsely elevate the importance of his decision to force the Ratings Scheme on an unsuspecting America, a decision many are now criticizing as increasingly useless and manipulated by the industry itself.

In describing Will Hays, the first president of the MPAA in 1922, Valenti wrote in a self-congratulatory op-ed piece in 2005 that "Hays was one of those starched, high-on-the-neck, white-collar orators reeking of moral integrity."[8] High on the neck? Reeking of moral integrity? It's obvious that, to Jack Valenti, values and moral integrity served no other purpose than to "reek" instead of their very real capacity to "elevate." The truth is Will Hays was directly hired *by* the movie studios as the first MPAA president because he *did* represent morality and values, something with which the movie moguls were unfamiliar. His mandate was literally to clean up the image of the motion picture industry awash in sex scandals, drug overdoses, adultery, and even murder. And that was in 1922!

From his "ascension" to the throne in 1966, many years would pass before Valenti would reveal his agenda for "junking" the Production Code. It had nothing to do with giving parents and adults guidance or protecting children. Jack Valenti's mission took on the form of a New Age philosophy that he proclaimed with a voracious, even occult-like, obsession. After all, his mandating mantra was the advent of a whole new era, "A New Kind of American Movie."[9]

Expanding on his urgent task to instill his philosophy on the public, Valenti wrote on the MPAA website, "The result of all this was the emergence of a 'new kind' of American movie—frank and open, and made by filmmakers subject to very few self-imposed restraints."[10] His all-consuming obsession was reflective of other morally vacant denizens who occupied the 1960's counterculture, including Timothy Leary, Hugh Hefner's "Playboy Philosophy," the "hippie movement," and the corrosive legacy of the Beat Generation of Jack Kerouac, Allen Ginsberg, and Edward Burroughs.

For decades the secret behind-the-scenes maneuvering of Jack Valenti between 1966 and 1968 were kept quiet as he toiled to undermine the Production Code as quickly as possible, and he was determined to achieve this by or before the end of 1968. Industry insiders would refer to this period as "the secret agreement." Critics referred to this time more aptly as the "Quiet Conspiracy" by four individuals of high profile and influence from both inside and outside Hollywood.

This "Gang of Four" was spearheaded by Valenti himself, who would be forever dubbed The Dark Prince of Hollywood, a diabolical individual whose mastery of double-speak, cunning, dishonesty, and manipulation would dominate and preside over the deterioration of Hollywood and ultimately the entire American culture as a whole.

THE QUIET CONSPIRACY AND THE GANG OF FOUR

In early 1966, Jacqueline "Jackie" Kennedy was the most recognized woman in the world. Less than three years earlier, she had become the most famous widow in the world after her husband, John F. Kennedy, was assassinated in 1963. Slowly emerging on the Manhattan social scene, Jackie was a fan of Broadway and eventually became acquainted with Mike Nichols, a brash young Tony-award-winning director of Neil Simon's plays. Jackie Kennedy's role in the Quiet Conspiracy would emerge as the most significant as she managed, miraculously, to conjure a voice from the dead.

This was also a landmark year for Nichols as he was being offered the opportunity to direct his first movie, the cinematic version of playwright Edward Albee's *Who's Afraid of Virginia Woolf.* And the offer was coming from none other than Jack Warner, head of Warner Brothers Studios. Warner, the once-polished studio mogul from the 1930s, was in his final days of motion picture production in 1966 and was now subject to extreme mood swings. Friendly, encouraging, and humorous at one moment, Warner could suddenly switch to a cursing, verbally abusive demon "from the dark recesses of his psyche."[11]

Inevitably, the finished movie version of *Who's Afraid of Virginia Woolf* would have to be submitted to Jack Valenti for approval in order to receive the coveted PCA (Production Code Administration) seal of approval. All four individuals, now known as the Gang of Four, would have met each other by early 1966, either professionally or through the Bi-Coastal Cocktail Party Circuit (BCPC). In fact, Jack Warner was one of the studio heads who approved the hiring of Jack Valenti as the industry's chief lobbyist.

Valenti tells part of the secret chapter of Hollywood's past, and many of the blanks and holes in Valenti's story were filled in by Mike Nichols in an interview buried in the back pages of a 1999 issue of *Newsweek* magazine. The Gang of Four would come together in a carefully orchestrated scheme of well-rehearsed lies, secret back-room deals, and theft; theft of the public trust in an industry that was now viciously determined to "define decency down" in the words of the late Senator Daniel Patrick Moynihan.

Valenti recounts the beginning of this period. "Within weeks of my new duties, I was confronted with controversy, neither amiable or fixable."[12] Valenti was faced with having to make his first decision about the content of a movie and its suitability for public viewing by theater owners and exhibitors across the nation, and inevitably, around the world. The new MPAA president didn't realize, or didn't want to admit, that an element of controversy was almost always a part of the process of submitting a film to the MPAA for the Production Code seal. Without the seal, theater owners would not show the film.

Approving and disapproving a movie for the Production Code seal was part of a process that had been in place for almost four decades. It may never have been an amiable process, but it was always fixable. In reality, the process of review by the MPAA's own Production Code Administration proved more flexible than the written code itself. The most strongly enforced restrictions related to depictions of sex, obscene language, violence, religious ridicule, ethnic insults, and drug abuse. Valenti was especially interested in lifting those restrictions, the sick results of which we are reaping today.

As Michael Medved observes, "It's very existence reminded moviemakers of the need to work within broadly accepted standards of decency and good taste."[13] In fact, the Production Code had ushered in the Golden Era of moviemaking from 1930 to 1968. Valenti was not faced with a controversy until he labeled the "situation" as a "controversy." He was not faced with a situation that was "neither amiable or fixable" until he declared it as such. Valenti was redefining the language and the dialogue to fit neatly into his scheme. After all, Valenti had a personal agenda to accomplish, and this would be his springboard. As for that last line as "one to remember," Valenti declared, "I determined to junk it [the Production Code] at the first opportune moment." Valenti's moment had arrived. How convenient was that?

The "controversy" concerned the finished film cut of *Who's Afraid of Virginia Woolf?* by director Nichols. The movie, based on Albee's play, was a deliriously depressing, sadistic, and masochistic bitter tale of a psychologically mangled university professor and his wretched wife (Richard Burton and Elizabeth Taylor) as they entertained a young new professor and his wife at the elder couple's home. The entire production was soaked in a haze of alcoholic dialogue of the most acrimonious, caustic, and sardonic lines ever spoken on the silver screen. But that wasn't the overall "controversy." Bleak films were becoming popular in the late 1960s as "darkness" was becoming "fashionable." And playwright Edward Albee, himself an alcoholic, knew how to dish out the lush-laden phrases that Nichols brought to life.

The trouble came when the final cut was screened at the MPAA's private screening room. Jack Valenti sat next to the unpredictable and hard-nosed Jack Warner, the youngest and last of the legendary Warner Brothers. Almost seventy-five years old, he was no stranger to controversy, usually of his own making. The cut that Nichols was showing that evening contained the phrase "hump the hostess" and the derogatory "screw." This was the first time that derisive sexually charged profanity had ever been uttered in a motion picture.

The fix was easy under the Production Code: cut the language or cut the scene. In fact, under the code, the script had to be submitted for approval first before something "controversial" happened in the screening room. Valenti never admitted to reading the script, and if he did, he knew that these scenes were in the film and they would serve to fulfill his "opportune moment."

Valenti, a seasoned politician as a former special assistant to President Johnson and as a former veteran ad agency hack from Houston, knew how to play the uncomfortable situation. To set the stage for, temporarily, "reeking of moral integrity," Valenti and his attorney, Louis Nizer, retreated to a back room with Warner and his top assistant Ben Kamelson. Nichols waited outside, hoping anxiously that the artistic integrity of such profound lines as "hump the hostess" and "screw" would not be left on the cutting room floor.

As Valenti discussed the meeting in his own words, "We talked for three hours and the result was the deletion of the word 'screw' and retention of 'hump the hostess,' but I was uneasy over the meeting."[14] Valenti wasn't uneasy over breaking the guidelines of the Production Code, or that he was developing a moral backbone with the consistency of jelly. Valenti stated his "unease" almost forty years later in his self-sanctifying op-ed in the *Los Angeles Times*. "How silly can it get? Two grown men discussing such things!"[15]

Maybe the Valenti-Warner decision was "silly" for "grown men," but certainly the discussion was necessary for "mature men." Valenti's failure to distinguish between the two would tarnish his worldview and every decision he would make up until the very end of his term in September 2004.

Despite the secret meeting and agreement between the two Jacks, word of the impending release with "racy" language was leaked to the press, and the Brooklyn-based Catholic League of Decency protested loudly. By 1966 the League (formerly the Legion of Decency) was no longer the powerhouse it had been in the 1930s and 40s, largely because Hollywood had followed the essence of the code, at least in regard to overt sexuality, obscene language, and over-indulgent violence.

The Production Code itself was the product of Catholic input from layman Martin Quigley and Father Daniel Lord. It was they, not Will Hays, who wrote the Production Code in 1930. But even in 1966, if a red flag was raised in regard to nudity, profanity, or violence, it was common courtesy from the movie industry to screen the film in question to the League's executive secretary, in this case, Monsignor Thomas Little.

The inevitability of this screening sent Jack Warner back to the editing room with scissors in hand. The mogul, now in a hot temper, literally locked Nichols out of the room and began to delete a few minutes of Nichols' perverse self-indulgent film adaptation. The fight over the "final cut" was as old as the motion picture camera and projector. Nichols wasn't about to have his film altered to suit audience sensibilities.

Eager to make a splash with his first major Hollywood movie, he stormed through the back lot at Warner Brothers until he tracked down Warner's assistant. Throughout his fledgling career, Nichols remained silent about his role in the Quiet Conspiracy until 1999, more than thirty years later, when he admitted to

Newsweek magazine his part in the plot. The story was barely noticed and little remembered due to its burial in a small boxed article on page 62, with the curious title, "Jackie to the Rescue."

As Nichols recounted the events that followed, he finally found Warner's assistant and told him, "You tell Warner that if he gets me back on the picture, Jackie Kennedy will be there when he screens it for the Monsignor. When it's over, she will say, 'What a beautiful picture, Jack (John F. Kennedy) would have loved it.' We made the deal and I got her to do a version of that. We kept it very quiet at the time."[16]

We made the deal . . . . We kept it very quiet at the time.

Nichols' "deal," which Warner accepted and Valenti approved, was a classic revelation into the dark underbelly of the Hollywood mindset and a sneak preview into the secretive, contemptuous, and shady dealings of an industry town unashamed to spitefully use the widow of an American president to promote a movie. More bizarre is Nichols' rehearsing a concocted dialogue of necromancy (conversation with the dead) with the famous widow as the "home run" line.

It should be noted at this point that Jack Valenti was using the two "controversial" phrases and wording to cover up another phrase that had never been "uttered" in motion pictures. Valenti would not speak about this in his historical revision on the MPAA website or the op-ed pieces in the press. Most likely, this phrase was at the center of the debate between the two Jacks in their "private" three-hour meeting.

The phrase in question was, and remains, the most offensive insult to Christians and Jews and even the secular community with a sense of decency; "god____n." This was Jack Valenti's version of a "New Kind of American Movie." Valenti would not discuss the true core of his fabricated "controversy" because he did not want to take the blame for his "legitimizing" a slap at Christians and Jews. His disdain for Christians in particular would reveal itself later in his career. In the meantime, Valenti sat back and let Nichols' "deal with the dead" run its course.

After the screening of *Who's Afraid of Virginia Woolf?* for Monsignor Thomas Little and a select group from the media, the elder Monsignor was caught off guard, just as Nichols had planned.[17] After Jackie recited her "lines" about how much "Jack would have loved the picture," Monsignor Little was dumbfounded. Did Jackie Kennedy also add, in a reverential tone, "Father, don't worry about the g.d. line. It's just a movie. Besides, Jack and Bobby used it all the time over at Frank's house in Vegas."

How could the kindly Monsignor possibly contradict the blessings of Jackie Kennedy, the popular, glamorous widow still in grieving over the brutal assassination of her husband barely three years earlier? And how would a negative opinion by the Monsignor be received by a nation still in shock over the untimely death of a popular president?

The forced silence of Monsignor Little was seen as a victory for the Gang of Four who felt their conquest was a mandate for a new moral disorder. In retrospect, the underhanded and juvenile actions by these four in permitting the Quiet Conspiracy of 1966 would be the first battle cry by Hollywood in the Culture War against America. Valenti's "validation" of "god____n" would also be the first insult, now referred to as "bashing," of the Judeo-Christian community in film history.

If the name Valenti became synonymous with the word "slippery," Nichols' name would be equally associated with "sleazy." One missing link in the story that neither Valenti or Nichols would talk about is how the brooding young Nichols came to be introduced to Jackie Kennedy, and why she was so willing to participate in this scheme. Again Valenti had bragged that he would "junk" the Code at the "first opportune moment."

Having literally created the controversy over which he sold out the country's morals, Valenti was now just out of the starting gate in his urgent mission to "free the screen" by breaking the Production Code. It would only seem natural that the former high-rent ad agency huckster would have to orchestrate the biggest and most secretive ad campaign in his career in order to leap the many hurdles that lay ahead in his path to eliminate the Code.

Jack Valenti had known Jackie Kennedy long before Nichols had been introduced to her. By 1961, Valenti was already serving as informal advisor to then Vice-President Lyndon Johnson, and social contacts during the Kennedy-Johnson administration offered numerous occasions to work with the Kennedy First Family. Valenti was even riding in the motorcade when Kennedy was shot and stood near the First Lady in the back of Air Force One as Johnson was being sworn in as president after Kennedy was pronounced dead.

Valenti maintained his friendship with Jackie Kennedy during his years as special assistant to President Johnson until resigning to accept the position of MPAA president in 1966. Valenti could keep Camelot alive by involving the former First Lady when it served his personal and political agendas. It is highly unlikely that Mike Nichols was the true originator of the "Jack said from the dead" trick on the Monsignor.

Only speculation would point to Valenti asking the former First Lady for a special favor. Jackie Kennedy, more a fan of Richard Burton and Liz Taylor than a close friend of Nichols, was obviously eager to participate in pulling the wool over Monsignor Little's eyes. Valenti was Catholic, as was the former First Lady, and what better way to deceive a Catholic priest than to enlist the most famous Catholic woman in America?

But what we do know now is that even though the word "screw" was left on the cutting room floor, the Gang of Four had reserved the term for what they did to the Catholic Church, the Christian and Jewish communities, and any other "self-appointed groups" that simply asked Hollywood to consider, at the very least, a basic morality in the exercise of the world's increasingly influential medium of communication. Throughout this entire period, Hugh Hefner was the quiet catalyst behind the scenes, pushing Valenti to drop the curtain on the Code so that Hefner could drop the skirts of "aspiring" actresses on the big screen.

SOUL SELLING AND CLOSING THE DEAL

Jack Valenti must have felt energized and fully validated for his backroom scheming when *Woolf* received international acclaim from the British Film Academy and the New York Film Critics, and was nominated by the Academy Awards with thirteen nominations and five awards. Nichols was not one of the winners, which must have infuriated the former "gang" member who worked so hard to deceive the quiet priest from Brooklyn.

Did the words "hump the hostess" and "god____n" somehow push the movie into Oscar territory? Would the absence of the risqué phrases that Valenti "approved" have taken the morbidly depressing movie out of contention? No one knows. And that is how Valenti worked—in secrecy, "unknowns," and contradictions.

Despite the rantings and ravings from the British Film Academy, the New York Film Critics, and the Academy Awards, the film was not a runaway hit among American audiences who would leave the theater and make famous the phrase, "Now that I'm totally depressed . . . ." The negative reaction would soon be felt by the entire film industry. Valenti was not concerned with audience reaction and he still had a long way to go before officially abolishing the Production Code and installing his Ratings Scheme. The following year, 1967, Valenti let the Production Code languish and Hollywood cranked out a number of anemic films that contained little appeal.

Since producers were now being allowed to use the letter "M" for "mature audiences," the confusion among the American audience, particularly the American family, was polarizing. The devastating effect at the box office should have been an indication for Valenti to reverse course—immediately. But he was blinded to everything except his "prophetic mission."

Titles and plots of films in 1967 seemed to emphasize sex, violence, and profanity more than any other year in previous film history. The result was quickly crippling Hollywood. In 1966, the year of the Quiet Conspiracy, movie attendance still hovered around 38 million weekly viewers. But 1967's plethora of largely dead-end movies caused the box office attendance to drop dramatically to only 17.8 million weekly viewers,[18] the largest one-year drop in history. In just one year, more than half of the movie audience vanished, many never to return again, especially after 1968 when Valenti effectually transferred the red-light district to Main Street U.S.A.

In 1967, Valenti had only one year left to install his Ratings Scheme on the American landscape with as little notice as possible by the American public until after it was firmly entrenched. Valenti's tone in describing this period shows a clear and intentional disdain for any open public debate about the merits and demerits of the Production Code and how it might be amended.

Instead, Valenti opted, as usual, for a secret and very rapid campaign to push the Ratings Scheme at all costs to avoid interference by those he would contemptuously deride as "self-appointed groups,"[19] code words for religious organizations and individuals of strong moral convictions who "reeked of moral integrity."

A main goal of Valenti's private agenda was to establish the Rating Scheme by or before November 1968. In the early summer of that year, Valenti was racing against the clock to get the *industry* on board. The *public*, the audience of individuals who purchased the tickets that supported the *industry*, didn't appear to play a role in Valenti's aggressive sales plan. A "business plan" that ignored consumer sales projections was simply a prescription for disaster.

MPAA MEMBERS OF 1968

- Walt Disney Company (now Buena Vista Pictures)
- Columbia (now Sony Pictures Entertainment)
- Metro Goldwyn Mayer Studios
- Paramount Pictures
- Twentieth Century Fox Film Corporation
- Universal City Studios
- Warner Brothers Entertainment

The Dark Prince quietly navigated inside industry circles and began to discuss his plot with the president of the National Association of Theater Owners and then with the governing committee of the International Film Importers and Distributors of America (IFIDA).[20] Valenti would later claim that "over the next five months I held 100 hours of meetings with these two groups as well as with actors, writers, directors, and producers, with craft unions, critics, religious organizations, and the heads of MPAA member companies of 1968."[21] Notice how Valenti squeezed "religious organizations" in between critics and studio moguls. To his death, Valenti never identified which "religious" organizations he met with.

Now let's do the math and determine how Valenti was launching this mammoth task of establishing "a new kind of American movie" with just 100 hours of meetings with *sixteen broadly defined "industry" and "religious" organizations* that doubtless consisted of thousands of individuals. Let us assume, for time compression, that Valenti's meetings were held back to back. Because he was in a hurry, perhaps Valenti was putting in ten hours a day of meetings. One hundred hours of meetings divided by ten-hour days comes to a grand total of ten days. Again, that's *TEN* days. And, of course, this is all hypothetical.

Now compare that with the establishment of the Production Code of industry self-regulation, which took ten years to conceive and establish. That period saw the input of a wide cross-section of the American public including educators, progressive reformers, social service organizations, artists, writers, community leaders, journalists, editors, publishers, and religious organizations—with the Catholic Church among the most aggressive. After years of "genuine" meetings, debates, arguments, conflicts, resolutions, concessions, and agreements, the Production Code was established.

The very openness of the debate of the 1920s was the very reason Valenti chose the covert campaign and "closed-to-the-public" policy of 1968. And that debate centered on the *import, immediacy,* and *power* of film and its overwhelming potential to influence the best and worst behaviors of the viewing audience. This power of film promotes an enormous capacity of persuasion. This capacity cuts across all cultural, social, economic, political, and educational boundaries. The images and messages movies project can and have changed human behavior and there are literally more than *three thousand* studies that confirm this very real power.[22]

While Valenti was greasing the wheels of the movie industry, the public remained largely in the dark; the same ticket-buying public that paid the industry salaries, bought the Beverly Hills mansions with the four-car garages, and paid the drug rehab bills and the occasional call girls.

In yet another pat-on-the-back description of his "slam-bam" sales job of the Ratings Scheme, Jack Valenti wrote a farewell op-ed for the *Los Angeles Times* on November 1, 2005, titled "Rated PG (Pretty Good)." He reflected again on that "intense" period convincing the industry to accept the Ratings Scheme.

"I met with the creative guilds—the actors, writers, directors, producers. I told them I wanted to 'free the screen' so no one could force them to change their movies . . . . But some films might end up restricted from viewing by children." Valenti concluded that "I thought it was a fair balance."[23]

Fair balance? Other than G, every other rating created by Valenti would result in today's system of PG, PG-13, R, and NC-17, offering an ascending degree of segregation for children of all ages up to seventeen. Valenti also boasted that "the movie industry would no longer 'approve or disapprove' the content of a film."[24]

This necessitates another translation for "Valentiism," a form of speech meant to persuade by chicanery. "Fair balance" can only mean what the Ratings Scheme has become and what was intended at its inception—the sacrifice of children for the pleasure of adults. For over seventy years, Hollywood produced tens of thousands of movies with no restrictions whatsoever and many from that period are classics unsurpassed even today.

As to when the American public was consulted about their ticket-buying choices of the future, the answer is: never. America was offered an "announcement" of the Voluntary Ratings System (Scheme) on November 1, 1968, the day Hollywood officially declared a Culture War on America. According to the MPAA, Valenti officially abolished the Production Code on the same day he announced the Ratings Scheme. That date also clearly revealed the apparent reason behind Valenti's urgency in ramming the scheme down the collective throat of the moviegoing audience.

Only someone like "slippery Jack" would calculate the announcement just a few short days before the election victory of President Richard Nixon over Hubert Humphrey, the Democratic vice-president under Johnson. By November 1, polls were showing that Nixon was likely to defeat Valenti's friend and Jack didn't want any interference from a conservative president who might have injected his own input about the true public temperature concerning the future of motion pictures.

With the country focused on the election and the war in Vietnam, the press release was generally relegated to the back pages of newspapers and periodicals and little mention was made on any of the three major networks. Also, Valenti wanted to push his scheme while his good friend and former boss Lyndon Johnson was still in office. The movie industry was not a priority for Johnson, a lame-duck president deeply occupied with the fiercest fighting of the Vietnam War. Johnson's only form of "entertainment" was listening to Walter Cronkite's nightly "opinion" of the pulse of the nation.

More cynically, Valenti had to know that the pulse of Johnson's heart was not working at its optimum pumping rate. Johnson was popping nitroglycerin almost daily at this time and probably didn't care that Valenti was about to crash the culture (Johnson would be dead in less than five years).

Valenti's announcement of November 1, 1968, would signal the selling of his soul and initiate the wholesale auction of every soul from that day forward who might be seduced into a counterfeit morality by the emerging dark side of Hollywood. A sold soul is always a contradiction and repository of lies and hypocrisy. To demonstrate the short-sighted self-importance that Valenti attached to himself, the president of the MPAA was asked many years later to speak at a nationwide convention of movie exhibitors. Addressing the pressing issue of *steadily declining* movie attendance, Valenti told the gathering quite adamantly, "We have to increase the theater audience—we just have to do it." Then he proceeded to give the prescription for success by encouraging Hollywood to "start pictures with less violence, less sexuality, and less raunchy language."[25] It was just another Valenti PR smoke screen.

As author and screen critic Michael Medved noted, "Of course, all the sympathetic statements by Hollywood honchos could be written off as so many pious but meaningless platitudes, calculated attempts to appease the industry's critics without making meaningful changes."[26] Obviously Medved was correct. Valenti's adamant appeal was made in 1993 and as the nation approaches the end of the first decade of the twenty-first century, screen content has declined even further into that ever-present, effervescent "moral sewer."

Medved also summarizes Valenti's Ratings Scheme by emphasizing that it "not only fails to provide essential information about the content of motion pictures, but it also advances horribly distorted ideas about what constitutes maturity."[27] Jack Valenti never discovered that becoming an "adult" necessitates a coinciding assertion of "maturity," and hopefully virtue. In 1993 Charles Barkley appeared in a Nike commercial broadcast nationwide in which he declared, "I am not a role model," which only made him more of a role model; a negative role model to a young adolescent generation searching for guidance and heroes.

The same holds true for Jack Valenti, who was never even close to epitomizing a positive role model as his words and actions had proven over the thirty-eight years of his reign before being replaced by Dan Glickman in 2004. As Pastor Bill McNeese of Harvestfamilychurch.com observed on Father's Day of 2004 concerning the refusal of adults, such as Barkley and others, to assume their positions as role models for future generations, he stated bluntly, "It's too late, buddy, you're already there!"[28]

As a member of the Association of Film Commissioners International (AFCI) I attended the annual gathering in Los Angeles in 1995 where Jack Valenti was one of the keynote speakers. As he mingled with the AFCI members after his speech, I asked Valenti if he thought, in hindsight, that abolishing the Production Code was a mistake. With his heavy black brows furrowed in anger, he gave me the stock answer that he delivered to anyone who dared to ask such a question. "We are constantly polling parents as to the usefulness of the ratings. Constantly they tell us that the ratings are very useful." I couldn't help making the unintentional interpretation of his claim when I told Valenti, "I'm sure it's 'useful' as far as warning parents not to expect much for their entertainment dollar at the local theater."

Valenti simply walked away and continued greeting the gathered crowd. This was just one of many colorful exchanges I would have with Hollywood's million-dollar lobbyist during the 1990s.

* * *

Ironically, Valenti simply replaced one production code with another. Producers squabble more now than they did pre-1968 over the content of their films. If a producer wants to reach a larger audience, but has been "slapped" with an R-rating, the producer must go back into the editing room in hopes of getting a PG-13.

But the irony of all ironies began fervently in the late 1990s when Hollywood began attacking Valenti on a regular basis claiming that ratings for movies was censorship at its worst! Valenti, the pioneer of the "free screen" was on the defensive from the industry he had "freed" from the slavery of the "odious smell" of the Production Code. Valenti would defend the Ratings Scheme by explaining that "rogue" producers just wanted to make more "adult" films. (The exact reason he abolished the Production Code.) Among Valenti's biggest critics was *Variety* editor Peter Bart who wanted ratings eliminated altogether. His solution was one rating for very young children and no ratings for the rest. Bart's problem was that he couldn't define the age of "very young children."

Despite efforts to demonize him by Valenti and others in Hollywood, Will Hays was actually the best friend of the motion picture industry when he was hired as the first president of the MPAA in 1922. Movies were facing hundreds of censorship boards across the nation and around the world, President Franklin Roosevelt threatened to establish federal control over Hollywood, and constant boycotts and threats of boycotts loomed larger every year as Hollywood was under siege even more than today.

The period between 1907 and 1934 might well be considered the "first" culture war between Hollywood and America as some critics saw Hollywood as an "exploitation market" more than an "entertainment industry." Many considered early silent films as a breeding ground for immorality, obscenity, perversion of morals, portrayals of depravity, criminality, lack of virtue, and demeaning depictions of citizens of race, color, creed, and religion. Some jurists on the U.S. Supreme Court in 1915 even branded Hollywood movies as "evil" and labeled films as "a business pure and simple."[29] This removed film from certain free speech protection, a ruling that would stand until the 1950s.

As author Gregory D. Black wrote in his comprehensive study of this very complicated period, *Hollywood Censored*, the Production Code ushered in by Will Hays at the MPAA probably saved the industry from its own over-indulgence. "This system of 'self-regulation' dominated film production during Hollywood's Golden Era of studio production," and the impact of this form of self-regulation "on the content, flavor, feel, and image of Hollywood films has not been fully understood or appreciated."[30]

Medved further observed that, "While many of the specific rules in the old Production Code look thoroughly ludicrous by today's standards, it is instructive to recall that Alfred Hitchcock and Howard Hawks, John Ford and Billy Wilder, George Cukor and Frank Capra and Orson Welles all somehow managed to create their masterpieces under its auspices."[31]

By encouraging the movie industry to adopt the Production Code, Will Hays promoted the industry's self-regulation as "designed to maintain the highest moral and artistic standards in motion pictures and to develop the educational as well as entertainment value and 'general usefulness' of motion picture production," and he simply told the industry that hired him that "No picture shall be produced that will lower the moral standards of those who see it."[32]

There was good reason why Hays was dubbed by the press as "A No-Man in Yes-Land."

Valenti took the opposite road and not only did it backfire on him, the entire culture continues to suffer as a result of his "deal" on November 1, 1968. This was the seminal event of the century that Tom Brokaw "conveniently" ignored in his two-hour documentary titled *1968*. Unfortunately, the name Jack Valenti will appear in almost every chapter from this point on as testament to his destructive and detrimental impact on the culture and the war that ensued.

This book will show how the choices and decisions of one man can affect the lives of millions of people and how one person can himself be negatively influenced by others with hearts of darkness. And if you should ever see a televised interview with Jack Valenti in a documentary or film retrospective, or read some of his "motivational" books or quotations, you might just be tempted to say, "He seemed like such a sweet old man." If that's the case, take it from me: You don't know Jack!

CHAPTER 3

THE WAR HEATS UP: HOLLYWOOD AND WASHINGTON

> *The affairs between Hollywood and the Democrats are conducted privately and denied vehemently, as though it were illicit.*
> —Charles Case, NewsMax

Even though Jack Valenti's Ratings Scheme of 1968 was never officially labeled a Culture War, the growing disenchantment of the American public with the product coming out of Hollywood was simmering throughout the 1970s and 1980s. The term was eventually applied to myriad social, economic, and educational issues by the late 1980s.

The American body-politic was becoming increasingly divided between conservative and liberal interpretations of public policy issues such as abortion, the definition of family, homosexuality, feminism, race, quotas, work ethics, and especially the teaching of "New Age" values to American school children. These issues began to be broadly branded as a "Culture War."

Hollywood certainly played a part by influencing the way values were being interpreted, or manipulated, through theatrical and televised "entertainment" with subtle messages and agendas inserted by writers, producers, and directors. Michael Medved's lecture "Popular Culture and the War against Standards" in 1990 would soon solidify "Culture War" in reference to the polar difference between the increasingly perverse culture of Hollywood and the traditional culture of the American family.

By 1990 an entire generation had been raised knowing nothing more about the moviegoing experience other than a multi-layered world of escalating exclusion. Parents began to realize that children were largely excluded from the entertainment experience by movies that were predominantly R-rated. The explicit, indecent, and callous nature of movies in general coming out of Hollywood seemed unnecessary and overly self-indulgent. After all, parents of this first "restricted generation" had grown up in a world when motion pictures were bold, fun, and exciting. Most important, nobody was excluded.

By 1990, the very thought of going to the movie theater on a Friday night was an exercise in trepidation and fear, not from anyone lurking in the parking lot, but rather an unexpected assault of grotesque and raunchy images attacking from the screen.

Television was still relatively "safe" and offered a wide variety of entertainment options without the oversexed and ultra-violent shock effect of theatrical feature films. For this reason, the entertainment industry did not register brightly on Washington radar screens until 1992 when the Culture War with Hollywood would begin to raise political and governmental eyebrows, especially when the public airwaves of network television entertainment began to brazenly inject Hollywood values into sitcoms, episodic shows, and TV movies.

The genesis of this contention began when a particular episode of a popular television sitcom prompted Vice-President Dan Quayle to comment on the episode in a speech about family values. The vice-presidential remark was an eight-second sentence in the context of a forty-minute speech. As CNN described the comment, "Vice President Dan Quayle ignited a firestorm of controversy when he criticized 'Murphy Brown,' the powerful, intelligent character in an eponymous sitcom, for having a child out of wedlock—and without any father in the picture whatsoever."[1] The eponymous hippopotamus at the center of the storm was played by left-wing activist Candace Bergen.

The actual eight-second sentence that Vice President Quayle spoke was, "It doesn't help matters when prime-time TV has Murphy Brown, a character who epitomizes today's intelligent highly-paid professional woman, mocking the importance of fathers by bearing a child alone and calling it just another lifestyle choice."[2]

The sound-byte was repeated continuously by the news media, and the entertainment establishment used the vice-president's words deceitfully to demonize him and portray him as mean-spirited as if he were marginalizing and diminishing single mothers around the nation. Ten years would pass before the former vice-president was given fair airtime to explain and defend his remarks in an interview with Wolff Blitzer of CNN at the ten-year anniversary of his much misquoted remark.

"The issue was not single motherhood: the issue was the absence of fathers. As you recall . . . I talk about mocking the importance of fathers. And that's what I really didn't like about the show. There was no father. The message was that fathers need not be involved; fathers can just be irresponsible; fathers can go ahead and have children, but they don't have to raise the children."[3] Barack

Obama made the exact same point in his Father's Day speech in June 2007 and was heralded as a cultural hero, though the hypocrisy of his past statements would catch up with him (see chapter 6.)

In addition to being ridiculed by the entertainment industry at the time of his 1992 remarks, the far left-leaning print media such as the *Washington Post* and *The New York Times* came to the defense of their Hollywood comrade, Candace Bergen, and made the vice-president's remarks the lead story in their next-day editions. Quayle did not have to apologize for his remarks as the media seemed to demand at the time, as the former VP explained, "I don't think I'd rephrase it . . . . The subject was the poverty of values, the breakdown of the family."

There existed, however, a more sinister reason for the unusually intense attack against the vice-president by the mutual alliance of the print and broadcast media along with the ongoing jabs by the network entertainment divisions. Lurking in the shadows of the presidential race that year was a man who shared the twisted philosophical bent of the mass media and would soon come to epitomize the very core of corruption, dishonesty, and the intentional neglect of the nation's own security. "Hollywood Bill" would redefine the word sleaze, especially as his relationship with Hollywood was inevitably exposed.

The "poverty of values" as spoken of by former Vice President Dan Quayle is at the very center of the Culture War with Hollywood. The vice-president's remarks would elevate the Culture War at all levels of society, and especially with Hollywood. The eight-second remark would catch the attention of politicians and elected officials across the broad spectrum of government, and Hollywood's political and social agenda would soon receive wider scrutiny than it ever anticipated or wanted.

BOB DOLE EXPOSES "SLIME WARNER"

If the vice-president of the United States ignited the conscience of Washington in 1992 with the "Poverty of Values" speech, Senator Bob Dole launched a major firestorm in 1995 that set the benchmark for America's growing outrage with the Hollywood poison-culture factories. In a series of events from June through September, Senator Dole would expose certain executive level entertainment industry leaders who were, and still are, the major manufacturers of slime in the guise of entertainment.

Bob Dole would be the Republican presidential contender challenging first term President Bill Clinton's bid for re-election. It was common knowledge by 1995 that the entertainment industry had largely backed Bill Clinton and was poised to lend even greater support for the star-struck president. According to the Center for Responsive Politics, of all contributions ranked by industry, "One group that clearly preferred [President Clinton] to his Republican challenger was the entertainment industry."[4] Clinton had to play "good cop/bad cop" on occasion when public disgust demanded it, but the industry knew that Clinton was in their collective pocket and they were preparing to renew the contract as millions of dollars would pour in for him and the Democratic Party in general.

Because President Clinton's position on cultural issues was never really known, due to his nature of duplicity and lying, Bob Dole saw an opportunity to latch onto the Culture War and take a stand on Hollywood's moral compass. The Culture War that had been percolating just beneath the surface would soon explode into an all-out assault from Senator Dole. This move by Dole could clearly be considered as the long-awaited counter-attack against the silent declaration of war by Jack Valenti on November 1, 1968.

"Bob Dole's Broadside against Sex and Violence in Popular Culture Sets Off a Furious Debate on Responsibility" blared the headlines in the June 12, 1995 issue of *Time*. "The Right Takes a Media Giant to Political Task" screamed the *Newsweek* headlines on the same day. In the Time article, writer Richard Lacayo confirmed the increased intensity of the Culture War by observing, "it's a safe bet that Campaign '96 will also be Murphy Brown II, a further chapter of the conservative assault on Hollywood that Quayle launched in 1992."[5]

The Associated Press headline was short and to the point, "Dole Raps Hollywood Deviancy." The industry that was once beloved around the world was now being widely labeled as "deviant," which would also explain its enthusiastic political support for someone who shared their values.

At a Los Angeles fundraiser in the entertainment industry's own backyard in June 1995, Bob Dole was joined by former Secretary of Education William Bennett when the two singled out media giant Time-Warner as the leading purveyor of "filth" in movies and music, citing in particular Warner's gangsta rap and its "violent and misogynistic" lyrics. Dole and Bennett had been picking up steam for the full-blown attack on the company now dubbed "Slime-Warner" after Bennett read an article in a March 1995 issue of *U.S. News and World Report* by former *Time* editor John Leo, an unapologetic journalist of moral integrity rarely seen in today's major print and broadcast media. In the article, Leo wrote, "Time-Warner is our leading cultural polluter."[6]

By the time Dole appeared at the fundraiser, his remarks took a sharp and decidedly pointed tone. Touching on topics in entertainment culture that have transcended party lines, Dole asked, "Is this what you intended to accomplish with your careers?" And further aiming his remarks at Time-Warner executives, Dole made the all-important point about the deeper nature of the Culture War with Hollywood. "You have sold your souls, but must you debase our nation and threaten our children as well?"[7]

Dole continued with the broader accusation that all of Hollywood was flooding the nation with "nightmares of depravity." The call to arms should not have been the only wake-up call for Time-Warner. At the time of Dole's speech, the major entertainment conglomerate was over $17 billion in debt.[8] That's "b" for billions. Obviously, soul-selling and debasing the nation had not proven very popular or profitable. Among the movies singled out by Dole was Oliver Stone's 1994 *Natural Born Killers*, a nightmarish blood-fest that spawned a series of copycat killings in the United States and Europe.

Time-Warner was shocked that it had been singled out as a slime factory. Michael Fuchs, head of the Warner Music Group, said, "We can't recall such a personalized, ad hominem attack on a single corporation."[9] And that statement only proved that he had been out of touch with the rest of the country, as is common among Hollywood execs and creative "trolls."

In a Time poll conducted by Yankelovich Partners during the same week as Dole's opening salvo, seventy-seven percent of those questioned said that they were "concerned" or "fairly concerned" about violence in the media; seventy percent said the same about media representations of sex.[10]

And if then Time-Warner Chairman Gerald Levin had his hands full with the Dole attack, it was Fuchs who was taking a large portion of the heat. Just two weeks earlier, William Bennett as head of Empower America and author of the best-selling *Book of Virtues* had teamed up with C. Delores Tucker, leader of the National Political Congress of Black Women, and brought their campaign against raunchy and gutter hip-hop/rap lyrics to the Time-Warner shareholder's meeting at New York's City Center.

The events that would unfold over the next four months would be a major victory, though limited, in the rapidly escalating Culture War. During the meeting, Tucker rose from her seat in the audience and delivered a seventeen-minute speech that pointedly attacked the extremely violent and misogynistic lyrics in songs recorded and performed by Time-Warner performers. The term "musicians" would be a stretch. Among the songs Tucker quoted were brutal lyrics from the now-deceased Tupac Shakur and Snoop Doggy Dog, now known simply as "Snoop Dog." (Hip-hop/rap artists are constantly in a state of identity crisis.)

After Tucker's dressing down of Time-Warner officials, a large portion of the packed audience rose to their feet in applause, including the son of Time's founder, Henry Luce III. After the shareholders' meeting, Levin and Fuchs hastily called together a meeting of company executives with Tucker and Bennett. Ms. Tucker asked that one of the Time-Warner execs read aloud the lyrics of "Big Man with a Gun" by the occult rock group Nine-Inch Nails. A sample from the song: "Maybe I'll put a hole in your head/You know, just for the f____ of it."

When company officials refused her request, she angrily walked out of the room. Bennett bluntly confronted Levin and Fuchs, asking, "Are you folks morally disabled?" When Time-Warner execs tried comparing rap to the phenomenon of Elvis, and Levin even recited the Hollywood line "art is hard to interpret," Bennett simply replied, "Baloney." And to that, Levin stalked out of the room.[11]

There would be no need for follow-up meetings. Tucker and Bennett had made their point. Bennett said later, "I was impressed with their lack of candor. It was extremely pompous. Here were these guys in four-thousand-dollar suits making us feel like we were lucky to be getting the time of day."[12]

Ms. Tucker told *Newsweek* after the meeting, "African-American women got tired of their children calling them 'hos, bitches, and sluts.'"[13] Levin had used the "art is hard to interpret" line earlier in the year when trying, in vain, to defend the violence-inciting gutter lyrics of Ice-T's "Cop Killer." But Levin's defense of their musicians' artistic freedom would no longer hold muster against an onslaught by the public and even many on Time-Warner's Board of Directors. Several board members, including Luce, former U.S. Trade Representative Carla Hills, and former baseball commissioner Fay Vincent agreed with Bennett's concerns and called a private meeting to express them to Levin.

Because Hollywood decisions are based often on fear and fear alone, it would be inevitable that Time-Warner would sell off its 50% share of Interscope Records, which became official in September 1995. But Time-Warner's fear was not so much about public backlash as it was about losing a "revenue stream" to a competing studio that would pick up the recording entity and reap millions.

Death Row Records, a producer/distributor under the Interscope umbrella, would have to find a new suitor for its hip-hop/rap trash heap. Death Row, an appropriate name for an offensive little recording label headed up by the foul-mouthed gun-toting convict thug Suge Knight, was showing interest in joining up with independent Priority Records, which distributed such groups as N. W. A. (Niggas With an Attitude). Interscope itself is now under Universal's corporate kingdom where it continues to generate a "revenue stream" of filthy sewage sometimes called music.

Dole, Bennett, and Tucker scored a victory, however brief, in at least exposing the record industry's agenda of enslaving generations of young, impressionable kids with a music that glorifies murder as "outlaw cool." The tragic truth is that hip-hop/rap is more a New Age religion than a style of music, and was originally foisted on urban youth by a rapper named Afrika Bambaataa in the 1970s.

Ironically, a few years before the Time-Warner debacle, Geffen Records, formerly affiliated with Time-Warner, decided not to distribute the Geto Boys because its lyrics praised the mutilation of women and engaging in sex with dead bodies of rotted flesh. The album was quickly picked up by another label, which also just so happened to be affiliated with Time-Warner. It was literally a "horizontal move."

As Time-Warner board member Henry Luce III noted accurately, "Some of us have known for many, many years that the freedoms under the First Amendment are not totally unlimited."[14] There are numerous First Amendment court cases that back up Luce's statement and are documented on a regular basis by New York-based Morality in Media.[15]

Richard Lacayo of *Time* magazine also pointed out the noteworthy distinction that "the First Amendment applies only to attempts by government to restrain expression. It says nothing about the decisions made by private media companies, and it does nothing to prevent them from choosing which songs or programs they will or will not promote. [In the 1980s] Simon & Schuster cancelled plans to publish *American Psycho*, the sado-chic novel by Bret Easton Ellis, after advance complaints about passages detailing the sexual torture and mutilation of women."

Martin Davis, then chairman of Simon & Schuster's corporate parent Paramount said, "It's our responsibility . . . . You have to stand for something."[16] As Lacayo noted, "This is just the sort of thing Dole [had] in mind: restraint on the part of producers and distributors."[17] And Davis continued, "I'm just saying sometimes you have to have corporate responsibility and remember the impact on children."[18] How often do you hear that from Hollywood?

Ultimately, Bob Dole would be fighting an uphill battle against President Clinton's re-election bid. With the Dick Morris strategy of "triangulation" Bill Clinton had learned to steal the agenda of any issue from his opponent if the polls showed a certain issue clearly held by the "enemy" camp. A better name for this strategy would have been "tristrangulation."

Unlike Bob Dole and Paramount's Martin Davis, Bill Clinton had no interest in "the impact on children" except at election time, after which he would cozy back up to Jack Valenti, who also held a private disdain for children and even their parents when he abolished the Production Code and handed the keys to the gates of hell over to Mom and Dad, in effect telling them, "*You* are now the gatekeepers."

Lacayo gives a brilliant synopsis about the effect of Big Media and giant entertainment conglomerates whose cross-section of perverse "creativity" intersect at America's Main Street. "Whatever is scabrous and saw-toothed and in-your-face is probably brought to you by the major labels and the big studios. For parents, the pervasive electronic culture can start to look like some suspect stranger who hangs around their kids too much, acting loutish, rude, and drunk."[19]

THE APPROPRIATIONS "BILL": VALUES FOR VOTES

Unfortunately for Dole, President Bill Clinton was already stealing the "values" platform early in 1995 when he gave a token slap on the wrist to Hollywood at the January State of the Union Speech. In one of the longest State of the Union speeches in recent history, Clinton devoted a one-sentence "plea" for Hollywood to "assess the impact of your work and understand the damage that comes from the incessant, repetitive, mindless violence that permeates our media all the time." Of course, no mention of "incessant" sex or profanity given his strong proclivity to both.

The strategy of "value theft" for short-term political goals was noted by Lacayo at *Time*. "Media company executives contributed heavily to Clinton's 1996 campaign and to Democratic coffers generally in 1994's congressional election. Even so, the Democrats appreciate the potential power of the cultural pollution issue and [hoped] to position themselves prominently before Republicans got a lock on it."[20]

Even First Lady Hillary Clinton, equally noted for her political hypocrisy, made the afternoon talk show circuit, a venue she had used infrequently to utter muted denunciations of Hollywood vulgarity. But when Dole placed the issue front and center, she pumped up the volume on media responsibility, especially on *Oprah*. Like her husband, she adopted the "tristrangulation" appropriation of the Republican platform.

Of course, everybody in Hollywood knew that neither she nor hubby "Hollywood Bill" were serious. Ten years later in April 2006, Tinseltown stars such as Cher, Billy Crystal, Jennifer Lopez, John Fogerty, and other celebrities gathered to raise one million dollars for Senator Hillary Clinton's re-election as senator from New York—or to a possible bid for President. Many of these celebrities knew that Hillary was devious and deceptive, if not more so than husband Bill. Her book *It Takes a Village* was actually written by author Barbara Feinman, whose contract stipulated a payment of $120,000 and an acknowledgement of Feinman's contribution to the book. Hillary Clinton reneged once the book was out, paying only $90,000 and giving Feinman *no credit whatsoever*.

Then President Clinton pushed Vice-President Gore out to step up the rhetoric against Hollywood in order to diminish Dole. As he told *Time* magazine in 1995, "Some of the decisions made by executives in the entertainment industry, the advertising industry, the creative community, have been obscene and atrocious."[21] (Of course, Hollywood knew he was grandstanding, especially when over 100 celebrities and twenty major entertainment companies later contributed to his failed 2000 bid for president. See Appendix II.)

The celebrity contributions listed in Chapter 4's "Honey Money List" for Clinton's campaign against Dole represent a cross-section of Hollywood's vast lunatic fringe. Some are very accomplished actors, producers, and directors. But almost all represent an irrational worldview that supports and aggressively promotes demoralizing behavior and vacant values.

It was only natural that the "entertainers" would have no problem supporting President Clinton for a second term; a man whose heart of darkness was greater than their own; a man being re-evaluated even now by the *new* media as the most corrupt president in the history of the United States, even as candidate Hillary flaunted him on the 2008 campaign trail as an "asset." Many of the Hollywood supporters were from the same left wing of the boomer generation, and they were ecstatic that America had elected the first dope-smoking, draft-dodging, post-hippie president.* The mutual love affair between the Clinton presidency and Hollywood was also due to Clinton being fully smitten and in full enamor of a false Hollywood glamour.

By the 1996 election between Clinton and Dole, it was common knowledge among even the casual observer of national politics that President Clinton had brought to the presidency a continuous legacy of his disdain for deeply held traditional American values, hatred of the military and the intelligence community, and lax unprofessional leadership. Couple that with his reckless personal life of flagrant adultery, habitual and continuous sexual harassment of women, long shadows of fraudulent land deals along with Hillary, and the extension of a "Clinton Machine" of close associates who spend their every waking hour targeting perceived enemies within the Democratic and Republican parties by waging vicious smear and slander campaigns of a personal and professional nature. Even as you read this book, the Clinton Machine is active in "opposition research" by destroying someone's life in order to continue exerting influence over American politics.

By Hollywood supporting a president whose past and present behavior was a poorly kept secret, Hollywood was sending a message that it endorsed Bill Clinton's behavior as much as his public policies, which few could actually identify if asked. More ominous was the Hollywood endorsement of an "eyes wide shut" foreign policy that ignored foreign threats coming to roost on American soil when the first bombing of the Word Trade Center was dismissed as a "criminal act."

A vote for Clinton was also an endorsement of Clinton's deconstruction of America as a superpower willing to engage or intervene in situations of urgent international crisis such as the 1994 genocide in Rwanda where one million people were slaughtered in fewer then 100 days. Samantha Power of *The Atlantic Online* wrote, "As the terror in Rwanda unfolded, Clinton had shown virtually no interest in stopping the genocide and his administration stood by as the death toll rose into the hundreds of thousands."[22]

Clinton visited Rwanda in 1998 and "apologized." He wanted to show he really did "care," much like his subsequent apology for slavery. As Power noted, with 10,000 people a day perishing under clubs and machetes, the Clinton administration was faced with a situation "to decide or to decide not to decide."[23] Clinton chose the latter.

"To decide not to decide" and a national security policy of "continuous inactive action" would return to haunt Bill Clinton in his second term with

---

* *This book differentiates between "post-hippie" and "ex-hippie." A "post-hippie" is still the reckless, rootless, wandering flower-child of the New Age whose only concession is shorter hair and conventional dress. An "ex-hippie" has renounced the destructive generational philosophies of that era.*

ramifications still reverberating to this day. This is the Bill Clinton that Hollywood supported again; a man after their own heart.

In August 1998, the Center for Security Policy reflected on the waning days of the Clinton administration. "History appears increasingly likely to remember the Clinton presidency as an era in which the world's only superpower lost its grip, . . . the international environment of Pax-Americana he inherited has given way to what one might characterize as 'Pack Up Americans.'"[24]

While Bob Dole lost the election, his full-scale assault on the entertainment industry exposed the Hollywood poison—word by word, scene by scene—to parents across America who were clueless as to the "nightmares of depravity" being sold to their children.

Some readers may ask why it is necessary to dissect the Clinton administration and its intersect with Hollywood. It is extremely important to reveal the results of America's first mutual admiration society between a corrupt, ruthless president and an entertainment industry that is out of control and promotes an agenda of value manipulation. The casualties resulting from this dangerous intersection need to be discussed so that the damage to the culture and to the very security of the American people will not be repeated.

The Clinton years were representative of the darkest days of United States international relations, and a sword in the prestige, honor, and stature of the office of the presidency itself.

As commentator and editor Richard John Neuhaus stated the issue best in 1999, "Ronald Reagan started in Hollywood and lived it down by living up to the presidency. Bill Clinton's achievement is to be accepted by a Hollywood responsible for a meretricious popular culture to which he has defined down the presidency."[25]

CHAPTER 4

"Hollywood Bill"

> *What a sad, pathetic man Bill Clinton is.*
> —Michael Moore, 1999

THE CAUTIONARY TALE:

A CLOSE ENCOUNTER OF THE FIRST KIND

My first and only encounter with Bill Clinton was by way of introduction through a mutual friend. It was brief, conversational, ultimately unsettling and bizarre—much like watching a short film with a distinctly obtuse worldview.

The setting was a Hollywood party at a Los Angeles hotel in 1987 hosted by an economic development authority of the State of Arkansas to promote locations for filmmakers to shoot their movies. The double-set of upper-floor suites was crammed with representatives from the state and local governments and a heavy presence from producers, directors, and actors who had filmed in Arkansas in the past and those who were considering doing so in the future.

The Hollywood types were easy to spot. Black was in from head to toe. For women, the cleavage descended to the navel. The men were sporting pony tails and three days growth of beards. I often believed the men used a special razor attachment that allowed them to constantly look three days late for a shave—the Yasser Arafat look. I knew many of them, and many of them I didn't want to know.

I spoke briefly with future Clinton hatchet man Harry Thomason and his producer wife, Linda Bloodworth Thomason of *Designing Women*. I told my friend that I had to leave and apologized for missing the "opportunity" to meet the governor. Just as I was stepping into the hall, Governor Clinton was on his way in, shaking hands and slapping backs with people trickling out into the hallway from the other entrance to the suite.

"Governor," my friend interrupted, "This is Michael Boyer from the Alabama Film Commission." I was almost as tall as Clinton, though I counted at least two of his inches in height to "high hair."

"Yes, Mike, . . . Great. Good to see you. What movies you shooting down there in Alabama?"

"Well, Governor, we're in preproduction for the last segment of *War and Remembrance*, but we recently wrapped on a little gangster film with Scott Glenn and Barbara Stock."

"Barbara Stock! Yeah, yeah . . . She's hot!" Clinton lit up, nodding to some Arkansas side-kick with a leisure suit and cowboy hat. "You should tell her to come on over."

"Well," I said with a laugh, somewhat surprised, "I have no idea where she is. That was a few months ago and—"

"She's always welcome over here." Clinton smiled broadly as my friend just rolled her eyes.

Before I could thank him for his hospitality, a staffer holding a walkie-talkie tugged at Clinton's coat, and he bent down as the young man whispered into his ear and pointed to another apparent staffer leaning against the wall behind him. Clinton spun around and put his left hand on the staffer's shoulder and with his right index finger began poking the young man in the chest repeatedly, as if to emphasize some mistake the young man had made.

Clinton let go of his shoulder grip and the embarrassed staffer rushed down the hall toward the elevator. Without missing a beat, Clinton turned on his broad smile and began shaking hands with an elderly couple waiting patiently for the chastisement to end, as though they had seen it all before.

I waved a quick good-bye to my friend as she turned back into the party, shaking her head. "She's a Brick House" was blaring from a boom-box inside the suite.

Pressing the button for the elevator, I was eager to get out of there. Pushing an elevator button three or four times has no effect on the arrival of the elevator. From the corner of my eye, I noticed the bearded cowboy with the old tan leisure suit walking toward me.

"Hey, buddy," he called with a beer in hand. "Buddy, how 'bout calling that pretty lady and invitin' her over to the party?"

I couldn't help but chuckle at the entire series of events that came cascading down on me in a period of five short minutes.

"Look, I really don't know where she is. I'm not a good friend of hers, and I only met her on the set a few times."

"I bet you could find her if you had to." He grinned with a final swig of the beer from a can he crumpled and tossed in the ashtray. I had the feeling he really wanted to meet her, or her best friend, or any woman with a set of large breasts and two legs.

"Sir, I really don't think you will have any problem meeting some pretty woman tonight. There's more beautiful women at that party down the hall than I have ever seen in one place at one time, ever!"

"Me? No, no, . . . I've got me a sweetie. I'm talkin' 'bout the governor. Didn't you hear him? He said she's welcome anytime. That means now! You know what I mean, . . . buddy?"

Fortunately, the elevator door opened and I stepped in—quickly—feeling a little unsettled. The door seemed frozen, probably because I kept jamming the "Down" button like a woodpecker.

The Clinton "sidekick" just stared at me and smiled.

"Listen," I said. "There's plenty of women in that room. He won't have any problem whatsoever . . . I'm sure . . . absolutely." And the door finally closed as I was running out of "running away" words.

* * *

At the Beverly Hills Hilton the next afternoon, I saw my Arkansas friend after the last meeting sponsored by the Association of Film Commissioners International (AFCI). We sat in the lobby to take a break before a group of us were to board a bus for an even bigger bash sponsored by Hollywood's new super-duo producers, and blood cousins, Menahem Golan and Yoram Globus of Cannon Films.

At this point I need to refer to my friend by her alias, Candace Roberts. She, like so many middle-level bureaucrats in Arkansas state government, had been threatened and intimidated for not doing the governor's "bidding" when it came to filling certain government personnel contracts. She remains in hiding to this day to avoid harassment from the current reincarnation of the Clinton Machine and its loose-knit web of George Soros funded smear merchants.

"Are you ready for a party of 3,000 people at MGM's biggest soundstage?" Candace asked, resting her head against the back of the overstuffed lobby chair.

"Anything has to be a welcome relief from that nightmare party you had last night," I said with a laugh. "I have to admit I wasn't real impressed with your governor. He seems like a smooth-talking letch."

"Michael, that's probably the nicest description I've heard about my boss in a long time. He'd consider that a compliment."

"So, I take it he's not popular back home."

"Oh, he's popular, don't get me wrong. You either love him or you hate him. But those who hate him are 'handled' quickly. So we all work and live under this uneasy consensus."

"Candace, when you say 'handled,' what exactly does that mean?"

"The Mud Room!" Candace said, laughing as she sat up and slapped her hands on her knees. "You mean you haven't heard about the Mud Room?"

"No. Never have. I'm sure you're going to tell me about it."

"Yes, I am!" She laughed again, this time slapping my knees. She was a good 'ol girl—and a feisty one—no nonsense honesty in a world of, in her words, "liars, whores, and thieves." Or, LWTs as she liked to call "them."

"You see, Michael, there's a FOB [Friend of Bill] who works full-time in this tiny little office in the basement of the state capitol with nothing more than an old desk-top computer full of dirt."

"Dirt?"

"You know. DIRT. MUD. Smear material. If anyone criticizes the governor, this guy will punch in their name. If there's no dirt on that person, they'll just make it up, issue a press release, and start a whisper campaign. A friendly newspaper prints the story, and the person's life is ruined. One, two, three, easy as do-re-mi, don't you see?" Candace was laughing so hard, she wrapped her arms around her ribs.

"Good gracious, Candace. Can't somebody get to the state Ethics Commission, or take it to the national press?"

"The Ethics Commission? You think they don't already know? Who wants their careers ruined by a phony whisper campaign or a professional mud machine? And the national press? They all have stringers or free-lance correspondents in Little Rock. They know what's going on. The problem is they all like the guy. They think he's going to be president one day and they want to go along for the ride." Candace sat back. "It's another world, like nothing I've ever seen."

"Be careful, Candace. Maybe it's best not to say anything, or somebody's going to make 'Cotton Candy' out of you. You don't seem too shy about telling the truth—which is good—but seems to me that could cause you trouble back in Little Rock."

"I really don't care, Michael. I'm already on their s____t list. No, let me clarify that. I'm on *his* s____t list. I'm sure they're cutting and pasting in the Mud Room as we speak."

"He didn't make a pass at you, did he?" I was certain that was the case, if the night before was any indication of the "brilliant young governor" from Arkansas. After all, Candace was a very beautiful woman, bright—and gutsy. I could hear an echo of Clinton's voice from the night before, "Yeah, yeah . . . . She's hot!"

"Oh, no! He knows better than that. I'd kick his ass across the river into Mississippi. I'm not a push-over like *all the other women* who fear for their jobs, or their reputations—what's left of them."

Needless to say, Candace was a gem and a genuine person who was not afraid of "The Machine." She was also a department director within Arkansas state government, a position of vulnerability where special political favors were often expected to be fulfilled at the risk of being fired for those who did not "obey."

"I know exactly why I'm on the list," Candace said, kicking her feet up on the glass coffee table. "One of Clinton's cronies told me that I needed to hire a *certain* person for my department and I said, 'I don't need anybody in my department.' The crony was blown away, telling me, 'But the governor insists.' I told him to keep on insistin', she wasn't qualified in the least."

"Who was she?"

"Some former bimbo weather girl turned nightclub singer."

"That's perfect," I said with a laugh. "That's exactly who you need in your office. Was she anybody you knew?"

"Oh, everybody in Little Rock knows Gennifer Flowers—lots of hair and hot air. She sings at the club where Clinton goes when he's in the mood to play the sax. And everybody knows he's boffing her, and has been for years."

"Boffing?"

"You know, . . . boffing!" Candace made a rather unique gesture interlocking her hands high above her head, which peaked the interest of the front desk clerk and the bellhop.

"Okay, Candace, I understand. Put your hands down." I began rubbing my temples. My head was throbbing. "It's a good thing the governor's not married. He'd really be in hot water."

"Not married?" Again she laughed. "Are you kidding? He's married to Dragon Lady Number One."

"What's that all about?"

"Nobody knows and nobody cares, Michael. I've pretty much figured it out. They have some kind of 'understanding' just beneath the surface of their 'love-hate' relationship. She's into power and he's into sex. That's what it's all about, Michael."

"Incredible . . . . But now you're pulling my leg."

"I'm serious. He can mess around all he wants as long as she pulls the strings on the 'big-ticket' political issues. Look, Bill Clinton is an old hippie, you know, one of those kind who just came along to smoke the dope and get the chicks. The only reason he became attorney general was to get the chicks. The only reason he became governor was to get *better* chicks. If he ever becomes president, it's only because he wants the *Hollywood* chicks. It's all about sex, power, and Hollywood."

I looked at my watch and realized it was getting late. And I had heard more than I really wanted to know. But I did have one more question.

"Okay, back to the 'bimbo.' I guess you had to hire her?"

"Not just no! But Hell no! That's why I'm on the list, percolating somewhere inside the Mud Room's computer. They just don't know when, or if, to make a move. Clinton's not giving up. He must owe her big time for all the boffing."

"But, Candace, how do you really know he's out to get you? Maybe he respects the fact that you didn't hire her in spite of looming retribution."

THE HOLLYWOOD CULTURE WAR

"Michael, you're making the all-too-kind assumption that he's a gentleman. Let me make it clear—he's a *whore*, nothing *more*. He personally let me know that I should, and I better hire Ms. Airhead."

"How so?"

"I was at a charity fundraiser at the governor's mansion, and everybody was lined up to shake his hand, and Hillary was right there beside him. When I put out my little hand, he grabbed it and started pumping it like an old cistern handle on momma's back porch. That's when he put on this 'evil eye' and said, 'Candace, I-understand-we-have-a-problem-in-your-department!' I looked over his shoulder, and Hillary was just zoned out, shaking hands with people who maneuvered around so as not to disturb his temper tantrum. She could hear him."

"And you said? . . ."

"First, I lifted my left hand over to pry his dirty crooked fingers off my right hand and said, very politely, 'Why, no, sir, there's no problem whatsoever,' and I walked right past Hillary on my way to the cheese sticks."

I must have looked a little deflated and speechless as Candace jumped up and gathered her purse to leave. Our shuttle would be pulling up in ten minutes.

"Don't let it get you down, Michael," Candace said with a smile. "There are bigger things in the world to worry about, like, well, how 'bout 'Bill Clinton, President of the United States of America.' That's when we're ALL going to be in trouble."

Candace tousled my hair as she walked away, laughing. "Ain't that right . . . good buddy?"

Candace was the last of the truly beautiful independently gutsy women who could genuinely be called "Southern," the likes of which had faded into memory by the 1990s as the internet, cable TV, and glossy periodicals had homogenized women into variations of Jennifer Anniston hair, olive-drab clothes, and paper personalities.

After that night I never saw Candace Roberts again, though she did stay in touch by phone for a few years. By 1994 she had already fled Arkansas and was living "somewhere east of the Mississippi" as she would say. Candace Roberts had, in fact, been harassed endlessly by anonymous phone calls that eventually became threatening to the point of finding the "signature warning" of a dead mockingbird on her front doorstep—on three different occasions.

Candace was an honest, tireless, good person with a straightforward, if somewhat colorful vocabulary. If Bill Clinton had appreciated the good, hardworking people that orbited just outside his jaded galaxy, his legacy may have been very different today. And he might have actually been a good president surrounded by good people, without axes to grind or mud to smear. But that was not to be the case.

On the night of Bill Clinton's election as president, there was a message left on my home answering machine.

"I told you so . . . . Now you know."

For a brief second, I caught one last sound of that rapid-fire, machine-gun laughter just before Candace hung up. Wherever she was "east of the Mississippi," she had to be better off than that suffocating pressure cooker she had been living under for so long.[1]

STAGE LEFT: CLINTON ENTERS THE CULTURE WAR

The year 1992 was a perfect time for Bill Clinton to run for president, especially considering the multiple "hot-button" issues that signaled the beginning of a new phase in the Culture War as we now know it today. The Murphy Brown/Dan Quayle confrontation had demonstrated a sharp split among viewers of entertainment, just as the Bob Dole/Slime-Warner showdown during the 1995 election would later testify.

Vice-President Quayle and Senator Bob Dole, had struck a notable chord among a growing segment of the American audience that strongly believed the entertainment industry was increasingly and aggressively pushing their private social/sexual/political agenda on the silver screen and television. Many Americans found the "free screen" philosophy of Jack Valenti as a distinctly troubling phenomenon.

Also notable earlier in the year, on February 1, 1992, Cardinal Roger Mahoney of the Archdiocese of Los Angeles gave a speech to an anti-pornography group at the Hollywood Roosevelt Hotel in which he delivered the following statement: "Perhaps the time is ripe for the entertainment industry to consider the advisability of having such a code,"[2] referring to efforts by Dr. Ted Baehr's Atlanta-based Christian Film and Television Commission to update and revise the Production Code that Jack Valenti had destroyed twenty-four years earlier.

Though Cardinal Mahoney didn't pronounce an official endorsement of any such effort, the very mention of "The Code" sent shock waves through the movie industry as entertainment rags such as *Variety* screamed in horror. But the mere mention of such a grand resurrection of a Golden Era institution spread debate across America. Clinton took note of both sides' reaction to the Cardinal's speech, just as he also weighed the reaction to Vice-President Quayle's statement on Murphy Brown.

The position of standards, values, morality, and character were not Clinton's values, but in a tight race for the presidency against sitting president George Herbert Walker Bush, Clinton would appropriate these issues as his own—temporarily and certainly without true conviction.

With Bill Clinton's election and inauguration, the dark underside of the chameleon president would start to show with such patronizing and disingenuous statements such as his *TV Guide* interview in November 1992. "The cumulative impact of the banalization of sex and violence in the popular culture is a net negative for America," Clinton proclaimed in a statement he could not possibly have written himself, and continued, "I think the question is, what can Hollywood do, not just to entertain, but to raise the human spirit?"[3]

What few people realized was that Clinton began voicing, practically verbatim, from Will Hays's own pronouncements in introducing the Production Code in 1930. Clinton's *TV Guide* statement also sounded very much like good friend Jack Valenti's plea to the industry in 1993 when he "passionately" urged Hollywood to start making movies with "less violence, less sensuality, and less raunchy language."[4] Of course, as we all know in hindsight, neither Clinton nor Valenti believed in their lofty pronouncements. It was all expedient theatrical politics for the moment.

Clinton's seemingly profound question, "What can Hollywood do, not just to entertain, but to raise the human spirit," was addressed in the early working elements of the Production Code of 1930. "Motion picture producers recognize the high trust and confidence which have been placed in them by the people of the world. They recognize their responsibility to the public because entertainment and art are important influences in the life of a nation." (See Appendix III).

As we now know all too well, Jack Valenti "freed" the producers from that "high trust and confidence" that enslaved them by "the people of the world." And then he couldn't understand why half the moviegoing audience disappeared twelve months later.

The underlying purpose of the Production Code, which Clinton was trying to echo but definitely not instill, was probably best summarized again by the fundamental statement in the Production Code's introduction, "No picture shall be produced which will lower the moral standards of those who see it."

But Clinton always counted on voter ignorance of certain issues that allowed him to appropriate (read: steal) the conservative leaning values of the swing voters. In 1980, Ronald Reagan's campaign strategists were the first to recognize the twenty percent "swing" vote; voters who often make up their minds in the final days leading up to the election. Reagan could count on a majority of that swing vote by simply standing on what he firmly believed, issues such as national security and positive moral values.

Because values, morality, and character are not monopolized by either party, but actually share a rare bipartisan consensus among the swing voters, Clinton could easily claim the high moral ground in the 1992 election, even though he embraced and lived in the low moral dust. This deception would not be fully realized by the swing voters until after Clinton's second term when the president began to flagrantly reveal his true colors as he spun out of control on both issues of values and national security.

According to the Progressive Review, many of Clinton's scandals, pathological lying, and aberrant behavior began during his years as a public office holder in

Arkansas and "the number of criminals with whom he associated before entering the White House."[5] That none of this was made widely public may be attributed to the fact that the majority of news media executives and individuals identify themselves as liberal or Democratic at the ballot box.

Also, many feminist groups championed by Hollywood were already aware of rumblings concerning Clinton's history of sexual harassment of women in and out of state government in Arkansas but said nothing, even though sexual harassment was and remains one of the key planks in the platform of the feminist movement. (Later in the Clinton presidency's second term when numerous women were coming forward to speak out about their victimization, including one who alleged rape, the press would most often question the motives of the accusers and the feminist groups were conveniently silent.)

It became apparent in the first and second Clinton terms that a mutual support system existed among the liberal press, left-wing organizations, and especially among Hollywood executives and celebrities. A common mantra among this coalition's cocktail party chatter was, "He may be a bastard, but he's *our* bastard."

Of all the secrets the press managed to downplay during Clinton's first run for president, one secret was so well known it became famous as "the best known secret" and managed to squeeze out of the Arkansas gridlock into the national limelight just before the election. "The best known secret" was the alleged long-term sexual affair with Gennifer Flowers. (Or as Candace Roberts described her, "the bimbo former weather-girl turned nightclub singer" who Clinton managed to "boff all the time.")

The CBS News magazine *Sixty Minutes* managed to arrange an interview concerning "the best known secret" that many believed would sink Clinton's chances for election due to the undeniable nature of the accusations. Appearing with wife, Hillary, in a cozy, softly-lit setting, the two sat close together holding hands and managed to put on one of the greatest stage plays ever performed in American political theater.

While never admitting to the affair, Hollywood Bill admitted that things were not always perfect with his marriage to Hillary. But before he could elaborate, a strange thing happened on the way to his network salvation. A strategically misplaced camera light came close to crashing down on Hillary Clinton's head. Husband Bill quickly rushed over to shield her from impending danger, covering her head and hugging her tightly.

The "accident" was not *supposed* to be part of the broadcast segment, but interviewer Steve Kroft felt that the segment would be "enhanced" by showing Bill Clinton's "true affection" for his wife. And in one of the greatest collusions between network news and the Democratic candidate for president, the "accident" was left intact in the interview that aired the following Sunday night.

The broadcast drew major sympathy from the twenty percent swing voters, or should it be said: from the swingers among the voters? A similar adulterous affair caused Democratic favorite Gary Hart to withdraw his run for the presidency in 1987. This redeemed Gary Hart as an honorable man as Clinton chose the road to deception that would mark almost every action and decision, and mainly indecision, of his presidency.

Clinton could thank CBS for his 1992 victory and other Clinton apologists who began to lower the character bar by whispering loudly, "It was only sex." That weak excuse would resurface years later in Clinton's second term as his appetite for sexual harassment drew international disdain when Hollywood Bill attended to issues of the flesh that took precedence over the president's supreme responsibility for the nation's national security; a grim harvest that the U.S. was forced to reap only nine months after he left office. And Hillary, the presidential candidate, promised America that if elected, Hollywood Bill would be a global ambassador to "restore respect for America." She truly believes in SMC (Short Memory Complex).

Knowing that the moniker "Hollywood Bill" was not necessarily an asset in a nation sharply divided over the entertainment industry's eroding content, Clinton tried to distance himself from any Hollywood-driven agenda by erecting a rather thin smoke screen. It was well known that Clinton made many trips to Tinseltown for fundraisers going back to his days as governor.

By 1993 Clinton had moved even closer in his friendship with record producer David Geffen, whose company, Geffen Records, produced some of the most nefarious and foul sounding noise that some mistakenly referred to as "music." He virtually created the suicide sound known as "Grunge" with Kurt Cobain as its poster child, complete with shotgun blast to the head. Geffen also promoted an angrier strain of rap music, lowering the values and standards of young African-Americans while raising the profits of his bank account.

When Clinton and his crew came to Hollywood, Geffen would throw lavish parties and fundraisers. Clinton, sometimes accompanied by Hillary, would stay at one of Geffen's gaudy mansions. And the favor would be returned when Geffen came to Washington, prompting Abraham Lincoln to roll over in his grave as David Geffen rolled over in his bed at the White House.

Geffen had sold his record company two years earlier in 1990 for half a billion dollars to Universal Pictures, headed by Lew Wasserman, considered to be Hollywood's most powerful and influential studio boss, friend to the mob, deal-maker and deal-breaker. Geffen was now the "G" in SKG Dreamworks along with partners Steven Spielberg and Jeffrey Katzenberg. The two would join Geffen at the Clinton fundraisers along with Wasserman, Barry Diller, Calvin Klein, and a large array of left coast entertainment producers, directors, and celebrities. The Hollywood fundraisers would net millions for Clinton and the Democratic Party. Geffen himself was one of Hollywood's single largest contributors to the Democrats.

Clinton was perpetually star-struck and apparently never took those fundraising opportunities to ask Hollywood to "raise the human spirit" as he publicly asked them to do in his *TV Guide* interview. He didn't want to offend his friends who were shoving more money into his campaign pockets than he had ever seen before. Clinton spent most of his breath saying "thank you" and "loved your last picture." After all, this was a "fun-raiser" as much as a "fundraiser."

As for Geffen, he had only recently "come out of the closet" and began proudly promoting homosexuality to the masses. Geffen was also developing a personal vision for America and was not shy about giving policy advice to Clinton.

President Clinton had begun his presidency with a demand to the United States military to end its ban on homosexuals in the armed services. However, Clinton was butting heads with the Joint Chiefs of Staff and other military leaders who believed the existing policy was sound and privately questioned the president's motive and the source of his urgent demand, David Geffen himself.

It would become apparent that the president was placing inordinate priority to issues of sexuality, which would plague him throughout his presidency. The American military commanders knew that they were dealing with a man who was still, basically, a hippie at heart, a draft dodger, a dope smoker, a pacifist, appeaser, with a fervently deep-seated hatred of the military. He was privately viewed as someone soft on national security as he began to gut the intelligence budget.

More frightening to not only the military, but also to the American people, was the sobering realization that Hollywood in general, and David Geffen in particular, could dictate the military policy of the United States. In Clinton's corrupt history of governing, those who pay can play the game of influence. Of course, there was no shortage of this game in national, state, and local politics.

But if David Geffen could dictate the hiring policy of the U.S. military, what were the chances that he could input foreign policy or impact decisions about national security? As the country would learn more acutely in Clinton's second term, everything in the people's government and its sacred assets would be up for sale, including the most secret and advanced nuclear technology intended for America's national security.

Eventually the Clinton administration and the military came to a compromise known as "Don't Ask, Don't Tell." The policy stated that homosexuals previously prevented form joining the armed services could join as long as they didn't "tell" their recruiters or future commanding officers about their sexual orientation, and the military in turn was not to "ask" an individual about his or her sexual orientation. However, those who "told" about their sexual orientation as homosexuals could be expelled from the military. The "Don't Ask, Don't Tell" policy was and remains as a bizarre legacy of Clinton's style of governing, which boils down to "Deciding to decide or deciding not to decide." And in this case, as were most policy dictates of President Clinton, the net effect was "deciding not to decide."

Bill Clinton's preoccupation with self-image, sexual obsessions, and being all things to all people would paralyze his presidency and distract him from his responsibility to protect the American people. Clinton's Hollywood values and his counterculture roots would come together to set the stage for one of the biggest tragedies in American history.

BIRDS OF A FEATHER STICK TOGETHER

President Bill Clinton's "Don't Ask, Don't Tell" policy would firmly brand the tag of "Hollywood Bill" as synonymous with "Slick Willie." Clinton's vague and contradictory value system was at least consistent with the same gainsay values held closely by the California post-hippies who were now running the entertainment industry. Together they represented the growing influence of a secular New Age belief system that continues to wreak havoc on the moral fiber of the nation.

In an article titled "Clinton and the Flower Children," David Limbaugh outlined this shared generational legacy. "What they are most known for is their idealism, love-ins, and nation shaking protests of the Vietnam War. What they ought to be remembered for is their self-indulgent narcissism that eschewed guilt and rejected traditional moral standards or anything else that got in their way of having a good time. The hedonistic culture of the '60s operated under the lofty moral principles that 'if it feels good, do it,' and 'I'm OK, you're OK.' Translation: Ego gratification is the noblest of pursuits, and unbridled tolerance the highest good.

"The problem with this counterculture psychobabble is that it is all based on a number of lies, such as: There are no moral absolutes, and the consequences of one's actions aren't as important as one's intentions. Bill Clinton is the model flower child, the quintessential protester. What a cruel irony that he became president of the nation he resents and commander in chief of the military he loathes . . . . But Clinton reached a new level of perniciousness when he put his own political self-intentions above our national security, above the very safety of our children."[6]

As the first Baby Boomer president, Clinton's self-destructive behavior had much in common with other "Darkside Boomers" in Hollywood, not just David Geffen whose own bizarre personal life may have motivated his proclivity for producing and promoting some of the '80s and '90s most demoralizing "music" and lifestyle behaviors. Harriet Rubin of *USA Today* analyzed some of the more prominent boomer behavior in Hollywood during the very public feud between Disney's former CEO Michael Eisner and his former Number Two Man at Disney, former super-agent Mike Ovitz. Stockholders sued over a severance package in which Ovitz was awarded a golden parachute of $100 million after less than a year on the job.

As Rubin states, it was more than a court battle, these boomers "are in their legacy years, when what matters most to chief executives is how they will be remembered. These are dangerous times for baby-boom leaders and the people and institutions they are entrusted with leading. The big, ego-driven actions they must take before their time in the sun is over are sparking outrageous, even childlike behavior."[7] The actions of left-wing baby-boomer leaders such as Clinton and his Hollywood counterparts involve egos, decimation, and drama, a reflection of the true legacy of their generation.

As Rubin notes, "Being the center of all this personal attention inspires deeds of ego-inflation and violent grandiosity, expressing itself in destructive acts. Throughout their careers, from the streets to the boardrooms, boomers have—true to their name—exalted in destruction. Call them the Ka-boomers."[8]

The public Bill Clinton was a well-rehearsed act of a man pretending to be president. What Clinton also shared with the Hollywood power brokers in private was a penchant for being crude, crass, loud, obnoxious, and manipulative. And manipulating values, as Hollywood was doing, was exactly what Clinton would do again in his re-election bid of 1996.

In order to trump the 1995 attack on Hollywood by Senator Bob Dole, the Republican contender for president, Clinton threw his insincere support behind the Telecommunications Bill adopted by Congress in February 1996. Hollywood Bill called a meeting of major media executives who acknowledged that they were accepting a system to rate televised entertainment programming even though they resisted the idea for years.[9] The Hollywood execs knew that in order to keep their boy president in office for another term, they would have to throw the public a token dog bone to make the whole charade appear as a moral crusade for Clinton.

Clinton even called in his secret admirer and good pal Jack Valenti to appear with him at the White House announcement with an enormous portrait of George Washington looming conspicuously in the background. Ironically, the announcement came almost thirty years to the day in 1966 when Jack Valenti orchestrated the Quiet Conspiracy to destroy the Production Code in favor of his Ratings Scheme.

If the Hollywood community acted reluctant to endorse TV ratings, one wouldn't know it by the celebrity contributions pouring into Clinton's campaign. As Charles Case noted, "the affairs between Hollywood and the Democrats are conducted privately and denied vehemently, as though it were illicit."[10]

President Clinton even stepped out so far as to make the lofty statement that the industry's commitment to TV ratings was tantamount to "handing the remote back to America's parents so that they can pass on their values and protect their children." The only reason children needed "protection" was due to the lurid Hollywood images and dialogue that were now going to be officially sanctioned by yet another "ratings scheme." Television's fall from grace also can be traced to a suspect series of events in the late 1970s and early 1980s involving a federal court and the National Association of Broadcasters. (See Chapter 8, The End of Television)

Hollywood crusader Jack Valenti played "bad cop" to Clinton's "good cop" at the White House press conference. But in the best tradition of Valentiism, he also played "good cop" to the industry's "bad cop" behavior. After all, they paid his million-dollar-plus salary. Initially, the industry opposed ratings preferring to sneak their private agenda into TV programming without a "warning label."

In the early fight by Hollywood against TV ratings, Valenti stated angrily that if the U.S. government made any attempt to interfere with Hollywood's right to produce and televise smut, "We'll be in court in a nanosecond."[11]

The TV Ratings Scheme was ushered in after three years of contentious Hollywood behavior. In 1999, two years after the TV Ratings Scheme became common practice on network and cable television, the Media Research Center's Brent Bozell held a bipartisan press conference with Republican Senator Brownback and then Democratic Senator Lieberman. Bozell gave the television ratings a resounding "F" for Failure.

Just one week before the Clinton-Valenti photo-op with George Washington, Senator Joe Lieberman made the now-famous assessment, "If you put a rating on garbage, it doesn't make it quality television. It's still garbage."[12] (During Senator Lieberman's 2006 bid for re-election, the George Soros Democrats (GSDs) not only dropped their support of Lieberman, they attacked him viciously with Clinton machine-like smears. Lieberman ran as an independent and won handily in November 2006.)

SCHOOL SHOOTINGS MAKE GOOD FUNDRAISERS

By far, the majority of the Baby-Boomer generation, those born between 1948 and 1962, did not represent the radical boomer attitudes of President Clinton and his Hollywood sympathizers. As mentioned earlier, Clinton and the Hollywood boomers came from a left-wing, drug-induced campus climate of perpetual protest. This group even held out a diligent sympathy for Communism as a model for some hazy future utopia.

From the beginning of Bill Clinton's second term as president until its end in 2001, he would begin slipping rapidly from the reality and responsibility of the world's most demanding job. Clinton's post-hippie boomer background put him out of touch with a series of tragic events in the 1998 and 1999 school shootings that exposed Hollywood Bill's cultural hypocrisy in his public and private association with the American entertainment industry.

Hollywood Bill's preoccupation with self, ego, reckless personal behavior, and a calendar growing heavy with investigations surrounding numerous individuals of compromised national security, theft, perjury, and unprecedented sexual harassment would cause his response to school shootings to appear as a blip on the radar screen of the administration's national agenda. Unknown to most Americans, President Clinton would engage in a series of repulsive "opportunities" to raise money for the Democratic Party from the very purveyors of grotesque and malevolent images of violence sold as "entertainment."

HOLLYWOOD BILL'S HONEY MONEY LIST

The Federal Election Commission (FEC) records all donations to candidates for the presidency in amounts of $200 or more. Many entertainment executives and celebrities hide their contributions through Political Action Committees (PACs) and special interest groups. According to Public Disclosure, Inc., these PACs may not always provide full information on their contributors due to a little known "Exception Clause" called "Best Efforts," a loophole in FEC reporting requirements that indicates the following "Sympathetic List" might be significantly longer if Hollywood executives and celebrities insisted on "Best Efforts," a loophole that many have taken advantage of.

CELEBRITY LIST 1: CONTRIBUTIONS TO GROUPS SYMPATHETIC TO BILL CLINTON IN 1996

Roseanne Arnold
Rosanna Arquette
Alec Baldwin
Kim Basinger
Meredith Baxter
Ed Begley
Annette Bening
Tom Berenger
Glenn Close
Tom Cruise
Peter Coyote
Tyne Daly
Rebecca DeMornay
Laura Dern
Danny DeVito
Michael Douglas
Fay Dunaway
Michael Eisner
Shelly Fabares

Lou Gossett Jr.
David Keith
Nicole Kidman
Jack Lemmon
Amy Madigan
Marla Maples
Marsha Mason
Rue McClanahan
Donna Mills
Joanne Woodward Newman
Paul Newman
Leonard Nimoy
Carol O'Connor
Sarah Jessica Parker
Gregory Peck
Sydney Pollock
Robert Redford
Robert Reiner
Jason Robards

Jane Fonda
James Garner
Shelly Hack
Larry Hagman
Woody Harrelson

Tony Roberts
Cybil Shepherd
Mary Steenburgen
Barbara Streisand

CELEBRITY LIST 2: DIRECT CONTRIBUTIONS TO BILL CLINTON IN 1996

Tom Arnold
Chevy Chase
Ted Danson
Marlo Thomas Donahue
Kirk Douglas
Richard Dreyfus
Patrick Duffey
Peter Falk
Sally Field

Jeff Goldblum
Melanie Griffith
Tom Hanks
Joanna Kerns
Mary Stuart Masterson
Jenny McCarthy
Ali McGraw
Rene Russo
Kathleen Turner

CELEBRITY LIST 3: CLINTON DEFENSE FUND 1998-2000

Tony Bennett	$10,000	Cheryl Saban	$10,000
Michael Douglas	$20,000	Robert Shaye	$10,000
David Geffen	$20,000	Betty Warner Sheinbaum	$10,000
Don Henley	$10,000	Paul Simms	$10,000
Robert Johnson	$10,000	Edith Wasserman	$20,000
Jeffrey Katzenburg	$20,000	Lew Wasserman	$20,000
Norman Lear	$10,000	Harvey Weinstein	$20,000
James H. Levin	$10,000	Peg Yorkin	$10,000
Haim Saban	$10,000		

From Public Disclosure, Inc., www.tray.com, 1995-1996

On June 13, 1998, President Clinton made an appearance in Springfield, Oregon, and gave a speech at Thurston High School where, only a few days earlier, a fifteen-year-old student had shot twenty-seven of his fellow classmates, killing two and injuring twenty-five.

Clinton would put on his most solemn face as he told teachers, students, and parents that he "felt their pain," a tired refrain he had used throughout his administration. Clinton cited the pervasive "culture of violence" that had contributed to the shooting at Thurston and other recent shootings at public schools in previous months, including the March 28th shooting in Jonesboro, Arkansas, in which two boys, an eleven-year-old and a thirteen-year-old, had shot and killed four students and one teacher in addition to injuring ten others. The "culture of violence" was also cited by Clinton in a special televised address after the Arkansas shootings.

Clinton ended his somber and hollow speech at Thurston High by suggesting that everybody gathered needed to get together and do "whatever" it takes to end this "culture of violence." Two years earlier, on the day President Clinton signed the 1996 Telecommunications Act into law, the president stated that the new law would give parents the tools and ability to "help them kick the degrading influence of excessive television violence and other inappropriate programming out of their house." Without a doubt, Hollywood Bill knew exactly who was producing the "degrading influence" that crept into American homes twenty-four hours a day.

In less than twenty-four hours he would be meeting with many of them, not to chastise their prostitution of values and perpetration of a "culture of violence," but with his hand out and a broad grin to collect money for the Democratic Party war chest for the upcoming congressional and presidential elections of 2000.

Clinton and his entourage rushed from Thurston High School to board Air Force One at the Springfield airport—next stop: Hollywood! Within hours of departing Air Force One in Los Angeles President Clinton arrived at the sprawling mansion of Lew Wasserman, then Chairman Emeritus of Universal Studios and its many subsidiaries including Geffen Records and the recently acquired Interscope Records, which Bob Dole had successfully kicked out of the "Slime-Warner" orbit in 1996. The two record groups were continuing to spew some of the most violent and hate-filled lyrics ever produced by a major Hollywood studio.

Clinton worked the room of Hollywood movers and shakers including Geffen, Steven Spielberg, Jeffrey Katzenberg, and over one hundred other producers and production executives responsible for "green-lighting" movies that enter the sewer pipe of distribution across America and around the world. Guests reported that Hollywood Bill was in the best of moods, backslapping and laughing with the moguls. When the night was over, the president walked away with over one million dollars for the Democratic Party.

According to one guest present, a producer from Universal, the subject of the school shootings never came up as Clinton expressed enthusiastic interest in the latest films in development and who was "starring" in them. It would be extremely naive to believe that Clinton did not know he was taking money from the very men and women who produced, perpetrated, and promoted the "culture of violence," especially in the case of the Jonesboro shootings.

At a special U.S. Senate committee called to explore the influence of gangsta-rap and other violent music, Jonesboro English teacher Debbie Pelley told the senators present about her observations of student Mitchell Johnson, the thirteen-year-old shooter in Jonesboro. Mitchell's favorite rapper was Tupac Shakur, the Universal-Interscope "artist" who was killed just one year earlier in Las Vegas.

"Mitchell brought this music to school with him, listened to it on the bus, tried listening to it in class . . . . He was far more into this music than anyone else his friends knew," Pelley told the senators. The Jonesboro English teacher had noticed Mitchell's behavior changing in the months just before the shooting. According to Pelley, Mitchell would openly sing along with the lyrics of Tupac Shakur and his hip-hop message about "coming to the school and killing all the kids."

Clinton never pulled his elderly host aside at the Beverly Hills fundraiser and said, "Look, you're almost eighty years old; it's time to grow up and take some responsibility." Clinton had no authority because he had not grown up himself and Hollywood Bill wasn't about to admonish a diabolical old tycoon who was handing over $40,000 on behalf of himself and his wife, Edith. And he certainly wasn't going to deliver the "culture of violence" campaign to a man of David Geffen's low state of debauchery who was anointing Clinton with a $20,000 gift. There was no Mrs. Geffen to match his "gift."

If the timing of the school shootings and Bill Clinton's shameful Hollywood behavior were not repugnant enough, he would prove even more revolting just one year later. On April 20, 1999, two high school students at the affluent Columbine High School in Littleton, Colorado, embarked on a Hollywood-inspired shooting rampage that left thirteen students dead and ended with the shooters, Eric Harris and Dylan Klebold, shooting themselves to death.

Appearing completely ignorant of the hypocritical performance he had played out before a national audience less than a year earlier, President Clinton pulled a less than successful public relations stunt in which he called on the major producers in the entertainment industry (his close friends and contributors) to come to the White House where they would receive a "stern" lecture on the production of irresponsible entertainment flooding out of Tinseltown. Many in the film and music industry failed to show, citing "schedule conflicts" that prevented them for attending. In other words, the guilty stayed home in order to polish their new scripts of unrelenting blood-letting and bodily dismemberment. After all, they bought and paid for this president; what more did he want from them?

On May 18, 1999, President Clinton brought the Columbine school shootings back to the forefront in his weekly radio address. In an article aptly titled "Clinton Nips, but Can't Bite Hollywood Hand," columnist Bruce Sullivan reported, "In his weekly radio address Saturday afternoon, President Clinton admonished the movie industry to curb 'gratuitous violence' in films and television shows."[14]

Clinton added, "There is still too much violence on our nation's screens, large and small." The president also found time to implicitly praise Jack Valenti's Ratings Scheme. Then in an amazing feat of symbolism lost on Hollywood Bill, the president would "fly over America" on his way to Hollywood, where he would appear again, only a few hours after his radio address, at a Beverly Hills fundraiser where Hollywood glitterati pooled together more than two million dollars to help the Democratic Party regain control of Congress and keep the presidency in Democratic hands in 2000. (They lost on both counts.)

The Hollywood fundraiser was held, appropriately, in a gloomy Victorian landmark known as Greystone, a location for movies such as *Witches of Eastwick* and *Ghostbusters II*. The event and its timing were defended heavily by new Universal Studios chief executive Edgar Bronfman Jr., who also headed up the Seagram liquor empire. Bronfman had finally shoved Lew Wasserman aside as Universal's new King of Sludge, overseeing and promoting the theme parks, movies, television, and the music division, which included the hip-hop/rap trash subsidiary of Interscope Records.

Sullivan noted that Bronfman rejected the linking of entertainment violence to the massacre at Columbine High School. But political analyst Sherri Jaffe of the Claremont Institute said, "The reality is that the movie industry understands that there is a valid argument that on-screen violence contributes to childhood violence."[15]

Senate Majority Leader Trent Lott (R-MS) took note of the tacky and morbidly insensitive timing of Clinton's money grab. "This weekend, the Clinton-Gore regime [was] begging for cash from one of the polluters responsible for our nation's moral decline."

The Hollywood extravaganza, Majority 2000, was hosted by the Dreamworks Studio trinity of Steven Spielberg, Jeffrey Katzenberg, and Clinton's military adviser, David Geffen. Approximately one hundred guests paid between $25,000 and $100,000 per couple to rub shoulders with President Hollywood Bill, the very same president who had chastised the entertainment industry earlier the same day for promoting "gratuitous violence" as opposed to the previous year's mantra of the "culture of violence."

Among the attendees were the usual clueless suspects such as Whoopi Goldberg, Meg Ryan, Dennis Quaid, and a smattering of Democratic congressmen such as Senator Dick Gephardt (D-MO) and Senate Minority Leader Tom Daschle (D-SD). As expected, Universal CEO Edgar Bronfman was present and never a word was spoken about Columbine or Interscope Records and the very real possibility of yet another connection between the foul sounds of Universal's recording subsidiary and one of the biggest school massacres in modern U.S. history.

This is largely because the mainstream media suspected the connection but refused to report it so as not to create an "anti-Hollywood hysteria." Because of that oversight, most people to this day have not known the dark and pervasive influence that yet another "bad boy artist" at Universal-Interscope music division had branded in the teenage minds of Eric Harris and Dylan Klebold, in addition to an Oliver Stone cult film by the folks at "Slime-Warner."

THE HOLLYWOOD CULTURE WAR

* * *

By 1999, the news industry had largely "gone Hollywood" due to corporate mergers between movie studios and network television, including their news divisions. This would appear to be a major violation of vertical Sherman Anti-Trust monopolization, but the trend picked up speed during the Clinton years and continued well into the first decade of the twenty-first century.

The soul-selling of the once-proud networks and their news divisions to become mere subsidiaries of Hollywood movie studios was unthinkable only twenty years earlier. Viacom-Paramount now owns and controls CBS. The Disney company had already swallowed ABC and Universal itself would soon be devoured by NBC. An excellent insight into this cross-dressing between entertainment and news is detailed in author James Hirsen's *Hollywood Nation*.

The worst fears of mass media conglomeration came true when *Brill's Content* magazine uncovered a plan by the Disney Company to kill a story set to be aired by ABC News. The controversy centered around a blistering exposé of Disney by Peter and Rochelle Sweitzer, authors of *Disney, The Mouse Betrayed: Greed, Corruption, and Children at Risk*.

The book uncovered, among other things, that Disney World officials had covered up on-site homicides, failed to report numerous sex crimes at the amusement park, and refused to fire a number of Disney employees who were caught peeping on guests in numerous changing room facilities. The book also exposed widespread pedophilia at the park. Former state attorney for Florida, Michael Gibbons, confirmed that the crimes were "enormously underreported." The elusive and bitter former CEO Michael Eisner, architect of Disney's downfall, responded to killing the ABC exposé by saying, "I would prefer ABC not cover Disney."

Despite the media's blinders, the unraveling of the connection between the Columbine killers and Universal-Interscope would be one of the first investigative reports to be undertaken by the new media of the internet, independent journalists, and media researchers. Just as hip-hop and rap music proved to be a murderous influence on Mitchell Johnson, the student shooter of Jonesboro, another Interscope "artist" would be revealed as the most repellent and monstrous individual ever promoted by a major entertainment conglomerate. He would also turn out to be Universal's official Number One Christian Basher from a studio with a long history of religious hatred from Lew Wasserman to Edgar Bronfman to Ron Meyer today. It is no surprise that *The New York Times* reported Universal's domestic box office ranked last out of the six major Hollywood studios in 2007.

A young man named Brian Warner had been influenced by his father who carried around a nude photo of Twiggy in his wallet and took young Brian to rock concerts by Kiss and other blood-drenched cloak-and-dagger bands of the time.

Soon young Brian was listening to Judas Priest, Ozzy Osborne, Black Sabbath, Iron Maiden, Megadeath, and other perverse "Satan Rock" groups that the record industry was pushing on troubled youth during the 1970s and 1980s. This was before hip-hop/rap usurped their core message of "demon devotion."

By the early 1990s, Brian Warner had reinvented himself as a deeply troubled transvestite who now called "himself" Marilyn Manson after Marilyn Monroe and his hero, Charles Manson. The pale, emaciated Manson began as his own record label when he started touring small gigs around the country. Manson would soon tap into disaffected youth around the country with his wickedly perverted stage shows and lyrics that glorified death, murder, sexual perversion, and violent hatred of all things "Christian." Souvenir hackers at concerts venues would sell T-shirts that encouraged "Kill Your Family, Kill Your Friends, Kill Yourself."

Of course, this prompted the bigger and sleazier record producers to take notice of Manson's antics and how they could promote him to a worldwide audience. The following description of a Marilyn Manson concert was well known by executives up and down the ladder at Universal who were planning to sign on new "artists" for the twenty-first century.

Manson would often start off his concerts in a crucifixion posture astride a series of television sets shaped like a cross. As he slid off the electronic crucifix, the television sets would explode as the rest of Manson's transvestite band rushed onto the stage. Often Manson would perform oral sex on one or another of the "trans-rockers" before jumping up to explode into a raunchy diatribe of hate-filled lyrics. While the band played on, Manson would begin to urinate into the open mouths of his submissive guitarists. But the teenage crowd was jealous and demanded more, so Manson turned to the mesmerized fans standing close to the stage with open arms and proceeded to urinate on them.

Things would only get worse, *much worse* than anything imaginable, except for the record promoters lurking in the shadows who saw the events unfolding as only getting *better, much better* in the dark vision of their own jaded imaginations. *Universal will love him*, they concurred.

A garish lectern appears onstage and Manson rises to the pulpit with a Bible in one hand and a painted image of Jesus Christ in the other. As the lights flash red and the noise level reaches fever pitch, Manson tears the Bible in half and throws it to the stage floor. Then, with both hands raised high holding the portrait of Christ, Manson smashes it against the lectern as it, too, falls to the soaked stage floor. Without missing a beat, Manson pulls down his spandex outfit and performs acts of unspeakable desecration certainly not worthy of describing in the text of this book.

As the drug-dazed audience of young teens cheered Manson's debauchery on, the androgynous rocker grabbed the microphone and, in a mock Billy Graham conclusion, asked everyone to come forward and renounce Jesus Christ and accept

Satan as their god. This isn't only a sick stage trick for shock value. Manson was one of the last "celebrities" to join the San Francisco-based Church of Satan before its founder, Anton LeVay, died in 1997.

In an interview for Spin magazine in 1996, Manson stated enthusiastically, "Hopefully, I'll be remembered as the person who brought an end to Christianity."[16]

This was just too good for Interscope Records, who would later sign Manson on as one of their own "discovered artists" with the full approval of the Universal CEO. The world's largest entertainment conglomerate could no longer feign ignorance of their own "talent" and the messages they send. Lew Wasserman had already established a twenty-year record positioning Universal as the number one Christian-bashing studio in Hollywood, with Time-Warner trying eagerly to gain the mantle.

What Lew Wasserman and his successor Edgar Bronfman didn't want the public to know was that the Columbine shooters, Eric Harris and Dylan Klebold, were big fans of Marilyn Manson. What Gerald Levin, CEO of Time-Warner, didn't want people to know was that the two teens' favorite movie, which they watched the day before the massacre, was Oliver Stone's *Natural Born Killers*.

Despite Bronfman's adamant denial that Hollywood-manufactured movies and music had influenced human behavior in connection to Columbine, the facts were not in his court. Regardless of Hollywood's denial of any link between "entertainment" and its influence on human behavior, there exist over *three thousand* studies that prove otherwise, beginning with the multi-volume Payne Fund studies of the Motion Picture Research Council conducted between 1928 and 1933.

If Universal and Time-Warner refused to cite the evidence, they were either extremely ignorant of the industry they controlled, or they were conveniently lying to cover their tracks. Of course this "ignorant lying" was a common misinformation campaign in the Hollywood community that was perpetuated equally by Valenti's MPAA, the Recording Industry Association of America (RIAA), and every producer who was ever accused of producing the overly violent and influentially malevolent "entertainment."

The industry line was unanimous, "Just don't watch it." If the product is that bad, then can Americans be blamed for responding, "Just don't make it."

There is every reason to believe that the party hosts of Clinton's "Columbine Fundraiser" had no idea that Clinton would deliver his "scolding" address to the industry over the airwaves just hours before showing up at the Hollywood fundraiser. This put Bronfman and others on the defensive, but it also had a reflex action of causing industry execs to dig deeper into their pockets.

Between Universal and Time-Warner alone, the two mega-conglomerates gave $3 million to the Democratic Party for 2000 (see Appendix I). This was a classic case of Clintonesque extortion, as if to say, hypothetically, to his hosts, "Don't worry, Bubba, I ain't gonna take any federal action—as long as you pay to play." In the meantime, the victims and survivors at Columbine were victimized twice: first by two murderous teens and second by a scandal-ridden president on the verge of a nervous breakdown extorting "guilt money" for the Democrats.

Just how connected were Hollywood and Columbine? Civil rights leader Johnny Lee Clary conducted an exhaustive study into the events of Columbine and the influence of Marilyn Manson on Eric Harris and Dylan Klebold. According to Clary, "Marilyn Manson is as guilty for the Columbine High School Massacre as the maniacs who pulled the trigger."[17]

Klebold and Harris were big fans of Marilyn Manson and had attended his concerts with friends, none of whom informed their own parents of their attendance at the sadistic concerts. The two were also consumers of the most violent video games on the market with sub-titles such as "Kill Your Friends Guilt Free." In the months before the massacre, Klebold and Harris had also embraced the "Goth" style of dressing in black, heavy attire. The Goth lifestyle was also a philosophy perpetrating a cult of "death fascination" and all things dark and dangerous.

The day before the massacre, Klebold and Harris would watch Time-Warner's *Natural Born Killers* over and over along with *The Basketball Diaries* by New Line Cinema, a division of Time-Warner. Both movies chronicle the disturbed characters of mass murderers, complete with the glow of slow-motion Technicolor death and candy-apple red blood.

On that April day in 1999, the two killers, whose minds were drenched with Universal's music and Time-Warner's movies, entered Columbine High School with their Goth-black clothing and proceeded to run through the hallways shooting everybody in sight. "Marilyn Manson Rules!" was their war cry as they moved form classroom to classroom and into the cafeteria.

That the two teenage killers were highly influenced by Manson's anti-God "Kill Your Friends" motto would become evident halfway through the killing spree when one of the shooters pointed his rifle at fellow student Cassie Bernall, crouched to her knees on the cafeteria floor. As she prayed underneath a lunch table, one of the teen shooters pulled the trigger and killed her.

Perhaps not wanting to give the police the opportunity to catch or kill them, Dylan Klebold and Eric Harris shot themselves to death. A New Line Cinema executive responsible for *The Basketball Diaries* was the only one in the Hollywood community to make the possible connection, explaining off the record, "It could be that our movie was the final moment of dark inspiration, the last straw that caused the crimes."

Could be? That same executive was at Hollywood Bill's Greystone Mansion fundraiser.

The actions of these Hollywood executives, producers, writers, and directors validate the American drumbeat that "Hollywood is out of touch." They are also, in fact, unindicted co-conspirators in the deaths of innocent people. The dark secret within the "creative" element of the entertainment industry is that these mentally disturbed moviemakers really do know the power of film. And they do know that a phenomenon does exist known within industry circles as "death by film." It is a dark circle of filmmakers who are not shy to brag about their "creative ability" to kill people through film. It is the darkest end of the spectrum in Hollywood known as "Value Manipulation."

Even Joseph Goebbels, Adolph Hitler's Minister of Propaganda once boasted, "Film is one of the most modern and far-reaching means for influencing the public that has ever existed." Goebbels worshiped film second only to Hitler himself. He elevated his devotion to occult status for which he sold his soul, shooting his wife, children, and himself within hours of Hitler's own suicide.

Among the members of Hollywood's "death by film" club is Clive Barker, the radical homosexual heterophobic creator of movieland's most lurid films. As Dr. Jason Kovar of the *Hollywood Unmasked* video series described Barker's strategy, the filmmaker "slyly uses his films to blindside his audiences with his own philosophies and usher a change into their lives."[18] As Barker himself gloats darkly, "I never used to care two hoots about the hero. I always used to side with the demons. I was interested in the dark mysterious creature that the hero faces."[19]

Another member of the "club" is Hollywood homosexual radical activist screenwriter Kevin Williamson, who partnered with the equally demented Wes Craven to produce the splatter movies such as the *Nightmare on Elm Street* series and the *Scream* movies. Actress Michelle Geller of *Buffy the Vampire Slayer* glowingly admires Williamson's blood-lust as "intelligent horror," rendering into the viewer "the thought of actually killing someone on the road, the thought of someone stalking you in your school or in your house."[20]

Clive Barker has responded to articles that claim his films invite violent acts that result in innocent deaths by arrogantly bragging, "That's my responsibility, to kill as many people as possible . . . . And some of that truth may not be possible to anybody. My responsibility is not to give a f____ about that. My responsibility is not to care."[21]

* * *

Though Clinton thought his macabre timing of "scolding" and "fundraising" had gone unnoticed, it became a drumbeat for genuine action by citizens who were weary of a president selling the soul and security of the country. Pressured by Congress, media watchdog groups, faith-based organizations, and the families of school shooting victims, President Clinton was in the spotlight and turned to Robert Pitofsky, chairman of the Federal Trade Commission (FTC).

Just weeks after returning from his "Columbine Fundraiser," Clinton asked Pitofsky to undertake a study in June 1999 to determine if the movie, music, and video game industry marketed violent content to young people in a strategy that undermined the industry's own ratings. If guilty of doing so, the commission was charged with determining if the target marketing was intentional.

Pitofsky's findings, released in 2000 as "The FTC Youth Violence Report," stated emphatically that the answer was "yes" to all three industry segments. Not only did Pitofsky say yes to the question of target marketing as intentional, but added that it was "pervasive and aggressive."[22] While Clinton was clever enough not to ask the FTC if violent content "influenced" behavior, Pitofsky had the fortitude to address the issue regardless, by inserting the statement, "Exposure does seem to correlate with aggressive attitudes, insensitivity to violence, and an exaggerated view of how much violence occurred in the world."[23] Certainly this was not what Hollywood Bill or his Tinseltown patrons wanted to hear.

Pitofsky went even further and offered the establishment of legal codes that, if violated, could incur sanctions against the distributors who conducted intentional target marketing to youth. But Clinton's hack legal advisors said that would smack of censorship. However, the First Amendment's right to freedom of speech is not without limits and is definitely not extended to obscenity, child pornography, or violations of the "incitement clause," all of which are illegal under federal law and not protected by the First Amendment. The FTC's findings actually provided a good case for violation of the "incitement" clause because the marketing of violence was "aggressive and pervasive." On the other hand, connecting "intent" with actual acts of violence could prove sticky, but not impossible as Oliver Stone discovered in a six-year legal battle against him for incitement surrounding his murder-fest film *Natural Born Killers*.

But the report didn't matter much to President Clinton when it was released in 2000. The report had no teeth, and Clinton could claim that "I tried." Clinton's response to the report was the same response to any national issue of urgent interest. Just like Rwanda, the decision was "to decide not to decide," the same strategy applied to avoid killing Osama bin Laden.

By the year 2000, Hollywood Bill and his administration were near their end, marred by a record number of crimes and scandals including his own impeachment, the first elected president in the history of the United States to be impeached, which he would pompously describe later as "a badge of honor." And Hollywood was behind him one hundred percent.

Clinton was now viewed nationally and internationally as a bad joke, garnering little respect, and consumed with the post-hippie ego of destruction that was blatantly immoral in the least and would prove to be extremely dangerous at most, which the world would discover with horror less than one year later. Fast forward to 2008 presidential candidate Hillary Clinton who was parading Hollywood Bill as "global ambassador" if "they" were elected.

Hollywood Bill would also earn the additional nickname "The MTV President" for trying to appear "hip" and "cool" among the new Generation X whose standards and values Clinton facilitated in lowering as a pathetic role model of mature adulthood. The MTV audience had important policy questions to ask such as, "What kind of underwear do you prefer?" And the most quoted presidential answer of all time came as a result of one question from the MTV audience, "Have you ever smoked marijuana?" Being all things to all people, the MTV President replied, "Yes, . . . but I didn't inhale."

This classic answer would not only be the brunt of many jokes, it would also set the Democratic party template of saying both "Yes" and "No" to the same question. When Senator John Kerry (D-MA) was asked during the 2004 presidential election if he supported the appropriation bill to fund the war in Iraq, he answered, "I voted for it before I could vote against it." That one answer basically cost him the election.

The terminology of ambiguity and contradiction became embedded in the English lexicon as "Clintonesque" and "Clintonian." Another Clintonian mistake by Kerry was his embrace of Hollywood as representing a "cross-section" of America. But Kerry was the second failed Democratic candidate for president after the end of the Bill and Hillary stronghold on the White House.

Vice-President Al Gore was expected to succeed Hollywood Bill as president, except that his lies were more grandiose, even if they lacked the Clinton touch of ambiguity and contradiction. The invention of the internet claim was over-the-top for even the swing voters—or the voters who were swingers. Al Gore did not seem to learn the Hollywood lesson, for he embraced them as openly as Clinton, taking all of their money and occasionally chiding them for their bad behavior.

While the election would be hotly contested for several weeks, well into December 2000, America would finally be free of the last vestige of the most corrupt president in American history. Clinton himself helped seal that distinction right up until his final days in office when he began an unprecedented act of issuing a record number of presidential pardons and commuted sentences of criminals across the wide spectrum of lawbreakers within the American criminal justice system; 181 separate executive orders on January 10, 2001.

Of those, Clinton commuted the sentences of thirty-seven convicted criminals and issued 144 pardons of criminal suspects awaiting trial including drug dealers, solicitors of child pornography, and major league embezzlers.[24] Law enforcement officials across the country shook their heads and wondered privately if they had chosen the right profession or if America had chosen the wrong president. The total number of pardons issued by Clinton during both terms exceeded 400. At the time, the Justice Department refused to investigate how many of the pardons were "bought."

But the "Clinton Machine" of Hollywood Bill and Hillary would, unfortunately, not disappear. A vast amount of money collected by Bill Clinton for the Democratic party, including his school shooting Hollywood fundraisers, would go to Hillary Clinton's bid for Senator from New York, which she would win and use as a stepping stone for her 2008 presidential bid.

The Clinton White House in exile would now move to the Clinton Presidential Library in Little Rock with offices in New York City and Washington. The special "agreement" between Bill and Hillary that Candace Roberts had described to me back in 1987 had proven to be a prophetic truth. He was into politics for the "chicks" and she was into it for the "power."

After two rounds of major open-heart surgery, Hollywood Bill decided to join with his wife in their quest to hold on to power at all costs and power for its own sake, even if it is only "the next best thing to sex."

Hillary Clinton's inconsistent and contradiction of conviction on any issue is evidence that the "will to power" is the only will for Hillary. On October 30, 2007, presidential candidate Hillary Clinton lied four times in five minutes during a Democratic primary debate. After taking flack from her fellow Democrats, Wolff Blitzer of CNN tried to restore her image two weeks later at the November 15th Nevada debates. Hillary's poll numbers would begin to dive the very next day and would never recover to their previous levels.

The "Mud Room" that Candace Roberts spoke about as the dingy little room in the basement of the Arkansas State Capitol has reached mammoth proportions. No doubt the repository of "official dirt" may reside now deep in the annals of the library with special access to ex-Clinton hacks and the senator from New York when "information" is needed to smear and defame an opponent or oppose a policy decision of national importance.

This dark, subterranean activity continues to this day with a big boost from the world's most notorious New Age atheist and power hungry "philanthropist" George Soros, whose goal is to "shape" the world in his own twisted and dangerous image. Soros injects millions of dollars into front groups on the internet, many employing Clinton cronies. From this vast network, a whisper campaign, a negative blog, a timely press release, and various other cloak-and-dagger activities are used to destroy the lives of anyone who would seriously challenge the Clintons or Soros himself. The names Ickes and Podesta are alive and well. Soros' flirtation with supporting Obama in the primaries was carefully calculated to throw his support to Clinton if Obama faltered.

That much of this activity has occurred just under the radar screen of the average American is intentional, but it is built around a cult of personality. As Ben Stein said, "We have a Democratic Party that worships, not likes, WORSHIPS Bill Clinton."[25] Barack Obama would eventually eclipse Clinton in the cult of personality worship. However, the Lying King and the Dragon Lady's agenda would surface above the national and international radar screen in the month of September 2006, when Bill Clinton exploded in a major meltdown on national television.

The roots of Hollywood Bill's meltdown can be traced to the first week in September 2006 when Disney-ABC announced the upcoming broadcast of the epic five-hour movie, *The Path to 9/11*. The film explored the escalating series of events that led to the attacks on September 11, 2001, by al Qaeda sponsored suicide pilots on orders from Osama bin Laden which left 3,000 Americans dead and counting as first responders continue dying from toxic air at Ground Zero.

As reports leaked out from an advance screening and 900 DVDs sent to people across the country, Hollywood Bill was given the lion's share of attention, if not all-out blame for numerous missed opportunities to capture or kill bin Laden. Clinton must have wondered why Hollywood was doing this to him, especially Disney, which had contributed more to the Democratic party and his 1996 re-election bid than any other studio in Hollywood.

The mass hysteria that burned across the Clinton Machine was probably best summarized by CNN radio correspondent Shelby Lynn, who reported on September 8, 2006, "The former Clinton officials are upset over the unflattering portrayal of their anti-terrorism efforts."[26]

Clinton had never even proposed any kind of censorship on television or the movies while he was president. But he was certainly going to impose censorship this time at all costs, and by doing so, would reveal the wide network of the Clinton Machine and the people who, as Ben Stein said, "WORSHIP Bill Clinton." His strenuous efforts to attempt censorship would push Hollywood Bill to the limit resulting ultimately in his angry September 24th encounter with network anchor Chris Wallace, better known as "The Clinton Meltdown Seen 'Round the World."

Less than a year later, one presidential candidate placed the blame for the 9/11 terrorist attack squarely on the doorstep of the one man *who purposely ignored ten opportunities* to kill or capture Osama bin Laden. On June 26, 2007, former New York City Mayor Rudy Giuliani directly accused Bill Clinton of not acting forcefully enough to the first bombing of the World Trade Center in 1993.

Giuliani made his remarks to over 600 business, corporate, and political leaders at Regent University, the college founded by Pat Robertson. Giuliani went on to explain that over 500 Americans were killed by Islamic terrorists *before* 9/11. Bill Clinton failed to respond to the first attack and that led to follow-up terrorist attacks on the Khobar Towers, attacks at embassies in Kenya and Tanzania, and on the U.S.S. Cole.

People ask, "What good does it do now to lay blame for past mistakes?" It is *very* relevant and *very* timely because a recent Democratic candidate for president just so happens to be the wife of the former president who "decided not to decide" when it came to fighting terrorism, and wife Hillary would have retreated to the same philosophy if allowed to enter the White House along with her husband, the new "global ambassador to the world." As Eli Pariser of MoveOn.org proclaimed, "Now it's our Party: we bought it, we own it." And they didn't care if their candidate was Hillary or Obama; they're both bought and paid for.

CLINTON'S MELTDOWN PATH TO 9/11

"Are there any men left in Washington, or are they all cowards?" asks Ahmed Shah Massoud, the charismatic leader of the Afghan Northern Alliance. Massoud is posing the frustrating question to a CIA operative named "Kirk" as the two peer over a rocky cliff into the Tarnak Farms enclave of Osama bin Laden.

Massoud is frustrated because Kirk can't get a "green light" from President Bill Clinton's National Security Advisor Sandy Berger, with whom he is talking by radio phone. With a simple "go" the Northern Alliance would sweep down into the camp and kill or capture Osama bin Laden, the "Most Wanted Man in the World."

But Berger flinches, and tells Kirk that if they want to go ahead and "accidentally" kill bin Laden in the raid, that would be fine. But by no means were they to "intentionally" kill bin Laden. Kirk must still get an official "green light" from Berger and CIA director George Tenet. When pressed for a yes or no, Berger is shown hanging up the phone. The next scene shows the bewildered CIA agent taking the hang-up as a "no."

This segment of the ABC miniseries *The Path to 9/11* would prove to be the most powerful and also the most controversial. Did Sandy Berger hang up on the CIA director, putting his men and the Northern Alliance in harm's way? Was there actually a CIA agent on the ground with Massoud, and were they both peering over a cliff directly into the camp of Osama bin Laden?

This was one small scene in a five-hour movie, without commercial interruption, broadcast on Sunday, September 10, and Monday, September 11, in 2006 on the five-year anniversary of the 9/11 terrorist attack on America. Marc Platt of ABC served as executive producer of the ambitious $40 million production with the script by Cyrus Nowrasteh (*Into the West*) and directed by David Cunningham (*To End All Wars*).

Nowrasteh based the mini-series on the "9/11 Commission Report," and two books, *The Looming Tower* by Lawrence Wright and *The Cell* by ABC correspondent John Miller. In addition, Nowrasteh interviewed a long list of people and operatives who worked in command and control capacities in the search for Al Qaeda and Osama bin Laden.

Senator Thomas Kean, Chairman of the 9/11 Commission, stated that the filmmakers made every effort to be accurate, especially considering the fact that an eight-year period beginning with the first World Trade Center bombing and ending with the 9/11 attack was compacted into a five-hour movie.

Kean was on the set constantly and even ordered re-shoots of scenes he deemed troublesome. (It should be noted that the use of technical advisors on fact-based films can be misused as "window-dressing" to authenticate a movie. In *Path to 9/11*, Kean had the rare power to order changes and his changes and advice were often heeded by director Cunningham.) "Other commission members said that the mini-series presented many facts in the 9/11 Commission Report," according to CNN Radio News.[27] Democrats on the committee would later disagree with Kean.

While the Berger "hang-up" scene appeared to be the most contentious and contested, the Clinton Machine began to show its face when reports of the advance screening described a scene in which President Clinton was "distracted" by the Monica Lewinsky affair at a time in 1998 and 1999 when the U.S. had the last two "best and clear" opportunities to kill bin Laden. According to Michael Scheuer, former chief of the bin Laden unit for the CIA's Counterterrorist Center, those two dates were specifically May 27, 1998, and February 11, 1999, sometimes referred to as the "Kandahar Opportunities" before bin Laden went into "Deep Cover." Scheuer added that these were clearly outlined in the 9/11 Commission Report.

But President Clinton appeared to have developed a bad habit of not answering the phone from the one person whose calls he should have always taken, the national security advisor who heads up the vast National Security Agency (NSA). It was also apparent to many NSA staffers that Berger was constantly frustrated with Clinton's refusal to take his calls or return his calls on matters of urgent split-second decision-making.

If anyone came off as "questionable" in the movie, it was the counter-terrorism analyst for the White House, Richard Clarke, who was himself a walking enigma and an artful dodger, and who was portrayed in the film as aggressively urging an attack on bin Laden before America itself was attacked. The filmmakers could only go by what Clarke stated in his 9/11 Commission testimony.

However, the most credible person in the real-life hunt for bin Laden would appear to be the CIA's Scheuer who was constantly on bin Laden's trail and knew all the players involved from the president to the operatives on the ground. Scheuer, author of *Imperial Hubris*, believed that Richard Clarke was actually a "risk-averse poseur" who did not take enough action to stop bin Laden.

No one could deny Scheuer's accurate assessment of ten clear opportunities to get bin Laden. And in each of the ten instances, senior policy makers in charge—Berger, Clarke, and Tenet—resisted taking action, afraid of collateral damage or reaction from the "Arab Street." That concern would prove fatal after bin Laden's terrorists attacked the United States with "collateral damage" as the target and not the risk.

And did the president's advisors, not to mention Clinton himself, not realize that hundreds of innocent people were killed and maimed in the "collateral damage" attacks of the two U.S. embassies in Africa? Another good source that backs up the administration's bungling is Richard Miniter's book *Losing bin Laden*. One can only wonder why the investigative duo of Woodward and Bernstein did not come out with *All the President's Men II*. The two liberal journalists were conspicuously absent until October 2006 when Bob Woodward wrote a book blaming President George Bush for the entire terrorism quagmire. And he even admitted that his "superiors" at the *Washington Post* told him not to release the book until a few weeks before the 2006 congressional election!

As for *The Path to 9/11*, the New York Times began to publicize the Clinton Machine's reaction to the film in an article published on September 5, 2006, and that's when the long arm of Bill Clinton would be revealed as he blustered and sputtered for the next three weeks until September 24th when the world witnessed his meltdown broadcast on television.

The Hollywood movie machine, which Bill Clinton had long worshipped, turned around and bit him in the rear, and he was not, as the old saying goes, "a happy camper."

The following is a timetable of Hollywood Bill's Meltdown Path to 9/11:

AUGUST 12, 2006

An advance screening of ABC's *The Path to 9/11* is shown to a large audience at the National Press Club. In addition, over 900 DVDs of the movie are sent out in a publicity package for the two-part, five-hour mini-series. The audience is impressed with the scope and depth of the series. Senator Thomas Kean, chairman of the 9/11 Commission and the film's technical advisor, said the movie was an "honest representation" of a number of failed attempts to capture Osama bin Laden. [28]

The ambitious mini-series proved a massive undertaking of research and production with 250 speaking parts, over 200 sets, and multiple locations. Director David Cunningham shot a total of 550 hours of film for the $40 million miniseries. ABC sets Sunday, September 10, and Monday, September 11, as the broadcast air dates.

During the question and answer period at the end of the movie's screening, 9/11 Commission member Richard Ben-Veniste rises to denounce the scene involving NSA Director Sandy Berger hanging up the phone on the CIA agent in Afghanistan waiting for the green-light to kill bin Laden. Ben-Veniste, a hardened and brash liberal Democrat who hovers on the outer edges of the Clinton Machine, was the only one of the ten member panel at this time to complain about the scene in particular or the movie in general.

Berger, the post-hippie former trade attorney turned National Security Advisor, was reached by phone after the screening and tersely replies, "It did not happen."[29] Some begin to question Berger's own version considering his previous conviction of theft of NSA documents from the National Archives just prior to the formation of the 9/11 Commission.

SEPTEMBER 5, 2006

For over a week, the mini-series has been discussed in detail over the internet and through hundreds of comments on the blogosphere. But publisher Arthur "Pinch" Sulzberger's *New York Times* waits until September 5th, the Tuesday before the national broadcast, to give the story full national attention with the *Times'* signature editorialized headlines, in this case, "9/11 Mini-Series Is Criticized as Inaccurate and Biased."

Former White House counterterrorism analyst Richard Clarke tells the *Times* that he found the scene mentioned by Ben-Veniste as "questionable."[30] (By now, however, Clarke's own version of the truth is questionable given his shifting positions on his role in the hunt for bin Laden as outlined in his book, interviews, statements before the 9/11 Commission, and his own portrayal in the film.)

Richard Ben-Veniste again airs his ardent objections to the Berger scene and to the movie. Senator Thomas Kean again restates his view that the film "is an honest representation of a number of failed attempts to capture Osama bin Laden."[31]

It should also be noted that during this period *The New York Times* was under heavy criticism for running front-page headline articles revealing details about U.S. government programs to trace the money trail of terrorists and also detailed revelations about the NSA's wiretapping of terrorist phone calls. The readership dropped so drastically that Sulzberger had to fire a large number of employees and he actually shrunk the size of the newspaper by an inch on each side to save paper costs.

SEPTEMBER 7, 2006

The internet chat and blogosphere begins running comments that the Clinton Machine is fuming, with Bill and Hillary personally corralling former cabinet members, staffers, and cronies to mount a full-scale offensive. Senate Majority Leader Harry Reid calls Robert Iger, CEO of ABC's parent company at Disney and strongly urges Iger to change or delete scenes from the movie.

Clinton spokesperson Jay Carson speaks up for former President Clinton and tells MSNBC that "it is despicable that ABC/Disney would insist on airing a fictional version of what is a serious and emotional event for our country."[32]

MSNBC learns that Clinton Library advisor Douglas Band had written letters earlier in the week to Iger expressing their "concern."

Joining the chorus of dissent is former Secretary of State Madeleine Albright who complains that she is misrepresented in a scene with CIA Director George Tenet in which she admits forewarning the government of Pakistan regarding a cruise missile attack on bin Laden's Afghanistan hideout. Tenet is furious after the failed attack and demands Albright explain her actions, especially in light of the common knowledge that bin Laden has sympathizers embedded in the highest levels of Pakistani government.

Curiously, Norah O'Donnell at competitor network NBC seems determined to extract a response from ABC to explain "what they're going to do" in response to the well-orchestrated uproar by the Clinton Machine. ABC releases a statement saying, "No one has seen the final version of the film, because the editing process is not yet complete, so criticisms of film specifics are premature and irresponsible."[33]

After an interview earlier in the day with writer/producer Cyrus Nowrasteh, Sean Hannity of Fox News announces on his TV show that ABC is "caving in" to the Clinton Machine demands and may be editing the film.[34]

SEPTEMBER 8, 2006

In what would become the busiest day in the Clinton meltdown countdown, Senate Minority Leader Harry Reid issues a new statement now calling for the entire movie to be pulled by ABC. He is joined in a photo-op with other de-facto members of the Clinton Machine currently serving in the Senate, including Senators Chuck Schumer, Dick Durbin, Nancy Pelosi, and others. Senator Hillary Clinton would chime in later in the day. Many believe she is responsible for the harsh Democratic Senate response to actually censor the *entire* movie. Former Clinton crony and Media Matters smear merchant John Podesta joined the chorus and is suspected to have helped spread disinformation about the movie.

The clarion call to pull the movie entirely is also endorsed by Clinton "Mud Room" administrator and presidential library chief Bruce Lindsey, Douglas Band, Madeleine Albright, Sandy Berger, and now John Podesta. Soros acolyte Harold Ickes is secretly working to undermine the filmmakers.

The former president is used to being properly maligned in numerous books throughout the years. But he knows those hard-cover political books have a limited readership, usually read among the "Metroliner" East Coast intellectual establishment. But the *Path to 9/11* movie will be shown on network television and broadcast to millions of people across the nation. Even worse, in Clinton's eyes, the movie will be broadcast simultaneously in several countries around the world and available in even more countries where people have access to satellite TV.

Clinton's biggest concern, according to insiders, is a scene taken directly from the 9/11 Commission Report showing the former president "distracted" with sexual matters instead of national security matters. In particular, a scene shows White House counterterrorism analyst Richard Clarke viewing the president's famous bent-finger press announcement claiming, "I did not have sexual relations with that woman—Miss Lewinsky," to which Clarke smirks and says to an aide, "Pathetic, isn't it?"

Disney CEO Robert Iger now insists that the ABC network will not pull the movie and it will be broadcast as planned. The Clinton Machine is burning furiously. E-mail and blog campaigns by George Soros funded MoveOn.org and other shadow front groups begin flooding computers across America urging people to refrain from watching the mini-series. Some e-mails claim the movie is "total fiction" and urge viewers "Don't waste your time."

As a result of Iger's refusal to pull *The Path to 9/11*, Clinton attorneys begin legal action. (One insider at ABC confides that certain implied verbal threats of future FCC oversight of the network will be increased in frequency if ABC does not pull the movie and comply with the Senate Democrats' demands.)

Senator Thomas Kean, chairman of the 9/11 Commission and the film's technical advisor releases another statement, "The filmmakers made every effort to be accurate. They even reshot an entire scene I had trouble with."[35]

Finally Bill Clinton himself spouts off by late afternoon on Friday, saying, "I just don't want any lies in there parading as truth." Hillary Clinton gives her own separate but equal assessment, "The truth is enough!" (Observers note the irony in the statements considering that the couple gave, inadvertently or not, a concise summary of their eight years together in the White House. Truth was morally relative to the Clintons and they could make these statements without flinching.)

FRIDAY EVENING, SEPTEMBER 8, 2006

By early evening on Friday other voices begin speaking up to counter the claims of "total fabrication," "pull the film," and "fictional storytelling and despicable acts" by ABC.

First, Robert "Buzz" Patterson, author of *Dereliction of Duty* and the former "hands-on" carrier of the "nuclear football," came on the Michael Savage radio show shortly after eight p.m. Eastern Time to clear up any misconception about whether Clinton had missed any opportunities to capture or kill bin Laden. Buzz Patterson was by Clinton's side most of the time with the secret codes for launching a nuclear strike in the event of an enemy nuclear attack.

Patterson saw the advance screening and said, "It was very accurate concerning Madeleine Albright's and Sandy Berger's behavior."[36] Patterson also revealed that he was personally aware of at least eight times that President Clinton had the opportunity to capture or kill bin Laden and passed on the opportunity every time. On one occasion, Clinton didn't want to be disturbed as he watched a golf tournament.[37] True to his position as carrier of the nuclear football, Patterson was always close to the real events, noting, "I saw a lot of *fumbling* by Clinton and Albright."[38]

Later Friday evening, former Clinton political strategist Dick Morris appears on television to give his thoughts on the film, which he also had an opportunity to preview. According to Morris, "Almost one hundred percent of the film rings true . . . . It is more fact than fiction."[39] From his close association with Bill Clinton throughout the presidency, Morris pointedly remarked that "President Clinton missed numerous opportunities to kill bin Laden."[40]

SEPTEMBER 10, 2006

ABC continues running promos for The *Path to 9/11* right up to the broadcast on Sunday night. For legal protection from the Clinton Machine attack campaign, ABC runs a disclaimer at the beginning of the movie stating that the mini-series is "not a documentary" and adding that "for dramatic and narrative purposes, the film contains fictionalized scenes, composite and representative characters and dialogue, as well as time compression."

Much to the dismay of the Clinton Machine, the movie was virtually intact from the original screened at the National Press Club. The shouting match between CIA Director George Tenet and Secretary of State Madeleine Albright over her reckless forewarning to the Pakistanis of a missile attack against bin Laden is left in place.

The lack of any credible response by Clinton to the bombings of the U.S. embassies in Kenya and Tanzania are depicted in the movie as well as the total lack of response to the bombing of the U.S.S. Cole, which further emboldens bin Laden. President Clinton's "sexual distraction" is also depicted at a time when the president had the clearest and best chances to capture or kill bin Laden. The same year as the "sexual distraction," bin Laden declares a fatwah, or Holy War, against America that goes largely unnoticed by the administration.

Even when Clinton's years of inaction bleeds over into the Bush administration, eight years of neglect to national security and defense bubbles to the surface. In a pivotal scene, Richard Clarke and George Tenet inform new NSA Director Condoleezza Rice that bin Laden has been spotted with a high-flying remote-controlled drone. When Rice asks if the drone is equipped with a rocket, the two Clinton leftovers simply look at each other, speechless. (Clinton had failed to authorize and appropriate the funding.)

According to those who saw the original version at the National Press Club and subsequently watched the broadcast version, only three minutes appeared to have been cut. And that was the scene where Berger was depicted as hanging up on the CIA agent. However, the scene of Northern Alliance leader Ahmed Shah Massoud and "Kirk" was left in the broadcast version showing the CIA agent with a blank look on his face after lowering the radio phone. That Massoud said exactly, "Are there any men left in Washington or are they all cowards," is known only to those who were closest to him.

After all, Massoud's relatively small band of fighters were instrumental in overthrowing the Soviet Army in the 1980s, forcing them to retreat all the way back to Moscow. Massoud was known to be leery and critical of Clinton's lack of assistance in addition to his lack of character. President Reagan had given Massoud anything he asked for in the fight against Russia.

Whether Massoud was peering directly over the cliff into the Tarnak Farm compound of bin Laden is known only to him. Regardless, the point was that Massoud was always within a few hours distance of being able to attack his arch-enemy Osama bin Laden, who had hijacked his country and his religion. What is known is that the Clinton administration would stall him continuously until Massoud was finally assassinated by bin Laden's men masquerading as, of course, television journalists. And that scene is depicted very vividly. Clinton's inaction not only led to bin Laden acting with impunity to attack U.S. interests, America's closest ally in Afghanistan was now dead and it was given passing notice in the mainstream media.

The Path to 9/11 only solidified the perception of the Clinton administration policy of "deciding not to decide," Observers of the movie take note that the mini-series may not have received much attention if Clinton and his machine had simply remained silent. The controversy and the smear tactics against the filmmaker by the Clinton cronies, along with Robert Iger's refusal to buckle to the machine politics, inevitably boosted viewership.

But the Clinton meltdown was only beginning, as he would prove two weeks later on September 24th. Clinton would remain furious at ABC and Iger, in spite of the fact that Iger is a strong supporter of Democrats. The disclaimer clearly indicated the production challenges of compressing eight years of story into five hours. The main message, according to Brent Bozell of the Media Research Center, is that "America's intelligence apparatus was woefully unprepared for 9/11 and remains dangerously inadequate today."

On the same night as the first installment of the mini-series, former CIA chief of the bin Laden unit, Michael Scheuer, tells Fox News what he has repeated previously, "There were clearly *ten* opportunities to kill bin Laden" under President Clinton and that they are all "outlined in the 9/11 Report."

The two men closest to the actual events, Michael Scheuer and Robert "Buzz" Patterson, began to emerge as the credible voices in contrast to the denial campaign being waged by Clinton, his former cabinet members, advisors, and Clinton Machine "operatives."

SEPTEMBER 11, 2006

On the afternoon of the second and final installment of the mini-series, the feverishly hypochondriac "news" magazine *The Nation* publishes a story by Max Blumenthal attacking the entire series from beginning to end as a "right-wing effort" to blame Clinton for the 9/11 attacks on America, and labeling the movie a "falsified version of events," and places "responsibility" for the "imaginative screenwriting" on a "well-known propaganda operation" that originated with a "network of little-known right-wingers working from within Hollywood," a group Blumenthal refers to as the "network within the ABC network."

Blumenthal foams viciously as he reaches out—way out—to describe the biggest conspiracy to overthrow the U.S. government in the history of America. He *even* calls the director a "Christian" and says that director Cunningham is part of a larger movement that "advocates stealth political methods to put the United States under the control of Biblical Law and jettison the Constitution."

Most of all, Blumenthal would assert that these "Christians" are out to "transform Hollywood from the inside out." (Imagine that!) Blumenthal goes on to viciously attack writer/producer Cyrus Nowrasteh as part of an emerging group of right-wing people "burrowing into the film industry with ulterior sectarian and religious agendas."[41] (Blumenthal's right-wing conspiracy theory assumes that Hollywood, as a whole, has no agenda and is a very objective group of moral high-grounders.)

SEPTEMBER 16, 2006

Jawbreaker author Gary Bernsten tells radio talk show host Glenn Beck that during the height of growing terrorism after the first bombing of the World Trade Center in 1993 the Clinton administration cut the clandestine operations budget by more than twenty-five percent, telling Beck, "There was an assault to cut clandestine operations." Bernsten was the CIA man-on-the-ground who cornered bin Laden at Tora Bora after the U.S. invaded Afghanistan in 2001. Unfortunately, his urgent pleas for more troops to close the holes were turned down by Washington Defense officials and bin Laden slipped into the no-man's land Waziristan.

SEPTEMBER 24, 2006

The Clinton meltdown begins. Chris Wallace, the highly respected host of Fox News Sunday, is granted an exclusive interview with former president Clinton after the ex-president gives a fund-raising speech for his new Clinton Global Initiative (CGI). For years Clinton had refused to ever give an interview to Fox

News. During the course of the interview, Wallace says that he received many e-mails when it was announced that he would be interviewing Clinton and many of the e-mails posed the question as to whether the ex-president could have done more to prevent 9/11 by capturing or killing bin Laden.

As the old saying goes, "That was all she wrote." Clinton went on the defensive in an escalating tirade including personal attacks on Chris Wallace, who would later comment that "Clinton could not control himself," and Wallace felt, as an interviewer, that he was standing at "the bottom of a mountain and looking up at the avalanche."

Clinton's hand was trembling in stark anger as he pointed his trademark bent index finger at Wallace, saying, "You did your nice little conservative hit job on me," and also told Wallace, "You got that little smirk on your face." Wallace did not roll over and simply asked Clinton about the U.S. response to the bombing of the American embassies in Africa and the attack on the U.S.S. Cole.

In a classic Clintonesque statement, the ex-president told a lie and a truth in the same answer. "I tried to kill bin Laden and I failed . . . . But at least I tried." According to the 9/11 Commission Report, Clinton didn't try very hard, and if anything, ignored clear opportunities to apprehend or kill bin Laden, even when the country of Sudan offered him up on a silver platter for the taking.

Clinton continues his tirade with a series of split-second lies that he could not retract and which would be deconstructed later by other news correspondents. Clinton tells Wallace in a red-faced heat that "I had battle plans drawn to go into Afghanistan and go after the Taliban and get bin Laden." But he quickly blames the CIA and FBI for not "certifying" bin Laden as the culprit.

Clinton then moves forward in his seat and asks Wallace if he had ever read Richard Clarke's book. Clinton claims that Richard Clarke passed a plan to the Bush administration about the key strategy for going into Afghanistan, "And what did they do?" Clinton demanded. "They demoted him!"

The ex-president leans forward again and with his bent index finger begins jabbing Chris Wallace at the side of his knee and asks, "How many Republicans have you asked these questions? Tell me! Tell me the truth, Chris!"

After the interview ends, Wallace reaches out to shake the ex-president's hand and Clinton, clearly fuming and shaken, hesitantly extends his limp hand for a curt, quick pump. Wallace thanks Clinton for "one of the more unusual" interviews he has ever done.[42]

SEPTEMBER 26, 2006

Senator Hillary Clinton tries to defend her husband's ignorance of the facts by claiming he was never shown a document that Osama bin Laden was planning an attack on United States soil (as opposed to an attack abroad). Senator Clinton says that President Bush was shown the document.

What Senator Clinton intentionally failed to mention was that the "assessment document" shown to President Bush was generated after Bush became president and could not have possibly been viewed by former President Clinton. This is the pathology of lying that the Hollywood media ignores.[43]

And Senator Clinton *did not* mention that her husband, as commander-in-chief, must have heard bin Laden's declaration of a Holy War against America in 1998. (Fortunately, the American people do not suffer amnesia to the extent that the Clintons would prefer when issuing ambiguous statements.)

Later in the afternoon of September 26th, former station chief Michael Scheuer responded to Clinton's meltdown statement that he "had battle plans drawn to go into Afghanistan and go after the Taliban and bin Laden." Scheuer says, "There were *no plans* to go into Afghanistan."[44] He also restated that the last clear and best opportunities to get bin Laden were May 29, 1998, and February 11, 1999. And the former president and the senator from New York failed to mention that those two dates happened to coincide with the avalanche of Clinton's sex scandals and his impeachment by Congress.

As to whether Chris Wallace ever asked "these questions" of Republicans, viewers of his Sunday news show know that he has a reputation for hard-hitting questions, regardless of party affiliation. As proof, Wallace replayed a taped interview with Donald Rumsfeld in which he asked even tougher questions of the Defense Secretary than he had asked Clinton.

Regarding Clinton's assertion that Richard Clarke's book validated the ex-president's "passing down" of battle plans for Afghanistan to the Bush administration, no such "passage" could be found. In a commentary broadcast on *Special Report with Brit Hume*, Pulitzer Prize-winning journalist Charles Krauthammer summed up the Chris Wallace interview and, in doing so, also summed up President Clinton's approach to terrorism and stopping bin Laden. "Clinton is an angry liar . . . . He had ten opportunities to get bin Laden, and he didn't."[45]

OCTOBER 22, 2006

A story appears in the *Weekly Standard* a few days after the Wallace/Clinton interview suggesting that Clinton "planned" to blow-up intentionally as a ploy to "set the record straight" after the airing of *The Path to 9/11* movie on ABC. After all, he never liked Fox News and even made an off-hand slur by telling Wallace to "look at the context—Fox News" where Clinton was being asked "these questions."

Throughout the whole period leading up to the *9/11* mini-series, all the way through the Clinton meltdown and still raging today is an ongoing conspiracy theory that, according to *Time* magazine, promotes the psychopathic belief that "The entire catastrophe was planned and executed by federal officials in order to provide the U.S. with a pretext for going to war in the Middle East and, by extension, as a means of consolidating and extending the power of the Bush administration."[46] That view, *Time* points out, was shared by thirty-six percent of people polled in an August 2006 Scripps-Howard poll. As Time staff writer Lev Grossman noted, "Thirty-six percent adds up to a lot of people." A Zoghby poll taken the same year put the percentage of conspiracy theorists at forty-two percent. The emergence of this mammoth lunatic fringe poses a threat to American cohesion on par with another cataclysmic terrorist attack.

As for the final word on *The Path to 9/11*, former CIA special unit director Michael Scheuer appeared on Fox News with Chris Wallace one week after the Clinton meltdown. Responding to the non-stop choir of denial from Clinton Machine front men and former administration officials making the talk-show circuit, Scheuer stated adamantly, "Bill Clinton, Sandy Berger, and the others are flat-out liars," and added, "I went to a Catholic school and I was told, 'If you're going to lie, don't lie about the facts!'" Whatever facts or fiction were presented in the ABC mini-series, *The Path to 9/11* managed to soon unravel events unanticipated by everyone. Once Bill Clinton exploded in anger two weeks later on national television, he perjured himself in the court of public opinion. The contention no longer surrounded the movie, it surrounded the veracity and credibility of, basically, two individuals: Bill Clinton and former CIA bin Laden Unit Chief Michael Scheuer. Clinton continued the fiction and Scheuer restated the truth.

CONCLUSION

The Hollywood that Bill Clinton had come to adore was now a source of deep disappointment for him. How could the industry that gave him so much money turn around and tell the American people that he "may" have been "sexually distracted" and that he "may" have missed a few (ten) opportunities to kill Osama bin Laden?

Hollywood Bill had delivered with his endorsement of TV ratings so that network programming could sink ever deeper into the gutter. The ex-prez had even signed a Telecommunications Indecency Bill that ended up with no teeth and an FCC that slept through thousands of complaints filed by individuals concerning lax enforcement of indecency and obscenity laws already on the books.

But Hollywood didn't abandon their favorite son for very long. In July 2007, *The Path to 9/11* writer/producer Cyrus Nowrasteh announced that the DVD of the film was supposed to have been released seven months earlier in January, but was put on hold "indefinitely." Disney CEO Robert Iger refused to return any phone calls. Nowrasteh strongly believes the Clinton Machine is behind the "delay." As this book was going to press in 2008, Iger refuses to release the DVD.

When I saw that now infamous bent index finger of Bill Clinton in the "Lewinsky Lie" video, and saw the same bent finger jabbing at the knee of Chris

Wallace, my mind drifted back twenty years to my brief introduction to then Governor Bill Clinton at a Hollywood party.

Our conversation was cut short so that he could scold one of his staffers by jamming his index finger repeatedly into the young man's chest. It occurred to me that Clinton's index finger was not bent at the time. But after twenty years, eight of them as president, he had apparently pointed and jabbed his finger at so many people that it was now bent, permanently. Or rather, it was . . . crooked.

As Candace Roberts told me that next morning in the lobby of the Beverly Hills Hilton, for Bill Clinton "it's all about getting the chicks." As the years passed, I became increasingly aware of how America's first post-hippie president and his "preoccupation" was eroding the country's stability. And it would eventually cost America the very real security it had enjoyed for many years.

The clarion Clintonesque justification for his sexual obsession from supporters would be the same when he left office as when he entered office. "It's all just sex." And Hollywood shouted the loudest with words and money. But that perverse excuse for presidential dysfunction would rarely be heard again after September 11, 2001.

Although Clinton committed no crime for ignoring the signposts to the largest attack on American soil, there were other acts of negligence that were more than criminal, they were treasonous. As the former first lady began her race for president, the "Dragon Lady" had some unfinished acts of negligence of her own to contend with.

That the true crimes of the "Bill and Hillary Show" have been largely forgotten or continually downplayed is a result of a "romance" between the mainstream media and Hollywood that was consummated during the dark days of the 1990s. With this "marriage," the Clinton's crimes were covered up, back-paged, and even promoted and redefined. Hollywood has a long history of embracing and supporting lunatic politics, especially if it contributes to the rapid decline of the nation's culture.

The dangerous intersection of Hollywood, the media, and Washington, along with the power of "infotainment" to endorse "their" candidate would politicize the arts and polarize the population, even now as the nation moves into the unknown territory of the twenty-first century.

Because the Clinton Machine continues to pose a danger to national stability and cohesion, the next chapter provides an opportunity for Hillary and Bill Clinton that they shouldn't ignore or miss—one time or ten times. There's even an address where Mr. and Mrs. Clinton can appear to help resolve their unresolved crimes.

First, a look at how the Hollywood-Media Defense Team began and its role, or lack thereof, in covering (or covering up) the most blatant crimes of any presidency in the history of America and the grim harvest we are now reaping.

CHAPTER 5

THE HOLLYWOOD MEDIA DEFENSE
"It's All Just Old News"

Christians are losers.
—Ted Turner

TO THE FRESHMAN CLASS OF 2012

If you are entering your freshman year of college in 2008, you were just two years old when Bill Clinton was elected president, and you were ten when he left office. Now that you can vote, it helps to understand how the leader of the free world governed the nation while you were learning to ride a bike. And you ask, "What does my first vote for president have to do with an ex-president who has been out of office for eight years?"

Because now that you do keep up with politics, you know that Hollywood Bill's wife, Hillary, was running for the presidency of the United States. And in case you missed the subtle news blurbs in April 2007, Hillary Clinton (who just happens to also be a Democratic senator from New York) announced that husband Bill would have been a great "global ambassador" in a Hillary presidency. Nepotism aside, Hillary declared enthusiastically at a campaign rally that "I can't think of a better cheerleader for America than Bill Clinton, can you?"

While everybody at the rally cheered, at least half of Americans who don't suffer amnesia became extremely ill to their stomachs. By 2008, even the amnesia victims were having second thoughts as Hillary's poll numbers began to slip.

Global ambassador? Was Hillary kidding? Unfortunately not. International Relations 101.

Now that you are old enough to think for yourself, there are some other major lessons to be learned from other indiscretions, even crimes, that were committed during Hollywood Bill's administration. In many cases, Hillary was not an innocent impartial bystander but often a full participant.

As authors, pundits, commentators, bloggers, and political operatives reflect on Bill and Hillary's actions and inactions during the 1990s, beware of the suspicious spinners of truth who tell you that bad news is "just old news." They'll even say "it's nothing new" and go so far as to relegate it all as "irrelevant." Hillary likes to say, "It's time to turn the page."

Before the major media jumped on the Obama bandwagon after he bravely threw his grandmother under the bus—not once, but twice—the mainstream media was still pushing a Clinton dynasty. But, they still cover for the dynamic duo as they fade, kicking and screaming, into the sunset.

What the biased liberal press won't tell you is that Hillary and Bill still carry "unresolved crimes" around their necks like yoked oxen as they attempted to drag their baggage back into the White House.

The New York Times won't bring the Clinton crimes back for public and peer review. *The Times* had already dubbed Hollywood Bill as Hillary's "Strategist in Chief." This comes from a newspaper that has broadcast advance warnings to al Qaeda about America's ability to track their phone calls and financial transactions. As "they" say in the movie business, "Are you getting the picture?"

In 1998 William Bennett, already a seasoned veteran of the Culture War, wrote *The Death of Outrage* as the Clinton Administration was winding down. Bennett analyzed the meaning of the Clinton scandals: "Why they matter, what the public reaction to them means, and the social and political damage they have already inflicted on America."

At the end of the book, Bennett listed a ten-point "Postscript" prediction of what might happen if Clinton's scandals are brushed aside by his defenders' exploitation of the natural tolerance of the American people. Again, this was written ten years ago. If these "arguments" sound conspicuously contemporary, that is no coincidence:

"In the end, perhaps the most important residue of the Clinton scandals will be pedagogical; that is, the lessons they will teach children—and their parents, too. If the arguments are left standing, if the justifications are left intact, it is worth considering the lessons that will be taught . . .

1. Character in our president doesn't matter. It's the economy, stupid.
2. Some powerful people are above the law. They don't need to play by the rules.
3. Adultery is no big deal. It's commonplace. Europeans don't care about it; neither should we.
4. It's okay to lie under oath.
5. It's okay to grope women as long as you eventually take no for an answer.

6. It's okay to close your eyes to wrongdoing when it's your own powerful friends and political allies who have done wrong.
7. A lot of people engage in misconduct, so it doesn't matter if you do, too. Everybody does it. This is especially true in politics.
8. A person hasn't really done anything wrong unless he's been convicted in a court of law.
9. If you do something wrong and people question you about it, do not voluntarily step forward, admit wrongdoing, and take responsibility. Instead, consider doing any or all of the following:

- Promise to give them answers soon, then stall by giving evasive answers or no answers at all. Maybe they'll get tired and drop it.
- Just feign ignorance about what you've done. Say you don't know what happened, you just don't have the facts.
- Attack those who are raising the questions. Try to dig up dirt on them. And intimidate them if you can.
- Play down and make fun of their concerns.
- Claim that people are conspiring to make you look guilty.
- Don't explain yourself.

10. The ends justify the means."

[Bill Bennett, 1998]

THE CLINTON'S HOLLYWOOD MEDIA DEFENSE TEAM

It is doubtful that without the help of the mainstream media, Bill and Hillary Clinton would have never set foot in the White House. And thanks to the megamedia consolidations of the mid to late 1990s, Bill Clinton would be elected a second time. The control of network news by the major movie studios would prove especially helpful to Bill and Hillary Clinton in "their" last term when the majority of scandals and crimes by the First Couple were being exposed or hatched, often simultaneously. By 2000, the Clintons had come a long way from the "innocent-looking" young couple who blazed into Washington in 1992 and projected, as Charles Krauthammer would say, "a young Dorian Gray portrait, long before the major sinning occurred."

Each time that an executive office scandal broke, or a suspected crime was being investigated, the mainstream media could be counted on to downplay, marginalize, erase, or simply not report the major malfunction of the First Family. There was at this time the visible emergence of a "common mindset" among the news media that had previously lingered just under the radar of most Americans.

By 1999 CBS News was already in the hands of Viacom-Paramount Studios. ABC News had been under the control of the Disney Studios since 1996. Warner Brothers Studios and the publishers of *Time* magazine had come together in 1989, but they would soon gobble up CNN, giving them a major print and broadcast mouthpiece. Finally, Universal joined NBC to complete the Hollywood merger with network news.

Even before the mergers, the members of the print, broadcast, and Hollywood communities were members of a much bigger club known as the BCPC, the Bi-coastal Cocktail Party Circuit. They were, and remain, elitist, left-wing, condescending liberals with a hatred for God and country, harboring a New Age vision of a vague America they can't quite define and don't really care to defend, either.

A poll released on October 31, 2006, by the Center for Media and Public Affairs confirmed the "common mindset" that had been growing and consolidating for almost thirty years. The poll was taken over a seven-week period leading up to the 2006 Congressional elections and measured the "favorable" and "unfavorable" coverage by the major network news divisions of the entertainment studios including CBS, NBC, ABC, and CNN.

The results found that seventy-seven percent of the reporting was broadcast in a light *favorable* to Democrats, while eighty-two percent of the reporting was broadcast in a *negative* light to Republicans.

Network news bias was first recognized by only a few in 1968 when CBS anchor Walter Cronkite made his infamous "personal" analysis that the Vietnam War could not be won. Cronkite made this sudden observation at the end of the Tet Offensive, a ten-day surprise attack by the North Vietnamese Communists and Viet Cong guerillas that, in reality, turned out to be the biggest defeat ever for the Communist North by the American and South Vietnamese armies. And that reality was apparent at the end of the battle by the American forces and by the Communist commanders.

Walter Cronkite made a completely false assessment and totally inappropriate comment, a shock to American forces, but a welcome surprise to the Communist North who could begin a propaganda war using the American journalists as their puppet pawns. Jane Fonda would be their crowning achievement in 1972. So incredibly gullible was the press, that on one occasion, *Time* magazine hired a North Vietnamese spy as a staff correspondent by the name of Phan Xuan An. They didn't know he was a spy at the time, but they definitely didn't conduct due diligence either. In a 2006 obituary for the Viet Cong "colonel," *Time* gave a glowing tribute to Phan as "a highly respected journalist while acting as a spy for the Communists—a double life he kept secret until the mid-80s."

As for Cronkite, his every word was followed by Lyndon Johnson who was more interested in Cronkite's view of the war than the military commanders he micromanaged. After Cronkite's totally flawed perception of the Tet Offensive,

Johnson said, "If we've lost Cronkite, we've lost middle-America," and five weeks later, Johnson announced he wouldn't run for re-election.

In 2004, at the age of 87, Walter Cronkite addressed the Commonwealth Club in San Francisco and told the audience that CBS News President Richard Salant pressured him to make the "assessment." Obviously, Cronkite wanted to remain on the invitation list for the Bi-coastal Cocktail Party Circuit. An apology would surely have dropped Cronkite from the cocktail parties by which he thrives.

By now, Cronkite had long been exposed as a deliberate deceiver who cherry-picked the news himself and always slanted liberal-left in an era when only three network news programs existed. His fatherly voice and grandfatherly appearance allowed him to pull the wool over three generations of American audiences who once dubbed him the "Most Trustworthy Man in America" when quite the opposite was true.

During the same speech at the Commonwealth Club, Cronkite came out as a pseudo-closeted homosexual heterophobe who admitted he would have "been happy to be married to several friends I had of the same sex" except that he had already married his wife, Betsy, "who just happened to be female." Cronkite made the statement in a Christian-bashing diatribe against those he labeled the "Christian Right."

The gross negligence of Walter Cronkite's reporting from Vietnam still reverberates today in a tragic way, a historical strategy lesson for America's enemies. In early July 2007, al-Qaeda leader Ayman al-Zawahiri announced that his militant following would be employing a "Tet Offensive-like" assault on America and the West to break the will of the people. Al-Zawahiri learned the lesson from Walter Cronkite, not the military. Cronkite, at age 90, continued to hob-nob the cocktail party scene and was spotted partying with band members of the Grateful Dead, minus Jerry Garcia, who really is dead.

One news "pioneer" who does not shy away from his hatred of all Christians, right or left, is the mentally unstable Mouth of the South, Ted Turner, who believes that God killed his father and sister and he doesn't want "anything to do with a God like that." Obviously Turner is misinformed as he waxes increasingly erratic with each passing year.

Turner is the persona of the news media mogul who was fully enamored by the movie business. And when the two worlds came together in a merger of the Turner Empire and Time-Warner, the stage would be set for the ultimate match between the manic-depressive and the hyper-neurotic.

And through the shared "common mindset" of a twisted moral worldview, the mega-media conglomerate would push their left-coast agenda and psychosis on "the rest of America" through twenty-four-hour news and motion pictures with a "message," a message that Senator Bob Dole would call "nightmares of depravity." Their merger would also accelerate the decline of news into its present-day format of "infotainment." In its coverage of politics and culture, the mainstream "old" media can inflict great harm and misinformation by the nature of its reporting, coined by Rush Limbaugh as "Drive-by Media."

By 2003 Time-Warner had managed to kick Ted Turner off the board and out of control. And "out of control" he has been ever since his swift ejection. In actuality, Turner is just more open about the demons that have controlled him for most of his life. Turner's story is a case study of how one man's contorted view of the world can be transmitted to his employees who then transfer their adopted philosophy into their individual interpretation of "reading the news." Though Turner no longer has "working" control over the twenty-four-hour news channel he started, his philosophical legacy remains intact at CNN decades after it began in 1980.

In October 2006, Turner railed publicly that the country was in danger of a president who was "a reformed alcoholic" whose "finger is on the nuclear button." Turner failed to mention if his own personal drinking habits had hindered him at CNN or the Time-Warner board. Sweating profusely at a ceremony honoring him for "global understanding," Turner took the opportunity to promote family disintegration and sing the praises of adultery. He even suggested that the Ten Commandments should be reduced to nine, reflecting his New Age worldview. (Turner had become the darling of Hollywood in the early 90s when he declared, "Christians Are Losers.")

Ted Turner also admitted he's not sure whose side he's on in the war on terror. He also blustered loudly that Iran should have a nuclear bomb and should have even more, as fast as they can make them. In October 2007, Turner made a serious announcement that the Iraq war was actually hatched at the headquarters of Fox News. This "assessment" was made as new ratings data showed CNN's viewership falling behind the Fox News Channel.

With Turner's words broadcast worldwide and his old CNN still intact with the "Turner mindset," the producers and editors of the news division "cut a deal" with a group of Islamic terrorists to broadcast "their side" of the war. The result: The terrorists eagerly supplied CNN with videotape footage of Americans being shot by snipers. The tape was not only grotesque in its propaganda intent, but was narrated by a CNN reporter who provided a voice-over for the shootings in a manner not unlike a sportscaster describing a crucial putt for par by Tiger Woods.

Perhaps CNN has no concept of "aiding and abetting the enemy." More likely is the case that they do have a concept of aiding the enemy after hearing their founding father's indecision about whose side he's on in the war on terror. Regardless, the producers, editors, and executives at Time-Warner should be held accountable in a court of law for treason and sedition.

CNN has now effectively become the American network division of Al-Jazeera. And the terrorist videographers, no doubt proud of their "international debut" on CNN, were eager to set up even more devastating carnage of American slaughter to help CNN boost its ratings. It is no coincidence that bombings of Humvees by IEDs increased dramatically after the "CNN Deal."

In an interview with Lynne Cheney, wife of Vice-President Dick Cheney, Wolff Blitzer was caught off guard when asked by Mrs. Cheney, "Who gave you the film?" Blitzer fumbled and stumbled long enough to change the subject and suddenly—a commercial break. This is the tragic result of Hollywood news. One of the few voices with a moral compass on the CNN staff is Mike Galanos; the other 98% are post-Turner zombies.

The only time ratings spike at CNN is when Glenn Beck is on the air. Beck displays independent courage, which was on display when he aired the documentary *Obsession*. The film exposes the ever-present threat from the extreme fascist elements of Islam and their eagerness to kill as many people as possible.

As for the left-leaning liberal bias begun by Walter Cronkite, the "fever-pitch" era became more apparent in the 1990s when the major network news divisions and Turner's CNN cable news began an endless parade of the Clinton agenda, unchallenged, and at the same time carefully downplaying his crimes. Turner was in control of CNN during this time and the cable news channel's coverage was so slanted toward the Clinton agenda, and adept at marginalizing his crimes, that the call letters, CNN, became synonymous with the Clinton News Network.

It was in this environment of politically biased news, now under the thumb of Hollywood studios, that Bill Clinton had virtual carte-blanche from a media that soft-pedaled the president's blatant negligence, leading to acts of theft, threats, bribery, sexual harassment, and high treason involving the largest wholesale auction of top-secret high-tech and nuclear technology to the last mega-Communist country on earth in exchange for illegal contributions from foreign "interests." In a May 5, 2007 interview, Clinton's FBI director, Louis Freeh, told Sean Hannity that seven of his eight years as director were spent investigating his own boss, the president.

This romance between the Hollywood Media and the Clinton administration would cement the polarization of America straight down the middle between *right* and *left* (read: right and wrong).

UNRESOLVED CRIMES

Even before the network-manipulated *60 Minutes* interview that boosted Clinton's poll numbers going into the 1992 election, the media was well aware of countless scandals that were hanging over Governor Bill Clinton's head from his fifteen years in state government. But they kept silent because Clinton was "their" man.

As author and journalist Christopher Hitchens would write years later, "Not one—I repeat, not one—of Clinton's team in 1992 did not harbor the fear that a 'flaw' might embarrass and even humiliate everybody. Was this not a recognition of the character issue, however oblique? Some thought it would be funny money, some thought it would be 'bimbo eruptions,' a few guessed it would be a sordid combination of the two. All were prepared to gloss it over in favor of the big picture, of getting the job done, or getting a job for themselves."[1]

Americans discovered for the first time in the history of broadcast and print media as to the extraordinary length and conspicuously boisterous effort that the mainstream press would endeavor to promote a candidate for president. In the same vein, the media's efforts to cover up and protect a president's many crimes was undertaken with the same ferociousness as it undertook to destroy a president in the 1970s.

Because the Clinton Machine continues to exert ruthless power behind the scenes of national politics and desperately tried to "reoccupy" the White House at all costs, and by any means necessary, it remains relevant and expedient to remember some of the "unresolved crimes" of the Clinton administration that the media continues, desperately, to attempt to bury from the eyes of the American conscience.

According to the *Progressive Review*, the official tally of guilty pleas and convictions of Clinton Machine individuals and businesses currently stands at forty-seven. The number of indictments and misdemeanor charges now total sixty-one. These include racketeering, extortion, bribery, tax evasion, embezzlement, fraud, conspiracy, kickbacks, money laundering, perjury, obstruction of justice, and many more violations and investigations. (See: "Hollywood Bill and Hillary's Traveling Crime Show" at the end of this chapter.)

If these statistics sound new, or at least startling to the reader, it is probably due to underreporting by the press, burying stories on page twenty-seven in a handful of newspapers, or television news producers who felt the crimes did not "merit" airtime on the evening news. What major coverage was given by the major media was slanted in the Clinton Machine's favor and generated by a "vast right-wing conspiracy" to quote the former first lady herself.

Nevertheless, there remain five major breaches of justice (read: crimes) that linger and should be resolved before the major Hollywood-controlled media bar their very mention on the airwaves or in newsprint. Some of their crimes will cause, and are already manifesting, an international shift in power and influence that threatens the United States as much, or more, than extremist Islamic terrorism.

UNRESOLVED CRIMES

1. The Clinton Pardons
2. Stolen FBI Files
3. Sexual Assaults and Abuse of Power
4. High Treason One
5. High Treason Two

STOLEN FBI FILES

Sometime during the first term of President Clinton, a young former nightclub bouncer from Arkansas by the name of Craig Livingstone had been given the unofficial title of White House Security Consultant, among other titles he would be granted on an "as needed" basis. An FBI document and sworn testimony revealed that Mrs. Clinton was responsible for hiring the large shaggy-haired thug. And U.S. Secret Service logs confirmed his frequent comings and goings at the White House.[5]

Surely, Mr. Livingstone's qualifications as a bar bouncer with unlimited access to the White House should not have raised any eyebrows as far as the Clintons were concerned. It just so happened that shortly after his hiring as another Clinton Machine stooge, a job he would soon come to regret, Mr. Livingstone "came into possession" of more than 900 classified FBI "personnel clearance" files on former members of the Reagan and first George Bush presidential offices as well as hundreds of files that included federal government and elected officials, many still serving across the broad spectrum of federal government.

The fiasco, which still reverberates today, was actually well-planned and executed because the information obtained would be later made accessible to select members of the Clinton Machine and the Democratic Party as additional "pay dirt" for the growing computer files of the Clinton "Mud Room," available at the click of a mouse to uncover confidential information to smear, slander, and destroy anybody who got in the way of the Clinton's quest for perpetual uninhibited power.

The whole affair would become known as "Filegate" and this scandal alone, not to mention the others percolating simultaneously, should have been enough to shrink Watergate to a footnote, except for the fact that the Hollywood media and the press "back-paged" the story. Where was Woodward? Where was Bernstein? Where was the 1970s investigative media out to uncover unbridled presidential abuse of power? It would appear, in hindsight, that nobody in the media wanted to be kicked off the White House cocktail party invitation list.

The average person has little or no memory of such an event of theft, lying, and intimidation that haunts Washington even today. The media went beyond just "back-paging" the story; it took the creative Hollywood approach of making the whole White House scandal appear as some vague Republican plot.

As an example, the following is a headline generated by the Hollywood mega-media giant Time-Warner's print news division, better known as *Time* magazine, from July 8, 1996: "A Funny Thing Happened: Scandal Hungry Republicans Hoped to Get Bill and Hillary But Were Waylaid by Low Level Bunglers." Besides being the longest headline in the history of *Time* magazine, it served two purposes; one, to cover up the crime, and two, to project the entire story in the headline for "scanners" who wouldn't bother to read the story, as biased as it already was. The strategy of the Hollywood defense is clever and deceptive: When the subject comes up at the water cooler the next day, the "scanner" pipes up and declares to his fellow workers, "I hear it's all a Republican plot." End of story. It's the same method Hollywood employs to create "buzz" about a new movie release.

And the ploy apparently seemed to work because, initially, nobody seemed to care. Furthermore, with Attorney General Janet Reno serving as the de-facto defense attorney for the Clintons, no substantial investigation would occur and the press had no reason to question her lack of interest.

To put the crime in perspective, during the Watergate probe, Nixon White House aide Charles "Chuck" Colson went to prison for "coming into possession" of *one* classified FBI file. Another fact lost to amnesia and apathy from the media was the First Lady's experience twenty-five years earlier as an aide to the Watergate investigative committee in Congress. She had a first-hand lesson in how files could be stolen. Combined with her background as a lawyer and pathological capacity for captivating lies, the whole affair would just fade away—or so she thought. By 1999, so many scandals were swirling around the Clintons, even special prosecutor Ken Starr did not have the time or staff to pursue the matter. "Filegate" was brought to light by the legal eagles at Judicial Watch under director Larry Klayman who filed suit on behalf of many of the people whose confidential FBI files were stolen.

And "a funny thing happened" on the way to the courthouse. Through pre-trial discovery, Judicial Watch uncovered Hillary Clinton's direct link to the "Filegate" controversy.[6] On behalf of those individuals whose privacy rights were violated under the Privacy Act of 1974, a federal case titled Alexander et. al. v. FBI et. al. was filed by Judicial Watch. Among the defendants listed in the case was First Lady Hillary Clinton. This would place her in the lone category of the first and only First Lady in history to come under criminal investigation.

The depositions obtained by Judicial Watch would read like a Who's Who of the Clinton Machine: James Carville, George Stephanopoulos, Paul Begala, Bernard Nussbaum, Harold Ickes, William Kennedy III, Eleanor Stacey Parker, Anthony Marceca and the Clinton's own private "investigator" and mud collector, Terry Lenzer.

Though named as a defendant, the only person missing from the list of deposed defendants was Hillary Rodham Clinton, who claimed that she was too important to give a deposition. Mrs. Clinton filed a questionable "legal" document known as a "sworn declaration" in which she claimed no involvement in accessing classified FBI files. In the "declaration," Mrs. Clinton stubbornly contended that "as a general proposition, high-ranking government officials are not subject to depositions" and that she must "have time to dedicate to the performance of [her] government functions."[7]

Even though the White House further compounded their legal problems by launching a cover-up and failed to turn over documents as required by subpoena, nobody went to jail in the largest theft of classified FBI files in the history of the country. The Clintons were setting milestones of malfeasance at a record level. As usual, the Clintons delegated responsibility (blame) to others. And the Hollywood media covered their backs.

However, one person who gave a subpoena that directly linked Hillary Clinton to the stolen files was Linda Tripp. Her testimony would show that there was an "extra special" motive for obtaining the FBI personnel clearance files of certain people. The motives Linda Tripp uncovered would lead directly to the next set of "Unresolved Crimes" of the Clintons: "Sexual Assault" *and* "Abuse of Power." A pattern began to evolve in the White House of dark deception as the frequency and consequences of lies increased dramatically with each passing year.

In the meantime, the Clinton motto ruled: "Admit nothing, deny everything."

SEXUAL ASSAULTS AND ABUSE OF POWER

Only in the hyper-eccentric decade of the Clinton-dominated 1990s could a series of impeachable crimes coincide and overlap with such velocity and ferocity that the American public, and even Clinton's supporters, began to develop an "I just don't want to talk about it" glaze in their eyes.

The two crimes in this section can only be described simultaneously because of the deadly mountain generated by bigger and broader lies to overshadow the previous lies. This would be the legacy of the Clinton presidency and the practice continues today within the purposely vague network known as the Clinton Machine and the deflated presidential candidacy of Hillary Clinton.

The exception to the "glaze" would be Hollywood producers, directors, actors, and other entertainment industry executives and creative individuals who would show their support in words and money. Never mind the fact that Bill Clinton had amassed a twenty-year history of sexually assaulting and harassing women by the time of the Monica Lewinsky affair in 1998.

During the federal investigation leading up to the impeachment of President Clinton, the special prosecutor was besieged with more victims of the president than he could keep up with. This, and confidentiality, led to the reference of such victims as "Jane Does" with a running counter of Number One, Number Two, Number Three . . . ad infinitum. The women who were stepping forward, or were handed a subpoena, not only found themselves the center of international attention, but also a target of the Clinton smear machine that would work overtime to discredit any woman claiming the president had made "improper sexual advances" toward them.

And this is where the stolen FBI files would play a part in the "formative information" needed to spread slander sheets and "talking points" to a media eager to defend "their" president. (The Clinton Machine had not yet mastered the internet or blogosphere method of cyber-smearing that they employ today, with the help of George Soros.)

It would be left up to Larry Klayman's Judicial Watch organization to make the connection, noting that, "In an effort to discredit the women who charged President Clinton with sexual misconduct, personnel files and papers were illegally obtained and released. The courts found, under the Privacy Act, that the privacy of Linda Tripp and Kathleen Willey had been violated."[8]

This is the same Judicial Watch that had established the connection between Hillary Clinton and the stolen FBI files, even listing her as a defendant in the case, even though she was *too important* to give a deposition. Did that imply that the First Lady was actually involved in harassing women who stepped forward, creating "formative material" from their files to intimidate them? Throughout the 2008 campaign, Hillary dodged questions about the release of presidential papers from the National Archives that could show her level of involvement in persecuting these women.

According to Candice E. Jackson, Hillary Clinton was very actively involved in the ensuing smear campaign against "Bill's Women." In her book, *Their Lives*, author Jackson chronicles the lives of seven different women and describes how both Bill and Hillary Clinton, along with their machine cronies, used their political power to "bribe, coerce, harass, intimidate, and terrorize" the women who got in "their" way.[9]

The president's defenders even took on the freakish task of defaming numerous dead presidents for their "alleged" philandering as if this was a common and expected trait of being an American president. Unfortunately, the dead presidents had no opportunity to reply to their accusers, which is how the Clinton Machine prefer their debates be conducted. As Christopher Hitchens noted, "For all the talk about historic 'philandering,' it is hard to recall any other White House which has had to maintain a quasi-governmental or para-state division devoted exclusively to the bullying and defamation of women."[10]

Also notable was former Clinton political advisor Dick Morris who told CNBC that during the 1992 campaign, "There was an entire operation funded with over $100,000 of campaign money, which included federal matching funds, to hire private detectives to go into the personal lives of women who were alleged to have had sex with Bill Clinton. To develop compromising material—blackmailing information, basically—to coerce them into signing affidavits saying they did not have sex with Bill Clinton."[11]

Hitchens notes that, "'Having sex' was the most fragrant and presentable way of describing the experience of certain women, like the Arkansas nursing-home supervisor Juanita Broaddrick, who was raped by Bill Clinton while he was state attorney general in 1978."[12] Broaddrick had an impeccable reputation and NBC correspondent Lisa Myers produced and taped a long interview that was scheduled for airing as the sole segment of the January 29, 1999, edition of *Dateline*.

As was common among the elite media club of Clinton admirers, a "sudden delay" was announced by NBC, deciding to air the interview in a shorter version "sometime" in February. It was obvious to most observers that the president's machine appeared to be intervening at top levels. Even Tim Russert was at a loss for words to explain the "delay." Of course, NBC was no different than CBS, ABC, and especially CNN in their biased reporting in Clinton's favor. NBC, like CNN, was known to be a "hot-bed" of Clinton defenders.

By the time the interview was postponed again in February 1999, Juanita Broaddrick and her husband had second thoughts about the mishandling and manipulation to which they were being subjected. Lisa Myers tried to console Broaddrick by explaining, "The good news is you're credible; the bad news is you're very, very credible."[13]

By early March when the interview was being "contemplated" by NBC for another *Dateline* broadcast, the NATO bombs began dropping on Kosovo and the network's priorities conveniently changed, killing the Jane Doe number five story forever. However, Juanita Broaddrick's sworn affidavit was secured in the evidence room of the House of Representatives during the Clinton impeachment debate and not a single Democrat exercised their right and duty to read the evidence surrounding Clinton's brutal rape of Mrs. Broaddrick. But Tim Russert read the transcript from the cancelled *Dateline* segment and would volunteer that Clinton's action against Broaddrick had caused him to become literally "sick" to his stomach. (To the Class of 2012: Raping a woman *is a crime* punishable by life in prison.)

Especially noticeable during this entire time period was the almost audible silence from women's rights groups. Gloria Steinem and N.O.W. Director Patricia Ireland accomplished disappearing acts that would make David Copperfield envious. The two had spread the issue of sexual harassment to a nationwide audience during the 1980s and 1990s, causing effective change in workplace personnel policies. But the White House in general and Bill Clinton in particular were apparently exempt from the abuses of sexual harassment.

According to Kathleen Willey, whose privacy was violated in the theft of the 900 FBI files, the Clinton Machine would put her through "a true nightmare" as she described the second offensive against her. After all four of her car tires were flattened with nails, and her cat came up missing, a mysterious jogger approached her and began asking about her children—by name. He then asked about the cat and the tires and was said to have asked, "Don't you get the message?" Poor little kitty-kitty.

Again the mainstream Hollywood media was more than happy to give the microphone to Clinton's official and unofficial "apologist-defamers." From the Machine itself, the rajin' cajun James Carville came out screaming, "Lies! Lies! Lies!"

More grotesque was the Hollywood media's plan, with no protest from the White House, to dig deep into the bowels of Sunset Boulevard and roll out America's king of bottom-feeding pornography, Larry Flynt, to defend the President of the United States. Again another record-setting low point for the Clinton administration. This was the man of low estate who began publication of the world's sleaziest porn magazine *Hustler*, which was the natural evolution of all the *Playboy* spinoffs to push Hugh Hefner's envelope.

In one issue, Flynt published a "photo spread" of human genitalia in the advanced stages of venereal disease. This was his version of the "fold-out." Paralyzed from an assassin's bullet, Flynt would appear as a talking head on numerous "news" shows with his slobbering retort to the effect of "C'mon, people are just hypocrites. It's all just sex." Flynt is a hero of director Oliver Stone who even made a movie about the sleaze-king as a "champion" of free speech.

Hard as it may be to believe, Hollywood rolled out more dangerous cannons of defense for President Clinton. When Rep. Henry Hyde pounded the gavel to send the articles of impeachment over to the Senate, Hollywood roared with indignation. Alec Baldwin, already an actor of questionable mental stability, made the indirect and insane threat of political perversity, noting that "in other countries, we would go in and kill all the senators, their wives, and their children." President Clinton never distanced himself from such remarks.

To the contrary, the convergence of all the stolen files and the Clinton Machine running in overdrive would manifest itself in a smear campaign against Rep. Hyde himself—right in the middle of the impeachment proceedings. The Hollywood media was more than anxious to carry the dirty water of Larry Flynt, Alec Baldwin, and other "entertainers" when "reports" began to mysteriously surface that Rep. Hyde once had an "inappropriate relationship." And others were being lined up for the same treatment.

This "purely coincidental" smearing of women accusers and congressional legislators in the midst of the impeachment process would eventually backfire. Erik Tarloff, a former speech writer for Clinton and Vice-President Gore, was disgusted with the never-ending abuse of power. "Notice how they always trash the accusers . . . . They destroy their reputations!"[14]

Finally, in 1999, the U.S. Congress voted to impeach President Clinton on two counts: "Providing perjurious, false, and misleading testimony" regarding Paula Jones, and "obstruction of justice" for the Monica Lewinsky affair in an effort to "delay, impede, and cover up evidence." The Senate voted to acquit the president along mainly party lines.

President Clinton would go down in history as the first elected president to be impeached in the Senate. Nixon had resigned long before his imminent impeachment in 1974. That same year, a young Bill Clinton was making his first failed attempt at running for office in Arkansas and sounded off on Richard Nixon by strongly suggesting that any president who lies should resign from office. But that was twenty-five years earlier and what was true for Nixon was not true for him. The Clinton Machine had counted on American amnesia over his silly "youthful" remarks. More importantly, to the Clintonites, was the nature of the lies; Nixon lied about a third-rate burglary and Clinton was only "protecting his family" about . . . sex. It's only sex. Larry Flynt said so. As Henry Hyde said shortly before his death in 2007, "It was all about perjury and the rule of law, not sex."

Meanwhile, in the glaring heat of the Afghanistan desert, a tall, bearded maniacal terrorist was patiently planning the largest attack on American soil while this presidential pornography played out on television every night. By now Osama bin Laden knew that Bill Clinton was the best friend he ever had.

Another issue the Hollywood media defense team missed entirely in its "adults-only" oriented reporting was the impact of the president's behavior and inevitable impeachment on children and families. Julie Berry, a mother of two, ten and eight years old at the time, said, "Suddenly, I'm faced with having to explain something to my children that I had set to do at the right time and the right place. Now I'm faced with a crash course on the subject and, to confound matters, having to explain it in the context of the misbehavior of the president of the United States. He became the poster 'child' of how *not* to behave—and he was the *president*. You can't find role models at the movies, at the ballparks, and not even at the White House."

For adults old enough to remember only twenty years earlier, Jimmy Carter almost lost his bid for the White House after giving an ill-advised interview to *Playboy* magazine in which he had admitted "lusting in his heart" at times in his life. Two decades later, the Senate acquittal of Bill Clinton sent a new message about presidential conduct: It's quite okay for a United States president to lie and cheat, intimidate, sexually assault, and even rape women and remain in office. Senator Daniel Patrick Moynihan lived long enough to see his own Senate body "define decency down." Way down.

And that was just fine with Bill Clinton. Hollywood came to the rescue in the form of Steven Spielberg, a major financial and moral supporter of presidential corruption. The director graciously invited the Clintons to "unwind" at his sprawling estate in the Hamptons. That was the least Spielberg could do for his favorite president and First Lady. After all, the Clintons had allowed Spielberg to stay in the Lincoln bedroom overnight for the bargain donation price of only $236,000. That really was a bargain compared to the $389,000 for an overnight stay by Clinton's military advisor and Spielberg partner, David Geffen.

* * *

However still and quiet the Congressional chambers became after the adjournment of impeachment, there remained that audible silence, again, of something left unattended. Something much bigger was breezed over in the press as sort of a necessary side-show distraction.

Christopher Hitchens wrote an essay about the apparent lack of attention to the most important and relevant determination factor for impeachment. This "factor" was overlooked even as it was playing out during the course of the impeachment proceedings. Hitchens was apparently the only journalist among the lonely few in the otherwise "half-dead left and liberal press" with the courage to note the lack of priorities for the true necessity of impeaching President Clinton. His research showed "the failure of all political forces to examine the most crucial, and the least scrutinized, of the federal counts of impeachment. That count is "Abuse of Power."[15] These actions by the president became known as "wag the dog" bombings of remote locations to sway the easily diverted attention of the media away from his mounting sex scandals and "localized" smear campaigns.

It would appear by the sequence of events that Clinton may have actually taken a direct cue from Hollywood. Many months before any of the president's "distractionary bombings" occurred, and just before the Lewinsky affair became public knowledge, director Barry Levinson premiered his feature film *Wag the Dog* at a private screening hosted by Robert DeNiro. *Wag the Dog* depicted a fictional president starting a fictional war on a Hollywood soundstage to distract the public and press from his extramarital sexual proclivities.

Eight months later, President Clinton acted almost on cue and as scripted from the movie. "Is there only a Hollywood link between Clinton's carnality and Clinton's carnage? Was our culture hit by weapons of mass detraction?" Hitchens asked. The difference between Clinton's mini-wars and the movie was that the fictional president created his war on a soundstage and the *real* president created his war on *real* countries with the effect of killing *very real* people.

On the same night that Monica Lewinsky was returning to the grand jury for further testimony on August 20, 1998, President Clinton ordered missile strikes on the El Shifa Pharmaceutical Company in Sudan. At the same time, cruise missiles were sent flying into remote areas of Afghanistan. The "urgent" bombings also occurred just three days after the president's bent-finger pointing denial of "sexual relations with that woman—Miss Lewinsky."

These "sudden" orders of attack quickly raised red flags, not from the press or broadcast media who believed that Clinton had discovered an imminent threat. The raised eyebrows came form the intelligence community and Louis Freeh, the FBI director who had been kept out of the loop concerning the "bombshell" bombings.

The pharmaceutical plant, as it turned out, was a completely bogus target. The Clinton administration "line" was explained to the effect that the facility manufactured a precursor agent for the nerve gas VX. Unfortunately for the administration's "sexual distraction team" there was not a trace of evidence that the bombed-out location produced anything close to nerve gas. One lonely soul who happened to be near the building that night was blown away, an anonymous sacrificial lamb to a distant and dysfunctional president of a once great nation.

As Hitchens noted, "But many more have died, and will die, because an impoverished nation has lost its chief source of medicine and pesticides."[16]

On the same night of the Sudan attack, cruise missiles rained down on Afghanistan in what was supposedly a "window of opportunity" to hit Osama bin Laden that just so happened to have occurred on the very night Monica Lewinsky was returning to deliver more testimony to the grand jury investigating presidential malfeasance. This "window" was not one of the eight to ten opportunities spoken of in the last chapter by Richard "Buzz" Patterson or CIA Special Unit Chief Michael Scheuer.

The flurry of cruise missiles did not manage to hit any targets, if there were targets, and the only known casualties were among Pakistani intelligence officers who were training and equipping guerrillas for their ongoing decades-old clashes with rebels in the northern province of Kashmir. And unlike General Stormin' Norman Schwarzkopf, who relished in showing video-taped air assaults, before and after, there would be no pictures of any kind showing the devastated "targets," or craters in the desert.

With such positive coverage in the Hollywood media, Clinton would not hesitate to launch even a *third* "sexual distraction" strike on December 15, 1998, just forty-eight hours before the House impeachment debate in Congress. Clinton unleashed another volley of cruise missiles into Baghdad for violations over inspections by the UN investigating weapons sites.

Despite the fact that violations had been ongoing for over seven years, and despite the lifting of any Security Council objections in early November, President Clinton decided "tonight's the night" and, as Clinton had hoped, the important debate was delayed again. The Hollywood media rallied behind the bold action of the president with very scant mention, if at all, of the curious timing. And to the relief of the Congress, actor Alec Baldwin never showed up to kill Rep. Henry Hyde, his wife, or his children.

But the bombing of Baghdad didn't stop the debate for very long. By Saturday, December 15th, the House impeachment vote was conducted and the bombings were called off by President Clinton a few hours later. And again, the Hollywood media defense team made no mention of possible innocent death from Clinton's rush-hour decision to bomb Baghdad.

Most likely, the first to die in the Iraqi capital were the late-night cab drivers, third shift workers, and lone janitors mopping the linoleum floor of some bland sand-colored governmental building as Saddam and friends partied 300 feet underground.

These actions were clearly the Abuse of Power and even War Crimes articles that should have been included in the counts of impeachment against Bill Clinton. As Hitchens concluded, "If a president who committed war crimes to distract public attention from blackmail of female witnesses cannot be dismissed for Abuse of Power, what must he do to be told to go?"

Congressman Patrick Kennedy (D-RI) used the Clinton intimidation technique of threat, defeat, and destroy when the young son of Senator Teddy announced that any mention of a connection between bombing Baghdad and delaying impeachment "bordered on treason." Of course, inheriting the Kennedy trait of amnesia, the brash young congressman from Rhode Island forgot to mention that President Clinton had already committed high treason himself three years earlier by selling off some of America's most classified military, technological, and nuclear secrets to Communist China with a wink and a nod from the broadcast media and short-summary back-page coverage in the nation's major liberal newspapers.

And through all this, Clinton asked for nothing in return except money. He didn't even hint to the Chinese that it would be a nice gesture to stop killing and beating Christians and other "illegal" religious groups who meet in the privacy of their homes. Or maybe even an appeal process for the Chinese assembly line executions of condemned prisoners within hours of their convictions. (Only recently, in November 2006, Chinese judicial activists convinced China to reform their judicial system. The new policy is called "Kill fewer, kill carefully.")

By the beginning of President Clinton's second term, the Hollywood media defense team was quite comfortable with the Clinton motto, "Admit nothing, deny everything."

HIGH TREASON ONE

President Bill Clinton must have felt invincible by 1996 for obstructing justice and setting in motion the largest illegal transfer of America's most secret and advanced technologies. The series of blatant transfers came to the public's attention as Clinton was leasing sections of the White House for fundraising to the Democratic party and, inevitably, his own campaign for re-election. Nothing was sacred or off-limits to Bill Clinton, and breaking the law was now routine for Clinton after the president "had a talk" with Attorney General Janet Reno about her "future" as Attorney General.

After renting the Lincoln Bedroom for "sleep-overs" to Hollywood celebrities, media executives, and major Democratic contributors, Clinton turned his attention to fundraising "coffees" in various meeting rooms of the White House, such as the Map Room. Over forty of these illegal fundraising coffees were held during the month of August alone in 1996. The "expectations" were clear; in order to meet and greet the president, money would be handed over for the president's re-election. Often the money changed hands right before or right after the coffees. In some cases, envelopes passed between donors and Clinton "handlers."

Amazingly, the White House taped these coffees on video and the tapes would later be the center of a Senate inquiry into the massive breach of campaign finance laws. But using her usual gift of glitch, Attorney General Janet Reno did not "expand the inquiry" at the stated deadline date, and that which was illegal became legal, allowing President Clinton to escape justice again. No blaring headlines in *The New York Times*. The Chinese donors, however, would not escape justice.

Many of the videotapes were made public out of the "good graces" of the administration, who practically invented the word "transparency" to show there was nothing to hide. Nothing to hide except for one particular videotape that was oddly absent of audio and that one tape just so happened to show President Clinton shaking hands with Chinese fundraiser John Huang. "Johnny" was very familiar to the Clintons and very familiar with the direct pipeline to the Communist military command in Beijing.

While the major media did not bother to connect the dots to the biggest transfer of military applicable technology overseas, watchdog organizations and publications didn't take long to uncover a host of illegal donations flowing rapidly into Democratic coffers from the Communists. John Huang would not be the only "emissary" to gain unabashed access to the presidency. Many other "front men" would come and go very openly without any semblance of secrecy or shyness. After all, this was a very "open" administration, in more ways than one. That is, until they were caught.

According to the *Telegraph* of London, John Huang was even given Top Secret clearance at the Commerce Department by the administration in which he received thirty-seven intelligence briefings and maintained access to fifteen classified field reports, mostly dealing with China. And there were many other now infamous and still mysterious Chinese donors with a long leash to Communist China, such as Charlie Trie and Johnny Chung. As the *Telegraph* stated, "Bill Clinton is responsible for creating an atmosphere in which the Chinese imagined it possible to buy what they wanted." And they got almost everything they asked for, including Top Secret nuclear weapon technology as detailed in the next section, High Treason Two. And Bill Clinton says he wants to "restore" America's image?

The Communist Chinese were not working alone without already establishing connections to the firms whose high technology they wanted to buy, with the president's permission. The most flagrant of these associations that the Chinese established was with Loral Space and Communications CEO Bernard "Bernie" Schwarz, one of Bill Clinton's largest financial supporters.

Up until the mid-1990s, Chinese missile tests looked magnificent at takeoff, but floundered far from their targets. Schwarz, a former parking lot owner who had worked his way up the ladder to head an *aerospace* firm that developed and perfected a unique missile guidance system, was happy to do business with the Communists and pay off the president for permission. For the small price of only $450,000, Bernie Schwarz bought the permission he needed through channeling the single largest individual, and illegal, campaign contribution to an American president.

To transfer sensitive technology, the president needed cabinet-level approval from the Defense Department and the State Department, both of which issued a firm "no." Surely Janet Reno at Justice could give the okay, but even she refused. Clinton's shopping of permission would end with good friend and crony Ron Brown at the Department of Commerce who gladly "certified" the permission to transfer the Loral technology to the Chinese.

By the late 1990s, Chinese missiles were hitting their targets—on time, every time. With Iran and North Korea as major military arms "customers" of the Chinese, it is very likely that Clinton enabled terrorist and rogue nations to sharpen their aim. The wheel of fortune would come full circle ten years later as Iranian sponsored Hezbollah terrorists surprised the Israeli government in 2006 with a direct hit on a military Israeli ship using a mysteriously well-guided rocket.

While the Hollywood media ignored high treason as being news, only a handful of responsible media followed the fallout. Shortly after Bill Clinton left office at the end of his second term in January 2001, the U.S. State Department moved swiftly against Loral and charged the aerospace company with passing advanced military technology to the Chinese Army and fined Loral $20 million. As reported by Charles Smith of NewsMax.com, the Loral Space and Communications Company filed for bankruptcy in 2003.

As a special favor to Hollywood Bill, the Communist Chinese allowed the popular website YouTube to operate in the country with one exception: no anti-Clinton video clips allowed. They are blocked before they can even download.

HIGH TREASON TWO

If that breach of security wasn't enough, there would be a case of espionage during the Clinton presidency that was so complex and baffling, it remains a mystery to everyone except those involved in the theft and the investigation. The theft, *this time*, was not classified guidance systems for long-range missiles. The theft was the largest transfer of U.S. nuclear arsenal technology in the entire history of America's nuclear research, development, and deployment. So vast was this theft, or "transfer," America's fifty-year nuclear advantage was virtually erased overnight.

Even *The New York Times*, *The Washington Post*, and other print media services covered the story with a unique perspective gained from a source in the federal government who knew of the theft, but felt the affair was being covered up at the highest levels of the Clinton administration's Cabinet and advisors. The center of the storm was a Taiwanese-born nuclear scientist by the name of Wen Ho Lee, an employee of the Los Alamos U.S. Nuclear Laboratory in New Mexico.

The series of events that would lead up to the arrest of Lee in December 1999 began in 1995 when a Communist Chinese double-agent walked into the CIA offices in Taiwan with a document marked "Top Secret" that contained detailed descriptions of all seven of America's classified nuclear warheads, including the newly-developed and most advanced warhead known as W-88.

The information about the compromised nuclear secrets was passed on to National Security Advisor Sandy Berger and then passed on to the Department of Energy and finally to Attorney General Janet Reno at the Justice Department.

The FBI began an investigation to trace the source of the documents that landed in the lap of the Communist Chinese government. By early 1997 the investigation was closing in on the U.S. Nuclear Laboratory in Los Alamos and directly to the desk of Wen Ho Lee. And by this time, none of President Clinton's top level Cabinet members had informed him of the *theft*. That's not to say Clinton was not informed of the *transfer*. In a presidential Cabinet top-heavy with lawyers, including Clinton himself, parsing of words meant all the difference between "right" and "wrong," or "innocent" and "guilty."

As early as 1995, the Cox Report had identified Clinton appointees and fundraisers with direct ties to the Communist Chinese Army and intelligence community. The report would also reveal that MIRV encryption satellite and ICBM secrets were "given away" or "sold" in the case of "Bernie's Secret Guidance System." And what good is all that technology if you can't top it off with reliable nuclear warheads that can wipe out millions of people in the blink of an eye?

Lee maintained that he had done nothing out of the ordinary duties of his position. However, the FBI discovered that Lee had downloaded "restricted data" from computer tape files to a separate computer network that could be accessed from virtually any computer. The FBI would also discover that a local computer inside a public library in Los Alamos had been used by someone to access the "specialized network" on at least forty different occasions. But because the library did not keep user logs on their computers, the identity of the mystery user was never identified.

When the FBI gave Wen Ho Lee a polygraph test, the results showed at least two major "indicators of deception." One involved a trip Lee made to China in the 1980s when he was approached by Chinese scientists to assist them in working for their nuclear program. Lee confessed that he was approached, but didn't "cooperate." The second "indicator of deception" concerned questions as to whether Lee passed classified information to outside sources. Apparently the polygraph needle began to zig and zag.

By December 1999, Wen Ho Lee was arrested and put into solitary confinement when the extent of his actions were discovered. Lee still maintained he had done nothing illegal. However, in the course of the investigation, the FBI learned that Lee was almost fired one previous time in 1996 for his handling of sensitive data at Los Alamos.

Lee, along with certain groups within the Asian-American community, began to cry "racism" and "profiling" because of his ethnicity. Never mind the fact that the federal case against Lee eventually involved fifty-nine charges against him. As early as April 1997, eight months before his arrest, the CIA released the findings of a special investigation into Wen Ho Lee's "error of judgment" and an assessment of damage to national security. According to the CNS News Service, "This scientist, suspected of spying for China, transferred huge amounts of top secret data from computer files at Los Alamos to a widely accessible network compromising virtually every nuclear weapon in the United States Army."[17] This included the top secret and highly advanced W-88 nuclear warhead.

When the report was released, President Clinton could no longer claim ignorance of the Wen Ho Lee affair. Also, at the time of the report, journalists began to question why Lee wasn't already under arrest, given the extent of the polygraph results and the enormous gravity of the CIA assessment report. The *New York Times* and the *Washington Post* were working on "deep throat" tips from a government insider in order to report the developments in the case. NSA Director Sandy Berger would claim that he had recommended Lee's arrest many months before, but nobody "acted" on his requests. And aging hippies like Berger aren't very keen on follow-up.

That claim would all depend on whether Sandy Berger's word could be trusted. He was, after all, a self-conflicted central player in the failed attempt to catch or kill Osama bin Laden and would later be convicted, himself, of document theft from the National Archives.

Furthermore, no one in the presidential Cabinet level would definitely confirm to what extent Clinton had been "briefed" in the ongoing investigation, even in 1998, three years after the revelation by the Chinese double-agent in Taiwan. Attorney General Janet Reno was prosecuting the case with "apparent" vigor and had authorized the FBI investigation. But Reno maintained the dubious ability to initiate and stifle and investigate at the same time, as she would prove the following year in the Clinton pardon of the sixteen FALN Puerto Rican terrorists.

After Lee was finally arrested and imprisoned, the cries of "racism" and "profiling" increased. The various Asian-American associations began to protest loudly to the White House and Justice Department. The fact that Lee was placed into solitary confinement was just "too much" for all of them to tolerate, but it was an appropriate move considering the fact that Lee had communications inside Los Alamos even after his security clearance was revoked just before his arrest.

The defense of Wen Ho Lee became so ridiculous at the time, it was even suggested by some in the Asian-American community that if Lee had actually downloaded sensitive material, it was only "insurance" to "be used" in case the Los Alamos Lab attempted to fire him as they had contemplated before in 1996. If that was the best defense they could come up with, they should have called it by the proper term: blackmail. Also, some began to question who was organizing the Asian-American groups to come to Lee's defense with fifty-nine charges against him and especially after the CIA damage assessment. Could this have been a well-organized public relations ploy by known "Clinton appointees and fundraisers with direct ties to the Chinese Army" as noted in the 1995 Cox Report?

Lee became so arrogantly cocky that he was threatening to sue *The New York Times*, the *Washington Post*, and other news organizations over their secret source in the federal government. His threats came closer to reality in August 2000 when Lee was called to stand before U.S. District Judge James Parker in an extremely bizarre twist of events.

A plea agreement was worked out where Wen Ho Lee could admit to one felony count of "mishandling" nuclear secrets, and the government would allow the other fifty-eight counts to be *dropped*. Again, that's *fifty-eight counts dropped*. On top of that, Lee would be allowed to walk free even after admitting guilt to one *felony* count.

For reasons unknown even today, Federal Judge Parker took the extraordinary step of apologizing profusely for the way that Wen Ho Lee was treated, even going so far as to say that government officials had "embarrassed the entire nation" with the handling of the case. This conclusion came from a sudden "admission" by the FBI that they had "bungled" the case. This is the same FBI over which Attorney General Janet Reno had ultimate authority to determine the validity of the government's case.

In classic Clintonian administration style of good cop/bad cop, Reno told reporters that she would not apologize for the government's prosecution of Lee, even though the FBI "admitted" bungling the case. How does an agency like the FBI "bungle" fifty-eight out of fifty-nine charges of malfeasance in Wen Ho Lee's "handling" of the U.S. military's *entire nuclear arsenal*? Didn't the polygraph test, the CIA damage assessment, and numerous unauthorized actions by Lee count for anything? Or, perhaps, someone higher up in the administration "told" the FBI they had "bungled" and they needed to "suck up and shut up."

About the only memorable quote from President Clinton was that he felt "troubled" by the affair.[18] No, Clinton wasn't troubled about the theft of five decades worth of nuclear secrets including the most current weapons technology of the United States arsenal. President Clinton was "troubled" about the treatment of Wen Ho Lee.

How could this fair and just nation put such a kindly, humble nuclear scientist in solitary confinement? How embarrassing! Clinton's "troubled" feelings were conveyed before Lee's surprising release in September 2000. A convenient and all too conspicuous signal at the height of the presidential election between Vice-President Al Gore and George W. Bush.

The Asian American vote just might help sway a very close election, in fact, one of the closest presidential elections in over a century. After all, President Clinton knew how to manipulate ethnic voting patterns, just as his clemency for Puerto Rican terrorists would throw the Hispanic vote for wife Hillary. But Clinton thought clemency for a Chinese immigrant with fifty-nine charges against him might be pushing the envelope. Judge Parker lifted that "burden" from him. Furthermore, Clinton's conspicuous lack of outrage over the nuclear theft suggests Wen Ho Lee was possibly part of a much larger "transaction" between the president and Communist China, as his more blatant earlier dealings demonstrated.

An excellent book that details the Wen Ho Lee affair was written by former Department of Energy intelligence head Notra Trulock titled *Code Name: Kindred Spirit*. The Clinton administration, as was their modus operandi, decided to blame Trulock for the case going south. But Trulock offers compelling evidence that the administration was curiously playing the whole affair down and strongly suggests that Lee and his wife may have at least been Chinese double-agents.

Judge Parker's long-winded statement and "apology" at the release of Wen Ho Lee made clear—abundantly, and suspiciously frequently—that his decision did not reflect the "other branches" of government, including "the executive branch." Judge Parker made it clear that he represented "The Third Branch of Government" in his capacity as a federal judge. Wen Ho Lee even received a bonus one-million-dollar settlement in 2006 from newspapers and magazines that refused to name their source in the federal government that revealed the potential administrative cover up of the nation's largest "theft" of military and nuclear secrets. Or was it a "sale?"

By the end of President Clinton's second term, Americans had become numb to the non-stop roller coaster of scandals emanating from the White House. There was a sense among many Americans that the Clintons operated in a purposely confounding parallel universe that was distinctly opposite the traditional values of work, family, religion, and culture that had built America into a great nation. Another segment of the population developed a peculiar yellow apathy and even tolerance of a president that was secretive, manipulative, and already proven as a willing and even eager accomplice in selling the very soul and security of America.

In 2006, a Quickbird satellite captured an image of China's new nuclear submarine, the Jin-class (Type 094), which replaced the unsuccessful Xia-class (Type 092). Log onto Google Earth and see for yourself what a difference a decade makes when "the price is right." A special FBI update released in November 2007 said that there are more foreign spies operating now in the U.S. than during the period of the Cold War. The Maldon Institute also reported that the Chinese have stolen over $24 *billion* worth of secrets, largely through a network of 3,000 "front companies" set up by the Chinese in the U.S. for the sole purpose of conducting espionage. Oh, . . . you didn't read about that?

* * *

Both Bill and Hillary Clinton maintain an extreme left-wing philosophy still shared by the liberal wing of the baby-boomer generation that deeply believes that America should not be the world's only superpower. The "hippie" faction of the baby-boomers, which Bill and Hillary dabbled in frequently, were not merely anti-war protesters of the Vietnam War.

It should be remembered that Los Alamos was the target of Julius and Ethel Rosenberg in the 1940s as they gleaned nuclear bomb technology from Ethel's brother Paul Greenglass, an employee of Los Alamos. The Rosenbergs passed the technology on to the Soviets as the good Brooklyn Communists that they were.

Hillary Rodham Clinton was fascinated with Communism and interned with the head of California's Communist Party, Bob Truehaft, as he was defending the ultra-violent Black Panthers. Now, that's a good choice for a resume builder. Adding to that, Bill Clinton found Communism so compelling, he traveled to Moscow as a college student in 1970, just months after a six year battle to avoid the draft.

Julius and Ethel Rosenberg were executed for violation of the Espionage Act for treason less than the breach of national secrets that President Clinton allowed in his second term alone.

It was no coincidence that Communist North Vietnamese flags were present at most anti-war demonstrations in the 1960s. They were not "Made in America" and they were not purchased at the Berkeley campus bookstore. As you will read in the chapter on Jane Fonda, the Soviets and the North Vietnamese admitted in the 1980s to their operation of a well-organized propaganda campaign in America and the "hippies" fell in—hook, line, sinker. Much of the hippie counterculture were not merely anti-war, they were pro-Communist. The Clintons don't like to discuss their days in celebration of "flower-power," for good reason.

Perhaps the lack of groundswell outrage and legal action, then and now, can be traced to the theft of the 900-plus FBI files that occurred early in the Clinton administration at the alleged direction of the former First Lady and presidential candidate. The "Mud Room" that once existed in a dingy basement room of the Arkansas State Capitol now resides on the discs and hard drives of select Clinton Machine lap-dog laptops. This new high-tech "Mud Room" is the likely repository of the 900 names stolen from the FBI in addition to hundreds more obtained during the intervening years. No elected official, government agent, law enforcement officer, or military personnel wants their names, reputations, and careers dragged from, and through, the "Mud Room" in the form of some anonymous blog or internet chatter that could be released at the wink of an eye from Hollywood Bill and the Dragon Lady.

Senator Barack Obama found this out early in the campaign on January 19, 2007, when the internet news service *Insight Magazine* posted a story titled "Hillary's Team Has Questions about Obama's Muslim Background." The story said that Obama was not forthcoming about his education in a radical Muslim school known as a Madrassa when he was a boy in Indonesia. The next day on January 20, 2007, Senator Hillary Clinton formally announced her exploratory committee to run for president of the United States. Coincidence or business as usual?

The catastrophic effects of Bill Clinton's reckless administration are still being felt today as the United States tries to rebuild its intelligence gathering capacity. As *Sabotage* author Rowan Scarborough noted, the U.S. capacity for gathering foreign intelligence was chipped away during Clinton's administration, a point also noted by *Jawbreaker* author and former intelligence officer Gary Bernsten and others.

And Hillary wanted to make hubby Bill a global ambassador? Please, spare us another tragedy!

A TIME FOR CLOSURE

This perspective of the past and present is important for understanding the prospects for the future. Under President Clinton, the American culture took a deeper dive than any other time since Jack Valenti "invented" the Ratings Scheme in 1968. This can be attributed largely to the fact that Clinton was the first "Hollywood President." Though Ronald Reagan came out of Hollywood, he gracefully lived it down. As Jack Valenti noted, "The movie business is a dazzling, unpredictable world—like politics—and naturally Clinton is drawn to that."

Hollywood loved the First Couple because they hailed from the good old days of "sex, drugs, and rock-n-roll." Hollywood also appreciated Clinton's FCC, which became very lax in enforcing thousands of broadcast indecency and obscenity complaints that were filed during his administration. There are laws governing both, they just weren't enforced. And that's how Hollywood liked it, unlike President Bush's FCC, which has levied over three million dollars in fines against sleaze producers and networks. Tinseltown preferred the Clinton enforcement policy of "deciding not to decide."

Also, network entertainment executives were privately very pleased with the TV Ratings Scheme that Clinton ushered in, with Jack Valenti's help, under the

THE HOLLYWOOD CULTURE WAR

guise of "greater parental control." In reality, TV ratings solidified the "red-light district" reputation of most cable offerings and gave the networks equal sleaze status to the signals beamed directly into your living room.

When the far-left bias of Hollywood was revealed to the masses at the movie theater after 1968, the same bias bled into television "entertainment" and "news" to the point where millions of viewers have tuned out completely. It is not uncommon to hear people young and old remark, "I don't watch much television anymore, except for the Discovery Channel, Animal Planet, HGTV, Turner Classic Movies, the Food Channel, Outdoor Channel, or Fox News." Most viewers would rather watch reruns of *When Good Pets Go Bad* before watching raunchy episodic dramas or sitcoms.

The mere mention of Fox News rankles the liberal left so much that pock marks appear on faces of those so affected. For decades the nation had become so accustomed to one side of every news story on broadcast reports that the novel idea of a cable news organization providing two sides of every story caught the network nation by surprise. As Ann Coulter noted in *Godless*, concerning American media before and after Fox News, "There were only three TV stations, three major newspapers, and a handful of national magazines, all run by liberals.... The appearance of Fox News Channel nearly drove liberals berserk: they were supposed to control 100 percent of news dissemination."[19]

So shocking was the prospect of hearing another perspective on national and international news stories that many people branded the upstart news channel as part of "a vast right-wing conspiracy." The phrase was coined by none other than the former First Lady and Democratic presidential candidate Hillary Rodham Clinton.

Fox News is the only channel that provides news programming free of Hollywood influence, even though it is a division of the massive 20th Century Fox entertainment empire and Rupert Murdoch's News Corporation. Joseph Farah's *WorldNetDaily* and Christopher Ruddy's *NewsMax* on the web and in print have also revolutionized the dissemination of the news that was once the domain of *Newsweek* and *Time*.

Unfortunately a growing number of young people are getting what they perceive as "real news" from comedians such as Jay Leno, David Letterman, Conan O'Brien, Bill Maher, Stephen Colbert, and Jon Stewart. Producer Ken Burns discovered how clueless the "Y" generation is when he disclosed that many recent high school graduates believed America fought *with* the Nazi army to defeat the Soviets in World War II!

But the time has come to realize that the Hollywood nation is here and intends to continue the manipulation of your values. As Appendix I and II demonstrate, Hollywood is steadily increasing its financial contributions to the political process in every election cycle, especially to the Democratic party and particularly to the far left elements within the party.

Again, "tristrangulation" would be employed to appropriate, temporarily, the moderate and conservative values of the country to sneak the far left wing of the Democratic party into the mainstream. This was accomplished in November 2006 by the Democratic congressional campaign coordinator Rahm Emmanuel, former Clinton administration official, Clinton Machine shadow member, Soros operative, and current congressman. Hollywood now knew the strategy and would be able to better focus its cash pipeline to Washington.

Forget the fact that former al Qaeda leader Abu al Masri of Iraq praised American voters for choosing Democrats, a sentiment shared by other middle-east terrorist groups such as Hamas, Hezbollah, and the glorious ayatollahs of Iran. The Democrats have already floated more than ten proposals and bills that would have alerted al Qaeda to be patient, their victory is near and they can count on the sage presidents of Bill Clinton and Jimmy Carter to defend "terrorist rights" to attack America. Best of all, the terrorists may return to making phone calls without the fear that America is listening in. This *will* happen in a Democratic presidential victory, especially an Obama victory.

And Hollywood will do its part to further the extremist terrorists' twisted crusade. As Iraqi war veteran Staff Sergeant David Bellavia explained after returning home, "They judge us by our primetime television." And he's not just talking about entertainment. In a November 2006 ad campaign by NBC to bring viewers back into the one-sided fold of network news, a scolding Brian Williams is rebuking President Bush, "You've apologized for the damage. What about the damage to your presidency! . . . It's enough to make one spiritual all over again!" This one tirade by NBC should be enough to tell you why people are abandoning network news by the millions, and even more so as a percentage of America's 300 million plus population. This is the same network that censored its own interview with Clinton's "very reliable" rape victim. Brian Williams and former anchor Tom Brokaw didn't express any rage about that. It was just sex.

* * *

Perhaps radio talk show host Jay Severin was not too far off base when he declared to Tucker Carlson on MSNBC that "Hillary is the devil," after the Senator from New York appeared, opportunistically, at one of Billy Graham's last revivals in 2005. The devil? No. A disciple? Well . . .

Because the Clinton Machine has desensitized the nation to corruption, scandal, and treason on a scale unprecedented in this country, we can only offer closure to a long drifting albatross that has choked America for almost two decades and continues to hover just above the surface.

During the peak of the presidential impeachment debate on December 10, 1998, Democrat David Schippers of the House Judiciary Committee Counsel concluded that President Bill Clinton "has lied under oath in a civil deposition, lied under oath in a criminal grand jury. He lied to the people, he lied to his Cabinet, he lied to his top aides, and now he's lied to the Congress of the United States. There's no one left to lie to."

And Hillary Clinton followed her husband's example in perfect lock-step in her quest for all-encompassing power. Few remember, or never even knew, that Hillary Clinton demanded to occupy the historic office space reserved for the vice-president when the Clintons were moving into the White House in 1993. Only upon the heated protest of Vice President Al Gore did she relent. It would be one of Gore's few victories earned as vice-president, pre global warming guru.

To further demonstrate the "admit nothing, deny everything" team solidarity of Mr. and Mrs. Clinton, William Safire summarized Hillary Clinton best when he penned the essay "Blizzard of Lies" in which he wrote, "Americans of all political persuasions are coming to the sad realization that our First Lady . . . is a congenital liar."

With this in mind, it is time for Americans to reach out and offer the Clintons a chance. A chance for a new beginning because of their service to this country, to justice, and their dedication to each other. The following address has been provided to Mr. and Mrs. Clinton so that they can help resolve the "Unresolved Crimes" of their eight-year co-presidency:

The Federal Bureau of Investigation
New York Field Office
26 Federal Plaza
New York, NY 10278

Again, it *is* time to give the Clintons this chance. Of course, that depends on what the definition of "is" is.

Because Hillary Clinton will not be reading this book, the only assignment for the freshman graduating Class of 2012 is to write Senator Clinton and let her know you have completed International Relations 101. In your letter, write down the FBI address above and let the Senator know that you want to get on with your life without any distractions from her or Bill. Be kind when writing the Senator from New York and send your letters to the following address:

Sen. Hillary Clinton
4420 North Fairfax Dr.
Arlington, VA 22203

Once you have sent your letter, you will have passed your course with flying colors. Congratulations!

MICHAEL VINCENT BOYER

Hollywood Bill and Hillary's Traveling Crime Show
(Crime statistics of America's Most Corrupt First Couple)
CONTRIBUTIONS TO THE CULTURE WAR

ALL TIME RECORDS SET:

- The only elected president to ever be impeached
- The only president ever impeached on grounds of personal malfeasance
- Most number of convictions and guilty pleas by friends and associates
- Most number of cabinet officials to come under criminal investigation
- Most number of witnesses to flee the country or refuse to testify
- Most number of witnesses to die suddenly
- First president sued for sexual harassment
- First president accused of rape
- First first lady to come under criminal investigation
- Largest criminal plea agreement in an illegal campaign contribution case
- First president to establish a legal defense fund
- First president to be held in contempt of court
- Greatest amount of illegal campaign contributions
- Greatest amount of illegal campaign contributions from abroad
- First president disbarred from the U.S. Supreme Court and a state court

THE STARR-RAY FEDERAL INVESTIGATION OF CLINTON CORRUPTION:

- Number of Starr-Ray investigation convictions or guilty pleas (including one governor, one associate attorney general, and two Clinton business partners): 14
- Number of Clinton Cabinet members who came under criminal investigation: 5

CRIME STATS:

- Number of individuals and businesses associated with the Clinton machine who have been convicted of or pleaded guilty to crimes: 47
- Number of these convictions during Clinton's presidency: 33
- Number of indictments/misdemeanor charges: 61
- Number of congressional witnesses who have pleaded the Fifth Amendment, fled the country to avoid testifying, or (in the case of foreign witnesses) refused to be interviewed: 122

SMALTZ FEDERAL INVESTIGATION OF CLINTON'S AGRICULTURE SECRETARY:

- Guilty pleas and convictions obtained by Donald Smaltz in cases involving charges of bribery and fraud against former Agriculture Secretary Mike Espy and associated individuals and businesses: 15
- Acquitted or overturned cases (including Espy): 6
- Fines and penalties assessed: $11.5 million
- Amount Tyson Food paid in fines and court costs: $6 million

CRIMES AND CONVICTIONS OF "THE CLINTON MACHINE":

- Drug trafficking (3); racketeering, extortion, bribery (4); tax evasion, kickbacks, embezzlement (2); fraud (12); conspiracy (5); fraudulent loans, illegal gifts (1); illegal campaign contributions (5); money laundering (6).

OTHER INVESTIGATIONS BY SPECIAL PROSECUTORS, CONGRESS, AND INVESTIGATIVE JOURNALISTS:

Bank and mail fraud, violations of campaign finance laws, illegal foreign campaign funding, improper exports of sensitive technology, physical violence and threats of violence, solicitation of perjury, intimidation of witnesses, bribery of witnesses, attempted intimidation of prosecutors, perjury before congressional committees, lying in statements to federal investigators and regulatory officials, flight of witnesses, obstruction of justice, bribery of cabinet members, real estate fraud, tax fraud, drug trafficking, failure to investigate drug trafficking, bribery of state officials, use of state police for personal purposes, exchange of promotions or benefits for sexual favors, using state police to provide false court testimony, laundering of drug money through a state agency, false reports by medical examiners and others investigating suspicious deaths, the firing of the RTC and FBI director when these agencies were investigating Clinton and his associates, failure to conduct autopsies in suspicious deaths, providing jobs in return for silence by witnesses, drug abuse, improper acquisition and use of 900 FBI files, improper futures trading, murder, sexual abuse of employees, false testimony before a federal judge, shredding of documents, withholding and concealment of subpoenaed documents, fabricated charges against (and improper firing of) White House employees, inviting drug traffickers, foreign agents, and participants in organized crime to the White House.

4,052 CASES OF AMNESIA:

Number of times that Clinton figures who testified in court or before Congress said that they didn't remember, didn't know, or something similar:

- Bill Clinton: 250
- Bill Kennedy: 116
- Harold Ickes: 148
- Ricki Seidman: 160
- Bruce Lindsey: 161
- Bill Burton: 191
- Mark Gearson: 221
- Mack McLarty: 233
- Neil Eggleston: 250
- Hillary Clinton: 250
- John Podesta: 264
- Jennifer O'Connor: 343
- Dwight Holton: 348
- Patsy Thomasson: 420
- Jeff Eller: 697

Source: The Progressive Review, http//prorev.com/legacy.htm

CHAPTER 6

The Rise and Fall of the Obama Nation
starring
DAVID GEFFEN • JESSE JACKSON • GEORGE SOROS

> *Everybody lies in politics, but the Clintons do it with such ease it's troubling.*
> —Producer David Geffen

To best understand the *true* Barack Obama is to look back at the actions of the Illinois senator and the people he associated himself with during the Democratic primary race. As a master of verbal nuance and subtle condescension, Obama's modus operandi is to dismantle and dissipate criticism of his empty oratory and Chicago leftist politics by rendering any opposition as "irrelevant" through dismissive sarcasm or thinly veiled hints of public "intolerance."

More than any other phrase in the marketplace of free ideas, Obama literally *hates* the term Culture War because it is one battle he can't seem to win. In July 2007, Obama tried to extinguish the phrase when he declared, "I am absolutely convinced that the Culture Wars are just *so* 90s." Like . . . for real? At the same time he was proposing mandatory sex education to four and five-year-olds in kindergarten while simultaneously bashing Ambassador Alan Keyes, a favorite pastime.

Obama's double-entendre far-left attacks made him a favorite of the Hollywood crowd which entitles Obama to this special chapter in *The Hollywood Culture War*. His first major collective contribution of one million dollars came by way of a Hollywood fundraiser in February 2007. And this is where the story of the Obama candidacy began and the people who supported him.

Tom Fitton summarized the Geffen tirade of February 2007 best when he commented, "Maureen Dowd wrote a column that contained quotes from an interview with Hollywood mogul and former Bill Clinton fundraiser David

Geffen (who supported Obama during the primaries) chastising the Clintons for their corrupt record. He even referenced Bill's adulterous behavior! Yes, you read that correctly. Someone from Hollywood called the Clintons corrupt and dishonest."[1]

Geffen's "everybody lies" quote was especially noteworthy for a man who has been variously described by people inside and outside the entertainment industry as "unfair," "untrustworthy," "deceitful," "liar," and a "con artist" of "bendable honesty." (For the larger list, see Chapter 20, The Velvet Mafia: Fact or Fiction?)

And there lies the irony in the not-so-strange bedfellows of producer David Geffen of Hollywood and Senator Barack Obama of Washington. Geffen sponsored an enormous fundraiser for Obama at the Beverly Hills Hilton with over 700 invited guests from a list carefully cultivated by the former record producer turned movie mogul. Each guest was expected to contribute $2,300, the federal maximum individual contribution. The final tally came in just under one million dollars.

As a friend of mine opined the day before the event, "My wife and I get this invitation from Geffen to attend an Obama fundraiser. We know nothing about Obama but we know everything about Geffen. If we don't send in twenty-three hundred dollars for *each* of us, we know that David will keep a little black book with a list of who gave and who didn't. And a person's status in that little black book could negatively affect a project we may be working on with someone who is friends with David or his partners Spielberg and Katzenberg. This is more than just a fundraiser for Obama. It's another opportunity by Geffen to blackmail somebody who didn't ante-up when he held his hand out."

Many others felt the same way, though there were undoubtedly a few genuine Obama supporters who fell into the "usual suspects" category such as Oliver Stone, Demi Moore, Norman Lear, Ben Affleck, Halle Berry, Matt Damon, and George Clooney who said he would do anything for Obama, even if it meant "staying out of sight." However, the big news was Geffen's post fundraiser tirade at his sprawling Hollywood mansion and its fifty-foot bar where he spewed the venom of the two-headed snake that he is. Geffen used typical movie lingo to say that Hillary was *overproduced* and *overscripted*. Geffen doubted that "Bill's behavior" had changed in the last six years, as if Geffen was a pillar of morality; quite the opposite.

Geffen was acting in typical Geffen fashion. He had raised over $18 million for Bill Clinton and the Democratic party in the 1990s and he gave generously to Clinton's legal defense fund to protect "Bill's behavior." Geffen, a petty personality of low estate who once ended a long friendship with agent Sandy Gallin over comments about a leather chair, was only behaving true to form—a form of beast.

Geffen claimed that Bill Clinton's refusal to pardon Hollywood's favorite criminal poster child, Leonard Peltier, was the reason for the split from the

Clintons. Peltier is serving time for murdering two FBI agents, but Geffen noted one of Clinton's other pardons as "less deserving."

David Geffen personally lobbied for Peltier's release for his noble act of killing two members of *the establishment*. Clinton's pardon frenzy at the end of his term included Marc Rich. According to Geffen, "Marc Rich getting pardoned? An oil-profiteer ex-patriot who left the country rather than pay taxes or face justice?" Not that Marc Rich was any role model either, but Hollywood loves an underdog cold-blooded killer who took on the law and took two agents out in the process. (Who cares about the victims' families?)

Geffen either saw a little or a lot of himself in Obama, an ambitious politician who will say and do whatever it takes to get the prize at the end of the road. Even if it means lying, something Geffen is familiar with. The little movie mogul, no doubt, had been listening to the young senator and liked what he heard and liked what he saw.

This was Obama's first major exposure to Hollywood fundraising. Obama and his staff would later become infatuated with the young "hip" Hollywood crowd that graced the tabloid covers. One of his covert fundraisers in Hollywood was held at a trendy-trashy Tinseltown nightspot for up-and-coming alcoholic and drug-addicted celebrities.

At the time of the Hollywood Hilton fundraiser, word was beginning to leak out from the press that Obama's earlier 1995 "autobiography" was turning out to be a clever piece of fiction by a fractured personality who was desperately trying to rewrite his life history into the most convincing of personal fantasies. Obama was painting himself as obsessively fixated on discovering his true identity in a world of racism that tried to oppress his rise to the top. The *Chicago Tribune* conducted more than forty interviews with former classmates, friends, teachers, and neighbors and what emerged was a portrait of a man less fixated than he *pretended* on discovering his racial identity.

It was all turning out to be a lie from Obama, but that is exactly why David Geffen liked him. Anyone as deceptive and manipulative as David Geffen was worthy of the mogul's full support. Besides, Geffen wanted another shot at influencing national political policy much the way he had operated as Clinton's de-facto Secretary of Defense.

Geffen appreciated Obama's stealth ability to mix and match gender agendas and other viewpoints in a single sentence that really didn't make any point other than to demonstrate that Obama was and remains "all things to all people." Especially moving for Geffen was Obama's declaration, "We coach little league in the Blue States and, yes, we have gay friends in the Red States." Obama also attacked conservative black pastors and their congregations as "homophobic."

Shortly after Geffen's endorsement, Obama hired the West Hollywood "gay power couple" of Jeremy Bernard and Rufus Gifford to tap into the "L.A. homosexual money pot" to help finance his campaign. According to the *L.A.*

Weekly, Bernard was "surprised" that Obama voiced his "federal gay agenda" talking points virtually verbatim at public events. Bernard also had suggestions for the kindergarten sex-ed proposals that Obama hopes to initiate.

Barack Obama was rapidly gaining a reputation of mastering double-speak by proclaiming open-ended statements that combined arbitrary issues that are not assigned values and then declaring his "openness" and "hope" for the future results of a stand he hadn't taken and never would take. These became known as "Obaminations."

Hollywood also appreciates Obama's ability to inject God into anti-American proclamations such as his 2004 declaration at the Democratic National Convention. "We worship an awesome God in the Blue States and we don't like federal agents poking around libraries in the Red States."

Obama is a staunch opponent of the Patriot Act and other measures to intercept terrorist plots to launch more attacks on Americans. Obama called American troops who gave their lives in defense of freedom as "wasted" instead of "patriots." He was also a "no-show" on a vote in July 2007 that would provide protection for "John Doe" whistleblowers who suspected terrorist activity in America. It is Obama's perversion of basic American values of security and safety that excites Geffen, a reckless individual who revels in bashing America's belief in faith and family.

Perhaps Geffen sensed that Obama is also easy to control because he has no true compass or sense of direction. In the timeline of Obama's myth-making anthology, he demonstrates his inability to focus. As Joe Klein of *Time* magazine noted, "But the tendency is so pronounced that it almost seems an obsessive-compulsive tic. I counted no fewer than fifty instances of excruciatingly judicious on-the-one-hand-on-the-other-handedness in *Audacity of Hope*."[2]

Obama's identity complex and personality disorder have raised hushed concerns among current and would-be supporters, especially after watching Obama change his pentameter and rhythm of speech to pander to specific audiences. More troubling to some was Obama's own admission in his book that, "I am even robbed of the certainty of uncertainty."

Could Obama be appealing to the "pity me" vote, which can be substantial. Author Rousas J. Rushdoony profiled candidate models just like Obama more than thirty years ago in his book *The Politics of Guilt and Pity*.

As writer and film critic Steve Sailer asked, "Which Obama is real? Or is that a naive question to ask of such a formidable identity artist? William Finnegan wrote in the *New Yorker* of Obama's campaigning: ' . . . it was possible to see him slipping subtly into the idiom of his interlocutor—the blushing, polysyllabic grad student, the hefty black church-pillar lady, the hip-hop auto-shop guy.' Like Madonna or David Bowie, he has spent his life trying on different personalities, but while theirs are, in Camille Paglia's phrase, sexual personae, his specialty is race personae."[3]

Obama critic Andy Martin sees deeper unresolved problems that are rooted in Obama's childhood of abandonment. Martin references *High Risk: Children Without a Conscience* in which the authors describe children who suffer from incomplete bonding and carry over certain behaviors throughout their adult life. "Obama is such a person. He can lie about the facts because reality is meaningless to him.

"His fantasy world is what controls. And because of the hope, and guilt, that have surrounded his political climb, his supporters and his audiences have failed to confront Obama over his confusion of fantasy and reality."[4]

As is common with many liberal leftist Democrats, the guilt card is a favorite at the political table, especially at election time. Obama manages to manipulate the card in ways that people are not even aware they are being used by an emerging master of social and political subterfuge. Author Shelby Steele, who writes extensively about the psychology of race, noted Obama's skill with each crowd he addresses. "White people are just thrilled when a prominent black person comes along and doesn't rub their noses in racial guilt."[5] At least not *blatantly*.

Not only was Barack Obama successful in designating victimhood on millions of Americans who didn't know what hit them, by March of 2008, Obama was portraying himself as a victim, according to columnist Matt Lewis. This would garner the Illinois senator a sizeable number of the "pity vote" from American voters who fell for the deceptive campaign ploy.

That is Obama's most subtle use of the guilt card. The more direct form was on display at Brown's AME Chapel in Selma, Alabama, where he told the congregation that his grandfather was a "boy" for the British, which had a trilateral effect. First, it was a lie. Second, he defamed his grandfather's legacy, and third, he viewed the Selma congregation contemptuously by pandering to the worst stereotypes concerning African-Americans.

Obama even squeezed in a fourth weapon of guilt in the same sentence by hinting at class warfare. His grandfather, Onyango, actually prospered very well under the British colonial system of the early twentieth century and became a wealthy farmer and landowner whose legacy is still remembered today in Kenya. But instead of portraying his grandfather as a success story to the captive audience in Selma, Obama wrote him off as a "boy" for the British. (More in Obama's defining "Selma Stage Play" later in this chapter.)

While Obama handles the subtle manipulation of race, David Geffen had hoped that the sexual reorientation guilt card was played also. This is a strategy which has been used for almost forty years within the Democratic party as well as outside the party line. Author E. Michael Jones refers to this tactic as "liberal guilt cookies."

As Jones explains, "Guilt has not only become endemic, it has become a powerful political tool. Liberalism, as currently practiced, is the politics of guilt. Guilt is the engine that pulls the liberal train. We all know that racism and misogyny are wrong: what we are interested in here is the political grammar of those ostensibly involved in righting these wrongs.

"The Democratic party is a good example of how all this gets brokered. The women blackmail the liberals, who feel guilty about the sexual revolution, and the feminist power block comes into existence. The homosexuals blackmail the feminists, who feel guilty about abortion and so compensate by allowing the homosexuals to become officially dedicated victims, so that the feminists won't have to face the real victims—their own aborted children. Guilt becomes the power base for each of these movements. It becomes the medium of exchange in the political marketplace. In order to play, you must first get yourself designated as a victim."[6]

Guilt, mythology, and fantasy all drive Obama's raw ambition to seek power. And his inability to acknowledge truth rivals that of both Bill and Hillary Clinton combined. As Steve Sailer observed, "His personal passions routinely war against his acknowledging unwelcome truths, even to himself."[7]

Barack Obama's almost pathological ability to express or redirect truth has been carefully covered up by the media, again excusing his snafus as "emotional truths" or simply "rookie mistakes" that anyone running for office the first time are bound to make. The problem is, it's not the first time he has run for office.

The press had a vested interest in covering up for Obama. Just like Bill Clinton, Obama was their original pick for president. He was officially "nominated" for president by *Time* magazine and writer Joe Klein on October 23, 2006, when they placed Barack Obama's face on the cover with the caption overlaid in carefully ascending typeface "Why Barack Obama Could Be THE NEXT PRESIDENT."

Just as the mainstream press turned a blind eye to Bill Clinton's well-established fifteen-year record of lying as an Arkansas politician, the same template was being followed with Obama. Only *WorldNetDailey* gave any national coverage to State Senator Barack Obama's perversely adamant support of infanticide in Illinois between 2001 and 2004.

The media and Hollywood have been Obama's enablers. As Andy Martin notes, this cover-up trickles down to his supporters who serve as his enablers at the grass root. "The more he lies, the more he gets away with. The bigger the lie, the less he is called on it."[8] Obama and his top advisor David Axelrod have already resorted to calls of "racism" when they cannot or will not answer substantive questions or give a response to even the most basic articles of constructive criticism.

Again, the early cast of characters who came to support Obama at the starting gate speaks volumes about Obama himself for embracing some of this nation's most abominable human beings who, in lack of judicious investigation or aggressive prosecution, are walking the streets when they should be sitting in a prison cell.

If this sounds familiar, it should. Barack Obama was surrounding himself with the same den of thieves who were there for Bill Clinton in 1992. Obama had not realized that these individuals were not joining *his* team. Rather, Obama had been invited into *their* team, by accepting their money and their endorsements. The club's name has not changed since the early days of Bill Clinton; The League of Extraordinary Liars, Thieves, and Con Men.

A closer look at the cast of David Geffen, Jesse Jackson, and George Soros will shed light on three of the most truly malevolent men in modern American history.

DAVID GEFFEN

By the age of eighteen, David Geffen was already a thief, stealing his mother's Social Security check after his father had died. By the time he was twenty-one, Geffen had lied about his nonexistent education from the UCLA Theater Department on an application for employment with the William Morris Talent Agency in 1964.

After being hired based on that fraudulent information and another lie that he was Phil Spector's cousin, Geffen quickly learned in his new mail room job that all applications would be double-checked for accuracy. Frantic, he arrived early at the agency every morning until he saw a letter arrive with a UCLA return address. Naturally, Geffen had been exposed as a fraud in the letter.

Geffen would instantly transition from thief and liar to forger as he pleaded with his attorney brother, Mitchell, to help him forge yet another lie in the form of a letter to William Morris that he had, in fact, graduated form UCLA. As biographer Tom King stated in *The Operator*, "In the surest sign yet that Geffen's moral compass was off kilter, he did not believe he had done anything wrong . . . and he proudly boasted about it throughout his life."[9]

David Geffen would operate on that morally vacant template as his career guide from that point onward. He would eventually work his way up the ladder to become an agent and record producer with his own company, Geffen Records. His climb was marked by vicious, ruthless power plays, backstabbing, vengeance, and even violent encounters with rivals in alleys and restaurants.

More bizarre was Geffen's sick habit of mixing conversational sexual conquests with business negotiations that unsettled more than a few clients and musicians who signed with him. It was not uncommon for Geffen to warm up to a new record group or agent by breaking the ice with a quick chat about sleeping with a homosexual prostitute or a barely legal boy he picked up at a party.

Without hesitation or the blink of an eye, Geffen would effortlessly segue into deal making. While many were shocked initially with this behavior, most new clients felt Geffen could definitely be trusted since he was so open about his predatory life. Many were sadly mistaken and disappointed after signing on the dotted line.

In his early record producing days, Geffen became noted as the driving force behind such groups as Crosby, Stills, and Nash, and the Eagles among others in the late 1960s and early 1970s. But by the early 1980s, Geffen was helping to create, promote, and publicize some of the music industry's most horrific and offensive "artists" such as Guns-n-Roses heavy metal trash and the suicidal "grunge" of Kurt Cobain and Nirvana. Worst of all, David Geffen was the ultimate industry epitome of the white record company executive helping to push the most violent, profane, and vulgar new sounds of hip-hop and rap, including the Geto Boys, who later moved to another division and popularized "necrophilia" hip-hop.

Geffen used to brag about his rap groups and the money he pulled in by "pushing" their music on American youth. But after selling Geffen Records to Universal in 1990, he seldom mentioned his association with the hip-hop music he helped to produce, preferring instead to recall the glory days with Joni Mitchell, David Crosby, Cher, and others.

By 1994, Geffen joined with Steven Spielberg and Jeffrey Katzenberg to form Dreamworks SKG movie studio. Two years earlier he had ingratiated himself with Bill and Hillary Clinton and would raise millions of dollars for them politically and personally. That same year, 1992, he had announced his homosexuality at an AIDS benefit in his honor in Los Angeles.

When Geffen boasted arrogantly at the 2007 Obama fundraiser that the Clintons lied so effortlessly it was "troubling," most people inside the industry laughed at Geffen's hypocrisy. Most people outside of the entertainment industry knew little about Geffen's easy access to the White House in general, and a particular meeting specifically, where he instructed President Clinton on the fine art of "spinning the press" when it came to getting publicity.

Hillary Clinton had called Geffen to help arrange a surprise forty-eighth birthday party for the president. Geffen was more than happy to comply and even brought along President Clinton's favorite band, Crosby, Stills, and Nash, to perform. The band was also happy to oblige, even though they were aware that the malignant backstabber Geffen had recently referred to them as "old fat farts."

Geffen also brought along his new boyfriend, thirty-year-old competitive diver Todd Mulzert, in order to impress him. After the impromptu concert at the White House, Geffen and Mulzert met privately with the president in the Oval Office. According to biographer Tom King, "[Clinton] was angry at the news coverage his policies had gotten and frustrated at his failure to spin the media." It was premature paranoia. He forgot, the media had "spun" him into office.

Apparently Clinton had asked the master manipulator and veteran Hollywood liar about a subject he knew well. "Geffen launched into a forty-five minute lecture on how to spin the media."[10] Geffen even concluded his free lesson in deception with a plea for Clinton to curry more support from some of the "more liberal" elements of the Democratic party. (Without fail, he would eagerly give Obama the same advice in early 2007.)

As Geffen and Mulzert entered a waiting car to take them back to the airport, a grinning Geffen turned to Mulzert.

"How was I?"

"What do you mean?" Mulzert replied, a bit puzzled. "You were great."

"I did that for You," Geffen explained. "Imagine," he continued after a pause. "*Me* . . . giving the president advice!"

"It's a little scary actually," Mulzert deadpanned. "As a citizen of the United States, it's not something I wanted to see."[11]

Geffen will not say what boyfriend he was trying to impress back in 1992 when he "ordered" Clinton to de-heterosexualize the military. David Geffen forgot to tell Maureen Dowd that little history lesson during his post-fundraiser euphoria for Obama.

If only Barack Obama knew what David Geffen *really* thinks about him.

JESSE JACKSON

"I was there from the beginning," Jesse Jackson used to say. He doesn't say it much anymore because the "beginning" bears no resemblance to the present life of Jesse Jackson, one of a very small handful of people known as a Quadra-Pleader (Paper Pastor Poverty Pimp). We won't refer to him as "Reverend" in light of numerous unreturned phone calls I made to his organization, Operation PUSH.

All I was asking was where Mr. Jackson "earned," or perhaps "learned," to place the title of divinity before his name. Since he had originally endorsed Barack Obama in March 2007, it only seemed logical to ask the question for biographical purposes. The Obama Chicago-based Headquarters didn't return my calls either, because they don't know or they don't want to know.

The "beginning" was 1968 in Memphis, Tennessee, with the very real Reverend Martin Luther King, Jr. Jackson, a Chicago native, had recently joined the Southern Christian Leadership Conference (SCLC) to help Rev. King's outreach into the northern urban areas where racism, especially as demonstrated in Chicago, was more entrenched and institutionalized than the media had ever previously revealed.

On April 4, 1968, Rev. King was in Memphis to support a strike by the city's sanitation workers. Rev. King, Rev. Ralph Abernathy, and Jackson were waiting near the second floor balcony of the Lorraine Motel when a shot rang out striking Rev. Martin Luther King. As he lay dying, Rev. Abernathy and Jackson held his head up as other members of the group pointed in the direction where the shots were heard.

With his own shirt sufficiently soaked with blood, Jackson would revert back to the Chicago hustler he had always been from the real beginning. Jackson wore the same shirt for almost two days as he arranged numerous television interviews in which the blood on his shirt was specifically pointed out, cameras zooming in. People who didn't know who Jackson was before that day, certainly would remember him from that day on.

The "bloody shirt" tactic would forever remain a source of tension between Jackson and King's widow, Coretta Scott King. She knew what Jackson was trying to do in anointing himself with the blood of her dead husband. Jackson thought surely this was a sign of divine intervention, or financial opportunity, and played it to the hilt.

Rev. Ralph Abernathy, who had been with King since the 1950s in Alabama, was the vice-president of SCLC and was the natural successor to King. However, between 1968 and 1971, Jackson squabbled frequently with Abernathy as he tried to exert his Chicago militant philosophy of administration at SCLC headquarters. By 1971, Abernathy had enough and fired Jackson for "administrative improprieties" and other repeated "insubordinate" behavior.

Jackson organized PUSH that same year and has been the organization's sole Emperor Jones for over thirty-five years. For a short period of time in the 1970s, he tried to be an "empowerer" instead of "emperor," but discovered that shaking down corporations was more profitable. Jackson really wanted to be president, but the millions he was making by lifting cash out of the pockets of American businessmen was too lucrative.

Doubtless, as a Chicagoan, Jackson was familiar with the local author and evangelist of corporate guilt shakedowns, Saul Alinsky, who wrote *Reveille for Radicals* in 1945 and *Rules for Radicals* in 1971. Alinsky "performed" the first guilt-ridden race shakedown in 1967 with the Eastman Kodak Company of Rochester, New York. Money was often "donated" to his Industrial Areas Foundation in Chicago, tax free.

While Jackson was perfecting the Alinsky model of corporate shakedowns, fellow Chicagoan Barack Obama was mastering the art of "emotional shakedowns" of potential voters to pity-party his way up the political ladder. The March 2007 love embrace between Jackson and Obama was only natural.

In both men's strategies, guilt and victimhood had to be established in order to receive money or votes. Though both pretend to champion a pluralistic society, victimhood is essential. Jesse Jackson would display his tactics more blatantly by using threats of mass boycotts by African-Americans in order to receive a "settlement" for "alleged" discrimination by a business or corporation. By continuing to paint African-Americans as victims, he has essentially created a perpetual culture of poverty that has kept a large segment of the black population in a constant state of repression and separatism, not too different from the rantings of Obama's former radical Chicago pastor, Dr. Jeremiah Wright.

John H. McWhorter, a linguistics professor at Berkeley wrote *Losing the Race* in which he demonstrates how African-Americans are damaging themselves when they embrace images of victimhood. He convincingly asserts that the black separatist philosophy and anti-intellectualism is robbing African-Americans of their motivation and ability to be successful in a multi-cultural American society.

While the mainstream Hollywood media refused to report on Jackson's antics, partially out of their own collective guilt and fear, author Ken Timmerman wrote an extensive exposé that explains in detail how Jackson stalks corporations for millions of dollars in "contributions" to Operation PUSH, not to be confused with Operation EXTORT. In his book, *Shakedown*, Timmerman also demonstrates how Jesse Jackson contemptuously uses African-Americans in his game-plan strategy.

After reading *Shakedown*, Jamaal Michaels of Baltimore noted that, "As a black man, I've always been disgusted by the hypocritical, racist actions of Jesse Jackson Sr. Unmistakably, this vicious scam artist has done more to set back race relations in the U.S. than the KKK ever dreamed of.... Hopefully the U.S. Justice Department will read this book as well and feel compelled to finally indict Jackson."[12]

Also, Jackson's actions put into question, again, the nature of his divinity degree. His hypocrisy, mass deception, and collective distribution of victimhood and guilt has devastated the lives of many people, black and white. Jesse Jackson is not a Christian, but a charlatan parading as a Christian—much like Jane Fonda who distributes Gnostic social/sexual/political guilt.

This places Obama in the same category; a charlatan who is parading as a Christian because he "has to" in order to be accepted on the larger American stage. He was thirty-one when he "converted" and did so only because it was required at the time in order to marry his wife, Michelle. He knew the double benefit included the increasing chances of being elected to office as a "Christian," of which he frequently waxes incoherent concerning even basic Christian beliefs. This is done intentionally to comfort the atheists.

While people have debated the definition of Christian for two thousand years, one constant truth which Obama, Jackson, and Hillary Clinton all deny is the Christian freedom from guilt, pain, sickness, despair, and sorrow.

This charlatan litmus test was masterfully elocuted as far back as 1970 by Rousas J. Rushdoony in his perceptive book *The Politics of Guilt and Pity*. "In the politics of guilt, man is perpetually drained of his social energy and cultural activity. He will progressively demand of the state a redemptive role. What he cannot do personally, i.e., to save himself, he demands that the state do for him, so that the state, as man enlarged, becomes the human savior of man. The politics of guilt, therefore, is not directed, as the Christian politics of liberty, to the creation of Godly justice and order, but to the creation of a redeeming order, a saving state. Guilt must be projected, therefore, on all those who oppose this new order and new age."[13]

That's why there is really very little difference between Jackson, Obama, Bill and Hillary Clinton, and the likes of Al Sharpton. All have become New Age "Christian" sham artists questing for raw power for its own sake and serving phony platitudes to the masses, many of whom allow themselves to be dragged through this mud of obliquity.

Speaking of ubiquitous charlatans, Quadra-Pleader Al Sharpton and Barack Obama had been circling each other like sharks in a ritualistic dance of pretenders to the throne of who should speak for black Americans along with Jesse Jackson. While Obama had been losing his character by associating with the likes of Geffen and Jackson, his "playful" appearance with Sharpton at the National Action Network (NAN) conference in April 2007 showed how low Obama would stoop as he groveled in front of Sharpton, putting on his best Harlem-jive personae.

The backdrop on the stage was emblazoned with Sharpton's NAN slogan, "No Justice-No Peace," which was the battle cry of the street thugs during the Rodney King riots in which more than fifty people were killed in less than forty-eight hours. It is important to pause here and explain, briefly, that Al Sharpton readily admits being a big fan of Jesse Jackson and learned his own tactics from Jackson.

Everyone needs to know that Sharpton holds a Screen Actors Guild (SAG) card. He has appeared in a handful of bit parts in both feature films and television shows. It could be argued that Sharpton is a frustrated actor who only shakes down corporations, local and state governments, and others to supplement his floundering career as a "leading" actor. It is another reason why he won't hold the major record companies to the same standard as Don Imus when it comes to race, rap, and hip-hop. The record companies are owned by the movie companies and he wants to remain on the casting call list as well as the Bi-coastal Cocktail Party Circuit (BCPC).

There is one major difference. In almost every major media event where Sharpton inserted himself, someone has died. Al Sharpton is the most infamous mass killer by proxy freely roaming America.

In 1987 when fifteen-year-old Twana Brawley claimed she was abducted, sexually abused, and wrapped in a garbage bag, Sharpton and two others arrived and accused the police of assaulting her. What the mainstream media almost always leaves out in their brief footnote to Sharpton's involvement is this: after the police were exonerated and Brawley, et. al., were discovered as frauds, a part-time police officer had become so distraught, he committed suicide.

A Hasidic Jew was stabbed to death after Sharpton riled up his followers in the Crown Heights riot of 1991. Not satisfied with the blood of two people on his hands, Sharpton raised the temperature of violence again in 1995 by accusing a "white interloper" of raising rent in Harlem at Freddy's Fashion Mart. Shortly after, a "shooter" entered Freddy's, ordered all blacks to leave, and began shooting everybody in sight and burned the building. Total dead: seven innocent people plus the shooter. Total death toll over two decades: Nine people. And this is the man Clinton and Obama were both courting?

Another important factor that most people outside the Obama-Jackson relationship are unaware of is the "official" hip-hop/rap vote. Jesse Jackson is deeply involved in helping to sponsor Russell Simmon's Hip-Hop Summit Action Network (HSAN) which stages rallies in large urban areas featuring some of hip-hop's most vulgar "artists" as entertainers.

With a captive audience, Simmons puts out a call for everyone eighteen to thirty years old to register to vote at tables set up onsite. The young voters are basically told "who" to vote for by proclamation of an "endorsement" from Simmons. Jackson can usually persuade Simmons who to endorse at the right time and "the word" is put out on the HSAN website and sympathetic radio stations.

In effect, Obama could receive the hip-hop vote without asking anything in return, such as "requesting" that the music industry expel all rap artists who rant about the joy of "killing niggas" and "slapping hos." "Christian" Obama can call for Don Imus to be fired without forgiveness, despite the fact that the Rutgers University Scarlet Knights accepted his apology and forgave him. On the other hand, Obama is able to "excuse" his pastor and "overlook" rap lyrics because both send out the same message.

However, Barack Obama doesn't possess the intestinal fortitude to stand up against even more horrific speech, if speech control is his agenda, for fear of losing the hip-hop vote of blood, violence, misogyny, and racism. As E. Michael Jones wrote, it's the politics of "brokering" guilt and blackmail that runs the Democratic party. And now Obama has become a slave to Hip-Hop Hollywood.

GEORGE SOROS

The young teenager George Soros was excited about his new assignment as the German Nazis occupied his home country of Hungary in 1944.[14] A "special" Jewish Council was set up by the Nazis and given the name *Judenrat* in which its members were given exclusive privileges if they helped betray fellow Jews.

Soros, the son of "non-practicing" Jews, was recruited to hand out leaflets to deceitfully persuade fellow Jews to report to a particular synagogue with only the clothes on their backs, a blanket, and two days worth of food. What the leaflet didn't tell them was that the little boy Soros was giving them a one-way ticket to the gas chambers and human ovens of Eastern Europe. Young George knew what the leaflets meant. His father, Tivadar, asked his son if he understood what he was doing and the consequences for those who followed the leaflet's orders.

"I can guess. They'll be interred," George said.[15] Tivadar told his son to continue delivering the messages, but to be sure and warn people that they were receiving a deportation summons. But Tivadar soon told the boy, George, to quit running errands for the Nazi-backed *Judenrat*.[16] George obeyed his father despite the fact that he "had liked the excitement" of being a messenger of death.

Tivadar knew it was just a matter of time before their number would come up, practicing or non-practicing. To the Nazis, after all, a Jew was a Jew. Tivadar took his family into hiding by creating false identities as Christians. He then split them up, provided them with forged papers, and bribed Gentile families to take them in.

Young George went to live with an official of Hungary's Nazi-collaborating government. The bureaucrat, Baumbach, was assigned the lucratively evil job of confiscating Jewish property and delivering direct deportation notices to the Jews.[18] There would be no more *Judenrat* charades. Now, at the age of fourteen, George followed along as Baumbach confiscated estates, large and small, throughout much of Hungary. For George Soros, there was no regret or remorse about his actions, even to this day.

Soros recounted the events with cool detachment in an interview with Steve Kroft of *60 Minutes* in 1998. After admitting to Kroft that he willingly assisted in the theft of Jewish property, Kroft replied, "I mean, that sounds like an experience that would send lots of people to the psychiatric couch for many, many years. Was it difficult?" Soros answered, "Not at all." Kroft probed a little deeper, "No feeling of guilt?" Expressionless, Soros answered, "No."[19]

In one degree or another, George Soros continued deceiving people and eventually entire nations through his subversive predatory social and financial manipulations. He continues doing so to this day. George Soros never got over the juvenile thrill of stealing property and sending men, women, and children to their deaths.

Soros first gained widespread attention in 1992 when he was nicknamed "The Man Who Broke the Bank of England." As head of the Quantum Fund, an international hedge fund that profits from currency fluctuations, Soros actually manipulated the entire currency of England so that the British were forced to devalue the pound by twenty percent. Millions of Brits saw their earnings, savings, and retirement shrink virtually overnight. In the meantime, Soros pocketed a cool $1 billion. To George Soros, it wasn't any different than sending Jews to be burned alive in concentration camps fifty years earlier.

Soros attempted a similar financial coup in France but was charged and found guilty of securities violations. He stayed out of prison by paying a few million dollars in fines—pocket change—and moved on to disrupt another country.

By 2005 Soros was rapidly sweeping through the former satellite countries of the Soviet Union. As the U.S. military began to pull out of Uzbekistan after Saddam

THE HOLLYWOOD CULTURE WAR

Hussein was overthrown, former Georgian president Eduard Shevardnadze warned Uzbek president Islam Karinow that Soros was on his way to wreak havoc. Soros had already made illicit inroads into the former Soviet state of Georgia and was cutting a swath through Kazakhstan, Turkmenistan, Tajikistan, Adjaris, and South Ossetia.[20]

A decade before cutting this swath through Central Asia, Soros had already dumped on Russia in the early and mid-1990s when America could have made a positive difference in the region after the collapse of the Soviet Union. Unfortunately, Bill Clinton gave George Soros wide latitude in dealing with Russia and he proceeded to financially rape the Russian people.

Journalist Anne Williamson wrote, "Soros not only expanded his fortune under Bill and Hillary, but he also fit in with their countercultural zeitgeist. Through them, Soros found a public platform to espouse his wacky politics. With Bush in power, Soros no longer has that kind of influence. That's a big part of what's driving him crazy."[21]

Soros' hatred for President Bush is what catapulted the name George Soros into the national spotlight in 2000 and 2004 as he spent millions of dollars trying to defeat Bush by supporting Al Gore and later John Kerry. In addition to money, Soros helped create and fund numerous smear websites such as MoveOn.org and many others in a no-holds-barred attempt to bring Bush down.

His failure to do so has only caused Soros to teeter on the verge of a nervous breakdown. As revenge, and as part of his backdoor de-facto support of terrorism, Soros is now spending enormous amounts of time and energy disrupting America's effort to fight terrorism abroad and at home. Much of the congressional discord among Democrats can be traced to political manipulation by Soros. Shortly after receiving a hefty contribution from Soros, presidential candidate John Edwards called the War on Terror "a bumper sticker." Soros also failed in smearing General David Petraeus through his slander website MoveOn.org.

Soros has hired Aryeh Neir and Morton Halperin to work for his global fantasy organization, the Open Society Institute (OSI), to help undermine America's war in Iraq. They are well-suited for the task since they worked behind the scenes to defund the Vietnam War, even though America had pulled out ground troops and was successfully providing air support to the South Vietnamese.

George Soros also profited handsomely from the September 11, 2001 terrorist attack on America. While investors were pouring money into the market, Soros was short-selling U.S. assets, saying, "I don't think you can run the market on patriotic principle." Soros then proceeded to announce that he *didn't* support a counter-attack on the Taliban.[22]

It should be made clear that not all multi-billionaires have reached out to the long arm of Mephistopheles, but it should be clear by now that this one has not only reached out, he continues to hug tightly. Soros, a die-hard atheist since his days as a young teenager tricking Jews into death camps, also hates Bush for daring to invoke the name of God in public places. In Soros' "World of the Future," there will be no god. That is OSI's goal number one. It was also the goal of Karl Marx.

In fact, Soros' atheism is the driving force behind the increasing advocacy and urgency of his "God complex" desire to control the world. For an atheist, there is no life after death, so he wants to see global results now. This is the same reason Soros hired a number of aging radical secular hippies to run OSI.

In his book *Slouching Towards Gomorrah*, Robert Bork points out this sixties counterculture mindset with a quote from the era repeated by Professor Todd Gitlin, a former leader of the Students for a Democratic Society (SDS), the "rock bottom fact that life ends."

As Bork explains this realization on the young secular hippies, "To adolescents without religious belief, that realization can be devastating. Radical politics can then become a substitute for a religion, a way to seek meaning in life, and even, one can hope, a form of immortality. To lead or be part of a movement that changes the world is, perhaps, to be remembered forever. For many, modern liberalism is a religion."

This also explains why Soros has supported Bill Clinton, Hillary Clinton, and Barack Obama. And those are the kind of people he works with best. As a Jewish Nazi war collaborator, Soros knows a charlatan when he sees one. He has first-hand experience. As Soros rapidly approaches eighty years of age, his patience is wearing thin. His tireless capacity to wreak havoc around the globe is not only formidable, it is already under way.

The shadow government of Communism that was rooted out of America in the 1940s and 1950s has, in some way, returned with a vengeance in a New Age virtual political party referred to as *The Shadow Party* by David Horowitz and Richard Poe in their book by the same name. The authors have compiled the most comprehensive and intricately researched book on the "party" and its mystical leader George Soros, who "remains cryptic and elusive, his goals and activities obscured by a smoke screen of denial and calculated misdirection," and "Like Lenin, Soros excels at waging revolution form 'above'—through manipulation of economic and political forces at the highest levels. However, Soros also resembles Lenin in his diligent cultivation of insurgent forces from 'below.'"[23]

Horowitz and Poe point out that this strategy was co-opted by Soros from a Communist strategy outlined in 1957 by Jan Kozak, a Czech Communist Party theoretician who explained how this road map to an *undemocratic* power grab was achieved in Czechoslovakia.

Unknown to most Americans, Soros has continued toppling leaders and disrupting nations around the world. If Soros isn't toppling governments, he is disrupting national economies and devaluing currencies to profit his Quantum Fund investments. As Horowitz and Poe explain, Soros is effecting his global revolution under the umbrella of the Open Society Institute and related foundations which "have facilitated coups and rebellions in many countries, always ostensibly in the interests of 'democratization.'"[24]

In an early display of bravado, Soros told an interviewer for a 1995 *New Yorker* profile that "the 'subversive' mission to his Open Society network has required him to wear a variety of masks through the years. In some countries, he would adopt a pro-Communist pose while in others he would play the anti-Communist," according to Horowitz and Poe. The authors also note that, "Before Soros can transform U.S. society into a socialist Utopia, our Constitution will need to undergo a great many 'evolutionary' changes."[25]

If this sounds hard to believe, consider the fact that George Soros has already established himself as a major contributor to "The American Constitution Society," which is studying "a progressive view of what the Constitution ought to be." The American Constitution Society is but one of many "front groups" that Soros controls and funds to promote his secular nightmares, not unlike a studio CEO in today's Hollywood.

Soros' vast network of "independent" front groups span the globe in more than forty countries and the untold number of such groups operating in the U.S. has already been chipping away at the American democratic system for more than a decade. Among the goals of Soros to be achieved through this shadowy web of organizations is the legalization of drugs, prostitution, taxing churches, legalizing same-sex marriage, reducing and eliminating most criminal penalties.[26] The jailhouse doors will swing open.

Allen St. Pierre of the National Organization for the Reform of Marijuana Laws (NORML) has cited Hollywood's positive portrayal of drug use on TV and the multi-plex as evidence of how "we're able to *capture*—and to demonstrate the change in culture." NORML receives a huge financial boost from Soros. This New Age incarnation of Lenin is a big fan and user of marijuana who says he has tried it and "liked it."[27]

Barack Obama takes his marching orders directly from Soros. Not only has Obama refused to address the need for fighting drug abuse during his presidential run, he even told a group of Northwestern University students that marijuana should be decriminalized. Instead of lifting young people out of the bondage of drug abuse, Obama drags them down, at least long enough to get them to float into the voting booth. Even more dangerous, in January of 2008, Obama told the editorial board of *Ebony* magazine that the mandatory minimum sentencing guidelines for crack dealers and users should be drastically reduced. In February, U.S. Attorney Gretchen Shappert testified before the Senate that long sentences for crack addicts had freed neighborhoods of dealers that were also brutal murderers, burglars, and thieves with long criminal records. In other words, an Obama presidency promises a never-ending *Night of the Living Dead*.

Former House Speaker Dennis Hastert once said of Soros that he "doesn't know where his money comes from," hinting strongly that George Soros is a major global drug runner. Columnist Cliff Kincaid wrote on October 27, 2004, that the Soros Hedge Fund is chartered and located in the Netherlands Antilles, a *self-governing* federation of five Caribbean islands. Kincaid reported that a CIA fact book describes the region as "a trans-shipment point for South American drugs bound for the U.S. and Europe, and a money-laundering center."[28]

Soros was outraged, but not as much as his secular-progressive billionaire partner Peter Lewis, the former CEO of Progressive Insurance. The ultra-leftist New Age contributor to the ACLU and MoveOn.org was arrested in New Zealand for importing drugs including hashish and marijuana. Despite Soros' outrage at being called one of the world's major drug dealers, he and his family found time to donate $60,000 to Barack Obama's 2004 Senate campaign. Obama would be back for more—much more. The Chicago school of politics teaches that dirty money spends just as easily as clean money, a lesson learned from terrorist friend William Ayers.

In America, Soros has concentrated his focus and fortune into infiltrating the Democratic party and by forming even more front groups that carry the Soros OSI message through "position papers" and slick internet websites. Subordinates of Soros are also not above the swamp tactic of vicious campaigns to achieve their goals. Among the people leading some of these groups on the extended Soros payroll are John Podesta, Harold Ickes, the Halperin family, and others who also happen to be de-facto participants of the Clinton Machine. Soros is adept at playing Obama and Hillary against each other in order to force them back with their hands out for more money like puppets on strings.

As Horowitz and Poe point out, Soros is *the* architect of the Shadow Party, "which operates much like a network of holding companies coordinating the disparate branches of this movement, both inside and outside the Democratic Party, and leading them toward the goal of securing state power. Once attained, that power will be used to effect a global transformation—economic, social, and political—a post-Berlin Wall reincarnation of the old radical dream."[29]

There are no clearly defined long-term goals of the OSI as Soros maintains a contradiction in philosophy and deception of operation. The catch-phrases and words like "front groups," "secretive," "infiltration," and "smear campaign" sound all too familiar. As Horowitz and Poe write in *The Shadow Party*, "Like Karl Marx and generations of socialists, Soros prefers not to offer a blueprint of the promised future, even as he works to dismantle the present."[30]

As Bill O'Reilly warns in *Culture Warrior*, "His secular approach would drastically diminish Judeo-Christian philosophy . . . . We ignore him at our own peril."[31] Soros is the ultimate secular progressive.

His occult-like following puts George Soros in a category not too different from the twentieth century's most evil man, the mystic Aleister Crowley, who coined the phrase "New Age" in 1904. By 1923 the British tabloid *John Blow* famously labeled Crowley as "The Wickedest Man in the World." It is now official that George Soros has inherited that title.

It's not only the people Obama embraces as his major money supporters that should concern voters, it's also the people he refuses to denounce who are carrying out the street level thug tactics against anyone who would not support his candidacy for president. In early 2008, Representative Emanuel Cleaver of Missouri was outraged at the high level of vicious harassment being waged against African-Americans who chose not to support Barack Obama for president. Emanuel said opponents were being "bludgeoned verbally" with "Uncle Tom" catcalls in addition to threats of very real harm. "It's really sad because Senator Obama is talking about a new kind of politics. But some of his supporters are practicing a1950s style of politics," said Representative Emanuel, referring to the racist intimidation of old Missouri machine politics.

Representative John Lewis only came over to Obama's side after an Atlanta pastor angrily threatened to run the veteran civil rights leader out of office during the next election if he didn't support Obama. In addition, an aide to Lewis said the congressman's office was being bombarded with telephone threats, including a strongly worded death threat. If a candidate's supporters reflect the culture of the candidate, who refuses to condemn these actions, is this an early indication of an Obama presidency?

Author Tavis Smiley was called out with the "hater, sell-out, traitor" mantra of the Obama supporters who were curiously using the same wording in their nationwide threats against black leaders. Obama did address Smiley's complaint in a peculiar, but no less south side Chicago response, as reported in a CBS.com article on February 16, 2008, "I'm going to have to call Tavis up and *straighten him out* on this." Smiley said his mother and brother were also being targeted. Obama's response came during the same week he told a *US Weekly* interviewer that his choice of boxer or brief underwear didn't matter because, "Either way, I look good in both."

Ohio Democratic Congresswoman Stephanie Tubbs Jones lent credence to the increasingly radical nature of the threats against anyone who wouldn't support Obama. "There are some black elected officials who have earned their stripes, who've had to change their phone numbers two or three times because of the calls being made to them about the positions they are taking in the election. *Shame on us! Shame on Us!*"

Barack Obama didn't respond to the other accusations as he basked in the long shadow of Saul Alinksy and his Chicago School of Social Chaos and Intimidation. Obama is simply practicing a new version from the textbook of the legendary socialist mobster.

By early summer of 2008, the frequency and intensity of attacks, smears, and violent threats against any opponent of Barack Obama began to follow a pattern that became suspicious by the repetitive use of words, phraseology and even the bullet-point order of the viscously verbal tirades. This suggested to many observers that the threats against opponents were not coming from a loose network of grassroots supporters, but rather from the Obama campaign office itself which scripted the attacks. More suspicious was Obama's refusal to denounce the attacks or even to acknowledge them. Campaign spokesmen David Axelrod, Ben LaBolt and Bill Burton all refused to return my calls concerning this strategy. According to a former Obama staffer that was very close to the strategy, the "anonymous attack" campaign by Obama will rely on these tactics in the general election against Senator John McCain including a number of fabricated mass e-mails that will attempt to portray non-existent white-supremacist groups as supporters, forcing McCain to apologize and denounce something for which he knows nothing about.

THE AUDACITY OF A CHILD'S HOPE

Johnnie finally saw light at the end of a long journey one December morning in 2003. He couldn't quite open his eyes, but the world of darkness with only the sound of his heartbeat was about to enter an exciting new phase. Johnnie could hear other people talking "outside" and there was a lot of excitement that a new day was about to dawn. Someone grabbed both of his feet with the clutch of a giant hand that felt like a rubber band.

The light was very bright now and Johnnie couldn't wait to take his first breath and open his eyes to this brave new world. His heart beat faster as the voices grew frantic. A woman screamed, "No! No! No!"

A man's voice piped up, "calm down. We'll take care it." And another set of hands wrapped around Johnnie's feet as he felt the cool air of a hospital corridor swirl around his body. No more voices—only footsteps—and plenty of light shining through his pink eyelids.

Johnnie's heart beat even faster as his back pressed against the freezing cold metal shelf of a storage room closet where he was "laid out." A door slammed and there was no more light. No more footsteps. No more voices. If only Johnnie could catch that first breath. If only someone would help him. There was a faint sound of a whimper and another sound of wheezing. Maybe there were other little Johnnies in the room who could help him.

But Johnnie's heart finally slowed down . . . slower . . . slower. Nobody was coming. But Johnnie held out hope . . . the very audacity of hope . . . that someone cared. But no one cared, at least not in this cold building of empty souls where saving life was the occupation of the staff.

And Johnnie spent three hours shivering, gasping for air, turning blue until finally his heart stopped beating. Hope died that day for Johnnie in a Chicago hospital where babies were born and left to die on a routine basis because they were never wanted in the first place.

Did anybody at the hospital speak English? Could anybody pronounce the two words—adoption agency? No wonder Johnnie can't read and write. He wasn't even allowed to live past the age of three . . . hours!

Johnnie was an infant victim of murder. In Latin, *infanticida*, or in English, infanticide, a process of allowing a child to die once it is born alive and then refused medical aid, oxygen, or food. Virtually unheard of in Western civilization, and certainly not discussed when it is practiced, Johnnie was not the first baby swept under the carpet, nor would he be the last.

So who killed little Johnnie and snuffed out his post-natal audacity of hope? Was it the mother, the doctor, or the nurse with the squeaky footsteps who laid Johnnie on a dirty metal shelf in a hospital corridor utility room?

Perhaps it was lack of any "governing legal authority" by the Illinois state legislature that addressed the issue of killing newborn babies in a ritual assembly-line manner. The doctors had their own code which provided a wide highway of discretion. The State of Illinois had no specific "law on the books" preventing infantile murder of live newborn babies. But not for lack of trying by people who still maintained a conscience. A very large group of Illinois citizens were trying to pass legislation called Born Alive Infants Protection Act, or BAIPA. Similar bills were being passed in other states and the U.S. Congress would pass a federal BAIPA bill in 2002 which was signed into law by President Bush. The legislation states that all live-born babies are guaranteed the same constitutional right to equal protection, whether or not they are wanted.

But there was a problem in Illinois. One state legislator, Barack Obama, was obsessively transfixed with blocking the local legislation from being passed; not once, not twice, but on three separate occasions. Nobody is exactly sure how many babies were killed in Illinois hospitals and clinics while Obama stalled legislation in 2001, 2002, and 2003 to stop the barbarian act of killing newborn babies.

The bills brought before Obama had nothing to do with abortion. They also had nothing to do with religion. Former nurse Jill Stanek gave personal testimony before Obama, recalling, "I testified in 2001 and 2002 before a committee of which Obama was a member. Obama articulately worried that legislation protecting live aborted babies might infringe on women's rights or abortionists' rights. Obama's clinical discourse, his lack of mercy, shocked me . . . . And Obama voted against the measure twice."[32]

Stanek recalls a third attempt to pass a bill preventing the killing of newborn infants. "In 2003, as chairman of the next committee to which BAIPA was sent, Obama stopped it from even getting a hearing, shelving it to die much like babies were still being shelved to die in Illinois hospitals and abortion clinics."[33]

One of Obama's typically dubious arguments was that there was no documentation that hospitals were actually doing what was alleged in testimony before him in committee. Obama also claimed that the whole debate was motivated by religion.

Apparently Obama had his iPod in when Stanek testified, "As a nurse at an Illinois hospital in 1999, I discovered babies were being aborted alive and shelved to die in soiled utility rooms. I discovered infanticide.... I don't recall mentioning religion when I testified against live birth abortion. I was only describing a *live* aborted baby I held in a soiled utility room until he died, and a *live* aborted baby who was accidentally thrown in the trash."[34]

Obama showed no emotion, much like his good friend and major money contributor George Soros, who found that leading children to their death was simply following orders, minus the tear-drop of remorse.

The Illinois BAIPA bill did not pass until after Obama left for Washington in 2005. The most passion Obama ever showed for a single issue or piece of legislation while a state senator in Illinois was his vehement support of infanticide, which has left many people, including supporters, questioning his source motivation to this day.

After all, this was the "gentle" senator who fought so strongly against the death penalty for convicted criminals, but didn't blink an eye at the rate of babies being killed in Illinois hospitals and clinics. As Stanek noted, "Even if a pre-viable baby survives an abortion, the pregnancy has been terminated. The mother gets what she wanted. What more does Obama need, a dead baby? Yes."[35]

Obama never spoke about crisis intervention centers for pregnant mothers and was deathly silent about the hundreds of adoption agencies that would not have any problem finding loving parents. Stanek was right. Obama had officially joined the culture of death.

Of course there are complex ethical challenges that will inevitably be faced. In rare cases, a newborn may display a rare form of fatal deformity such as anencephaly, or lack of brain tissue. Or there may be such an extreme condition of which there is no medical procedure to save the infant's life. In such cases, most hospitals have a policy of "comfort care" where the newborn is kept warm and fed until the infant dies, which in such extreme cases may be a few hours or a few days.

Supporters of BAIPA have demonstrated that infanticide has been practiced in cases where there were no fatal abnormalities, or that the abnormalities were not life-threatening to the baby or the mother. In a congressional debate in 2003 over another controversial procedure, partial birth abortion, Senator Rick Santorum (R-PA) showed visual aids depicting babies at various stages of development. Senator Hillary Clinton, whose views differ little from Obama's, protested loudly, "Where are the swollen heads?"[36]

THE HOLLYWOOD CULTURE WAR

What Hillary Clinton and Barack Obama have demonstrated is their support for eugenics, the "perfecting" of the race by "selective infanticide," something the Dutch government is considering even as this book went to press. Such a move was considered unthinkable in civilized Western societies, especially in light of the fact that eugenics was widely practiced by Adolph Hitler.

Under Hitler, babies that were somewhat deficient were marked, therefore, as unwanted. "Deficiency" might be an infant with seven fingers out of ten, or one leg shorter than the other. Regardless, they were all "eligible" for death under German law.

The Dutch debate to allow infanticide sparked outrage from Italian Parliamentary Affairs Minister Carlo Giovanardi, who compared the move in the Netherlands as nothing less than "Nazi legislation and Hitler ideas" and was a revival of the evil practice of "how to kill ill children."[37]

However, Obama's bold move not to budge from infanticide has put him squarely in Phase One of a dangerous New Age revival of the eugenic infanticide movement that is "under study" in the United States. With generous grants from Lawrence Rockefeller and the Ira W. DeCamp Foundation, Princeton University hired Dr. Peter Singer to head its Center for Human Values. If the Center for Human Values represents the New Left definition of "values," then we have reached a dark, even diabolical, cultural low.

Singer proposes strongly that parents should have the right to *kill* their babies at any time from the moment of birth up until twenty-eight days! In his book, *Rethinking Life and Death*, Singer draws the moral equivalency between killing a baby and that of a fish, writing, "Since neither a newborn infant nor a fish is a person, the wrongness of killing such beings is not as great as the wrongness of killing a person."[38]

You read that right. "*Killing such beings*," from the director of Princeton's Center for Human Values. Obama argued in the Illinois Senate that allowing a newborn to live against *its* mother's wishes was an infringement on women's rights. A newborn is an "it."

Obama's motivations are extremely bizarre, and yet, the source for his actions may lie closer to home than many people previously realized. When asked about influential members of his inner circle in the campaign for presidency, one name that trumps all others is his wife, Michelle, who Obama himself describes as an "activist" wife and partner.

Michelle Obama has not only been a lifelong supporter of abortion, but particularly a supporter of partial-birth abortion and did not discourage husband Barack from pushing the limits to infanticide, or "fetuses born alive," as the Obama supporters in the media refer to "babies."

Jill Stanek recalls a February 2004 benefit in which U.S. Senate candidate Barack Obama's wife, Michelle, sent a fund-raising letter with the "alarming news" that "right-wing politicians" had passed a law that would stop the killing of babies as they're being born (partial birth abortion), a practice she proclaimed as "a legitimate medical procedure." With that explosive intro, Michelle Obama asked supporters to pay "$150 to attend a luncheon for her husband, who would fight against 'cynical ploys' to stop it."[39]

In April 2007, the U.S. Supreme Court voted to ban the practice of partial-birth abortion, much to the chagrin of the Obamas.

In a crafty pre-emptive diversion tactic to deflect any last minute reminders of his Illinois Senate infanticide crusade, Obama delivered one of his typical hypocritical "obaminations" on Father's Day in June 2007 when he "chided" black men for impregnating black women and then abandoning them, saying, "Responsibility does not end at conception." That's a crude disingenuous flip-flop. Of course responsibility ends at conception; according to Obama it can even end if the aborted baby is born alive. Just put it on a cold metal shelf to die.

So horrific was Obama's insistence on blocking anti-infanticide legislation, it became the sole issue in the final days of his U.S. senatorial campaign against Ambassador Alan Keyes. The lopsided outcome in Obama's favor showed the apathy concerning the issue, especially among the Chicago metropolitan voters who really didn't care about an issue that didn't *directly* affect their lives.

Keyes was so passionate about the issue, he was painted by Obama and his supporters in the press as a virtual lunatic. As Obama would write in *The Audacity of Hope*, "All I had to do was keep my mouth shut and start planning my swearing-in ceremony."[40]

But Keyes had hit a note inside Obama, especially concerning infanticide, and he never really recovered in the sense that he was unable to explain his actions in the Illinois State House and his perpetual lack of commitment to anything other than broad platitudes of style without substance.

"I found him getting under my skin in a way few people ever have," Obama would write. "I was mindful of Mr. Keyes's implicit accusation—that I remained steeped in doubt, that my faith was adulterated, that I was not a true Christian."[41]

Obama then made one of the biggest mistakes of his young career by taking a broad petty and personal swipe at Keyes by comparing him in a sweeping derogatory manner that reflected his true disdain for over one-third of America's population. ". . . he came off as a cross between a Pentecostal preacher and William F. Buckley, Jr.," complete with "hooded eyes."[42] Obama, still unable to counter Alan Keyes's devastating exposé of Obama's state senatorial record, resorted to mere childish mockery of Keyes's facial and physical appearance. However, as has become his strategy, Obama managed to drag those he really disliked through his subtle-single-sentence jab that he knows, as a lawyer, will plant a subliminal seed in the mind of the reader.

This one statement, completely missed, intentionally or not, by the media, carried a lot of pent-up baggage that Obama needed to drop on unsuspecting toes. And it is worth looking at closer because Obama's verbal discourses are often loaded messages intended to divide the audience, completely contrary to his proclamations of unity, reconciliation, common ground, and renewal.

The famed San Francisco semantics professor and former U.S. Senator S. I. Hayakawa referred to these types of subtle smears spoken by one individual against another as "purring," a form of disguised snarling using words and phrases with strong affective connotations. Again, unable to rebuke his opponent's accusation, Obama chose to dismiss Keyes in a juvenile attack that inflicted collateral condescending contempt on millions of Americans who he considered fodder for "derision by association."

Impotent to repudiate Keyes, Obama chose instead to declare his deep-seated hatred for 20 million Americans who call themselves Pentecostal and, at the same time, "purr" his scorn for the 120 million Americans who consider themselves conservatives, a virtually extinct political philosophy until the emergence and perseverance of William F. Buckley Jr.

It is important to analyze this one sample of "Obamaspeech" in order to understand that his sole manner of speaking is intended to confuse and persuade at the same time, something only Bill and Hillary Clinton have ever accomplished before in the executive levels of American government.

First, the Pentecostal smear. Obama's comparison of Keyes to a "Pentecostal" preacher was not meant to be taken in a favorable light. In fact, Obama has made it clear in his book and in his Sojourner's Call to Renewal Speech of June 28, 2006, that there are certain evangelical leaders that are "my friends," and there is a larger group of Christians that are on his enemies list.

Barack Obama's severe misconception of Pentecostals may have come from a jaundiced stereotype character portrayed by Hollywood, no friend of Christians. Or Obama's prejudice may have certainly originated with his secular mother who would "entertain" young Barack with wild-eyed tales of angry preachers and "church fathers who chiseled their workers out of every nickel . . . ."

What Obama's mother and Hollywood did not get across to Obama is that Pentecostals are among the most generous and giving people on the face of the earth. Pentecostals volunteer wholeheartedly to give of their time and energy to those in need and their evangelical call is to spread the Word of freedom and liberty through salvation with charitable missions worldwide.

In 1998, *Christianity Today* reported that twenty-five percent of the world's two billion Christians, almost half a *billion*, were Pentecostal or Charismatic and growing at a rate of 19 million believers a year.[43] The 20 million plus Pentecostals in America are among the fastest growing affiliations in the country with a rich, century-long history that includes many of the world's most influential and charitable evangelists.

Pentecostals were among the first to declare, "God is a Good God" in the early twentieth century when many denominations were teaching that God is *always* angry, mad, and ready to punish. This was a revolution in Western Christianity which Obama has failed to learn.

Pentecostals represent the vast spectrum of the world's races, with many churches maintaining multiracial congregations who believe in miracles, healing, and an abundant overflow of praise through the indwelling of the Holy Spirit. Obama finds this a little questionable and highly embarrassing.

Obama likes to talk about his conversion to Christianity happening in a very orderly "walk down the aisle" and that his choice came not as "an epiphany. I didn't fall out in church," implying that those who do must be off their rockers. Obama has much more in store for the Christian Church if he becomes president. Obama and his Christian socialist supporters want to engineer a total reorganization of American Christianity, a New Age Christian Reformation, which will be thoroughly discussed in the next section.

As for the other half of Barack Obama's two-sided smear of Alan Keyes, the junior senator from Illinois may have found some consensus within segments of American conservative voters, which quickly evaporated after his broadside against Buckley, who Obama had never liked.

Obama is looking for "unity" and "common ground" between liberals and conservatives as long as it fits "his" vision of unity, which just shows that Obama's kumbaya "can't we all get along" rhetoric is about as sincere as Rodney King's pronouncement.

Barack Obama might have learned some valuable life lessons from reading William F. Buckley's *God and Man at Yale* that propelled him into the national spotlight. He has been referred to as the father of modern American Conservatism and even Libertarians. According to the Battle Ground poll, about sixty percent of Americans of voting age consider themselves "conservative" or "very conservative."[44] Of the 300 million people in America in 2008, roughly 200 million are of voting age. That sixty percent accounts for over 120 million eligible voters.

Perhaps Obama will think twice before his vindictive smearing of his political opponents takes on mammoth consequences. His actions and words are not unlike those of Bill Clinton in the early 1990s, a truly Hollywood president who took his cues form Tinseltown instead of the voters and citizens of the country. There is every indication that Obama wants to be the second Hollywood president someday. Obama even admits that around age ten he began to take his life lessons directly from the television tube and at the movie theaters. "TV, movies, the radio; those were places to start. Pop culture was color-coded, after all, an arcade of images from which you could cop a walk, a talk, a step, a *style*."

And that is the answer to the million dollar question: Why is Obama all style and no substance? Because he learned to "cop a walk" and "a style" from the shallow world of early 1970s network TV. Barack Obama is the poster child of the first generation that grew up in the post 1968 world where movie houses "rated" movies according to Valenti's Scheme. Barack Obama may be a good example of the multi-polar personality that resulted from a fractured entertainment industry that imposed age limits on its audiences, ushering in the era of "forbidden fruit" that children were naturally expected to pursue.

This TV Land upbringing may also explain why Obama has no real identifiable personality and a total lack of humor. As Steve Sailer noted in his article "Obama's Identity Crisis," the presidential candidate "Obama himself is a bit of a drip, a humorless impaired Holden Caulfield whose preppie angst is fueled by racial regret. Obama has a knack for irony, but a strangely humorless flavor."

Obama's weak attempt at humor by slamming a broad spectrum of Americans clearly indicates he grew up watching cheap PG-13 teen comedies and third-rate skits on fourth-season episodes of *Saturday Night Live*.

America didn't deserve its first Hollywood president and it certainly doesn't deserve a second one.

OBAMA'S NEW AGE CHRISTIAN REFORMATION:

Evangelical Left vs. Evangelical Right

"No matter how religious they may be, people are tired of seeing faith used as a tool of attack. They don't want faith used to battle or divide," declared Senator Barack Obama as keynote speaker at the Call to Renewal's Building a Covenant for a New America conference in 2006. The Sojourners/Call to Renewal is an organization directed by Jim Wallis, author of *God's Politics: Why the Right Gets It Wrong and the Left Doesn't Get It* and clearly an Obama supporter.

Wallis appears more intent on pleasing liberal journalists than promoting the *true* Word of God. On the first three pages, including the cover, are glowing reviews from America's most liberal, left-wing newspapers, including the first review by America's worst newspaper, *The Atlanta-Journal-Constitution*, who calls Wallis' book a powerful "battle manual" in the fight against "conservative leaders." A good review from the *Journal* is a bad start.

Obama has become the "social justice" enthusiastic front man for a virtual Christian Evangelical Reformation. Again, he was not satisfied with his burning desire *just* to be president, he wants to shake up the Christian community, and not for the better. For a man who is adamantly against any semblance of religion in politics, though he acknowledges its place and origin, Obama adamantly wants to *reform* Christianity to *conform* to his personal Chicago-leftist politics; a bold and reckless move that not even the likes of Bill Clinton attempted.

And despite Obama's call for "unity" and "common ground" among people of all faiths and those "with no faith at all," he squarely has his sights on a vindictive, truly circuitous campaign against the emerging power of those who the media disdainfully refer to as the Religious Right. Obama's opening remarks at the Sojourners conference was yet another back-handed jab at his old nemesis Alan Keyes, the man who Obama described as "looking like a cross between a Pentecostal preacher and William F. Buckley, Jr."

While Alan Keyes was able to move on with his life after the 2004 defeat in the Illinois senate campaign, Obama continued to hold a nagging grudge, despite being the winner, that he is channeling by a targeted campaign against a major portion of the American Christian community.

The following quote is printed with emphasis added to demonstrate Obama's New Age plan to reorganize and appropriate Christianity to fit *his* worldview instead of God's worldview. "If *we* truly hope to speak to people where *they're at*—to communicate *our* hopes and [our] values in a way that is relevant to *their* own—then as *progressives*, *we* cannot abandon the field of religious discourse." Obama has been known to inject class warfare, but never before has a candidate for president called for religious warfare within Christianity itself. Obama, ungrounded himself in faith, is a dangerously divisive figure.

Obama's harsh words for Alan Keyes and his apocalyptic call for an American Christian Reformation that should fit his vision of Christianity probably didn't bother many at the Sojourners' Call to Renewal Covenant for a New America. As Jim Wallis had already prematurely declared, "The Religious Right's dominance over politics and evangelists has come to an end. I would say the Religious Right has lost and the Secular Left has lost."[45]

If that sounds like socialist pseudo-religious cant posturing as Christianity, it is. But conspicuously absent in that statement by Wallis is the tern Evangelical Left, which is the name being applied to the Sojourners movement, which resembles a California New Age political agenda with only a sprinkling of Christianity for flavor. Many of the Evangelical Left ignore the fact that Obama, in his book *Dreams From My Father*, wrote compassionately of his interest in the Communist system and also his admiration for the college professors who extolled the *virtues* of the Communist ideology.

Any reports that Obama smiled broadly upon hearing of Rev. Jerry Falwell's death were quickly squashed by Wallis who waged political damage control by praising Falwell on the internet for Falwell's Ministry Home for Alcoholics, The Center for Tutoring Inner-City Children, The Liberty Godparent Home for Unwed Mothers, and countless programs over the last forty years to help the poor, sick, and needy. Of course, Wallis forgot to mention that *no* government money was spent, unlike Wallis and Obama's dream of a "nanny state" America.

Some refer to the Evangelical Left as the Religious Left or Liberal Evangelicals. And in his polite self-contradictory fashion, Obama plans to *use* the Evangelical Left to smash "conservative Christians," a term he uses derisively. "If we [liberal Democrats] don't reach out to the evangelical Christians and tell them what *we* stand for," Obama declared, then the conservatives including the "Alan Keyes" of the world "will continue to hold sway."[46] Apparently in his seventeen-year Christian walk, he has learned nothing about unconditional forgiveness and Heaven is *wishful thinking*.

And there is the Obama dilemma, contradicting himself only a few minutes into the speech after telling the Sojourners, ". . . people are tired of seeing faith used as a tool of attack." Even Hillary Clinton envied the ability of Obama to say one thing and mean another.

Not surprisingly, Obama then contradicted himself within the same sentence, which has come to be seen as a trademark in his speeches and interviews. "When we shy away from religious venues and religious broadcasts because we assume that we will be unwelcome—others will fill the vacuum, those with the most insular views of faith, or those who cynically use religion to justify partisan ends."[47]

Certainly, Senator Obama was not at this large gathering of Leftist Christians for any *cynical* use of religion for his *own* partisan ends. After all, he wouldn't be announcing his run for presidency for another seven months, but he most certainly would call upon the Sojourners and their constituents to help raise money. Obama could always justify his repeated pleas for money from the Leftist Christians because he didn't "come and clap off-rhythm to the choir."

Obama continued his keynote address by despairing about problems of race and poverty as if this were 1957 instead of 2007. Particularly strange was Obama and the Evangelical Left emphasis on poverty in broad ambiguous tones.

Obama began his speech by saying, "As you all know, we can affirm the importance of poverty in the Bible."[48] Michael Gershon, former speech writer for President Bush, said that those Christians were more likely to consider themselves "pro-life and pro-poor."[49] (Remember: guilt and victimhood.)

Tom Kruttenmaker of *USA Today* said that he considers himself among those evangelicals who support "poverty relief."[50] The insinuation being falsely promulgated by the Evangelical Left is that the so-called Religious Right doesn't care about the poor and never did. In truth, the so-called Religious Right teach the *overcoming* of poverty as the next step *after* poverty relief, for which they have over a century of experience.

Those counted as the Religious Right correctly read from the Bible verses and directly from the words of Jesus, "I have come that you may have life and that you may have it more abundantly." (John 10:10).

They also teach directly from the words of Christ and his disciples who declare, "God is able to make all grace abound to you, that you, having *all* sufficiency in *all* things may abound to *every* good work." (11 Corinthians 9-8). The "Evangelical Right" teaches miracles, healing, and deliverance whereas the Evangelical Left de-emphasizes these promises from the Bible. Obama's vehement opposition to the Evangelical Right comes across as Evangelical Lite. Does the Evangelical Left believe people should be poor because it's good to suffer? That type of thinking prevailed for many centuries during the period known as the Dark Ages.

In early 2007, pastor Rick Warren, a self-described "poverty pastor," strongly denounced the teachings of pastor Joel Olsteen and many others who simply read directly from the Bible about the promises of abundance, prosperity, and good health. Warren said he didn't believe in the "name it and claim it" message from the Bible. So is the Bible better served as just a coffee table ornament or paperweight?

As Ed Vitagliano of the *AFA Journal* asked, "And while a Christian should certainly feel compelled to help the poor, is it *more* Christian to support an increase in entitlement programs or to cut the capital gains tax to spur more hiring?"[51] Obama and the Evangelical Left also find it convenient to ignore that charitable giving by churches, foundations, and individuals is at an all time high. In 2005 alone, charitable giving in the United States topped $260 *billion*.

That amount is almost as much as the $300 billion President Johnson spent on the various "War on Poverty" programs during the 1960s. Adjusted for inflation, charitable giving *in one year alone* is more than double the amount Johnson spent using your tax dollars. And as Senator Daniel Patrick Moynihan and others noted in the early 1970s, the government's war on poverty created new generations of poverty that came to expect handouts, having never been taught the work ethic.

In February 2008, editor Cliff Kincaid of Accuracy In Media revealed that Obama had secretly pushed legislation in Congress that could force the United States to contribute $845 *billion* to "reduce global poverty" by redistributing the income of the American worker into a monolithic giveaway to third-world countries run by dictators and thugs. What is certain is that the U.N. would run the program by "collecting" the taxes from the U.S. government, which Obama fully expects to fund by dramatically raising federal payroll taxes from worker's paychecks. The Global Poverty Act is fully supported by the Leftist-Socialist Evangelicals like Wallis and Warren. The *Reverend* Jim Wallis, a longtime Communist sympathizer (you know, the "God is dead" philosophy) would like to see more of your money given away to corrupt world leaders, perhaps as much as 15% of your income. Jim doesn't worry about that. His "organization" is tax-exempt and long overdue for a financial review.

"Social Justice" is a code term by Democrats and the Evangelical Left to keep people oppressed so that they will continue to rely on the government for all their needs. And more importantly, they will be reminded on election day just who it is that writes the checks. Also, when Democrats like Hillary Clinton and Barack Obama use the term "social justice," it is code for "class warfare," which both learned to foment as fellow Chicagoans in the Alinsky school of social chaos for partisan ends. So the Democrats, now with the assistance and support of Leftist Christians, have become the new plantation owners. The victims have been established, the guilt will be distributed, and blackmail will punish the disobedient.

Obama, Hillary Clinton, and most Democrats are supporting this social justice Christianity, again using it spitefully as if to insinuate the "conservative" Christians don't care about social *in*justice. This is a lie being spurred on by elitist "religious" groups, Democratic politicians, sympathetic pundits, and journalists who suddenly "got religion" on *their* terms, not God's terms, and squeezed in a tax increase along the way.

And Obama didn't feel any forgiveness was in order for himself after the media exposed Obama's Chicago mob ties to Alexi Giannoulis, who organized a $100,000 fundraiser for Obama. The "banker to the mob" has "loaned" enormous amounts of money to Chicago mafia figures such as "Jaws" Giorango, who runs illegal gambling and prostitution rings. Against the advice of Illinois' top Democratic leaders, Obama vouched for Giannoulis' run for *state treasurer*, which he won. Obama couldn't understand what all the fuss was about over his *good friend* Alexi Giannoulis. It's *social* justice.

The emergence of an Evangelical Left is a new twist in the Culture War as these groups tend to stoke fires of poverty and racism, phony tolerance instead of redemption, and embrace the "political science" of global warming. At the same time, this "Religious" Left has "de-emphasized or sometimes jettisoned issues like abortion, same-sex marriage, and the culturally polluting effects of the entertainment industry," according to Ed Vitagliano.

The increasing volume of the talking point strategy among the Religious Left and its counterparts in the media was echoed by Kathleen Kennedy Thompson, author of *Failing America's Faithful*, in which she says that the "Religious Right" has "shrunk God" to issues of "abortion, same-sex marriage, and stem-cell research," and have abandoned "social justice" by ignoring the poor. Again, Thompson is part of the broad multilateral campaign to smear a group that the media itself labeled "Religious Right." In truth, the Religious Left is shrinking God—virtually out of existence—as the Covenant for a New America begins to look and sound like a New Age Covenant for America.

After all, there already is a New Covenant, better known as the New Testament, which has been in effect for almost 2,000 years. The so-called Religious Right is not "narrowly focused" as the press would like to portray them. The problem is the press has "narrowly covered" this movement, which has preached Christian freedom from bondage in areas of sickness, poverty, despair, crime, and hunger for over a century beginning with the true evangelical revivals in England and America in the late nineteenth century.

Segments of contemporary American evangelism have focused certain urgency on some matters without neglecting the wider arena. As Vitagliano notes, " . . . It's probably understandable. More than 1.2 million unborn children are butchered in U.S. abortuaries *each year*, and radical gay activists are busily attempting to abolish the traditional family while propagandizing our children in public schools about the marvels of anal sex." Obama and his supporters refer to this promotion of teen "gay" sex as "a sense of reverence that all young people should have for the act of sexual intimacy."[52] And now Obama wants to extend his sexual agenda to four and five-year-olds.

Obama proceeded to lecture conservatives while at the podium of the Sojourners Conference by demanding what "*they* need to do" and what "*they* need to acknowledge" and what "*they* need to understand," which all boils down to the same Democratic "Progressive" lie that conservative Christians are trying to impose "state-sponsored religion."

It is only natural that Barack Obama and the Evangelical Left had bonded given recent revelations that Obama had shown an interest in radical far-left groups such as Socialists International (SI) and Democratic Socialist of America (DSA). Columnist Cliff Kincaid also revealed that Obama's boyhood mentor in Hawaii was a well known member of the Communist Party USA, Frank Davis.

The Evangelical Left also turns a blind ear when Obama speaks on behalf of Jesus about such issues as "gay marriage" and "gay unions," saying that "If people find that controversial, then I would just refer them to the Sermon on the Mount which I think is, in my mind . . . more central than *an obscure passage in Romans.*" You know, that *obscure passage* by Paul, the apostle to Christ, that says homosexuality is wrong. Obama forgot one of the most important messages from the Sermon on the Mount, "Watch out for false prophets. They come to you in sheep's clothing, but inwardly they are ferocious wolves."

Obama's Open Letter to the Lesbian, Gay, Bisexual, and Transgender (LGBT) community stated that "As your president, I will use the bully pulpit" of the office to *push* states to create a special status of civil unions that will be no different than marriage. Obama made this proclamation as a concession to David Geffen, who had held a second million dollar fundraiser for Obama in late 2008. The "gay producer" who castrated the military by paying off Bill Clinton has now managed to plant the seeds for the destruction of the American family by paying off Barack Obama.

Obama is the last person to be lecturing Americans on a new "Christian Reformation" given his affiliation with the urban radical Afrocentric "church" called Trinity United Church of Christ on Chicago's south side and formally pastored by Dr. Jeremiah Wright. Obama says he came to Christ by discerning the "attributes of the historically black church." True historical black churches cringe at the very thought of being associated with Dr. Jeremiah Wright's racist version of a church that promotes separation instead of inclusion. This alone should ring loud alarm bells among any supporters of Barack Obama.

The mission statement on the church's website declares, "We are a congregation that is Unashamedly Black and Unapologetically Christian," in that order. At the Call to Renewal keynote speech, Barack Obama said that problems of racism are rooted in "societal indifference and individual callousness." But do these calls of racism and discrimination apply to *his* church?

Trinity Church had adopted a "12-point" doctrine known as the "Black Value System" that "must be taught . . . wherever Blacks are gathered."[53] Among the blatantly racial precepts is the curious Precept Number 8, which proclaims a "Disavowal of the Pursuit of Middleclassness." This might explain Obama's declaration of "the importance of poverty" statement at the Sojourners Call to Renewal speech in 2006.

It would appear that any attempt to approach the middle class in economic or social status would be an affront to the joys of poverty. (Of course, Dr. Wright and the Honorable Senator Obama are excused from this precept.)

African-American writer Erik Rush first brought the revelations about Obama's church to the public's attention in his February 21, 2007, article "Obamanation" in which he wrote, "To say that the Trinity United Church of Christ is Afrocentric in the extreme would be a gross understatement. It's not simply Afrocentric, it's African-centric. In fact, one could argue that their organization worships things African to a far greater degree than they do Christ, and gives the impression of being a separatist 'church' in the same vein as do certain supremacist 'white brethren' churches—or even Louis Farrakhan's Nation of Islam."

In addition to the 12-Point Precepts of the Black Value System, Erik Rush notes that "Trinity United Church of Christ's congregation also claims to hold a '10-Point Vision' which is similarly Afrocentric, or if you will, separatist. Again, like the Nation of Islam, a white separatist church or the Branch Davidians, Trinity United more resembles a cult than a church. Only this one has as one of the most prominent members a serious contender for the White House."[54] On March 17, 2008, Trinity quietly removed the Black Value System from its website.On the same day, a link to the Black Panthers appeared on Obama's website.

Trinity also practices a form of Kawaida, an African philosophy of never-ending questions about being "African" *and* "human." It was developed by former radical Black Nationalist Ron Karenga of US (United Slaves), a rival of the Black Panther Party in the 1970s, and implicated in the murders of two Black Panther members. Karenga was also the founder of Kwanzaa in 1967 as a holiday that he demanded be practiced and celebrated as a secular event, free of African mythology and American Christianity.

Karenga developed Kawaida after serving federal time for assaulting two United Slaves associates, Gail Davis and Deborah Jones, in 1971. Ms. Jones told the *Los Angeles Times* in a May 14, 1971 article that Karenga and other members put a hot smoldering iron in Ms. Davis' mouth, and that Karenga also forced toxic chemical cleaning detergents in their throats with a hose.

Whether Karenga was officially declared insane at the time is still unclear. What is clear is that Karenga "developed" his secular Pan-African Kawaida philosophy during his idle time in prison. As Erik Rush concluded, "Gravitation toward an Africanized year-round Kwanzaa-based pseudo-Christianity seems less a solution than the aforementioned socialist stranglehold in the black community." Rush adds, "And George W. Bush's born-again status scares people?"[55]

Jeremiah Wright is a student of James Cone's radical New Age black liberation theology which states, "If God is not for us and against white people, then he is a murderer and we better kill him. The task of black theology is to kill gods who do not belong to the black community." How bizarre is that? But as African-American pastor Jesse Lee Peterson observed, "If you say you support your pastor, who is a racist, people need to know. Christianity is not about color."[56] In March 2008, Obama announced that Pastor Wright would be "retiring" in the coming months. Timing is everything. Obama's church is affiliated with the radical branch of the United Church of Christ (UCC) with 1.2 million members nationwide. UCC is not to be confused with the loose confederation of Southern Churches of Christ. Also many of UCC's own nationwide membership do not subscribe to the leadership's increasingly Left Wing socialist president, John Thomas. David Roozen, director of the Hartford Institute for Religious Research FACT study, noted that "the national church's pronouncements are often more liberal than the views from the pews."[57] After Trinity's new pastor continued pandering for publicity and guest pastor Father Pflegler put on a racist sideshow, Obama finally resigned from the church for the same reason he joined; because "he had to."

THE HOLLYWOOD BIBLE

The great debate between the Evangelical Left and the Evangelical Right is only possible because we live in a country that constitutionally assures freedom *of* religion as opposed to freedom *from* religion. In the Judeo-Christian tradition, the debate will inevitably center around the book which is the foundation of faith, the Bible.

But in the last thirty years, the Bible has been "re-released," like an edited Hollywood movie, into numerous "new" *versions*, not to be confused with *translations*. And with each consecutive version of these contemporary Bibles, the revisions have been so extensive that some Bibles bear little resemblance to the original English version.

Obama and the Evangelical Left have come to rely on those "contemporary" versions with unquestionable reliance. In doing so, they are being increasingly misled by consecutively "new" versions that continually dilute the Bible's original meaning. As Cathy Lynn Grossman of *USA Today* wrote, "For Christians, every word change is measured against the scripture's purpose: to guide the reader's life in this world by the light of God and to give the readers the prospect of eternal life by bringing them, through Jesus, to salvation.

"Because each verb, noun, and pronoun shapes the vision of God and humanity, errors are like miscalculating the path of a rocket: One tiny navigational shift can send everything spiraling in the wrong direction."

Some of this clamor began mildly in the 1960s with *The Living Bible* and in 1978 with the *New International Version* (NIV). However, many of the changes were viewed as single word "upgrades" that did not change the meaning of the Biblical verse.

But everything changed dramatically with the release in 2002 of *Today's New International Version* (TNIV) and the *Gender Neutral Bible* (GNB). The TNIV truly was an international version—of controversy. One hundred eighteen theological critics from around the world signed a letter that listed their numerous complaints. Most comprehensively, the theologians complained that these new versions not only updated language, they tampered with theology, more specifically, the true original *meaning* of words and phrases by the original author, God.

Ben Irwin, who heads the Bible publishing division that created TNIV said the *Bible* was aimed at the "under-35" crowd. Now, even the Bible is age-rated much like any episodic TV series or feature length motion picture. This would make sense considering the fact that the TNIV publishing company is owned by a major Hollywood entertainment conglomerate, hence the euphemistically appropriate term "Hollywood Bible."

According to Wayne Grudem, author of *The TNIV and the Gender-Neutral Bible Controversy*, "The change is not only unnecessary, it undermines the most essential quality of a Bible translation—trustworthiness." He adds, "How would you like to read a Bible when you don't know which words you can trust? People memorize the Bible. They pray on it. They want to trust every word."

The most egregious and ridiculous version of the Bible is the *Gender-Neutral Bible*, fueled by the radical feminist movement, which wants the very mention of the word "man" eliminated from the worldwide lexicon. That anybody bothered to publish a *Gender-Neutral Bible* demonstrates that some people have way too much time on their hands.

What the feminists and the revisionists apparently do not understand is that the first *comprehensive* translation of the Bible into English was carried out at the order of King James I, who instructed learned scholars of language translation to begin with the most original text of the Bible as it was written in the international language of its day, which was the *Stephen's Greek Text of the Holy Bible*.

This was an enormous challenge due to the fact that the Greek language contains many synonymous words that were often translated as a single English word. "Man," for example, originates from *six* separate Greek words. In order to understand which meaning is applicable, the verse and chapter have to be cross-referenced in an English-Greek concordance, which many of the New Left find too cumbersome to use and, God forbid (no pun intended), too accurate.

What the feminists and the obviously uneducated Bible revisionists failed to do is compare their revisions with the original Greek texts. Chances are that most of these modern revisionists can't even speak Greek and apparently have a hard time understanding simple English.

The *TNIV* threw all these distinctions out and the "editors" invented a new English-language oxymoron called the "singular they." In other words, the *TNIV* is a misleading mess of massive proportions. It officially debuted in a full-page ad that appeared in *Rolling Stone* magazine in 2005. Enough said.

These steps in the evolutionary process of dumbing down the Bible can be seen in its extreme with the release in 2006 of a Dutch Bible published under the auspices of the Western Bible Foundation. The Dutch Bible didn't just edit parts of the Bible, they literally cut out entire sections that the Foundation felt were no longer necessary or "relevant." According to the Foundation's chairman, Mr. DeRijke, "Jesus was very inspiring for our inner health, but we don't need to take his naive remarks about money seriously. He didn't study economics, obviously."

The well-known Christian publisher Bijten & Schipperheijn had discarded passages from the Ten Commandments, sections of Isaiah, Proverbs, and the Sermon on the Mount.

However, as *WorldNetDaily* reported on October 20, 2006, the new "versions" turned out to be a joke, which produced "more anger than humor" among Christians. But the "Dutch Bible" hoax was an example of just how easy it would be for New Age Evangelists to produce a "condensed" Bible to match their liberal politics. And with the *TNIV* and *Gender-Neutral Bible*, those early steps have already taken place. These "new" Bibles have rendered words, verses, and entire chapters virtually meaningless.

No wonder Barack Obama admitted that his conversion to Christianity left him with many unanswered questions. He may very well be reading a Hollywood novel that just happens to be titled "The Bible."

DREAMS FROM MY HOLLYWOOD FANTASIES:

Daydreams and Fables

By early 2007, journalists pouring over Barack Obama's *Dreams from My Father: Race and Inheritance* began to discover that there was more fiction than fact in the book promoted as an autobiography. His biggest defenders, the Hollywood-dominated media, would dismiss his "creative memory" losses as trivial. But taken as a whole, Obama's fantasies of his youth have spilled over into his present habit of glazing over facts, creating false images of himself, and basing his future ambitions and agenda on a cacophony of past lies. Obama desperately wants to be the second Hollywood president someday and is writing the screenplay himself.

At the outset, most readers of *Dreams* have completely overlooked the Preface to the book, especially the strategically placed last paragraph, which states, or warns, depending on your perspective: "Although much of this book is based on contemporaneous journals or the oral histories of my family, the dialog is necessarily an approximation of what was actually said or relayed to me. For the sake of compression, some even appear out of precise chronology. With the exception of my family and a handful of public figures, the names of most characters have been changed for the sake of their privacy."[58]

Having spent more than twenty years in the movie business and reading over 2,000 scripts, I recognized that wording as classic boilerplate language often used on page two of docudramas and historical mini-series. This provided Obama with an easy "legal out" just in case he decided to run for political office one day. *Dreams* is the main reason he quickly penned *Audacity of Hope* in hopes of erasing the nightmare fiction he spewed in *Dreams*. But in doing so, he only perpetuated his gauzy "hope" for America in sweeping terms that was structured with good narration and absolutely no substance.

Perhaps his fan base doesn't mind that he lies, as long as he does it "lovingly." *Audacity*, however, only complicated Obama's personae as an individual who is incapable of taking a stand, which could be a major problem for someone who may have to make quick decisions under pressure.

The first fib that started the cascade was an incident Obama recounted in *Dreams* as a "revelation," a kind of "violent" awakening that would forever and "permanently" alter his future. As a nine-year-old living in Indonesia with his mother, Obama recalled on more than one occasion about visiting the U.S. Embassy and coming across an article in *Life* magazine about a black man who suffered "disaster" after trying to whiten his skin using chemicals.

"I felt my stomach knotted; the type began to blur on the page."[59] Obama had confronted the ugly truth of racism for the first time in his young life and the ugly problems it produced. The only problem for Obama is that he told a lie, a trait that he would carry into adulthood.

The *Chicago Tribune* approached Obama and told him that *Life* magazine archivists could find no such story. Obama suggested that the article might have been in *Ebony*, "or it might have been . . . who knows what it was?"[60]

Obama was clearly irritated that he had been caught in yet another lie. *Ebony* archivists tried to find the article also, but to no avail. However, Obama wrote of the incident in such intensity as if it happened yesterday and said the event "permanently altered" his "vision."[61]

Washington Post columnist Richard Cohen came to the rescue to "excuse" Obama's lies, which began springing up like daisies in the spring of 2007. Cohen suggested that "Obama may be manipulating facts in order to wrap race ambition in the gauze of a larger cause." Cohen proceeded to outwit Obama's own audacity when he suggested that "emotional truth" trumps "intellectual truth."[62] This twisted thinking is actually being used by the Obama campaign to "explain" the proliferation of "double-defined-truths" and outright lies.

For many, Obama's "emotional truth" sounded all too familiar to Hollywood Bill's "emotional tale" of black churches being torched when he was a child growing up in Arkansas, even though historical records could not produce any such instances of church burnings at the time. The sum whole of Obama's *Dreams* is the yearning of a young man in search of his racial identity. The "autobiography" depicts an Obama obsessed with the torment of finding his father's ancestors and struggles against racism back in America.

But as writer Steve Sailer noted, after reading *Dreams*, "Obama has led a fairly pleasant existence, with most of the suffering and conflict taking place within his own head as he tries to turn himself into an angry black man." Sailer adds, "Obama's gift for restructuring the past into emotionally and aesthetically satisfying patterns made for an uneasy hybrid of fact and fiction, with composite characters, clearly made up dialogue, and even preposterous dream sequences."[63]

For Obama, matters of his integrity, honesty, and his "emotional truths" only grew more intense after his appearance on March 4, 2007, at Brown's AME Chapel in Selma, Alabama, when he proceeded to tell one premeditated myth after another in hopes that no one would notice or dare to question his "emotional truths" of dubious authenticity. The first tale told by Obama was one of the most disturbing because it was a basic repeat of the tale he spilled at the 2004 Democratic Presidential Convention in which he perpetuated a false history of his African family in demeaning terminology in hopes of stoking audience outrage.

Obama told the gathering at Brown's Chapel that his grandfather Onyango, to his last days, was a "boy" for the British in colonial Africa. At the Democratic National Convention, Obama had at least referred to him as a "domestic servant." And he referred to his own father, Barack Sr., as a "herdsman" for goats. Obama Jr. had in effect defamed his ancestors and insulted the intelligence of his Selma hosts. Obama must have genuinely believed in his stereotyping strategy that he was speaking to a gathering of sharecropping cotton-pickers who would, therefore, identify with his father's and grandfather's oppression by "whitey!"

Onyango was, in fact, a very well-respected, prominent and wealthy farmer in Kenya. He adopted the customs and Western education of the British colonial system. His prosperous legacy remains to this day and he was profiled extensively in *The Nation of Nairobi* newspaper in Kenya in 2004. He was also identified as one of the first Muslin converts in his village, something Barack Obama seems distantly ashamed of, despite his call for religious unity in America.

His father, Barack Sr., was born into privilege and received a superior education by way of a scholarship to the University of Hawaii in 1958 where he met and married Obama Jr.'s mother, Ann Dunham, in 1960. He left her less than a year after Obama Jr. was born in 1961 so he could pursue another prestigious scholarship, this time from Harvard. They separated two years later.

But the Selma audience didn't hear that part of the story, in other words, the true story. Barack Obama talked down to the Selma audience as if they couldn't or wouldn't appreciate the fact that opportunity to excel was available to all people. Obama didn't want to sound too "middle-class." After all, that was something his own pastor, Dr. Jeremiah Wright, frowned upon.

So Obama did what Obama does best—he lied.[64] And he was just getting started. Obama began swinging his head back and forth and assumed the best impersonation of a Deep South Alabama pastor that he could muster. Hillary Clinton was doing the very same thing just down the street at the Baptist Church where she was putting on an equally pathetic and condescending minstrel show.

Obama's next major faux pas is best described by writer Mike Allen. "Consider Obama's stirring tale for the Selma audience about how he had been conceived by his parents, Barack Sr. and Ann Dunham, because they had been inspired by the fervor following the 1965 'Bloody Sunday' voting rights demonstration that was commemorated March 4, 2007. 'There was something stirring across the country because of what happened in Selma, Alabama,' he said, 'because some folks are willing to march across a bridge. So they got together and Barack Obama Jr. was born. So don't tell me I don't have a claim on Selma, Alabama. Don't tell me I'm not coming home to Selma, Alabama.'"[65]

One of the pleasures of living deep in the Black Belt of Alabama is the convenience of travel to the "sacred triangle" of Selma, Montgomery, and Birmingham to attend civil rights anniversaries, commemorations, and speeches by visiting dignitaries as they struggle to rub a little bit of Alabama history into their shirtsleeves. Sitting in the church that day, I realized that the views from the pews *are* much different than the news, which completely ignored Obama's mythical stump speech. It was also another example of Obama's Evangelical Left reformation as he was able to effortlessly delete "Thou shalt not lie" from the Ten Commandments that guide the Selma congregation.

Concerning Obama's "claim on Selma," an elderly gentleman asked me, "Does the senator from Illinois have any idea that this is the forty-second anniversary of the march across Edmund Pettus Bridge? Does he also think that we are ignorant in Alabama and unable to read, and that all of us already know he is forty-five years old?" Laughing out loud, he added, "Now who's going to go up and ask him how he is the offspring of an immaculate misconception?"

Among the national press, only the *Chicago Tribune* and *The New York Times* called him to the carpet of honest confession, which was not forthcoming. Obama told *The New York Times*, "I meant the whole civil rights movement."[66] One of Obama's spokesmen told the *Tribune* that Obama was speaking "metaphorically."

This is the heart of the problem that is Barack Obama. His every move and word in public pronouncements and town hall speeches appear as "metaphors" to a lie he has been living for so long, it is truly difficult for him to separate fact from fiction. The not-so-accidental primary appearance of Sen. Hillary Clinton in Selma on the same day as Sen. Obama brought back memories of another famous teller of tall tales. In 2006, Hillary Clinton made the comment that she was named Hillary by her parents after the famous mountain explorer Sir Edmund Hillary. The only problem was Sir Edmund Hillary was virtually unknown to everyone in America when Hillary Rodham was born in 1947. Sir Edmund Hillary did not become a household name until May 20, 1953, when he and his guide, Tenzing Norgay, reached the peak of Mount Everest. Hillary Clinton's "handlers" tried to explain that tale by claiming her parents "meant well" when "they" told her that story.

Much of Obama's blind ambition and disconnect with reality may have more to do with the very abandonment by his father and for a short time by his mother who sent him to live with her parents in Hawaii. He lived with his grandparents very comfortably and received a first-rate education. This is another period he rarely talks about, not wanting to give the impression that his life was ever comfortable. Obama is painting his legacy as a *victim* to instill *guilt* and sympathy with the American electorate. As author E. Michael Jones noted in *Degenerate Moderns*, guilt "becomes the medium of exchange in the political marketplace. In order to play, you must first get yourself designated as a victim." Jones adds, "The Democratic Party is a good example of how all this gets brokered."

Syndicated columnist Linda Chavez wrote that Obama's pain comes not from the racism Obama claims, but rather from his parental abandonment. Abandoned children usually create fantasy worlds in which the absent parent is a fantasy figure.[67] Gradually, as a child becomes an adult, the fantasies and pretenses morph into self-deception and then outright lies. The scars of abandonment will follow many children throughout their entire adult life.[68]

One might be able to argue that this sense of abandonment can explain Obama's strident and adamant stand to fight against laws that would prevent infanticide when they came up for a vote in the Illinois State Senate in 2001, 2002, and 2003. At his keynote address to the Sojourners in 2006, Obama said that young "girls and boys" should be given information on contraception to "prevent unwanted pregnancies, lower abortion rates, and help assure that every child is loved and cherished."

Obama's statement seemed oddly out of context with the body of his speech, but it may have unintendedly revealed more about Obama's carefully concealed bitterness toward his own abandonment and why he lacked total emotion or concern at the revelation of live babies being shelved to die in Chicago hospitals and clinics.

In his Sojourners' speech, Obama implies that only those children that are not aborted or shelved to die should be assured love and cherishment. He says nothing about promoting adoption agencies where there are more couples wanting children than there are children "available."

Again, Obama says nothing about crisis intervention centers where pregnant women may be encouraged to give birth to their babies to either raise on their own or be offered for adoption. In Obama's tortured, morbid cultivation of his personal culture of death, if a baby isn't wanted, the baby is better off dead—even if born alive. Anyone reading Obama's statements for the public record in the Illinois State Senate during the 2001 through 2003 sessions will find his opinions heartless, shallow, and, to be sure, representative of a sick mind.

Those who have watched Obama's rise in politics certainly should notice the disturbing trend in his ability to change personae when convenience calls, from ghetto stride and "street talk" to Ivy League government-speak and sure-footed gait, all accomplished at the drop of a dime or blink of an eye. As writer Steve Sailer asks, "Which Obama is real? Or is that a naive question to ask of such a formidable identity artist?"[69]

THE RULERS OF THE DARKNESS OF THIS WORLD

Totally missed by the mainstream media was a cut and paste quote from the Bible Obama used in Selma to shamelessly pander to his audience. "I'm in Washington. I see what's going on. I see those powers and principalities have snuck back in there."[70] Obama was referring to lobbyists and special interest groups from which he claims to be immune, as if a single lobbyist or special interest group has never even attempted to contact this saint who is "above" all that. And how many times has that image been tried in American politics?

As with all Obama statements, they are packed with multiple meanings, intentional or not. Obama's "powers and principalities" proclamation in Selma revealed much more about the senator from Illinois than any statement he has made since taking a wrong turn on his Road to Damascus.

On the lighter, but no less serious side, it revealed his hypocrisy and ability to happily confuse and mislead his audience. As Mike Allen noted about "those powers and principalities" sermon in Selma, "It was fine populist riff calculated to appeal to Democratic audiences . . . . But not only did Obama vote for the Senate's big energy bill in 2005, he also put out a press release bragging about its provisions, and his Senate website carried a news article about the vote headlined, 'Senate Energy Bill Contains Goodies for Illinois.'"[71]

So it appears the "powers and principalities" have a very good working relationship with Obama. More disturbing, however, is Obama's selective usage of Bible verses to support his habitual shading of the truth and outright lies. As the political darling of the Evangelical Left, Obama's game of shadows with Biblical verses is indicative of the movement's ambivalence in Biblical reinterpretation. Obama's pride in his Christian animosity and his bendable value system explains why he has no problem in twisting the truth and absolutely no problem with twisting The Truth.

In Selma, Barack Obama was cherry picking with Ephesians 6:12, "for we wrestle not against flesh and blood, but against principalities, against powers, against the rulers of the darkness of this world, against spiritual wickedness in high places."

According to E. W. Bullinger, one of the Western World's most respected theologians, the Apostle Paul wrote Ephesians around 62 A.D. shortly after finishing the book of Philippians. Paul was exhorting Christian believers how to defend themselves against "spiritual wickedness in high places." Bullinger translates directly from the Greek: "These are the wicked spirits of the evil one."[72]

It's very uncomfortable for Obama to read the verse in its entirety because he thinks people have a hard time putting two and two together. There is good and there is evil in this world. Both sides have their authors who collide in the five senses world (touch, taste, sight, sound, and smell), but more frequently in a world invisible to the human eye. Paul explains how to fight against "spiritual wickedness in high places." Obama considers this very extreme. It is because it is extremely true.

Also, any discussion of evil at this level would reveal to most Americans that Barack Obama has surrounded himself with some of the very people who occupy those dark spaces "in high places," chief among them being the world's most prominent atheist and radical socialist who literally wants to reorganize the world into his perverted mindset. That Obama accepted his endorsement and ultimately the Soros machine's web of deception, lies, and smears tells you everything you need to know about Obama.

Barack Obama's association with the "God complex" obsessed megalomaniac provided the young senator with a lesson in developing his own "Christ complex." In October 2007, Obama startled a South Carolina church congregation when he proclaimed, "I am confident we can create a Kingdom right here on earth." Jesus Christ will be establishing the "Kingdom of Heaven" to which Obama was vaguely alluding.

Unless Obama is a Scientologist, he is definitely showing his impatience with Jesus and plans to build the Kingdom himself, or as John Gibson remarked, this will happen for Obama " . . . if you just vote for me. I will lead sinners from the wilderness with smart legislation, impeccable judgment, etc., etc."

In early May 2007, Oprah Winfrey played the race card by throwing her support behind Barack Obama during the primaries in an appearance on the *Larry King Show*. Oprah said Obama was her "favorite senator." When King asked Oprah why she was throwing her support behind Obama, Oprah answered that she likes "what he stands for."[73] But when pressed, Oprah could not name *anything* that Barack Obama truly stands for. Appealing to celebrity worshipers, Obama invited Oprah to join him on the campaign trail in 2008. When pressed again about Obama's credentials, Oprah said, "I know him well enough to believe in his moral authority." She offered no comment on Obama's propensity toward dishonesty.

Oprah can also claim to be part of the Evangelical Left—as in FAR LEFT. In reality, Oprah Winfrey abandoned Christianity years ago and is known best now as the Queen of the New Age. The Watchman Fellowship, Inc., of Birmingham, Alabama, has followed Oprah's slide into the nefarious world of New Age thinking for over a decade. They note that Oprah "is clearly in the process of deconstructing Christianity and reframing it into a New Age perspective."[74]

Part of the Evangelical Left's impetus for swinging along with the New Agers is an ongoing movement in the Protestant Church known as the "new understanding." To listen to Barack Obama, he is lockstep with this movement and this explains why he not only wants to be president, he also wants to "reorganize" Christianity into this bogus image. With Oprah Winfrey's support, he will join her in literally deconstructing Christianity into a New Age blend of people who worship crystals and Jesus simultaneously.

Of this "new understanding" advent and New Age collusion, Oprah declared, "As I read more of Shirley MacLaine, crystals and *The Aquarian Conspiracy*, it seems to me to say what the Bible has said for years."[75] Odd, Oprah, I couldn't find any similarity to Shirley MacLaine and crystals anywhere in the Bible. Remember, it was Shirley MacLaine who proclaimed "I am god" in her book and TV movie *Out on a Limb*.

With Obama's campaign slogan of "A New Kind of Politics," he is signaling a "New Age" for not only politics, but for American religion. With Oprah's help, Obama believes that he can gain the support of everybody on the faith-based scale from dedicated believers to hardened atheists. Obama has also pandered to the worst stereotypes of African-Americans when he tried to show he was "black enough" by introducing subtle threats of race riots if the underserved are not quickly brought up to speed, speaking about the poor in general. But he was specifically addressing the post-Katrina response, threatening that "quiet riots" of rage were prepared to explode. And he's not above firing the starter pistol.

As Bill Cosby once said, "I don't know the key to success, but the key to failure is to please everyone."

Perhaps Obama's delusion into believing he is invincible took a reality check when he concocted yet another ruse to elevate himself as candidate and victim. Just three days after Oprah's endorsement, Obama requested Secret Service protection citing "hate mail, calls, and other threatening material," according to a report by Anderson Cooper.

Obama cited these vague threats and the "growing crowds" at his appearances, despite the fact that recent appearances, including the Tampa fiasco, produced substantially fewer crowds than the campaign hoped for. Even though the Secret Service could not identify any specific threats, he was granted protection by Homeland Security. The strategy, orchestrated by campaign manager David Axelrod, was a staggering success. By the summer of 2007, crowds at Obama rallies tripled as throngs of curiosity-seekers scrambled to catch a glimpse of the candidate who could become "the new John F. Kennedy."

The Obama campaign also orchestrated a press release shortly after the July 4, 2007 holiday claiming that a laptop computer with *important* information had been stolen from campaign headquarters. However, it apparently wasn't important enough to file a police report. The Obama campaign attempt to fabricate another Watergate scenario fizzled.

In the 1996 piece, "Blizzard of Lies," columnist William Safire called America's First Lady Hillary Clinton "a congenital liar." Eleven years later, columnist Andy Martin, who has been covering Obama's political tracks since 2004, called the Illinois senator "a congenital liar."[76]

As a young man in his thirties, Obama had the opportunity to watch Bill Clinton lie repeatedly while running for his first term and again for his second term. Seeing no firestorm of outrage from the voters or the press, Obama just keeps on lying in the same mold as Bill and Hillary Clinton. In the moral relativism of a Hollywood nation, lying appears to be just another inflection of speech. After all, Obama's Hollywood mentor, David Geffen, said, "Everybody in politics lies. . . ."

One Hollywood president for America was enough. A second Hollywood president or even a Hollywood vice-president would precipitate a disaster for the United States, nationally and globally. And "globally" is the problem for Obama. In his first attempt to pose a genuine policy stand after eight months of touchy-feely empty rhetoric, he proved how out of touch with reality he is. In mid-July 2007, Obama was talking about the need to pull all of our troops from the war on terror and engage in talks with tyrants and dictators. Within ten days, on August 1, Obama made a statement about the need to attack sensitive ally and nuclear nation Pakistan to weed out al-Qaeda. In a GOP debate five days later, presidential candidate Mitt Romney summed it up best. "In one week, he went from saying he's going to sit down for tea with our enemies, but then he's going to bomb our allies. He went from Jane Fonda to Dr. Strangelove."

If Obama ever succeeded to becoming president at some point in the future, everyone should consider the consequences of that nightmare scenario:

ADVISOR: President Obama! America is being attacked! New Orleans has fallen to the enemy!
PRESIDENT OBAMA: Have we established their religion? How about their race? Have you determined if they feel in their heart that America owes them something? Let's not be judgmental. Let's be open to dialogue.
ADVISOR: Mr. President, the enemy is already moving up the Mississippi River. Can we attack now!
PRESIDENT OBAMA: Let's not jump to conclusions.... You said the Mississippi River?
ADVISOR: Yes, sir!
PRESIDENT OBAMA: Well, there you go. My good friend Charlie Rangel said, "Who the hell wants to live in Mississippi?" Let's just give it to them. A peace offering. Tell Haley Barbour to bail out. Get Soros on the phone and tell him I avoided military action to defend America. I promised him that much.
ADVISOR: But ... sir, well ... what about ...
PRESIDENT OBAMA: What are you stuttering about? Just get me David Geffen on the phone!
ADVISOR: Yes, sir.

UNSOLICITED ENDORSEMENTS FOR BARACK OBAMA

Bernadine Dohrn - American terrorist implicated in 1981 Brinks muders.
William Ayers - American terrorist leader. Bombed Pentagon, U.S. Capitol.
Louis Farrakhan - Racist leader of NOI and visitor to UFO "Mother Wheel."
Rashid Khalidi - Informal supporter of violent PLO and terrorist sympathizer.
Ahmed Yousef - Ultra-violent political director of Hamas, "We like Obama."
Mailik Shabazz - Virulent racist, supremacist leader of New Black Panthers.
MoveOn.org - Official smear, slander, & defamation site for George Soros.
P. Diddy - Promoter of profane, violent music and uncut porn video for HYPE-TV in association with Playboy. Motto: "Obama or Die !!"

CHAPTER 7

The Ratings Fiasco

*If you put a rating on garbage,
it doesn't make it quality television.
It's still garbage.*
—Sen. Joe Lieberman

By the early 1990s, dissatisfaction with the content of broadcast and cable television was reaching a fever pitch from the American public, media watchdog groups, and even a large segment of the U.S. Congress that transcended party lines. With overwhelming bipartisan support, the Congress was proposing a radical challenge to the television entertainment industry to clean up its act or face a new federally mandated system to rate the programming that permeated every television set in America, leaving a foul odor that lingered in the home long after the OFF button was pressed.

The prospect of ratings, whether government mandated or industry mandated, was a controversial proposal in itself. Supporters felt that ratings would help parents and adults decide what was suitable not only for their children, but also for themselves. Critics could easily point to the effect ratings had inflicted on motion pictures at the neighborhood theater. Family viewing was almost eliminated, with the audience fragmented into age groups. Also, the Ratings Scheme of Jack Valenti had given gratuitous sex, violence, profanity, and raunchy behavior a "legitimate" venue with a de-facto industry stamp of approval.

Ratings for television seemed to be the only option to fill the vacuum created by the abolishment of the Television Code of the National Association of Broadcasters (NAB) in 1982. The content guidelines set down by the Television Code was a guide for basic standards and practices regarding content in programming that was the broadcast world's equivalent of the Production Code for feature films that Valenti abolished in 1968. In the case of the Television Code, the NAB was "forced" to abolish its guidelines by a federal court case that remains murky even today.

Filling this void became an exciting challenge for the sleaze merchants of Hollywood television production. Even before 1982, TV producers were pushing the envelope with the incremental creep of "Jiggle TV" and the tag-line favorite "T and A programming." The formula was simple and the plot incidental; lots of bulging cleavage that would swing, sway, and jiggle with every corresponding motion of facial expression. The term "headshot" gave way to the term "boobshot."

But after the abolishment of the Television Code, producers started to slowly edge their personal social/sexual/political agendas into programming. So pervasive was the lowering of the moral bar, network and cable television by the mid-1990s represented a series of whorehouses on an Amsterdam street with each channel trying to one-up, or one-down, each other's content.

By 1995, momentum from the public, critics, and outspoken elected officials from the federal, state, and local level would result in the adoption of a key component in the Telecommunications Act of 1996 that would require television manufacturers to install a computer chip in new TV sets. This would allow consumers to block shows electronically for "objectionable" content.

The original term for the computer chip to be installed into new televisions was the C-Chip (C for Choice). However, Democratic Rep. Edward Markey began to coin the term V-Chip (V for Violence), as if escalating violence was the only concern of Americans. The term change was seen as a way of placating Hollywood concerns that too much "choice" might lead viewers to block out ninety percent of their content, or worse, block out virtually everything except the local news, sports, and weather.

Hollywood couldn't deny or fight the fact that extraneous and exploitative violence was having an effect on the culture, and they just might be willing to participate, even though they felt the whole idea of a V-chip was "censorship" and "anti-democratic." The truth was, the chip was very democratic. Allowing viewers at least a semblance of choice instead of trash; except the viewers still paid for the garbage.

By June 1995, two Democratic senators, Joe Lieberman of Connecticut and Kent Conrad of North Dakota, had pushed the measure through the Senate for passage. In the House, Rep. Markey along with Democratic Representative Jim Moran of Virginia and Republican Representative Doug Bereuter of Nebraska pushed a similar measure for passage.

With the mandated V-chip language intact, the Telecommunications Act was passed by a whopping 414-16 in the House and 91-5 in the Senate. It was clear that Americans of all political persuasions were tired of being fed "nightmares of depravity." The provisions of the new act required TV set manufacturers to install the chip in all new sets by 1998, later extended to the millennium year 2000.

But the hard part of implementing an ambitious system of this magnitude was just beginning. Deciding what was "objectionable" would take over a year to outline, and would result in a system that remains controversial to this day.

The Telecom Act called on the broadcast and cable industry to develop a ratings system to coincide with the V-chip technology so that viewers could block out certain programs or entire channels based on the content code. All this could be accomplished with a special electronically coordinated remote control. Broadcast and cable executives acted reluctant to participate at first. But as Ted Turner said at the time, "We got the message. Either we were going to do it or someone was going to do it for us."[1]

The pressure on the industry came as a dual result of the new Telecom Act and election year politics. The presidential race of 1996 was already heating up between Republican Senator Bob Dole and President Clinton, which set the stage for the contemporary phase of the Culture War with Hollywood, as we discussed in detail in Chapter 3. In fact, in early June 1995, Senator Dole was defining himself and the Culture War more strongly than ever before and gained widespread support as a result.

According to *Newsweek*, Dole took on Hollywood by "bombing and strafing some of the entertainment industry's more sordid trash purveyors to very great effect."[2] And as a refresher to Chapter 3, *Newsweek* reporter Larry Reibstein outlined the defining moment when the Culture War hit an all new up-tempo phase. "Senator Bob Dole and former Education Secretary William Bennett singled out Time-Warner, Inc., as the leading purveyor of what Bennett called 'trash.'"[3]

With pressure from both sides of the political aisle, the television industry called in the Dark Prince from the feature film industry, Jack Valenti, the MPAA president who started the whole ratings snowball three decades earlier. Critics had mixed feelings. After all, it was Valenti's establishment of the feature film Ratings Scheme that put the cautionary stamp of approval on some, it not most, of Hollywood's increasing output of "trash," as Bennett termed it.

Clinton was already planning to co-opt the Dole agenda and make it his own, the values-for-votes strategy. Valenti didn't want ratings for TV but he knew it was going to be a make-or-break issue for Clinton in order to win re-election. And Clinton didn't care about TV's slide into the gutter until it became politically expedient to care about it.

Clinton needed Hollywood money and Valenti needed a corrupt president so the two would be joined at the hip for the following year. Hollywood was flooding the campaign with millions of dollars in contributions (Appendix I) with the larger percentage going to the Democratic Party. It was hoped that the Congress would accept a "soft" ratings system from the industry, and money was funneling into congressional races as well as the presidential race.

Valenti and industry leaders promised President Clinton that a voluntary ratings system (again, "scheme") would be in place by January 1, 1997, and Clinton could claim the moral high ground, even though he was already waist deep in the moral low ground and political swamp of assaulting women and selling military secrets to the Communist Chinese.

Dexter Anstrom, president of the National Cable Television Association, and Edward Frits of the National Association of Broadcasters agreed to work with Valenti to develop the new ratings scheme for television programming. Valenti and friends waited until after Clinton's re-election victory to release the details of the new system. This was typical Clinton-Valenti strategy; promise the world before election and deliver the crumbs after the votes are cast. Sen. Joe Lieberman, the level-headed former Democrat from Connecticut, would make his summary assessment of the new system announcing, "They've produced a turkey."[4]

What Valenti had delivered, and what many had expected, was another scheme based largely on his 1968 Movie Ratings Scheme, a letter grade of ascending exclusion: G, PG, TV-14, and M. The public and Congress were not happy, to say the least. As *USA Today* reported on Friday the thirteenth, December 1996, "Clinton snared a political victory when network and Hollywood studio leaders came to the White House and vowed to create the code. What [Clinton] will say about the result is unclear."[5] Nothing new there. The president would soon disappear from the whole affair.

A poll released a few days earlier by the Media Studies Center/Freedom Forum found that seventy-three percent of respondents preferred additional "content descriptions" and only fifteen percent preferred an age-based-only code. Valenti had to continually remind people—it's a system, not a *code*—lest anybody harkens back to the Production *Code* Administration or the Television *Code*. Of course, the new television ratings were nothing more than a *scheme*.

Unlike 1968 when Valenti cleverly sprang the Movie Ratings Scheme on America after his "Quiet Conspiracy," the American audience was witness to the craftiness of Valenti this time and they were fighting back against the Dark Prince. Valenti didn't like the heat. Jack Valenti vented his anger at Congress and the American people, vowing that any attempt by the federal government to amend "his" scheme would force him "to be in court in a nanosecond."[6]

Larry Garrett, a parent from Hurricane, West Virginia, roared back, "Who is movie industry official Jack Valenti that he can insult parents by telling them it is their responsibility to filter out filth?" Mr. Garrett expressed the concern of many parents and adults. "How can a parent know what is suitable without first viewing it? Should we record each program, then judge what is decent enough to allow in our homes?" The Television Code of the NAB and the individual network "Standards and Practices" divisions used to do just that before they flushed their conscience and values down the drain.

In January 1997, the age-based ratings system made its debut on American television sets. However, the reception from the American viewing audience was less than lukewarm, and they let their representatives in Congress know, as Jack Valenti would say, in a "nanosecond."

To gauge "middle-American" opinion, the House Telecommunications Subcommittee traveled to Peoria, Illinois, in May 1997 to determine how the four-month-old system was being received. The old saying coined by early movie moguls, "How will it play in Peoria?" was now going to be asked by Congress to a group of local residents gathered in a town meeting hall. Jack Valenti was dragged along as the whipping boy he would soon become.

"I am horrified at what I watched last week on television," exclaimed one mother to a round of applause from the audience. "I could not believe some of the things I saw on television and the ratings they were given."

Another mother in attendance asked, "How could you let TV go so far?"

Jack Valenti was not accustomed to mingling with the "common folk," especially in lieu of cocktails, and proceeded to pander his sympathy for the Peoria audience, "I am utterly flabbergasted, as you are, about some of the programs that I see . . . . We're trying only to rate what is on the screen, so you have advance information."[7]

Valenti's usual ploy of playing both sides of the debate did not sit well in Peoria. Nor did it sit well with Congress, despite all the money Valenti's MPAA had spread around for the past thirty years since he "assumed" the throne. Furthermore, Valenti and Hollywood executives should have taken the hint from the Peoria audience that the entertainment industry had been out of touch, generally, for three decades. People in Peoria did not use Hollywood snob terminology like "utterly flabbergasted." No, they were simply "horrified." What part of "horrified" did Jack Valenti not understand?

House Telecommunications Subcommittee Chairman Billy Tauzin (R-LA) took the Peoria message to heart, saying, "generally they don't like a lot of what they see on TV and they want some help." Rep. Edward Markey said that supporters of the four-month-old system "are so hard to find that they may qualify for protection under the Endangered Species Act."

With that message ringing loud and clear, the television industry grudgingly caved in to add a "Content Description" based system that would take effect on October 1, 1997, only eight months after the age-based-only system was set in place. The Dark Prince would have to pull up to the table and eat his words about refusing to ever make any changes to his original proposal.

What followed, and remains in effect today, is one of the most ambiguous and fallacious systems ever designed by the entertainment industry to educate (read: confuse) the American television audience. The original four age-based ratings would now be expanded to six: *TV-Y*, all children; *TV-Y7*, directed to older children; *TV-G*, general audience; *TV-PG*, parental guidance; *TV-14*, parents strongly cautioned; *TV-MA*, mature audiences only. That's right, the television industry that once brought you the Ed Sullivan Show had now degenerated into an adult movie house, complete with its own version of the X-rating.

But wait, it would get even more confusing for the viewer. Added to each age-based rating was a list of five additional content descriptors such as V-Violence, S-Sex, L-Crude Language, D-Suggestive Dialogue, and FV-Fantasy Violence.

Parents and adults with V-chip equipped television sets would be able to block certain programs using a grid such as this:

THE V-CHIP RATING SCHEME

TV-MA	V	S	L	D
TV-14V	V	S	L	D
TV-PGV	S	L	D	
Y7	FV			

Source: U.S. Congress

Simple math demonstrates that this grid is capable of producing hundreds of rating combinations. In truth, the combinations are virtually endless due to the MPAA further *redefining* TV content descriptions for *each* age-based rating. Confused? You should be. That's what Hollywood intended, to dull your senses to the point that you eventually zone out the ratings and watch whatever the industry flushes into your television.

For example, under *TV-PG*, the content letter D stands for "some suggestive dialogue." But under *TV-14*, the letter D stands for "intensely suggestive dialogue," and under *TV-MA*, the same letter D stands for "crude indecent language."[8]

These are the extrapolated definitions according to the MPAA's website under "TV Parental Guidelines." The TV Ratings Scheme is separate and different from the MPAA's Ratings Scheme for theatrical films.

The most outlandishly ludicrous example of TV ratings is the MPAA's confounding definition of content under the category *TV-Y7* for programming "Directed to Older Children." Under this category, the parental guidelines make a special note, "For those programs where fantasy violence may be more intense or more combative than other programs in this category, such programs will be designated "*TV-Y7-FV*." The obtuse nature of the TV Ratings Scheme has rendered the V-chip virtually worthless as it does not distinguish between ever changing content descriptors. And this was the "pay back" revenge of Hollywood to override the technology by overloading it.

Evidence of this was made more apparent by the fact that the MPAA allowed each television network to rate their own programming. What might pass for

TV-PG at CBS could be labeled *TV-14* by NBC. Take your local television station guide and count all the stations and channels available in your area. That's how many interpretations of the TV Ratings Scheme exist. That's why the TV ratings combinations are not only endless, they are useless.

You may ask yourself, "How did television manage to exist, grow, and thrive for thirty-four years without ratings?" It did, until 1982 when the NAB was "forced" to abolish the Television Code. (The true story behind that secret is detailed in the next chapter.)

Once that happened, the spill-over effect from the feature film industry infected television entertainment like the plague. This was another major example of the ancillary effect that Jack Valenti unleashed on the culture when he abolished the Production Code Administration in 1968. It was no coincidence that the television industry brought him in to help define down the deviance of TV programming.

Media Research Center Chairman Brent Bozell strongly predicted that the TV Ratings Scheme would backfire. In a 1999 press conference, Bozell released a report on the status of the television ratings titled "TV More Offensive Than Ever." Bozell reminded the press that "some irresponsible members of the entertainment industry would see the opportunity presented by the ratings system to insert even edgier content into their shows."

Standing with Bozell at the news conference were Sen. Joe Lieberman, former Democrat of Connecticut, and Sen. Sam Brownback, Republican from Kansas. Just two years earlier Lieberman saw the flaws in a "system" that basically was a warning to viewers that the programming on television would be defective and intentionally divisive on families.

"The public, and parents especially, want more from television than better labels on programs," Lieberman stated. "They want higher quality and lower amounts of what might be called 'must-flee TV'—feel-good killing, talk-show debauchery, bed-hopping without consequences, and general 'anything goes' mentality that pervades too much of today's programming."

In the same year that TV ratings began, 1997, the *Los Angeles Times* conducted a national survey on entertainment programming in the television industry. Sixty-five percent of respondents believed that the quality of programming had declined in the previous ten years compared to only seventeen percent who thought it had improved. Seventy percent told the pollsters they have "very different values" than those values portrayed by the television entertainment industry.

In the same year, the Opinion Research Corporation asked a wide cross-section of Americans if they agreed with the following statement: "I watch less TV than I used to." The result was a staggering seventy-one percent who agreed.

Research polls on the "quality" of television programming are becoming less frequent since the Ratings Scheme was installed. The reason is simple, the quality of "entertainment" *programming* is so low it is no longer quantifiable. And that's how Hollywood wanted the outcome. It is part of the end result of "value manipulation" by Hollywood.

THE CROSSOVER DECEPTION:
The Movie House to Your House

The Ratings Scheme for television, a jungle maze created by Valenti with the approval of the broadcasting and cable industry, was intended for programming specifically produced for television such as episodic shows, sitcoms, movies, and other formats. Again, the ratings designed for television are different from the ratings designed for movies.

So, you ask, what happens when movies produced for theaters make their debut on television? This scenario was already anticipated by Valenti and company. Any movie or other production originally released at a movie theater would be re-rated according to the TV Ratings Scheme. And that rating would depend on which network or cable station debuted the movie due to the "Standards and Practices" department of that particular channel.

As useless as the Ratings Scheme is for theatrical movies, when the crossover to television occurs, the new ratings grid becomes a virtual joke on the audience due to the endless combinations of age and content descriptions.

But in the ever-changing world of communication delivery technology, entertainment venues such as feature films can be downloaded to home computers, laptops, cell phones, and other portable hand-held displays. In these situations, the "understanding" from the MPAA is that the original MPAA rating applies, though age identification and enforcement are sketchy gray areas.

The most popular and challenging crossover from the movie house to your house is the purchase and rental of movies and other productions on DVD. In this case, the home television set serves simply as a portal of the production on the DVD. With this being the most common scenario, the MPAA expects the consumers to follow the ratings they give to titles released on DVD. But the age-based ratings enforcement would no longer be the ticket-taker; the clerk at the video rental outlet or the cashier at the mass market retailers would serve as the intermediate gatekeeper.

In the early days of video rental stores, beginning in the early 1980s and followed by the popularity of video purchases beginning in the mid-1990s, the distribution arms of the major movie studios were counting on lax enforcement in order to "push" their product. The retailers were not bound by the same agreement that exists between the MPAA and National Association of Theater Owners (NATO), which requires age verification for ticket buyers.

For more than a decade, it was a common practice by video retailers to blink or look the other way when renting or selling videos to underage buyers. It was in the best interest of the retailers and the studios to "move" as much product as possible. And that's where the whole sad chapter of rating entertainment really hit home. Movies would become as potentially dangerous as tobacco and alcohol, requiring identification to prove the consumer was "adult enough" to handle a tape or DVD of "entertainment." Just another notch on the legacy of Jack Valenti and his dark vision of American culture.

The distribution arms of the studios did not mount major "awareness" campaigns to video retailers encouraging strict enforcement of the age-based ratings, first on VHS tapes and then the new DVD format of today. In fact, the Hollywood entertainment machine actually fostered a "temptation" strategy of marketing movies at both the movie theaters and at the rental level.

This strategy became known among industry promoters as the "forbidden fruit" marketing plan, supported enthusiastically by industry insiders such as veteran child-hater and *Variety* columnist Timothy Gray, who declared, "Tykes don't want to be protected—nothing is as enticing as forbidden entertainment—and it's not clear they need to be protected."[9]

That attitude was being shared by video retailers and the multi-plex theater operators, except on rare occasions where responsible ownership prevailed. The very creation of the multi-plex theater with eight, twelve, twenty or more screens was a desperate attempt by exhibitors to save money with the era of unpredictable or declining attendance.

But it also provided a convenient "opportunity" for underage children to buy a ticket to a PG movie and then slither into the long corridors and dart into an R-rated film. After all, the theaters were, and remain, understaffed with tickets being taken only at the front door, and not in front of the dark individual hallway entrance to the theater itself.

But a red-hot poker in the form of public outrage after the Columbine massacre proved a wake-up call to exhibitors, video retailers, and the Hollywood denial department of the MPAA, who would come together to make a "flabbergasting" announcement.

While refusing to acknowledge that movies had any influence over the Columbine teen killers (the two shooters had watched Oliver Stone's *Natural Born Killers* like a non-stop video-loop the night before the massacre) Jack Valenti was summoned to Washington by President Clinton. The president was eager to put a new face on his dwindling reputation shattered by impeachment.

Jack Valenti, forced to face the consequences of his "free screen" movement, appeared with President Clinton on June 8, 1999, to announce that the National Association of Theater Owners and its members were going to *start enforcing* movie ratings, focusing special attention on teenagers. Identification would *now* be required if teens "looked" under seventeen and tried to buy tickets into R-rated films. Video retailers were "expected" to follow the example of the theater owners.

This was a classic example of just how "out of touch" Jack Valenti had become with the American public. Wasn't the Ratings Scheme intended to conquer and divide families, individuals, and children into constricted and enforced age groups in order for Valenti's "New Kind of American Movie" to prevail? And didn't he make that announcement back in 1968, some thirty-one years prior to this June day in 1999?

As Ellen Goodman of the Boston Globe noted in her column that same week, "We've had more panels and debates about Hollywood than premieres. Now, with enough hype to rival Star Wars, major theater owners have announced their new plan: They're actually going to enforce their old ratings code."[10] What a shock! And we were so stupid to think they were doing so all along.

To their partial credit, some theater owners continue to be extra vigilant about asking for IDs. But again it's only at the front door and not the back door to the individual theaters where it really counts. Retailers also began to crack down on lax enforcement with more pressure from parents and media watchdog groups than Valenti's hollow pronouncement.

Wal-Mart stepped up to the plate with a strict policy for checking IDs at the register. Going the extra mile, Wal-Mart programmed all the registers in their stores to ask for an ID anytime an R-rated DVD was scanned. This program is known today as Wal-Mart's "Mature Merchandise Policy." Other mass retailers and video rental outlets followed Wal-Mart's example. Up until the early 1990s, Wal-Mart would not sell R-rated movies and record producers are still forced to cut "special cleaned-up" versions of raunchy music.

One last bastion for Hollywood to break the rules is the corner convenience store and local grocers. DVD sales racks have been springing up at thousands of locations around the country with little or no enforcement of ID checks.

Hollywood was relentless in its eagerness to override the roadblocks at the larger retail level. By 2005, some movie titles were showing up on retail shelves absent any rating on the back of the DVD cover jackets. At the same time, some studio distributors were shipping DVDs to retail outlets with the phrase "No Rating" or "Unrated" in tiny wording on the back covers of DVDs. Most of these "Unrated" DVDs were originally released in theaters as "R" movies. Wal-Mart immediately picked up on the scam and reprogrammed the scanners to display the "Check ID" warning on the register screen. Other mass retailers such as Target, Sears, and dozens more followed suit.

Knowing that their short-lived stint at deception was a bomb, the studio distributors returned to the "forbidden fruit" plan and began releasing DVDs with "Unrated" as part of the title on the front cover. Titles such as the Brad Pitt and Angelina Jolie flop *Mr. and Mrs. Smith* were now being released and sold as Mr. and Mrs. Smith: UNRATED.

In the slasher-film genre, the gore-fest remake of *The Hills Have Eyes* was now being sold as *The Hills Have Eyes: The Unrated Version*, as if the original blood-by-the-gallon version wasn't enough. And today Hollywood cannot find enough words to sell "entertainment" titles on DVD that contain extra footage included to appeal to the viewer's "inner base" temptation, courtesy of an industry that lives in an "outer base" world.

The longest title of those "special" raunchy DVDs has to be *The Girl Next Door—Unrated Edition—What They Couldn't Show You In the Theaters*. Walking through the video aisles of any retailer is not much different than strolling through P. T. Barnum's New York freak shows of the late nineteenth century. Most consumers have no clue that Hollywood clings religiously to P.T. Barnum's dictum, "There's a sucker born every minute."

But, strict enforcement wouldn't last long. According to Dr. David Walsh, enforcement of ratings on video games from the big-box retailers rated a "D" and the smaller retailers and rental outlets rated an "F" according to "secret shopper" research conducted in late 2007. The major exceptions were K-Mart, Hollywood Video, and KB games and toys.

The popular mail-order DVD service NetFlix provides a special service where parents can set a "privacy account" that allows an account profile to be set so that their children can order DVDs. But the parents can customize the access controls so that their children will not be allowed to order R-rated movies.

All of this begs the question: Does being an adult warrant the viewing of entertainment that you don't feel comfortable letting your children watch? As Ellen Goodman noted in the wake of Valenti's 1999 enforcement announcement, "Meanwhile, the ID requirement implies that anyone *over* 17 is unaffected by violence. Remember the study showing how sexually violent films desensitized men to rape?"[11]

WHO EXACTLY IS RATING THE MOVIES?

Now that we know how television programming is arbitrarily rated since the inception of television ratings in 1997, the next logical question is: Who has actually been rating the feature films shown in movie theaters around the world since Jack Valenti's Ratings Scheme revolution of 1968?

Within the MPAA organization, an office exists with the kindly acronym CARA, which stands for the Classification and Ratings Administration. According to the MPAA website, "The Classification and Ratings Administration is funded through fees submitted by filmmakers who participate in the voluntary rating process. It is comprised of ten to thirteen parents, chosen from different demographics, who are hired to screen the films as a Board, and apply the ratings they think the majority of American parents would find most appropriate. Raters are parents of children between five and seventeen when they are hired. The Rating Board searches for people who have good parental judgment and are from various backgrounds geographically."

The tricky language is a legacy of the Valenti years and the challenge of replacing one rating system like the Production Code Administration (PCA) with another one called CARA in order to validate his ratings scheme. And CARA is the heartbeat of that scheme. Reading between the lines of the CARA mission statement is fairly easy:

VOLUNTARY RATINGS PROCESS

The filmmaker's participation in the "voluntary" system implies that filmmakers have the freedom to submit, or not to submit, their films for a rating. However, if they don't, their movies cannot be shown in a major theater owned by any of the handful of major theater owners that control the majority of movie screens in America and belong to NATO.

According to the original 1968 scheme laid out by Valenti and the National Association of Theater Owners, a movie must have the MPAA seal on it before a NATO affiliated theater will agree to exhibit the film. In order to obtain the seal, filmmakers must have a rating on these films or they end up on the "art house" circuit of theaters. These art houses are typically not members of NATO and their numbers have steadily dwindled over the years, almost always guaranteeing a money losing release.

This is virtually the same system that existed pre-1968 when the PCA was still in existence. Instead of submitting a movie for a rating to the CARA board to receive the seal, movie scripts were submitted to the PCA staff to determine if the projected film met the basic guidelines set forth in the Production Code. (See Appendix III)

In both the Code administration days and the current system of ratings, the respective boards maintained a great deal of flexibility in giving a film the green light of the MPAA seal. The main difference is that the old Production Code maintained a higher standard of content values while the current systems maintains a philosophy of "anything goes" as long as it has a rating attached.

But in both the old and the new systems, producers and directors did not, and do not now, maintain control over the "final cut." The MPAA has the *final* say over the *final* cut.

FUNDED THROUGH FEES

As the description of CARA indicates, their administrative function is funded by fees "submitted by filmmakers." In addition, it is important to remember that the MPAA itself is funded by the major movie studios who have a vested interest in seeing their films receive the seal of approval. While CARA is semi-autonomous, it does allow "fee paying" filmmakers to appeal the rating bestowed upon their films. Filmmakers may also resubmit their films for review again after edits have been made.

In the perverse mindset of many Hollywood producers, the R-rating seems to be the goal for "serious" filmmakers, or at least a PG-13. In the left-coast philosophy of contemporary film writers, producers, and directors, a heavy dose of splattered blood, F-bombs, decapitations, dismembered bodies, and pornographic sex are the hallmark signs of a film their "peers" will approve. In today's Hollywood, the filmmakers aim to please their fellow movie-makers first and the audience comes in second. None of them want to be laughed at or ridiculed at a Beverly Hills cocktail party for cranking out a PG movie or, God forbid, a G movie.

A large number of films submitted to CARA originally received the truly dreaded NC-17, the softball rating created by Valenti in 1990 to replace the X-rating. After making the necessary cuts recommended by the board members of "good parental judgment," the film is resubmitted until the "acceptable" rating of R is granted. This is a carefully orchestrated ruse.

The moviemakers learned long ago how to manipulate the CARA board. By the late 1980s and early 1990s, filmmakers had dramatically stepped up the amount of blood, gore, profanity, and sex to a level never before seen by the moviegoing audience. Each level of audience desensitizing is met by a new generation of filmmakers with a higher threshold of perversity.

Instead of submitting a film to CARA as producers and directors would like to see them exhibited, the filmmakers submit a "loaded" print with extra helpings of all the offensive material guaranteed to warrant an NC-17. When the board at CARA stamp the film with the adults-only NC-17 rating, the producer spits and curses, declares the unfairness of this "censorship" process and the infringement of their rights under the First Amendment of the Constitution of the United States of America!

Then, calmly, the producer returns to CARA with the print of the film that was "intended" for submission in the first place. After some token wailing and gnashing of teeth, the board members of "good parental judgment" give the film a reluctant R.

Ironically, R-rated movies are almost always money losers. Even the MPAA noted on its website that of the top twenty films of 2005, eighty-five percent were rated PG or PG-13. The Dove Foundation has conducted surveys for the past fifteen years that continually indicate that G and PG-rated movies make considerably more money than R-rated films. But many of today's filmmakers are on a single-minded mission: Losing money for their investors.

What the public receives today as a PG-13 movie is basically an R movie. And R movies of today are basically NC-17 movies; in original terminology, X-rated. The whole idea of Valenti's Rating Scheme of 1968 was to define decency down, and CARA, with its rotating members of "good parental judgment" ensure that the definition of decency continues to be lowered. This is the natural outcome of a board of parents, or bored parents, that become accustomed to annually increasing displays of carnage, rape, scattered body parts, nudity, and profanity and begin to view these scenes as just another "artist's" depiction of life in America.

These board members of "good parental judgment" know they are being manipulated. But it's easy to get tired after watching up to 900 movies a year, most containing some degree of desensitizing and hypnotizing offensive content. At the end of the week, they just want to pick up their paychecks and go home. For some, invitations to the Hollywood cocktail party circuit could be too much to resist. As a de-facto jury, these individuals might not be beyond the capacity to be "swayed," not to be confused with "bought." But for that reason of potential corrupting pressure from the studios, the names of the actual raters at CARA are carefully kept secret.

Have you ever wondered why NC-17-rated movies are rarely released anymore? They're actually out there, right now, in the theaters and on DVD. They've just been "dumbed down" with misplaced ratings courtesy of the good folks at CARA.

GOOD PARENTAL JUDGEMENT

According to the MPAA, the ratings board at CARA is comprised "of ten to thirteen parents, chosen from different demographics, who are hired to screen the films" and then, happy with the extra income, proceed to "apply the ratings *they* think the majority of American parents would find most appropriate." The description continues by enunciating these anonymous and nameless people as "parents of children between five and seventeen" and also possessing "good parental judgment."

First, what kind of "good parental judgment" is exercised by a father or mother who watches a movie such as Saw, Silent Hill, or Natural Born Killers and gives the film an R instead of an NC-17? In movies like these and thousands of others reviewed by CARA, human limbs are sawed off with the camera up-front and personal to show the severed bone and blood vessels spraying the room ruby red while the victim screams bloody murder (sorry). And then there are the eyeballs gouged out, revealing dark empty sockets to the brain.

In other films, human bodies explode spontaneously in mid-air while human organs fall to the ground only to be stomped on by some semi-conscious evil zombie who is the "star" of the film. Or there's the "classic" where a young couple go on a killing spree shooting, stabbing, and chopping too many bodies to keep count. In the end the happy young couple ride off into the sunset as heroes. Heroes because they "got away" with no one to punish them at the end of the road.

It should not have come as a surprise that thousands of Los Angeles residents lined the streets to cheer O. J. Simpson on as his white Bronco weaved in and out of traffic in "cold" pursuit, and was later found "not guilty" of killing his wife and Ron Goldman to the sheer delight of his fans.

What people of "good parental judgment" would want movies of such horrific content seen by adults, much less children? And if, at least, the CARA parents give movies like these an R-rating, it only means children under seventeen can't be allowed to watch the movie unless accompanied by a "parent or adult guardian." In April 2007, the MPAA did take the extra step of adding language to the R-rating that read, "Generally, it is not appropriate for parents to bring their children with them to R-rated motion pictures."

The R-rating is still a joke containing a wide-open loophole for "fun-loving" big brothers and sisters, or friends eighteen and older who have no problem taking their younger friends and siblings to see the sickness of Hollywood splashed on a once silver screen.

Also, many parents of movie-going children were not even born when the Valenti Ratings Scheme was concocted in 1968. Many of the parents grew up on debauched entertainment and see a big problem in "censoring" their kids' "rights" to read and watch anything they can get their hands on.

Other parents who were wise to resist the "New Kind of American Movie" are the ones who have organized and participated in any one of dozens of media watchdog groups that have sprung up to counter on-screen mayhem. With more detailed information about the contents and consequences of movies, television, music, and video games, these organizations have virtually replaced CARA as a source for accurate information on content now available to a whole new generation of entertainment consumers. To their credit, the MPAA site now links to a couple of alternative sites that give far more information on entertainment offerings. (These sites and more than a dozen other excellent sources are listed in the Entertainment Resource Guide at the end of this book.)

In most cases, the current "crop" of CARA board members of "good parental judgment" were themselves also not even a gleam in their mothers' eyes when the Ratings Scheme was sprung on American audiences. The fact that this current "crop" has accepted a defined-down standard of decency, values, and morality can be seen in the progression (read: regression) of film ratings over the past four decades.

In 1969, *Midnight Cowboy* and *Carnal Knowledge*, among others, received X-ratings. By the mid-1980s, these same movies released on video and cable had been "defined down" to R-ratings. Obviously, the parents in 1968 were exercising "good parental judgment" because they held a higher and grounded standard for what is and what is not harmful to young viewers.

And what kind of adult of "good parental judgment" would give an R-rating to the *Passion of Christ* and an R to the feature film about Robert F. Kennedy called *Bobby?* It's the same adults of "good parental judgment" who gave an R to *Saw III* in which body parts are graphically dismembered and subsequently devoured.

The first example supports the theory of anti-Christian bias by CARA, discussed in the next section of this chapter. As for *Saw III*, the "good parental judgment" would have been to refuse a rating altogether, preventing the film from being released in mainstream theaters, relegating it to the "straight-to-video" marketplace of bloodsuckers produced exclusively by bloodsuckers.

As Ellen Goodman noted in her article, "It's not the *Private Ryans* that do the most damage, it's movies in which force that goes unpunished is portrayed as justified."[12]

According to CARA Chairman Joan Graves, "As always, we urge parents to find out as much as they can about the movies they want their children to see, and any questions or concerns people have are welcome."[13] Parents have long ago taken the chairman's advice and have located numerous other sources and sites for accurate and specific information about entertainment titles. And in doing so many consumers have also uncovered the true agenda fueling the Hollywood entertainment industry.

As for questions, who are the members of the CARA board? What are their personal political persuasions? What are the religious beliefs of the board, if any? Why are they not allowed to be interviewed by the press concerning their decisions? Who actually hires the board members? Are the board members of "good parental judgment" friends of any employee of the MPAA or its member movie studios? Why all the secrecy?

Again, according to an article in the April 10, 2007 issue of *USA Today*, "MPAA officials say board members names are undisclosed to prevent pressure from studio executives and filmmakers." If anything, the MPAA is now more concerned about the radical filmmakers who want no ratings at all. The newly identified raters could become targets for the "anything goes" school of directors who want to vent their rage against the people who put a "warning" on their productions, or slip some cash under the Country Club table.

However, these board members of "good parental judgment" receive a paycheck from the MPAA. The MPAA is supported by the six major studio conglomerates through their hefty membership dues. The studios receive their profit from the tickets *you* buy at the box office, better known as their "revenue stream."

But for many moviegoers today, the price of a ticket allows you to swim in a one-way "stream" that offers "trips to hell" as Wilbur Crafts once declared. And that's about the extent of your "input." Remember, the Hollywood entertainment machine is one of the very, VERY few retail services that does not offer a money-back guarantee.

As the Ratings Scheme has constantly lost credibility over the years, despite the loaded polls by MPAA showing otherwise, the MPAA decided to follow the example of the TV Ratings Scheme by adding "content descriptors" or "rating reasons" which have only perpetuated the uselessness of the MPAA Movie Ratings Scheme, but has added some much needed humor to the whole sad affair that is the Classification and Ratings Administration.

Known as "The Red Carpet Ratings Service," the MPAA announced in the summer of 2006 that it was providing "Rating Reasons" by adding content descriptions. Furthermore, the MPAA thought it was doing a service by making this information easily downloaded to your computer, cell phone, or other hand-held electronic device.

The following chart is a list of film ratings issued by the MPAA for selected movie and DVD titles. The new service provided by the MPAA offers the consumer three categories: Film Title, Rating, and Rating Reasons. We added a fourth column, Our Questions, which highlight the hilarity of the MPAA's expanded service of "Red Carpet Ratings."

SAMPLE MPAA RATINGS INCLUDING "RATING REASON"

The MPAA will list "content descriptors" or a "Rating Reason" in addition to the letter rating. This is part of their "Red Carpet Service" online. We added the "Our Questions" category.

Film Title	Rating/Rating Reason	Our Questions
A Good Year	PG-13 For language and some sexual content	"Some" sexual content? Like? . . .
Harsh Times	R For strong violence, language and drug use	"Pro-Drug Use" or "Anti Drug Use?"
The Return	PG-13 For violence, terror, and disturbing images	"Disturbing?" Like what?
Stranger Than Fiction	PG-13 For some disturbing images, sexuality, nudity, brief language	"Sexuality" as opposed to "sex?" "Brief?"

Come Early Morning	R	For language and some sexual situations	"Sexual situations" as opposed to "Sexuality?"
Copying Beethoven	PG-13	Some sexual elements	"Elements" as opposed to "Situations?"
Fur: An Imaginary Portrait	R	For graphic nudity, some sexuality, and language	"Some?" as opposed to "Situations" or "Elements?"
Borat	R	For pervasive crude and sexual content, graphic nudity, language	"Content?" Not "Elements" "Situations" or "Some?"
Flushed Away	PG	Some crude humor and some language	In other words, "Toilet humor?"
The Santa Clause 3	G	(Blank)	No Reason for a G rating?
Saw III	R	For strong grisly violence, gore, terror, torture, nudity, language	Why was this movie made in the first place?
Conversations with God	PG	For thematic elements, some language	"Thematic" means God or Jesus deserves a PG
Death of a President	R	For brief violent images	"Images" with an "s." How many? How violent?
Shut Up and Sing	R	For language	What kind of language? "French?" "Foul?" Or are they one and the same?

This list is just a small sample of the thousands of movies that have been rated, with thousands more to be re-rated, with "Rating Reasons." It only takes a quick glance to come away with the uneasy feeling that the Ratings Scheme has shown its true colors with the addition of content descriptions.

Except for the Our Questions column, this is what you find when looking up movie ratings on the MPAA Red Carpet Ratings Service website. Seen in their new context, it would appear that the "ratings" are more or less "warnings." Again this is the trickle-down, way down, legacy of Jack Valenti's "free screen" movement. Just read the Rating Reasons column alone as one continuous sentence and determine for yourself if most motion pictures are worth your entertainment dollars.

Legendary director Frank Capra of *It's a Wonderful Life* and scores of other classic films from the 1930s and 1940s was one of the Golden Era directors whose life transcended the cinema earthquake of 1968. His 1971 autobiography describes the period that ensued immediately after Valenti "liberated" the movie screen, and Capra's subsequent refusal to participate in the "new" Hollywood.

> "There was dancing in the streets among the disciples of lewdness and violence. Sentiment was dead, they cried. And so was Capra, its aging missionary. *Viva* hard core brutality! *Arriba* barnyard sex! *Arriba* SHOCK! Topless-shock, Bottomless shock! Mass intercourse, mass rape, mass murder, kill for thrill-shock! Shock! To hell with the good in man. Dredge up his evil-shock! Shock!"[14"]

In 1984, I had the opportunity to meet Mr. Capra through an introduction made possible by director Robert Wise. Capra, rubbing his temples to relieve a relentless migraine, told me, "Jack Valenti never asked my opinion about abolishing the Production Code. Nor do I remember him asking the American audience. Did he ask you, Bob?"

Wise shook his head, adding, "Four years after I won an Oscar for *Sound of Music*, the Academy gave the Oscar to an X-rated movie called *Midnight Cowboy*."

Capra concluded, "He [Valenti] broke the sacred trust with the audience."

Three more questions for CARA board members and their qualities of "good parental judgment" as determined by their employer, the MPAA. What kind of mature role models are you setting for the children of America in general and your own children in particular? What kind of role model are you for even giving a rating for demented subhuman shock films? Have you thought about turning the tables upside down at the MPAA by refusing to give ratings until the movies return to, at least, a basic level of sanity instead of grading the levels of insanity? As John Kasich would say, "Stand for something!"

There's no reason to spend much time discussing video game ratings since they are now basically set up on the same model that Valenti laid down for movies and television. Starting out with four basic age-based ratings, the video game Ratings Scheme then expanded to five, and has now joined the other Ratings Schemes by adding content descriptors of endless ambiguous language.

The video game ratings, administered by the Entertainment Software Ratings Board (ESRB), actually warranted a recent "FTC Consumer Alert" by the U.S. Federal Trade Commission titled "Video Games: Reading the Ratings on the Games People Play."

In the special alert, a sub-section informs consumers about "Decoding the Descriptors" by explaining that "According to the ESRB, Animated Blood means discolored and unrealistic depictions of blood, while Blood refers to depictions of blood, and Blood and Gore means depictions of blood or the mutilation of body parts as well. Sexual Violence refers to depictions of rape or other violent sexual acts, and Intense Violence refers to graphic and realistic-looking blood, gore, weapons, and depictions of human injury and death. Sexual Themes indicates mild to moderate sexual references or depictions, and possibly, partial nudity. Other content descriptors refer to alcohol, comic mischief, crude humor, drugs, gambling, language (profanity), mature humor, nudity, and the like."

That represents less than ten percent of the "FTC Consumer Alert" on video games. If you can stomach the rest, log on to www.ftc.org. The FTC even offers a phone number to file a complaint. The video game ratings are so bad and ineffective that Dr. David Walsh's National Institute for Media and the Family rated the system "F" based on research by the Media Family Guide under CEO David G. Kinney.

CHRISTIAN MOVIES WILL BE RATED ACCORDINGLY

In the summer of 2006, Rep. Roy Blunt (R-MO) brought the nation's attention to a small Christian-themed movie titled *Facing the Giants* by Destination Films. The story was classic Americana about character, challenges, choices, right versus wrong, and victory over defeat with a theme of Christian faith and values in the plot.

The MPAA gave the movie a PG rating, which means "Some material may not be suitable for children." Rep. Blunt and the film's producers were understandably taken aback by the rating on the movie intended for family viewing. Making the talk-show circuit, Blunt surmised from the MPAA that a mention of "pregnancy" warranted the PG rating. However, Blunt and the filmmakers discovered that the rating may have been applied due to the "Christian content," or as Blunt described it more accurately, "Too openly or overtly Christian." This would indicate what many have speculated as the New Age set of values by the current board at CARA who exercise "good parental judgment" as part of their job descriptions.

This kind of bias by the board would explain why *The Passion of Christ*, with its scenes depicting the scourge of Jesus, received the same R-rating as *Silent Hill* in which a possessed freak orchestrates the explosion of bodies levitating inside a sanctuary with human organs splattering down on the stone floors and against the stained-glass windows.

Rep. Blunt was curious as to how the MPAA came about applying ratings to movies and promptly set up a meeting with new MPAA president Dan Glickman, a former congressional representative and colleague of Blunt. The congressman was clearly dismayed that the CARA board appeared to be morphing into deeper social and political activism when Christian "themes" became a criteria for a restrictive rating along with "smoking cigarettes."

Whether a coincidence of timing or a reaction to Blunt's criticism, the MPAA announced in late July 2006 that it was unveiling a new service called "My Movie Muse." The new internet interactive service has enlisted 15,000 participants from various age and income levels to participate in ongoing surveys by the MPAA to gauge viewer input on the movies Hollywood releases to the public.

It's too early to gauge the effectiveness of this service, but if the past four decades are any indication, the Hollywood movie machine really doesn't care about audience input. The exceptions are the blockbusters Hollywood turns out to mass appeal, only to turn around and use the profits to cover the losses incurred by their social/sexual/political "agenda" films.

As Rep. Blunt remarked before his meeting with Glickman, "We shouldn't let Hollywood's set of values drive the new ratings system." Blunt was discovering what Jack Valenti and the Hollywood producers intended all along, the manipulation of American values by dragging the rest of the country down to its level.

As discussed earlier in this book, the Hollywood cultural agenda has affected virtually every aspect of American culture, to its detriment and not to its credit.

With more Christian "themed" movies being produced with bigger budgets and intended for distribution in NATO affiliated theaters, the MPAA has continued to "rank" Christian or religious themes as a "rating criteria" alongside sex, violence, profanity, and general mayhem.

Another recent example following in the footsteps of *Facing the Giants* was Triumph Film's *The Second Chance*, which examines the challenges facing an African-American minister and his white counterpart in a central-city church. Like *Facing the Giants*, the movie contains a Christian theme of redemption and the overcoming of fear with faith. As a result, the MPAA gave the highly inspirational film a PG-13 for "some material may be inappropriate for children" as opposed to the lesser "Not suitable for children" under the PG rating.

According to the content descriptions, this rating was due to a "reference to drugs." Unlike most Hollywood movies, the message was "anti-drug" as opposed to the casual "pro-drug" recreational depictions in most Hollywood films. Most likely, the hidden agenda of the ratings board found this film, like *Facing the Giants*, as "Too overtly Christian."

Director Otto Preminger's gripping 1955 movie *The Man with the Golden Arm* depicted drug use from beginning to end with Frank Sinatra portraying a heroin addict spinning out of control. The Production Code did not prevent the movie from being made because the film accurately depicted the dangers of drug abuse. Hollywood took out the "ab" and redefined all references as "drug *use*."

As for the "Christian theme," even Warner Brothers' 2006 Christmas feature film The Nativity Story warranted a PG for "Some violent content." The film's creators, including Christian writer Mike Rich, indicate that scenes depicting the crucifixion and tribal massacre "may" have played a part in the rating.

Now let's look at some "Judeo-Christian themed" movies produced pre-1968 before Valenti abolished the Production Code. *Samson and Delilah*, 1949; *The Ten Commandments*, 1956; *The Robe*, 1953; and *Ben-Hur*, 1959. All of them depicted not only "some violent content" but rather "a lot of violent content," and some included Biblical-scale massacres along with vivid depictions of crucifixions. Under the Production Code, these films were determined as suitable for all ages because of the context of the content.

The critics of the Production Code in 1968 cried "censorship." But a careful look at today's Ratings Scheme as applied to religious "themes" suggest a true censorship is now taking place in the name of Valenti's "free screen" movement. And some of this Christian censorship has been more subtle than overt. For almost two decades, during the 1980s and 1990s, *The Robe* practically vanished from its traditional showcase on television during Easter. This was considered an annual holiday favorite since its first debut on TV in the 1960s.

In a rather curious twist of fate, I discovered one man's opinion as to the mystery disappearance of *The Robe* from its once sacred slot as a seasonal TV special. After leaving dinner with friends at the Beverly Wilshire Hotel on a cool March evening in 1987, an elderly man with thick grey hair approached me, gripping a set of rusty jumper cables. "Can I get a jump?" he asked, indicating with a nod to an aging Chrysler New Yorker parked directly in front of the hotel.

After connecting my rental car battery to his, we stood in the brisk wind while his battery charged. No amount of years could erase the distinctive features of this time-tested actor from Hollywood's "Golden Era." If anybody knew the answer to the fate of this particular movie, I was sure he knew something. "For years I would look forward to watching *The Robe* on TV at Easter. Whatever happened to your movie? I haven't seen it for years."

The old actor was shivering, even with an old, long suit coat. "Keep it as a memory. You may never see it again. The young guys out here say it's just not 'sexy.' That's all this town is about anymore," he said with a chuckle. "Besides, when was the last time you saw a movie with an actor kneeling at the base of a cross?"

The man had a point. He was one of the last actors I could recall kneeling before a cross. After disconnecting the jumper cables, Victor Mature shook my hand graciously, adding, "Thanks for remembering. Most people don't anymore."

The massive old Chrysler lumbered away down Wilshire Boulevard with Demetrius and Samson, as one, behind the wheel. And he had given me the straight story on God and Hollywood. In Tinseltown, God was not "hot, cool, or sexy."

In the world of television, there is a different form of bigotry known as "Crucifixion by Omission" which Tyler Perry discovered when proposing a sitcom for the networks. "Did you know you can't say 'Jesus" in a sitcom?" Perry, the most successful writer, producer and director working in the film industry, told his fans about the meeting with the pony-tailed producers. "If you don't want my God, you don't want me either."

* * *

On November 1, 2006, the MPAA released the results of its annually commissioned poll to determine the "usefulness" of the Ratings Scheme. According to the press release, "This year's poll, conducted by the Opinion Research Corporation, showed that eighty percent of parents found the ratings system to be fairly to very useful in helping them make decisions about what movies their children see."[16]

The poll, and its interpretation, is deceptive on many fronts. True, the Ratings Scheme is "useful" in helping parents "make decisions about what movies their children see." But the truth that is not conveyed is that the Ratings Scheme mainly helps parents decide there really isn't a good selection of movies for their children to watch. And for that matter, there are not many movies that merit the attention or patronage of mature adults. In that respect, it is very useful.

But the wording and interpretation of the poll by the MPAA sounds like a ringing endorsement of their efforts. The poll has been taken every year since the 1968 Ratings Scheme revolution. A review of the poll results over the last forty years indicate that the outcome has been largely the same, especially given the fact that the MPAA comes to its "usefulness" conclusion by combining the "fairly useful" and "very useful" categories together. In this scenario, the math is clear: Information + Interpretation = Manipulation.

Even Jack Valenti, co-conspirator with the Gang of Four and the Quiet Conspiracy of 1968, used this same poll as "vindication" of the Ratings Scheme by referencing a similar outcome upon his retirement in 2004. As a master of hype and illusion, Valenti went so far as to claim the results of the poll showed a favorability "rating" toward his scheme that was higher than the average ruling of the U.S. Supreme Court.[17] Right up to his death, the Dark Prince of Hollywood truly believed his actions and deceptions from 1968 to 2004 left a positive stamp on American culture.

As for the true legacy of the Ratings Fiasco, no one has ever described it more accurately than Senator Joe Lieberman (I-CT). The senator from Connecticut enjoys wide bi-partisan support in Congress due to his character, honesty, kindness, and a genuine heart-felt belief in the capacity of the entertainment industry to bring out the best in mankind and instill a cultural environment that fosters constructive cultural growth for present and future generations.

As for the Ratings Scheme, Lieberman's sentiment is shared by millions today as much, and even more, than his declaration a decade ago. "If you put a rating on garbage, it doesn't make it quality television. It's still garbage."

Director Quentin Tarantino summed up Hollywood's feeling about the Rating Scheme and the American audience as a whole when he told *USA Today* on April 10, 2007, "I actually think the MPAA has a very hard job and does it as well as they possibly can. The alternative would be every jerkwater county in America having their own obscenity laws." Does that include the "jerkwater" county he lives in? This typically condescending view of America is why movies and television productions largely flop with viewers, including his last movie *Grindhouse*. Tarantino needs to realize that there are 3,077 individual counties in America with a total population that surpassed 300 million people in 2007. Tarantino translation: America is a country with 300 million "jerks." At the next meeting of the National Association of County Commissioners, the top priority should be for each individual county in America to set up their own censorship boards and watch Hollywood and Quentin Tarantino teeter on the verge of a nervous breakdown when negotiating with all of us "jerks" out here in America who have been paying their salary in the past, but definitely not in the future.

HOW FILMMAKERS CHEAT FOR RATINGS

Quentin Tarantino's condescending remark about "jerkwater" Americans is shared by most people in the Hollywood entertainment industry. His association with sleaze merchant producer Harvey Weinstein only amplifies his disdain for the American audience. After Weinstein produced director Tarantino's movie *Grindhouse*, he was certain that the MPAA Ratings board would give the ultra-violent film an NC-17 rating. The caustic and vulgar producer had battled with the Ratings Board on too many occasions and decided that Tarantino would have a better chance lying to the board. Weinstein is damaged goods whose word carries about as much trust as David Geffen.

As Scott Bowles of *USA Today* wrote in the April 10, 2007 issue, "So he let fast-talking Quentin Tarantino pitch the movie as mainstream art." As Weinstein explained, referring to past clashes, "When I go, they make me take chunks out of my movies. Quentin, they love." Tarantino got his R-rating through persuasion of personality and the "it's art" lie, which proves how easily the MPAA Ratings Board can be swayed. The film bombed anyway. Weinstein had usually resorted to lawsuits and threats of lawsuits if he didn't get the rating he wanted. Harvey Weinstein produced director Kevin Smith's profanity-laden exercise in perversity movie *Clerks* in 1994 and promptly received an NC-17. Weinstein sued and the Ratings Board caved in and gave the film an R.

Ironically, it was Weinstein who sued the MPAA and Jack Valenti in 1990 for giving his cannibal-sex film *The Cook, the Thief, His Wife, and Her Lover* an X-rating. This angered director Peter Greenaway and especially Weinstein. On behalf of his Miramax film company, Weinstein felt it was his duty to destroy the X-rating forever because the audience was given the "wrong impression" that the X stood for "depravity" instead of "art."

Valenti and the MPAA actually won the lawsuit to keep the X-rating, but Valenti mysteriously went ahead and created the "friendly" sounding NC-17 for "No children under 17." Many insiders believed that Valenti encouraged the suit because he never wanted an X-rating as part of the original Ratings Scheme he created. Only at the insistence of the National Association of Theater Owners did Valenti add X along with the other letter age-based ratings in 1968.

Blood and guts splatter-director Rob Zombie is another mentally deranged director who gives advice to his fellow bloodsucker filmmakers on how to lie to the MPAA Ratings Board. *Time* magazine's Rebecca Winter Keegan explained in the October 30, 2006 issue how *Saw III* director Darren Lynn Bousman was shocked that the MPAA might give his hard-core torture-based installment an NC-17 due to the "tonality" of the film being "too dark."

"It's a horror movie!" screamed the perverted member of the Splat Pack group of organ-grinding Hollywood directors. Rob Zombie explained calmly to Bousman to go back to the Board and "Explain why the extreme violence is necessary to tell the story in a way that's more socially responsible."

As *Time* writer Keegan added, "When pressed, Zombie admits he doesn't actually care what's socially responsible. He just wanted to help out a kindred spirit, another guy who understands the unique beauty of a properly lighted viscera shot." The most horrific film in recent memory received an R-rating after Bousman took Rob Zombie's advice on lying, cheating, and stealing. Now Rob Zombie wonders if it's "socially responsible" to be tested for hepatitis considering the enormous amount of tattoos that cover his entire body.

CHAPTER 8

THE END OF TELEVISION

> *I just give people what they want.*
> —F. Scott Fitzgerald
> *No, you just give people what they'll take.*
> —Zelda Fitzgerald

"It'll take a host of heroes to save this season. As happy as the network may be to put a disastrous summer behind them, they face a fall that may not be much brighter with a new crop of shows that is their least interesting and inspired in years." That's how *USA Today* columnist Robert Bianco described the 2007 television offerings. Not only is television uninteresting and uninspired, it continues to engage in programming that limits what families can watch together and has shocked even adults by the high levels of depravity being broadcast.

In order to understand the devastation to American television that resulted in "age appropriate ratings," it is imperative to understand the deeper, darker, and more sinister forces that were in play behind the scenes to bring down the last vestige of a moral safe-house for entertainment: the American living room.

In 1969, the year after Jack Valenti unveiled the Ratings on an unsuspecting public, the weekly attendance at the box office dropped by more than half the number of people that attended movie theaters in 1965, the year before Valenti's arrival on the Hollywood scene. That amounted to a real loss of more than 27 million people weekly, many of whom would never return to the movie theaters again. This represented one of the biggest drops in the history of weekly movie attendance up until that period.

So, you ask, where did everybody go? Families and individuals simply went back home and turned on the television for entertainment that was every bit as thrilling, dramatic, and humorous as the fare at the local movie house. Sales of home popcorn makers and stove-top poppers soared. Not only was home television entertaining, it was free.

The specter of Jack Nicholson smashing plates and cups on a diner floor while screaming at a waitress for an ill-prepared chicken salad sandwich in *Five Easy Pieces* just didn't appeal to most people. Neither did the story of dysfunctional homosexual urban cowboys pimping themselves in the gritty streets of New York City in *Midnight Cowboy*.

However, the window of opportunity at home would be short as cracks began to appear on the home TV screen. The picture at home began to blur so rapidly during the 1970s that the same fate that brought down the Golden Era of motion pictures would soon drag down home television entertainment with equal ferocity of perversity.

In 1971 CBS production executive Fred Silverman became known as a hatchet man with an agenda for blood when he initiated the now famous "Massacre of '71" in which he axed the network's most popular shows. The entertainment programs he chopped were the very shows that had propelled the network to the top of the charts and earned for CBS the title of "The Tiffany Network."

The year before the massacre, network executives tried a quiet phase-out of classic variety shows and the beheading of their veteran hosts who were household names, not just in America, but around the world. After eighteen years the "rotund one," Jackie Gleason, bid farewell as his stage lights went dark and "Melancholy Serenade" fell silent.

Red Skelton, the comic genius who ended his shows with "May God Bless," was promptly kicked off the air after twenty years on television. No prime-time variety entertainment show on the air today has lasted as long.

By 1971 Silverman was ordered by CBS "brass" to finish the hit job by cutting the rest of the network's hit shows, such as *Hogan's Heroes, Hawaii Five-O, Family Affair, Green Acres,* and *The Beverly Hillbillies*. Most stunning of these ruthless cancellations was the final curtain call on a twenty-three-year Sunday night tradition known as *The Ed Sullivan Show*, which had been on the air since television began broadcasting nationwide in 1948.

For those of you who were not around at the time of the infamous massacre, it is important to note that these were not ratings losers. Neither were the rest of the popular pack that would be killed off before the end of the decade such as *Mission Impossible, Gunsmoke, My Three Sons, Mannix,* and the last true prime-time variety show in television history, *The Carol Burnett Show.*

Only one replacement show became a ratings hit at CBS after the massacre. In truth, the massacre had more to do with social agendas, advertising time, and new sponsors. CBS was determined to rid the network of what it termed condescendingly as "rural comedies." The first step was to introduce "edge" programming, what executives would call "a new kind of American television." Sound familiar?

THE HOLLYWOOD CULTURE WAR

That one hit show that provided the new edge at CBS was *All in the Family*, telecast in January 1971 to coincide with the ongoing massacre. Carroll O'Connor played Archie Bunker, a prejudiced blue-collar shipping foreman who lambasted every ethnic group on earth with abrasive dialogue and references to "jungle bunnies," "Spics," "Chinks," and "Pollacks." This one show set the tone for many situation comedies to follow, known by the shortened term "sitcom."

There was more to this dark comedy than most people realized at the time. *All in the Family's* producer, Norman Lear, was an avid ultra-radical liberal with a sinister two-edged marketing strategy. His "comedy" dealt with social issues that had rarely been approached by episodic or sitcom programming. Contrary to television critics at the time, television had a long history of tackling social issues going back to the *Playhouse 90* live dramas of the 1950s and 1960s and many other long-format televised programming.

Lear cynically played both ends of the show's audience appeal by reaching out to the bleeding heart liberals eager for "reality" TV. At the same time, the character of Archie Bunker was an attractive stereotype that drew in a segment of society that "related to" and "relished" Archie's slamming of racial and ethnic groups. This same audience segment also cheered Archie on as he berated his wife, daughter, and son-in-law (Jean Stapleton, Sally Struthers, and Rob Reiner).

As television reviewers Tim Brooks and Earle Marsh explained the show's eventual, though short-lived, popularity, "Liberals and intellectuals could cite it as an example of the absurdity of prejudice while another larger segment of the viewing audience could agree with Archie's attitudes and enjoy him as their kind of guy."[1]

For all its fanfare, *All in the Family* began to slide in ratings after just five years. Unfortunately, the show opened the door for other TV sitcoms and episodic series that would push the envelope for other agendas of the advertisers and the new breed of Hollywood's young perversity producers, writers, and directors. These "ground-breakers" would set the standard for shows more attuned to "shock" value than social "awareness," much less entertainment.

Mary Hartman, Mary Hartman would soon follow in the "new ground" of television beginning in 1975. But its comedy was crude and uncomfortable and was broadcast as a syndicated show only in late-night time slots, setting the stage for television's "indecency" time period of 10:00 p.m. to 6:00 a.m.

Family was another peculiar and discomforting comedy that, like *Mary Hartman*, contained persistent obsessive undercurrents of sex. While *Family* aired on prime-time by the network, many local affiliates (more in tune to their audience than Hollywood) delayed the show into the late-night indecency slot, later re-named "Safe Harbor," as in safe for trash.

This pattern of late-night relegation of the "absurdity shows" continued well into the 1970s and early 1980s, leaving the normal "waking hours" available for family viewing. And the new prime-time viewing was diverse, it just wasn't perverse. But that would come to an end in 1982.

The reason television's Golden Era lingered a bit longer than their movie theater counterparts in the feature film industry was due to the existence and voluntary enforcement of the "Standards and Practices" departments maintained at the major networks. While each network maintained their own department staffed with individuals who reviewed programming for content, they also adhered to the Television Code administered by the National Association of Broadcasters (NAB). The Television Code, based on the 1930s Radio Code and revised for TV in 1952, laid out basic minimum guidelines for content in programming and advertising.

While the system was always voluntary, the NAB maintained a program for station compliance if the affiliate programming was to receive the coveted NAB seal of the polished parallel fig leaves. This system was very similar to the agreement between the MPAA and NATO.

The MPAA seal was an elongated world globe with a film reel in the center and the seal had to be present on a movie in order to be exhibited in a NATO affiliated theater. That system is still in existence for theatrical feature films today. The only change to the system came when Jack Valenti defined decency down so that deviant films could also receive the seal. That same scenario would soon be replayed in the world of television.

In the broadcast television industry, part of the NAB compliance for seal approval was related to a cap on commercial time allotments in addition to minimum content decency guidelines. For every thirty minutes of program broadcasting, commercial time was restricted to roughly three minutes and forty seconds, with flexible variations allowed. As veteran television producer Sheldon Leonard remembered, "We had to deliver precisely twenty-six minutes and twenty seconds of film to the network; the thirty-minute spot was filled out with commercials and credits."[2]

Leonard was a strong believer in the Television Code for both its content requirements and commercial time allotments. Otherwise, Leonard knew that television programming could be swallowed up by excessive commercial time and producers' perverse self-indulgent fantasies. Among a few of his classics were *I Spy, The Andy Griffith Show, The Dick Van Dyke Show, The Danny Thomas Show,* and *Gomer Pyle.*

Leonard's personal life was reflected in his professional life. He was one of the few in Hollywood who could boast of a sixty-five-year love affair with his own wife. However, like Frank Capra, Sheldon Leonard would live long enough to see the industry he loved fall apart as it, too, would define decency down. In a bizarre twist of governmental interference, the U.S. Justice Department under President Jimmy Carter began an anti-trust motion against the NAB's Television Code.

The motion, supported wholeheartedly by Carter, claimed that the Code and its advertising guidelines artificially limited the amount of commercial time per television program and, by doing so, maintained an "artificial" monopoly on setting ad rates. The Carter Justice Department claimed that this restriction actually raised the price of per-minute commercial time.

This was a judicially argumentative bogus claim considering the fact that television ad rates were basically set by Nielsen ratings for individual shows. Regulated or not, networks could set ad rates based on "projected" viewership for special programming. The Super Bowl is a prime example where the sky is the only limit on how much networks can charge advertisers.

THE MYSTERY PHONE CALL

The subject of the NAB Code's demise is shrouded in secrecy, political and professional agendas, ambiguous motivations, and federal government strong-arming, in addition to NAB infighting and paranoia. In four years of research for this book, I found only one comprehensive printed source concerning this cataclysmic event that turned television into a House of Horrors. John Summers, former senior executive vice-president of the NAB wrote an article titled "The Judicial Death of the NAB Codes," published in the obscure, short-lived Gannet Center Journal in the winter 1988 edition.

Summers remembers a phone call in early 1979 from the Antitrust Division of the U.S. Department of Justice under President Jimmy Carter and Attorney General Griffin Bell. The Justice Department attorneys were requesting a routine discussion of various aspects of the NAB Code. As Summers recalled, this was not unusual. "It was customary for the department to inquire periodically about certain provisions of the code." One passing subject brought up that day touched on provisions in the code dealing with prohibitions on alcohol in advertising and programming content.

The NAB attorneys did not hear from the Justice Department again until June 14, 1979, when U.S. Antitrust attorneys called to inform the NAB that a lawsuit was being filed in twenty minutes against the broadcasting association and would be entered into the court dockets of the D. C. District Court in Washington. The "twenty-minute warning" from the Justice Department is often a sign that secret agendas are at play within the Beltway. This kind of alert caught the NAB by surprise, giving them little time to appear for a response, though the NAB would receive a copy of the complaint to challenge or settle.

What struck former NAB vice-president John Summers was the lack of any publicly filed complaint and no effort by the Justice Department to simply ask the NAB to reconsider the "offending" sections of the code. The lawsuit centered around the aforementioned commercial time limit provisions of the code.

The lawsuit complaint alleged that the limit on the number of commercial minutes per hour was a violation of the Sherman Anti-Trust Act. The NAB had always acted in the "public interest" so as not to "clutter" programming with excess commercials. Again, the Justice Department thought the limitations increased the cost of advertising time and locked out others who wanted to advertise on TV.

If that was the case, the NAB reasoned, why didn't they just call to meet with NAB officials and ask for voluntary revisions. The specter of a lawsuit, again, raised concerns that a particular industry was working behind the scenes in order to break the back of the code in order to flood airtime with commercial advertising. These "suspected" special interests wouldn't have minded bringing down the entire code including content provisions. This raised suspicions that perhaps networks and their program producers were looking to produce "edgier" and "offensive" material and play the "cutting edge" promotional card. Somebody other than "basement bureaucrats" at Justice had to be behind this move.

The NAB Code was effective in dealing with content ethics in programming as well as commercials. There were guidelines on fraudulent and deceptive advertising including weight reducers and toys. Programming content touched on a variety of subjects such as depictions of alcohol, violence, drugs, gambling, obscenity, profanity, the occult, astrology, hypnotism, and special sensitivity to insure no racial insults or ridicule of those with disabilities.

But the Antitrust Division of Justice was apparently interested only in the commercial time requirement. The case came before D.C. District Court Judge Harold Greene, who the media dubbed as a "one man regulatory agency." Judge Greene sided with the Antitrust Division and the NAB prepared to appeal. But within a week the NAB decided to drop all provisions of commercial time limitation in the NAB Code.

The NAB decided to settle via a consent decree with the Department of Justice on November 23, 1982. The content provisions of the code would remain intact—but only for a few months. According to Summers, "The case cast a fear of liability like a pall over NAB codes." The "lawsuit paranoia" excuse seemed a little premature. And in one of the most controversial and baffling moves by any self-regulatory agency, the NAB executive committee decided to sack the entire NAB codes altogether, including content provisions.

As Summers concluded, "Fifty-five years of industry programming and advertising standards came to an end . . . . A small dose of bureaucratic common sense could have averted the code's demise. And the public, in the end, would have benefited." Summers also reflected that "In my twenty years with the NAB, the work of the codes stood above all else . . . . They served the public interest. They deserved a better fate."

The judgment by D.C. Judge Harold Greene outraged both parties in Congress. Congressman Peter Peyser stated, "To make the punishment fit the crime, I wish

I could make the Antitrust Division's Mr. Anderson sit through a solid hour of dog food, upset stomach, feminine hygiene, and hemorrhoid commercials. He thinks we can save the taxpayer money by increasing commercials. I think we can save the taxpayer money cutting appropriations of this division of the Justice Department."

Art Buchwald devoted an entire column to the absurdity of the lawsuit. "The beauty of government in Washington is that they are always willing to help American citizens, even when you don't want them to."

Remember how this whole affair started? Summers described a phone call from the Justice Department to review provisions of the code. One of their questions concerned descriptions of and prohibitions on alcohol consumption in programming and advertising. Twenty-five years later, television is so awash in alcohol advertising and deranged content that the *Wall Street Journal* published an article on July 20, 2007, titled, "Drinks, Drugs, Dysfunction Star on Summer Cable TV."

If the NAB Code were still in place, there would be no rap musicians singing the praises of "killing cops," "beating hos," and "slappin' niggas." In its purest sense, those phrases are actually a violation of the "incitement clause" of the First Amendment.

Norman Lear was also a key player in destroying the last hour of TV known as the "Family Viewing Hour." He called it a violation of his First Amendment Rights. Lear left television in 1980 to form the deceptively titled "People for the American Way" for the sole purpose of fighting against evangelical Christians, according to his website.

The whole cloak and dagger surreptitious sacking of the NAB content code would not only be a major blow to television decency, it would also explain why most viewers must now put up with six, seven, and eight minutes of commercials per thirty minutes of programming.

Television shows that once ran for twenty-seven minutes per half hour after compensating for commercials may now run for a mere twenty-two minutes. The hapless production crew members whose names appear in the credits now go largely unrecognized as the credit scroll runs at warp speed to a compressed half-screen while TV commercials continue to run unabated on the other half. Between 1985 and 1987, the number of *network* TV commercials alone increased from 1800 a week to 5400 according to former Westinghouse executive Dan Ritchie.

The over-commercialization of television that Sheldon Leonard feared is now a reality. Even during the shortened segments of programming, tiny, fully-animated pop-up ads appear in the lower corners of the screen to advertise the next program in the line-up. This compressed time frame for television broadcasts may also explain the condensed hyperactive pacing of contemporary sitcom characters and storylines.

Whether this unusual move by the Carter Justice Department was motivated by "well-intentioned" regulators or by political pressure from advertisers remains a mystery to this day. Some have even speculated that the NAB itself may have privately initiated the Code ban to free up more space for ad dollars to benefit its member networks. In an attempt to unravel the mystery, we placed a series of phone calls to the Atlanta presidential White House in exile of Jimmy Carter. Neither he nor his representatives returned our calls. During one of the last attempts to contact Jimmy Carter, we discovered that most of his presidential library advisory board had resigned in protest over Carter's increasingly reckless behavior toward Israel and the Palestinians.

In another attempt to contact the former president, we were told that Carter was busy "monitoring" the "free and fair" election of Hugo Chavez as the clown president of Venezuela. Since leaving office after his bitter defeat by Ronald Reagan in 1980, Carter has developed a radical left reputation for "monitoring" pre-rigged elections of third-world dictators, apologizing in person to Communist leader Fidel Castro for the isolation of his country by America (while swallowing a twelve-course seafood dinner courtesy of Fidel), and now lobbying for the extension of American constitutional rights to foreign terrorists that are hell-bent (or virgin-heaven bound) on killing you and me.

With a busy schedule such as his, we surely understand that he has no time to discuss his contribution to the decay of American culture. We do know that Jack Valenti maintained a close working relationship with Carter. Hollywood adored and supported Carter simply because he was AOTN (Anyone Other Than Nixon).

What is certain is that broadcasting executives were beginning to look for ways to increase ad revenues and ad time on network television. The popular consensus among the broadcasting community is that the 1971 CBS massacre was driven by pressure from deep-pocket Madison Avenue ad agencies who wanted to appeal to younger "sophisticated" viewers by selling youth-oriented products. The sacking of the NAB Code in 1982 was just the "legal" icing on the cake.

These advertisers were willing to pay premium ad prices if the "entertainment" was "edgier" in order to attract the affluent low-life lemmings who thrived on "cutting edge" comedies and drama. If CBS would just drop its line-up of popular shows, the agency hacks reasoned, then the rest of America would eventually come around to their way of thinking and buying. It was long-term value manipulation.

Madison Avenue and network execs were also not too shy about blatantly stabbing their own loyal audience in the back, claiming that its own programming had largely appealed to an older and "graying" audience. That condescending contemptuous philosophy was flawed on a number of counts.

First, this "rush to the graveyard" strategy assumed that older viewers no longer deserved to watch television programming that they enjoyed. Second, it assumed that older viewers did not possess buying power, when quite the opposite was true. And it is far greater today than in 1971, which brings us to the third flawed strategy of the networks; the failure to realize that many "baby boomers" and "war babies" were already approaching their mid-thirties, the age advertisers consider "getting older." And eventually, this group would make up the majority of the "older" audience, which is happening now.

What is "older?" According to the networks, the 18 to 49 demographic is the ideal age group to buy products advertised on television. In other words, over 49 is "over the hill." When Jackie Gleason last said, "And away we go," little did he know that CBS would say, "And don't ever come back."

During a location scout I conducted with producer Dorothea Petrie in Atlanta in 1993, the veteran TV producer was lamenting to me about the change in television movies from the time she started producing in the 1970s.

"The networks used to give us twenty-eight days to shoot a movie. Now its twenty-one days," she moaned. "They used to give us $4 million. Not it's only $3 million. Advertisers will spend that much money on a 60-second commercial." Petrie seemed sadly resigned to her new plight. "I think I've been reduced to producing low-rent productions of WIP movies to sell fast cars and tight jeans."

The WIP movie Petrie was speaking about was TV industry lingo for "Women in Peril." As a location coordinator, the job for me was easy. Find a hospital, a courthouse, and a jail. Most TV movies follow the same formula: A beautiful woman is either in trouble or she *is* trouble. In Act II, the woman in peril or her attackers end up sick in the hospital. Legal action forces everybody into a courtroom in Act III and the bad person, either the star or the co-star, end up in jail. Simple as 1-2-3. Most made-for-TV movies still follow some version of this three-penny opera.

And Petrie was right. Corporations that produced fast cars and tight jeans would dictate what viewers watched, not what you wanted to watch. Have you ever wondered why slick auto commercials show "sexy" men and women driving 120 mph through deserted urban landscapes? As television guru Marshall McLuhan declared famously in the 1960s, "The medium is the message."

Today the pharmaceutical companies have moved in to dictate what the viewer is going to watch on television. So the message now is simple. After three decades of tight jeans and fast cars, we are now depressed, anxious, attention deficient, overweight, and unable to get a good night's sleep. And all of that is understandable after watching just thirty minutes of almost any prime-time programming.

*   *   *

Most TV viewers are totally unaware of an event that takes place every spring in New York City known as UpFront. The affair is the largest gathering of television programming executives commingling with media-buyers from Madison Avenue ad agencies that represent the fast cars and fast drugs. The network and cable executives use this opportunity to "pitch" their shows to potential advertisers in order to secure funding for their programs. At the same time, media buyers use this opportunity to tell the TV execs what "they" would like to see play across the home television screen. Where do you, the viewer, fit in? Apparently, nowhere. You're not invited.

But you might be interested in knowing what you've missed in recent years. Back in 2005, the content being pitched by producers ran the gamut of Hollywood's innermost nightmares packaged as entertainment. Among the themes being promoted were stories heavily-laden with the occult, aliens, and supernatural phenomena. The media-buyers, on the other hand, were looking for another *Desperate Housewives*, with a little blood in addition to more sex.

By 2007, the gathering of ad agency hacks and TV execs felt that another good "reality" show like *Survivor* or hybrids like *Lost* could be a prefect fit for viewers with short attention spans and drug companies that could increase that span. These reality shows have moved beyond sex and violence and have promoted the "virtue" of lying, cheating, and stealing in order to "make it" to the top of the dung heap. It wasn't rocket science for Hollywood to come up with this formula considering that these traits are a fact of life in Tinseltown.

With more than two decades having passed since the sacking of the Production Code by the NAB, the tone and tenor of television programming and advertising seem to support the speculation that the major ad agencies and network executives may have lobbied heavily to overthrow the Television Code by pushing for anti-trust laws as a ruse to cover their true intentions.

While Jimmy Carter was too busy trying to secure softer mattresses for Taliban and al Qaeda detainees, I was able to get through to the NAB to ask about the fate of the now defunct Television Code. Though NAB President David Rehr was unavailable, a high-ranking assistant volunteered some limited insight on condition of anonymity. I felt as though I were speaking with a spy who just came in from the cold, with one foot wedged in the door frame. When asked if he had a copy of the old Television Code that I could review for this book, the NAB spokesman said, very frankly, "I have a whole stack of the Code sitting right here behind my desk. But I'm not going to send any copies out."

When I asked why, he casually blew off the whole affair of twenty-five years earlier. "It's old news. It's history. That was a long time ago. We don't feel it is relevant anymore." The NAB spokesman also volunteered that he personally receives two to three calls every week from authors, professors, media activists, think-tanks, and politicians who would like to revive the Television Code and perhaps rewrite it in accordance with today's rapidly changing television market and technology while restoring some "standards and practices" at the same time.

"When government agencies call us," the spokesperson added, "we just laugh out loud. It was the government that forced us to drop the code in the first place."

This was a curious statement. If the audience and the federal government are now reaching out to possibly embrace and support segments of the Production Code that the NAB supposedly treasured, why all the laughter and secrecy? This is a new generation reaching out to the NAB and they are biting the fingers of the hands that feed them.

While the 1971 massacre set a precedent and the abolishment of the Television Code removed content guidelines, the networks were set free to move into unchartered territory with a frenzy. The "indecency time period" of 10:00 p.m. to 6:00 a.m. would now be extended to twenty-three hours of a twenty-four-hour day. Through a very generous gift of network goodwill, one hour would be set aside as "The Family Hour." And that would disappear by the mid-1990s.

The last glimmer of the Golden Era of television had vanished. The viewing audience would soon see the likes of even raunchier and irreverent fare starting, this time, in prime time with *Roseanne* and *Married with Children*. These shows and their imitators quickly earned television the nickname of "Trash TV." The daytime line-up had been a lost cause years earlier.

While reflecting the true personal values of the Hollywood creative community, network television producers were also under the impression that they were in a self-deceiving race to "catch up" with their competition on the other side of the spectrum in cable television. In reality, these producers were "reaching down" into the red-light district of cable TV as it then existed before "How To" and "Educational" channels arrived.

By 1980, cable television offered viewers as many as ten to fifteen new channels in addition to the major networks. In order to access these additional channels, viewers had to subscribe by paying a fee. The choice of channels was considered astounding at the time and some viewers complained of "too many choices." By 2008, viewers would have access to over 500 channels and growing with digital cable and satellite TV.

Most of these new channels in 1980 appealed to a broad audience and were rarely offensive. Even MTV in the early '80s was actually entertaining before the advent of its "dark phase," which persists today, and negatively influenced other music video channels. MTV aggressively promoted and continues to promote the most dysfunctional social, psychological, and sexual behavior that has tarnished three generations of youth. Tattoos, body piercing, and bald heads are the hallmarks of MTV slaves.

But what concerned the networks most at the time was the arrival of an additional cable component known as "Pay Channels." While viewers already had to pay for the extra cable channels beyond the network universe, this was yet another tier that would drive up the cost of watching television entertainment.

These extra "Pay Channels" offered and produced exclusive "uncut" movies, a code term for sex and violence. The two behemoths in 1980 were HBO and Showtime in a rivalry that continues unabated today. Because cable and pay channels were not regulated by the FCC, these two pay channels could show movies as they were meant to be seen in theaters.

Feature films shown on HBO and Showtime provided "adult" viewers heavy doses of extreme violence, gore, sex, and non-stop profanity. None of this raunch content had ever streamed through the home television before. Parents who subscribed to these services were proving to be poor role models by introducing the "forbidden fruit" dilemma into their own living rooms.

HBO and Showtime were not content in just showing "uncut" movies straight out of the theaters. Both channels soon began making their own movies with the intent to give audiences more of anything that the broadcast networks wouldn't allow. Late-night programming at HBO would turn the pay channel into a virtual porn site with "staged reality" series like the taxi driver who video-taped patrons having sex in the back of his cab.

By the 1990s, the pay channel would roll out *Sex and the City* as a weekly drama about a group of Manhattan women whose only preoccupation in life was having sex with friends, strangers, and more strangers. *Sex and the City* was basic soft-core pornography to attract the sex lemmings away from the networks. In a low point for America's mail delivery service, HBO even contracted with the U.S. Post Office to place six-foot tall stand-up theater placards in major post office lobbies to advertise their line-up of "uncut" movies and "tailor-made" sex shows.

HBO decided to bring in the blood and reignite Hollywood's twisted love affair with the mafia by creating a series called *The Sopranos*. The series followed the daily life surrounding a functionally impaired New Jersey crime family led by the mentally impaired manic depressive patriarch Tony Soprano. Amidst the psychotherapy, profane family feuds, Italian food fights, and other mob "attractions," the family would not shy away from its obligation to shake down businesses and kill when duty called.

The TV critics and award ceremonies applauded the efforts by the pay stations to bring "adult" drama to the small screen. The critics, like the Hollywood producers, have no concept of the differentiation between "adult" and "mature."

Fortunately, Showtime did not debut *The Bodeckers* about a functionally impaired Louisiana Klan family led by the mentally impaired manic-depressive patriarch Billy Bodecker. Amidst the psychotherapy, profane family feuds, fried food fights, and other Klan "attractions," the family would not shy away from its obligation to spit on the sidewalks and lynch "negroes" when duty called.

For a period in the 1990s, HBO was expected to dole out the violence and Showtime would dole out the sex. It was the "adult" thing to do.

Again, the neurotic executives at the networks were under the distinct impression that the pay channels were usurping their audience. Instead of providing quality uplifting fare, the networks took the downstairs basement trail to reel in their zombified sex addicts back to prime time.

The network's answer was *Desperate Housewives*, a sex in the suburbs version of HBO's sex drama. Shallow women with too much time, money, and cleavage on their hands, or in the hands of others, would cause endless problems for themselves and their neighbors by trying to "outsex" each other. Then, fearing that the networks were co-opting their monopoly on sex, Showtime rolled out a new farce in 2007 called *Californication*.

Other network offerings would provide the blood and violence "allure" with crime dramas such as the *CSI* series and the *SVU* series. In the *CSI* series, crime scene investigators spend a lot of time in the morgue discussing the pathway a sharp knife leaves after slicing through layers of the adipose tissue of a rotting corpse.

By the late 1990s and into the first decade of the twenty-first century, the pay channels countered by actually producing some quality offerings such as the *Earth to the Moon* series and *Band of Brothers*. Whether these channels were struck by a bolt of decency or a threat of regulation is unclear. From 2000 up until the present, legislation had been discussed and even introduced in Congress to bring cable and pay stations under the purview of the FCC, which currently only has oversight of the networks.

In the hoped-for future of true a' la carte cable service (currently being debated in Congress) viewers will be able to pick and pay for only the channels they want. This will be the true democratic face of television's future. Combined with the new innovations in wide-screen high definition television, the American audience will be able to tailor-pick their own channels and create the home theater of their choice.

Viewers are fleeing pre-packaged entertainment in the forms of sitcoms, episodic, and televised movies in favor of special interest programming that has arrived in the expanding cable universe. Certainly, some people will use this new choice to create a virtual hell room of gore, ultra-violence, and gratuitous sex courtesy of the contents that flew out of Jack Valenti's Box of Pandora.

On the other hand, the wise and discerning viewer will discover entertaining choices that maintain character, value, and even the capacity to educate. In a cable choice future, the "mature" adult and parent will be able to change the face of television as it now exists and revive a new Golden Era of crystal clear high definition programming consisting of both quality and quantity.

Former FCC Chairman Newton Minnow was a few decades premature in his 1961 speech to the NAB in which he said, "When television is good, nothing—not the theater, not the magazines or newspapers—nothing is better. But when television is bad, nothing is worse . . . . I can assure you will observe a vast wasteland."[3]

Minnow spoke those words in a three channel network universe and a universe in which stations promptly shut down at midnight. The "wasteland" Minnow was referring to probably reached its peak thirty-five years later when the television industry was forced to adopt the Valenti-designed Ratings Scheme to officially divide families and the masses into "appropriate age groups."

In the meantime, the television industry continues to give us what "they" want us to watch. And the American audience has every right to get "hooked" on "trash" as Senator Lieberman described the current wasteland. But the television industry is capable of doing better and the audience should not only expect better, but demand it.

Perhaps the best analogy of the entertainment offerings from both the movie industry and the television industry can be gleaned from a conversation that took place at a sidewalk cafe in Paris. The story was told to me in 1983 by Francis "Scottie" Fitzgerald, the only child of F. Scott and Zelda Fitzgerald.

"Mother and Father were having lunch with a young Ernest Hemmingway in Paris, about 1925, and the subject of literary 'integrity' came to fore. Mr. Hemmingway asked Father if he was writing from the heart or writing for the money.

"Father said, 'I just give people what they want.' But Mother, of course, quickly corrected him. 'No, you just give people what they'll take.'"

More than eighty years later, the same can be said of Hollywood.

CHAPTER 9

The Big Lie and Value Manipulation

> *There's a group of older people who will never accept it. But there's a lot of empty cemeteries, and when they're filled, the world will be a whole lot more tolerant.*
> —Tim Doyle
> Writer and creator of *Ellen*

"Films are one vast reflection of every image in the stream of contemporary life."[1] This was one of the earliest recorded statements of "The Big Lie" that feature film and television producers continue to use today to justify content in their productions that audiences have found increasingly offensive, debasing, exploitative, and increasingly laced with an aggressively defined left-coast agenda of social/sexual/political persuasions and perversions. Or, as the Media Research Center's Brent Bozell accurately observed the industry output as simply "rapidly escalating raunch."

The statement of film as a reflection of society was a collective declaration made in 1929 by the most powerful studio moguls of their day, the Warner Brothers, B. P. Schulberg of Paramount, Sol Wurtzel of Fox, and Irving Thalberg of MGM. The statement was a carefully worded bullet-ridden lie that was intended to deflect criticism of the film industry during the first Culture War against Hollywood within the first three decades of the twentieth century. The moguls were trying desperately to ward off the growing movement of community leaders, social reformers, elected officials, and the clergy who were unifying to encourage, if not force, the movie business to establish a basic code of ethical content for motion picture productions.

Despite a number of classic movies between 1900 and 1930, a large percentage of silent and early sound films were a licentious lot of exploitation movies delving into adultery, prostitution, "white slavery," drug abuse, deceit, and the promotion and glamorization of promiscuous behavior. The bulk of the remainder were simply bad films intent on dazzling the audiences with black and white images that actually moved on a flat white screen.

The moguls had been using the Big Lie for years as an excuse and "apology" for "reflecting society." In reality, the moguls were largely projecting their daydream fantasies and nocturnal nightmares on spontaneously combustible silver nitrate film. As early as 1921, Governor Nathan Miller of New York had already grown tired of the Big Lie. "The motion picture people say now that they will be good, but you have heard that old story before."[2]

In 1930, one year after the collective declaration by the studio moguls, the major motion picture studios decided to accept the Production Code drafted by Daniel Lord and Martin Quigley for the MPAA office under Will Hayes (Appendix III). The unanimous decision may have had more to do with the Great Depression than with a Hollywood moral awakening.

If the movie industry wanted to survive, it would be imperative to put on a "good face" and bring in the fence-sitters and theater boycotters by actually producing quality entertainment, if somewhat bowdlerized in its politics and sociology. But the power of cinema was universally recognized as a shaper of values as witnessed by the opening preamble of the Code. "Mankind has always recognized the importance of entertainment and its value in rebuilding the bodies and souls of human beings. But it has always recognized that entertainment can be of a character either HARMFUL or HELPFUL to the human race."

Between 1930 and 1934, however, the major sleaze elements of the studios tried to test the Production Code by producing some of the most alien and lurid films in movie history. As author Thomas Doherty noted, "For four years, the Code commandments were violated with impunity and inventiveness in a series of wildly eccentric films. More unbridled, salacious, subversive and just plain bizarre than what came afterwards, they look like Hollywood cinema but the moral terrain is so off-kilter they seem imported from a parallel universe."[3]

There was Congo Picture's *Ingagi* in 1930 fraudulently masquerading as an expeditionary film projecting the "strange traffic" of forbidden sexual liaisons between gorillas and native women. And there was the cruel exploitation of carnival side-show performers in Tod Browning's 1931 *Freaks*.

According to author Doherty, the cast of *Freaks* would "make for a colorful pageant in the studio commissary. Nursing a wicked hangover, the journeyman screenwriter F. Scott Fitzgerald looked up from his meal and beheld the Siamese twin sisters from *Freaks* ordering lunch . . . . Fitzgerald bolted to the bathroom and vomited."[4] Perhaps Fitzgerald became ill over the fact he had arrived in Hollywood contrary to his dedicated comments to Zelda six years earlier about "giving people what they want." It was clear, now, to Fitzgerald that he would have to give people the nightmares of perverted Hollywood studio moguls, producers, and directors.

This four-year "cheating" period came to an end when the Production Code was enforced by a special office called the Production Code Administration under the MPAA. Will Hays appointed the ironclad Catholic "no man" Joseph Breen as the administrator who, along with his staff, would approve or disapprove of scripts before cameras ever rolled. This was the system of "dual understanding" and "moral compensating values" that ushered in Hollywood's Golden Era spanning almost four decades until the arrival of Jack Valenti.

After the 1968 abolition of the Production Code, producers of film, television, and the entire entertainment industry itself quickly revived The Big Lie and the creative industry began to sink again into a moral abyss and an even darker parallel universe from which precious few gems have managed to emerge.

"Movies are just a reflection of society" or "Entertainment is a mirror" are the shortened versions today of the 1929 studio mogul declaration of deception. A second "apology" for entertainment trash is the slightly revised version of F. Scott Fitzgerald's 1925 Paris sidewalk cafe commentary. "[We're] just giving people what they want."

The conventional wisdom of today's Hollywood is the blended version: "We're just giving people what they want because what they want is a reflection of society." That would make sense if it were true. But it's still a lie—The Big Lie. The entertainment cranked out by Hollywood is a reflection of their world. And that is not giving people what they want as the annually declining box office figures of today indicate.

Remember the first sentence in Chapter One? "Hollywood, and everything it stands for, hates you and everything you stand for—with a few notable exceptions—very few." I know this for a fact because I heard their vitriol for twenty years while scouting locations with the industry's most influential producers, directors, writers, and actors. Hollywood has a long-term plan to impose their culture on the nation and around the globe.

This deep-seated hatred of the American audience *is* true and is spoken about sparingly and only when it is convenient to advance the cause. Though once discussed only in "inner industry circles," the "movers and shakers" in Hollywood are becoming more vocal in recent years out of frustration over the slow pace of their "cultural revolution" begun by Prince Jack.

"Hollywood influences society" is what the entertainment community *really* means when it talks about "reflection" and being a "mirror." This is known by a term in Hollywood that nobody wants to use, at least publicly: Value manipulation.

After the Quiet Conspiracy of 1968, Hollywood has been on a mission to desensitize America to Hollywood values with "glamorous" portrayals of drug abuse, infidelity, bed-hopping, divorce courts, head chopping, profane retorts, gutter humor, and ultra-violent gore fests. In addition, Hollywood productions often portray "alternative" solutions for achieving success such as lying, cheating, stealing, and even killing. And in today's Hollywood, there are fewer and fewer consequences and moral compensating values in stories that stem from the demented minds of the screenwriter. The redemptive element in storytelling is what made Hollywood great. The lack of redemption in contemporary filmmaking is destroying Hollywood and the nation.

And the real-life dysfunction of movieland character is paraded by the Hollywood types themselves across the pages of countless celebrity magazines that would cease publication if adultery, philandering, alcoholism, drug addiction, child abuse, anorexia, rehab, face lifts, and numerous breakdowns came to a halt in Tinseltown. Hollywood *is* influencing behavior both on screen and off.

The Big Lie and value manipulation excuses are thrown around so loosely that industry leaders constantly contradict themselves by tripping over these terms on a regular basis. The most glaring example of Hollywood's insecurity of purpose and sense of place in this world occurred in editorial comments of the 1997 and 1998 anniversary issues of *The Hollywood Reporter*.

Published each November, the anniversary issues often focus on the "impact" of the entertainment industry. Former *Hollywood Reporter* publisher Robert Dowling boasted in the 1997 issue that "It will forever be a part of the entertainment portfolio, as entertainment is a reflection of our society." Just one year later in the November 1998 anniversary issue, Dowling declared, "There is virtually no part of the world that has escaped the influence of Hollywood."

One year Dowling is rehashing the old line that Hollywood is a "reflection" of society. But the following year Dowling is declaring Hollywood as a powerful "influence" on society. Not only is the industry an influence, but *"no part of the world has escaped the influence of Hollywood."*

The tone is straight out of *Invasion of the Body Snatchers*.

Not only is the 1998 issue a contradiction of the 1997 issue, it is a foreboding muscle-flexing warning that, as much as you and I try, the world will not be able to "escape" the doctrine of darkness and all-consuming power of Hollywood—the "influence" of Hollywood.

Is Dowling saying that there will be absolutely no escape clause for citizens of the world who might find Hollywood entertainment not only demoralizing, but downright destructive and harmful? Apparently *The Hollywood Reporter* and *Variety* are on the same page with this philosophy as we visit once again with Hollywood's favorite child-hater Timothy Gray, writing in *Daily Variety* that " . . . showbiz is the religion of the masses, and the devout are constantly declaring war on entertainment they consider harmful . . . . Perhaps harmful TV fare is good for children, preparing them for the wicked realities of life."[5]

What *Variety's* veteran child-hater failed to mention is the role played by Hollywood in influencing the creation of "the wicked realities of life." Children will most often face the wicked realities of life when they are exposed to trash TV, corrosive movies, ultra-violent video games, profane music, and flashes of lurid pop-up sex on their home computers while innocently scanning the Encyclopedia Britannica Online. (All compliments of the Dark Prince.)

The use of entertainment as "reflection" or "influence" is selective by the industry as it sees fit, again, for convenience or defense. When Oliver Stone's *Natural Born Killers* or New Line Cinema's *Basketball Diaries* were linked by some critics to numerous acts of murder and even school shootings, the movie industry adamantly denied that movies "influence" behavior and that they were merely a "reflection" of society.

On the other hand, when the National Center for Health Statistics reported in November 2006 that almost forty percent of children are now born to out-of-wedlock mothers, Hollywood celebrities took "credit" for influencing the "liberation" of women from the need for mates and marriage. Of course, celebrity-hugging reporters never mentioned how much money Madonna, Rosie O'Donnell, and Angelina Jolie spend on nannies or how much time they spend away from their children.

But by most accounts, the favorite Hollywood term is often the "reflection in the mirror" excuse, still in use more than seventy-five years after the studio moguls tried it on for size in 1929. George "Looney" Clooney used it at the seventy-eighth annual Academy Awards ceremony in 2006, and longtime UCLA Screenwriting School Chairman Richard Walter used it the same year during a debate with former congressman Joe Scarborough. According to Professor Walter, movies are "more a reflection than a shaper of the world."[6]

It would only make sense for Professor Walter to use the "reflection" excuse as he wouldn't want to be accused of fostering scripts that "influence" behavior. Among scripts written by students of Walter include *Seed of Chucky* and *The Simpsons*. Publisher's Weekly even described Walter as a "prolific hack writer" who has worked for most of the major studios and all of the television networks. It would be a stretch to take Walter's words to Joe Scarborough seriously. In other words, it's once again a lie—the Big Lie.

A contrary opinion to The Big Lie defense strategy was written by *Wall Street Journal* columnist Ellen Graham who noted accurately that movies and televised entertainment are not merely "a national mirror of human events, but a shaper as well; of national values, family, life, politics, and consumption habits."[7]

WHY WALT DISNEY ROLLS OVER IN HIS GRAVE

Unfortunately, the real victims of The Big Lie and value manipulation are children—the future adults, parents, and leaders of our country. The current "adults" in control of the film industry have already proven themselves as largely unworthy of providing images of "maturity" in the form of role models. In fact, the very core strategy of Valenti's Ratings Scheme is a carefully crafted revision of a child's rights of passage and coming of age.

A child of today learns early that the older he or she becomes, the achievement of true "adulthood" (as defined by the MPAA) lies in their journey to an R-rated movie without their parents or an "adult guardian."

Boston Globe columnist Ellen Goodman nails the point home about the Ratings Scheme's true agenda of value manipulation. "The industry offer [of ratings] is designed to help the studios more than the kids. It's fine to control who gets into movie theaters, but it's better to change what gets into the movie. This time, let Hollywood come of age."[8]

Brent Bozell points out the cynical, even diabolical, nature of the entertainment industry's snare tactics for children. "The industry doesn't care what children think. They understand that it's forbidden fruit for youngsters and they make it available as low-hanging fruit."

Of course, the industry has a different view as determined by *Variety* editor Peter Bart who once told Katie Couric in a 1999 interview that "It's sort of hip to see an R picture and somewhat sissy to see a G picture." Again, this is another fine example of an older "adult" Hollywood insider who has no concept of maturity.

Bart carries the movie industry's toxic water because his magazine could not survive without the glossy full-page color ads taken out by Hollywood's "hip" filmmakers. And that speaks volumes about an industry that spends more money on a single page ad in an industry trade magazine than it would spend in an average U.S. city newspaper to promote a film. Hollywood filmmakers are more concerned with impressing each other than with impressing their potential audience.

Ironically, the most prolific proponent of value manipulation was the Walt Disney Company under the two decade reign by one of Hollywood's most corrupt examples of moral leadership and financial administration, Michael Eisner. Taking control in 1984, it was Eisner who turned the once coveted studio name of Disney into a name synonymous with the most grotesque output of film and television production in Hollywood, complete with their new social/sexual/political agenda and a film division called Miramax that consisted of largely X-rated movie production.

There were the occasional animated gems that brought in the millions to fund the studio's money losing social agenda productions. Among those were the feature-length *The Lion King* and *Aladdin*. Because they brought in enormous amounts of money and appealed to the broadest audiences, Peter Bart would consider these "sissy" films.

So as not to be embarrassed at Hollywood cocktail parties, Eisner rolled out other "family" films such as *The Little Mermaid* and *Pocahontas* that were promoted with a subliminal sex subcontext, perpetuated by the perverts in the marketing department. The ploy was a sick trick to lure parents into buying an extra ticket for themselves so they would sit in the theaters with their children instead of dropping them off at the multiplex.

DESENSITIVITY TRAINING

Eisner developed a two-pronged strategy of value manipulation that was copied by some of the other major Hollywood studios. "Desensitivity Training" and "Strangulation Manipulation" often deployed in concert with one another or separately, depending on the production and the target audience.

First, an examination of Desensitivity Training, which was aimed at the audience. The strategy had roots that can be traced to Disney's *"Sensitivity Training,"* which was aimed at company employees regarding not only homosexual *tolerance* in the workplace, but also the *advancement* of an ultra-radical homosexual agenda under the umbrella of the Hollywood Sexual Reorientation Society (HSRS).

This would result in a wide array of movie and television productions with subtle, and not so subtle, private agendas that founder Walt Disney would never have tried to foist on the American public. By now, Walt Disney had already turned ninety degrees in his grave at the very mention of Eisner's name as Disney CEO.

Eisner's Disney Studio had already desensitized the American theatrical audience for his first ten years with a new and rapidly increasing output of gratuitous sex, profanity, ultra-violence, and cannibalistic gore. Television was the next frontier for Eisner to push the studio's seemingly endless obsession with sex.

With a much wider TV audience than its theatrical film divisions, the Eisner Disney Studios saw an opportunity to saturate the audience with sex, thus desensitizing the viewers. Then the Disney-owned ABC network would add sex with a twist. The sitcom *Ellen*, starring Ellen DeGeneres, would be the vehicle to bend the genders slowly into the heads of the mind-numbed TV audiences who still held out hope for some semblance of network excellence.

But "slowly" was not in the network's vocabulary. During *Ellen's* premiere year on ABC in 1994, the subject matter was routinely in-your-face sex talk about endless sexual encounters complete with detailed descriptions. Having saturated the audience with heterosexual "sex" dialogue and story lines, the lesbian and transsexual show writers, with Ellen DeGeneres' full endorsement, began to introduce plan B, the radically homosexual "action agenda."

When Ellen decided that the lesbian way was the only way, ratings began to drop dramatically. The show's ratings slipped to levels far below what most networks would tolerate before cancellation. But Eisner personally let the show play out so that Ellen could "come out" of the closet, both in her character and in reality. This episode was a revealing chapter into the Eisner empire's fascination with genitalia orientation.

Already facing a massive boycott by media watchdog organizations, civic groups, denominational and non-denominational churches across North America, the *Ellen* show was finally cancelled. The reaction by *Ellen* creator and writer Tim Doyle will go down in television history as one of the most telling insights into the mind of the more radical heterophobes in the Disney Television arena. "There's a group of older people who will never accept it. But there's a lot of empty cemeteries, and when they're filled, the world will be a lot more tolerant."

Meanwhile, despite the show's cancellation, the objective of desensitizing the audience another notch on the sexual obsession ladder was achieved. It would now be "no big deal" for heterophobic characters to parade across the TV screen spouting social/sexual/political agendas.

Because Eisner never apologized for Doyle's remarks, the American audience was given its first clue that Eisner wanted Walt's devoted old fans and family to "hurry up and die!" Despite falling ratings, profits, and the Ellen fiasco, Eisner's "New Disney" decided to roll out more homosexual heterophobic characters as "regulars" in two new TV shows in the fall of 1999.

Disney and Hollywood in general might be commended for bringing homosexual characters into mainstream TV and movie storylines. But in true Hollywood fashion, the characters are almost always presented and portrayed with an overt or covert attitude of simmering heterophobia; an inordinate distrust or disdain for heterosexuals.

The Disney studios hired radical homosexual activist producer Kevin Williamson to create a show called *Wasteland*, an aptly-named show about a group of brooding twenty-somethings wasting away in Manhattan. Williamson was hired because of his "courage" in introducing a homosexual teen character for the TV show *Dawson's Creek*. The other Disney-ABC heterophobe outing sitcom was *Oh, Grow Up*, about three dysfunctional roommates with a focus on their newest arrival, a man who left his wife after proclaiming he was a homosexual. Now, that's entertainment.

The Disney-ABC television shows were such low-rated bombs they were cancelled before the rot began to stink, and Disney's stock continued tanking rapidly between 1999 and 2000. But at least the Gender Bender Advocacy Department (GBAD) was getting their message out. That's really all that counted to Eisner and the "New Disney." More importantly, Eisner could continue to maintain his friendships and "open door" policy with Hollywood's Velvet Mafia.

Since homosexuality and heterophobia obviously wasn't going to be profitable, Eisner would turn to blood—and lots of it. Eisner again enlisted the deeply-troubled mind of Kevin Williamson who was not only a radical heterophobic artist, but personally maintained a heart of darkness that rivaled his idol, Wes Craven, whom he helped write and produce the disturbing slice and dice blood-fest *Nightmare on Elm Street* series.

Eisner's Disney now wanted to project more blood, guts, and gore than anything previously splattered on the silver screen. And the deviants in the marketing department wanted to tailor-make and promote the new blood-fests to adolescents and teenagers.

This new move into hard-core gore films was another plank in the Desensitivity Training and value manipulation of the American audience. Disney's aforementioned perversity-diversity marketing department set out to actually redefine genres by trading in the term "horror" for "fright films" and further clarify and legitimize the genre as "fear and *fun* films."

Disney's foray into gore was not necessarily new ground in Hollywood. The tempo of increasingly graphic bloodlust had already been in progress since the late 1970s and early 1980s with the Halloween series and the *Friday the Thirteenth* series. Tobe Hooper's *Texas Chainsaw Massacre* and George Romero's *Dawn of the Dead* were also eye-popping body-chopping films of the late 1970s that were so brutal theater owners would only exhibit them at midnight.

But Eisner's "New Disney" wanted even more graphic depictions of decapitations, bloody stabbings, bodily dismemberment, shattered skulls, and exploding human bodies. And it was to be a "fun" experience. Eisner could count on Williamson's sick mind to begin producing a portion of the desired results and deliver them to America's teens, which he did in the *Scream* series.

Dr. Jason Kovar, a consummate researcher into the media and culture of Hollywood, noted that *Scream* contains "numerous scenes of blood and gore which just fifty years ago would have been condemned as depraved."[9] But depravity is what Eisner was seeking despite the very negative and harmful consequences of this destructive form of value manipulation.

Scream would help spur the promulgation of "heavy gore" films of recent years, such as the *Saw* series and the *Grudge* series, to name only a few. There has now arisen in Hollywood a new breed of sicker and increasingly deranged filmmakers who specialize in "splatter" movies and are known collectively as "The Splat Pack" led by tattoo-laden slime-master with the very Hollywood name of Rob Zombie.

"The harmful effect is the cumulative impact," according to Professor Gary Smith of Dickinson College. Constant exposure to "frightening images of destruction or harm" doesn't always lead children to imitate what they see, but it does have a coarsening effect that makes children and even adults "more callous toward one another."[10]

This is how Eisner carried out Desensitivity Training by Disney studios, producing and marketing depravity until numbness set in. But the "New Disney" did not stop at Fright Films. Eisner's acquisition of Miramax Films, headed by the sleaze king brothers Harvey and Bob Weinstein, was the ultimate test in Desensitivity Training and the final nail in the coffin of Walt Disney.

Eisner was also apparently impressed with Miramax's 1990 X-rated feature *The Cook, the Thief, His Wife, and Her Lover.* After all, Leonard Maltin hailed the film as "another stylish, challenging piece of cinema from [director] Peter Greenaway that's set in a plush gourmet restaurant and details the various relationships between the title characters."[11] Caryn Jones of *The New York Times* called the film "something profound and extremely rare: a work so intelligent and powerful that it evokes our best emotions."

But enter the honest and determined movie critic Michael Medved who said, without wavering, that the movie was "... in short, unrelieved ugliness, horror, and depravity at every turn. Naturally, the critics loved it."[12]

And so did Eisner's "New Disney," which was becoming about as popular as New Coke. With output like this, Eisner could join his fellow Hollywood moguls in defining decency down. Best of all, Eisner wouldn't be called a "sissy" by Peter Bart at Hollywood cocktail parties.

Medved, understanding audience sensibilities in direct contradiction to the Miramax view of the audience, noted that "The film just made me sick, but the reviews made me angry. The glowing notices for *The Cook* gave prospective moviegoers no indication of the intensity of the horrors they would experience if they went to see the film."[13]

The movie was probably one of Hollywood's most grotesquely baroque undertakings in film history. The two-hour cinematic nightmare was an endless orgy of offenses against the senses reveling in toilet sex, necrophilia, slicing and dicing of children's body parts, sex amidst maggots, and the eating of human limbs by the main character.

This was the film that was given "Two Thumbs Up" by Siskell and Ebert. And Eisner was so impressed, the sleaze brothers Weinstein began a long-term relationship for the House built by Mickey Mouse.

The Cook also set a precedent in redefining decency and obscenity, at least in the eyes of the MPAA. Harvey Weinstein sued the MPAA for its application of the X rating, claiming that it put his movies into an "illegitimate" category. Weinstein certainly didn't want his film to be associated with pornography. After all, this was simply human cannibalism.

Eisner and his two new street gutter associates would continue to desensitize audiences with such films as Larry Clark's *Kids*. The desperately depressing film follows the bleak and dismal lives of very young and aimless adolescents roaming New York City streets as they engage in rape, violence, drug abuse, and alcoholism. The pedophile overtones did not go unnoticed by some critics, especially considering the fact that underage "kids" were used to "act out" director

Larry Clark's urban nightmare visions. By now Eisner must have thought that the American audience was pretty stupid and never connected the dots between Miramax and Disney. But just in case, a third company called Excalibur was created for the purpose of distributing the film.

It was Eisner who created the multi-layered Disney empire with its subsidiary production and distribution units such as Touchstone, Hollywood Pictures, Buena Vista Distribution, Walt Disney Pictures and Miramax. Touchstone Pictures was the subdivision used to release *Splash* in 1984, the first Disney picture with profanity and sexual innuendo.

Having explored cannibalism, pedophilia, and gender-bending, it would only be a natural next step for Eisner's "New Disney" to take on the Christians. As a virulent Christian basher, Eisner welcomed the release of *Dogma*, where the heroine of the story is a descendant of Mary and Joseph who works in an abortion clinic.

Dogma would also overlap in Eisner's two-pronged strategy of value manipulation: "Strangulation Manipulation."

STRANGULATION MANIPULATION

By the late 1990s, Disney's reputation as a Palace of Dark Dreams was well known around the country and around the world, and Eisner was not ignorant of the fact that he was losing millions of dollars for Disney stockholders. But he was such a master of deception that Eisner may have been deceiving himself.

In the late 1990s, I ran into Michael Eisner as he was leaving an awards ceremony for longtime Disney employees at the Biltmore Hotel in Los Angeles. After introducing myself, I asked Eisner what he thought of recent Wall Street analysts' announcement of a whopping thirty-six percent drop in earnings over the previous year.

Scratching the back of his ear, Eisner cracked a faint smile and said, "I think this is a very good period for Disney." Eisner suddenly disappeared in the shadow of a three hundred pound body guard who had been summoned by the ear-scratching "signal." I found the incident totally hilarious and typically Eisner as I looked up at the three hundred pound gorilla in the room whispering into his lapel mike. A longtime friend of mine, a production executive at Disney's Burbank headquarters, said that was an Eisner ploy to escape "pedestrian" criticism, though he was known to tell taller tales at stockholder meetings. My friend also explained the Strangulation Manipulation prong of value manipulation and how it worked in conjunction with Desensitivity Training.

Strangulation Manipulation was a very *strange* marketing ploy of widespread deceit that made no common sense in a capitalist free-market economy. Eisner was one of many moguls who employed the practice of purposely killing good

"G" rated movies by withdrawing advertising and promotion dollars, guaranteeing a failure at the box office. When family-friendly critics would complain about the lack of quality movies, the studios would spit up the industry line, "We try to make family pictures, but nobody comes." And the movie critics would take their cue and regurgitate the talking points all the way to the press room.

A classic example of this form of Strangulation Manipulation was seen in the release of the Warner Brothers animated feature *The Iron Giant*. The story centers around a young boy who befriends a mysterious giant hiding in the forest. The dialogue between the two actually plays out as a morality play dealing with timeless themes of problem-solving, values, alienation, ignorance, love, fear, and making responsible choices. The film had wide appeal to children and adults alike. All Warner Brothers had to do was give it a "wide release," which industry lingo dictates as 1,000 theaters or more. Instead, Warner Brothers released the movie to just 300 theaters, which would amount to *six* screens for every state in the country.

Before the movie even had a chance to get legs, despite Warner's refusal to promote it, the studio quickly pulled the film and released it as a "kiddie video." As if in lock-step with the whole strategy, *USA Today* movie reviewer Mike Clark wrote, "People say they want good family entertainment, but apparently they don't given the horrifically brief theatrical run."

It's a sad fact that many print and broadcast movie critics accept junkets to Vegas and cruises on the Caribbean from Hollywood's major studios. Certainly, that wasn't the case at *USA Today*.

That is an example of Strangulation Manipulation from A to Z. And Eisner was on board to do the same at Disney. The strategy had two goals: first, diminish the idea that a movie could transcend the age restrictions imposed by Jack Valenti's "age-appropriate" Ratings Scheme; second, maintain the "adult" status of most movies because only "serious" filmmakers could bravely drop F-bombs, cut off limbs, depict explicit sex acts, and explode heads while still managing to deliver a far-left political message.

The Strangulation Manipulation theory was inadvertently revealed recently when spokesman John Feehrey of the MPAA appeared before Congress to decry and browbeat companies that had popped up to provide family-friendly movies on DVD by editing out the "adult" language and scenes. In his statement to the House Subcommittee on Commerce, Feehrey used typical MPAA manipulation language to "clarify" the MPAA's destruction of American family movie viewing. "But not all films are appropriate for the entire family, and I trust you would agree that all movies should not be geared to an audience of five-year-olds."[14]

What Feehrey failed to mention is that before 1968 all movies approved by the MPAA were accessible to all ages. That did not prevent "mature" themes, it did not prevent Academy Awards, and it certainly didn't deny profitability.

THE HOLLYWOOD CULTURE WAR

Was *Casablanca* geared to five-year-olds? Was *To Kill a Mockingbird* geared to five-year-olds? Was *On the Waterfront* geared to five-year-olds? Whether you were five or ninety-five, movies were accessible to everyone. They made money and they earned awards. And they still play on television today. Does that make people who watch them "sissies" as *Variety* editor Peter Bart suggests?

Feehrey's statement to the Congress needs translation. "I trust you would agree" might as well be, "If you don't agree, don't expect anymore campaign money to be given to you in the next election." But the main reason people such as Feehrey and the trendsetters at the MPAA make those public statements is the hope that we'll all forget there used to be a Golden Era of filmmaking, which the MPAA destroyed, and that era was largely free of Hollywood's self-indulgent perversions.

Eisner's favorite shot at Strangulation Manipulation was the release of two movies with completely different world views. One was uplifting, humorous, and decidedly inspirational, and the other film was profane, indecent, and decidedly sacrilegious. Eisner put his money on the second film. Eisner not only wanted to bolster the "adult" offerings and diminish the age-inclusive movies, he was on a revenge attack on faith-based organizations around the country that had mounted one of the longest and most successful boycotts in entertainment history. As a result of Eisner's morally bankrupt tactics, Disney would take a double hit—at the box office and the stock exchange.

In the first week of December 1999, Disney positioned two films for exhibition at theaters during the crucial Christmas movie season, *The Straight Story* and *Dogma*.

Veteran actor Richard Farnsworth was the featured actor in The *Straight Story*, based on the true life of Alvin Straight, an elderly Midwesterner who had not spoken to his ailing brother in decades. When Straight discovers that his brother's life may be coming rapidly to an end, he powers up an ancient John Deere riding lawn mower, hooks up a small hand-made wagon, and journeys over 360 miles to be with his brother and make amends.

Denied a driver's license due to his poor eyesight, the tractor-mower is his only means of transportation. Despite the long journey, Straight encounters a colorful cast of characters spanning the rainbow of time that has passed him by. After dark, Straight camps out in vast cornfields under stunning starlit nights where the vast landscape offers a setting for reflection on better days as a younger man without grudges or bitterness. The World War II veteran realizes that too much time has lapsed without reconciliation.

The mark of any good movie is the value of redemption. *The Straight Story* is a masterpiece of redemption. But there was one problem. Even after unanimous glowing reviews by the usually cynical film critics, Disney failed to actively promote and advertise the film, except for a thumbnail mention on its website. Disney failed to promote *The Straight Story* even after news flooded out of Hollywood that Farnsworth was being considered as a leading contender for Best Actor at the Academy Awards. He had already received a Best Actor award from the New York Film Critics.

Disney failed to promote the movie because it released the film in only 153 theaters across America, fewer than half the number of theaters than the pathetic ultra-limited release of *The Iron Giant* by Warner Brothers. God forbid *The Straight Story* might have been a hit at the box office; then the boycotters would have been justified by an extra notch.

In a 2007 DVD release review, *USA Today* wrote, "This may be the best live-action G-rated movie since the current movie ratings system began in 1968."

But forbidding God was the true intention of Eisner's Disney. The same week in December that *The Straight Story* was playing in 153 theaters, Disney was showcasing its "Christmas feature" called *Dogma* in 1,287 theaters.

Eisner and the largely atheist employee base at Disney knew that *Dogma* would cause a stir and they intended it as a big stir with a blatant message to the faithful. *Dogma* would be a vicious slap in the face of Jews, Christians, and anybody else who dared boycott the Walt Disney Company under the vengeful and neurotic chairmanship of Michael Eisner. And sleaze-king Harvey Weinstein would serve as executive producer for the Disney/Miramax assault film.

In *Dogma*, God is played by a woman who comes to earth as a *man* to play a game of carnival skeeball. At the same time, a profanity-spewing thirteenth apostle, played by maggot-mouthed "comedian" Chris Rock, comes back to earth and complains that he was killed for revealing the sex lives of the other twelve apostles. The "woman/man/god" and the profane thirteenth apostle form a "holy union" to rescue the movie's heroine, the abortion clinic worker who claims to be a descendant of Mary and Joseph.

Eisner and the veteran Christian-basher Weinstein must have had a field day toasting drinks under an inverted pentacle as they laughed their way trough the holiday season. They certainly didn't laugh all the way to the bank. Both movies bombed as a result of Eisner's total lapse from reality as his retribution train teetered on the verge of yet another nervous breakdown. The Disney board was taking note, as were the stockholders. When Desensitivity Training and Strangulation Manipulation are combined in this extreme example of value manipulation, everybody comes out a loser.

Donald Wildmon, founder and president of the American Family Association (AFA) proudly wears the title "The Most Hated Man in Hollywood." During this period of Disney's Culture War counterattack on "fly-over country," Wildmon remarked, "At times Disney appears to be trying to win back families. Meanwhile they continue to produce and market trash. Until Disney makes up its mind, I think the boycott will only grow."

Even the NAACP threatened a boycott when the Disney Corporation distributed promotional giveaway gardening tools by the name of "The Black Hoe." Civil rights groups found the term offensive because of a historically racist connotation to black prostitutes. Though the Disney Corporation apologized, the NAACP promised a limited boycott. However, Disney Studios saw no reason to apologize to Jews and Christians who were purposely humiliated during the Christmas season of 1999. So much for Disney's "tolerance" and "inclusion" policies.

When Wildmon said "the boycott will only grow," it was an understatement. Though Eisner dismissed the AFA and its one million plus supporters as "little Hitlers," the financial picture grew increasingly red, a deeper red than the blood Harvey Weinstein splattered on the silver screen. By January 1999, Disney's stock price had already fallen nearly thirty percent from the previous year. During a meeting with stockholders at this time, Eisner described company profits as merely "flat."

The Disney board debated the CEO's future and decided to punish Eisner by trimming his annual bonus to a mere $5 million and temporarily freezing his salary at only $764,000. Before the stock fell further, Eisner was allowed to exercise the sale of stock options worth over half a billion dollars. Total take for the Disney chairman during the company's stock free-fall: $575 million.

DeWayne Wickham, who broke the story, noted sardonically, "Not bad" for the leader of a major entertainment conglomerate with continuously slipping profits.[15]

And the news only grew bleaker for the Disney Company. Three months later, on March 31, the *Wall Street Journal* reported a net income drop of forty-one percent for the first quarter and average earnings estimates for the same three-month period fell fifty percent below analysts' predictions.[16] But Eisner continued his snow-job on the board, blaming everything and everybody but himself for one of the largest profit freefalls in recent corporate entertainment history.

Despite the lack of good news, nobody within the Disney corporate structure criticized the high level of raunch content of Eisner and Company's excruciating campaign of value manipulation and contempt for the American moviegoing public. However, the *Wall Street Journal* noted that the problems at Disney were not industry specific as a whole, but were definitely "Disney specific."[17]

The entire dark era of Eisner's desecration of the Mouse House played out like an endless video loop from a bad "fright film" where Eisner exhumes the body of Walt Disney and stabs the poor dead soul in the heart while screaming, "It's not your company anymore . . . . It's mine!"

It is worth noting that the Federal Election Commission recorded the Walt Disney Corporation as the single largest entertainment industry contributor to the Democratic Party in the previous election cycle prior to Eisner's 1999 reign of destruction. While a number of Democrats sat on the Disney board, nobody can say for sure if Eisner's contributions to the Clinton Democrats ranked higher on the board's priority list than the company's bottom line and the public's desire for quality entertainment, which ranked zero on Eisner's personal list.

Regardless, Eisner was finally forced out and left Disney in September 2005 and *only* after the Disney board voted forty-three percent disfavor with Eisner. The reason was not a conflict with content. The Disney board was furious with Eisner for granting a golden parachute worth almost $100 million to Eisner's former friend Mike Ovitz, whom Eisner himself fired after barely ten months as a do-nothing Disney executive. Eisner defended the payoff during a stockholder lawsuit against him by declaring to a Delaware court that he feared Ovitz "might commit suicide" if not properly compensated. So far, no reports of an Ovitz suicide.

The good news is that Disney is experiencing a revival with Eisner's departure. New CEO Robert Iger is considerably more level-headed and responsive to audience expectations. He has helped to re-establish ties with animation giant Pixar, which has helped put Disney back in the profitable and popular throne of animation, the birthright of the Disney Studios. The 2006 sequel to *Pirates of the Caribbean* not only helped push Disney back toward the black, it partially helped pull the entire motion picture industry out of a record three-year financial slump. (Unfortunately, Iger's refusal to release *Path to 9/11* on DVD makes him a puppet for the Clinton Machine.)

The sequel, *Dead Man's Chest*, might have even become the biggest blockbuster in recent history if not for Johnny Depp's loose lips sinking ships. In 2003, Depp called Americans "dumb puppies" and sparked the growing boycott of Johnny Depp movies. The true credit for the movie can be given to Walt Disney himself, who "green lighted" the pirate concept movie just before he died in 1966, according to Neal Gabler in his book *Walt Disney*. In the end, Walt Disney got the last laugh as Michael Eisner walked out the door.

Eisner's Disney was only one example of the thousands of similar scenarios being played out even now in Hollywood by the people who are working day and night to reshape the way you and I think by the manipulation of our values at the movie house and at your house.

AVERSION TO PERVERSION

Movies and other entertainment products do not manifest themselves out of thin air. As Michael Medved described the process, "Every commitment to produce a movie, TV show, or popular song involves an element of conscious or unconscious value judgement."[18]

Dr. Jason Kovar has studied the Hollywood agenda for decades and is producer of the *Hollywood Unmasked* DVD series. Concerning value manipulation,

Kovar noted that "Research from George Washington University found that Hollywood's producers, writers, and directors view themselves as 'crusaders for social reform in America. They see it as their duty to restructure our culture into their image.'"[19]

And if that image is not social/sexual/political, it is often simply sick to the core of the screenwriter's dark heart. Consider the plot of a 2006 movie titled *Sick Girl* in which a young female lab assistant takes a job with a prominent female entomologist who happens to be a lesbian.

Naturally, as Hollywood would have it, the prominent lesbian lab director seduces the young lab assistant into a lesbian love affair. But since America is used to that old story, the producers of *Sick Girl* take a new leap by transforming the lab assistant into an insect after she is bitten by a strange little creature in a box. The lab director is "turned on" and she proceeds to have sex with the insect-lesbian humanoid.

This video was on the shelves of many "big box" retail discounters until I pointed it out to a number of store managers who took the initiative to yank the DVD to file in the trash can. Is it any wonder that astute individuals with a moral backbone developed the Production Code in 1930 to prevent mentally ill screenwriters, producers, and directors from projecting their self-indulgent bottomless pit nightmares onto the world movie market?

Now with an "anything goes" sick and shock approach to entertainment, the sordid content of Hollywood is piped directly into your home living room and is available for viewing on the latest version of any widescreen HDTV home theater complete with surround-sound.

Writing about the lack of decent television programming, columnist George Will described the defunct TV series *Action* as "evidence of how frantically producers now strain in search of something that can startle—never mind shock—America's desensitized audiences." Desensitivity training is a never-ending continuum that must be fed by ever increasing bolts of shock and insanity. It won't stop at lesbian sex with insects or maggot-infested French kisses.

MTV is a good example of the shock continuum and the effect of value manipulation over three generations as witnessed by MTV babies having MTV babies. It is not hard to identify MTV zombies by their dress, behavior, and even individual speech patterns. The "MTV Effect" was best summarized by the late humorist Lewis Grizzard, who gave me an advanced colorful reading of his column over lunch at Manuel's Tavern in Atlanta in 1992, shortly before his death:

For those people out there who don't know, MTV is a cable channel that shows very strange things called rock music videos. Rock groups and rock stars bellow their cacophonies while doing such things as having sex with seventeen other people, not to mention an occasional duckbill platypus or two. Your children watch this, and that is why they have rings in their noses and resemble duckbill platypus more than human beings."[20]

Bill Cosby even joined the chorus by poking fun at the entertainment industry's ongoing refusal to acknowledge that they influence anybody's behavior. Appearing at a conference in Minneapolis with psychologist David Walsh, Cosby told the audience, "The networks say they don't influence anybody. If that's true, why do they have commercials? Why am I sitting there with Jell-O pudding?"

There are other voices within the entertainment industry who are speaking out against Hollywood's campaign of viciously debauched value manipulation as the Culture War escalates into the twenty-first century. After more than forty-five years together, Peter, Paul, and Mary released a CD titled *Don't Laugh at Me* with lyrics that teach respect.

According to Peter Yarrow, "Something has crept up on us that I don't think we're fully aware of," citing trash entertainment and prime-time TV plots. "Kids learn disrespectful behavior is okay, so why are we surprised they act that way?"

The problems caused by Hollywood's malicious mayhem and perspiring perversity are not just local, state, and national. They reach around the globe and are very often cited as one of the main aggravating reasons for America's low image around the world. Former Undersecretary of State, Karen Hughes, told the Associated Press that America's "sex and violence" culture is so rapacious and the damage so vast that repairing it is "going to be the work of years and maybe decades.

"One of the things I hear a lot, particularly in deeply conservative societies, is that parents feel assaulted by American culture. The sex and violence that they see on television and movies, . . . some of the lyrics of our music."[21]

In all its abhorrent arrogance, Hollywood continues to push its aggressive necrosis onto the world market under the auspices of a liberating cultural army of enlightenment and freedom. Hollywood has never been too keen on international cultural sensitivities. As the industry has created a Hollywood nation, it seeks nothing less than the creation of a Hollywood globe.

I wouldn't argue that Hollywood should shape up for the sake of satisfying extremist elements that are hell-bent (literally) on destroying America. It would be a minor miracle if Hollywood could exercise good taste at least for America's own sake and, by example, prove that this country can be a moral leader on the international scene. Unfortunately, in Hollywood morality is equated with moronity.

Rome did not fall in one day, one week, one month, or one year. But decades of complacent citizens of the ancient empire spent morning, noon, and night in a drunken haze at the Coliseum, the Circus Maximus, and the Hippodrome. The saloons, gambling dens, and the whorehouses were open when the gladiators slept.

THE HOLLYWOOD CULTURE WAR

Entertainment then, as now, was twenty-four hours a day, seven days a week. The barbarians at the gate simply walked in and set up shop as new citizens of Rome, abstaining from the crass diversions created by Rome's theatrical writers, producers, and directors. Eventually, the drunken citizens of Rome awoke to find their swords had rusted and they wondered aloud if their "movies," their "video games," and their "casinos" were worth the loss of their morality and liberty. The ancient Romans once aspired to a golden era of entertainment before Nero, Claudius, and Caligula (the studio moguls of their day) "freed" the Roman entertainment world of its constraints and promoted "nightmares of depravity" to rule the theater. And the rest, as *they* say, is history, and history has been repeating itself since 1968.

William B. Brown, former editor of the *Montgomery Advertiser*, wrote about how he learned moral lessons "at a matinee" in the days before the Quiet Conspiracy. Brown remembered that "The plots of all of them could be summed up simply: An appealing character strives against great odds to achieve a worthwhile goal . . . . Come to think of it, that's the plot of countless tales dating back to the dawn of time. The cynical will argue that those are simply myths, but myths are powerful things that not only explain our behavior but also *shape* it. The ancient Greeks and Romans knew that well."

Today, with very little accurate knowledge of history by the contemporary creative community in Hollywood, the march is on to make spineless consumers of American audiences in the entertainment marketplace. Perhaps the most malicious strategy of value manipulation was the "cradle to grave" strategy announced by CBS President Les Moonves on the occasion of the network's merger with Viacom.

As one of the largest mega-mergers of Hollywood studios with an American television giant, the new mega-conglomerate demonstrated how one combined entertainment monolith could ultimately control content and manipulate values across a broad spectrum of the culture. Under one umbrella, controlled by master mogul manipulator, Sumner Redstone, the merger brought together Paramount Studios, CBS Television, MTV, VH1, CMT, *Wheel of Fortune, Jeopardy, Oprah Wynfrey*, and many more programs and channels at the time.

As an example of "compromised values" in such a merger, CMT (Country Music Television) started as a showcase of America's best and emerging country artists such as Alabama, Clint Black, Randy Travis, Alan Jackson, Trisha Yearwood, Alison Kraus, and *many* more, combined with the best cinematographers to create an endless stream of pastoral dreamscapes of small-town America and front porch country serenity music videos.

Almost overnight, the back-drops changed to Malibu beaches and even Manhattan rooftops in New-York-City. Obviously, the mega-monolith asked the directors at MTV to help change the scenery and the tone of "fly over country." A ghastly example of this change was a music video with Shania Twain riding a heavy-metal super-sonic motorcycle through dark video-game landscapes as she battled and evaded a fire-breathing dragon. Good-bye Grand Ol' Opry—Hello Hollywood. Few people know that CMT is now actually a "division" of MTV and has no independent identity.

A corporate entertainment mega-merger of this magnitude should have been judged illegal under the Sherman Anti-Trust vertical monopoly laws. But considering that Sumner Redstone's Viacom ranked No. 3 in federal campaign contributions during this time, the jury is out. (Appendix I). And new corporate partner Les Moonves of CBS brought his own political football to the field in the form of golfing buddy and good friend President Bill Clinton. Again, birds of a feather do definitely stick together.

The "cradle to grave" strategy unleashed by Moonves at this time reflected the CBS president's exuberance for controlling a large portion of the American audience. The strategy was all about increasing total viewership in order to charge higher ad dollars to television commercial buyers, "We'll get them from the time they're two until the time they're eighty."

Notice carefully that Moonves didn't say, "We'll get everyone *between* the age of two and the age of eighty." Moonves is talking about the long-term plan of replacing an entire generation with a "new" generation that has been "desensitized" to the current sad state of televised entertainment. This is the generation that has no memory of CBS, television, or movies in general before the "Massacre of '71" and the Quiet Conspiracy of 1968.

If the current generation of middle-aged and older viewers do not like what they see, Moonves' declaration fits like a hand in the glove with *Ellen* creator Tim Doyle's statement about "a lot of empty cemeteries" just waiting to be filled. As for children coming into this world void of any responsible parents with a moral compass and sense of boundaries, Hollywood's plan is to "capture" them at age two and take them on a dark journey through the twisted minds and fantasies of shallow, vicious hearts that have been creating "nightmares of depravity" for forty years.

As you will discover later in this book, these entertainment values do not only "startle—never mind shock" as George Will observed, they have the power to literally kill. And you'll read more true-life examples of filmmakers exercising their malevolent power of "death over life" than anyone thought imaginable from the American Dream Machine. It is value manipulation at its bleakest. But more importantly, you'll learn how American audiences are fighting back against the dark underbelly of the monolithic Hollywood Juggernaut.

Finally, the core source of this value manipulation was summarily traced and dissected by an unlikely source, computer scientist David Gelernter, who was one of the victims of the decade-long terror by the Unabomber. In his book, *Drawing Life: Surviving the Unabomber*, Gelernter squarely places the source of American moral chaos on the intelligentsia.

THE HOLLYWOOD CULTURE WAR

U.S. News & World Report contributing editor John Leo wrote an excellent review of Gelernter's book and the simmering Culture War that the Yale professor discovered during a period of reflection over an extended convalescence. As Leo points out, "Gelernter weaves together the story of his painful recovery with a series of inspired outbursts about our morally deregulated culture." The author, who was severely wounded by one of the Unabomber's mail bombs, was particularly outraged by the media's treatment of the Unabomber, particularly the "intellectual" press and the entertainment industry rags.

Why would such a despicable character even receive coverage in the personality cult press of Hollywood? "Worse," as Leo continues, "*People* magazine named the Unabomber as one of the 'most intriguing' people of 1996. Presumably, Mengele and Adolph Eichman would have been eligible for the 1944 fascination list along with Bob Hope and Bing Crosby if *People* and its sensibility had been around at the time."

"Gelernter, who wrote an earlier book on the 1939-1940 World's Fair and the mental world of that period, asks how America could have deteriorated so quickly from a stable and orderly world into our current chaos of fatherlessness, illegitimacy, divorce, violence, and anything goes mentality."

All of which begs the question of how America descended into this moral abyss. Gelernter points the finger at the condescending elitist intellectuals, sometimes known as the "Eastern Establishment" but now includes all like-minded people in academia, the media, and their counterparts in the left-coast entertainment industry.

As Leo gleans from the professor's book, the "anti-bourgeois intellectuals and artists have always been outsiders with a predictable set of attitudes: opposition to 'organized religion, the military, social constraints on sexual behavior, traditional sex roles and family structures, formality or fancy dress or good manners, authority in general.' But those attitudes now dominate the popular culture, he says, because the old elite has given way to a new intellectualized elite or intelligentsia that chopped away at tradition and won."[22] Of course, the press and mass media are part of the problem, a major part, because they worship the elitists and carry their tainted water in newsprint, television, and at the movies.

"The elite naturally resists open scrutiny of its power, but we are moving ever closer to the inevitable examination of the extent to which the elite's role is manipulative and antidemocratic."[23]

And there you have an inside view of the very source of Hollywood's manipulative strategy to change your values, headed by an army of elitist Tinseltown producers. As humorist Fred Allen observed, "You can take all the sincerity in Hollywood, place it in the navel of a firefly, and still have enough room for a producer's heart."

CHAPTER 10

Springtime for Stalin: Roots of Hollywood Radicalism
(Or, Why Jane Loves Hanoi and Clooney Hates McCarthy)

> *I think Joe Stalin was a guy that was hugely misunderstood.*
> —Ed Asner

During my twenty years in the film industry, I was never more perplexed, and at the same time amused, by the Hollywood fascination with Communism. During hundreds of location scouts with members of Old Hollywood and New Hollywood, I often heard the common thread philosophy that united the two generations of filmmakers. And as far as I was concerned, it was a very thin thread that was laughable at its least, pitiful at its worst.

The stories shared with me were so common, I could fill in the blanks for any who suffered memory lapses during their doctrinal discourses to me about the "persecution" of many "brave independent thinkers" who were hounded and "censored by the government" simply for exercising their "freedom of speech."

There is an old saying, "I do not suffer fools gladly." However, during those long tedious location scouts, "I gladly allowed the fools to suffer" as they rambled on and repeated such mythological reinterpretations of "The Blacklist" and the bestowing of virtual sainthood on "The Hollywood Ten."

Those Communist sympathizers were also the very industry people who invented self-serving terms like "Red Scare" and "McCarthyism" as ways to denigrate or demonize anyone who didn't agree with their left-coast Hollywood mind-set. Basically, the Communist sympathizers were repeating lies so often, they actually believed in the spider webs they were so cleverly weaving.

But what I couldn't understand was how so many of these Hollywood Communist sympathizers, or "Hollycoms," lionized a totally corrupt political and social system that would have put an iron clamp over the very creative juices that dribbled from their lips. If these Hollywood creative types ever lived under that Communist "utopia" they described, they would be forced into propaganda film factories or face the firing squad.

A few, very few, stage and screen artists made the move to the "glorious" Soviet Union in the 1930s and were never heard from again, likely victims of any one of Joseph Stalin's vodka-induced nervous breakdowns, also known as "purges." But the Hollywood elites didn't dwell on those forgotten few. They agreed with smooth-talking Soviet emissary Vladimir Pozner who explained that "there were no dissidents; they were shot before they ever came close to dissenting."

Freedom of speech was applied selectively on a one-way street during these day-long and week-long location scouts I conducted. They talked, I listened. Any opposing opinions to their political monologues might be viewed as "subversive," placing my job and career at stake.

This was not true of all Hollywood insiders I worked with. One such person who encouraged open debate was Oscar-winning production designer Paul Sylbert. Long before winning his Academy Award for *Heaven Can Wait*, Sylbert had worked as a production designer and art director on movies such as Alfred Hitchcock's *The Wrong Man* in 1956 and Elia Kazan's *A Face in the Crowd* in 1957.

Even earlier, Paul Sylbert, the twin brother of production designer Dick Sylbert, had begun his journeyman days in the entertainment business by designing and building sets for the early days of live television and also backstage on Broadway. It was the New York theater scene that became the hotbed incubator of Communism in "the industry" going back to the late 1920s.

My chance to talk freely with a true Hollycom had arrived. While scouting locations for Truman Capote's *The Grass Harp* in 1995, I sat down with Sylbert over dinner at Kat-n-Harry's restaurant in Montgomery, Alabama. Sylbert spoke nonchalantly about the "Red scare" days and how he, too, had been targeted as a Communist "fellow traveler" or "popuchiki" in Russian. The fellow travelers were sympathizers to Communism without being card-carrying members.

"They tried to blacklist me, but I kept working anyhow. It was the heyday of *McCarthyism* and *they* wanted to take me down." The emphasis-added are mine to illustrate the casually common code words of a genuine Hollycom fellow traveler. *They* was usually meant to convey "the U.S. government."

Without questioning his own politics, I asked Sylbert, "Did it ever cause you any problems working alongside others who were card-carrying members?"

Sylbert brought up a point missed by many whose understanding of the Hollycom infiltration is confused strictly with ideology. "It was very simple, Michael. In those days, if you didn't 'go along,' you didn't work."

This was true on Broadway and in Hollywood. The Communists wanted to control the labor unions and the labor dues. Entry into the craft unions meant a pledge of loyalty to the Communist bosses who controlled or influenced many of the unions. These Communist bosses were in direct opposition to the American labor union movement and to gangsters who also wanted union control.

Sylbert was more interested in working than promoting Stalinism in America. But his words did reflect a certain long-lost youthful romance with "the cause." Sylbert didn't use the term "Communist" often. This was 1995 and speaking the "C" word was even more out of favor since the collapse of the Soviet Union only four years earlier. *It* became synonymous with Communism.

Sylbert didn't have a problem with selling his soul to the most brutal ideology on the planet in order to work in the entertainment industry, noting, "I never had a problem with *it*. After Kruschev blew the whistle on Stalin's screw-ups [the slaughter of millions] *it* pretty much fell out of favor. I really don't have any regrets," Sylbert said casually between bites of pasta.

Sylbert had largely answered my long-perplexed curiosity with Hollywood's fascination with a system that would have swiftly stifled their creative freedom. It was about work—about "getting in the business." However, a part of Sylbert was overly sympathetic to the man who murdered more people than Adolph Hitler.

"But, Paul, didn't you have any second thoughts about the 50 million people who Stalin executed, starved, tortured, and worked to death in the labor camps?"

Sylbert looked up from his pasta plate with his trademark sidewinder smile, "It was pretty well accepted that 'you can't make an omelet without breaking eggs.'"

Only a true Hollywood fellow traveler could quote that line with a smile, referring to the sick justification of forced mass starvation of five million Ukrainian farmers by Joseph Stalin in the 1930s along with hundreds of thousands more during one of Stalin's purges (nervous breakdowns) of government and civilian workers.

The phrase quoted by Sylbert was coined by *New York Times* reporter Walter Duranty who traveled to Russia to cover the flimsy show trials of those who were about to die. His cover-up stories of the Soviet starvation and "omelet" remark won him a Pulitzer prize, which proves that *The New York Times* has maintained an enduring love affair with America's enemies that pre-date their current romance with radical Islamic terrorism by six decades.

THE HOLLYWOOD CULTURE WAR

Sylbert also felt it necessary to correct my mass-murder death toll of Stalin's reign of terror. "And, Michael, it was more like 20 million killed, maybe 30 at the most."

"But, Paul, 10 million here, 20 million there, pretty soon you're talking about real people," I said, paraphrasing Daniel Moynihan.

Again, from Sylbert, only a grin.

On a different location scout two years later with director John Frankenheimer (*Birdman of Alcatraz, The Manchurian Candidate*) I discovered another facet of Hollywood's fascination with Communism. Though not a former member of "the Party" or even a fellow traveler, Frankenheimer—like so many in Hollywood—held some fraternal sympathy for the Hollycoms and their masters in Moscow.

"You have to give them credit," Frankenheimer told me enthusiastically as we traveled the road to Selma. "They were the first world leaders to take God out of the picture. Now, that takes real courage."

By now, I had developed a much clearer picture of the secular entertainment industry's love affair with Communism. It was really all about the hatred of God; officially sanctioned and written into law. For many, it was part of the Faustian deal for "getting in the business." That's why there was no groundswell of Hollywood movies during or after the period of 1989-1991 when dozens of Eastern European and Baltic countries freed themselves from the stronghold of Communism, including the internal collapse of the Soviet Union.

But by Hollywood's account, you would have never known that the Cold War had come to an end after decades of oppression, starvation, and human extermination. Surely, there are least a thousand and one noble stories of sacrifice, resistance, and victory over the darkest "experiments" of social engineering in the history of the planet.

To understand the roots of Hollywood's radical love affair with Communism is to better understand the current ultra-left social/sexual/political radicalism that has consumed the entertainment industry to a much greater degree than the relatively short Hollycom heyday between 1930 and 1955.

Actor George Clooney is but one of many examples of the new "Lunatic Fringe" that has largely embraced Hollywood's Culture War agenda since Jack Valenti's Quiet Conspiracy of 1968. Clooney, eager to escape his role on the TV show *ER* began to sputter and spit a variety of left-coast political opinions in order to impress the power-brokers in the Hollywood feature film community. Soon he was being offered a number of movie roles in films that were not particularly profitable or memorable.

In order to please the "really big boys" at the studios, Clooney escalated his "looney" liberal agenda by attacking conservative Americans and conservative leaders. His one bold move that helped push the desperate actor up the ladder was a sick, shameless, and repeated attack on Charlton Heston, one of Hollywood's

239

unabashed conservatives and all-around gentleman who did not engage in bashing his fellow actors.

When Heston was diagnosed with Alzheimer's in 2002, Clooney jumped at the opportunity to kick Heston while he was down, saying "Charlton Heston announced again that he is suffering from Alzheimer's."[1] Clooney would repeat the "joke" often on camera and especially on the Beverly Hills cocktail party circuit where "influential" producers heaped praise and approval on his cruel political astuteness.

When asked what he thought about the remark, Heston remarked quite clearly that "It just goes to show that sometimes class skips a generation."[2] And what the Hollywood media machine didn't report is how Clooney's wicked remarks came back to haunt him.

During the filming of the pro-terrorist movie *Syriana* in 2005, Clooney slipped and hit his head on a concrete floor, tearing open his dura-mater, the fibrous tissue covering the brain and spinal chord. After spinal fluid leaked continuously from his nose, doctors performed surgery and implanted numerous plastic bolts to stabilize his spine, leaving him in a state of permanent physical disability and pain.

As Clooney learned, it's bad enough to make fun of Charlton Heston, but it's much worse to make fun of Moses. For his attacks on Heston, for his deteriorating spinal condition, for the refusal of insurance companies to cover him, and for his phony self-serving platitudes on the genocide in Darfur, Sudan, the American Cinematheque granted George Clooney an award for, apparently, just being George Clooney.

Clooney and his lunatic fringe behavior have their philosophical counterparts that can be traced back to Hollywood's silent era. But his misguided social/sexual/political agenda operating in today's Hollywood is the natural evolution of the liberal Communist adulation that swayed a large part of Hollywood for more than twenty-five years and maintains a sentimental sympathy among Hollywood's current New Left.

The very term "Left" comes from Karl Marx himself, the founder of Communism. In the late 1840s, Marx was associated with a group of "revolutionaries" who were living in Paris. They referred to themselves as Hagelins, or "The Left" as they preferred to be known.

As Hollywood actively tries to whitewash the dark period between 1930 and 1955, a summary insight into the truth will open your eyes to the birth of Hollywood radicalism and its twisted allegiances to deviant, dark, and destructive causes that continue today with the intent to drag you into the snare of deception.

WELCOME TO THE PARTY

"Of all the arts, the cinema is the most important," Vladimir Lenin declared after he conquered Russia in 1917 and transformed the country into the first

Communist nation in the world.[3] The Hollywood film industry must have felt honored. It would be a quote they would never forget.

In the eyes of the young industry with an already over-inflated ego, somebody had arrived (certainly not elected) to create the perfect world, the perfect society—right here on earth—and Lenin declared how useful Hollywood could be in creating the new utopia where everybody would live in peace, harmony, and equality.

Forget that people working in the motion picture industry were "useful idiots" as Lenin was fond of saying. And forget that Lenin put into law the Nietzsche philosophical declaration that "God is dead."

Indeed, believing in God just might earn a Russian citizen the right to have a bullet shot into their head; if they were fortunate. Even worse, they might be spared with a one-way ticket to a far-away life-long vacation as guests of the Gulag Archipelago where "throwaway" citizens were worked to death. That really didn't matter to the people who worked in sunny Hollywood, California. The film industry would just go about their business of making movies while Lenin and his sidekick Joe Stalin did what they had to do in order to create Shangri-la.

Charlie Chaplin was all for Communism, so it couldn't be all that bad in the eyes of a growing number of sympathizers in Hollywood and the New York stage. "They say Communism may spread all over the world. I say so what?" proclaimed The Tramp almost twenty years after Stalin took power upon the death of Lenin in 1924.[4]

By the time of Chaplin's statement, more than 20 million people had perished during the brutal Russian Civil War, the forced famines, and political purges of the 1930s.[5] In little more than a decade, that number would more than double by the time of Stalin's death in 1953. Scholars estimate that between 40 and 50 million people died as a result of Joseph Stalin's actions and inactions.[6] But as Ed Asner said many years later, "Joe" was simply "misunderstood."

Charlie "The Tramp" Chaplin fled the United States in 1952 after being denied re-entry to America as he was returning from a trip to London. Chaplin's full support of the blood-thirsty Soviet Union was unwavering during the three and a half decades of starvation, massacres, political purges, terror killings, proxy wars, labor camp deaths, genocide, random mass murder, and even mass executions of Soviet war veterans. Chaplin couldn't turn his back on a country that "loved" him so much they even built a museum in his name. In other words, a tribute pay-off for his years of propaganda support.

Chaplin, who never became a citizen of the United States, railed bitterly against the country that gave him the freedom of opportunity to achieve wealth and fame. Chaplin, like so many effete and pompous actors, forgot that millions of Americans bought a ticket to see every film he made and he failed to acknowledge their dedication.

The little hypocrite Tramp sailed to Switzerland, vowing never to return to America "even if Jesus Christ was president."[7] Chaplin did, however, manage a trip back to Hollywood twenty years later in 1972 to accept an honorary Oscar, despite the fact that Jesus Christ was not president. (Ironically, Chaplin died five years later on Christmas Day 1977.)

What happened in Hollywood during the three-decade reign of Joseph Stalin can best be described by the same quote Winston Churchill used to describe the Soviet Union itself in 1939 as "a riddle wrapped inside a mystery inside an enigma."

Nothing could be more important in the study of Hollywood's current radical occult fascination with the darker passages of life than to take a look back at the entertainment industry of the 1930s and 1940s. Though by no means was the entire industry under the spell, nevertheless, thousands of people employed on stage and screen embraced Communism either formally as a member or as a sympathetic fellow traveler.

To understand the warped hypocrisy of these individuals is key to understanding why Hollywood is still an industry of malcontents and low-estate misfits who often display a collective mindset. This peculiar collective Hollywood worldview is necessary in order to please the contemporary studio bosses, producers, directors, and casting agents who do the hiring and firing.

These major players are the High Priests of Perpetually Malevolent Malcontent, or PMM for short. Only now, the like-mindedness of the industry insiders is not blind loyalty to Communism, but rather a devoted loyalty to a neurotic hybrid New Age social/sexual/political agenda.

Those who share the dark philosophical identification with this far-left neurosis will not only get invited to both the Beverly Hills and Bel-Air cocktail parties, but they will be rewarded with lucrative production and casting deals. The difference between "then" and "now" is the ownership and management of the entertainment industry corporations. Today's entertainment conglomerates not only share, but also shape, the thinking of the industry workers. That would be fine if the Hollywood entertainment leaders of today maintained deep-seated bedrock values that uplift and inspire instead of degrade and devour.

In the Communist adulation era, the management and the ownership of the studios originated from the classic American work ethic. They were a testament of the American dream and opportunities of a free-market economy. This mindset was different from the back-lot Hollywood studio employees who were experimenting with mind-bending politics that resembled drug addiction and held an attraction that actor Sterling Hayden once described as "occult-like."

Thousands of volumes, articles, studies, stories, speeches, and biographies have accumulated over the years in an attempt to chronicle this Hollywood era. More disturbing, until recently the history of this era was being constantly rewritten and reshaped by some of the very participants in the Hollycom movement with the full support and help of their contemporary admirers. The strategy has been evolving since the Hollywood Communist era came to an end more than fifty years ago. "Their" script is an attempt to recast the players as "victims" of a "witch hunt" by the big bad U.S. government intent on squashing the First Amendment rights of Hollywood.

Fortunately, the elevated absurdity of this hysterical revisionism was discovered by Kenneth Lloyd Billingsley, editorial director of the Pacific Research Institute, who sat through the ultimate Hollywood propaganda stage retrospect. The occasion was the fiftieth anniversary of the House Committee on Un-American Activities (HCUA) hearings on Communist infiltration of the motion picture industry. It was a multi-media extravaganza titled "Hollywood Remembers the Blacklist" held on October 27, 1997, at the Motion Picture Academy of Arts and Sciences theater and produced by the major show business guilds and backed by the Association of Motion Picture and Television Producers.

As Billingsley observed, after the revisionist production was over, "Fiftieth anniversaries tend to be the last celebrated, and the audience got the feeling that this show intended to be the final, authoritative, and above all official entertainment industry last word.

"What the show revealed was interesting, but what it concealed was crucial, and no one knew that better than those who had performed so convincingly onstage. When the carefully contrived emotional payoff had faded, even casual observers could not help noticing that something was missing. As they moved out onto Wilshire Boulevard, many people knew full well that what they had seen was full of secret passageways and escape hatches and gaps vast enough to swallow entire decades."[8]

This rewriting of history was and continues to be an amazing display of creativity from a community that earns its living by writing and producing fantasy. Billingsley proceeded to write the consummate "correction" of Hollywood revisionism and filled in the "gaps vast enough to swallow entire decades."

Within a year of the industry production "honoring" the members of the "Blacklist," Billingsley published *Hollywood Party: How Communism Seduced the American Film Industry in the 1930s and 1940s*. The highly informative and well-researched book should be required reading for anyone interested in Hollywood's ability to twist the truth and its inability to separate fact from fiction.

Part of the fraudulent rewriting of the Hollywood period by sympathetic authors, past and present, summarily portray the Hollywood creative industry insiders as persecuted victims by the U.S. Congress under Senator Joseph McCarthy. The "persecuted" included former members, then-current members and fellow travelers of the Communist Party (CP) who were "blacklisted" *by the government* from ever working again. All of this, supposedly, began and ended with the actions of the House Committee on Un-American Activities (HCUA).

The very name of the acronym was changed by Communist sympathizers to give the committee a pronounceable yet provocative Big-Brother spin known as "HUAC" for *House Un-American Activities Committee.* This was not the name of the committee and HUAC does not stand for anything other than another footnote victory by the sympathetic revisionists.

The whole freedom of speech breach and *government* "blacklist" was and remains one of Hollywood's most clever retelling and whitewashing of the true extent and intent of Communist involvement in the movie industry. The Hollywood argument is basically another industry lie of mythic proportions.

The HCUA was actually created in 1938 by an act of Congress and was originally chaired by Texas Democrat Morton Dies to investigate subversive groups that may have been inclined to initiate the violent overthrow of the U.S. government. This was precipitated largely by the emergence of pro-Nazi groups in America.

The sight of American protestors being beaten by Nazi "guards" would become a little too much for a free America to stomach, especially since the beatings took place at Madison Square Garden in New York City. As for Joseph McCarthy, he was not even elected as a senator until 1946, fully eight years after the formation of the HCUA. And then, he concentrated his investigations on the Washington federal government power establishment—not Hollywood.

What the Hollywood revisionists fail to explain in their constantly evolving script of "stolen freedom" is the constitutional prohibition against the violent overthrow of the United States government. The Communist ideology is *all about violence*, preferring violent "revolution" as the method of choice to invoke societal change.

Not wanting to alienate mainstream America by bringing this central theme of the Communist Manifesto to light, the Hollywood Communists and fellow travelers had to paint America as the "bad guy" like some despicable character in a low-budget script. For this reason, the Hollycoms came to invent the now famous terms "Red scare," "anti-Communist hysteria," "witch hunt," "McCarthyism," "McCarthyite," "McCarthy Era," and many more.

As for the most commonly butchered term, "blacklist," Billingsley explains, "Though it was the industry, not the government, that blacklisted writers and performers, the blacklist legend allowed studios to pose as victims, themselves, a cover-up too intoxicating to pass up."[9]

And not only were studio bosses and management engaged in blacklisting their own employees, a much larger blacklisting campaign was being carried out by Communist Party front organizations that were battling for control of Hollywood's vast network of film unions. These shadowy organizations would call for nationwide *boycotts* of films made by writers, directors, and actors who dared to cross Communists-backed picket lines or refused to support their "cause." In other words, the Communists themselves, were among the most prolific blacklisters.

The June 15, 1945 headline of the *Hollywood Studio Union News* blared out in bold black letters, "Stars Face Blacklist: 51 Movie Greats Risk Strikers' Wrath if They Go On Shooting." This was a time when nobody in Hollywood ever heard the name Joe McCarthy, because he was finishing up his wartime duties as a tail-gunner.

One such Communist Party front group was the Conference of Studio Unions (CSU), which, as Billingsley explains, "openly blacklisted actors and actresses, no matter how famous, who crossed [CSU] picket lines to work."[10] Among those actors and actresses were Rosalind Russell, Robert Montgomery, John Wayne, Lucille Ball, Van Johnson, Clark Gable, Maureen O'Hara, Bette Davis, Humphrey Bogart, and Barbara Stanwyck.

The CSU and its supportive unions told their members nationwide to boycott films in which these stars appeared, especially since they weren't "Red" stars. These are the *real* blacklists the revisionists don't want you to know about.

By the 1940s, the HCUA began to focus on Communist influence into American institutions in addition to Nazi influence. The committee soon discovered an incredible amount of CP members, front groups, and fellow travelers embedded throughout the entertainment industry. This was also confirmed by the California Joint Fact Finding Committee on Un-American Activities headed by former Leftist and sympathizer State Senator Jack Tenny.

The HCUA began to focus on two areas of concern regarding the Communist presence in Hollywood:

1. *Communists were rumored to be planting subversive messages into Hollywood films, and*
2. *Communists were discriminating against unsympathetic colleagues in the industry guilds and labor unions.*

There was plenty of truth in both areas of focus. But the domination of Communists and fellow travelers in the labor unions and their increased violent strategy to take control of the unions from anti-Communist liberals drew the sharpest attention and calls for action.

THE SEEDS TAKE ROOT

The infiltration and infatuation by Communists into the entertainment industry entered both coasts at about the same time. The rabid Communist V. J. Jerome was considered the Communist cultural commissar of the New York theater stage scene. With the headquarters of the Communist Party USA located in New York City, Jerome was in a good position to radically influence stage production content.

Before CP front groups began to take on more patriotic sounding names in the 1940s, to deceive the public, the 1930s was peppered with front groups designed to influence varying segments of society. Jerome was head of the not-so-subtly named National Agitation and Propaganda Commission. And despite that "agitating" title, Jerome managed to apply for and receive grants from the U.S. funded Federal Theater Project, a New Deal program that generously funded cultural projects.

According to Jerome's mission and vision for the performing arts, the powerful dramatic setting of the stage was a perfect weapon and plays would be staged to teach social lessons with a palatable, but no less revolutionary punch. Jerome believed that Western society at the time was corrupt to the core and beyond any repair or redemption by peaceful means. Jerome was a strict Stalinist up and down the board, and he maintained close ties to CP members who ran espionage and spy rings for the Soviet Union.[11]

Actors and stage workers desperate for work during the Depression had no problem embracing Communist ideology. Indeed, refusing to embrace Stalinistic Communism would most likely prevent employment under the undue influence being exerted by Jerome.

Some of the early Communist playwrights, directors, and actors would make the transition to Hollywood, such as Elia Kazan (*On the Waterfront, A Face in the Crowd, and A Streetcar Named Desire*). Kazan even taught classes at the New Theatre League, a CP front organization. Others making the transition were actors such as John Garfield, Phil Loeb, and many others.

The transition to Hollywood by former theater stars would also bring the Communist ideology. According to author Billingsley, "Federal Theater Director Adolph Hecht, who went on to work for the Goldstone [Talent] Agency in Hollywood, explained that party affiliation was a kind of political casting couch. If the choice came down to dismissing a Communist or non-Communist, he was expected to get rid of the non-Communists regardless of talent."[12]

A parallel to today's casting environment can be found in this highly selective process, minus talent. The Communist criteria for getting an acting part has now been replaced with the now familiar tri-lateral requirements of social/sexual/political correctness as the key detriment for prime acting roles. And homosexual orientation adds two points to the score.

Without a doubt, sexual orientation has replaced Communist affiliation on the Hollywood casting couch. Researchers Stanley Rothman and Amy Black conducted a poll that indicated almost eighty percent of Hollywood decision-makers agreed that homosexuality is an acceptable lifestyle.[13] And these are the individuals that are inserting their agendas into the popular entertainment culture with the intent on influencing social behavior, proving that sexual politics have replaced Communist politics as the Number One Hollywood priority. And V. J. Jerome, the cultural commissar from New York, planted the early seeds.

Jerome would eventually pack up for the left coast as Communist theater dwindled and film became the dominant medium. Others would also be descending on Hollywood, including Willi Münzenberg, the Soviet's special envoy to the Hollywood film industry who declared, "One of the most pressing tasks confronting the Communist Party in the field of propaganda is the conquest of this supremely important propaganda unit, until now the monopoly of the ruling class. We must wrest it from them and turn it against them."[14]

Münzenberg's "ambassador" to the film industry was Otto Katz, a dashing character who split his time in Hollywood between bedding starlets and recruiting new members for the Communist Party, sometimes conducting both tasks at the same time. Katz's fate, which will be described at the end of this chapter, is a classic example of the dark unbridled insanity of Hollywood affections and Communist affiliations.

By the time Jerome, Münzenberg, Katz, and others were arriving in Hollywood, during the 1930s, the fantasy image of a far-away utopia had already taken root in the hearts and minds of many in Hollywood, especially writers, directors, and a fair number of actors. Billingsley refers to the revisionists' efforts to rewrite the history of this period as "The Chronicle of Some Mythical Kingdom," quoting director Phillip Dunne.

Hollywood was awash with Communist organizations, sub-organizations, chapters, "special sections" within guilds, unions, talent agencies, and maintained at least fingertips in just about any group that conducted business with the Hollywood studios on a regular basis.

With innocent sounding names like Progressive Citizens of America, Conference of Studio Unions, the Screen Story Analysts Guild, and the American Veterans' Committee (AVC), these groups were propaganda stealth organizations pumping the party line into the movie industry. For many, especially writers and directors, there was not only hope, but an opportunity to squeeze their leftist message into the movie storyline for general public consumption.

One of the AVC's favorite speakers was the young actor Ronald Reagan, eager to fight the fascism that Hitler and Franco were unleashing on the world. As a member of the Screen Actors' Guild (SAG) board and its next president, Reagan showcased his superb speaking abilities on the AVC speaking circuit.

However, Reagan soon realized that the speeches written for him and the audiences he spoke to were not always of his own choosing. He also felt that he was being "steered" on more than one occasion. Billingsley describes one speech where he was given rousing applause until he passionately denounced Communism and the room fell instantly silent.[15]

Reagan had inserted some of his own beliefs into the speech "prepared" for him. Reagan realized he had been duped and soon discovered the CP influence in a multitude of other groups such as the Film Audiences for Democracy, Associated Film Audiences, and the Peoples' Federation Center. The most blatant and vocal of these front groups was the Hollywood Independent Citizens Council of the Arts, Sciences, and Professions (HICCAP) indicating that Hollywood was drowning in a Communist conspiracy of "alphabet soup groups." To say that the Communist influence in Hollywood was minimal at best is not only an understatement by the modern day revisionists, it is a blaring lie.

After Soviet Hollywood envoy Willi Münzenberg settled in Hollywood with more money and organizational instruction, the Communist liaison realized that the screenwriters and directors could have the most effect on spreading the Communist message through the medium of film. Among the CP favorites were some of the biggest names of their day such as Dalton Trumbo, Edward Dmytryk, Ring Lardner Jr., Budd Schulberg, and many others.

Screenwriter Ring Lardner Jr. had already been given a "guided" tour of the Soviet Union in 1934 and was fully convinced that heaven on earth was being created by benevolent comrade Joseph Stalin. Dalton Trumbo was not only a prolific fellow screenwriter, he also wrote speeches for many of the Communist front organization speakers.

This is when the HCUA concern "Number One" would delve its investigative arm; the belief that Communists were planting subversive messages into Hollywood's films. There were only a handful of Hollywood films that this trend could be found in, at least *overtly*. The most obvious film in this category was *Mission to Moscow*. However, there were other notable Party messages in films such as *North Star*, *Song of Russia*, and *Tender Comrade*, written by Trumbo himself and directed by Edward Dmytryk, two party faithfuls.

Where the party faithful and their fellow travelers exerted the most influence in this area was *covertly* by following CP instructions of subtle incrementalism and following an artistic Hippocratic Oath to "First, Do No Harm," translated: Do no harm to the Communist cause.

Because of their influence in the Writer's Guild and working relationships with directors, this close knit group of Communists, headed by Trumbo, demanded to review all scripts being submitted for possible production. The key for Trumbo was to make sure there were no *anti*-Communist or *anti*-Soviet messages being written into films, a secret censorship by omission. These same radical writers and their contemporaries in Hollywood would grudgingly gripe about the "censorship" of the Production Code Administration (PCA), also known as the Hays Code.

This was the height of hypocrisy and deception in the Hollywood creative community, traits still present in today's jilted and jaded movie industry. These influential Communist screenwriters were rewriting the scripts of aspiring new writers on the film scene so as to maintain a squeaky-clean image of the CP line and maintain the divinity of Stalin and the new utopia.

Screenwriter Walter Berry admitted years later that he and director Robert Rossen would deliberately insert left-wing views into scenes of movies they collaborated on at Columbia. Harry Cohn, president of Columbia, would view the final cut, recognize the propaganda, and snip the scenes out.

More than influencing content, the congressional investigation began to realize the depth and numbers of Communist Party members in the entertainment industry and how they worked together as a "United Front" to push the party message to all corners of the industry and inevitably to community front groups. The Communists in Hollywood were among the most vicious, deceptive, and aggressive promoters of their dark doctrine in a town where being vicious was, and is, a virtue.

Again it was the Communists in Hollywood who invented the blacklist. If one didn't cooperate with the Hollycoms, a smear campaign would quickly follow. On the labor side, violence and threats of violence loomed at every corner.

The popular 1940s actor Adolphe Menjou was a liberal, but ardent anti-Communist who found himself the victim of a CP smear campaign when the party's inside machinery started a whisper campaign that Menjou was sympathetic to Hitler. As Billingsley noted, this was "an effective smear with Jewish producers, who would quickly put out the word to other producers. Such actors found themselves out of favor but never knew what hit them."

This smear tactic was particularly ironic given the fact that the Hollycoms remained faithful to the Communist Party even when Stalin and Hitler signed a Pact of cooperation in 1939, which only lasted two years due to Hitler's invasion of his "peace partner" in the Soviet Union.

As easily as the Hollycoms could be vicious and deceitful, they were equally adept at the clever back-handed art of welcoming new talent to Hollywood. Newcomers to Hollywood who faced difficulty in finding work were welcomed with gracious handshaking, dinner invitations, and ultimately, invitations to the Communist Party.

The Hollycoms promoted newcomers with the old favorite seductions of Hollywood as a land of glamour and sex. When newcomer Marc Lawrence joined the CP in hopes of getting new roles, fellow actor Lionel Stander told Lawrence quite frankly that "you will make out more with the dames."[16]

Ring Lardner Jr., the Communist screenwriter who would eventually be known as one of "The Hollywood Ten," even went so far as to pen the Hollycom recruiting slogan, "The Most Beautiful Girls in Hollywood Belong to the Communist Party." Not too original but it apparently worked for some.

As an indicator of this period in Hollywood as the root of future entertainment industry radicalism and "New Age open-mindedness," veteran film critic Pauline

Kael observed that "When Stalinism was fashionable, movie people became Stalinists the way they later became witches and warlocks."[17]

One of the HCUA committee's findings was again the subtle message of the Communist Party. One very strict taboo discovered by the HCUA was the command by CP enforcers that businessmen were not to be shown in a positive light whenever possible."[18]

This is a taboo that appears to have survived and manifests itself today as Hollywood screenwriters and directors continue to demonize businessmen and women as wretched characters, or, in their minds, "capitalist pigs." The demonization treatment today is even extended largely to depictions of families, marriage, ministers, the military, and especially actors portraying Republican politicians.

The HCUA's concern "Number Two" was the creeping Communist discrimination against unsympathetic colleagues in the industry guilds and labor unions where CP influence was dominant. Much of that concern overlapped with the first concern of the committee about "subversive messages." Discrimination through favoritism and threats of smears have been covered in the previous pages, at least as it manifested in the studio creative guilds. These same tactics were more brutal in the industry labor battles where fear, intimidation, and violence were common.

Today's radical Hollywood took its cues from Hollywood Communists and routinely smears not only fellow members of their own industry, but anyone in America who doesn't agree with their private agendas. Those who engage in private and public smears include Sean Penn, Johnny Depp, George Clooney, Alec Baldwin, Chris Rock, Bill Maher, Rosie O'Donnell, Oliver Stone, Whoopi Goldberg, Matt Damon, Tim Robbins, and literally hundreds of others on both sides of the camera.

The events surrounding the infighting among Hollywood labor unions and Communist Party infiltration drew the most attention, and the resulting violence inevitably led the HCUA to hold the now famous hearings of 1947 and 1951. A brief review of the back lot Communist maneuvers in 1945 and 1946 will show how the tyrannical Hollycoms became their own worst enemy.

The myriad film unions directly had their hands full dealing with jurisdictional infighting, splintering, and the usual demands and concessions between management and labor. On top of these disputes, the back lot labor unions constantly wrestled with organized crime and gangster interference within their ranks. Added to this already volatile mix were the almost demonic attacks and infiltration by Communists, and the back lot pot heated above and beyond the boiling point.

Against this complex backdrop, two major figures emerged that came to represent the film labor unions led by Roy Brewer on one side, and the aggressive and violent tactics of the Communists on the other side headed by Herb Sorrell.

The International Theater and Stage Employees, better known as the IA, was the umbrella organization for many Hollywood Unions, and remains so today. In 1945, Brewer was appointed as the IA's new representative negotiator in Hollywood. The young union projectionist from Nebraska had a good reputation for being both an honest and fair labor negotiator, a rare trait in the rough and tumble world of Hollywood labor. Brewer was about to enter the fight of his life and take center stage in the struggle against Communist infiltration of the film unions and their radical plan to gain control over all union dues.

The rumpled, unshaven Sorrell was planning at this time to negotiate new contracts for his newly formed Communist-dominated Set Decorators Union on behalf of the larger Communist-dominated Conference of Studio Unions (CSU). The CSU and the IA were about to clash over contractual negotiations with the studios, and the clash would bring to light just how deeply and violently the Communists had infiltrated almost every layer of the entertainment industry.

Among the first wave of assaults by Sorrell would target Disney's labor and animators at the Burbank studio. Sorrell threatened Walt Disney himself, saying, "I will smear you and I will make a dust bowl out of your plant."[19] Disney would later recall the threat verbatim at the HCUA hearings.

In March 1945, the CSU under Sorrell's leadership, turned up the heat to fever pitch by calling for a walkout of its members unless the studios negotiated with him instead of "the hayseed lunch bucket" from Nebraska, as Sorrell and others referred to Roy Brewer. Hollywood's condescending contempt for middle-Americans in "fly-over" country had its roots in the likes of Sorrell and other left-wing malcontents.

When the major studios refused to negotiate with the Communists, Sorrell soon decided to call for strikes at all studios, including the B-film studios known as Poverty Row. More devastating, he would also call for strikes at the film processing labs such as Technicolor. If film couldn't be processed and duplicated, there would be no movies released into theaters.

As Billingsley explains this tense period, the royal studio moguls who often expected royal treatment from their subordinates as they exercised authority from their lofty offices, were humbling themselves by picking up the phone and calling Roy Brewer personally. Their dire hope was that the "rustic" union man from Nebraska could fill in the rapidly decreasing labor force with skilled technicians. Unskilled labor would only botch the entire moviemaking system.

Brewer became an overnight sensation for filling thousands of positions, restructuring sub-unions, pulling charters of others, and by doing so, managed to keep the studios running, all without raising his voice or inciting a single violent act.

By 1946, Sorrell was planning all-out attacks with picket lines and threats of violence. He had already told Communist union faithful around the country to boycott over fifty films, and Sorrell proceeded to smear and *blacklist* hundreds of actors and directors. With his brass knuckles polished for another blood fest, this time Sorrell indicated that some men "might die."

This is the romantic First Amendment-loving Communists that Hollywood lionizes to this day for their great "courage."

REAGAN RISING

Roy Brewer was working overtime and around the clock to keep the studios running while Sorrell was corralling over 9,000 union members for "combat duty." The strikes started with violence outside the MGM studio in Culver City where blood would spill on the streets. Very shortly violence was raging at every Hollywood studio. Herb Sorrell donned his brass knuckles and took great joy in breaking jaws and beating anyone who crossed picket lines.

Even with his carefully organized intelligence network, Brewer was finding it increasingly difficult to keep ahead of Sorrell's snake-infested network. But Brewer's reputation as the level-headed negotiator from the IA was gaining him allies among studio management and labor. One of Brewer's newest and strongest allies would be liberal Democrat Ronald Reagan.

During the 1946 studio strikes, Sorrell's men were smashing automobiles, dragging people out of cars and beating them with pipes, and threatening even more workers and actors. Sorrell was pumped up with his own ego and Communist encouragement from the party faithful. At a meeting of the American Federation of Labor, Sorrell ran into Ronald Reagan and boasted that when all was said an done, "There'll be only one man running labor in Hollywood and that man will be me!"[20]

Sorrell's biggest mistake, not only for himself but for the entire Communist Party, was to threaten Ronald Reagan with a facial bath of acid.[21] Reagan, who was serving at this time as president of the Screen Actors Guild, was working with anti-Communist groups to negotiate contracts with the studios. The acid threat was a major turning point for Reagan who would later cite the incident as the catalyst for his conversion from a Hollywood liberal to a conservative Republican. The news of the acid threat made the rounds at the Hollywood studios and people began to see the true face of the Communists in their midst.

Forty years later, President of the United States Ronald Reagan would be the driving force behind the collapse of European and Soviet Communism. By that time, the name of Herb Sorrell was forgotten by almost everybody except President Ronald Reagan.

As Roy Brewer continued filling slots left vacant by strikes, the pickets began to lose steam as their incomes dropped off and court injunctions picked up. Hundreds were arrested and their trials upheld. CSU members began to go back to work, crossing their own picket lines. The Conference of Studio Unions began to weaken and the Communist battle for the back lots was lost. Roy Brewer, the former Nebraska theater projectionist was now the most famous man in Hollywood.

And the focus would soon shift to Washington in 1947 where the first of many hearings would be held on Communist influence in Hollywood. With nine newsreel cameras running throughout the sessions, the often raucous hearings would highlight for American audiences the belligerent Hollycoms at their worst.

The contemporary revisionists and sympathizers in Hollywood began to refer to these hearings as witch hunts. Fellow traveler Arthur Miller would write a play at this time called *The Crucible*, which was meant as a parody of the hearings with the Salem witch hunts of the 1600s as a backdrop. A movie version of the play was produced more than fifty years later and proved to be a major Hollywood flop.

As director Elia Kazan's wife Molly once said, "Those witches did not exist: Communists do."

SHOWTIME IN WASHINGTON

The House Committee on Un-American Activities (HCUA) had been a standing committee in the Congress investigating subversive activity across America since 1938. The specter of undue Communist influence in the motion picture industry took center stage from 1947 on and lasted well into the early 1950s.

Many in the movie industry were looking forward to testifying, with the hard-core Left looking for a confrontation. As Billingsley described this period, many of the heavyweights "longed for a showdown with the hated Committee, a phenomenon Norman Mailer dubbed 'subpoena envy.'"

The HCUA selected forty-five film industry individuals of various political leanings for testimony. Being a Communist was not against the law. The Communist Party, after all, had maintained its headquarters in New York City on 12th Street for two decades.

What was against the law, and remains so today, is the violent overthrow of the United States government. Whether the Hollycoms or their fellow travelers ever advocated such a move could never be fully ascertained. Nonetheless, many did not want to answer questions about their political associations, citing First Amendment freedom of speech and association. This would become the hallmark defense of the first wave of trials in 1947.

Many opponents of the Hollycoms saw this slithering under the rock of the First Amendment as a convenient cop-out and turtle shell cover for the morally bankrupt political philosophy for which they shamefully could not defend in good conscience. Contrary to sympathetic revisionists, nobody inside or outside the government advocated the "suspension" of the First Amendment.

In fact, one HCUA committee member even asked at the outset, for clarification, if the Communist Party USA should be outlawed. It was then purposely not acted upon because the House of Representatives believed wholly in the First Amendment and freedom of speech and association. But the question of Communist Party legality sparked some of the most colorful testimony from the movie industry itself.

Of the forty-five individuals selected, nineteen indicated that they would not cooperate. This group became known as "the unfriendly nineteen," including the far left Communists like Dalton Trumbo, Ring Lardner Jr., Bertolt Brecht, Albert Maltz, and Waldo Salt. Veteran director Billy Wilder made the famous quip that only a few were talented and the rest were simply unfriendly. Among the "friendly" testifiers were Walt Disney, who told the committee about the smear campaign and threats against his company by brass-knuckled Communist front labor leader Herb Sorrell. Louis B. Mayer of MGM, the highest paid man in America, attacked Communism with a vengeance.

Jack Warner gave the famous termite-Communist analogy testimony. "Ideological termites have burrowed into many American industries, organizations, and societies . . . . Wherever they may be, I say let us dig them out and get rid of them. My brother and I will be happy to subscribe to a pest-removal fund."[22] (Ironically, this is the same Jack Warner that twenty years later would be counted among the Gang of Four and the Quiet Conspiracy to destroy the Production Code and unleash truly dark cultural termites from which Hollywood and the American culture have never fully recovered.)

Actor Robert Montgomery gave one of the most impressive speeches against the Hollycoms, which he said had been present in the talent guilds since 1933. "I consider the German American Bund (Nazis) a subversive group."[23] He then proceeded to lambast the Communists. Ronald Reagan testified that as much as he disliked Communism, he did not believe the CP should be banned, saying, "I still think democracy can do it."[24]

Director Leo McCarey made one of the most central points of contention about Communism that was never fully explored by the committee, the press, or commentators of the day. Unlike the Soviet Communist system, which not only banned the belief in God, but was continuously demolishing cathedrals and churches with thunderous demolitions, the U.S. Constitution expressly allows for the free expression of religion.

McCarey's two most popular film classics starred Bing Crosby in *Going My Way* and *The Bells of St. Mary's*. McCarey said the Communists had objected to a character in both films.

"Bing Crosby?" asked Congressman Robert Stripling.

"No, . . . God," replied McCarey.

Parnell Thomas, the cigar-chomping gavel-banging chairman of the HCUA, asked McCarey if he believed the Communist Party should be outlawed. "I certainly do," replied McCarey, "and I hope something is done about it because at this time it is a very dangerous thing."[25]

For the first time, the American moviegoing public was given a first-hand peek into the motivations and operations of people working for the film industry. What the public saw was an industry that was either highly secular in nature or even atheistic at its core. While many in the American public had referred to Hollywood as the modern Babylon as far back as early silent days, the revelation of so many industry insiders as followers of "the Godless ideology" of Communism came as a shock.

The HCUA was itself shocked to uncover the fact that as many as 300 Communists belonged to the Hollywood talent guilds alone, not to mention hundreds more on the back lots and a sizable number of members in the Los Angeles branch of the Communist Party.

* * *

This would give credence to the HCUA's second major concern in holding the hearings: discrimination against unsympathetic colleagues. The political casting couch made famous in the Communist theater groups in New York had taken on a much larger role in Hollywood.

Veteran actor Adolphe Menjou, who had been smeared by Communists inside the industry, told the committee, "We have in California what I call a lunatic fringe, the political idiots, the morons, the dangerous Communists, and those who have yet to be convinced." And Menjou had no problem blasting Stalin, whom he readily compared to Al Capone on a major scale. "He committed the murders and then killed the witnesses."[26]

Unfortunately, one of the most effective witnesses could not testify because she was in an asylum after suffering a series of nervous breakdowns brought on largely by constant harassment from the Hollycoms. She would not appear again on the public scene until late 1950.

In her 1972 biography, *Will There Be a Morning*? Frances Farmer wrote quite openly about her scorn for the card-carrying Communists who she recalled "lied through their teeth," referring to the "nineteen unfriendly" witnesses. Farmer added, "I would have no doubt provided the rope to hang many of the industry's luminaries." The 1982 movie *Frances*, starring Jessica Lange, was one of the early screen attempts to rewrite this period of manipulative Communist influence in Hollywood, which was the first step to later rewriting the HCUA hearings as "anti-Communist hysteria" and then reinvent the past as "The Chronicle of Some Mythical Kingdom."

Nowhere in the movie *Frances* is there given a portrait of the headstrong actress as she very directly rejected the Soviet Union as a dead nation on life support. And any viewers of the "biography" will not see the relentless pressure exerted as Hollywood Communists blacklisted her from working. Again that's Hollywood Communists who blacklisted her from working. The tactics of the Hollycoms became a major contributing factor to her breakdown. And then Jessica Lange comes along more than thirty years later to abuse her again by participating in the whitewash.

After the 1947 HCUA hearings began with mainly "friendly" testimony from industry leaders, the "nineteen unfriendlies" gave their testimony, and true to their word, they remained defiant and obstinate. Dalton Trumbo, the most virulent pro-Stalinist of the group, would not admit if he was even a member of the Screen Writers Guild, much less admit being a member of the Communist Party.

Trumbo began a tirade against the committee and screamed out, "This is the beginning of an American concentration camp," as he was lead away to the now famous banging of Chairman Parnell's gavel seen in the grainy black and white film footage of the day. Trumbo's rather bizarre outburst was an allusion to Nazi concentration camps, not to his beloved Soviet leader's labor camps where hundreds of thousands had perished and would continue to perish long after Stalin's death in 1953.

Playwright Bertolt Brecht was also called to testify. Brecht, one of the most ideologically brutal individuals among the Communists, was a friend of the New York cultural commissar V. J. Jerome, the Communist theater producer who believed drama should be a "weapon." Brecht at this time had become infamous for his commentary about the massacres and purges in the Soviet Union, for which he observed, "The more innocent they are, the more they deserve to be shot."[27]

Eventually, the "nineteen unfriendlies" were whittled down to eleven, and then to ten after the monstrous Brecht fled to East Germany to join his comrades in the Cold War against the West. The group that was about to be immortalized as "The Hollywood Eleven" officially became "The Hollywood Ten."

In November 1947, HCUA Chairman Parnell Thomas held a special session in the House concerning the need for funds to stop Stalin's expansion in Europe. At the same session, in a fit manner of timing, Thomas asked for a citation of contempt against one of the ten, Albert Maltz, for his refusal to answer questions. The vote in favor of contempt was one of the biggest landslide votes in U.S. congressional history, 346 to 17. The nine others were also charged with contempt and received similar landslide votes of support.

As author Billingsley wrote, "In the last speech before the vote, Congressman Richard M. Nixon said that the only two relevant issues were whether the Committee had the right to ask questions and whether the witnesses had refused to answer such questions."[28] That statement, to determine the enduring legitimacy of the vote, would forever seal leftist Hollywood's hatred for Nixon.

Before the beginning of the 1947 hearings, Director John Huston formed a group of Hollywood heavyweights to lend support to all individuals testifying. Members of the Committee for the First Amendment included Frederic March, Charles Boyer, Judy Garland, Groucho Marx, Gregory Peck, William Holden, Lucille Ball, Sterling Hayden, Burt Lancaster, Frank Sinatra, Edward G. Robinson, Joseph Cotten, Humphrey Bogart, Lauren Bacall, John Garfield, Danny Kaye, and Gene Kelly.

Huston decided to send twenty-nine members of the group to Washington, D.C., where they would give news conferences offering rousing support for their Hollywood colleagues. But cracks in the Committee for the First Amendment would appear before the last bang of the gavel. During the hearing, a newspaper reported that Sterling Hayden was a former member of the Communist Party.

Hayden responded by telling the HCUA, "I had become susceptible to and, in a sense perhaps, a victim of the idea that they had a form of democracy in mind." And in a revelation of the dark power the Communists used in Hollywood and elsewhere, Hayden added, "I found the belief is that they have the key, by some occult power, to know what is best for people, and that is the way it is going to be . . . . I decided to get out and I got out."[29]

The revelation about Hayden and the vulgar performances of the unfriendly witnesses had stretched the limits of Bogart's already short temper. He confronted Danny Kaye later and shouted, "You f____ s sold me out!" Bogart was not alone in his feelings and many former supporters began to fade away.

THE BLACKLIST MYTH

Matters for The Hollywood Ten were about to get much worse. Shortly before the contempt citations, the studio moguls had gathered quietly at the Waldorf-Astoria in New York and issued a public statement for release to the press after the contempt citations were handed down, declaring, "Members of the Association of Motion Picture Producers deplore the actions of the ten Hollywood men who have been cited for contempt by the House of Representatives . . . We will forthwith discharge and suspend without compensation those in our employ and of the ten until such time as he is acquitted or has purged himself of contempt and declares under oath that he is not a Communist."[30]

The statement proceeded to declare, "We will not knowingly employ a Communist or a member of any party or group which advocates the overthrow of the government of the United States by force or by any illegal or unconstitutional methods." And with that statement, Hollywood began another in a long line of blacklists, a method invented by and used by the Communist dominated labor unions against "unfriendly" actors and directors and soon employed by the studio moguls themselves—not the U.S. government.

The contemporary myth, aided over the years by the surviving and then dying Hollywood ten and their sympathizers, would paint the now famous scenario that Joseph McCarthy chaired the HCUA hearings, compiled a little black book of Hollywood Communist insiders, and finally passed a law that forced the studios to refrain from hiring anybody on that list. That scenario and anything vaguely resembling it is a complete and well-orchestrated lie that only Hollywood could concoct. The very rewriting of history shows the Orwellian nature of the entertainment industry; those who control the past control the future.

Joseph McCarthy was a *Senator* and not a *House* congressman. McCarthy had no interest in Hollywood and concentrated his investigations solely on the Washington power establishment. But the revisionists count on the short memory, or no memory, of the moviegoing audience. And those historical revisionist wizards proceeded to transfer the ghost of Joseph McCarthy into a setting for which he never sat.

The revisionists then invented creative terminology to make the linkage believable like "witch hunt," "Red scare," and the ever popular Hollywood favorite, "McCarthyism."

Bogart's famous "sold out" statement would be the understatement of the entire HCUA period from 1947 to 1953. Before the next major hearing on Communist influence in Hollywood began in 1951, the cultural, political, and social atmosphere around the globe had changed so dramatically that any attempt to cling to the fictional kingdom of a Soviet heaven on earth would indicate a severe case of blind ignorance, hopeless neurosis, cowardice, or the uncompromised darkened heart and occult worship of Joseph Stalin as God.

In 1948, former high-profile Communist leader Arthur Koestler wrote *The God That Failed* in which he described the Communist journey as a virtual religion that promised utopia and ended as a road to hell scattered with bodies of the dead. In that same year, theater box office ticket sales sank dramatically. Hollywood was not looking forward to another round of investigations that would certainly expose more of the dark underbelly of the entertainment industry.

Also in 1948, the Berlin Blockade began with Joseph Stalin attempting to literally starve the free citizens of West Berlin to death, prompting Truman to order an airlift of food and supplies. Churchill had already made his famous Iron Curtain speech in Fulton, Missouri, revealing that Stalin was aggressively imposing his man-eating "utopia" on the eastern nations of Europe after the end of World War II. Executions were rampant, especially in Poland and in Czechoslovakia.

The fearful prospect of a nuclear winter or atomic Armageddon began promptly on September 27, 1949, as Joseph Stalin, the world's most notorious mass murderer of all human history, exploded an atomic bomb. This was accomplished by secrets stolen from the U.S. and Britain by Communist spies such as Klaus Fuchs, Harold Gold, and the Rosenbergs.

An even bigger bomb was the overthrow of China in the same year by Stalinist devotee Mao Tse Tung, who would surpass Stalin as the earth's worst mass murderer. The two world-class butchers would appear together in the now famous photograph of Stalin's seventieth birthday party.

The following year, in June 1950, North Korea's Stalin-hugging dictator invaded South Korea with the full support of Stalin and Mao. The war claimed the lives of over 50,000 Americans and tens of thousands of democratic allies. To this day, the war has never been officially declared over with only a tense armistice in place and North Korea now controlled by the mentally ill Kim Jong Il, the failed former filmmaker who passes time by watching Hollywood movies, pornography, drinking Johnny Walker, and raping young children. In 2006, he found the spare time to test a nuclear bomb.

Throughout the colossal events of 1948 to 1950, the Hollywood Ten remained defiant and appealed their convictions all the way to the Supreme Court, which upheld the contempt sentences. The Hollywood Ten behaved like beasts of burden with blinders on, unable to see the reality that was encroaching from all sides.

The Hollycoms blindly denied or defended the atrocities of Soviet Communism and more, including the Moscow show trials where thousands perished, the five million dead farmers in the Ukraine, the Soviet's pact with Hitler, the invasion of Finland, the execution of Jewish Communists, the Soviet massacre of every officer in the Polish army, the mass execution of former Soviet POWs, and the slave labor camps where people were worked to death.

The Hollywood Communists carried the CP's dirty water all the way to the bitter end. As Billingsley wrote in *Hollywood Party*, the Hollywood Communists continued to sing the praises of Stalin and "did all this while earning a good living, substantial fortunes in some cases, in the very country they attacked as repressive and fascist."[31] Sound familiar?

* * *

The 1951 hearings did not parade the theatrics of the 1947 hearings, but the questions asked would provide a new dilemma for witnesses. Committee members would again question Hollywood insiders about their Communist Party affiliations, but they would also ask witnesses to name other individuals whom they knew to be members of the Communist Party.

Some had no problem with providing the Committee with names, usually individuals whose Communist association was no longer a secret. Others, including most of the Hollywood Ten, refused any such overtures. Whereas the 1947 witnesses claimed *First* Amendment and freedom of expression protection, the 1951 witnesses relied on the *Fifth* Amendment protection against self-incrimination.

One of two major bombshells that would explode during the 1951 hearings was the testimony of director Edward Dmytryk. One of the original "Hollywood Ten," Dmytryk had second thoughts as international events had unfolded in the previous few years, especially the invasion of South Korea and particularly the open testimony of the famous American actor-singer and Communist activist Paul Robeson.

Robeson declared that he would not fight for the U.S. if a conflict ever arose between the Soviet Union and the United States. Especially disturbing to Dmytryk was the fact that Stalin had not only tortured and murdered Robeson's best friends in Russia, he was on another gruesome persecution and killing spree that included Russia's most talented entertainers, writers, and poets.

Robeson, perhaps one of the brightest men of the twentieth century, fluent in twelve languages, the arts, cinema, song, and a star athlete who excelled in football, baseball, track, and basketball, was also becoming known as the Soviet's biggest dupe and absolutely the most "useful idiot" as Lenin might have dubbed him. At Stalin's death, Robeson praised the mass murderer for his "wise understanding" and "deep humanity."

His blind devotion and the increasing violent expansion of Soviet Communism disgusted Dmytryk who arranged a meeting with Ronald Reagan and IA union veteran Roy Brewer. Dmytryk had decided to publicly oppose and expose the Communist Party, and did so in an article titled, "What Makes a Hollywood Communist?" which was published on May 19, 1951, in *The Saturday Evening Post*.

Dmytryk became a target of smear campaigns by the hard-core Communists who could not see the writing on the wall. Dmytryk and other friendly witnesses were being peppered with catcalls and insults such as "stool pigeons," "singing canaries," and "snitch."

By 1952, the second most explosive testimony came from one of Hollywood's most acclaimed and talented directors of all time, Elia Kazan, whose films included *Streetcar Named Desire, On the Waterfront, Gentleman's Agreement,* and *A Face in the Crowd*. Though not one of the original Hollywood Ten, Kazan had been a Communist in his earlier days and was under heavy pressure from the Hollycoms not to cooperate. But Kazan was fed up and had enough intimidation from the liberal left occult stranglehold of the increasingly blind Communist community in Hollywood. As Kazan said at the time, "I had enough regimentation, enough of being told what to think and say and do, enough of their habitual violation of the daily practices of democracy to which I was accustomed."[32]

The remainder of the HCUA hearings brought out a who's who from the Hollywood Communist heyday. V. J. Jerome, the cultural commissar famous for his "theater as weapon" dictate, would appear at the later hearings, but remained evasive and eventually faded into the obscurity of "has-been Communists."

Herb Sorrell, the scruffy brass-knuckle-wielding leader of the Conference of Studio Unions, would also appear and give a confusing speech that dropped his credibility and cost him his union leadership position. Sorrell "found God" shortly after this period, which effectively made him "persona non grata" among the heathen Communists.

Sorrell returned to painting houses around Los Angeles and died in 1971. He didn't live long enough to witness fully the effects of his acid-throwing threat against Ronald Reagan. Largely because of Sorrell, Reagan became a Republican, was twice elected President of the United States, and crusaded wholeheartedly for an end to Soviet Communism, which he witnessed between 1989 and 1991.

Otto Katz, the dashing young cultural ambassador who recruited members for the Communist Party both in and out of bed, could not be called to testify due to the fact that his body had assumed room temperature in 1952. Katz had joined the Communist Czech government and was brutally tortured and eventually executed during one of Stalin's many nervous breakdowns (read: purges).

As Ronald Radosh and Allis Radosh wrote in *Red Star Over Hollywood*, "A loyal communist to the end, he was accused of being a 'Jewish bourgeois nationalist and spy.'"[34] Lillian Hellman, the fellow Communist writer with whom he had an affair, knew he was innocent, but kept silent. It was becoming obvious that the Hollycoms were a sanctimonious group of ungrateful hypocritical sadomasochists. In other words, fair weather friends.

Though only a year away from his death in 1953, Stalin lived long enough to see the CP crumble in Hollywood. A big fan of Hollywood gangster films, naturally, Stalin had been kept apprised of Communist activity in Hollywood and no doubt got a good chuckle out of his "useful idiots" putting a pretty face on his non-stop slaughter of human civilization.

Stalin was, however, disappointed that some of his orders fell through the cracks such as the planned "assassination" of John Wayne for the actor's ardent and vocal opposition to Communism.[35] Pete Seeger, the popular songwriter of 1960s hits "If I Had a Hammer" and "Where Have All the Flowers Gone," left the Communist Party in 1950 and apologized long ago for not realizing the despot that Stalin was. In 2007, at age 88, Seeger wrote "The Big Joe Blues" about the horrors of Ed Asner's "misunderstood" buddy.

Upon his release form prison, Dalton Trumbo continued writing scripts under a pseudonym while living in Mexico. He would quickly return to his habits of alcohol, uppers, downers, and relishing his role as an angry, vicious backstabber of former friends such as director Otto Preminger and actor Kirk Douglas. As master of deception and double-speak, Trumbo would live long enough to help rewrite the dark legacy of himself and others as the persecuted "good guys."

Ring Lardner Jr., the profane whore-mongering screenwriter, would also emerge from jail and work under pseudonyms. He would write the script for the 1970 movie *Mash,* which spawned the popular TV series. What most viewers of the movie never realized is that Lardner's script was an anti-American attack on the nation's war against Communist North Vietnam.

The setting was changed to Korea during the Vietnam War to veil Lardner's pro-Communist dialogue masked as American buffoonery at a remote medical aid station. Lardner's love of profanity was evident as he became the first screenwriter to introduce the F-word to motion pictures with the full support of director Robert Altman and Jack Valenti of the MPAA. The F-Bomb, as it is now known, is uttered frequently on the silver screen and the television screen and has entered the American lexicon as a common figure of speech. Such is the legacy of an unrepentant and unapologetic Stalinist supporter of mass murder who went to his grave in 2005.

Mikhail Gorbachev, the Soviet leader who initiated "glasnost" for openness and "perestroika" for economic restructuring, cut off the last dribble of subsidy to the Communist Party USA in the 1980s after CP American leader Gus Hall called "Gorby's" plans "old democratic thinking class collaboration . . ."[36] Gorbachev would reign over the collapse of Eastern Europe and the dissolving of the Soviet Union almost seventy-five years after it began. Belief in God was again "legalized" and the country is once again known as Russia.

Gorbachev apparently didn't have any real problems with capitalism. By the late 1990s Mikhail Gorbachev was making commercials for Pizza Hut. In 2007, he appeared in glossy *Vanity Fair* ads as the face of Louis Vuitton luggage.

Other than my dinner with former fellow traveler Paul Sylbert, I did have another encounter with a former fellow traveler, actress Lee Grant. During the second round of hearings by the HCUA, Grant refused to testify against her husband, playwright Arnold Manoff, citing her Fifth Amendment rights. Though the *studios* blacklisted her, she continued working on Broadway and returned to television and movies by the early 1960s.

During a location scout with Lee Grant in 1991 for a TV movie she was planning to direct, Grant talked about her persecution by the Government and revised history by insisting that the HCUA and McCarthy himself hounded actor John Garfield to death. "He died of a heart attack right after the hearings," she explained. But I knew different, as Hollycoms love to parade Garfield out as the sacrificial lamb to the HCUA hearings.

"The way I understand it," I explained to Grant as we drove the country roads north of Atlanta, "is that Garfield had a lifelong history of heart problems, probably related to the scarlet fever he contracted as a child. While he didn't name names, he didn't have to. His wife, Robbe, was a well-known member of the Communist Party and she should have been testifying.

THE HOLLYWOOD CULTURE WAR

"He had just finished filming *He Ran All the Way* in 1951 and the following year landed the leading role in *Golden Boy* on Broadway, a role he had sought for years. He was even planning another movie under his own company, Enterprise Productions, when he moved into the Warwick Hotel after months of fighting with his wife. She was always nagging Garfield to join every left-wing cause that came along and he finally just darted out from the house. Against doctor's orders, Garfield went on a three-day binge of no sleep while drinking, smoking, and eating to excess with former showgirl and actress Iris Whiting, in whose bed he was found dead in May of 1952. He had a massive heart attack and was only thirty-nine years old.

"He apparently was tired of the endless political harangues of his wife and enjoyed the company of a woman who cared less about the Communist Party. That's the way I understood Garfield's death."

Lee Grant glared at me from the passenger side of the car. "And just where did you get that understanding?" Grant demanded.

"His close friend, director John Berry told me that verbatim during a location scout for a TV movie he was producing called *Sister, Sister*."

Grant changed the subject and went into her own harangue bashing Rush Limbaugh, who was celebrating his three-year anniversary as a syndicated talk show host.

Howard Fast, a staff writer for the *Daily Worker*, perhaps summed up Hollywood's morbid fascination with radicalism and Communism. In his book, *The Naked God*, published in 1957, Fast described how these elite and arrogant sympathizers were, at best, "the mental revolutionaries, the parlor pinks, the living room warriors, the mink-coated allies of the working class."[37]

Actor Sterling Hayden's admission that communism perpetuated an "occult-like" attraction says much about the shared mindset of Hollywood and Communism. As Fast explained, the Communist Party was "based on pseudo-religious cant, cemented with neurotic fear and parading ritualistic magic as a substitute for reason."[39]

The Hollywood fascination with Communism would lay the roots of the "radical chic" of later decades and "limousine liberals" where entertainers and artists like composer Leonard Bernstein would host swank Manhattan parties for the violent Black Panthers. Actress Jane Fonda would revive interest to Stalinism in Hollywood in the early 1970s as she and her own fellow travelers supported the Communist massacres of the democratic people of Southeast Asia.

While the revisionists revel in the rewriting of history about the "blacklist," they may have better served themselves and future generations by telling the truth about the "death list." According to Stephanie Courtois' *Black Book of Communism*, between eighty-five and 100 million deaths worldwide during the twentieth century could be attributed to the Marxist-Lenin-Stalinist view of the world.

But as actor Ed Asner reminds us, poor "Joe" Stalin was just a "hugely misunderstood" kind of guy.

HOLLYWOOD HOLDS A GRUDGE

In the entire history of Hollywood filmmaking, there were only a few directors as prolific as Elia Kazan in scope, artistry, and conscience. His movies were among the best to ever come out of the Golden Era of Hollywood, such as *East of Eden* (1955), *On the Waterfront* (1954*), A Streetcar Named Desire* (1951), and *A Face in the Crowd* (1957) to name only a few.

A committed left-leaning liberal, Kazan won an Academy Award in 1947 by confronting anti-Semitism in *Gentleman's Agreement*. Earlier, in 1945, Kazan directed *Pinky*, a pioneering critique of racism in America.

But he apparently just wasn't liberal enough for the Communists creeping around every corner of the Broadway stage or hiding under every rock inside and outside the Hollywood Studios. In his open letter printed in *The New York Times* on April 12, 1952, Kazan urged his fellow liberals to break loose from the maddening mind control of the Communists.

In a statement before Congress, Kazan said, "The American people need the facts" because Communism was both mentally and physically brutal and Kazan was one of the first to express outrage at the revelation of Stalin's massacres. "The last straw came when I was invited to go through a typical Communist scene of crawling and apologizing and admitting the error of my ways," Kazan told Congress in 1952.[40] The Hollywood Communists would run Kazan and others through childish gauntlets of political correction.

Fast forward to 1999, almost half a century later, and Elia Kazan was about to receive a Lifetime Achievement Award from the Academy of Motion Picture Arts and Sciences. The Academy agreed to the award at the urging of friend and actor Karl Malden. What Malden didn't realize was that Kazan was about to be put through another childish gauntlet from some members of the Academy who would be sitting in the audience. These would include old Communist fellow travelers and contemporary sympathizers who were angry with Kazan for exposing the truth about the industry supporters of mass murder, executions, genocide, starvation, and slave labor. The Hollycoms were alive and well and waiting for the moment when Kazan, the man who betrayed poor Joe Stalin, would walk up to the podium.

The event seemed to arouse more anxiety and excitement than the 1999 Academy Awards ceremony itself in another ordinary and lackluster year of Hollywood movies. Crusty eighty-eight-year-old Communist writer-director Abe Polonsky was asked what he thought of the award. "I hope somebody shoots him. It will be an interesting moment in an otherwise dull evening." The typical

Communist retort from the ultra-radical leader of the Hollycoms proved that old Communists die hard—but not soon enough.

Just short of his 90th birthday, Kazan was accompanied to the podium by Martin Scorsese and Robert DeNiro. Before formally announcing the award, DeNiro quietly admonished the audience to be on their "best behavior," revealing that contemporary fellow travelers were lurking in the audience.

After introducing Kazan as the recipient of the Lifetime Achievement Award, DeNiro and Scorsese quickly walked backwards in a visibly mock tip-toe fashion, in poor taste, giving the impression that a mob hit was about to take place. Perhaps old Abe Polonsky himself would enter stage "Left" and do the dirty deed. But the only revelation came from the audience reaction.

As the camera panned the audience at the Kodak Theater, fully three-quarters of those present gave Kazan a rousing standing ovation including good friend Karl Malden, Lynn Redgrave, Meryl Streep, and ultra-liberal Warren Beatty (of course, Beatty would later explain that the only reason he was applauding was out of respect for Kazan directing him in his first film, *Splendor in the Grass*.)

The camera also revealed the contemporary fellow traveling sympathizers such as Ed Harris, Amy Madigan, Holly Hunter, and Nick Nolte, who literally sat on their hands to protest Kazan's defense of democracy. Some attendees joked later that they were merely constipated and didn't want to embarrass Kazan by walking out to use the bathroom.

More disappointing were the non-reactions of Paramount president Sherry Lansing, who sat stony-faced as if to hex Kazan for his betrayal of Hollywood Communism, and Steven Spielberg, who remained seated and engaged in hard, slow obligatory applause that facially pained him to the core. Spielberg would later reveal his Communist allegiance to Cuba's Fidel Castro.

Ironically, eight years later at the 79th Annual Academy Awards in 2007, the now retired Lansing was receiving her own honorary Oscar and bragged about her new social causes and how "we work in a culture where we are encouraged to speak out." Apparently, in Sherry Lansing's world, that applies to everybody except Elia Kazan.

Perhaps these silent protesters did not even realize they were affirming Elia Kazan's defense of American democracy as they expressed their First Amendment freedom of expression, or lack thereof, by demonstrating that Vladimir Lenin could still count on the "useful idiots" of Hollywood to carry the message of Soviet Communism, which had died long before this night at the opera.

Kazan spoke briefly and thanked the Academy and its members for the award and for the opportunity to direct movies and tell stories that may not have otherwise made it to the silver screen. Kazan quietly left the stage to the same ovation as when he was introduced. What the television cameras didn't capture was the drama being played out on the street in front of the theater. Becca

Wilson, whose father Michael Wilson was one of the "blacklisted" members of the Writers Guild, held up a sign that read, "The Academy seems to have learned nothing from collaborating with McCarthyism." Obviously, Wilson was one of the hysterical revisionists as her placard revealed. However, across the street was another gathering holding up signs that read, "Thank You, Kazan, For Not Being Silent."

Elia Kazan had explained decades before that he felt it was in the best interests of the country and his own liberal beliefs to cooperate with the U.S. government's investigation into Communist infiltration in order to counter Communists who were co-opting the liberal agenda.

Kenneth Lloyd Billingsley summed up Hollywood's morbid seduction with radicalism and Communism by quoting Richard Grenier. "In the dialectic of the Hollywood Left capitalism is evil—except for the three-picture deal with Paramount, the Malibu mansions, the swimming pool, tennis court, and the Mercedes Benz."[41]

AS FOR MCARTHY

Though Senator Joseph McCarthy was not involved in the Hollywood hearings of the House Committee on Un-American Activities, his name would become synonymous with revisionist terms like "virulent anti-Communist," "Red scare," and "Red-baiters." Hollywood needed terms, phrases, and catch-names with extreme, ominous, and foreboding sounds to tag their persecutors and cover their tracks.

Even though McCarthy had no interest in Hollywood, there was a parallel in that Communism was being fought on two fronts domestically—Hollywood and Washington. The infiltration of Stalinist agents in Washington reached all the way into the White House and was uncovered in a way that only McCarthy could achieve.

At the time, the Hollywood Communists were serving Moscow as the unofficial public relations arm in America to paint a pretty picture of the Soviet Union as Shangri-la. While Hollywood was conducting cosmetic damage control for the Communists, McCarthy discovered that the real damage was taking place throughout the U.S. federal government and had been ongoing for almost a decade. It is a testament to his effectiveness that Hollywood would turn his name into a common slur.

One of the foremost scholars on Joseph McCarthy, Professor Arthur Herman, took a fresh look at the much demonized senator in his book *Joseph McCarthy: Re-examining the Life and Legacy of America's Most Hated Senator*. As Herman stated in a January 17, 2006, interview, "The fact is that he got a lot of things right. He didn't always arrive at them with the best methods and the most direct methods, but he knew something was really wrong taking place, especially in the federal government during the New Deal years, during the World War II years, by penetration of Stalinist agents and supporters of Stalin in government. He wanted that rooted out and he pursued them by any means necessary. And those means moved in a way to destroy him—destroy him personally and destroy his reputation."[42]

Like many elected officials after World War II, McCarthy felt a sense of shock that by 1950 about a fifth of the world's population was under Communist control with Stalin pulling the Iron Curtain around Eastern Europe. China had fallen under control of the world's worst mass murderer, Mao Tse Tung, a tyrant of horrific proportions, who would eventually kill more of his own people than Joseph Stalin. And with the test of a nuclear bomb by Comrade Joe Stalin just four years after America dropped two nuclear bombs on Japan, the suspicion thermometer was raised to its highest level.

Senator McCarthy exposed a vast network of Soviet agents in the Justice Department, State Department, and the Defense Department, many of whom had been embedded in these sensitive agencies since the late 1930s. And when McCarthy dug into the Executive Branch and the vast array of presidential advisors, he discovered some of the Soviet's top-level agents were working on the U.S. payroll. As Jack Warner had quipped, the fellow traveling "termites" were burrowed deep. Many others in the federal government were simply "sympathetic" to Communism.

Harry Hopkins, a close advisor to President Roosevelt, was a key emissary between the White House and the Soviet Union. As Roosevelt's health began to deteriorate in 1944 due to congestive heart failure, Hopkins' influence on the ailing president became more pronounced.

In the waning days of the war, President Roosevelt, Winston Churchill, and Joseph Stalin met in Yalta in 1945 to map out a post-war Europe. At the conference, Churchill appeared openly surprised that Roosevelt seemed overly anxious to give Stalin whatever he wanted. As author Billingsley noted, "Hopkins would have given the Russians the key to the White House if he could have sent it."[43] Hopkins was a major mole for the Soviets.

Just before the Yalta Conference in 1945, a Justice Department official named Alger Hiss suddenly "transferred" to the State Department where he and his "associates" drafted some of the policies of the Yalta Conference, which in effect deeded almost all of eastern Europe to Stalin's Soviet Union. Hiss turned out to be another mole embedded at the highest levels for many years.

Old film clips of the Yalta Conference show a visibly ill and easily distracted Roosevelt turning his head from side to side in a vain attempt to follow the negotiations. Churchill is seen carefully keeping his temper in check, especially after discovering that Roosevelt and his "aides" had met secretly with Stalin. As Billingsley noted, "While Hopkins did plenty of damage, Soviet agents such as

Henry Dexter White and others were funneling information to Moscow. Soviet moles in the Manhattan Project were giving Stalin secrets to the atomic bomb."[44] These intricate subversive plots went virtually undetected until McCarthy revealed how deep the network's Communist termites had bored.

Joseph Davies, Roosevelt's ambassador to the Soviets, had declared earlier that Stalin's "purge trials" in Moscow were authentic and "genuine," despite the fact that he must have known to the contrary that Stalin's purges were truly "show trials" to kill thousands of Communist party members solely for the sheer bloodlust of Stalin. Davies helped to downplay the slaughter due to his influence with the media and the top tiers of federal government.

Davies even wrote the book *Mission to Moscow*, which Dalton Trumbo adapted as a screenplay and Edward Dmytryk directed as a movie in what became Hollywood's most glaring and glowing portrait of Joseph Stalin. Billingsley noted that many at the time dubbed the film *Submission to Moscow*.

As for Yalta and its devastating effect on international relations, Billingsley explains that "Roosevelt's openly stated policy was to give Stalin everything he wanted, without asking anything in return, in the hope that by some mysterious means, Stalin would somehow become an amiable democrat."[45]

The revelations of Communist infiltration into the Roosevelt administration proved a huge embarrassment among Roosevelt and Truman Democrats as the security breaches were being uncovered by McCarthy during the 1950s. Adding to this embarrassment were revelations by the press that Roosevelt's vice-president, Henry Wallace, was deeply involved in the occult with Russian mystic Nicholas Roerich, who Wallace referred to as "Guru." Roerich was a devotee of the black magic New Age art of H. P. Blavatsky.

Wallace was vice-president to Roosevelt from 1941 to 1944 and was then bumped down to Secretary of Agriculture, an office he continued serving under President Truman. However, when Wallace publicly declared acceptance of a Soviet Communist sphere of influence in Europe, Truman fired him immediately in 1946. Of course, this made Wallace popular among the Hollywood crowd. Not only was Wallace a fellow traveler, he was a New Ager also, complete with his own Black magic yoga guru.

The following year Truman began to feel the heat of the Communist infiltration into all levels of government and issued his controversial "Loyalty Order" in March 1947. With an urgency to purge the government of Communists and sympathizers, over six million individuals were investigated and hundreds would lose their jobs.

McCarthy's dogged perseverance did not stop at Soviet Communist expansion. The Wisconsin senator wanted to know how China could have fallen to Communism so quickly after World War II, especially in light of America's hard fought effort with American blood to rid China of Imperial Japanese occupation.

The ongoing investigation into the State Department and White House revealed that close Roosevelt advisor Laughlin Currie was a long-time Soviet spy. His close friend was revealed to be Owen Lattimore, a key advisor to the State Department and America's foremost "expert" on Central Asia. Lattimore was also an aid to New Age Vice President Henry Wallace and was a key target of McCarthy's investigation into the fall of China to Communist despot Mao Tse Tung.

Lattimore was a prime suspect in passing secrets to both the Soviet Union and the Communist Chinese. Amazingly, he received much support from liberal Democrats during McCarthy's investigation. Lattimore himself denied doing anything more than "advising" State Department and White House policymakers. Lattimore is even credited with inventing the term "McCarthyism" to direct attention away from his actions by making himself appear as a victim of slander. Hollywood can thank Lattimore for his creative terminology.

But FBI files read at the McCarthy hearings stated that Lattimore was a Communist and should be detained in the case of a national emergency. According to J. Barry O'Connell, "Laughlin Currie, John Stewart Service, and Owen Lattimore were all players in a conspiracy that engaged in espionage for the Communists and manipulated U.S. policy to their benefit.

"They maneuvered to cut off aid to the Chinese Nationalists in order to help Mao win control of China. Their efforts succeeded and the Nationalists fled to Taiwan in 1949."[46] A recent book would appear to support the myth that Mao's "Long March" to Peking, marked with heroic battles against the Nationalists, never actually happened. Mao and his Communist army marched the 6,000-mile trek without incident because there was nobody in their way to oppose them. No one was more surprised than Mao himself when the Communists marched into Peking.

According to authors Jung Chang and Jon Halliday of *Mao: The Unknown Story*, the duplicitous schemer and blood-thirsty thug took the podium to declare the Peoples Republic of China with nervousness, constant throat clearing, and offering no agenda whatsoever for the Chinese people."[47] What Mao did say was that "Half of China may well have to die."[48] Fortunately, for most of China, Mao lived long enough to kill *only* 50 million of his own people.[49] Chung and Halliday put the estimate at 70 million.

Owen Lattimore lived long enough to witness the effects of his subversion of the U.S. foreign policy and the massacre of innocents unlike any killing spree in the history of the world. Many of Lattimore's close friends were later revealed as Soviet *and* Chinese spies. After retiring from John Hopkins University, with his pipe and cardigan, Lattimore continued writing about Pacific affairs until his death in 1989.

As Professor Herman noted, Joseph McCarthy was a flawed individual whose relentless pursuits eventually moved to destroy him. And there is no doubt, in an investigation of massive proportions, that some innocent individuals were targeted. Yet, without McCarthy's tireless pursuit of foreign enemy infiltration, the representative government of the United States and the fabric of the nation itself may have been transformed into a state unrecognizable by the freedoms we still enjoy. The America we know today may very well have survived, but its policies, domestic and foreign, could have been dictated by a shadow government operating just beneath the radar screen. And with today's largely biased press, it would be easy to maintain.

And what does all this record of carnage and Communist espionage have to do with Hollywood? Again, the constant rewriting and cover-up of the twentieth century's greatest failure of devastating proportion, Communism, is continually and curiously carried out by Hollywood, as witnessed by 2005's *Good Night and Good Luck*, the story of the classic battle between Edward R. Murrow and Senator Joseph McCarthy. The movie was full of inaccuracies and omits many facts already presented in this section.

But ruthless industry climbers devoid of a grip on reality, like George Clooney, know that the more McCarthy can be demonized, the more they can please the major producers and studio chiefs who still harbor a sick romance with Communism. And in pleasing their masters with fictionalized history, people like Clooney will receive the Academy awards and the big parts as he sells his soul in honor of the true demons that slaughtered more than 100 million people in the twentieth century.

George Clooney is but one example of the fellow travelers that are alive and well in Hollywood. During the 2006 Academy Awards, filmmaker Paul Haggis picked up two Oscars for *Crash*, including Best Picture. After accepting the awards, Haggis quoted the Communist playwright Bertolt Brecht, declaring "Art is not a mirror held up to society, it is a hammer by which to shape it." This is the same Bertolt Brecht who said that all of Stalin's victims deserved to die even if they were innocent.

The specter of a shadow government operating today became more apparent in December of 2007 when three "analysts" of the National Intelligence Council issued the year-end National Intelligence Estimate which stated that Iran had stopped pursing nuclear weapons in 2003. It was a lie in the best tradition of U.S. government entrenched fellow travelers. Only this time the philosophical fellow travelers appeared to side with the most dangerous strain of extreme Islamic terrorism.

Ken Timmerman, author of *Shadow Warriors*, identified these three men as Thomas Fingar, Kenneth Brill and Vann H. Van Diepen. All had a history of "redirecting" national foreign policy, incompetence or harboring what Ambassador John Bolton would describe as possible "hidden policy agendas." Combined with the *Shadow Party* of George Soros and his increasing control of the Democratic Party, the termites have again bored deep into American government.

Some of Hollywood's current fellow travelers who greatly admire Communism even as it dies on the vine are Oliver Stone, Jack Nicholson, Chevy Chase, Danny Glover, Spike Lee and even Steven Spielberg who was spellbound after personally meeting with Fidel Castro, a brutal dictator who has murdered thousands of his own people.

As Professor Arthur Herman concluded, "We won the Cold War in Eastern Europe and Russia, but we may have lost the Cold War in Hollywood. The goals that the Communist Party set for itself in the 1930s and 1940s have become very much realized there in the contemporary Hollywood scene now."[50]

As further evidence of Hollywood's defense of a dead ideology is the complete lack of film projects centered around the fall of Communism in 1989 throughout Eastern Europe and the demise of the Soviet Union in 1991. If the creative community cannot produce even *one* true story of heroism, endurance, struggle, reunion, and triumph in Poland, Czechoslovakia, Hungary, East Germany, Romania, Bulgaria and the provinces of the Soviet Union, then you have an industry truly perverted by the darkness that dwells deep within the Hollywood heart. Besides, to make such a film might justify the HCUA hearings into Communist infiltration of Hollywood. And nobody wants that; it would spoil their "Chronicle of Some Mythical Kingdom."

When the Berlin Wall fell, literally, Hollywood exhausted a collective yawn and proceeded to make films about space aliens, mutant creatures, and Ninja turtles.

CHAPTER 11

Jane Fonda: The Enemy Within

We have in Hollywood what I call a lunatic fringe.
—Adolphe Menjou

"Every day our leaders would listen to world news over the radio at 9:00 a.m. to follow the growth of the American anti-war movement. Visits to Hanoi by people like Jane Fonda and former U.S. Attorney General Ramsey Clark and ministers gave us confidence that we should hold on in the face of battlefield reverses," said Vietnamese Communist General Bui Tin on August 3, 1995, in an article in the *Wall Street Journal*.[1]

According to Russian government defector Stanislav Lunev, "The GRU and the KGB helped fund just about every anti-war movement and organization in America and abroad.... What will be a great surprise to the American people is that GRU and KGB had a larger budget for anti-war propaganda in the United States than it [the Soviet Union] did for economic and military support to the [Communist] Vietnamese."[2]

These quotes by prominent and well-placed officials from North Vietnam and the Soviet Union demonstrate that as recently as 1972, twenty years after The Hollywood Ten, the Soviet Communists could still count on Hollywood to conduct its evil agenda in America and on the battlefield.

Whereas The Hollywood Ten and their fellow travelers were helping Stalin cover up the massacre of his own people, Jane Fonda's new brand of Hollywood Communism "caused the deaths of American fighting men and the deaths of our own allies," according to author Mark Holzer.[3] For almost forty years Fonda has proven to be the most overtly subversive enemy of the United States. While that may sound like an oxymoron, half of that label definitely applies to Fonda.

Her contradiction and blurred vision of reality, facts, and truth places her in the same category of "the useful idiots" that Lenin loved to employ to spread lies and deception in order to control "the people." In other words, Kill the People.

The dilemma of Jane Fonda and her continued destructive influence in the American Culture War can best be digested by examining the two major factors that comprise the "Jane Fonda Problem."

Number One: TREASON, SEDITION AND LIES

Jane Fonda is technically still at large for committing high treason by giving "aid and comfort" to an enemy at war with the United States.

Number Two: APOLOGIES, DENIALS, AND LOST CAUSES

Jane Fonda has apologized on several "convenient" occasions for being "inconveniently" photographed sitting atop a Communist North Vietnamese anti-aircraft gun laughing and applauding. She has never apologized for pro-Communist anti-American statements and acts that aided the enemy.

To better understand the most dysfunctionally destructive woman to come out of 1970s Hollywood untouched by her own delusions, we must first take a look at Number Two: *Apologies, Denials, and Lost Causes* before delving into Number One: *Treason, Sedition, and Lies,* which is unparalleled in American history. It is important to note the dates and corresponding sequence of events.

APOLOLGIES, DENIALS, AND LOST CAUSES

Military veterans of Vietnam and other wars along with a groundswell of Americans have felt that Jane Fonda should apologize for a trip to Communist North Vietnam in 1972 in which she viciously disparaged both America and U.S. soldiers fighting the war. The most recent of the carefully-worded "apologies" came in the spring of 2005 as she made an appearance on *60 Minutes* and was also quoted in *The New York Times* and other venues.

The apologies at that time related to photographs taken of Fonda sitting in the seat of a North Vietnamese anti-aircraft gun in 1972 that was used to shoot down American planes. Assuming Americans had short memories, Fonda also claimed her mission was strictly to "promote peace."

As for the photos on the Communist anti-American-aircraft gun, *The New York Times* quoted Fonda from her autobiography in which the actress-activist says she absent-mindedly sat down in a moment of euphoria with her Communist hosts and added, "That two-minute lapse of sanity will haunt me until the day I die."[4]

On *60 Minutes*, Fonda said "sitting on the gun was a betrayal. It was like I was thumbing my nose at the military."[5] Walter Inge wrote a letter to the editor at the *Atlanta Journal-Constitution* in which he declared, "Writing that it was 'a betrayal' and a 'lapse of judgment' is a confession, not an apology."

These series of public apologies took place between March and April 2005. In Fonda's fellow traveling strategy to rewrite history, she fails to mention that her trip to North Vietnam in 1972 was more extensive than a two-minute photo-op on a Communist anti-aircraft gun. Fonda and her then-husband, radical Leftist Tom Hayden, spent *two weeks* "touring" Communist North Vietnam and making pro-Communist anti-American propaganda speeches including radio broadcasts on Radio Hanoi that were recorded and played continuously throughout the remainder of the war.

Jane Fonda pointedly did not apologize for her whole-hearted endorsement of Communism and the North Vietnamese struggle to defeat democratic South Vietnam. As the record shows, Fonda supported the violent overthrow of South Vietnam and, as a result, the killing and slaughter inflicted by the Communists. Jane Fonda was, and remains, a dedicated member of what Adolphe Menjou described as "the lunatic fringe" in the movie industry.

The carefully orchestrated apologies just happened to coincide with the release of Fonda's massive autobiography *My Life So Far*. Publicists knew that a large potential market would be women, and many women in America are wives of military veterans past and present. She was "softening the market" as one bookseller noted.

Barely eight weeks later, after her barrage of semi partial apologies, Jane Fonda appeared at the Director's Guild theater in Los Angeles for a special restored-print screening of her 1972 antiwar film FTA (F____ the Army). According to a report by AlterNet news service writer Ed Rampell, "The feisty two-time Academy award winner also showed herself to be as antiwar as ever."[6] Veteran drug-addict, conspiracy theorist, and director Oliver Stone was in attendance, calling the thirty-five-year-old film "the highest form of free expression we've seen in America in a long time." Director David O. Russell called the film a "very spirited pinnacle of the counterculture."

Fonda's antiwar film was a degrading spoof of Bob Hope's USO tours and starred Fonda fellow-travelers Donald Sutherland and Peter Boyle. The filmed version of her traveling 1972 freak show was intended to encourage military personnel to desert, even on the battlefield. (The film was so bad that Fonda was never able to secure a consistent distributor.) Of course Oliver Stone volunteered his "theory," saying, "Calls were made from high up, *possibly* the White House, and the film just disappeared."[7] In other words, it's all Richard Nixon's fault.

Fonda discussed possible new venues with her audience for distributing the old film along with another "Hate America First" diatribe called *Soldier's Pay*.

Some audience members suggested the internet as a way to reach a worldwide audience. Half-tuned-in to her audience, Fonda suddenly switched gears and began a rant against President Bush and descended into bad-mouthing every recent Republican president declaring, condescendingly, "Today Nixon and Reagan are looking pretty good. I think this is the scariest time I ever lived through."

Fonda, pumped up with her own delusionary revolutionary banter, proclaimed to the audience, "It's a dying beast that is always the scariest and most dangerous."

The audience at the DGA theater was clearly encouraging Jane to jump on the Iraq antiwar bandwagon and the seventy-year-old actress and post-toasty hippie came alive. "Just below the crust of the surface is the volcano ready to erupt. It is our job to create critical mass and ignite it."

As she pondered incoherently, Fonda offered that Iraq is "more complicated than Vietnam.... There was no Saddam during Vietnam." Because Jane Fonda's memory is short, selective, or fading, we'll take this opportunity to remind her that there was a Saddam in Vietnam. His name was Ho Chi Minh, and he died shortly before Fonda's visit to North Vietnam in 1972.

In fact, Ho Chi Minh, the Communist leader of the North, and Saddam Hussein were both members of the exclusive Twentieth-Century Million Plus Club; tyrants who, by their action or inaction, have caused the deaths of one million people or more. Other members of the Twentieth-Century Million Plus Club include such Fonda heroes as Joseph Stalin, Mao Tse Tung, Pol Pot, Kim Il Sung, and his son Kim Jong Il. Of these mass murderers, only the frustrated failed filmmaker and porn collector Kim Jong Il is still alive.

Fonda proceeded to wrap up her appearance at the Director's Guild theater by telling everyone gathered that she was only spit on once during her five week book signing tour and then blew that off by saying it was "a vet spit on me."[9] She then reminded the audience there were plenty of her new books in the lobby. Jane Fonda missed another opportunity to apologize and instead treated the audience to another performance of denials and lost causes.

But this appearance was only a warm up for Jane Fonda's traveling circus side-show book signing tour. In an article by Kathleen Parker of the *Independent Women's Forum* in July 2005, Fonda was reported proclaiming to a Santa Fe, New Mexico, audience, "I've decided I'm coming out. I have not taken a stand on any war since Vietnam."[10]

Fonda was on a fast track to becoming "Hussein Jane." As Parker noted in Fonda's announcement, "Her newest foray into anti-war territory feels like a cartoonish parody of her former self. Jane Fonda playing Jane Fonda. In her newest version of me, myself, and I, Fonda will segue book tour to anti-war tour via a cross-country trip on a bus that runs on vegetable oil."[11]

Of course, Fonda has no solution for ending the war. "So what's the point of an anti-war, vegetable oil bus tour? After the trip, Fonda may need a small island to accommodate the baggage she'll accrue," Parker concludes. As Michelle Malkin said, "She has contracted an acute case of Aging Celebrity Hippie Syndrome—and it's going to land her tell-all memoir on *The New York Times* best-seller list in no time."[12]

Five months after Fonda's barrage of semi-apologies and non-apologies, the aging celebrity hippie made a bi-polar decision to schedule herself to appear with controversial British parliamentarian George Galloway in Madison, Wisconsin, on September 17, 2005, where they would jointly condemn America's war efforts in Iraq as illegal and immoral. Galloway is the leading advocate for a de-facto alliance between Western Leftists and radical Islamists.

Galloway is an avid admirer of the executed Stalinist dictator Saddam Hussein, once telling him personally, "I salute your courage, your strength, your indefatigability."[13] Galloway even compared Hussein favorably with Stalin and added that the day the Soviet Union fell was the worst day in his life. In the billion dollar oil-for-food scandal at the United Nations, documents revealed that Galloway was on Saddam's payroll to the tune of half a million dollars a year. Galloway would even remark that the assassination of former British Prime Minister Tony Blair would be justified.[14]

When Galloway appeared in Madison, Wisconsin, on September 17, 2005, he informed the gathered crowd that Jane Fonda would be unable to attend due to recovery from *hip surgery*. But Galloway "assured" the radical storm gathering that Fonda was with them in spirit and the crowd roared with applause. The conveniently scheduled *hip surgery* also put an end to Fonda's dream of an anti-war tour on a vegetable-oil bus.

Seven months after the cancelled appearance with the ultra-radical George Galloway and fully one year from her pre-publicity book tour apologies for the famous anti-aircraft gun photos, Fonda announced on April 17, 2006, that she would not be joining the Iraq war protests. Appearing on *Good Morning America*, Fonda said, "I wanted to do a tour like I did during the Vietnam War, . . . but then Cindy Sheehan filled in the gap, and she is much better at this than I am. I carry too much baggage."

The month before, the Georgia State Senate overwhelmingly rejected a resolution honoring Fonda, an Atlanta resident, for work she performed in preventing teen pregnancy, donations to universities and charities, and as a goodwill ambassador for the U.N. Fonda had just returned from a fishing trip in Argentina with former husband and veteran Christian-basher Ted Turner. Fonda added cheerfully, "He's my favorite ex-husband." Obviously, the Mouth of the South was also telling his ex-wife to keep her lips zipped about any apologies.

For the record, Fonda's first recorded "semi-apology" occurred in 1988 during the on-location filming of *Stanley and Iris* in New England. Veterans groups protested so badly at the set that production was halted and a hastily called interview with Barbara Walters was arranged for airing on the weekly news show *20/20*. Most veterans recognized the interview immediately as a gambit to get them away from her production trailer because she began by apologizing first to "the veterans of New England" and then to the *other* "men who were in Vietnam who I hurt."

The second recorded apology occurred twelve years later in the June issue of Oprah Wynfrey's magazine *O* and rambled so incoherently that columnist Jonah Goldberg noted that "Her *O* interview is so top-heavy with New Age treacle and secrets of the Ya Ya Sisterhood touchy-feeliness, it's hard to tell whether she's apologizing, looking for sympathy, or offering advice for crystal worshippers."[15] In both cases, Fonda was only apologizing for hurting the veterans' feelings, and was not apologizing for being a traitor against the U.S.

The motive? Industry insiders said that the entire Jane Fonda workout videos were in the process of being copied and re-released on the new DVD format for worldwide sales to a new generation. Among potential customers: wives, daughters, family, and friends of vets, past and especially present. Fonda's defenders ask, "What more do you want Jane Fonda to do?" What most vets note is that she has never addressed her whole-hearted commitment to Communism, which would go against her supposed new-found born-again Christian faith.

The truth is Jane Fonda will not retract her support for Communism, the godless ideology that has been drying up for almost twenty years. More specifically, Fonda has not addressed honestly her turning a blind eye to the obvious torture of American airmen who were paraded before her. Nor will Fonda honestly address the propaganda radio campaign that vehemently demonized America and Americans while at the same time giving homage to Ho Chi Minh, one of this planet's major tyrants and mass murderers.

The bottom line is Jane Fonda's semi-apologies are all timed and motivated for personal gain, publicity, and money. Her romance with Communism has even overshadowed her career in movies which spans five decades and over sixty films. Ask anybody what movies they associate Fonda with and *Barbarella* comes to mind. Ask anybody what single memory stands out about Jane Fonda, and "Treason" comes to mind.

The following section will discuss the treason of Jane Fonda because of its horrific impact at the time and the damaging example it set for the contemporary generation. This is must reading because Fonda chose to ignore the treason in her 600-page biography that deals with more pressing memories in her life, such as orgies, sexploits, neurotic husbands, alcoholism, adultery, drug use, and other "high" points in her otherwise "low" life.

More than any other member of the entertainment industry, Jane Fonda is possibly heading down the hall of shame for having committed the most horrendous forms of treason against the United States during wartime. Fonda could have taken a page from the playbook of Edward Dmytryk and Elia Kazan and exposed the slaughterhouse that was North Vietnam and its bloody sponsors in the Soviet Union and China. But Fonda doesn't want to risk a possible embarrassment at a future Academy awards ceremony where fellow travelers might sit on their hands out of protest or to prevent flatulence. The dilemma for Fonda is she would never know the true reasons why she wasn't applauded for her lifetime lack of achievement.

As for Jane Fonda's apologies or lack thereof, Michelle Malkin summarized it best. "This isn't about making amends. This is about making money."[16]

TREASON, SEDITION, AND LIES

By 1970, Jane Fonda had become the official poster child face of the New Left movement that had been stirring up "anti-war" protests on college campuses and urban settings since the mid-1960s, and would continue well into the 1970s.[17]

With a pretty face on a secretive agenda by a relatively small group of shadowy radicals, Jane Fonda would help usher in the wholesale Communist slaughter of more than *three million* Vietnamese and Cambodian people throughout the mid to late 1970s. What Communist Hollywood could not achieve in the 1930s and 1940s was finally realized in the actions of one radical activist. The Communist playwright Bertolt Brecht would have been proud that his words lived on in Fonda, "The more innocent they are, the more they deserve to be shot."

The New Left, which would eventually morph into the counterculture or "hippie" movement, had its roots in 1959 when Aryeh Neier created a radical group called Students for a Democratic Society (SDS). Its illusionary name was reminiscent of the patriotic-sounding "front groups" for Communism that popped up in Hollywood during the 1940s. One of the earliest members of SDS, joining in 1962, was Tom Hayden, future husband of Jane Fonda.

The demonstrations Americans watched unfolding on their television screens during the 1960s were not spontaneous gatherings of "young people" who came together casually at the campus coffee shop and discovered their mutual hatred of American democracy. The "riots in the streets," as Jack Valenti referred to the anti-war demonstrations, were a well-orchestrated activity as part of a larger campaign, very covert, to exert "pressure from above and below" in a radical undemocratic power grab in America that was intended to aid the Communists overseas, as described by David Horowitz and Richard Poe in their groundbreaking expose *Shadow Party*.

As the two authors described the early phase of the Leftist strategy, "During the Vietnam War, SDS was the student group most responsible for fanning the flames of unrest on U.S. campuses."[18] Not surprisingly, SDS founder Neier would start working for the American Civil Liberties Union in 1963 and would serve as its director between 1970 and 1978.

While Neier had the distinction of helping fan the "Phase One" leftist flame "from below," as ACLU director he subsequently fanned the "Phase Two" revolution of exerting pressure "from above" by being the first to call for the impeachment of President Nixon in an October 4, 1973, resolution. The mainstream media, long a supporter of the New Left agenda, did not and will not discuss the deeper roots of Nixon's demise beyond "what he knew and when he knew" of a bungled third-rate burglary.

Neier followed exactly the 1957 strategy of exacting radical non-democratic change from the Czech Communist theoretician Jan Kozak. In need of a new cause and new paycheck twenty years after the Leftist defeat of Nixon, George Soros came along and hired Neier in 1993 to head up his shadowy international subversive Open Society Institute (OSI). Soros also hired fellow Nixon consultant-turned-critic and later ACLU member Morton Halperin in 2002.

As Horowitz and Poe followed the radical Leftist trail right up to today, they note that Soros "has elevated to positions of the highest authority in his Shadow Party two of the men responsible for the political efforts that helped engineer America's defeat in Vietnam. Today, under Soros' leadership, Neier and Halperin are hard at work on a new project—undermining America's war in Iraq—a task for which their experience uniquely fits them."[19]

The two cryptic radicals even tried to start the drumbeat "from above and below" for the impeachment of President Bush. They opted instead to concentrate on the new Democratic controlled House under Nancy Pelosi and the Senate under Harry Reid, who declared, "The war in Iraq is lost," on April 19, 2007. Though he was cheered by the OSI radicals, his fellow members of the Senate were so outraged, Senator Reid "amended" his statement, much to the chagrin of his patron George Soros. One can almost smell the marijuana in the air.

And the media is more openly Leftist now than it was in the 1960s. Morton Halperin's son, Mark Halperin, once held the unique position of "Political Director" for ABC News and may be remembered as the Soros mole who issued a memo to his reporters in late 2004 urging ABC reporters to slant their news in favor of Democratic candidate John Kerry, the Soros favorite for president.

Jane Fonda was more than a Communist sympathizer, she was a full-fledged activist supporting the Communist military slaughter of South Vietnam civilians, its military, and the U.S. military service men and women. Transcripts of Fonda's deceptively violent collaboration on Radio Hanoi are readily available on the internet. She has never retracted her words.

On the domestic front, the counterculture radicals took a more subversive, false patriotic stance in their staged American demonstrations, drawing from the playbook of Saul Alinsky, who also happened to be the mentor to a young campus activist named Hillary Rodham. As Horowitz and Poe point out, the key to the decade-long deception was simple, at the same time it was destructive. "The radicals slogan was not 'Support a Communist Victory in Vietnam,' which would have been rejected by the American people out of hand. The radicals slogan was 'Bring the Troops Home Now.' This slogan did not proclaim the radicals desire that the Communists would win the war—but created the illusion that the anti-war movement cared about America's troops, which it most certainly did not."[20]

This was evidenced by U.S. troops being spit on when they returned home, a tactic supported by Jane Fonda. Senator John Kerry is a major player in the current subterfuge to undermine America's war on terror. Kerry is finding it hard to revive his old role as a radical in the era of a patriotic all-volunteer military of young soldiers who are perplexed by the protests of aging hippie lawmakers and news anchors who seem determined to undermine their efforts and even put their lives in peril.

When Tom Hayden married Jane Fonda, he had more than a "useful idiot" to put the Hollywood face on his New Left Communist agenda. Fonda was not ignorant of the bloodlust union she was wholeheartedly embracing. While the massive death toll of Mao was only suspected in the late 1960s, the megamillions of deaths by Stalin were fairly well known. Ho Chi Minh was a Stalinist Communist who received his earliest aid directly from the mass murderers of Moscow. Any casual student of Vietnam could have discovered this in the campus library. By 1970, Fonda was appropriately starring as a prostitute in the feature film *Klute* and introducing her revolutionary hairstyle known as the "Shag" to a new generation of Fonda wannabe schoolgirls across the country.

Jane Fonda would soon come to symbolize the counterculture as "fashionable" at the same time she demonized almost every aspect of American life while propagating a Communist utopia in Indochina. In a university appearance in 1970, Fonda stated defiantly, "I, a socialist, think that we should strive toward a socialist society, all the way to Communism." On November 21st that same year, Fonda told a University of Michigan audience, "If you understood what Communism was, you would hope, you would pray on your knees that we would someday become Communist."[21]

Fonda obviously never read former Hollycom author Howard Fast's book *The Naked God,* in which he states that "If one were to understand Communism, one must begin not with social science, but naked terror, awful brutality, and frightening ignorance."[22]

By the early 1970s, Jane Fonda was considered a de-facto agent of Communist North Vietnam. As First Cavalry medic John Dennison described Fonda's aggressive efforts on behalf of North Vietnam, "[An] agent is any person who works to obtain the goals of another nation either for money or for their own political beliefs."[23] To again quote former Russian agent Stanislav Lunev, "The

KGB helped fund about every anti-war movement and organization in America." And North Vietnam Communist General Bui Tin said that the extensive *anti-war movement* and its *speakers* were "essential to our strategy."

Now let's do the math. Communist Soviet espionage money plus Communist North Vietnam political accommodation equals Communist American agent, also known as "fellow traveler," also known as "traitor," also known as "accessory to mass murder." Just how much Communist money went into Fonda's traveling FTA shows to encourage military desertion is unknown. Fonda also refuses to discuss if she was reimbursed by Vietnamese or Soviet Communists for her extended stay at the Hotel Especen in July and August 1972.

Just twenty-five years earlier, Jane Fonda's father, Henry Fonda, joined the International Rescue and Relief Committee, along with many other celebrities, to give aid and comfort to *victims* of Communism. Much to his dismay, he watched in quiet horror as his only daughter engaged in giving aid and comfort *to* the Communists.

Fonda's individual statements and acts of treason while in North Vietnam are too numerous to list here. However, Mark Holzer, co-author of *Aid and Comfort: Jane Fonda and North Vietnam*, has carefully catalogued the massive extent of Fonda's treason, acts that perversely made her a cult hero among the young Turks taking over the movie industry in the 1970s. Her actions would also reinvigorate the Communist sympathizers for the "blacklist" Hollycom entertainers of the 1930s and 1940s. Fonda's radical treason would set the tone for Hollywood's misguided and radical social/sexual/politics of today.

What is certain, according to author Mark Holzer in an interview with Joe Scarborough, is that by committing high treason Fonda "exploited and misused American POWs. She gave the North Vietnamese Communists, with whom we were then at war, propaganda that American POWs endured unimaginable torture not to give them—she gave it to them free. And, indeed, she caused the deaths of American fighting men and the deaths of our allies as well."[24]

The most specific acts of Fonda's treason were centered around her eight separate live radio broadcasts in English, read from obviously scripted Communist propaganda, which were intended for U.S. soldiers. Some of the most outrageous statements concerned the condition of POWs, whom she described as appearing "healthy and fit . . . and all of them have called publicly for an end to the war and signed a powerful anti-war statement."[25]

Another bizarre statement was intended for the democratic South Vietnamese troops in a pitiful attempt to stir their sense of injustice at American morality by explaining that female members of the military were clearly present to "service the men."[26]

In addition to the radio broadcasts, Fonda toured the country with high-ranking officials of the Communist North Vietnamese government and even met privately with North Vietnamese Vice-Premier Nguyen Duy Trinh. During her visit, Fonda gave at least ten pro-Communist, anti-American speeches and press interviews.

But Fonda's declaration that the POWs were treated well received the most scrutiny in her relentless betrayal of Americans. One of those prisoners who was isolated and tortured for refusing to tell Fonda what the Communists wanted her to hear was an American civilian POW named Michael Benge who was forced to kneel over while holding a metal bar behind his back for three straight days.[27] Navy Captain David Hoffman was also reportedly tortured for refusing to meet with Fonda for a Communist propaganda stunt.

With the passage of time, there were a few stories about prisoner abuse and torture that turned out to be false. One involved F-4E Colonel Jerry Driscoll who was rumored to have been dragged from his cell to stand in line with the other seven POWs, and when he refused to tell Fonda about his "humane treatment," he subsequently spit on her and was then beaten unconscious in front of Fonda and dragged away.[28] Contacted years later, Colonel Driscoll denied the internet rumor and said he never even saw Fonda. He did add, however, he had no love lost on Jane Fonda and her acts of treason.

Jane Fonda would report later that there was no systematic abuse and torture of American POWs in Ho Lo Prison. A returning prisoner named John McCain from Arizona strongly disputed that claim. The future senator from Arizona was horribly tortured when his captors literally pulled his arms out of his shoulder sockets.

When the prisoners were released in 1973, the stories about the brutal torture were made public and well-documented. Upon hearing the POW's accounts, Fonda literally went into a raging hysteria, screaming that the returning soldiers were "liars, hypocrites, and pawns." She based her pathetic accusations on the fact that "Tortured men do not march smartly off the planes, salute the flag, and kiss their wives. They are liars! I also want to say these men are not heroes."[29]

Although Nixon had largely ended America's ground force troop involvement by 1973, Jane Fonda was not finished. Along with husband Tom Hayden, Fonda established a front group called the Indo-China Peace Campaign (IPC) that lobbied vigorously and continuously to cut off all funds, even of a support nature, to the free people of South Vietnam and Cambodia. Fonda claimed that this lobbying effort was fully funded by "supporters" including herself. But former Soviet agent Lunev's statements since his defection and the timing of Fonda's lobbying at the height of America's negotiating advantage at the Paris Peace Talks would put her claims into suspicion. Nobody bothered to follow the money trail of IPC's "supporters."

Fonda's strategy was taken directly out of the radical playbook of Czech Communist Jan Kozak and *Rules for Radicals* author Saul Alinsky in the stealth tactic of applying "pressure from above and below." The closer America and her allies came to victory over the Communists, the louder and more shrill came the protests from the streets and the campus (pressure from below).

By 1972, President Nixon had forced the Communist North Vietnamese back to the peace table after bombing Hanoi relentlessly. The very thought of an American victory over the Communists outraged the New Leftist radicals who were having to work double-time to coordinate the corresponding government pressure (pressure from above).

During this time, the FBI discovered that Nixon consultant and Leftist mole Morton Halperin was secretly discussing political strategies for sabotaging the war effort by "de-funding" the military effort. This took careful coordination with powers "from above" in Congress and the media. Walter Cronkite was already on their side, having declared America's greatest victory of the Vietnam War, the Tet Offensive, as a stunning blow and defeat of America's efforts. This report stunned the American military more than anyone else considering the fact that Cronkite's report was a blatant lie. Former Defense Department employee Daniel Ellsberg, who had clearly violated the Espionage Act of 1918, was perversely transferred into a hero by none other than America's worst enemy, *The New York Times*.

Fonda's IPC continued its tenacious and persistent attack to de-fund the war-support effort and completely abandon the free people of Southeast Asia to certain slaughter at the hands of the Communists. At the same time, others were working to disrupt the leadership of the Commander in Chief in the United States.

Horowitz and Poe called the strategy of "pressure from above and below" as Phase One and Phase Two as tested successfully by the New Left radicals and their counterculture revolution of the early 1970s. "Phase One is to undermine America's will to fight by fostering a spirit of defeatism regarding the war and by casting doubt on its morality. Phase Two is to deprive Americans of their war leader. During the Vietnam War, this was accomplished by forcing President Nixon's resignation."[30] As Horowitz and Poe continue, "It was the resignation of Richard Nixon that encouraged the North Vietnamese to break the Paris Peace Accords by invading and conquering South Vietnam, and the Khmer Rouge to do the same in Cambodia."[31]

By 1975, Fonda's "lobbying" efforts paid off as Congress abruptly cut funding to even the *basic* support of the free people of South Vietnam and Cambodia, effectively endorsing the four-year slaughter of more than three million people. While the elite New Left radicals and their counterculture allies celebrated on the east and west coast cocktail party circuits, blood was overflowing in the streets and villages of Southeast Asia.

These revelers in America were the people author Howard Fast called "the parlor pinks, the living room warriors . . . sick people who had seen no other death than a painted corpse in a funeral parlor."[32] The Radical Left had become the Radical Chic and the "Limousine Liberals" who now work for George Soros and the liberal wing of the Democratic Party who are attempting to pull off the very same charade in America's war against terror in Iraq, Afghanistan, and even at home in America. The radical's newest hope is Barack Obama.

In his book *Schmoozing With Terrorists: From Hollywood to the Holy Land*, Aaron Klein discovered that extreme Islamic terrorists are very familiar with Fonda's success in aiding America's defeat in Vietnam. However, Fonda may be their only Hollywood idol. As terrorist leader Muhammed Abdul-El told Klein regarding two other celebrities, "If I meet these whores, I will have the honor to be the first to cut the heads of Madonna and Britney Spears."

In one of her 1972 radio broadcasts from Hanoi, Jane Fonda pulled a cruel hoax of seduction in a statement addressed directly to the soldiers of South Vietnam. "We read with interest about the growing number of you who are understanding the *truth* and joining with your fellow countrymen to fight for *freedom* and *independence* and *democracy* [i.e., with the Communists] . . . . We think that this is an example of the fact that the *democratic, peace-loving, patriotic* Vietnamese people want to *embrace* all Vietnamese people in *forgiveness*."[33]

With even the most basic, essential back-up support withdrawn by the democratic, peace-loving, patriotic U.S. Congress, the Communist Khmer Rouge took over Cambodia swiftly on April 17, 1975. Thirteen days later, the Communist North Vietnamese troops stormed into Saigon.

There was no embracing. There was no forgiveness. How many South Vietnamese soldiers, as they were being blindfolded by their executioners, asked, "But what about the promise of that American actress who said . . ." and then the lights went out forever?

Within a few months of the Communist takeover, Fonda returned to Hanoi with her newborn son, Troy, for a special celebration in honor of her treason against America. Fonda was lionized as a Communist goddess for all the propaganda and lobbying work she had contributed with her Hollywood celebrity status to ensure Communist victory. While there, her newborn son was given a "Communist christening" in the name of Nguyen Troi, a Communist assassin who was executed in 1963 for attempting to kill U.S. Secretary of Defense Robert McNamara. Fonda was thrilled.

The screaming sounds of mass human slaughter and executions were too far away for Fonda to hear, not that she would have cared. Even before Fonda arrived back in Vietnam, the Communists were executing the people of the south on a daily basis. Hundreds of thousands of people were being herded into "re-education" camps where many faced, according to author R. J. Rummel, "rapid death."[34]

The rural economy was being quickly reorganized and landlords were being massacred much like Stalin's and Mao's bloody landowner massacres. Owning land was evil and punishable by death, except for Jane Fonda, because she was a "hero." The North Vietnamese were so pumped up with their victory in defeating the South Vietnamese, the Communist military fomented war in Laos and were setting the stage for an invasion of Cambodia.

The Cambodians were too busy killing their own people to take notice. The Cambodian rebels were killing at a rate that would have made Ho Chi Minh red with envy. Pol Pot would soon take on the title of the twentieth century's most brutal tyrant. As a percentage of the population, Pol Pot would kill more people in less time than Stalin killed in thirty years.

Meanwhile, back in America, hippies donning John Lennon glasses were celebrating the Communist victory in their dilapidated apartments while listening to Pink Floyd and smoking pot at the same time Pol Pot was killing his fellow countrymen, often for no other reason than possessing an education or simply wearing glasses.

As Fonda and baby Troy were leaving Hanoi to return to their California mansion, could she have missed looking out the plane's window to notice thousands of tiny man-made boats floating off the coast of Vietnam? Did Jane Fonda not ask herself why two million "boat people" were so desperate to leave their country? After all, this was the new country that Fonda herself had promised them just three years earlier as overflowing with "freedom, independence, and democracy" and a country where "peace-loving patriotic Vietnamese people" were just waiting to embrace "*all* Vietnamese people with forgiveness."

From the time of Fonda's honorary celebration by her Communist hosts in 1975 until the end of 1990, at least three million Southeast Asian people would be massacred by the "peace-loving" Communists. Of the two million boat people who fled Southeast Asia after the war, approximately 250,000 drowned at sea.[35] Many of these people obviously knew the risk of taking their rickety crafts to an open and vicious ocean with only the hope of being picked up by a passing ship or landing in a friendly country. But for many, dying at sea was probably a better option than dying in a forced labor camp. And Jane Fonda did absolutely nothing to help these poor souls, the victims of her misadventure and "experimentation" with Communism.

Fonda has never apologized for her Communist affiliation and collaboration. To do so would be an admission that she truly did something wrong. Inevitably, celebrities like Jane Fonda are, in the words of Kenneth Lloyd Billingsley, "not up to admitting that [they] had played a role of what Lenin called 'useful idiots,' duped and bilked by militant Communists."

In August 2007, a War Crimes Tribunal commenced in Cambodia to try the perpetrators of Southeast Asia's worst genocide. Perhaps Jane Fonda should be called to testify about "what she knew and when she knew it."

Collectively, Hollywood itself could not come to admit its blind eye during this whole period and afterward. The films about Vietnam were carefully calculated deceptions about the reality of the New Left's involvement, and battle movies almost always portrayed the American military as villains. The more evil the portrayal of Americans, the better chance the film would have of winning an Academy Award. This was best epitomized by "the first-hand account" of a soldier in Vietnam and his reaction to battle in director Oliver Stone's *Platoon*.

Stone conveniently casts Charlie Sheen as a young Stone who is quickly and stoically shocked by the vicious actions of his fellow platoon members during combat. The movie is a highly fictional and hazy account of Stone's service in Vietnam. In reality, Oliver Stone loved to "get high" on LSD and marijuana before putting his fellow platoon members at risk during firefights with the enemy. For Stone's drug-infested, anti-American vision of battle in Vietnam, he was awarded an Oscar for Best Director in 1987.

Another Hollywood portrait of deception was 1984's *The Killing Fields*, about the genocide in Cambodia. Naturally Hollywood waits for the four-year killing spree to stop before making a movie about "what went wrong."

Because the movie was based on the memoirs of liberal, left-wing reporter Sidney Schanberg of *The New York Times*, the blame for Pol Pot's genocide of millions of his own people can be placed squarely on the shoulders of the United States for supporting democracy in Cambodia. You figure that out and maybe, just maybe, you too can win a Pulitzer Prize.

Of course, the movie won a couple of Oscars including Best Supporting Actor for Dr. Haing S. Ngor, a real-life refugee of the Cambodian genocide who played Schanberg's translator, Dith Pran. The movie Hollywood has yet to make is the ironic fate of Dr. Haing S. Ngor who, as a resident of Los Angeles, the film capital of the world, was gunned down outside his home as an anonymous victim of a drive-by shooting.

Even Jack Valenti used the carefully orchestrated demonstrations by the Leftist radicals to dictate his decision (excuse) for "junking" the Production Code and installing his Ratings Scheme. As one of his "reasons" for establishing his Ratings Scheme, Jack Valenti boasted on the MPAA website that it all boiled down to "insurrection on the campus, riots in the streets," and further rambled on to justify his vulgarization of the silver screen. "It would have been foolish to believe that movies, the most creative of art forms, could have remained unaffected by the change and torment in our society."[37]

Long after he left the presidency, Richard Nixon wrote *No More Vietnams* in which he summarized the media deception surrounding Vietnam. "No event in American history is more misunderstood than the Vietnam War. It was misrepresented then and it is misrepresented now. Rarely have so many people been so wrong about so much. Never have the consequences of their misunderstanding been so tragic."

Nixon further noted how the media and Hollywood continued to perpetuate the Leftist radical bias into portrayals of that era. "The great majority of these [movie] efforts have erroneously portrayed many myths about the Vietnam War as being facts."[38]

That Nixon was a target of the Leftists for a long time was confirmed to me by director John Frankenheimer during our location scout of 1996. Speaking of the Vietnam War and Jane Fonda's involvement, Frankenheimer made a curiously boastful remark. "It took us twenty-seven years, but we finally got him," referring to Nixon.

"We?" I asked.

Frankenheimer simply smiled and remained silent. The Hollycoms and the Leftists had been chasing Nixon since his vocal 1947 vote of contempt against The Hollywood Ten, his prosecution of Communist spy Alger Hiss, his vigorous defense of capitalism in a debate with Kruschev, and especially his aggressive waging of war against the Communist North Vietnamese despite the Communist-backed demonstrations in America. Nixon knew who was pulling all the strings, and so did the media. The problem was the media was part of the puppet act, then and now.

President Gerald Ford, who was never really liked by the press because of his Republican credentials and his pardon of Nixon, suddenly became one of their favorite presidents when he died in late December 2006. Almost every reporter in the mainstream press cited Ford's "moderation" and "civility" as opposed to "Nixon and Bush." It was the most shameless coverage of a president's death and funeral for the sole purpose of advancing a liberal agenda.

The lessons of Jane Fonda's treason, lies, and denials are important because of the role she played in a much larger movement of undermining national unity through undemocratic "organized chaos." Sadly, the same people who undermined an American victory over Communism in Vietnam are back purposely orchestrating America's defeat at the hands of terrorists.

On January 3, 2007, "anti-war" activist Cindy Sheehan showed up outside the U.S. Capitol with a newly "selected" group of demonstrators shouting a ritualistic chant about "bringing our boys home." (She neglected to mention the service women.) She screamed for "defunding the war." Three days later, new House Majority Leader Nancy Pelosi and Senate Majority Leader Harry Reid began planning a series of legislative acts to defund the war on terror in Iraq. Both have failed, but they have not given up on legislating America's defeat.

Unable to stay away from the spotlight, Jane Fonda led an "anti-war" rally in Washington on January 27, 2007. The only two people, besides herself, that were smiling broadly that day were Osama bin Laden and Mahmoud Ahmadinejad of Iran. Throughout the entire war on terrorism, Jane Fonda has not given a dime to the families of those who gave their lives and those who have been wounded severely in support of her freedom to give aid and comfort, again, to the enemies of the American people.

Fonda might try following the examples of actors Gary Sinise and Denzel Washington who have given generous donations of time and money for the Fisher Houses that support the families of America's wounded warriors. Nor has she even contemplated contributing *anything* to Sinese's "Operation Iraqi Children."

After the rally was over, a field producer for Bill O'Reilly asked Fonda the question no one else in the media has managed to ask her in the thirty-five years since her first treason: what did she think about the fact that three million Indo-Chinese people were killed shortly after America abruptly pulled out of the region, to which she replied casually, "It's too bad we [USA] caused it to happen."

It all sounds too familiar. Horowitz and Poe note the events are well orchestrated, calling the New-New Left strategy as "Watergate II and Vietnam II." There will be increasing "pressure from above and pressure from below." And the new Jane Fonda is Arthur "Pinch" Sulzberger, the publisher of *The New York Times*.[40]

JANE FONDA IS A GNOSTIC, NOT A CHRISTIAN

No, I didn't say Jane Fonda is an agnostic; I said Jane Fonda is a Gnostic, the heretical band of Christian pretenders who attempted to rewrite the life of Christ through perverse books that were a mix of Greek and Oriental philosophies. "Claiming that Jesus is the *only* way to salvation felt like Christian imperialism,"[41] Fonda proclaimed in her exhaustive, self-indulgent 2005 biography. Obviously, she believes that Ho Chi Minh is another possible "choice" for salvation.

Contrary to popular belief, Jane Fonda never converted to Christianity, and she certainly didn't become a born-again Christian. All of this resulted from a series of articles that circulated in 2000 and 2001. Because Fonda would not comment on the stories until her autobiography came out five years after the "supposed conversion," journalists and even those close to Fonda could only speculate.

For those who saved their valuable time by not reading her autobiography and for those people who, again, are fortunate enough not to read *The New York Times*, those are the venues Jane Fonda chose to reveal her fraudulent chicanery. About the same time she was releasing her autobiography, Jane Fonda and "Joe" Stalin's friend Ed Asner bought a full-page ad in *The New York Times* in which they contemptuously ridiculed Christianity in a weak and pitiful attempt to rouse anti-Christian bigotry.[42] The ad was signed by a Who's Who of Hollywood celebrities.

It was becoming clear by 2007 that Jane Fonda's "experiment" with Christianity was just that, an experiment no different than dabbling in New Age philosophy, trying drugs, and group sex, all while maintaining her devotion to Communism. To quote Jonah Goldberg again, listening to Jane Fonda is like sitting through a diatribe of "New-Agey treacle and Secrets of the Ya Ya Sisterhood touchy-feeliness."[43]

THE HOLLYWOOD CULTURE WAR

A little background is needed to explain how Jane Fonda took a few more steps down into the increasingly darker hole she has dug for herself. By late 1999, Jane Fonda's friends in Atlanta had begun to talk very publicly about Fonda's path to becoming a born-again Christian. Fonda herself would not comment on the reports that she was "exploring" becoming a Christian.

While many of her "Peachtree Street" and "Buckhead" friends were witnessing to Fonda, her chauffeur had invited Fonda to his congregation at Providence Missionary Baptist Church where she "reportedly" made the confession of faith in Jesus Christ; but she never really did so and in her book she not only omits any such profession of faith, she very openly admitted rabid distrust. Some members at Providence were flattered, but a little confused, when she quickly turned her interest toward the African-American artwork by some members of the congregation. While she attended a few Bible studies, she was also busy collecting folk art and her interest in Christianity waned shortly thereafter.

She did keep the fire going just long enough to tell her world-class Christian-bashing husband, Ted Turner, who was so repulsed that he couldn't stand the thought of remaining married to her. They separated immediately and divorced a year later. A source close to Fonda speculates that part of Fonda's Christian ruse was intended to incite Ted into divorcing her. Her divorce settlement would be larger if he initiated the divorce. In Fonda's book, she practically describes Ted Turner as a whoremonger of epic proportions given to "quickies" with various women before jumping in the limo with Jane for lunch.

Fonda knew which buttons to push and the Christian button was sure to set him off, as Turner hated Christians more than any individual or group on the face of the earth. He once proudly declared, "Christians are losers," which one pastor claimed was very true, and that is why they come to Christ—to be saved.

In 2008, Turner finally apologized for his Christian-bashing. At the same time, he claimed Americans would become "cannibals" and start eating each other in just thirty years due to "global warming."

For the secular reader, a primer is needed to better understand Christian Evangelism, salvation, and being born-again.

The word "evangel" comes from the Greek word evangelion, meaning "good news, gospel."[44] Specifically, the four books that make up the "Gospel" section of the New Testament—Matthew, Mark, Luke, and John—is the noun form of "evangel." The "good news" as recorded in the four books outlines the birth, ministry, and crucifixion of Jesus. It is the foundation of all books that follow in the New Testament known as the Epistles, teachings from the apostles and the Resurrection of Jesus as the Christ and Ascension to Heaven.

Many people mistake "evangelical" as a denomination in the Christian church. Evangelism is a movement, not a denomination. There are many "mainline" denominations that maintain an evangelical element to their ministry such as

Methodists, Baptists, Catholics, and hundreds of Christian denominations. There are also nondenominational Christian churches in which "evangelical" is their sole identification, which is spreading the Word of God to those who have not heard the "good news" before, or to those who have not heard enough to understand fully the accuracy of the Word.

It was widely believed that Fonda's *New York Times* ad was a direct attack on evangelicals, which she and her Hollywood friends very incorrectly called "narrow and hateful," when quite the opposite is true. What other group would reach out their hands of forgiveness and love in light of Fonda's record of treason against her country and aiding and abetting the enemy's ability to kill Americans and open the door to the genocide of millions?

Just five years after the Christian community reached out to her, she turned around and bit the hands that fed her. Fonda never admitted to being a born-again Christian. It would ruin her career and it would mean the denunciation of Communism. Fonda is a malignant narcissist who revels in bringing people down in order to elevate her ego.

"Born Again" Christians subscribe to the confession of faith in and of Jesus Christ as put forth by the Apostle Paul during the first-century in the book of Romans 10: 9, 10. Not only is Romans 10: 9, 10 the central confession of faith for born-again believers, it is the central core belief for the Christian church. All the Apostle Paul is asking is that the reader "believes" what they are reading.

The companion verse that accompanies the confession of faith is John 3: 3, in which Jesus announces, "Verily, verily, I say unto thee, except a man be born again, he cannot see the kingdom of God."

First, Jane Fonda denies making the confession of faith, so she has no need to "believe" in anything she didn't confess. This is the danger of someone like Jane Fonda, who sets out to make a mockery out of people's sacred beliefs.

Second, Jane Fonda has a problem with John 3: 3 because it mentions "man" and "he" and no mention of "women" and "her." Had Fonda stuck with her Bible study long enough, she would have learned that the English bible was translated from the Stephens Greek Text. The Greek word for man here is *teleios*, which means "one who has reached maturity." Another Greek word for man is *anthropos*, which means "a human being as distinct from animals."[45] In other words, the verse refers to *all* mankind. In other verses, the term is gender specific.

Out of her 642-page autobiography, Jane Fonda devoted a total of one page to the subject of her "spiritual" journey. And it is clear from her description that she is adamantly not a "born-again Christian" or even at the least an "almost" Christian. It is personal interpretation that has caused the division of the Christian Church into thousands of denominations. Add one more denomination: The Church of Jane Fonda.

As only one immersed in a Hollywood social/sexual/political lifestyle could describe it, Fonda's first mention of her "spiritual" quest began as a "psychic lucidity, that was allowing me access to something beyond consciousness." Then, just as suddenly, Fonda describes her "spiritual journey" as coinciding with her need for a "new" form of sex that she required, centered on a "soul to soul" basis and not sex strictly based on "performance."

When Fonda does finally delve into the single page description of her interest in being "Christian," which she is determined to enclose in quotations, the reader is left wondering why Fonda even bothered devoting one whole page to a phenomenon most believers consider a life-changing experience worthy of an entire book.

In her brief mention of "Christianity," Fonda proceeds to describe her true conversion down the dark path of radical Gnostic feminism in her "impression" of the Bible as interpreted by Jane Fonda. Not only is she repulsed by the idea of Jesus Christ as "the only way to salvation," Fonda takes another feminist stab at the Bible, declaring, "Nor can I accept woman as the cause of man's downfall."

What Jane failed to learn when she walked out of Bible study in search of folk art is that "woman" didn't cause the downfall of man, it was the Devil himself—or is it "herself." How about "itself?" Better still, how about the Devil as "serpent" just as it says in the Bible. That way no genders are offended, the perception of which seems to be Fonda's only interest in the Bible.

The problem with Fonda is the same problem experienced by most people who use the Bible deceitfully. People of deception, like Fonda, read verses out of context, connect verses together out of order, and then skip over entire sections that connect the dots. Adding insult to injury, to themselves and others, people like Jane Fonda proceed to inject their personal bias into Bible verses. Even Jane's earthly father, Ho Chi Minh, once believed that Jesus was the original Communist. He obviously didn't read "the rest of the story," as Paul Harvey would say.

The major problem in Fonda's "spiritual" quest is that she veered into the Gnostic books that were left out of the Bible, such as The Gospel of Mary, the Pistis Sophia, The Book of Thomas, and other books. It is only natural that Fonda would be attracted to these books because of the air of secrecy and conspiracy that people have injected into them.

It would seem as though Fonda never really read the Bible, but picked up a copy of *The DaVinci Code* instead. Fonda blames the exclusion of those Gnostic books from the Bible on a male dominated church (sexism again) in an attempt to suppress the role of women in spreading Christianity. There is nothing secret or mysterious about the Gnostic books that were left out of the Bible. Not only were they very poorly written, there is no Divine Revelation or edification concerning the Truth of God's revelation.

Fonda has obviously not even read the Book of Thomas, which might change her thinking about Gnosticism very quickly. In one verse, Simon Peter *supposedly says*, "females do not deserve life" and proceeds to "quote" Jesus as saying, "For every female who makes herself male will enter the domain of Heaven."

Is there any doubt why the early church elders threw these books on the "speculation" stack? These writers were the first to attempt to destroy the Bible as Divine Revelation and create their own New Age sect, which remains to this day in numbers of believers you could fit on the head of a pin. But what really fascinated Fonda was that these secret books were authored by writers "who saw themselves as seekers rather than believers."[46] Yet another reason why these books were not included in the Bible. For New Age Fonda to actually *believe* in something *true* would take away her "adventurous" side, and life would be just so . . . well, boring.

The prophetic apostle Paul recognized early that there would be plenty of Jane Fondas in the world, and for that reason he wrote about such skeptics in his Second Letter to Timothy in Chapter 3, verse 7, concerning the restless wanderers who reveled more in *searching* than they did in *finding,* "Ever learning, and never able to come to the knowledge of the truth."

Fonda also expressed amazement that some of her "early" Christian friends were shocked to find out that she gave a speech at a pro-abortion rally (Fonda called it "pro-choice"). What would have shocked Fonda's "early" Christian friends even more was Fonda's *$12 million* contribution to a shadowy abortion rights group called "Pro-Choice Vote" in September 2000, shortly after her so-called conversion.[47] This was an early sign that Jane Fonda was not "saved," as the "born-again" usually do not terminate the "un-born."

While Fonda observers noted that the aging actress' interest in Christianity quickly waned, Fonda told readers in her long-winded biography, "But with my discovery of early Christian *interpretations* [Gnostic] and having found a community of *feminist* Christians, reverence is humming back to me."[48] Reverence for what? For whom? How about a reverence for "Hummmmm?"

Since Fonda is always "seeking" she will have no problem finding "interpretations" that will justify her devotion to the ultimate anti-God religion of Communism, justify her betrayal of America, her contribution to the massacre of innocents, and, ultimately, justify her perverting the Bible itself. She has also found "interpretations" that allow her to further denigrate and export her morally impoverished view of American culture and promote a traveling circus act in which women sit in a chair on an empty stage and talk ad-nauseum and infinitum about their vaginas.

Yes, Jane Fonda signed on as a carnival barker and participant in Eve Ensler's traveling off-Broadway show known as *The Vagina Monologues* in which women who have no other central focus in their life except an obsession to bloviate endlessly about their vaginas. Even worse, Fonda has helped to take the show international where it was performed in India and Pakistan, further ensuring America's image around the world as a bottomless pit hellhole.

In early 2008, Oprah announced that she would be joining the 10th anniversary of The Vagina Monologues, which Jane Fonda now refers to simply as The C____t.

Of course, Fonda's "new" Gnostic feminist friends have convinced her that God is smiling down on her. Hummmmmm.

REFLECTIONS ON A LIFE WELL-WASTED

As for Fonda's autobiographical mention of her role in Vietnam, it is worth noting that she gives that section of her book a whopping twelve pages with the title "Framed." At first glance, I thought that Jane Fonda had come to the revelation that she was, indeed, framed and duped by the Communists in North Vietnam.

But no, slap my head. How could I have thought something so improbable for even a moment. What Fonda was referring to by the title is how she was framed by observers in America (you and me) who "misinterpreted" the famous photo of her smiling, laughing, clapping, and sitting firmly in the seat of a Communist North Vietnamese Soviet-built anti-aircraft gun intended for the sole purpose of killing Americans. It's the photographic image that always haunts Fonda, as if nobody read her inflammatory radio address and fierce anti-American (you and me) propaganda from her perch at Hanoi's Hotel Especen. Her statements about POWs were glazed over as "misunderstandings."

In her autobiography, Fonda said she was only trying to "stop the killing on both sides." Not true. By very actively promoting North Vietnamese and Khmer versions of Stalinist Communism, overseas and domestically, Jane Fonda was aggressively promoting the inevitable killing of millions, which is exactly what happened. Fonda "framed" the whole period much as she did in 1972. The whole war, the whole situation in Indo-China, every problem in America and the entire world was all Richard Nixon's fault—no more, no less. It was apparent in her book that all she was apologizing for was the fact that she got caught.

Those early supporters of Fonda who thought she had become a Christian foresaw a grand opportunity for Jane to travel back to Vietnam as a great witness for Christ in a country that had now renewed relations with the United States. But as her "spirituality" waxed feeble, her very presence could have started another cataclysm in Vietnam. She served her purpose and she was discarded. Besides, President Bush beat Jane Fonda for the opportunity to push for more openness in religious expression in Vietnam.

On June 21, 2005, Vietnam Prime Minister Pham Van Khai visited the White House to meet with President Bush and signed what President Bush described as a "landmark agreement" with the Vietnamese Prime Minister that would make freedom of worship easier for the people of Vietnam. And when President Bush visited Vietnam in 2006, he and the First Lady made a point to attend worship services during their stay.

During this time, Fonda was traveling the world to discuss her vagina with strangers willing to pay the price of a ticket. But, if Fonda and former hubby radical Tom Hayden heard the statement read by the Vietnamese Prime Minister Khai, they no doubt were hurling their lunch onto somebody else's lap as Khai declared, "We believe that America can find in Vietnam a cooperative partner. We have a population of 80 million people, which means a huge market for American business . . . . And they are working hard to achieve the goal of building Vietnam into a strong country with wealthy people and a democratic and advanced society."[49]

Advanced? Markets? Wealthy? That certainly didn't sound like the anti-materialistic, anti-capitalist, bloodthirsty leadership that Jane and Tom had collaborated with four decades earlier. The lesson here is simple. Not only did Americans never lose a battle during the Vietnam War, America, in all reality, actually won the Vietnam War. Prime Minister Khai was speaking words that would have cost him his life if Ho Chi Minh had overheard such talk of "wealth" and "markets" and "worship."

As to the original question at the beginning of this chapter: Is Jane Fonda a born-again Christian? The answer is no. Is she "any kind" of Christian? The answer is no. In Fonda's one-page discussion on the matter of being "Christian" (her quotations), she *very* pointedly denied that Jesus is "the *only* way" to salvation.

In her autobiography, Jane Fonda spent more pages discussing her vagina than discussing the idea of being "Christian." Is it too late for her to become a Christian if she chose to do so? No, it's never too late. One only needs eyes to see and ears to hear, both of which she has closed.

Finally, a special warning to residents of Georgia. In her book, Fonda explains that her reason for settling in Atlanta was based in part on the decision to escape the elitist Hollywood view of looking down on mainstream America. However, she notes, once she came to Atlanta she "realized" there was a "lot of truth" in that condescending view perpetuated by her Hollywood friends. As Queen of Hypocrisy, this is what makes Jane Fonda a dangerous person. She revels in tearing down the morals and deeply held faith-based values of people as a sinister sport. She projects her own guilt on everyone but herself.

Fonda has formally announced she will stay in Georgia and "effect change" where it is "needed most." She admits that making Georgia (and the South, for that matter) into a paradise as "bucolic" as Hollywood will be a daunting task, but she's going to give it her all.

With that in mind, residents of Georgia may want to consider the Fulton County Probate Office to search for the proper procedures for having the seventy-year-old Norma Desmond look-a-like returned to Sunset Boulevard, preferably in a comfortable nursing facility where she will be cared for with all due respect, dignity, compassion, and loving kindness.

Because of her darkly malevolent capacity to wreak havoc upon the face of the earth with her quadra-polar personality and the failure from decades of therapy to become a productive citizen and positive role model, Jane Fonda is rapidly becoming a danger not only to herself, but to everyone around her.

If extraditing Fonda back to "bucolic" Hollywood by legal means is not feasible, the good people of Georgia may want to organize a "radical" demonstration in front of her Atlanta home, since this is the only language she understands. By paraphrasing a popular 2004 campaign slogan, "the people" should shout, "Jane Fonda can take her tax-hiking, government expanding, latte-drinking, sushi-eating, Volvo-driving, *New York Times* reading, body-piercing, Hollywood-loving, left-wing freak show back to California where it belongs. And take Ted and Jimmy with you."

MODERN-DAY HOLLYCOMS

Even in the twenty-first century, the Hollywood fascination with a "cultural communism" continues to hold sway with a majority of people in the entertainment industry, despite the continuing collapse and dissipation of Communist governments and political power around the world. The basic Communist tenet of being able to tell people what to do and what to think is very attractive to the Hollywood creative community because of their over-inflated sense of power, arrogance, and unbridled ego.

Also, the ability to instill urgent unreasonable fear and the specter of imminent death to a broad audience is a deeply-seated perverted mindset among the Hollywood crowd. This is currently being manifested in the global warming alarmist movement perpetrated by Al Gore and Hollywood sidekick Leonardo DiCaprio, whose reckless tactics have already caused a new generation of children to live in a constant state of fear and anxiety over a looming and suspicious albatross of the world's end before they even reach puberty.

The "carbon offset" program is a fraudulent guilt-ridden shake-down not too different from paying Communist Party dues if you want to "stay connected" to the politically correct network. In August 2007, Al Gore gave another angry, foreboding speech in which he declared that *anybody* who didn't believe in global warming was being *controlled* by special interests. Heidi Cullen of the Weather Channel demanded that any meteorologist who didn't believe in global warming should be fired. This isn't pseudo-Communism, this is Stalinist Communism complete with payoffs and punishment. John Coleman, founder of the Weather Channel, had heard enough by November 2007 and called global warming the biggest hoax in the history of the world.

George Soros and his one-world vision of one-way thinking is also cultural communism at its worst. His Open Society Institute is attempting to undermine democratic societies around the globe and replace them with Soros' personal politics of destruction. After a short stint as a Nazi collaborator in World War II, where he lured fellow Jews to their death and confiscated their property, he told his father he wanted to go to Moscow. When his father, Tivadar, asked him why, young George said, "That's where the power is."

Dr. Ted Baehr and Dr. Tom Snyder have traced the origin of the American brand of Communist chic and the radical left "secular progressive" counterculture back to Germany shortly after the end of World War I. An atheistic, pseudo-intellectual leftist political ideology originated with the Frankfurt School. According to Baehr and Snyder, this school of thought "was started in Germany in 1923 by a group of Marxist intellectuals and modeled after the Marx-Engels Institute in Moscow. When Hitler came to power in 1933, the Marxists fled to the United States to teach at famous colleges such as Columbia, Princeton, and the University of California at Berkeley. Eventually they became founders and powerful leaders of the counterculture revolution in the 1960s. This revolution started the movement for 'political correctness' in America.

"America's education system, its government, its popular culture, its military, its business community, and its news media have been transformed by this insidious Fifth Column of 'Cultural Marxism.' We are now suffering the consequences of this quiet political correctness invasion. This is what the current Culture War in Hollywood and America is all about."[50]

These Frankfurt school professors were also the "hosts" for the influx of Soviet Communists who infiltrated Hollywood and Washington. As Baehr and Snyder noted, "political correctness has its direct roots in Soviet Communism and set the stage for the Culture War." And as Baehr and Snyder declare, "It is a Culture War that must not be lost" to Hollywood.

CHAPTER 12

OLIVER STONE: NATURAL BORN KILLER?

"Sadly, Hollywood will have to be forced to shed some of its own blood before it learns to police itself."
—John Grisham

"I'm trying to reshape the world through movies," Oliver Stone once boasted, disproving "The Big Lie" perpetrated by Hollywood since the 1920s that "film is a reflection of society."[1] Of all the angry and tormented filmmakers who are trying to reshape the world in the vision of their darkened soul, none are more dangerous than the true mirror reflection of evil, Oliver Stone.

The longtime addict, intermittent alcoholic, screenwriter, producer and director has been involved in numerous Hollywood productions including *Platoon, Wall Street, The Doors, JFK, Nixon, Midnight Express*, the hip-hop cult film *Scarface* and the box-office bombs *Alexander* and *World Trade Center*. His biopic on George W. Bush was crashing even before its release.

If he's not trying to rewrite history, Stone is fascinated with portraying the degradation of humanity without any hope of redemption; substituting bloodlust at it's worst. That movies have the ability to negatively influence people's behavior is an understatement in the dark catalog of Stone's filmography. The best evidence out of this collection is Oliver Stone's film *Natural Born Killers*, released by none other than Warner Brothers in 1994.

Natural Born Killers would also be cited as a major influence in the numerous copycat acts of cold-blooded murders and monstrous massacres throughout the 1990s including two of the worst school shootings in American history; Paducah Kentucky and the Columbine High massacre in Littleton, Colorado. The most notorious of the "copycat killings" would center around the 1995 murder of Mississippi cotton gin owner William Savage and the subsequent shooting of convenience store clerk Pasty Byers, who was paralyzed from the neck down. The shooters were two 18 year old "acid-heads" named Ben Darras and Sarah Edmonson who were also addicted to watching *Natural Born Killers* on videotape more times than they could count. It was the last viewing that "hit a nerve" and the two Oklahoma teenagers jumped in their car on a shooting spree into the deep south.

The trial that followed resulted from a lawsuit filed by the Byers family against the two teenagers and would soon be expanded to include the film's distributor Time-Warner and even director Oliver Stone himself. The charges would eventually cite the violation of the incitement clause of the First Amendment by Stone and others involved in the production and distribution of *Natural Born Killer*, which would be referred to as *NBK*.

Never before in the 100 year history of filmmaking had a legal case against a filmmaker and his distributor reached such legal heights and advanced stages of alleged liability. Before the dust settled after a six-year legal battle which left Hollywood holding it's breath of death, even the long dark shadow of Jack Valenti would rear his ancient head directly into the proceedings.

Stone's defense of the indefensible and the industry colluding to cover its bloody footprints would mark one of the lowest points in Hollywood's campaign of value manipulation.

* * *

First, a thorough background of Oliver Stone's unending love affair with highly dangerous and illegal drugs is warranted. The lesson and dilemma of Oliver Stone is two-fold; not only can films have a negative and even deadly influence on their audience, but the personally destructive drug addicted behavior of the filmmaker is now part of the corrosive creative input into the movies. This drug-induced desire by filmmakers to put their nightmares on the silver screen has become known as the "Oliver Stone Effect."

Also, Stone's ability to run you down in his car on a street in Los Angeles is a very real possiblilty, depending on the quality and quantity of drugs he is washing down with alcohol. The fact that Stone serves no jail time or is even sentenced to produce public service announcements renouncing his behavior is not lost on the Hollywood hugging culture, who interpret this as a sign of privilege and influence in an era where "becoming rich" and "becoming famous" are now seen as the two most popular goals for adolescents.

Before delving into the dark lifelong motivations of Stone's behavior and resultant impact on the culture, it is important to note that during the 1980s and

1990s, the world of entertainment and the world of sports were beginning to merge in a confluence of mutual interest, especially in the areas of "star" promotions. Sports stars and movie stars as well as their high-energy managers and promoters were collectively being labeled as "celebrities." Both industries are plagued with drug abuse far worse than is reported in the press. This chapter will go into detail as to how pervasive it is in the film industry and what can be done to bring it under control with the goal of putting an end to it.

In a time when the International Olympic Committee and the professional sports industry is increasingly scrutinizing the rising illegal drug use among athletes, trainers and the league officials who turn a blind eye, now may be the time for a clarion call to mandate drug testing for celebrities and all employees of the Hollywood entertainment industry. The industry can thank Oliver Stone's highly destructive behavior on screen and off for the mandating of such a broad and comprehensive initiative. The bimbo eruptions of Paris Hilton, Nicole Richie, Lindsay Lohan and Britney Spears have amplified the urgency of dealing with this problem as a new generation follows in the footsteps of their Hollywood elders like Stone.

After all, the Hollywood creative community has become increasingly popular due to the exhaustive coverage it is given by the mainstream press, more so now than at anytime in broadcast or print history. And, it's not only coverage of celebrities in front of the camera. Never before has the "action" behind the camera become more popular than the present day in the age of "infotainment," especially when every major network news entity and many cable channels are owned by a movie studio or entertainment conglomerate.

Entertainment news segments are now as regular as sports and the weather. The thought of Huntley and Brinkley devoting even two minutes to entertainment during the evening news of the 1960s would have been considered ridiculous. Impressionable children, adolescents and adults are intrigued by the moviemaking process and their appetite for information from the world of Hollywood is voracious at the same time it is pitiful, considering the poor examples of role models that the entertainment community offers.

Just as sports fans look up to the top point earnings and salaries of all players, they also have become keen to the management and coaching of pro and amateur teams. With sports becoming entertainment and entertainment becoming sport, movie fans are also savvy to the actions and behaviors of producers and directors in the same way they lap up movie star celebrity news.

When professional sports and entertainment celebrities are apprehended or detected with drug-related violations and crimes, the public often see fines imposed that are considered pocket change for the offenders who laugh all the way home. However, that approach is changing rapidly in Olympic, professional, amateur and college sports. With the Olympic committee and Major League sports increasing drug oversight of its athletes and trainers, it's now time for Hollywood to step up to the plate. Oliver Stone will be just one example of many that necessitate the long-overdue initiative of mandatory drug testing in Hollywood.

OLIVER STONE: THE DRUG ADDICT

As a role model, Oliver Stone has obviously adopted the old Charles Barkley declaration, "I'm no role model." Not only do his movies portray dark lies, deceptions, conspiracy theories, personal vendettas, perversion, drug abuse and total human dysfunction, his own personal life has become the perfect role model—the role model of a director gone mad—whose mind has been seared by 40 years of constant drug and alcohol abuse for which he is unapologetic in the least, and at the worst has put the lives of innocent people in peril; not just the Beverly Hills pedestrians who have been blessed not to be rolled over by one of Stone's drunken, drug-hazed night rides. Also in peril are the American audiences who have become impaled by Stone's bleak worldviews projected on the screen; the Oliver Stone Effect.

Not only does Stone's professional and defiant personal behavior as a proud drug addict portray adulthood in Hollywood as insanity rewarded with a new movie contract, Stone's behavior as a father of three children should have landed him in the "care" and monitoring of social workers for defacto child abuse years ago. Why?

In a "60 Minutes" interview in the early 1990s, Stone stated that he was no longer addicted to drugs. More disturbing than that public relations lie, when asked if he would object to his children "experimenting" with drugs, Stone stated that it would all depend on what kind of drugs they were interested in "trying." That's a classic example of "Hollywood logic."

More than a decade after his "denial" interview, Stone was pulled over again on May 29, 2005 for drunken driving and drug possession in Beverly Hills. According to police spokesman Sgt. John Edmonson, Stone was spotted driving erratically and pulled over just before midnight while "cruising" Sunset Boulevard.

Stone, just shy of his 60th birthday, was charged with DUI and possession of an undisclosed amount of drugs. After posting $15,000 bond, Stone managed to avoid jail time.[2] How he managed this is known only to the office holders of Beverly Hills justice. His avoidance of any kind of punishment is especially noteworthy in light of the fact this was not his first "bat out of hell" driving incident.

In 1999, in the middle of the ongoing litigation against him for complicity in the copycat killings perpetrated by Oliver Stone movie addicts Ben Darras and Sarah Edmonson, Stone was pulled over in Beverly Hills and later pleaded "no contest" to DUI and guilty to drug possession. After a brief stay in one of

Hollywood's many "quickie rehab" programs, he was out again and returned to drinking and drugging.

In a letter to Playboy columnist Marc Cooper, a reader commented, "It does not surprise me that he has a drug problem because all his recent movies are [expletive] acid trips. Too much drugs, God, isn't he too old for that?"[3]

Stone's behavior is consistent with his personal idols from the 1960s such as Timothy Leary, as Stone explains, "I was doing a lot of drugs, grass and acid. I was into Timothy Leary . . ."[4] Stone was also fascinated with Jim Morrison of the music group *The Doors*. Morrison was a self-professed occultist, drug addict and believed he received his music from "Satan."

Dr. Jason Kovar, a respected scholar of the occult and New Age philosophy's influence on the entertainment industry noted, "Stone's initiation into the New Age mindset is reflected in his work at practically every level."[5]

Stone's close friend Richard Rutkowski tried to explain the machination of Stone's dark, dreary cynicism. "It [film] is an exploration of what's going on inside him. He's analytical to a point, but he doesn't have control over it. I think that's what he's looking for—how to control it. He has control over the medium, but I don't think he has control over his mind . . . He's constantly trying to explain that and put those demons on celluloid—writing and filmmaking are his psycho therapy."[6]

Stone was, and still is completely mesmerized by Jim Morrison's occult-like presence inside the director's deep-fried mind, "I believe in Morrison's incantations. Break on through. Kill the pigs. Destroy: Loot. F___ your mother. All that s___. Anything goes. ANYTHING."[7]

"Anything goes," "Destroy," "If it feels good, do it" and "there are no consequences" are popular chants among the Hollywood film industry that have their origins in one man who has been virtually idolized if not worshiped by many members of the movie and music industry. Aleister Crowley's influence on the contemporary entertainment scene cannot be underestimated.

Crowley declared "The New Age" is 1904 with the motto: "Do what thou will shall be the whole of the law." He has directly and indirectly influenced thousands of people in the entertainment industry and popular culture including Oliver Stone. Others influenced by Crowley's occult philosophies include Stone's idol Jim Morrison, John Lennon, Paul McCartney, Jack Valenti, Timothy Leary, Hugh Hefner, Mick Jagger and the founder of Hollywood's secretive religion, Scientology, L. Ron Hubbard, to name a few. Conspiracy theory? No. Just the truth.

Oliver Stone is just another strand in the long dark thread which runs through the Hollywood entertainment machine.

* * *

In an interview with Marc Cooper, Stone talked openly about his passion for illegal drug abuse and the "fun havoc" it has ravaged on his mind. Like most aging post-hippies, Stone has blamed most of the world's problems on Richard Nixon. This is particularly sad as these graying hippies approach the ages of 65 and 70 and the only thing that still unites them is a mutual hatred of one man.

Cooper asked Stone point blank, "Drugs seem to be a theme in every one of your movies. Were they a central part of your life?"

Stone, like so many radical baby-boomers tried to lessen the sting of the question by trotting out the well-worn and untrue rationalization that *everybody* from his generation was taking drugs. That is a media myth perpetrated for over 40 years and Stone is the poster child of that ruse, "I think drugs were very much a part of my generation's experience . . . we were the drug generation. And marijuana, with its origin in the sixties, was good. It was a force for good. As was acid. It transformed consciousness. And in Vietnam, it certainly kept us sane."[8]

Stone requested frontline combat duty during the Vietnam War and "attempted" to sum up the sentiment among his fellow soldiers by injecting *his own* sentiment about combat with the enemy, "I'm here man; I'm gonna smoke dope and I'm gonna make it and I'm gonna survive and I'm gonna make a lot of money. And the dope was great."[9]

In the interview with Cooper, Stone boasts about smoking marijuana on the day he earned the Bronze Star. "Yeah, I had been stoned that morning and the firefight was that afternoon. But it wasn't really a big deal. There were so many acts of valor from other guys . . ."[10]

And it was the "many acts of valor" from the "sober" members of the platoon that saved Stone from being killed. Soldiers like Oliver Stone were a major liability to the platoon who had their hands full keeping an eye on the enemy and another eye on the drug addicts in their own formation.

My own father, Edgar Boyer, served in Vietnam during the same time as Oliver Stone and was almost killed by a sniper's bullet during the Tet Offensive. His sentiment about Oliver Stone was reflected by the others he served with in Qui Nhon, South Vietnam, "When a firefight starts, the last person you want to depend on is an acid-head like Stone who is in 'la-la' land when bullets are flying past your head. The only reason I survived Tet as I was running across the street is because a completely sober, sharp-eyed soldier picked off the sniper before he could squeeze off another round. Besides, Oliver Stone doesn't tell you about the soldiers who might have died and did die because he was "passed-out" when he should have been on the "look-out."

For years, rumors have circulated that *Platoon* was an attempt by Stone to paint himself in a positive light during his Vietnam War years, especially in light of accusations circulated around the UCLA campus that Stone had participated in murder while in Vietnam. Cooper asked Stone point blank if he had ever participated in the random killing of civilians.

Stone was quick to answer, "No, I saved a girl from getting killed. I put that in the movie too, the rape. They would have killed that girl." No one serving with Stone has ever come forward to corroborate Stone's depiction of the incident.

Cooper asked specifically if he hated his superior officers and if Stone had "seen" any fragging (murder) of officers. Stone admitted to "hating" virtually all commanding officers, but stopped short of admitting any direct involvement in witnessing or participating in the murder of combat officers by offering a post-war dance of an answer.

"I heard about it. But some people have suggested that I really participated in some of the scenes in *Platoon*, I should be tried for war crimes—a pamphlet was sent around UCLA saying that I'm a war criminal. So *I'm not going to be any more specific* [emphasis added]." Then without taking a breath, Stone gives Cooper a "how to" lesson in killing a fellow comrade or officer, "You kill somebody during a battle, you just put your M-16 on somebody and you just do him. Nobody's going to see it."[11] This is the man who once volunteered to assassinate President Nixon, or "do him" in Oliver Stone lingo.

Stone admitted that his increasing appetite for drugs was based on shear indulgence and not on any wartime post-traumatic stress. Stone even slipped drugs to his own unsuspecting father, much like a doper teen who gets a thrill from blowing smoke in the pet dog's face.

"I took drugs to excess. I was using as much LSD as anybody. Even slipped it into my dad's drink once . . . My usage became heavier, but not for a purpose. It became an indulgence." Slipping LSD into his own father's drink says much about Oliver Stone's total lack of responsibility, then and now, not only to his own father, but to members of the audience who watch his movies that are laced with conspiracies, lies and subliminal messages.

Whereas the elder Mr. Stone survived young Oliver's "slip," many viewers of Stone's *Natural Born Killers* did not—killing their friends and often themselves, as we will explore in the next section. And Stone laughs at the very real destruction and deception his films cause, much like he must have laughed when his father was struggling for sanity against a stroke or heart attack induced by Ollie's acid. The motive that Stone fails to admit is that he could have been in line to inherit his father's estate in the case of "sudden death."

"I started more acid, and grass, I suppose in the beginning. And then I touched on some other things here and there . . . cocaine, certainly . . . cocaine is what took me to the edge."[12] At least Stone admitted that Hollywood was awash in drug abuse unlike anything he had seen before, which probably explains why he chose Hollywood as "home." When Stone arrived in Hollywood, he said the industry there "was in a kind of cocaine craze."

Stone was first busted for drugs after leaving the military when he was thrown into the San Diego jail for smuggling marijuana. His father paid off his court appointed attorney in order to get him released. The incident would inspire Stone to write the script for *Midnight Express* for which he received an Oscar in 1978 for Best Screenplay. But, his past experience with buying justice seemed only to embolden his escalating drug use. Certainly any thoughts about killing his father quickly dissipated when he realized how "useful" he could be in another stint behind bars.

Joe O'Har, the veteran location scout, told me about his hair-raising experience of working with Oliver Stone during this time. As location scout for "Midnight Express," O'Har explained that Stone insisted on tagging along for the scout with him and director Alan Parker.

"The screenwriter rarely comes along during a location scout and Oliver Stone was the one person I didn't feel comfortable with during our travels. He had already developed a reputation as a doper, but Parker insisted on Stone's 'input.' We were looking for the Turkish prison location by scouting active but older prisons throughout the southwest and southeast U.S.

"Stone was carrying a briefcase that never left his side. I just figured he was carrying copies of the script and the blue-paged rewrites. We stopped at a gas station and he opened it up right next to me and there was a virtual pharmacy of every conceivable drug in the world packed in special little bottles and baggies. I said 'what the [expletive] are you doing? We're walking in and out of federal prisons as the guests of law enforcement and you're carrying enough drugs to kill the entire population of a small town.' Stone just laughed and Parker was sleeping off a hangover from drinking too much the night before. It was the last time I worked for either one of those [expletives]."[13]

* * *

In the interim period between his first drug bust and his first Academy Award, Stone landed in New York where he attended NYU Film School, ironically under the G.I. Bill. His mentor at the film school was the equally dark and mendacious Martin Scorcese. By now a regular addict, Stone was also showing an interest in the occult and was playing the role of the angry young man who found a soul-mate in the bleak visions of Scorcese's urban nightmares.

Stone described himself as "an anarchist. Radical. Very much like Travis Bickle in *Taxi Driver*. A walking time bomb. Hateful and suspicious."[14] Stone was equally open about his hatred for Richard Nixon and his very real intention to assassinate the president. Stone told Cooper at the end of the interview, "I thought, why don't we get a gun and just do Nixon, you know? I'll do him. Laughs, You know, 'Let's go kill man.' I thought if you want to have a revolution, let's [expletive] have one. Let's kill cops . . . I was feeling pure anger. Hatred. Well, actually, I'm right . . . That's the only way revolution is going to occur."[15]

Finally, Stone ended the interview with his own New Age solution to fight drugs, "I mean, the way to beat it is to legalize drugs out and out. Legalize heroin, cocaine, marijuana. Yeah. Let kids try it . . . get it out of their system . . . Make it available. People kill to get it."[16]

Obviously, with Oliver Stone's 1999 and 2005 arrests occurring more than a decade after his Marc Cooper interview, the "kid" still hasn't got it out of his "system." Stone is the lowest form of role model for American children, adolescents, adults, the moviegoing audience in general and his own three children in particular. Stone is the true epitome of Hollywood's darkside; a man whose deep-seated hatred and fantasies of killing sprees would soon be realized.

As a paranoid conspiracy theorist, confirmed anarchist, failed radical and assassin, possessing a mind severely ravished and damaged through decades of drug abuse, Oliver Stone would create and direct a film that would demonstrate the true power of film as a force of evil at it's worst; a film that would be tied to the death of more than twenty people in America and abroad.

The phenomena would become labeled as "copycat crimes." And, the author of the original "copy" sought his inspiration through persistent drug abuse for which he still practices as, in his words, "an indulgence." Where was the Writers Guild of America? Where was the Director's Guild? Whose side did they take in the epic case of "Death by Film?"

OLIVER STONE: DEATH BY FILM

In the early days of silent movies, shortly after the dawn of the 20th century, urban reformer Jane Addams of Chicago called the curious amusement of motion pictures "a veritable house of dreams" for America's children. Film historian Gregory D. Black noted that "Addams was convinced, like so many in her day, that movies were a more powerful influence on the minds of children than any other form of communication or education. She believed that what they saw on the screen directly and immediately was transformed into action. If children saw crime movies, they would become criminals."[17]

While not all children, obviously, who watch crime movies grow up to become criminals, the influence on the behavior of children and adults has been demonstrated in over 3,000 studies beginning with the Payne Studies of The Motion Picture Research Council between 1928 and 1933. The very advent of this first study may well have prompted the major movie moguls to make their "Big Lie" proclamation of 1929 that movies were "a reflection of society," not an influence.

Eight decades later, Oliver Stone would prove that Jane Addams was at least partially correct in her assessment that movies were "a more powerful influence on the minds of children than any other form of communication or education."

He accomplished this by directing a movie whose basic plot line revolves around a young couple who travel the country on a killing spree that leaves 52 people dead in three weeks. In the end, the young couple ride off into Oliver Stone's golden sunset of glory having never been apprehended or punished.

Stone may have preferred to title the film *Natural Born Heroes,* for that is how he portrayed the murderers in *Natural Born Killers, or NBK.* Remember, this film is from a man who described himself as an anarchist, hate-monger, revolutionary, drug addict and as a willing and eager volunteer to assassinate the president of the United States.

On March 5th of 1995, less than a year after NBK's release, Sarah Edmonson and Ben Darras, both 18 at the time, would spend the evening together in a cabin in rural Oklahoma. Both were taking acid-based drugs, much like Oliver Stone has publicly advocated for kids to try.

The two teenagers were planning a much bigger "trip" the next morning by driving to Memphis to watch a live concert by the ancient original hippie rock group "The Grateful Dead," headed by drug addict Jerry Garcia, himself a scorched-brain acid addict who led tens of thousands of teens and young adults into drug abuse and early death during the 1960s and continuously until his own death by consumption in August of 1995. Darras and Edmondson decided to stay up all night watching *NBK* over and over again on their VCR until the sun rose over the horizon the next morning. With no sleep, brains singed by LSD and the continuous images of murderous carnage burned into their minds from *NBK*, the two teenagers left for Memphis carrying a .38 caliber pistol.

Not surprisingly, the two arrive in Memphis only to discover that they are a day early for the concert. With no place to go and fresh memories of *NBK* replaying in their heads like an endless video loop, Darras decides that the two would drive into Mississippi to "kill time."

Darras and Edmondson stopped just outside the small crossroads town of Hernando, pulling into a cotton gin on the main road. Inside, owner William Savage was sitting alone behind his desk when Darras and Edmonson entered and asked Savage for directions. Before he even had a chance to stand up, Darras pulled out the .38 pistol and shot Savage in the head. He then fired a second shot to make sure Savage was dead.

Darras was pumped up and excited. He was just like the Woody Harrelson character in *NBK* killing his first victim. The young couple decided to skip the concert in Memphis. They were on a new mission and the road south led to New Orleans. "Party City" was their new destination and they planned to pave the road with blood.

Just across the border in Ponchatoula, Louisiana Darras and Edmonson pulled their Nissan Maxima into the parking lot of a convenience store. Darras handed the .38 to Edmonson and told her "it's your turn." Walking calmly into the store,

THE HOLLYWOOD CULTURE WAR

Edmondson pulled out the pistol on unsuspecting store clerk Patsy Byers and shoots her in the neck, paralyzing her from the neck down.

Unphased, the two Oklahoma teenagers traveled further south toward New Orleans. Ben Darras and Sarah Edmondson seemed intent on rivaling the shooting spree of their two heroes in *NBK*.

Fortunately, the teenager's crusade of imitating a movie-inspired killing spree was cut short when they were apprehended after the surveillance cameras captured the grainy image of Sarah Edmondson's face. She was recognized and identified by fellow students back in Oklahoma where the tape was broadcast on local television news. It was an ironic triumph of real-time video-tape technology that captured the killers who had been fueled by the video fantasies and deviated cerebrum of another acid-head, Oliver Stone.

As Stone's friend Richard Rutkowski said, " . . . I don't think he has control over his mind."[18] However, Oliver Stone would not be able to plead insanity in the six year legal battle that was about to unfold. Dr. Jason Kovar did, however, make note of the chilling statement made by a wide-eyed Oliver Stone after an initial screening of his film, boasting with euphoria, "this movie is great. It makes you want to go out and kill somebody."[19] Statements like this and others quoted in *The New York Times* came back later to haunt Stone.

Store clerk Patsy Byers survived the shooting by Sarah Edmondson, but was left permanently paralyzed and bedridden with no feeling or movement below the neck. She would die two years later in 1997. But, before her death, Patsy Byers and husband Lonne, along with their three children, filed suit in Louisiana State Court on July 26, 1995 against Edmondson and Darras for damages Byers and her family sustained as a result of the shooting (Patsy Ann Byers, et al. v. Sarah Edmondson, et al.)

The Byers retained longtime Louisiana attorney Joe Simpson as their lawyer in the case to be tried at the parrish county seat of Amite, Louisiana. And then, a curious thing happened on the way to the courthouse.

In March of 1996, Simpson amends the Byers lawsuit adding Time-Warner Entertainment, Oliver Stone and others associated with the production and distribution of the film. All would join Darras and Edmondson as defendants. The amended petition alleged, in the words of attorney Simpson, that the Hollywood defendants "knew or should have known that the film would cause and inspire people . . . to commit crimes such as the shooting of Patsy Ann Byers."[20]

Insiders at the Warner legal department were rumored to have *laughed* out loud at the thought of being added to the lawsuit. Hadn't those little people in that two-bit, two-lane town ever heard of the First Amendment and freedom of expression? But, Warner's raucous laughter would be short-lived and quickly muffled.

Ironically, the first man to be shot and killed, William Savage of Hernando, Mississippi had a good friend who was a regular writer and contributor to the

Oxford American magazine. The writer explained and defended Simpson's additional strategy that would argue movies "should be considered as a product." In a 1996 issue of the *Oxford American*, the writer shared attorney Joe Simpson's concept of product liability, "Think of a movie as a product brought to market, not to dissimilar from, say Ford Pintos. If something goes wrong with the product, whether by design or defect, and injury ensues, its makers are held responsible."

The writer of the article had a keen knowledge of the law as a practicing attorney, and was an accomplished author who also maintained an excellent working knowledge of the movie industry. John Grisham not only wrote for the *Oxford American*, he was a co-founder of the bi-monthly magazine. By 1996, Grisham was already an instant best-seller of legal thrillers and his films were coming to the screen on an annual basis.

Grisham first met William Savage in 1983, describing him as "active in local affairs, a decent Christian and solid citizen who believed in public service and was always ready to volunteer."

Cold hearts don't bleed and Stone offered no condolences to the bereaved families. After all, it would imply guilt for the alleged crimes that he committed. And now, Stone was engaged in a war of words with Grisham after the author ravished the demented director in the *Oxford American*. Stone, whose capacity for vendettas and revenge is well documented, angrily called Grisham a hypocrite because his stories also contained violent content.

Grisham made the point that his stories contain a moral underpinning whereas Stone's movie did not. Stone admitted as much when he bragged openly about the horrific influence of *NBK*, boasting in an April 1996 issue of *The New York Times*, "The most pacifistic people in the world said they came out of this movie and wanted to kill somebody."[21]

Stone also made a cavalier statement about the special "director's cut" in which he was alleged to include even more scenes of carnage. Commenting on the death of a character played by Tommy Lee Jones, "He is impaled. All of his limbs come off. It's very funny actually."[22]

Concerning the case against him, Stone suffered a foot-in-mouth incident in which he said, "An elementary principle of our civilization is that people are responsible for their own actions."[23] He obviously didn't consider himself to be one of those "responsible" people.

By now, Warner's lawyers and Stone's own attorneys were telling the brain-fried alcoholic director to keep his mouth shut. Stone was teetering on the fence of the First Amendment's "incitement exception," most popularly described, ironically, as falsely crying fire in a crowded *movie house*.

Attorney Joe Simpson's argument for treating movies as a product had legal precedent in the Supreme Court going back to the early days of silent movies in 1915. That year, the Supreme Court upheld an Ohio State law that required movies to pay a licensing fee in order to be shown in the state. Film approval for exhibition in Ohio required that a film exhibit "moral, educational, amusing and harmless characters" and exercising that discretion would fall into the hands of the film review board for the State of Ohio.[24]

Mutual Films, a movie distributor, had challenged the Ohio state law claiming movies were a form of the free speech, similar to the press. The U.S. Supreme Court rejected Mutual's argument, stating that the extension of unfettered free speech to movies could open the doors for abuse of the medium in which movies "may be used for evil" and continued by saying that certain things "should not have pictorial representation in public places." The U.S. Supreme Court's final judgment was handed down that movies were "a business pure and simple."[25]

This would be the law of the land for the next four decades until being overturned in the mid 1950s. Because the 1915 Supreme Court Mutual decision was overturned, family attorney Joe Simpson did not have current case precedent and the jury trial court dismissed the lawsuit against Stone and Warners on January 23, 1997; however, the Byers family immediately appealed the decision up to the state appeals court.

By May of 1998, Stone and Time-Warner were becoming frustrated that the case against them was continuing into its third year and contended that the case against them should be barred because *NBK* was protected by the First Amendment guarantee of free speech. The Byers family and attorney were saving their new argument for the appeals court by presenting *NBK* as a film that fell squarely into the incitement exception to the First Amendment protection of free speech.

The incitement exception states that in cases where speech advocates the use of imminent force or unlawful action, and is likely to produce such conduct, the state may indeed forbid free speech. The Louisiana State Appeals Court determined on May 15, 1998 that the Byers family allegations that Stone intended for his movie to incite people to commit violent crimes and because it also stated a valid cause of action, the parties would be allowed to go to trial.

By October 1998, Stone and Time-Warner were becoming desperate, fearing that not only may they lose their case, but a new law could, in reality, rise from this case that could restore elements of the 1915 Supreme Court case that would restrict Hollywood's production of movies "used for evil." Furthermore, a new law may attempt to limit depictions on film of base, vulgar, bloodlust, ultra-violent content and perhaps even adversely affect the increasing pornographic content creeping into mainstream movies and television.

The entire movie industry was shuddering at the prospect of having to "clean up" their act after 30 years of Valenti's "free screen" movement that allowed rape, pillage, random murder, sexual deviancy, drug abuse and profanity to become "entertainment" without consequences. Stone began drinking more heavily and indulging in frequent illegal drug use—again.

In the meantime not a single individual or group in the Hollywood entertainment industry stepped forth to extend even the most basic form of sympathy and condolence to the Byers or family of William Savage. The Hollywood cop-outs were reviving The Big Lie at fever pitch saying that Stone's movie *NBK* was "a reflection of society."

* * *

On October 9th of 1998, the Louisiana Supreme Court declined to review the Court of Appeal's decision at the request of Stone and Time-Warner. And, the big shocker to the Hollywood defendants arrived on March 8, 1999 when the Supreme Court of the United States refused their appeal to have the case thrown out.

Even Hollywood's Dark Prince Jack Valenti stormed onto the scene from his lofty offices of the MPAA *demanding* that the case be *thrown out* without exception. Valenti had a lot at stake. He had worked long and hard to make moviegoing a more dangerous and malicious experience and he wasn't about to support any attempt to protect the public from mentally deranged and drug-addicted movie directors and producers.

The U.S. Supreme Court decision was a green light for the trial to continue back at local court in Amite, Louisiana. The Byers' family lawyer was now in a position to request viewing of any documents related to the case including not only production notes, but private journals and even unused footage. Joe Simpson could now take a deposition from Oliver Stone and the director would be forced to answer questions.

Simpson would ask salient and specifically relevant questions such as "What did you mean when you said that?" "Did you decide it after you saw the final cut?" Simpson also stated publicly, "If Stone thought that people were going to go out and murder people, he should have never released the film."[26]

By the summer of 1999, both sides in the Patsy Byers wrongful death lawsuit would begin presentations for a long trial that would not begin until the end of the year. In the meantime, the case was receiving national and international attention. The trial was being viewed by many as a legal test case in the Culture War to determine whether Hollywood would be allowed to act in a reckless manner to such an extent that people's lives could be put in peril.

Legal analyst Greta Van Susteren, then a CNN reporter, said at the time, "there's a climate of wanting to teach Hollywood a lesson . . . the courts are one place where that's happening."[27]

And, rumors about Stone spinning out of control with drugs and alcohol were validated when the director was arrested in Beverly Hills, again for DUI and possession of hashish. Stone would later plead guilty in the fall of 1999 to drug possession and "no contest" to DUI.

Stone would be checked into a quickie rehab center program and released, driver's license intact. Stone's rampant drug and alcohol abuse was not allowed to be entered into court evidence, but his arrest made national news. Warner Brothers was not happy.

When the trial resumed, Simpson and other plaintiff attorneys who had joined the case faced a major hurdle, even though they had come so far down a long and winding legal road. In order to win the case, the plaintiffs would have to prove that Stone and Time-Warner actually intended to "incite" viewers of *NBK* to commit crimes such as the type committed against Byers.

To this point, the Louisiana Intermediate Court of Appeals determined that the Byers family's allegations that Stone intended for his movie to incite people to commit violent crimes *did* state a valid cause of legal action. Stone's production was determined to fall within the "incitement exception" to the First Amendment. In effect, this stage of the ruling was held up by the Louisiana Supreme Court.

Now, the Byers family and their attorneys would bring in additional ammunition. The legal team produced results from a recently compiled Federal Trade Commission Study in early 2000. Chairman Robert Pitofsky stated that "target marketing to children of entertainment products with violent content is pervasive and aggressive."[28]

While promoting violence to children didn't imply intent to commit violence in the Byers vs. Stone case, FTC Chairman Pitofsky did make special mention in his report that "exposure does seem to correlate with aggressive attitudes, insensitivity to violence and an exaggerated view of how much violence occurs in the world."[29]

Stone's own statements such as his *New York Times* quote that people who saw his movie "wanted to kill somebody" were also introduced to his deposition which was full of Clintonesque "memory lapses," which the president cited over 250 times in his own deposition the year before.

None of this was convincing enough to Judge Robert Morrison, even in light of the fact that Oliver Stone once boasted, "I'm trying to reshape the world through movies." And that is exactly what he did with *NBK w*hen the movie's number one fan, Ben Darras, reshaped the living body of William Savage into a dead body and Sarah Edmondson reshaped the vibrant world of Patsy Byers into a quadriplegic unable to move anything except her mouth and eyes.

In addition, the Byers family attorneys argued that *NBK* violated federal obscenity laws. While "indecency" is afforded limited protection by law, "obscenity" is *not* protected by the First Amendment, proving that there is no such thing as "unfettered" free speech. (For definitions of "indecency" and "obscenity" see Appendix IV.)

Not only was *NBK* clearly obscene, Sarah Edmondson admitted under oath that *NBK* directly influenced her actions in shooting Patsy Byers. The defense cried foul, calling Edmondson's assertion a "cop out" and an attempt to shift personal responsibility for her actions to a vague *death by film* excuse.

The dilemma of charging the film as obscene was unfortunately plagued with the age-old judicial levity regarding determination of interpretation which can swing either way depending on who is "judging" the obscenity charge. (See www.moralityinmedia.com for examples of judicial hypocrisy and enforcement failure of obscenity laws).

Faced with the three "I" argument of incitement, intent, and interpretation, Louisiana Judge Robert Morrison dismissed the wrongful death lawsuit against Oliver Stone and Time-Warner. Stone walked away smiling, much like he had done more than thirty years earlier when his wealthy father "paid-off" a San Diego court-appointed attorney and the judge released Stone suddenly from his drug-smuggling charges "for the intent of justice."

John Grisham wrote in the Oxford American, "Sadly, Hollywood will have to be forced to shed some of its own blood before it learns to police itself. Even sadder, the families of Bill Savage and Patsy Byers can only mourn and try to pick up the pieces and wonder why such a movie was allowed to be made." The family should have asked Jack Valenti. The reason a movie like *Natural Born Killers* was made is because Jack Valenti wanted movies like this made. Again, it cannot be restated enough that Jack Valenti wanted to usher in a "New Age" of movie making "frank and open, made by filmmakers subject to very few self-imposed restraints."[30]

Not only did Jack Valenti destroy the production code in 1968 (which would have never let this project fly off the printed page), he also went the extra mile to throw the full support of the MPAA behind Stone and Time-Warner's right to incite violence and death.

Jack Valenti was one of Washington's top 10 lobbyists who dispersed millions in campaign contributions to candidates and elected officials at all levels during his 38 year reign as president of the MPAA. It is very important to make clear, right here, that there is no "physical" evidence that Jack Valenti influenced the outcome of the court decision against the Byers family, even despite the fact that people in Hollywood were ribbing Stone by saying "who's your daddy, now?"

Maybe the Louisiana courtroom of Judge Robert Morrison dismissed the Byers' case solely for lack of intent. But, other courts including the U.S. Supreme Court left standing a lower court ruling that *NBK* did "incite" violence. It is worth noting the rare judicial courage of Judge Brady Fitzsimmons of Louisiana's First Circuit who very adamantly took Hollywood to task, strongly chastising "those who would for profit or other motive, intentionally assist and encourage crime then shamelessly seek refuge in the sanctuary of the First Amendment."

By the time Oliver Stone was arrested again for DUI and drug possession in 2005, *Natural Born Killers* had been implicated in the violent deaths of at least

20 Americans and severely injuring scores of other innocent people since the film's release in 1994 with the MPAA "seal of approval." To this day, as you are reading this, distributors continue to push the movie at retail outlets, video rental stores and over the internet. Jerry Garcia of the "Grateful Dead" died just five months after the shooting spree of Darras and Edmondson. The cause of death was due to a massive heart attack. Press reports did not list drugs as a "direct" cause, even though they mentioned Garcia "struggled" with LSD, marijuana, heroin, cocaine, peyote, pain-killers, barbiturates and amphetamines. President Clinton declared Garcia "a national icon." Were these the "adult role models" for Darras and Edmonson?

NBK DEATH TOLL . . . AND COUNTING

- In 1994 a 14-year-old Texas boy was accused of decapitating a 13-year-old girl. In a report filed by the police department, the boy told officers he "wanted to be famous like the natural born killers."
- In 1995, four young people from Toombs County, Georgia—all in their twenties—watched *NBK* 19 times in one sitting and then began a rampage that was cut short after the four abducted a truck driver, killing him brutally and stealing his truck. They were all caught shortly after.[31]
- Also during 1995, in the quiet town of Newnan, Georgia, a 15-year-old boy named Jason Lewis loaded his father's 12 gauge shotgun, walked into the family living room and shot both his parents to death, blowing their faces off. Police reports stated that Lewis told friends he wanted to live out the story of *Natural Born Killers*.[32]
- Another 1995 killing of an 82-year-old man in Massachusetts made national headlines when one of the accused, 18-year-old Christopher Smith shouted into the news cameras, "I'm a natural born killer!"[33]
- In Salt Lake City, 17-year-old Nathan Martinez obsessed with *Natural Born Killers* viciously murders his stepmother and half-sister. Martinez had shaved his head and was wearing round tinted glasses like the Woody Harrelson character in *NBK*. After being arrested, he would say, "It's nothing like the movies. They're just dead."[34]
- In 1997, a 14-year-old boy is accused of killing three students in a Paducah Kentucky high school. The boy cites *Natural Born Killers* among other movies and video games as his inspiration. Attorneys for the parents of the victims file a lawsuit against certain motion picture studios and video game manufacturers. The suit goes nowhere.
- In April of 1999, fully five years after the release of *NBK* and as the Byers trial raged on, the most atrocious of the copycat crimes was committed when Erik Harris and Dylan Klebold went on a shooting spree

at Columbine High School in Colorado, killing 12 students, one teacher and then shooting themselves for a total of 15 dead and injuring even more. Classmates would say later that Harris and Klebold were obsessed with *NBK* and the *The Basketball Diaries* by Time-Warner subsidiary NewLine Cinema headed by exploitation king Robert Shaye.[35] Universal's Satan-rocker Marilyn Manson has also been cited as an influence.

The Columbine massacre was the defining incident that prompted then President Clinton to give a radio address "chastising" the movie industry for its pervasive violent content. As we discussed in detail in Chapter 7, it was also at this time that President Clinton immediately boarded Air Force One for a Democratic Fundraiser in Beverly Hills by David Geffen and other celebrities including Time-Warner execs.

Even more disturbing to the dark drug infested legacy of Oliver Stone is a double copycat effect that was discovered in March of 2006 when three separate plots were uncovered from Kansas to Alaska where certain high school students were planning a mass slaughter of fellow students in April as a "commemoration" of the Columbine shootings.

Time magazine predicted this type of ongoing threat to the American school student in a March 19, 2001 article titled "The Columbine Effect." School systems across the country will continue to undergo Columbine-like tragedies as the progeny of Harris and Klebold will attempt to reenact a horrendous new social ill—school shootings.[36]

Part of the "Columbine Effect" is hard for parents of a different era to grasp. Their children face an ongoing specter of constant fear just at the thought of walking into their school building. The proper term for this should be "The Oliver Stone Effect."

THE OLIVER STONE EFFECT

"I think America has to bleed. I think the corpses have to pile up . . . Let the mothers weep and mourn."[37] This is Oliver Stone's favorite quote. It's also an indication of how mentally ill he has been for a long time and how Hollywood has enabled and fed his drug habit. As we will learn later in this book, Oliver Stone is also involved with darker demons than alcoholism and drug addiction. And Stone is but one example of thousands in the Hollywood entertainment industry who have eagerly and unapologetically engaged in the dangerous combination of alcoholism and illegal drug use combined with an ego-driven "power of entertainment" to "hammer down" the moral edification and cohesive value system of the nation.

Since 1960, thousands of celebrities have been arrested, indicted, jailed or admitted to rehab centers with such names as "Wonderland" in Laurel Canyon.

THE HOLLYWOOD CULTURE WAR

The substance abuse runs the gamut of anything that will alter reality such as alcohol, heroin, cocaine, LSD, marijuana, amphetamines, pain killers, ecstasy, uppers, downers and in-betweeners.[38]

In an industry that produces fantasy, Stone has found the perfect outlet to vent his drug-induced fantasies on the screen. In many cases, he will portray biographical stories loaded with his personal brand of hatred and vengeance for "powerful" people using scripts with totally false content to punish the successful people in American society that he could never become. Stone's "inspiration" comes largely from the deleterious effects of brain decay from forty years of substance abuse. And, as Oliver Stone is a barely breathing example, his abuse is shared and embraced by thousands more behind the camera from the executive suites of the studios to the on-location dressing rooms and "honey-wagons."

On both sides of the camera, both sides of the musician's microphone and in virtually all levels of the entertainment industry, hundreds of people have died from overdose, drug-related accidents and suicide. Yet the media and the industry itself often treat these individuals as footnotes in the "glamorous" world of Hollywood. The entertainment media will rave about the "input" and the "output" of a celebrity's contribution to the craft of entertainment, but inevitably, the obituary will close with the only thing the entertainer will truly be remembered for, such as "unfortunately *Your Name Here* succumbed to a lifelong struggle with *Your Drug Here."* And that's all she wrote.

In my twenty years in the movie business, I have actually been told by studio executives, producers, directors and actors themselves, that they have no problem with "recreational" drug use (translation: addiction) because it actually "fuels creative juices," and produces "exceptional performances." I once scouted locations with an individual who was an associate producer on *The Blues Brothers* and he very casually repeated these well worn lines of drug abuse alibis.

I asked him if he thought John Belushi was a "recreational" user of drugs. "It's all relatively relative, man, you know?" I told him, "All I know is he is very relatively dead, man . . . you know?" This is known as "The Belushi Factor" which explains how the entire entertainment industry enables and encourages drug use, despite all of the dead bodies and rehab re-admissions that pile up every year. It is important to understand how the Belushi Factor and the Oliver Stone Effect operate so that you have a better understanding of how Hollywood enables drug abuse and death among its own and why mandatory drug testing in Hollywood is needed not only to protect industry workers, but also to protect you as a member of the entertainment audience from the nightmare images and twisted dream fantasies fed to you by Tinseltown, or worse, being run over at a pedestrian crosswalk by Oliver Stone or Lindsay Lohan, Nicole Richie, Paris Hilton, Courtney Love, Nick Nolte, Gary Busey, David Hasselhoff, Kiefer Sutherland, etc., etc., and of course, etc.

MICHAEL VINCENT BOYER

THE BELUSHI FACTOR

"Coke please?" John Belushi was fond of saying on the set of 1980's *The Blues Brothers*, a star-studded cameo-filled movie with Belushi and Dan Aykroyd "on a mission from God" to raise money quickly for their doomed former orphanage.

Belushi would always shake an empty can or bottle of Coca-Cola and put on a sad face for anyone who heard his plea in between takes. Someone usually arrived within 20 minutes or less and Belushi would disappear into his location trailer or dressing room and emerge a new man. There was no sign that he now had a full bottle or can of Coca-Cola because it was all part of Belushi's off-camera antics to "summon" a new supply of cocaine. And someone always "came through."

The 1984 book *Wired* by journalist Bob Woodward chronicled "the short life and fast times of John Belushi," a drug abuser of mammoth proportions who even made Oliver Stone pale in comparison. Belushi, who would die two years after the movie's completion at the age of 33, was considered a comic genius and a "hot property" in Hollywood, meaning that his appearance in a film almost guaranteed a certain box-office profit for the studio.

An entire generation has come of age and have children of their own who know nothing about Belushi other than what they see on reruns, DVD's or what they read in books. Anybody who has read *Wired* wonders why he was ever allowed to appear on television or in films. The reason is simple. Hollywood is a very sick industry run by very sick people. Its potential to entertain is enormous and is occasionally realized at its best. But, to a large degree, destruction is the price of fame in today's Hollywood more than at anytime in its history. To have a death wish, to be surrounded by enablers and to die of drug induced internal combustion is the Belushi Factor, as opposed to the Oliver Stone Effect where the goal is to kill the audience, directly or indirectly.

The main reason John Belushi was a major "star" was due to the fact that his "genius energy" came solely from drugs, specifically cocaine and heroin. And Belushi's drug abuse was fueled and encouraged by everybody he worked with from the studio executive suite to the hotel master suite.

The Belushi Factor is the best example of how one person's substance abuse in Hollywood is almost always linked to a complex chain of "enablers," drug-wise and otherwise, who are constantly giving each other mixed signals about surviving in the industry. If one is not always "up" then that certain creative individual may very easily be on their way "out."

Woodward's book shows a hypocritical entertainment industry that makes public service announcements against drugs with their left hand and supply drugs to their fellow entertainers with their right hand. Canadian psychologist Dr. Emma Pivato, who studied the Belushi Factor, stated that "drug use is endemic and considered normative in Hollywood."[39] In reading *Wired,* Dr. Pivato demonstrated how many people were involved in keeping Belushi "up" and "wired" so that he could give his most outrageous performances.

Not only did every "below the line" cast and crew member know that Belushi was "coked up," the "above the line" producers and directors also knew and they expected him to be "up" even if it meant cocaine on demand day or night.

Only 30 years old at the time of filming, Belushi had become "accustomed" to his abuse and addiction and saw it no differently than someone who drinks tea or coffee all day. He also knew, in the darkest recesses of his mind, that he was nothing without cocaine—as far as Hollywood was concerned. Belushi's "super agent" Mike Ovitz knew, but intervening in Belushi's cocaine life might cut into his percentage he earned off Belushi.

Blues Brothers producer Bernie Brillstein didn't have any interest in intervening either, especially not during production. He might actually sober up and destroy the "comic pacing" of the picture. There is a reason for the old saying "the show must go on." Brillstein's cavalier attitude about Belushi's drug use was legend. "When there was idle time, John would go get drugs, three pizzas, [sex] or a nap."[40]

The Blues Brothers movie set was brimming with enablers, enforcers, and "faucet-handlers." Morris Lyda, hired as the Blues Brothers Band road manager, noted that it was his job to keep Belushi jolly and to make sure he was supplied with enough drugs to keep him functional during the filming. As Woodward noted, "he was both facilitator and regulator of John's drugs: it was an impossible contradiction."[41]

During production of the movie in Chicago, crew members also supplied Belushi with "diluted cocaine" in an effort to control the "faucet" of the seemingly endless pipeline of cocaine for the increasingly bloated Belushi. Crew members considered their actions "benevolent."

While cocaine was literally blowing in the wind on the set, there were some who refused to give Belushi cocaine when he demanded it. Not because they were concerned about Belushi's health, but, as Dr. Pivato noted, "Many of Belushi's associates avoided offering cocaine to him, by *pretending* they didn't have any, because of his tendency to use up all that was available."[42] *How could John be so selfish,* they must have thought to themselves?

Dr. Pivato also observed that, "producers and directors turned a blind eye to his drug abuse whenever possible . . ." confirming Brillstein's fear about a production slowdown.[43] However, a Chicago physician named Dr. Bennett Braun saw a major slowdown just over the horizon. Braun was coordinating medical support for the movie.

After a brief physical of Belushi, Dr. Braun told Belushi straight "You're burning out." Braun went to Robert K. Weiss, one of the film's producers and said, "You've got to get him off drugs . . . if you don't, get as many movies out of him as possible, because he has only two to three years to live.[44] As Woodward noted, "there was no putting any kind of leash on John, and it was precisely that absence of control, that daredevil quality that made him such a box office hit."

Producer Weiss obviously opted for the doctor's second opinion, to squeeze as many movies out of him. After all, Weiss was not only a producer; he was John's "friend." And he was one of Belushi's cocaine suppliers.[45]

It's worth mentioning some of Belushi's other "friends" who helped keep John's "creative juices" flowing. Tony Hendra, an off-Broadway producer, was "credited" with introducing Belushi to cocaine in 1972. After that, Belushi had no problem getting cocaine, often from "friends" who freely offered *their* "stash" for him to snort. Friends, such as Chevy Chase, Dan Aykroyd and *Saturday Night Live* writer Michael O'Donahue. *SNL* producer Lorne Michaels had also shared plenty of cocaine with Belushi.[46]

Right up to Belushi's last hours of life in the seedy Chateau Marmont of Sunset Boulevard, Belushi was in the company of "friends" such as Cathy Smith, one of his favorite "suppliers". Robert DeNiro and Robin Williams stopped by to use some cocaine on that early morning of March 5, 1982.

What is so disturbing in reading about Belushi's last hours is how Woodward describes the reactions of DeNiro and Williams, as if they were somehow disconnected as fellow enablers. The concentration of the two actors focused more on their impressions of Cathy Smith, the drug dealer in the room.

Before Robin Williams took his turn with the cocaine, Woodward describes how "Williams had never seen John with such a crusty woman." And Robert DeNiro "found Smith trashy and was surprised that John was with such a woman."[47] Of course, neither one had any problem snorting the "trashy" and "crusty" woman's cocaine. Belushi would be dead within hours. DeNiro reportedly started crying. Robin Williams decided to "re-evaluate" his own lifestyle, which resulted in his 2006 announcement 24 years later, that he was going to finally give up drinking. Some things take time in Hollywood.

It is interesting that Woodward's book, written more than twenty years ago, lists the names and sometimes the addresses of over 200 people interviewed for *Wired*. Many of them are drug dealers, suppliers or regular users. One section casually mentions the fact that Jack Nicholson keeps two kinds of cocaine at his house, the "downstairs" variety for casual friends and the "upstairs" supply for lady friends.

The book is a roadmap for law enforcement officers to raid and arrest scores of people. But, I cannot recall since the book's publication two decades ago that anybody has been investigated or arrested. Where was the Los Angeles County Sherriff's Department? They are sitting on the largest supply of drugs in the United States. It should have been a drug interdiction gold mine.

But where was the Screen Actor's Guild? More important, where was and where is the MPAA? The Oliver Stone Effect and the Belushi Factor are still daily facts of life in the industry. There is much to learn from the advances in drug testing among the sporting world, which is even larger than the entertainment industry. But first, the MPAA needs a history lesson before it can again actively set the tone of zero tolerance for drug abuse, one of the main reasons for its own creation in the 1920's.

CHAPTER 13

STEPPING UP TO THE PLATE: THE MPAA'S MANDATE FOR DRUG TESTING

> *"The movie business is a little like the drug business. We are the pushers, and our customers are the users."*
> —Greg Laemmle—President
> Laemmle Theaters

The one organization that should take control of the narco-plague being spread by Hollywood is the Motion Picture Association of America (MPAA), which is supported and funded by the major entertainment conglomerates, known collectively as the "Hollywood" industry.

While the MPAA has been performing exceptionally well at clamping down on the multi-billion dollar piracy of its member's movies, domestically and internationally, it has largely neglected and forgotten the reason why it came into existence. And that reason was widespread drug abuse across the entire spectrum of the Hollywood motion-picture industry—plain and simple.

And, because Hollywood and the MPAA's memory is short and selective, we'll take just a couple of pages to remind them of their mandate and responsibility to the industry and to the audiences around the world.

SPECIAL THANKS TO FATTY ARBUCKLE

Originally created in 1922 as the Motion Picture Producers and Distributors of America (MPPDA), the organization later known as the MPAA was formed as a result of the Hollywood film community drowning in alcohol, drug abuse, overdoses, sudden death, and even murder—behavior which "confirmed for critics that Hollywood was the modern Babylon."[1]

The major moguls of the day had decided that the industry needed a collective clean-up of the motion picture industry's image after a series of these scandals rocked the movie business, beginning with the death of actress Virginia Rapp in an alcohol and drug-fueled party frenzy hosted by silent comic star Roscoe "Fatty" Arbuckle at the St. Francis Hotel in San Francisco. Arbuckle was second only to Charlie Chaplin as the most famous comedian of the era.

In another case, silent film director William Desmond Taylor was found murdered in his apartment and a series of front-page stories revealed his double life of drug abuse and clandestine affairs. To this day, his murder remains unsolved and there are active web sites by historians and film buffs attempting to solve the crime. In yet another incident, one of the silent era's most famous matinee idols, Wallace Reid, died from complications resulting from drug abuse. His death led to investigations uncovering widespread abuse throughout Hollywood.

Even Jack Valenti described the roots of the MPAA's organization by saying "there was outrage in the land, and Arbuckle's trial along with several other simultaneous sex, drug and death scandals, led to attacks on the movie industry's indecency and its alleged promotion of immorality."[2] Valenti went on to state that the MPAA's task was "to restore a more favorable public image for the motion picture industry."[3]

It's a classic case of Valentiism and his unique use of double-speak. He acknowledged the reason for the MPAA's inception and then boasted later about dismantling the Production Code, which has created the current culture crisis drowning America even deeper than 1922. Valenti's Ratings Scheme proceeded to erase the "favorable public image" the MPAA had worked so long to restore.

Until Valenti's abolishment of the Production Code, the movie studios and the industry made extraordinary efforts to control the out of control behavior of its stars and "creative types." At the very least, the studios, producers and agents covered up the movie industry's indiscretions because of the poor role models being portrayed to the nation's youth by high-profile celebrities.

This is not to say that drug abuse and alcoholism in the entertainment industry stopped suddenly in 1922, but it was made known to industry personnel and celebrities that there was no glamour to be gained from dysfunctional and self-destructive lifestyles.

When Valenti destroyed the Production Code in 1968, not only did on-screen behavior begin to immediately glamorize drug abuse, but off-screen mayhem followed suit as the "let it all hang out" cry of the counterculture became "hip" in Hollywood. (Even the word "hip" has roots in the drug culture of 19th century opium dens in San Francisco where "operators" told their "clients" that the effect would last long if one laid sideways on their "hip.")

And, since 1968, the personal malfunctioning behavior of the industry's substance abuse, at all levels, is far more prevalent than even the celebrity-addicted tabloids report. As we've shown, The Belushi Factor describes how the abuse is destroying lives within the industry and The Oliver Stone Effect describes how the audience is being abused by the abusers. That today's "entertainment" is often the product of drug-riddled minds is, again, a single and significant strand in a long dark thread that runs wide and deep in the entertainment industry's worldview.

* * *

Knowing how the harm that substance abuse has and continues to inflict on the culture, the time for mandatory drug testing in the entertainment industry has arrived. In fact, drug testing in the entertainment industry is long past due. And the testing should not be limited to celebrities, but should encompass everyone in the creative *and* administrative process, both "above the line" and "below the line," Hollywood lingo for "management" and "labor."

Because Hollywood's casual and "tolerant" behavior of drug abuse is now rampant across the broad spectrum of the entertainment community; the MPAA would certainly want to take the lead in eradicating this abuse for the sake of individual health and increased entertainment industry productivity.

For an industry that helped usher in "smoke-free" environments and is leading the charge against "greenhouse emissions" in the fight against "global warming," putting a stop to drug abuse and addiction within the industry will *surely* garner the support of everybody.

To help provide a model of administration for the MPAA to emulate, let's take a look first at how the world of sports is tackling this issue.

SPORTS AND DRUG TESTING: A PAGE FROM THE PLAYBOOK

In order to implement drug testing in the entertainment industry, one need look no further than the boundless world of sports—Olympic, professional, amateur, collegiate and high school. Though still in its relative infancy, the sporting world's fight against drug abuse and its increasing use of testing within an organized model of administration can shed light on the scope and scale of an effort that Hollywood needs to take up immediately. The individuals and organizations involved in amateur and professional sports is far greater than those employed full and part-time by the entertainment industry.

If the world of sports can take on the task of widespread drug abuse, so too can the world of entertainment. Detractors of Hollywood drug testing say

THE HOLLYWOOD CULTURE WAR

there is no comparison between the two, using the old "like apples and oranges" comparison excuse. The truth is the world of sports and the world of entertainment have everything in common—talent and abilities.

In sports, the talent and abilities are athletic, requiring concentration, focus, mental and physical sharpness to excel in achieving the best performance humanly and naturally possible. The process involves everybody from league affiliation, owners, coaches, union members, judges for awards and the athletes.

In entertainment, the abilities are athletic, requiring concentration, focus, mental and physical sharpness to excel in achieving the best performance humanly and naturally possible (sound familiar?) The process involves everybody from production company affiliation, producers, writers, directors, craft guilds, union members, technical crew, judges for awards and actors.

To use sports drug testing as a model, let's take a brief look back at drugs as they emerged in sports competition, most notably during the Olympic games of the 1930's when international Olympic officials and competing international teams began to complain quietly that certain athletes from Germany and some eastern European countries appeared to demonstrate an unfair advantage.

Most of these early assessments were made simply by observing the size of the athletes during competition in relation to their size in the time period between the four-year span of Olympic events. It was a time when men were men and women were, well, almost men.

Anabolic steroids were largely a European invention as were amphetamines. Little was known about the steroids in Olympic competition until the 1950's, but amphetamines, were already becoming widespread, especially among Nazi German athletes. Adolph Hitler himself was an amphetamine addict by the early 1930's and was receiving daily injections by the late 1930's. Nazi troops and Luftwaffe pilots would take amphetamines during intense battles and long sieges.

Facing the unfair advantage of drugs in sports would be largely an Olympic endeavor and by the 1980's spot testing was becoming common by Olympic authorities. The tests would often be administered randomly to competition winners directly after the athletes won a certain event. This is when blood levels of steroids would be at their highest. Track star Ben Johnson from Canada would be among the first well-known athletes to test positive and relinquish his title in 1988.

Coaches and trainers often knew of their athlete's usage and, in many cases, they were the facilitator and provider of the athlete's performance enhancing drugs, not to dissimilar from The Belushi Factor. But, coaches and trainers were rarely implicated or punished. The haunting specter of being tested and detected positive, especially after winning an event, was a powerful deterrent and kept illegal drug use to a minimum. But, by the late 1980's new and undetectable drugs were appearing on the Olympic sports scene.

Some athletes were using drugs that even Olympic officials did not know existed or they had not developed tests to detect. Some were the basic component in antihistamines, such as pseudoephedrine and others were tagged as "pro-hormones" or "designer steroids."

The pro-hormones were engineered by chemists to be one or two molecules less than an "official" steroid. The world of performance enhancing drugs was rapidly escalating in new directions and becoming increasingly complicated as certain athletes and their sponsors vied for the gold medal, the "Oscar" for the world's best athletes.

Also, "doping" was becoming popular among endurance sports. The original definition of doping refers to the method of withdrawing vials of an athlete's blood, re-oxygenating it through a complex process and injecting it back into the athlete for a boost of energy. It was doping allegations that dogged Lance Armstrong throughout his competition in addition to testosterone boosters.

The term doping would soon be used to include all performance enhancing drugs and its proliferation initiated the formation of the World Anti Doping Agency (WADA), which would compile a comprehensive list of all performance enhancing drugs to be banned in Olympic competition.

At the same time, American sports from the high school level all the way to professional team sports would be affected by the explosion of pro-hormones. Because they were not legally steroids due to their molecular component manipulation, the drugs were considered natural supplements and were showing up at health food stores and even over-the-counter at pharmacies around the country.

When pro-baseball player Mark McGwire admitted using androstenedine, the suspicion of many fans and competing teams was confirmed. As a record-breaking athlete, McGwire's admission would begin the long road to drug testing among professional athletes including football, baseball, hockey, basketball and tennis. However, most of the testing was conducted by the particular sport league or association in a random manner, and often only during training season.

By 2000, the press coverage of illegal and "barely legal" drug use also implied that not only were the athletes involved, but knowledge and "enabling" of drug use had to be known and tolerated across the spectrum from league officials, team owners, and coaches. Again, the Belushi Factor. Too many loopholes were made available for athletes to jump through and those who tested positive were given mild penalties.

The government would become increasingly involved as Congress began to investigate the widespread epidemic. Representative Joe Barton, R-TX, of the House Commerce Committee described the steroid policies announced by the major professional sports leagues as "grudging, modest and late."[4]

Anticipating congressional action, major league baseball began a stricter and more professional drug testing policy in 2003. By 2004, Senator John McCain,

R-AZ, introduced a bill that passed both houses of Congress banning the sale and possession of pro-hormones. The law took effect in January of 2005 and overnight the sale of pro-hormones came to an end.

It was the first time that lawmakers had to intervene to accomplish what the pro sports leagues wouldn't tackle or couldn't control. The official list of banned substances exceeded 100 different chemical combinations of pseudo-steroids and placed their legal status in the same class as full-scale illegal anabolic steroids. Anyone selling or even possessing the "designer" drugs would face stiff jail penalties.

An interesting parallel to the Belushi Factor and the double standard for illegal drug use in the entertainment industry can be found in Bob Woodward's book *Wired*. As mentioned in the earlier chapter, Woodward actually names Hollywood drug dealers, suppliers and regular users of even more dangerous, extremely addictive and highly illegal drugs with penalties stiffer than steroid sale and possession. Among those addicts and abusers are the biggest names in contemporary Hollywood entertainment. I ask again: No investigation? No arrests? No trials? No jail time? Perhaps that will change, sooner than the industry would like.

After Congress banned the designer steroids, the shrinkage in athletic size and performance was noticeable from the major leagues to the high school athlete. However, rogue players and trainers continued to test the limits. Lance Williams, co-author of the 2006 book, *Game of Shadows,* estimated that drug use in professional baseball ranged between 50% to 80% of players. The increased federal emphasis on banning drug use among athletes was given increased urgency because of the revelation of more players testing positive and the poor example of role models that pro athletes were setting for young people. The Mitchell Report of December 2007 stated that, next to parents, children looked to athletes as role models. Some have argued that Hollywood celebrities come in a close third, perhaps even tying for second place with athletes.

Major League Baseball (MLB) was the first to receive heavy scrutiny when Barry Bonds, Gary Sheffield, Jason Giambi and Rafael Palmeiro were all implicated in steroid use. In the case of Bonds, his personal trainer was convicted for his involvement in a steroids distribution ring. Frequently, Bonds and Palmeiro were booed at stadiums when they came to the field, indicating fans were not happy.

Jason Giambi turned out to be baseball's true voice of honor when he told sportswriter Bob Nightengale, "I was wrong for doing that stuff. What we should have done a long time ago was stand up—players, ownership, everybody—and said we made a mistake."

There are some, like sportswriter Andy Nesbitt, who see nothing wrong with out-of-control drug use among athletes, especially Barry Bonds. He boils it all down to the Hollywoodization of sports, "any time he comes to the plate, a Giants game in April suddenly becomes must-see television. It's better than *Seinfeld* in the late 1990s or the *Soprano's* whenever it is on . . . We turn to television for entertainment."[5]

Nesbitt begins to sound like Variety's veteran child-hater Timothy Gray who believes "forbidden fruit" is good for children. Nesbitt concludes by saying "Remember, cheering for Barry Bonds can be fun. Its like watching an R-rated movie when you were eleven years old and your parents were out for the night. You knew it wasn't the popular decision, but it sure was a good time."[6]

Is new MPAA president Dan Glickman taking notes? In the tawdry adulation of Barry Bonds, even as a suspected drug abuser, Nesbitt forgot to mention the story of one young Barry Bonds admirer named Rob Garibaldi. In high school, even at 150 pounds, Rob was beginning to excel in baseball. He pushed himself hard by injecting steroids to gain weight and soon found himself as one of the nation's top 100 baseball players at the University of Southern California.

Not long after he was drafted by the New York Yankees, Rob's life began to fall apart. In order to enter the major leagues, he would require a physical and that meant no evidence of steroids. He tried to ease off the drugs he had been taking for a long time but became very depressed and began to suffer hallucinations and sleep disorders. He eventually had to admit to his parents that he was using steroids because he was just trying to be like his hero Barry Bonds. He told his father, Ray, that steroids were the only way to make it in the major leagues and it was common knowledge that the high achievers were using steroids.

Unable to shake the depression and physical side effects, Rob took a .357 caliber pistol and committed suicide by shooting himself. The day after Bonds beat Hank Aaron's record, two-time National League MVP Dale Murphy said Bonds is a "terrible example for our kids" and that Bonds used performance-enhancing drugs "without a doubt." Then Surgeon General Richard Carmona told the AP, "If youngsters are seeing their role models practicing this kind of behavior and it seems acceptable, then we need to do something about that." The glamorization of drugs on screen is equally a problem and potentially affects far more people than sports drug abuse.

On November 15, 2007, Bonds was finally indicted by the grand jury for perjury and obstruction of justice after three years of deliberation. If convicted of all counts, Barry Bonds could spend more than 40 years in prison. But, Bond's indictment was only a prelude to the much bigger revelations to come by the Mitchell Report on drug use and Major League Baseball.

Professional football also received heavy scrutiny by the House Government Reform Committee after CBS News reported three Carolina Panthers ball players had purchased drugs just days before the Super Bowl of 2004. The trickle of America's drug-addicted role models was turning into a flood.

Of baseball, Congressman Barton of Texas added, "Steroids and other illegal drugs have tarnished baseball for a generation of fans, including this one."[7] Representative Cliff Stearns of Florida said "steroids are the tools of the cheater."[8]

In April 2005, Congress was ready to implement even tougher penalties by introducing legislation that would create a national standard for steroid drug testing for all professional sports. (Imagine a similar move implementing a national standard for drug testing for all segments of the entertainment industry?) Under the proposed bill, athletes in baseball, football, basketball, hockey and other pro sports in the U.S. caught using performance enhancing substances would face the same stringent penalties as Olympic athletes. The World Anti-Doping Association (WADA) includes "drugs of abuse" as well as performance enhancing drugs. This is what makes the WADA protocol important as a possible model for Hollywood.

In a 2005 interview with the *San Francisco Chronicle*, MLB Commissioner Bud Selig stated that he would prefer to see baseball clean up its own drug problems, but was open to legislation that would help in that effort. "I've said it before. Number one, we need to tighten up our policy. We need a much tougher program" Selig said. "But would I be amiable to federal legislation? Yes I would . . . My point is the best way to do it is to do it on our own."[9] Many critics say Selig was far behind the curve when it came to cracking down on well-known abuse in the league. But, in 2006 alone, 221 major and minor league players were suspended after testing positive for banned substances.

In a purely hypothetical scenario, re-read the above paragraph and replace "MLB Commissioner Bud Selig" with "MPAA President Dan Glickman" and replace "baseball" with "movie industry."

On November 15, 2005, lawmakers in Congress were again just hours away from imposing drug testing and penalty requirements on all major league sports when a deal was reached between leaders of Major League Baseball and the players union agreeing to require baseball players to submit to several tests each year, during and between seasons, and would also impose lengthy supensions for steroid and amphetamine use.

Repeat offenders would be banned for life. The testing would also be conducted by a professional not connected to management or the player's union. In addition, the independent professional administration would schedule and supervise the tests, which previously were administered by a joint management union committee.

"This is about the integrity of the game and particularly kids," said Jim Banning, a Kentucky Republican and Hall of Fame pitcher.[10] Congress agreed to hold off on legislation for the time being, but called on other professional sports leagues to follow baseball's lead. The National Association of State High School Associations surveyed their members and reported an increasing number of schools adopting drug-testing programs.[11] The NFL has the strongest policy of all pro leagues.

At the same time, the testing of Olympic athletes continues to be updated and enforced. There are opportunities for appeals and sometimes the process can get complicated. In June of 2006, track athlete Marion Jones was found to be positive for EPO, a new performance-enhancing drug that is sometimes undetected. To avoid possible mistakes, a second sample is always taken, known as a "B" sample, which turned out to be negative. Though Jones seemed to have escaped detection again, the track star made a tearful surprise announcement on October 4, 2007 in which she admitted using steroids before the 2000 Sydney Olympics. She pleaded guilty two days later in U.S. federal court for lying to government investigators. In 2008, Jones was sentenced to a stern prison term in a federal detention facility.

Detractors of Hollywood drug testing like to point to the case of Tour de France cyclist Floyd Landis who was determined to have a positive finding of confirmed doping; not once, but twice. Tour de France director Christian Prudhomme no longer considered Landis the winner in 2006, but the ultimate decision as to strip Landis of his title was transferred to the International Cycling Union (UCI). And, under UCI rules, the determination of whether or not a cyclist violated drug rules must be determined by the cyclist's national federation, in Landis' case, that would be USA Cycling, which transferred the case to the U.S. Anti-Doping Agency (USADA) for the "final determination." Ultimately, Landis was stripped of his title in September of 2007 after arbitration determined he had used synthetic testosterone. The heated and contentious hearings lasted over a year.

Again, Hollywood detractors point to the multiple layers as "time-consuming." That's what Olympic athletes, trainers, and sponsors once said about Olympic testing. In reality, these same multiple layers of authority would exist in the entertainment industry. But, there would have to be an ultimate authority to make a "final determination," and that is where the MPAA comes in. In the world of cycling, these extra steps of due diligence resulted from the fact that every Tour de France winner between 1996 and 2006 either has admitted to, been charged with, or accused of using doping products and techniques.

In the world of pro wrestling, which is more Hollywood than sport, the raucous organization of World Wrestling Entertainment (WWE) announced on December 5, 2005 that it would start random drug testing to detect "illicit" drugs such as steroids and prescription drug abuse among its "players." The decision came after wrestler Eddie Guerrero was found dead in a Minneapolis hotel room shortly before a show. The popular wrestler had a long history of drug abuse, not unlike John Belushi. He was only 38 years old.

The controversial and flamboyant WWE chairman Vince McMahon told wrestlers that the new policy would involve frequent, random tests conducted by an independent agency. This was quite a change for McMahon considering the fact he was charged on more than one occasion for putting pressure on his athletes to bulk up on steroids in 1994.[12] Besides, the bodies were piling up including the 2003 cocaine overdose of Curt "Mr. Perfect" Henning and the sudden 1997 heart attack of former NFL player-turned-wrestler Brian Pillman after emptying a bottle of painkillers.

But, apparently, McMahon's testing protocols were not quite up to par. Or, the wrestlers were trying to wiggle through the system. On June 24, 2007 word had spread across the country that one of the WWE's most prominent wrestlers, Chris Benoit, was found dead in his suburban Atlanta home hanging from a weight-training cable. But, more horrific than his suicide, Benoit had first murdered his wife and young son.

The extent of steroid and other drug defenders became clear over the next few weeks as many ex-wrestlers practically sang in harmony, "It just couldn't have been the steroids—he must have been upset over something." But, when the police report was released, steroids were found in his house and toxicology reports found drugs in his blood stream. Benoit was not only taking steroids, he was on painkillers, uppers and downers. Benoit was definitely a victim of the Belushi Factor—always trying to stay "up" for fear of being "out." As *Blue Brothers* director John Landis noted shortly before Belushi's death, "You can't make money off a corpse."

The Benoit tragedy revealed statistics that showed just over 70 pro wrestlers had died before the age of 45 in little more than a decade. Just one week before Benoit's murder-suicide, "Marvelous" Sherry Martel had dropped dead on the porch of her mother's Birmingham home.

As for the wrestling world, Brian Sammartino, who held the World Wrestling Federation title for eleven years in the 1960's and 1970's refused to be inducted into the Wrestling Hall of Fame in 2005 because he expressed disgust that *the contemporary wrestling scene had become outrageously vulgar and a bad influence on children*. Who, in the history of Hollywood ever refused to have a star on Hollywood Boulevard because the entertainment industry has become *a bad influence on children?*

Even in sports, Mark McGwire didn't refuse to become a member of the Baseball Hall of Fame, he was simply voted out by the Baseball Writers Association of America. Imagine, for a moment, if the sponsors of the Golden Globes (The Hollywood Foreign Press Association) or the Oscars (The Academy of Motion Picture Arts and Sciences) decided to shed their backbones of jelly and actually refuse to give awards on the grounds of the nominees being drug abusers. A press release in advance of the nominations for Best Actor might read as follows: "The Academy voted Jack Nicholson out as one of the nominees due to his ongoing use of marijuana and cocaine."

One Hollywood insider said to me, "that would exclude 90% of Hollywood." How bad would that really be? The well-known drug addict and British pop-singer Amy Winehouse was told she would have to take a drug test before she could get a visa to attend the 2008 Grammy awards where she received six nominations for the CD *Back to Black*. Her most famous lyrics became the industry's biggest joke, "They tried to make me go to rehab, I said 'No, No, No.'" But the law and her father stepped in and said "Yes, Yes, Yes." Why doesn't the Grammy board save her the trouble and revoke her nominations and awards much like Mark McGwire was refused admission into the Baseball Hall of Fame? Universal Music Group would not even admit her well-publicized addiction until she was videotaped smoking crack.

* * *

Experts predict that in the near future, all professional and amateur sports will follow the guidelines put in place by the World Anti-Doping Association (WADA) and its counterpart in the United States, the U.S. Anti-Doping Agency (USADA).

In 2004, the USADA announced an updated process of drug testing and penalties for Olympic athletes. The list of banned ingredients includes hundred of substances from steroids to "drugs of abuse." The WADA will maintain and update that list periodically.

The MPAA may want to study the following chart by the USADA as a possible template for their own anti-doping division under the umbrella of the MPAA. Just as the Classification and Ratings Administration (CARA) is a division under the MPAA that decides ratings for movies, the proposed Entertainment Anti-Doping Administration (EADA) can take the noble and long overdue steps to clean up the entertainment industry.

The USADA's Process Behind Drug Testing for Olympic Athletes
A TEMPLATE FOR HOLLYWOOD?

The U.S. Anti-Doping Agency is breaking ground in its attempt to sanction athletes for drug violations based on evidence other than a positive test. Though the process is unprecedented, the protocol will be the same as for a positive test. Many professional sports organizations are looking to the USADA process as a reference point model for their own drug testing administration process.

1. The sending of notice letters is the first step towards determining whether sport anti-doping rules have been violated. USADA will follow its process, on an expedited basis where necessary.

2. An independent review board, consisting of experts with legal, technical and medical knowledge of anti-doping matters, will consider the alleged violations and make a recommendation as to whether USADA should proceed with a formal charge. Under the USADA protocol, those who are notified of potential violations are innocent unless and until a formal charge has been brought and they accept the sanction or a panel of arbitrators, after a full hearing, determines that a doping violation has occurred. The review panel's recommendation will be forwarded to the athlete, the sport's national governing body, the U.S. Olympic Committee, the international federation and World Anti-Doping Agency.
3. Within 10 days after being notified of a sanction, the athlete must notify USADA in writing if he or she desires a hearing to contest the sanction. If an athlete accepts the sanction proposed by USADA, it then will be publicly announced.
4. Or an athlete can choose arbitration. Athletes have two choices for the hearing, to be held in the USA:

   A. Selecting the American Arbitration Association (AAA). A single arbitrator will rule, unless either party wants a three-arbitrator panel. Arbitrators come from a pool of the North American Court of Arbitration for Sport (CAS) arbitrators.
   B. Or an athlete can choose to go straight to CAS for a single, final hearing. The CAS decision shall be final and binding on all parties and shall not be subject to further review or appeal.

Source: U.S. Anti-Doping Agency; USADA protocol for Olympic testing.

This table only deals with the protocol to be followed after a tested individual is found positive for drug use. A sample testing procedure for Hollywood is proposed under "MPAA AT THE FOREFRONT" later in this chapter.

As an example to Hollywood of how serious drug abuse is taken by the American and International sporting community, consider the following: On February 8, 2006 the testing totals for the previous year were announced by the USADA in a press release stating, "The USADA performed a total of 8,175 doping control tests in 2005 in 67 Paralympics and Pan American Sports, including 7,675 domestic tests.[13]

Internationally, the WADA stated in 2004 that all major sports organizations in the Olympics and fifty governments around the globe have agreed to the World Anti-Doping Code and 23 more governments have already committed. Dr. Jacques Rogge, president of the International Olympic Committee (IOC) stated that "there will be no place in Olympic Games for any government or federation that does not accept the code." Richard Pound, President of the WADA said, "this brings the fight against doping to a new level."[14]

An example of the benefits of uniform and universal drug testing is the sport of tennis, which has signed on to the IOC's Anti-Doping Program by setting up the Tennis Anti-Doping Program which covers Men's Professional Tennis (ATP), Women's Professional Tennis (WTA), and the International Tennis Federation (ITF).

The Tennis Anti-Doping program has set up a system of rules, penalties, and testing protocols, which is reviewed annually, compiles a list of banned substances and publishes annual statistics, all in accordance with the World Anti-Doping Agency (WADA).

Who benefits? The official website of the Tennis Anti-Doping Program states that the goals of the program are: ONE—Ensure equal and fair competition on the field of play, and TWO—Protect the health of professional tennis players.[15]

Hypothetically, again, suppose such a system applied to the motion picture and entertainment industry and the goals would read as follows: ONE—Ensure equal and fair competition in the production of motion pictures and entertainment products, and TWO—Protect the health of professional filmmakers, musicians, and entertainment personnel.

Certainly, the motion picture industry in particular and the wider entertainment industry in general would welcome the goals of fair treatment and good health for all employed across the spectrum. According to a 2006 economic survey cited by the MPAA, over 1.3 million people earn a living, directly and indirectly, in the movie industry alone.

HOLLYWOOD'S TURN: WHO SHOULD BE TESTED?

The entertainment industry is every bit as competitive as professional and amateur sports. Filmmakers hope that their movies will earn at least a nomination, if not an award, at the Golden Globes and especially the Academy Awards. Members of the television industry also vie for Golden Globes and the most coveted, an Emmy Award. Music producers and musicians believe their worth is profound to the point that a Grammy Award would be their crowning achievement. And, the Tony Award is sought by all segments of the Broadway theatre stage as a sign of excellence in their art and craft.

Whether winners or losers, production companies and everyone involved in the creative process of the entertainment industry deserve "equal and fair" treatment in order to reach their goals and the key decision-makers should play a major part in "protecting the health" of everyone involved in the production of quality entertainment.

As "The Belushi Factor" and "The Oliver Stone Effect" proved, drug and alcohol abuse is prevalent, tolerated or known by people from all levels of production from the studio chiefs to the assistants on location. In the case of Belushi, "protecting the health" of the crew was not a priority for the producers because many of them were equally addicted and even served as "pushers."

In the case of Oliver Stone, executives at Time-Warner knew he was a well-publicized drug addict and alcoholic with a recent bust under his belt when hired on to direct *NBK*. The deadly collateral drug-induced influence of that movie is still reverberating to this day. Even in the middle of the wrongful death lawsuit against him, Stone was busted again for drugs and alcohol. Time-Warner *and* the MPAA under Jack Valenti continued to defend Oliver Stone's "First Amendment" right to self-destruct and his right to influence others to commit deadly crimes.

* * *

I can tell you from my very own personal observations after twenty years in the movie business and from what I continue to hear from friends inside the industry, the substance abuse taking place today dwarfs the already massive abuse demonstrated by John Belushi and his enablers over 25 years ago.

For all the carnage, broken bodies and fractured minds, one would certainly expect that Hollywood is looking forward to the day when people enter a corporate entertainment headquarters building and read the sign "This is a Drug Free Environment." The benefits to the entire industry will have productive and positive effects, not only on the health of the individuals, but hopefully, also on the quality of entertainment emanating from Hollywood.

Again, this should not be difficult for an industry that touts environmental purity, smoke-free spaces, pesticide-free vegetables, farm-fed fish, animal rights and bottled water at room temperature. What better place to set an example for America and citizens of the globe than the very doorsteps to the entertainment capital of the world? Without a doubt, this is the industry to promote what the ancient Greeks termed "A Sound Mind in a Sound Body."

Perhaps the price of movie tickets, DVDs, CDs, concert tickets, cable and satellite television will match normal inflation rates instead of surpassing the national average. That is another benefit to the members of the audience who will no longer be forced to subsidize the drug habits of the entertainment industry.

Just as baseball fans want to know if a batter's record is tainted by drugs, the audience would like to know if performers on screen or stage are tainted by drugs. And, because the creative industry is increasingly turning out more product in 3-D (darkness, despair, and death), it only makes sense to conduct mandatory random drug testing in the industry lest more people fall prey to the dark side of entertainment and its already proven capacity to wreak havoc on society.

As Dr. Jason Kovar noted, "Sadly, the moral decline of our country in the 1960s was primarily facilitated by Hollywood's elite who, through *active personal lives*, set the trend for immorality among millions of people, thereby destroying families, marriages and all things sacred."[16]

Kovar isn't talking just about the celebrities like Britney Spears who vomits on her boyfriend's lap or Paris Hilton who throws-up on the Las Vegas stage (adding to global warming), he is also referring to the very publicized lives of the arrogant power brokers at the top levels who proudly pronounced their love affair with drugs. Drug guru Timothy Leary was and remains, an "icon of liberation" who somehow justified their *active personal lives*.[17]

SAD BUT TRUE

In my two decades in the movie business, issues with substance abuse affected almost every production that I came upon. One of my early assignments was to ensure that Lou Gossett, Jr. woke up on time every morning and arrived at the make-up trailer on the set of *Benny's Place*, a 1982 CBS television movie.

The producer who gave my instructions was concerned that Gossett was doing too much cocaine and drinking too much, especially after a nationally publicized bust of Gossett caught him using cocaine in front of his very young children. A week later, the producer approached me and wanted to know where he could get some cocaine for himself! I said "Don't ask me, ask Lou." This addicted producer would win an Oscar for "Silence of the Lambs" ten years later.

On another occasion, during an Atlanta location scouting trip with a director from Universal, I had to stop the van in front of the Georgian Terrace Hotel at 8:30 in the morning so the young director could throw-up on the sidewalk of Peachtree Street. (Again, more global warming).

Along the Gulf Coast, I was checking on the progress of a low-budget film called *The Lost Platoon* shooting in the coastal pine forest. At first glance, I thought I had stumbled on a massacre. Everybody, except the director, was sprawled across a wide path in the trail, not unlike Jonestown before the bodies began to bloat. "It's okay!" the director assured me, "they all took too much acid last night and they're having a hard time getting started."

During the final week of shooting the mega-mini-series *War and Remembrance* director Dan Curtis imposed on me to approach 70-year-old actor Robert Mitchum to empty his admiral's uniform of miniature bottles of whiskey. The soundman was complaining about too many "clinking" sounds when Mitchum moved his arms.

As the legendary actor graciously emptied his multiple pockets of multiple bottles in a private room adjacent to the battleship set, he glanced at me sideways through his classic hooded eyelids, "Michael, you know what I learned after being released from the Betty Ford Clinic?" No sir, I said to the actor who had made me shudder as a child watching *Cape Fear* decades earlier. "I learned that whiskey tastes much better with ice."

Even on the last film I worked on, *The Insider*, the production was plagued by drug and alcohol problems. Shirley Crumley, the casting director and longtime friend came up to alert me that "the production might be delayed a day or two." Why's that? I already sensed by her look it was another drug problem. "Russell Crowe had enough. He was burned out. Last night he went on a binge and drove to New Orleans to get plastered. I think he's pretty sick." That turned out to be a mild understatement.

When child actors are pampered to the point that they are treated as adults, the signs of early death are planted quickly. During Disney's filming of *Tom and Huck* in 1995, 13-year old Brad Renfro was spending his spare time smoking pot and drinking alcohol. When I rushed to the set from my office in Montgomery, nobody took responsibility. The adult guardian was out of sight; the director pleaded with me "not to interfere with the boy's *talent,*" and so I told producer Barry Bernardi to straighten the boy out or the entire movie will be shut down by sunset.

There was no more trouble from Renfro until the movie wrapped. His life spiraled out of control until January of 2008 when he died of an overdose of heroin and cocaine. His death at age 25 was quickly overshadowed by the death of 28-year old actor Heath Ledger who also overdosed, accidental or otherwise. Sean Penn and Natalie Portman threatened Paramount Television if they showed actual video of Ledger on a cocaine and pot binge at Hollywood's legendary drug castle, the Chateau Marmont where the ghost of John Belushi roams the halls in search of one more "hit."

The hardest memory to shake was the five year period between 1988 and 1993 when I assisted the location manager for the popular television series *In the Heat of the Night*. During frequent travel to and from the set, I witnessed the slow death of actors Howard Rollins and Hugh O'Connor, son of Carroll O'Connor. They were good people with affable personalities who also happened to be very addicted to cocaine. During the five year run of production outside Atlanta, Hugh slowly wasted away and aged rapidly at the same time that Rollins became bloated beyond recognition and missed enough episodes that he was replaced with Carl Weathers. Hugh O'Connor would commit suicide in 1995 at age 32. Rollins died a year later at age 46.

After completion of the 1993 series, Carroll O'Connor returned to Georgia to scout locations in Savannah for a possible TV movie he was considering producing. He had been frustrated with the drug problem on the set throughout the series, which affected more people than just his son and Rollins. At the time, he told me, "The next project I do will be Zero Tolerance for drug and alcohol abuse. It's going to be a fresh start, even if I have to fight the unions. "Zero Tolerance" was, and is, a rare but effective practice of film production usually initiated by a conscientious producer—of which there a very few—who take control of cast and crew conduct. Having coordinated and scouted over two hundred feature and television productions in my career, I can recall only three who insisted on Zero Tolerance and their productions always finished on time and under budget.

O'Connor added an interesting thought during his 1993 scouting trip, "I read that the football players association will not object to a new policy of drug testing that will begin this year for the NFL. It's the first of its kind. Can you imagine the movie industry trying something like that?" Though I never saw O'Connor again after he returned to California, his question was worth more than imagining. It's worth more than considering. It's time to begin planning and implementing.

* * *

Increasingly disturbing, the film and music industry consistently view themselves as political "progressives" and are putting their messages in their movies and their music. How many of their messages originated from drug and alcohol impaired visions that ended up on screen and on stage?

The "Progressive Party" of the early 20th century had butchered the word *progressive* so badly by the 1920s, Democrats began to call themselves *liberal*, especially after the ACLU formed in 1920 as a "progressive" organization with their persistent attacks on Christianity. By 1940, Hollywood Communists preferred the word "progressive" until they fizzled in the 1950's. The radical left wing of the Democratic party appropriated 'Progressive" in the late 1990's and continue so to this day.

Certainly, the entertainment industry would prefer to have their "true" feelings written, produced and directed in a sober state of mind, especially with the sense of self-importance that these individuals view themselves. As Dr. Kovar noted, "Researchers at George Washington University found that Hollywood producers, writers and directors view themselves as crusaders for social reform in America. They see it as their duty to restructure our culture into their image."

With that said, the time for a reality check in Hollywood has arrived. In their quest to promote the unfettered tenets in their First Amendment freedom of speech and expression, the individuals in the creative community should be allowed to explore that freedom without the bondage of substance abuse and move forward with clear minds and healthy bodies.

MPAA THE FOREFRONT: EVERYONE BENEFITS

Now that the MPAA has been freed from Jack Valenti's 38 year reign as Hollywood's Dark Prince, new MPAA President Dan Glickman has a unique opportunity to re-energize Hollywood for the same reason the MPAA was created in 1922, to restore public confidence in the entertainment industry. The March

2007 revisions in the Ratings Scheme unfortunately amounted to nothing more than extra confusion and extra layers of "allowable" excuses for filmmakers to appeal for bad behavior permission rights by an industry rocking out of control and past the verge of a breakdown. It's already broken.

With the world of sports coming closer every year to following the uniform protocols and rules set forth by the U.S. Anti-Doping Agency (USADA), the entertainment industry has a timely opportunity to follow the examples set forth by Olympic professionals who have labored for over two decades to create and refine the system that is in place today. The USADA chart earlier in the chapter is a sample template and the protocol chart only deals with the tested participant *after a* "positive" determination of drug use is found. So, the next logical question is: How would the MPAA set up a system of testing across the Byzantine labyrinth of the entertainment industry?

Just as the Classification and Ratings Administration (CARA) is set up as a division under the MPAA with the authority to rate movies that are distributed by the six major entertainment conglomerates and movies shown in affiliated NATO theaters, another division can be dedicated to industry-wide mandatory random drug testing. An Entertainment Anti-Doping Administration (EADA) patterned after the USADA would be one possible model to fall under the entertainment industry's most powerful lobby. This would provide the central nexus and major starting point for which the rest of the entertainment community would participate.

Most of the same six major studio companies that fund the MPAA are the same studio labels that founded the MPAA in 1922 to clean up it's "drugs and death" image. Of course, all have been through corporate mergers, buyouts, takeovers or morphed into the consolidated mega-conglomerates that exist today; much larger in scope than their original corporate structures. What has changed very little is the coveted logos, which are recognized around the world.

Because of the broadened scope of the six members of the MPAA, the task at hand of ridding the industry of widespread substance abuse through random testing at all levels is actually enhanced. Now, a single movie studio may have a vast number of divisions to handle specific types of entertainment. There are divisions for theatrical releases, TV movies, and television shows. Many studios may even own a network or cable television station with a multitude of interconnected divisions falling under each one of these categories.

Some episodic and sitcom television shows are not only produced, but also distributed through the studio label. And, every studio has a music division, which controls a large share of the recorded music in every conceivable genre, which is produced and distributed throughout the world. There are further subdivisions under the studio that control music concerts and promotions.

Most of these mega-conglomerate entertainment studios maintain their own marketing departments, licensing divisions, DVD, CD and video-game distribution, advertising, event programming, radio station groups and even large-scale theme parks around the globe.

While the entertainment industry is virtually awash with so-called "independent" film, television and music production companies, virtually all of these disparate groups depend upon a formal or informal relationship with one or more of the major studios. If an independently produced feature, TV movie, episodic series, sitcom or music CD expects to receive widespread distribution, the major studios are the only entities with the distribution dollars and networks to make national or international marketing a reality for the independents. While the internet has opened up new avenues, only the studios maintain the power to punch out a "showcase" performance to the masses.

Because of the immense reach into the industry that a single studio maintains, the vast resources of all six members of the MPAA can exert enormous influence on industry individuals to respond to calls for participation in an MPAA sponsored program to "ensure equal and fair competition" and "protect the health of *all* the players."

CURRENT MEMBERS OF THE MPAA

1. Buena Vista Pictures Distribution (Disney)
2. Paramount Pictures
3. Sony Pictures Entertainment (Columbia and Tri-Star)
4. Warner Brothers Entertainment, Inc.
5. 20th Century Fox Film Corporation
6. Universal City Studios

(*MGM and United Artists are owned by a consortium that includes Sony.*)

The MPAA's "newly created" Entertainment Anti-Doping Administration would fall under the umbrella of the MPAA and would be headed by an executive director with the power to hire an Independent Administrator who would oversee the administration of tests, sanctions, and appeals process. Ideally, all member studios and their respective employees in all divisions and departments would be eligible for mandatory random tests.

Just like major league baseball's new protocol, the tests would be administered by the independent administrator and not connected to studio management, employee unions, guilds or the MPAA itself other than the association's EADA executive director. The Independent Administrator will have the power to schedule and supervise the tests in a professional manner that will reduce and prevent attempts at cheating and avoidance. To improve on baseball's testing, the movie industry would increase the frequency of testing, more along the lines of the NFL under Paul Tagliabue and now Roger Goodell.

The Independent Administrator will report directly to the MPAA's executive director of EADA who will report directly to the MPAA president. The EADA executive director will be in charge of promoting, informing and educating all member studios and personnel regarding the program protocol.

Ideally, the protocol established by the EADA and the Independent Administrator will be adopted by all six member studios of the MPAA. This should not be a problem for the Studios who *deeply care* about the health of their employees, increased productivity and reduced health care costs that will ensue.

One good starting place for the MPAA would be to study the procedure in place by the U.S. Anti-Doping Agency and arranging an exploratory meeting with the USADA director. But, before embarking on any drug testing program, the entertainment industry under the leadership of the MPAA should begin with a study that addresses the most commonly occurring issues and questions that will arise with a program of this magnitude:

ADDRESSING DRUG TESTING ISSUES

1. Benefits and drawbacks of drug testing.
2. What drugs will be tested.
3. Costs and accuracy of drug testing.
4. Who should be tested.
5. Independent administration of testing.
6. Sanctions and appeals process.
7. Effective recovery and rehabilitation
8. Legal implications.

These issues are addressed in one of the best books on the increasing practice of drug testing in private industry, workplaces, schools, organizations and sports. Author Robert H. Coombs, *Drug Testing: Issues and Options*, addresses the multi-layered procedures and difficult circumstances that require informed decision-making. Coombs' book introduces the reader to the complex world of drug testing and covers the wide range of substance abuse issues that arise in the American workforce.

Coombs explores drug testing methodology and offers guidelines for selecting the appropriate screening techniques. Relevant topics that are discussed include treatment and counseling of drug abuses in various workplace environments with diverse organizational structures. *Drug Testing: Issues and Options* is an informative starting point for policymakers, private employers and employees. For the MPAA, Coombs' book is a beginning reference that helps clarify the national debate about drug testing.

Coombs also authored *Drug Impaired Professionals*, which explores and uncovers the abuse of drugs in the upper level professional positions of American business and organizational structures. This would be especially relevant to the entertainment industry in which testing of the executive level is highly recommended.

MPAA President Dan Glickman undoubtedly wants to overcome the glaring problem of substance abuse that Jack Valenti turned a blind eye against and in a very real way, helped to promote the "openness" of drug abuse through his "free screen" movement. The MPAA also knows it can accomplish the task of comprehensive industry drug testing without government interference. As a former congressman, Glickman knows the long arm of federal regulation.

And, failure to pursue a viable drug testing program for the entertainment industry could potentially invite scrutiny, hearings and even investigations by congressional committees such as the House Government Reform Committee, the House Energy and Commerce Committee or the Commerce, Trade and Consumer Protection subcommittees. All of these congressional committees have investigated professional sports drug abuse and can exert oversight to the entertainment industry.

A point of interest: In the baseball drug probe, initiatives by Democratic Representative Henry Waxman and Republican Representative Thomas Davis forged a unique bi-partisan effort to investigate steroid and drug abuse among professional ball players. (Major League Baseball started drug testing in 2003 and their policy has been updated twice since 2004).

Representative Waxman, who is now chairman of the House Reform Committee as a result of the political power shift in 2006, is expected to keep up the pressure on pro-sports to weed out drug use. As Waxman proclaimed in an interview with the *San Francisco Chronicle*, "Caring for our kids health is not a partisan issue. It's something we all share."[18]

Waxman would be a natural leader for pushing reform of the entertainment industry's laxity on drug use for two reasons. One, as the *Chronicle* article mentioned, Waxman and his colleagues are " . . . well-versed in complicated investigations that, like the baseball and steroids probe, involve thousands of documents, difficult negotiations with witnesses reluctant to appear and lots of media attention."[19]

Second, Representative Waxman represents the very heart of the entertainment industry whose district includes Los Angeles, Beverly Hills, Bel-Air, Malibu and West Hollywood. Furthermore, MPAA President Dan Glickman is a former Democratic congressional colleague with Waxman when Glickman served in Congress. Also, Waxman is known for his "dogged" investigations into the tobacco industry. Clearly, therefore, he must be an advocate of good health.

"Don't you understand!?" I was asked by an old friend and vice-president of production at Disney. "The only reason Waxman is in office is due to Hollywood money. He is in the pocket of almost every entertainment entity and power broker out here. And Glickman? Why do you think Jack Valenti hand-picked him? Jack practically financed Glickman's re-election campaigns in Congress and Glickman knows where the skeletons are." "Now, don't be cynical!" I said to my old friend, "that sounds like an insult to the congressman from Hollywood and to the former congressman and current president of the MPAA. *Surely*, both of them have the health and welfare of not only the entertainment industry employees at heart, but also the interests of the American people who want to know that their entertainment dollars are not going to drug dealers on Sunset Boulevard that inevitably bankroll drug rings in South America."

Long before the dealers go to work on Sunset Boulevard, seven South American drug enforcement officers, two judges, and a prosecutor are shot to death by thugs from a drug cartel. *Surely*, Waxman or Glickman wouldn't want that. Right?" "Don't call me Shirley," my old friend said, shaking his head.

To demonstrate why the MPAA doesn't want the government to get involved, consider the ongoing situation with Major League Baseball. The U.S. Senate was only two hours away from imposing drug testing and penalty requirements on all major league sports when a deal was reached at the 11th hour. The senators, including John McCain (R-AZ) and Jay Rockefeller (D-WV) were "exasperated at what they viewed as foot-dragging."[20]

Though the original agreement forged by Major League Baseball only included steroids and amphetamines, it is widely believed that, eventually, baseball and all professional and amateur sports will adopt the World Anti-Doping Agency list of banned substances.

A report by Bloomberg.com demonstrates that Major League Baseball continues to undergo intense scrutiny. Danielle Sessa reported on June 18, 2007, "Former Senator George Mitchell told *major league baseball owners* that the U.S. Congress might get involved with a *steroids* investigation if *teams* don't cooperate with his own probe. Mitchell, appointed by *baseball commissioner Bud Selig* in March 2007 to investigate *steroid* use, said the federal government would use subpoena power he lacks to force them to talk."[Italics added].

Now, imagine the entertainment industry refusing to confront its overwhelming problems with substance abuse. Replace the italicized words in the Bloomberg article above so that it might read, "Former Senator George Mitchell told *Motion Picture Association of America studio owners* that the U.S. Congress might get involved with a *drug* investigation if *studios* don't cooperate with his own probe. Mitchell, appointed by *MPAA President Dan Glickman* in March to investigate *drug* use, said the federal government would use subpoena power he lacks to force them to talk."

Even NASCAR racing has not escaped scrutiny. In fact, the cars are scrutinized more than the drivers. Michael Waldrip was sanctioned during the

2007 Daytona time trials when race officials discovered his gas tank contained "unauthorized additives."

*   *   *

When the Mitchell Report on drug abuse in Major League Baseball was released on December 13, 2007, there was a sweeping reaction of disappointment and disgust across the wide spectrum of the sports audience from sports fans to the president of the United States. Former Senator George Mitchell released the names of more than sixty players, past and present, involved in illegal drugs involving steroids and other substances. Mitchell called the abuse "a collective failure" from baseball commissioners, player's associations and the players themselves through a mutual "code of silence."

According to a Zogby/MSN poll taken just before the announcement, 85% of sports fans believe leagues and government bodies should do "whatever is necessary" to rid sports of drug abuse "including lengthy suspensions and other forms of discipline." Representatives Henry Waxman and Tom Davis issued a statement that "Everyone in Major League Baseball holds some responsibility for the scandal." House Speaker Nancy Pelosi said, "Our children's heroes cheated the game." President Bush declared that, "Drugs in baseball has sullied the game."

One of Mitchell's recommendations called for outsourcing testing to a *truly* independent testing operation. Former baseball commissioner Fay Vincent said the drug problem was the most serious challenge to baseball since the 1919 Black Sox scandal of game-rigging by the players. Mitchell even suggested setting up a special investigative department within Major League Baseball that would include a "tip line" for people to report drug abuse. MLB Commissioner Bud Selig agreed to the proposal in 2008.

Suppose a similar investigation was conducted in the Hollywood entertainment establishment including studio administrators, producers, directors, writers and actors. It certainly would reveal a problem more serious than the 1922 drug scandals that initiated the very founding of the MPAA. Would fans, the U.S. Congress and the president issue equally stern language calling for the MPAA and government bodies to do "whatever is necessary" to rid the entertainment industry of drugs?

WHAT ABOUT NON-STUDIO EMPLOYEES?

As I floated the idea about drug testing in the entertainment industry to a friend of mine, a production executive at Sony, his first question was "What about the rest of the industry?" He was referring to the much larger group of independent producers, writers, directors, designers, creative personnel, crew and talent who are not in the direct employment of the major studios.

THE HOLLYWOOD CULTURE WAR

If the studios and all their employees are the only individuals participating in mandatory random drug testing, the equally large independent community would appear to have received a free pass to continue indulging in Oliver Stone or John Belushi related behavior.

After Heath Ledger's death, Tia Brown of *In Touch Weekly* appeared on Glenn Beck's TV show and made a simple statement that the industry does not have the courage to propose, "Unless they do something that prevents them from working, nobody is going to notice." It really is that simple.

One option for extending drug testing to these ancillary entertainment groups would be for the relevant guilds, craft unions, talent agencies and independent production companies to adopt similar anti-doping programs for their fellow members. Like the studios, the unions, guilds and agencies want to promote the best care and working condition for their members. The same is true for independent production companies because, inevitably, all of these groups are tied at the hip to the studios when it comes to ultimate distribution of their products and personnel services.

These would include the Writer's Guild of America (WGA), Directors Guild of America (DGA), The Alliance of Motion Picture and Television Producers (AMPTP), the Producers Guild of America (PGA), the American Society of Cinematography (ASC), the Screen Actors Guild (SAG), the International Association of Theatrical and Stage Employees (IATSE) and the American Society of Composers, Artists and Performers (ASCAP), to name just a few. Together, these groups represent well over 300,000 people. The DGA alone has over 13,400 members worldwide.

Those organizations may want to take a close look at the world of sports; their associations, unions and relevant drug testing programs and how they fit into the larger arena of their particular sport.[21] The aforementioned American Tennis Association's anti-doping program and their interdependent relationship to the larger Olympic Tennis' anti-doping guidelines is a good example.

Again, because most of the above-mentioned entertainment organizations are often connected to the studio system, directly or indirectly, the best proposition would be for the MPAA and its member studios to include anti-doping language in its contracts with independent production companies and revised wording in the studio's signatory relationships with the guilds, unions and talent agencies.

These revised relationships would be necessary in order to "green-light" production deals, funding, agreements and distribution for the vast array of entertainment products. These ancillary and interdependent organizations and businesses would be strongly encouraged to adopt the MPAA's protocol set forth by its internal office of the proposed Entertainment Anti-Doping Administration (EADA).

* * *

Finally, the mindset of drug abuse in Hollywood is far behind the pro-active attitudes and approaches to drug abuse in other industries and institutions. Much of this book will explain how drug abuse came to shape some of the most destructive, and widely followed, philosophies of our time and continues to influence each successive generation in a downward definition of deviancy and decency.

I learned first hand about this mindset during a location scout in 1987 with Michael Wadleigh, the producer-director of the *Woodstock* film in 1969. The movie did more to misrepresent the youth of that time and painted a disturbed picture of drug use and counterculture attitudes that the news media, movie industry and other "shapers" of the culture used as a reference point, even going so far as to label that period as "The Woodstock Generation." As Michael Medved noted, "to a remarkable extent, the nation's opinion leaders accepted that assumption, inexplicably assigning earth shattering significance to an overcrowded rock festival in upstate New York . . ."[22]

Wadleigh had enlisted my services to help scout locations for a second Woodstock that he was frantically trying to put together for a 1989 *20th Anniversary Woodstock Reunion*. We scouted for almost a week in search of the "right look" of a natural sloping field to serve as "nature's amphitheatre."

At the time, crack cocaine was just starting to become an epidemic among youth and adults across the nation. We were listening to a news report about the epidemic as we journeyed through the rolling countryside. Wadleigh, a kind-hearted individual who might even be described as a "gentleman hippie" with long gray remnants of hair growing beneath the skullcap baldness of age, reached over and turned the radio off.

"That just disgusts me," he said, obviously disturbed by the death toll the drug was beginning to take on America. "When we were young, we used to take drugs to expand our minds. These kids are just crazy!"

I was dumfounded for a second, sure that I heard a classic example of "the pot calling the kettle black."

"Now, think for a minute," I asked Wadleigh, "Don't you think these kids doing crack cocaine are hoping to expand their minds, too? They might call it 'getting high,' but they're definitely looking for something that will put them in a different state of mind, and it must be pretty mind-expanding; they're willing to rob, steal and kill to get more."

"Then they should just make it legal," Wadleigh responded with the typical post-hippie drug store "solution."

"Oh, that's right. Then they'll do even more crack and if they don't overdose and die first, they'll slam into a car and kill an entire family on their way back from the shopping mall." I was clearly stepping out of line in my capacity as a location scout who should never disagree with the politics of Hollywood or risk losing the project, but I went on.

"Michael, did it ever occur to you that these kids, and most likely their parents, watched *Woodstock* as frazzled half-naked kids danced whirling-dervishes in the mud while Jimi Hendrix jammed in the background on acid. I think that one movie did more to *popularize* and *romanticize* drug use than any other film in America. How many people have died, how many are brain dead in mental institutes, how many innocent people are robbed and killed so young people can expand their minds? Why in the world would you ever want to make another movie that drags the culture down another 17 notches?"

I knew I had blown this location scout as Wadleigh sat quietly in the passenger seat staring into the floor. "Look" he said softly, "The only reason I'm trying to put this Woodstock reunion together is because my in-laws are about to lose their ranch in Montana because of their property tax bill. I'm just trying to save the ranch."

We remained friends despite our differences. But, it was a valuable lesson in the motives of filmmakers. Sometimes "saving the family ranch" can result in destroying generations of people, young and old.

PRESS RELEASE: "SMOKING-BAD; DRUGS-OKAY!"

No press release ever issued by the MPAA drew more laughs from both inside and outside the movie industry than the May 10, 2007 announcement that depictions of smoking in movies would warrant a stricter rating. According to Glickman's release, "Now, all smoking will be considered and depictions that glamorize smoking or movies that feature pervasive smoking outside of a historic or other mitigating context may receive a higher rating." This action by the MPAA was considered necessary because "on-screen smoking impacts young people."

Of course, no mention of drug and alcohol glamorization. That would be asking too much. When the proclamation was announced on CNN by Paula Zahn, commentator Roland Martin laughed and asked if the MPAA considered the fact that the number-one killer of teens in America is fast-driving youth who end up in auto accidents. "Is the industry going to ban all car chases?" Guest Bill Donahue laughed, "Ridiculous! Smoking's bad. Sodomy is okay."

Hollywood was quick to pick up on the announcement—sort of. A headline in *The Wall Street Journal* said it best, "Drinks, Drugs, Dysfunction star on Summer Cable TV." As cable networks pump out more original cable programming, a surprising number of drug users and problem drinkers are wobbling into the summer line-up.[23]

AMC's *Mad Men* is filled with alcoholic martini-swilling hard-smoking ad agency hacks. Holly Hunter is an alcoholic, hard-smoking cop in TNT's *Saving Grace*. In the pilot episode, Hunter's character is shown having sex with a married man, pouring whiskey into her morning soda, and mowing down a pedestrian with her Porsche.

Somehow, Hollywood needs a villain like cigarettes to keep at bay while it indulges in all the other dysfunctional behavior that ultimately chases the audience away, which is what happened with FX's *Rescue Me* after the TV Series about alcoholic firemen lost about a third of its viewers in 2007.

Glickman claims Hollywood productions will not take tobacco money advertising for product placement, but apparently alcohol and even marijuana is another story. The makers of Jack Daniels whiskey made a "deal" for its products to appear in three episodes of *Mad Men*. And, alcohol glamorization is awash on television and the big screen more than it has ever been depicted in the past.

Showtime's *Weeds* stars Mary Louise Parker as a mom who turns to selling marijuana after her husband dies. Gary Strauss of *USA Today* summarizes the show's plot, "numbed by her husband's fatal heart attack, she struggles to keep her two sons focused as they deal with a fatherless household, school and ripening sexuality. Sixth-grader Shane experienced the pleasures of early puberty at a massage parlor last season while Silas impregnates his Princeton-bound girlfriend."

Showtime producer Robert Greenblatt and *Weeds* producer Jenji Kohan even "consulted" with "professional" drug dealers including one who has been a pusher since the 1970's. We tried to reach Greenblatt and Kohan by phone to discover how they were able to quickly locate so many drug dealers who actually came to the production office to "discuss pot" with the show's writers. Our calls were never returned.

The show is basically a comedy that features highly dysfunctional "family members." The Showtime series has more agendas at work than drugs, which are basically glamorized. Greenblatt and Kohan come across largely as anti-Christian bigots who depict a "pot-smoking Christian" played by Mary-Kate Olsen. The show is packed with Christian-bashing themes by Kohan, which keeps the producer on Hollywood's pro-drug A-list of de-facto pushers and bashers.

In between puffs of pot, characters are making Hollywood political statements such as a sixth-grader who blurts out, "Bush is the worst president ever." Co-star Elizabeth Perkins says that when the story ultimately ends, "it won't be like 'Everybody's life is fine.' Ultimately, it will end tragically." Perkins adds, "Jenji Kohan doesn't like happy endings." With guest stars like real-life drug-addict and convict Snoop Dogg, the tragic ending is just around the corner as the show bombs in the ratings.

Showtime's *Weeds* is a perfect example of how Hollywood sleaze producers of low-estate come together to promote their passion for illegal drug use. The TV series receives the theatrical equivalent of an R-rating. According to the National Center on Addiction and Substance Abuse, twelve to seventeen year olds who frequently watch R-rated films are more likely to smoke, drink and use drugs.

But don't worry about *Weeds*. The producers have made sure to keep cigarette smoking scenes carefully in check.

THE HOLLYWOOD CULTURE WAR

* * *

In a press release issued on January 10, 2007, MPAA president Dan Glickman announced "Now, more than ever, the MPAA is battling for the hearts and minds of policy makers in Washington, but also for those of consumers around the world." The way to reach the hearts and minds of consumers around the world will not be accomplished by pushing drug abuse or other gratuitous scatological behavior. The first step in the right direction is comprehensive industry-wide drug testing. Only then will the audience return in record numbers.

CHAPTER 14

INTERMISSION

I am one of the last generations who can recall the unique American experience of "going to the movies" before the Ratings Scheme was established in 1968. For people born after 1960, the chances of remembering that era will be slim or non-existent. I was eleven years old when the transformation took place and I can vividly remember how it adversely affected my family.

Most people can remember the first movie they ever saw as a child in a movie theater. Few can remember the first movie or program that flashed across their TV set because of its ever present nature and location in the living room. The TV set was another piece of furniture that involved no special fanfare in turning the knob on or off.

Going to the movie theater, however, was an experience held in high anticipation for weeks on end, especially after new releases were announced in the Thursday edition of our local newspaper. My first experience occurred on a warm evening in 1962 at the age of five. My brother Mark and I jumped into the back seat of our family's new 1962 aqua-green Plymouth with the high chrome tail fins.

Going to the movies at that time was an experience for all people; families, couples or single adults. The movies coming out of Hollywood were still guided by the Production Code, though I knew nothing about that at the age of five. Movie ratings were still six years away and none of us even knew they were on the horizon.

Our destination that night was the Lyric Theater on Washington Street in downtown Huntsville, Alabama. The marquee lit up the otherwise dark street complete with oscillating lights that framed a bright white sign with three-dimensional red letters that spelled out *TO KILL A MOCKINGBIRD*.

Once inside, we walked quietly to our seats. Though the theater was almost full, the audience maintained a collective hush, with only the occasional muted

THE HOLLYWOOD CULTURE WAR

whispers. The walls of the old theater were curiously painted with desert scenery complete with green luminescent cactus that glowed in the dark as the lights went down and the curtains opened. (Yes, the large screen was actually covered with a curtain and its opening was part of the experience of anticipation that even small town theater owners had choreographed with precision.)

* * *

Almost twenty years later, as a young college student, I would discuss with my mother the memory of watching *To Kill A Mockingbird* as a five year old. The movie I remembered seeing was quite different than the movie my parents saw on that warm evening in 1962.

That was the secret of the Production Code that allowed people of all ages and families to watch movies together without the haunting specter of "age-appropriate" content. With movies made under the Code, adults could pick up on the deeper themes of a film while children could usually comprehend the broader, general themes that only young minds could fathom; basically, good and evil, right and wrong. Director Robert Mulligan was a master of this art.

This was the underestimated brilliance of the Code, the projection of "dual understanding." Any "gray areas" of the movie could be discussed and resolved by the time the family car pulled in the driveway.

The movie I remembered seeing that night was a simple story, if a little frightening at times. Two children named Jem and Scout, not much older than my brother and me, ventured into the backyards, alleyways, and side roads of their dusty little neighborhood with all the zeal and excitement of explorers. Each day and night, they managed to rediscover a new world, or the same world, but always enthusiastic in the subtle revelations they encountered. And, fatherly-inspired caution guided their journeys every time.

Nothing fascinated Jem and Scout more than the darkened, unpainted house at the end of the street. This particular summer, the brother and sister duo were determined to catch a glimpse of the home's mysterious inhabitant, Boo Radley. Their childhood imaginations had conjured up images of the strange man whom they had never seen.

One night, the two children, along with a visiting neighbor friend, were confronted by the myserious man as the three stalked ever closer to the old house for a glimpse. They escaped in time and were later carefully chastised by their sage father, local attorney Atticus Finch. He was a good man with strong character who only wanted his children to respect all their neighbors and shun the temptation to make fun of other people.

In the end, Jem and Scout made friends with Boo Radley on a hot night at the end of a long summer that tested their father's strong will and reputation in the community. Jem and Scout took their father's advice to heart and reached out to their mysterious neighbor and discovered he was not so mysterious anymore.

That was the movie I remembered seeing as a five year old, though I had seen it many more times as a teenager and young adult. My mother proceeded to tell me about *To Kill A Mockingbird* as the movie she remembered seeing as an adult and young mother in 1962. It was quite different than the movie I saw as a child.

My mother described a story about racial prejudice, hatred and bigotry in a small town in which a morally courageous attorney and widowed father of two children named Atticus Finch was the sole defender of a black man named Tom Robinson who was on trial for rape. Despite all his efforts at defending the man, including sitting in front of the jail house door with a shotgun in his lap, Tom Robinson was ultimately killed.

While that outcome saddened my mother greatly, she also remembered the trial as the central most riveting part of the story. Even to this day, she finds the core plot of the story open for debate due to the skillful direction of Robert Mulligan who transferred Harper Lee's best-selling book into one of cinema's classic movies.

My mother remembered Tom Robinson being viciously and falsely accused of rape by a poor white girl named Mayella Ewell. But, as the story unfolded, mainly in the courtroom, allusions to other scenarios of Tom Robinson's plight varied widely according to the viewer's own perception or prejudice about such situations which only adults could comprehend because of maturity, age and education of the tangled webs that people weave or become ensnared.

For my mother, there were four possible scenarios as to how Tom Robinson became a captive of Mayella Ewell. One possibility was that Mayella Ewell seduced Tom Robinson after asking him to move a heavy chest of drawers. An unstable personality, Mayella may have been flushed with shame after the seduction was complete and cried rape in order to save her "honor." She would be vindicated because, after all, she was white and Tom Robinson was black and that's all the jury needed to know in 1920's Alabama.

A second scenario posed by my mother was that Mayella was caught in the act of seducing Tom Robinson by her father, Bob, the crusty little town drunk, also known in the southern class system as "white trash" or a "no-count." Mr. Ewell may have forced his daughter to cry rape in order to save his own honor, what little, if any, he maintained.

A third, more plausible possibility was that Mayella Ewell tried to exert her authority in an otherwise powerless life of poverty by trying to seduce Tom Robinson—only to be rejected by him—and causing Mayella to extract revenge by crying rape.

The fourth scenario appeared obvious to my mother in that Bob Ewell was having an incestuous relationship with his daughter, and any of the other three underlying plots could have overlapped with this ongoing abuse.

THE HOLLYWOOD CULTURE WAR

As a five year old watching the same movie, none of those scenes or plotlines registered in my young mind. The courtroom was a large place where adults had gathered to solve some kind of problem and I had no idea what the problem was. I do, however, remember the scene when a frustrated Atticus Finch was gathering his papers as the courtroom emptied. As he turned to leave, he glanced up to the balcony where the black members of the community were relegated. They all stood in solemn silence; the men had removed their hats in reverence. Whatever was going on in the courtroom, I knew that Atticus Finch was a "good" man. In the world of a five year old, discerning the "good" from the "bad" is a full time occupation.

Though my focus in watching *To Kill A Mockingbird* was centered on the adventures of Jem and Scout, in the end, I learned that people are not to be unfairly judged or accused, as Boo Radley had been by the children of Atticus. For my mother, the lesson was exactly the same, as the fateful story of Tom Robinson unfolded.

* * *

In 1990, twenty-eight years after my first experience at a movie theater, I had the opportunity to briefly scout locations with director Robert Mulligan and production designer Gene Callahan for *The Man in the Moon*, Mulligan's last feature film as director. I asked Mulligan if he felt *To Kill A Mockingbird* could have been filmed after 1968 in the post-ratings era.

Mulligan, then 65, said that it was possible, but interference from the young turk crop of producers may have demanded an unnecessary quota of salaciousness which in turn would have shut out an entire generation of children and adolescents. "Be thankful," Mulligan said, "that your first experience at the movies was prior to the era of ratings. That you learned a valuable lesson at the age of five says much about the brilliance of the Production Code, though it did have its limitations at times, it certainly didn't prevent *Mockingbird* from becoming a box office success and a major award-winning film; certainly my favorite."

Mulligan made a perceptive observation in how the Ratings Scheme served to take away the individual moviegoer's imaginative thought process that worked simultaneously with the projected image. "The producers of today greatly underestimate the mind of the audience and they are doing everything in their power to take away the individual's ability to think for themselves."

For the next three years after 1962's *To Kill A Mockingbird*, our family enjoyed going to the movies almost every weekend. We watched an all-star cast of Allies storm the beach in *The Longest Day* by producer David Zanuck and three generations moving west in John Ford's *How The West Was Won*. 1963's *It's a Mad Mad Mad Mad World* was the funniest movie we had ever seen, complete with inside gags like Jimmy Durante "kicking the can." In 1965, "The Sound of Music" was an Oscar-winner worth of a second visit to the theater, a rare occurrence reserved for the "best of the best."

Later in 1965, a crack would appear at the cinema that changed our family's movie nights forever. It appeared suddenly, like a split in the walls of a strong house whose foundation shifted dramatically.

It would mark the very early signs of a period that Michael Medved would term years later as the "Missing Moviegoers," a span of only four years between 1965 and 1969 when more than 60% of the weekly moviegoing audience would disappear. Not only did they disappear, according to Medved the "audiences fled from the theaters in horror and disgust."

EXODUS

I was only eight years old when the mass exodus from the theaters began as a trickle. I'm sure our family attended one of the few movies in 1965 that desperately pushed the envelope. Thursday's newspaper was the only newspaper that counted for children anticipating the upcoming weekend's slate of new movies. As my father spread out the paper across the dining room table, I didn't see any interest in his face over the new movies. In fact, for the first time, his brows furrowed in confusion. He called over to my mother as he pointed to an ad announcing the local premier of *Hush-Hush, Sweet Charlotte*.

I peered over the table as my father pointed to some small print at the bottom of the ad. It read: For Mature Audiences. "What do you suppose that means?" my mother asked. "I don't know. It has Bette Davis, Joseph Cotten and Olivia deHavilland," my dad answered, trying to sound assuring. "It can't be *that bad* if they're in it."

On Friday night all four of us were sitting in the Martin Theatre, right across from the Lyric, where just three years earlier we saw *To Kill A Mockingbird*. With popcorn and cola in hand, we nestled into our seats as the opening shot featured Louisiana's grand Oak Alley plantation with the background dialogue of a vicious argument raging between Victor Buono and Bruce Dern in a flashback segment that would set the stage for the movie.

Very soon into the film, a scene would take place that would forever change my life and the life of my family as our weekly journey to the movies would largely come to an end. In the scene, Bruce Dern was sitting at a small wrought-iron garden table inside the greenhouse behind the mansion. Dern was clutching a bouquet of flowers with his hand resting on the table. The only sound to be hard was the gentle wind chime of tubular bells ringing through the warm summer breeze.

As the screen door opened, Dern leaned forward, "Charlotte?" At that moment, the camera closed in on an enormous meat clever that came crashing down on the

THE HOLLYWOOD CULTURE WAR

garden table, slicing Dern's hand off at the wrist. As Dern grasped the bleeding stump, I could feel my father's hand reaching over and pushing at the back of my head so that I was staring into my bag of popcorn.

Just as the coast seemed clear, my father released his hold and I looked up at the screen only to see the cleaver descend again and slice straight through Dern's neck as his head tumbled off his shoulders. My father's hand was a little late, but, again I found myself staring into a bag of popcorn.

My brother was frozen in silence. I captured my mother peaking over my brother's head to "check" on me. With only the sound of wind chimes, the entire theater was abuzz with whispering as the tension of the screen had crept into the theater. A few people walked out.

The ride home was unusually silent. We usually engaged in lively discussions after a movie, all the way into the driveway. But, not this night, or any other night ever again. 1965 was the last time our family went to a movie. In fact, none of us saw a movie at a theater for another five years. My mother and father *never* returned.

The sound of tubular bells and wind chimes would haunt me from age eight to the age of thirteen. Going to bed every night was a judgment call. Do I leave my bedroom door open? Do I close it? Should I leave the window ajar? Should I keep it locked? The simple act of going to bed became an exercise in futility, preparing for some unseen horror that could fall as easy as a meat clever on a humid summer night.

Michael Medved was right on the mark when he wrote in *Hollywood vs. America* that "those disillusioned moviegoers have stayed away to this day." My father died in 1980 having never returned to the movie theater again. My mother, now 76, also never returned to the movie theater, preferring occasional television programming over anything that Hollywood parades at the multiplex.

Of course, none of us knew at the time that this 1965 to 1969 period was the gestation of Jack Valenti's Quiet Conspiracy by the Gang of Four. And, a fact that cannot be made often enough in this book is that the weekly attendance at the movie theaters has *never* returned to the level of 1965, despite the fact that America's population jumped from 200 million to 300 million in the last forty years.

It's hard to imagine the experience of "going to the movies" before 1968 unless you were there. The MPAA's secret agenda is to prevent that era from ever returning again.

Again, columnist Ellen Goodman put it best, "The rites of passage to adulthood are now defined by card-carrying access to alcohol, tobacco and big screen mayhem. What message does that send about what it means to come of age?"

CHAPTER 15

DAWN OF THE NEW AGE: THE LONG ARM OF MEPHISTOPHELES

> *"Aiwass, High Priest of Horus the Sun God, has called on me to proclaim the dawn of The New Age"*
> —Aleister Crowley, 1904

Mephistopheles—(mef 'a-stof'a-lez'),n.—a devil to whom Faust sold his soul for riches and power.

* * *

"*The Wickedest Man In The World*," as dubbed by the English tabloid *John Blow* in 1923, was born just before midnight on October 12, 1875. By the time he reached the age of ten in 1885, Aleister Crowley was not only developing a fascination, but also an obsessive occult-like identification with the enemies of God as his mother read passages of the Bible to him. He even developed a "kinship" relationship with the antichrist character from the book of Revelation.[1] By age 12, Crowley had graduated to a systematic and ritualistic killing of animals.

Between that time and his death in 1947, Aleister Crowley would come to influence generations of bohemians, artists, musicians and filmmakers who consciously chose to explore the dark side of life, embracing it as religion and expressing it in their work. In writing this book, no other decision was more difficult than choosing the location of this chapter within the context of all the others. At this point, it would be difficult to further explain the influence of the entertainment industry without referring to Crowley and those individuals and "movements" that he influenced.

If you have ever questioned the existence of good and evil—and specifically the origins—it is imperative to understand Crowley. Widely known among many in the music and movie industry, he remains largely unknown to the mainstream of American society. However, much of the discourse that has fueled the Culture War can be traced back to Aleister Crowley and those that followed his radical New Age secular philosophies during the 20th century.

Described variously as an explorer, teacher, writer and philosopher, by 1900 he was already being labeled as a guru, mystic, practitioner of black magic, occultist and chief promoter of Satanism in Europe and America. Aleister Crowley is the man who first coined and promoted the "The New Age" in 1904.

While we have mentioned a number of influential entertainment celebrities that represent a "strand" in the long dark thread that runs through Hollywood, Aleister Crowley is the dark thread that connects the disparate strands. There are many in the popular culture that can quote him verbatim to this day. Before finishing this chapter, and this book, you may be fairly surprised, or shocked, by who his devotees are in the world of entertainment. Much worse, these individuals have influenced millions of their own devoted fans who unknowingly have adopted the beliefs and mindsets of their entertainment idols.

* * *

Aleister Crowley's father had died at the same time young "Alick" had developed his love for animal torture and death. Aleister was left with a considerable fortune from which he would fund his education, explorations and inevitably, finance his own occult enterprise.[2]

Frustrated with his dark childhood endeavors, Crowley's mother would refer to him as "The Great Beast of Revelation" and this would greatly please the young boy—an adolescent Rosemary's Baby—as he grew older and enrolled at Trinity College in 1895 to study English literature.

During this time Crowley began a sex rampage that would continue for the rest of his life. While in college, the young beasty boy began to run with prostitutes and girls he picked up at local pubs and tobacco shops. But, this would bore him quickly, a trait he would carry throughout his life. Crowley took a quick leap into the dark underbelly of the homosexual underground in Cambridge at the turn of the century.[3]

Toward the end of his debauched university days in late 1896, Crowley began to enter larger open doors to the occult, fascinated with the darker, esoteric side of life. On New Year's Eve of 1896, during one of his homo-erotic experiences, Crowley claims to have come in contact with "an immanent deity" (an ever present power).[4] Soon thereafter, Crowley began to embark on a reading frenzy that coincided with his voracious sexcapades.

At every opportunity, when he was not having sex with young boys and prostitutes, Crowley was picking up books that dealt with mysticism, magic, the occult and especially alchemy (Author J.K. Rowling demonstrates a similar fascination with alchemists; pseudo-quack-scientific-spiritualists who believed they could turn base metal into gold).

Between 1896 and 1904, Crowley would join various secretive "magick" societies that were prominent in England and America at the time. (The "k" was added to magic to distinguish it as an occult practice as opposed to the "illusionist" variety.) These secret societies, some of which exist today, were deeply entrenched into ritualistic occult practices. Most of these societies engaged in worship of ancient Egyptian deities and demon idols, which totally fascinated Crowley.

By this time, Crowley had developed a nihilistic futility in pursuing the normal human endeavors and responsibilities of life. In 1898, Aleister Crowley decided to make contact with the devil himself.

In that year, Crowley had become a member of the Hermetic Order of the Golden Dawn, a secret society of mystics with highly ordered and deeply protected rituals involved with "accessing" the "dark powers" of the ancient deities. Crowley was a walking contradiction, something he would cultivate and teach to others. When it came to joining these secret societies, he would take oaths and break them with routine regularity. Crowley began demonstrating the secret rituals of the Golden Dawn in public and would be hounded for decades by the leaders of the mystic order. In the meantime, London bohemians and artists took note of Crowley's mystifying demonstrations.

Samuel Mathers, leader of the Golden Dawn, sued Crowley for infringement after Crowley spilled all of the secrets of the society for public consumption. Behind the scenes of the sensational court battles, both Crowley and Mathers claimed to have summoned armies of demons to fight each other.[5]

Crowley would later travel to Mexico and immerse himself in Raja Yoga and then Buddhism. But, the ever fluctuating Crowley would join other secret societies, the Silver Star and O.T.O. Again, Crowley was accused by Theodore Reuss, O.T.O. leader, of publishing the secret occult rituals for public consumption. Crowley denied this, claiming he never reached the "9th" degree within the organization. Crowley was later proven to have lied, a trait which he had mastered since childhood. In the meantime, the bohemians were collecting any tract or writings by Crowley, a man they considered a mystic traveler with secret powers and perverse sexual prowess; "attributes" they wanted to imitate.

Author B. Gary Patterson, whose ground-breaking book *Hellhounds on Their Trail* exposes the occult influence of Crowley on contemporary entertainment, admitted, "When writing the Aleister Crowley chapter late at night, I must admit that I had a few cold chills running up my spine . . ."[6]

THE HOLLYWOOD CULTURE WAR

* * *

Before going further, it would help in understanding the meaning of the word "occult," as it has been largely misunderstood. The word originated from the Latin "occultus," meaning "conceal" or "to cover." Webster's New World dictionary defines occult as: "hidden, secret, esoteric, beyond human understanding." It is also used inclusively to designate "mystic arts, magic, astrology, alchemy, etc." In Christianity, it is always considered to be in diametric opposition to God.

The seminal event for Crowley that would gain him a certain degree of international attention came in 1904 during a "vacation" to Cairo, Egypt. Though still involved with prostitutes and frequent pedophile trysts, Crowley had married in order to promote himself as a "family man." While in Cairo, Crowley's wife, Rose began to act in a strange manner which led Crowley to believe she had been possessed with some "entity." At Rose's direction, Crowley summoned the ancient Egyptian God Horus on March 20th. Crowley said a demonic voice spoke to him identifying itself as Aiwass, the High Priest of Horus.

Crowley claimed that Aiwass announced the arrival of a New Aeon (New Age) and Crowley would be the chosen scribe to spread the New Age religion. For the next month, Crowley would dictate the words spoken to him by Aiwass and collect the "proclamations" into a text known as "The Book of the Law." (Daryl Hall of the music group Hall & Oates owns a signed copy of the book and considers it one of his most coveted "possessions.")

The central guiding slogan from the *The Book of the Law* as written by Crowley is "Do What Thou Will Shall Be The Whole Of The Law." He would refer to this as a "true will," meaning that a person was free to do anything and there would be no consequences from an "all seeing, all knowing God." The bohemians took this as holy doctrine, releasing them from the "bondage" of morality and personal values. "True will" is not to be confused with "free will," which does imply potential consequences for "unrepentant" acts of wrong doing.

Within fifteen years of the "Egyptian experience," copies of Crowley's "bible" would circulate throughout Manhattan and the new Hollywood film industry. Crowley's central statement "Do What Thou Will" would become the guiding slogan behind numerous countercultural "movements" and philosophies that would culminate in the cascading decline of American culture. As the chart "Timeline of New Age Philosophies in Western Culture" demonstrates, Crowley's dark doctrines were not the first to chip away at Western culture, but they would become the most prominent, especially in the second half of the 20th century and continuing today. (See Appendix 5).

After basically accepting his "demon-inspired" marching orders to lead the New Age, Crowley would endeavor to learn and teach everything he could about every man-made religion and "mystical" experience by wrapping it up in one new "religious denomination" he termed "Thelema." This project to spread The New Age would reflect a deep influence from Friedrich Nietzsche, the original "secular liberator" who proclaimed "God is Dead" in the late 19th century. (Nietzsche's original quote was "once the sin against God was the greatest sin; but God died.")

The artists and "creative types" found a kinship in Crowley's teachings which basically said that the individual was God—something very appealing in Hollywood and the eastern establishment media. In his book, *The World's Tragedy*, Crowley confronted Christianity and how " . . . it is their God and their religion that I hate and I will destroy."[7]

Devotees of Crowley often fail to mention that Crowley's wife, Rose, was pregnant at the time she received "the voice" in Egypt in March 1904. In July of that year, Rose Crowley gave birth to a daughter whom Crowley named after another ancient Egyptian deity, Sappho Jezebel Lilith Crowley. Within two years the young girl was dead and Rose ended up in a mental institute.

Crowley established his Abbey of Thelema in Italy and began an "anti-monastery" where there existed no rules or laws; only "pleasure" consisting of drug use and orgies mixed in with intermittent worship of Egyptian gods. Not long after the temple was established, Italian authorities expelled Crowley from the country when his antics were exposed by the British press. Apparently, bestiality was also being practiced at the "Abbey."

Crowley adopted many occult and Eastern religions which he rewrote and formulated as part of Thelema and the broader New Age movement. Among these were mystic Buddhism, Indian Yoga, Chinese I Ching, Jewish Kabbalah (Madonna's current favorite), Taoism, O.T.O., Gnosticism (Jane Fonda's New Age choice), tarot, astrology (most of Hollywood), and conversing with the dead, known as necromancy (practiced by Oprah Winfrey). Also included in the Thelemic New Age religion was Crowley's pagan devotion to such ancient deities as Nuit, Hadit, Horus, Babalon, Choios, Baphomet and many more.

Aleister Crowley took great pleasure in the practice of witchcraft and sorcery and went to great lengths to rewrite new "spells" and "curses" that he and his followers would use to bring harm against their perceived enemies. Crowley was a sexual pervert of immensely demented proportions, promoting a type of occult ritual known as "sex magick" which had been practiced in America by the abolitionist Paschal Beverly Randolph and the Hermetic Brotherhood of Luxor; again, another secret society with ancient Egyptian allegiance.

The New Age "founder" was so obsessed with sex that he began writing numerous tracts and poems that combined pagan religious rituals with sexual imagery that was heterosexual, homosexual and pederastic (pedophilia).[8] Aleister Crowley's promotion of homosexual sex with young boys would later be embraced by "Beat Generation" founders Allen Ginsberg and William Burroughs who bragged quite openly about their support of sex with young children for which they promoted right up until their deaths. Crowley devotee Ginsberg was the "bridge" to forming the hippie movement of the 1960's and was an active member of NAMBLA (North American Man Boy Love Association). It is no coincidence that Ginsberg was one of George Soros' closest friends.

These are the "footnotes" of the countercultural secular New Age leaders that the mainstream press forgot to include in their articles of adoration for anybody who promoted the "unconventional." Along with Beat author Jack Kerouac, these three men followed Crowley's promotion of illegal drug use to the point of popularizing it into the youth culture of the 1950s and 1960s, from which it would metastasize into the epidemic it is today.

Crowley was mainly addicted to opium, but was also a regular user of heroin, hashish, peyote and cocaine. *The International Times* once declared Crowley as "the unsung hero of the hippies."[9] Like the bohemians of the early 20th century and the beatniks of the 1950s, the hippies felt "justified" in their deconstruction of American culture because they had a personal sage who had set the stage.

The popularization of drug use as advocated by Crowley would become well known in Hollywood by the early 1920s, more than a decade after he wrote *The Book of the Law.* Another book which made the rounds in Hollywood was Crowley's *Diary of a Drug Fiend* in which he chronicled the use of cocaine.

Not ironically, the book was published in 1922, the same year the MPAA was founded by the studio moguls to clean up Hollywood's drug-ridden image. Always the hypocrite, Crowley actually referred to Hollywood celebrities as "cocaine-crazed sexual lunatics."[10] Hollywood obviously took this as a compliment. Certainly Oliver Stone and John Belushi took it to heart.

Crowley's teachings would find a popular following among the young New Leftists of the early 1960s in more ways than promoting drug abuse. Crowley taught a form of personal mind control in which his students could focus their mental and behavioral habits to the point of switching political views and personalities at will. This trait can still be evidenced today in the politics of aging activists such as Jane Fonda, Sandy Berger, Bill and Hillary Clinton and Senator John Kerry who epitomized the practice in his famous 2004 campaign statement, "I voted for the war before I voted against it."

The modern incarnation of Aleister Crowley today is easily the multibillionaire hedge fund operator and political manipulator George Soros. Suffice it to say for now that he is the polished package version of Aleister Crowley, promoting the destruction of the traditional family, open and unfettered drug use, demonizing Jews and Christians, promoting legal prostitution, abolishing punishment for crime and initiating the rewriting of the American Constitution.

Soros promotes all this and more in the name of his Open Society Institute (OSI) which is pure Crowleian New Age philosophy taken straight from the "Book of the Law." The basic guiding slogan behind OSI is "Do What Thou Will Shall Be the Whole of the Law." The fact that Soros refuses to define OSI's mission is right in line with Crowley's dictum of secrecy and changing politics at will. The fact that Barack Obama and Hillary Clinton have both received endorsements from Soros says much about their willingness to enter into the Faustian deal and negates their claims to any semblance of a "proclaimed" Christian faith as they become members of the *George Soros Church of God is Dead*.

By 1934, Crowley was bankrupt after losing a libel suit against artist Nina Hammett for calling Crowley a "practitioner of magic" in her 1932 book *Laughing Torso*. It was not like the whole world didn't know and now Crowley was being consumed by the very evil he promoted. Almost sixty years old, Crowley had spent most of his fortune promoting the New Age through self-published books on the worship of false gods and demons.

However, Crowley's "anything goes" philosophy continued to spread among his loyal fans even though it was well known that Crowley was an anti-Semite. He fully supported the slaughter of Jews by Joseph Stalin at the same time he maintained a sadistic homosexual relationship with his Jewish lover Victor Neuberg. Crowley even offered his services to Soviet Communist authorities to help wipe out their Christian populations as well.[11]

As Crowley wasted away during the 1940s, he believed himself to be the reincarnation of the 19th century magician Eliphas Levi, who happened to die the day Aleister Crowley was born. Crowley also believed that he was Pope Alexander the VI, in a previous life.

When the verdict was handed down in the Hammett libel case, Judge Swift, a forty-year veteran of English law, stated from the bench, "I thought I had known everything which was vicious and bad had been produced at one time or another before me. I have learnt in this case that we can always learn something if we live long enough. I have never heard of such dreadful, horrible, blasphemous and abominable stuff as that which has been produced by the man [Crowley] who describes himself to you as the greatest living poet."

The judge was not shy about injecting value judgments in his judicial opinion from the bench. This would become known as "swift" justice.

As author Steve Turner wrote, "Crowley finished his life as a sick, wasted heroin addict given to black rages and doubts about the value of his life's work. His last words as he passed into a coma on December 1, 1947 were, "I am perplexed."[12]

The man who founded The New Age movement, which continues to grow with the secularization of society, spent the greater part of his life destroying the lives of others. These included his friends, associates and especially his own family. After the institutionalization of his first wife, his second wife also went insane. Five mistresses committed suicide and scores of his concubines ended in the gutter as drug addicts, wasted alcoholics or committed to mental institutions.[13]

If you are thoroughly depressed at this point, do not despair. It is proof that you have a heart and a conscience, unlike Mr. Crowley and all those who have followed him. And while you may have never heard of Aleister Crowley before you probably have heard the names of those who were influenced by him directly and indirectly.

In Chapter 18 "Hollywood's Road to Perdition," we will reveal how Crowley's motto of "Do What Thou Will" was appropriated by some of the major players in the desecration of American culture during the 20th century. These are the people who promulgated the Culture War by the very darkness of their hearts and the premeditated deceptions of their words and actions.

In the meantime, we'll give you a sample of Crowley's influence into contemporary music. Those mentioned here are the ones directly influenced by Crowley. When you consider the multiplier effect of others "inspired" by these musicians, a "corporate" flow chart begins that has no ending.

CROWLEY'S HOLLYWOOD CONGREGATION

"The whole Beatle idea was to do what you want . . . do what thou will . . ."[14] declared John Lennon in an interview with *Playboy* magazine. It was an appropriate format for Lennon to declare his open allegiance to Crowley. After all, Hugh Hefner's "Playboy Philosophy" boiled down to the same guiding slogan.

Lennon apparently had no problem convincing his fellow Beatles of the Crowlean New Age philosophy of sex and drugs. They expounded a little by adding the rock and the roll, hence the mantra of the 1960s "sex, drugs and rock and roll."

The Beatles paid homage to a hodgepodge of their cultural heroes when they released their best-selling album *Sergeant Pepper*. The cover of the album was a photo montage tribute to the oddball cast of characters who had shaped the group's attitudes and personal philosophies since their inception originally as "The Quarrymen" in the late 1950s. Prominent among the photos that graced the cover was a picture of Aleister Crowley. Paul McCartney would declare Crowley as one of the group's "heroes." Authors Geoffrey Giuliano and Denny Laine chronicled Paul and Linda McCartney's practice of Crowlean occultism throughout the 1970s in their biography *Blackbird: The Life and Times of Paul McCartney*. LSD guru Timothy Leary was a friend of Lennon's and a devout follower of Crowley, saying "I've been an admirer of Aleister Crowley . . . 'Do what thou will shall be the whole of the law' . . . It was a very powerful statement."[15]

In the late 1960s, Leary was contemplating running for political office in California and asked Lennon to write a campaign song for him. However, it didn't take long for Leary to be "convinced" that an "acidhead" like himself was not going to win political office—even in California. But, Lennon was as enthusiastic over Leary as he was over Crowley because of their mutual dream of an "open society" and he insisted on writing a song anyhow, a sort of "patron saint" accolade. The result was "Come together, right now . . . over me" meaning Leary and his whole "turn on, tune in, drop out" philosophy of life—a carbon copy cartoonish character of Aleister Crowley.

In 1960s "rock and roll," it doesn't even take seven degrees of separation to connect to Aleister Crowley.

With the Beatles on board as Crowley's voice from the dead, interest sparked among other early rockers. The radical homosexual filmmaker Kenneth Anger was a devout follower of Crowley among his contemporaries in documentaries and music more than anyone other than John Lennon and Paul McCartney.

Anger, also author of *Hollywood Babylon*, claimed that his films were "visual incantations" inspired by Crowley. Anger shared Crowley's deep-seated hatred of Jews and Christians and decided to embark upon the "ultimate" documentary to glorify his beloved Crowley. When the film was finished, Anger was in desperate need for a "rock" soundtrack to play throughout the documentary. Through mutual New Age occultists, Anger discovered that Mick Jagger of The Rolling Stones and Jimmy Paige of Led Zeppelin were also devout followers of Crowley's *Book of the Law* and both offered their services for the sound track.

Ozzy Ozbourne, the "Your Brain on Drugs" poster child was the "innovator" in the 1970s of "Satanic Rock" and called Crowley, "a phenomenon of his time."[16] Anyone needing to see the effects of embracing Aleister Crowley should buy or rent a DVD of the defunct MTV "reality show" known as *The Osbournes*.

Ozzy, as he is affectionately known by his wife and purple-haired children, wasn't even able to negotiate a simple sentence without drooling and stuttering like the sad brain-fried sub-human he became. He was already contributing to global warming as far back as the 1970s when he routinely "up-chucked" before each concert. This often preceded the performance of one of Osbourne's favorite songs, simply titled "Mr. Crowley."

Another "Satanic Rock" singer, Bruce Dickinson of Iron Maiden, was quoted in the August 31, 1984 issue of *Circus Magazine* as saying " . . . we've referred to things like the tarot and ideas of people like Aleister Crowley." Like Ozbourne, their ode to Crowley was a song titled "The Number of the Beast" with lyrics not fit for print here. Crowley's lifelong nickname was "The Beast."

The current "Satanic Rocker" promoted around the world by Universal Studios is the androgynous pervert Marilyn Manson, a major lunatic fan of Crowley's writings whose song "Misery Machine" is his dedication to Mr. Wicked with the lyrics "We're gonna ride to the Abbey of Thelema," which was Crowley's Italian drug/orgy occult temple.[17]

As mentioned earlier, Daryl Hall of Hall and Oates not only owns a signed copy of *The Book of the Law,* he is an avid reader of Aleister Crowley's many other writings including the long-winded diatribes against Christians and instructions in occult "magick." Probably the only other "rocker" who studies Crowley more than Daryl Hall is Sting, lead singer of the Police.[18]

David Bowie, close friend of Mick Jagger, is so enamored with Aleister Crowley that he named an album *The Man Who Sold the World* in which he refers "affectionately" to Crowley in his song appropriately titled "Quicksand."[19]

The musician, who Oliver Stone referred to as "a god" of rock music, Jim Morrison of the Doors, is seen posing next to a bust of Aleister Crowley on the back cover of his popular Doors 13 album. Morrison was enthralled with Crowley's drug use and emulated his narco-fascination to such an extreme that he died from a massive overdose on a night-club toilet seat, not in a bathtub.

Afrika Bambaataa, the founder of hip-hop music and patron saint to rappers does not admit to patronizing Crowley, but he credits the founding of hip hop to his trip to Egypt in the early 1970's and a fascination with the same ancient Egyptian deities which captured the interest of Crowley in 1904. G. Craige Lewis exposed hip hop as a religion devised by Bambaataa, a self-proclaimed "god' of the "Zulu Nation," who revels in dressing up in King Tut regalia and advocates the rewriting of the entire Bible at his direction and vision.

Bambaataa and his fellow rapper KRS-ONE began promoting hip hop as a "new" religion which, according to Lewis, advocates man as his own god and "anything goes, as long as you are feeling it."[20] This is, in all respects, the very same as "Do what thou will shall be the whole of the law." The hip-hop music is but one aspect of the "culture" dictated by "The Temple of Hip-Hop," as KRS-ONE calls it.

Pink Floyd, the perpetrators of "psychedelic rock" can thank Aleister Crowley for their drug-induced musical nightmares. Special credit can easily be traced to its first lead singer, Syd Barrett, who "disappeared" mysteriously in the early 1970s after countless acid trips that seemingly propelled him to the very "Dark Side of the Moon" which later became the band's light-splitting prism anthem to acid-heads.

As it turns out, Barrett had permanently fried his brain, shaved his head and eyebrows and bloated up with water retention after moving back in with his mother in Cambridge, England. The neighbors around town knew him as nothing more than an odd old Englishman who tooled around town on a bicycle and spent warm days working in his garden.

His death and life were perceptively noted in a Slate.com article by Judy Rosen posted on July 11, 2006, "Syd Barrett, who died several days ago (no one is sure exactly when) at age 60, was to say the least, a mess. The wire services are remembering the co-founder and first lead singer of Pink Floyd as a "troubled genius"—obit-speak for lunatic—and indeed his life was a lurid tragedy . . ." Rosen continues by noting that "had Barrett been born 30 years earlier, and done several thousand fewer hits of LSD, he could have made a fine living on Tin Pan Alley."[21] Barrett was Crowley's biggest fan.

The last casualty of this chapter is an example of the long arm of Mephistopheles as the Crowleian example reproduces exponentially into each new generation. Aleister Crowley was a cultural icon to beatnik kingpin and author William Burroughs who would take Crowley's message deeper into the music scene. Burroughs, Allen Ginsberg and Jack Kerouac were all heroes of the hippies who helped pave the way for the 1960's counterculture.

Burroughs, like Crowley, spent most of his life indulging in every form of drug available beginning in the 1950s and was an unapologetic child molester well into his 70's. He would exert his perverted influence in the contemporary music scene right up until his death in 1997.

As biographer Steven Davis would write, "Like Crowley, Burroughs was an urbane and genial Lucifer, a modern magus, legendary addict and activist whose influence extended far beyond literature to music, painting, and film."[22]

Burroughs was infatuated with every form of derelict music that streaked across the popular culture with great frequency from the 1950s on. He is even credited with coining the term "heavy metal" to that particular head-banging form of noise with no semblance to "music." Burroughs's biggest fan in the 1990s was Kurt Cobain of the band Nirvana whose "noise" was sometimes labeled, appropriately, "Grunge." Cobain became a devoted follower of the occult and sought out Burroughs advice on a regular basis. Another habit Cobain picked up and intensified with his Burroughs friendship was an immense appetite for illegal and extremely deadly drugs of every variety.

By April of 1994, Cobain's brain was so frosted from non-stop drug use that his multiple attempts at overdosing to death ended in failure. By April 5th of the that year, disappointed that he was still alive, Cobain vanished from public view and was found in the loft apartment of his parent's home with a shotgun blast to the head.

Like Syd Barrett of Pink Floyd, Cobain was "taught" by fellow culture critics that their life in the middle-class was a mundane existence of false serenity from which they must escape to "express themselves." Yet, as their brains literally dissolved over their brief flash across the music scene, somewhere deep in the cerebrum was the reality that L. Frank Baum would immortalize forever in the voice of Dorothy that "There's no place like home."

Aleister Crowley may very well be credited with lowering the average life span of musicians. *The World Almanac And Book of Facts* in 1997 listed the average age at death of rock stars as 36.9 years. The average age of death for all Americans was 75.8 years.[23]

THE HOLLYWOOD CULTURE WAR

From movie stars, musicians, artists and even presidential candidates, many continue to reach out to the long arm of Mephistopheles in the Faustian deal to gain power and prestige at the crossroads of good and evil. It is never too late to flee and turn against the darkness that Hollywood frequently serves up on the silver screen. Faust knows, even he was given another chance.

CHAPTER 16

CELEBRITY GODS

*"People who work in the
entertainment industry are mentally ill."*
—Michael Savage

"There's plenty of money to be made in Hollywood, but you practically lose your soul in the process," Alan Alda told me rather casually over lunch at Atlanta's City Grill during a location scout for *Betsy's Wedding* in 1990. Producer Lou Stroller was along from Universal as we piled back into the car for another long day of scouting. What I knew, for certain, is that Alda and Stroller were among the very few industry people I had met that did not "lose" their soul for success in the motion picture industry. The term "lose" was a diplomatic way of saying "sell."

But, they were the exception rather than the rule among the hundreds of producers, writers, directors and actors I had scouted locations with over the years. As the chief location scout, and driver, I was often the target of proselytizing from New Age celebrities that would preach everything from atom-bomb-toting aliens, spirit guides from the dead, crystal power, mystic Kaballah and more often than not, witchcraft and the occult.

Those who had not scouted with me before would be subject to a thorough debunking of their beliefs as I would deconstruct them word by word. This often caused many of them to fly into red-eyed ear-splitting defense of their New Age neo-pagan deities. Many of these Hollywood "true believers" were, I felt certain, truly possessed or tormented individuals.

In the summer of 1989, I was coordinating locations for a Turner Network Television movie, *The Rose and the Jackal,* starring Christopher Reeve in a loosely based docudrama on the life of Abraham Lincoln's Secret Service agent Allan Pinkerton. During a break in filming, I joined Reeve and other members of the crew for dinner at a downtown Macon, Georgia tavern.

THE HOLLYWOOD CULTURE WAR

Reeve began to praise the "virtues" of a deviated form of astrology known as astroyoga. I had never heard of it before, but Reeve assured me that many celebrities practiced astroyoga very faithfully. It all sounded very bogus to me and I asked him as politely as possible why he chose this particular "religion" to guide his life.

"Its all about overcoming fear," he explained. "There's too much fear in this industry, too much fear in the world. It's a source of peace, *if* properly practiced." He was absolutely right about fear, but I questioned his choice of "deliverance," for he didn't seem to be radiating confidence on this particular evening. In fact Reeve always gave the impression that a cloud was hanging over his head and no one could ever pinpoint why.

"Is there anything in life that you feel particularly afraid of . . . something that led you to astroyoga?" I asked Reeve.

"I think everybody's afraid of accidents, you know, car accidents or plane crashes—something devastating. I'm not talking about death. We're all going to die someday. But, my biggest fear would be incapacitation; not being able to care for yourself and having to depend on others. That is truly frightening."

Indeed it was. I have never forgotten that conversation. I remembered it word for word after hearing of his total paralysis from a horse riding accident. I heard it like a distant echo in my head on the day he died. I also remember the tone of his voice when describing astroyoga. If it was meant to erase fear, I don't think Christopher Reeve was truly convinced on that summer night in 1989.

* * *

This was the age of Shirley Maclaines's neurotic New Age epiphany only a few years earlier with the release of her self-indulgent book *Out on a Limb* and the TV movie by the same name a year later in 1987. Hollywood may have thought she was the new goddess of mysticism, but the book and the movie largely demonstrated just how unhinged Maclaine had become.

Even people inside the industry were more than a little surprised when ABC not only gave her a TV movie, but they gave Shirley Maclaine a five-hour miniseries to demonstrate her deeply-held beliefs in telepathic space aliens, astral projection, "Atlantis" power, crystal worship, reincarnation, demon possession and pyramid power, (the Egyptian connection again.)

Maclaine also plunged headlong into trances, séances and necromancy. Maclaine even bragged that she has allowed herself to be "possessed" before acting in a movie. The scene that shocked America from the ABC miniseries was her ocean-front declaration, with hands outstretched, proclaiming, "I am god . . . I AM GOD!" Hollywood lapped it up, if only because it was an affront to Christians *and* Jews. Hollywood was just beginning its twenty year attack on "Judeo-Christian" values.

Hollywood's fascination with New Age religions and general fruit-looped philosophies are not recent occurrences in the entertainment industry. Aleister Crowley's "official" declaration of the New Age in 1904 could not have arrived at a better time, less than a decade after the fledgling movie industry began to flourish in New York and New Jersey. Because Crowley self-published his works from the sizeable fortune he inherited, copies of his work passed hand to hand. This slow, arduous distribution among occult readers would not make an impact across the Atlantic into America until the early 1920s.

While Crowley had been largely unavailable, the writings of his New Age predecessor, Madame H.P. Blavatsky, had been readily accessible in New York and were widely circulated among the artsy bohemian crowd already established in Greenwich Village and other neighborhoods in Lower Manhattan.

Blavatsky had moved to New York from Europe and established a new pseudo-religious philosophy in New York in 1875 known as Theosophy. Madame Blavatsky was, in many ways, the true genesis of New Age secular thinking, though the New Age "label" would not be coined until Crowley's "Egyptian vision" thirty years later.

Blavatsky and Theosophy were widely described as a "spiritist" movement which ruminated endlessly on her self-styled hybrid mixture of eastern mystic philosophies and religions such as Buddhism, Khaballa and "selective" Christianity combined with the occult practices of trances, séances, conjuring of spirits and, the most dangerous, necromancy. Conversing with the dead would become a Hollywood favorite which continues to this day.

By the early 1920's evidence of Blavatsky pseudo-religious-cant in Hollywood was no secret as rising silent screen star Rudolph Valentino and his part-time lover and short-term wife, Natasha Rambova, embraced the occult teachings of spiritism, séances, and mediums and practiced necromancy on a regular basis. This was no secret to his fans and was widely reported in the popular press.

The studios and Valentino himself didn't mind this as it added to the "mystical" appeal of Valentino. Unfortunately, the idol worship over Valentino demonstrated the danger of celebrity influence for the first time as the public began to experiment with mysticism. Natasha was even referred to as a "Blavatskyite."[1]

While many of Valentino's fans knew of his love for séances and other mystic practices, few knew at the time of the Valentino's involvement with an ancient from of "demonic-induced" trances, especially as practiced by Natasha, in which she would become transfixed and engage in "automatic writing." While in this trance state, Mrs. Valentino's pen would be guided by a "spirit force" that produced some of Rudolph Valentino's story lines and scripts.[2] At that time, the term "ghost-writer" had an entirely different meaning, but that is where the term originated. Valentino would die at the age of thirty-one.

THE HOLLYWOOD CULTURE WAR

Between the silent era and the early 1930s, when atheistic Communism became the favorite religion for many celebrities, the New Age practice of "conjuring spirits" was practiced by some of the most prominent actresses of their day including Greta Garbo, Mae West, and Marlene Dietrich. Dietrich was one of the earliest adherents to the Crowlean form of New Age occultism as his writings were being circulated among Hollywood celebrities. She even considered his writings as her "formal" religion.

Kenny Kingston, the so-called "psychic to the stars" recalls that he first learned how to develop his "power" from his grandmother who taught him how to read tea leaves. Kinston also admits that, at the age of nine, Mae West taught him how to "listen for voices" and how to "pick up psychic vibrations."

Kingston, who has served as a medium on many occasions over the last five decades, is the biggest perpetrator of necromancy to the Hollywood industry. He was the originator of the "psychic hotline" concept which has many imitators today. Marilyn Monroe, a virulent Christian-basher in private, was considered *the* "sex goddess" of the 1950s and referred to Kingston as her "full time psychic advisor."

During the final days of filming 1961's *The Misfits,* Clark Gable died of a massive heart attack. For some twisted, morbid reason, Monroe felt she had somehow caused Gable's heart attack. Monroe immediately consulted Kingston and asked the Hollywood psychic to perform a séance so she could talk to Gable in the grave. According to Kingston, Monroe was initially afraid that Gable might be mad at her for putting him in such a position (horizontal and six feet under the ground).

Kingston reported that, during the séance, Gable spoke and "assured" Monroe he was not mad. Kingston also reported Monroe as saying, "I feel so much better."[3] She was dead less than a year later.

A decade earlier, Lawrence Olivier was eyewitness to a conversation between Monroe and close friend Paula Strasberg, who once told the rising star, "You are the greatest women of your time, the greatest human being of your time, any time—you name it. You can't think of anybody, I mean—no, not even Jesus—except you're more popular." According to Olivier, Monroe "lapped it up." By the way, Kingston claims to "stay in touch" with Monroe . . . and Elvis, too.

The early Hollywood New Agers who followed the Blavatsky Theosophic spiritism probably had no idea that one of history's most notorious madmen was a member of the Austrian-German occult branch of Theosophy known as the Thule Society. Dietrich Eckhart was known as a medium who frequently conducted séances, engaged in necromancy and had a reputation as an angry, hard-boiled occultist who practiced fortune-telling under self-induced trances.

After World War I, Eckhart inducted a wandering German soldier into the Thule Society by the name of Adolph Hitler. According to author Bob Rosio of

Hitler and the New Age.[4] Before dying in 1923, Eckhart said Hitler would be Germany's salvation. Twenty-two years later, the once wandering World War I veteran had started World War II and ended it by shooting himself in the mouth in April of 1945 after destroying much of the European continent with the blood of over 50 million dead on his hands.

Critics of author J.K. Rowling claim that Theosophic themes are prevalent throughout her writings. In one book, Rowling even describes an "author" by the name of "Vablatsky," a not too thinly veiled anagrammatic tribute to Blavatsky.

Some celebrities didn't dance around the occult bush and went straight to the source. Peter Sellers, Kim Novak, Tina Louise and Sammy Davis, Jr. were all regular devotees of Satanism through Anton LaVey's Church of Satan in San Francisco.[5] Sammy Davis, Jr. was so enthusiastic about his new-found buddy, Mephistopheles, that he would recruit fellow actors and musicians in Hollywood to "join the church." Apparently, the rest of "The Rat Pack" declined Sammy's fanatic overtures.

Jayne Mansfield was an even bigger promoter of LaVey's Church of Satan than Sammy Davis, Jr. For Mansfield, a meeting with a producer, director or casting director was also a two-way equal opportunity to recruit new members for the "church." Even the contemporary generation who never saw a Jayne Mansfield movie are familiar with her and especially familiar with her legendary demise.

* * *

Hollywood's fascination with the "curious arts" has continued unabated. In 1999, director M. Night Shyamalan released "The Sixth Sense" about a little boy necromancer who had regular conversations with dead people. The movie became very popular with the public and initiated many work place water cooler conversations such as "Do you think it really is possible to talk to the dead?" Shyamalan, a Buddhist remarked that "something" flowed out of him as he directed the movie, which he equated to a Buddhism state of mind. The young director also believed that his movie was guided by "supernatural means" and that talking to the dead, for him, was "pretty natural."

There is no doubt that these people do, sometimes, hear real audible voices, not echoes of insanity bouncing around in their otherwise empty heads. However, if any of these "communicators with the dead" could see the source behind the voices, they would flee in horror at rates approximating the speed of light.

Shyamalan did make a rather "intuitive" comment about how movies are individual altars to be worshipped, noting that "films can be a version of faith. You learn to believe."[6]

To demonstrate how "whacked-out" many celebrities are concerning their yearning for New Age experiences, Larry King interviewed Goldie Hawn in a

2006 TV interview and asked, as only Larry King could, "So, you're a Jew-Bu?" Hawn had to explain that although she is Jewish "as far as being a member of a tribe" she does practice various forms of Buddhism. King, rubbing a few extra creases into his forehead asked, "So you're more Buddhist than Jewish?" Hawn responded, "I'm not really more one than the other."[7]

As for Goldie Hawn's actress daughter, Kate Hudson, *Hollywood Nation* author James Hirsen noted that she not only inherited her mother's looks and talent, but "she got her mother's Miss Cleo gene as well."[8] Hirsen continues by explaining that "evidently, Hudson only gets a charge out of chitchatting with the dearly departed."[9]

Besides necromania, there are a number of contemporary film stars that engage in the equally dangerous practice of "inviting spirits" of unknown origin to enter their bodies. Among those "dancing with the devil" are Halle Berry, Robin Williams, Denzel Washington, Leonardo DiCaprio, Winona Ryder, Meryl Streep and Keanu Reeves who claims, "I can be possessed pretty easily."[10]

The actor of questionable mental stability, Johnny Depp, star of the *Pirates of the Caribbean* feature films and the actor who called Americans "dumb puppies" freely admitted, "I know I have demons . . . I'm thirty different people sometimes."[11] He is reported to have a "psychic bond" with director Tim Burton.

During the filming of *Gorillas in the Mist,* actress Sigourney Weaver said that she was guided and protected during the filming by the "spirit" of Dian Fossey. Weaver doesn't say whether Fossey was "invited" or not, so we can only assume that her experience is another hybrid New Age occult practice, perhaps known as "necromanical spirit non-invitational infestation."

Kevin Bacon doesn't necessarily claim to be possessed, but at the same time, he prefers to keep his "demons under the surface . . . keep them bubbling" in order to allow the "muse" to enter.[12]

Before his ashes were literally rocketed into outer space along with Timothy Leary's acidic remains, *Star Trek* creator Gene Rodenberry was fond of "calling out spirits." NASA officials may want to consider laws against polluting the outer rims of earth's atmosphere.

On any given movie set or concert stage, mingling among the production assistants, technical crew and various hangers on, it is not unusual to find a celebrity psychic or "advisor" standing at the ready. Some New Age necromancers are even on the production payroll. In the case of the CBS sitcom, *Ghost Whisperers,* one of the co-executive producers is a career medium named James Van Praagh who makes a living listening to and talking with dead people.

One of the more blatantly bizarre New Agers is actor Patrick Swayze, who must have been transformed by his performance in *Ghost* given the fact that he is now known for carrying a gem-studded "magic wand" when working on location. Swayze brags openly about his little friend, "It's my 'magic' wand . . . I put it into each person's hand and say that this is to bless the production and create an atmosphere of mutual good, devoid of ego."[13]

While there are many individuals in Hollywood practicing witchcraft, one of the few to openly admit dallying with the "craft" is Sandra Bullock who said, "the magic only exists if you allow it, if you open yourselves up to the possibilities of it." Bullock was promoting her movie "Practical Magic" at the same time she appeared to be promoting mystical magic and her desire to spread its practice by Hollywood's typical strategy of value manipulation. "I'm at a point right now where I want to change public opinion."

Psychics, mediums, soothsayers and "astrological advisors" are literally drowning the Hollywood entertainment community in the deep dark sea of the occult. Among those who regularly consult these advisors of the curious arts are Kim Basinger, Sally Struthers, Ted Danson, Valerie Bertinelli, Burt Reynolds, Brigette Nielson and Joseph Stalin's biggest fan, Ed Asner, to name only a few among many.

Some deceased followers of psychics and astrologers were Steve McQueen, Grace Kelly, Burgess Meredith, Marilyn Monroe and Princess Diana. All who were deceived not only allowed it, they invited it into their lives.

The divergent form of astrology that I spoke of earlier, astroyoga, is also practiced by Jessica Lange, Susan Sarandon, Glenn Close, Louis Gossett, Jr. Linda Gray, Darryl Hannah and Richard Gere.[14]

Some of Hollywood's better known crystal carriers are George Hamilton, Michael York, Cybil Shepherd, Stephanie Beacham and Elizabeth Taylor. Many of these celebrities feign ignorance to the fact that Aleister Crowley was the original "pusher" of this fraudulent New Age belief in his pseudo-religious philosophy called "magick" with a "K." Crowley claimed that the stones of certain "cuts" and substances gave off psychic vibrations that help tune the body to the proper "frequency" in order to contact "the god within." Perhaps this will help Dan Rather better understand his attacker's question, "What's the frequency Kenneth?"

* * *

Some Hollywood religions are created out of thin air by certain individuals who didn't make the final cut in the talent category. Failed torch singer Marianne Williamson created a trendy super fusion of Buddhism, Christianity, pop psychology and twelve step recovery philosophy. Biographer Albert Goldman remembers Williamson as "very profoundly confused and had no conception of what to do with herself."[15]

But, that didn't stop her from creating a nebulous left coast religion catering specifically to celebrities such as Cher, Louie Anderson, Rosanna Arquette, Linda Blair, Laura Dern, Darryl Hannah, Angelica Huston, Theresa Russell, Roy Scheider, Barbara Streisand and Raquel Welch.

THE HOLLYWOOD CULTURE WAR

The list of Williamson devotees has also included some major left-leaning power brokers such as David Geffen, Norman Lear, agent Sandy Gallin, the late Dawn Steel and even Bill and Hillary Clinton.[16] Of course, Hillary denied any such devotion shortly before announcing her candidacy for president.

Williamson owes her elevation as New Age guru to the *new* New Age queen of the middle American masses, Oprah Winfrey. The daytime talk-show host and part-time Hollywood actress is the richest and most influential woman in the entertainment industry according to *Fortune* and *Life* magazine. *Time* called Winfrey one of the most important people of the 20th century. *USA Today* reported that her television show is seen by 49 million people in the U.S. and is viewed by millions more in more than 100 countries.[17]

USA Today wrote in 2006, "She's no longer just a successful talk-show host worth 1.4 billion dollars . . . Winfrey has emerged as a spiritual leader for the *New Millennium,* a moral voice of authority for the nation."[18]

Chris Altrock, minister of Highland Street Church of Christ in Memphis said, "our culture is changing . . . the bulk of a new generation is growing up outside of religion." And writer Ann Oldenberg says "they're turning to the Church of Oprah."

Unfortunately, Oprah Winfrey is also becoming known as Queen of the New Age because of her embrace of a multitude of the Blavatsky and Crowlean offshoots of New Age religions. She is also the best known practioner of conversation with the dead.

According to Dr. Jason Kovar, "Oprah has admitted to coming into contact with what is called The Universal Hum.[19] Winfrey also claimed to have broken into "the other side" of this "Hum" and she was introduced to "spiritual guides" who just happen to be the voices of dead slaves. Roseanne Barr subscribed to "The Hum" for awhile, but apparently never "crossed over."

As *Time* magazine wrote of these spirit guides, "Oprah calls these her 'go to' moments, spiritual episodes of divine guidance that far transcend the chatty exchanges with her studio audiences. And sometimes the epiphanies carry the voices of Negro slaves—Joe and Emily Dara; Sue and Bess and Sara. Winfrey says she has come to know each of them personally and calls them in at will to guide her in her work."[20]

There is no disputing the great work that Oprah Winfrey has performed for millions of people. Among the many profound guests on her show who have helped to confront and battle personal and social problems, Winfrey has also brought in a troublesome array of "spiritists" of nebulous origin who use Oprah Winfrey's show as a New Age pulpit to preach very dangerous beliefs to a sometimes gullible public, worldwide, that will embrace anybody and anything with Oprah's seal of approval.

As director Jonathan Demme noted, during the filming of Toni Morrison's *Beloved,* "Oprah had explained to me when we originally met that it was her *goal* and *intention* to channel the spirit of Margaret Garner." Oprah was playing the part of Garner from Morrison's book about a woman who is haunted by the spirit of her dead daughter.

As Jason Kovar noted concerning Oprah's scene preparation, "Oprah freely confesses to demonic possession as a tool to enhance her influencing performances before the camera."[21] Prior to each day's filming, Winfrey said, "I tried to empty myself and let the spirit of Seth inhabit me ... Every morning, before my scenes, I lit candles and said the names of these slaves. I prayed everyday to the ancestors."[22]

Necromancy is a very real form of bondage that few people understand, but by which many have been deceived, and from which many have been set free—without any feared "loss of talent"—which is the real fear that drags Hollywood down into the "dark arts."

"THE SECRET" AND "THE PROMISE"

OPRAH vs. JESUS

Just when Oprah's fans say she has moved away from New Age dribble and "spirit invitations" to dead people, Winfrey manages to conjure up another New Age guru named Rhonda Byrne who seems infinitely harmless, until you peruse her book, *The Secret,* and realize that Oprah has taken a dive right back into the same old drowning pool of the dark arts. Unable to pull herself away from occult fascinations, Winfrey invited Byrne on her show and gave *The Secret* the official Oprah stamp of approval which sent sales of the book skyrocketing to the very top of the bestselling lists.

Byrne, an Australian television and commercial producer, came to the "realization" of *The Secret"* while sitting under a tree. She rounded up her video production friends and created a special video that could be viewed on the internet or purchased as a book for around $25.00. Since its inception in 2006, she has offered various packages that include the DVD, CD, book and even the soundtrack that can be yours for $149.00, more or less.

Originally, the website "teaser" offered a glossy intro video slapped together by her Aussie TV friends, complete with apocalyptic-style music and chanting choir. *The Secret* promises to show the road to *enormous* wealth, love, power, healing or just about anything as long as you believe. You can even believe for "negative" results! A narrator voice-over explains that *The Secret* has at various times been lost, stolen, forgotten, rediscovered, uncovered and lost again, until . . . Rhonda Byrne had an epiphany on a warm summer day.

The video montage scrolls a series of etchings across the screen depicting famous men like Plato, Shakespeare, Newton, Napolean, Beethoven, Edison and

Einstein—all of whom apparently knew *The Secret,* which the narrator explains is "the culmination of many centuries of *great* thinkers, scientists, artists and philosophers." (No women are depicted and conspicuously absent are any mention of notable religious leaders or Biblical scholars, which is intentional.)

The ominous part of the web video ends with a bold statement declaring *The Secret* as *a New Age for Humankind.* There seems to be little doubt that the whole strategy behind writing, producing and marketing *The Secret* was fashioned in a manner meant to, first and foremost, impress Oprah Winfrey. One of her camera operators even admitted as much. With her "blessing," they could simply schedule regular deposits at the bank from the sucker-money that would, and continues, to flood into their "secret" bank account. Byrne is no different than the carnival barkers who roamed the country in the last century.

The Secret, in reality, is a New Age religion created as a diametric polar opposite to "faith" in Christianity, which believers often refer to as "The Promise" of the Bible. Health, prosperity, sufficiency, comfort and freedom from fear are all contained in "The Promise." And, while *The Secret* claims to offer all of these promises and more, Rhonda Byrne can't deliver on the main attraction; eternal life. She hints vainly at "eternal youth," but can't quite describe what that means.

"The Promise" is offered as a *selfless* acceptance of an unconditional love from God that is not present in any other "belief system" in the world. *The Secret*, on the other hand, is a pseudo-religious New Age deception that is all about *selfish* and *excessive* self-indulgence. The choice between eternal life and eternal youth should be an easy one, but the "creators" of *The Secret* engage in seduction and a malevolent self-serving "law of attraction" of which the "teachers" openly boast.

Consider the testimony of one of the teachers, Jack Canfield, "My life has truly become magical—a life everyone dreams of . . . I live in a four-and-a-half million dollar mansion. I have a wife to die for."

To say that Canfield places a monetary value on his life is an understatement; not just four million dollars, but "four-and-a-half-million dollars" to be exact. Of course he has a wife "to die for" and with that kind of thinking, his wife wouldn't mind if he did die for her. Then, she could paint the bedroom the color she had wanted from the beginning. All she has to do is use *The Secret* and "poof," he'll be gone.

The truly diabolical message of *The Secret* is that you can believe for anything to come to pass, even if it has negative consequences; a "fact" that the producers of *The Secret* make *no secret* in their introduction.

The more you learn about *The Secret*, the more you realize it is deeply steeped in the occult, a major footnote that apparently didn't bother Oprah when she endorsed the book. In fact, the teachers of *The Secret* that Byrne had "employed" largely display a fraudulent "kinder-gentler" version of the Aleister Crowley dictum that *you* are god.

One of these teachers is Lisa Nichols who instructs, "You are eternal life. You are source energy. *You are God* manifested *in human form . . ."* That is *exactly* the message Crowley declared when he "officially" proclaimed the New Age from his Cairo hotel room in 1904.

That Oprah has no problem with this kind of endorsement is equally not surprising considering her friendship with Shirley Maclaine who shouted "I AM GOD!!" in her book and movie *Out On A Limb,* which is exactly where Oprah has put herself when it comes to choosing between eternal youth and eternal life.

On one show, Oprah asked Maclaine, "When you connected to the Higher Self . . . knowing that you can do anything you want to do—is it what other people describe as being 'born again?'" Maclaine, clueless, nodded her head, "Yes, probably." For people without a history or personal knowledge of Christianity, Oprah Winfrey and Shirley Maclaine become instant authorities as the camera pans the audience of lemmings shaking their head "yes." And, when you factor in the millions of viewers around the world, Oprah Winfrey and Shirley Maclaine did more to bastardize Christianity in three minutes than any two people ever attempted in the history of the world.

"Yes, but she gives free cars away to people all the time," her fans cry out. You do the math—is Oprah doing the greater good or the greater harm?

As for *The Secret,* consider one of the former teachers, Esther Hicks, whose New Age orientation is strict occultism. According to her bio on *The Secret* website, Hicks "communicates with a collection of *non-physical entities* collectively called Abraham." The main reason she left is because she and Byrne could not come to agreement on financial compensation. If all of this is *The Secret* that Napoleon once used, there is little doubt as to why he fell at Waterloo. Among the other teachers of *The Secret* are a hypnotist and a magician. What more do you need to know? Oprah's promotion of *The Secret* is a classic textbook example of how she is incrementally deconstructing Judeo-Christian traditions and foundations, which she accomplishes with a subtle smile and a purr.

Unlike the New Age trite of *The Secret,* why has Oprah never introduced "genuine" authors and innovators in personal growth and development that have a huge following and have a well known history in the popular culture for many decades? Since Norman Vincent Peale released *The Power of Positive Thinking* in 1952, the book has sold over 20 million copies worldwide and counting. What sets Peale's book apart from Byrne's book is that Peale actually quotes verses from the Bible such as "If God be for us, who can be against us?"

Though Peale is no longer living (he was almost 100 when he died), the Peale Center is thriving more now than at anytime in its history, publishing the popular *Guideposts* magazine. Why, in the twenty year history of her show, has Oprah never invited anybody from the Peale Center to appear? Could it be that the full title of the organization is The Peale Center for *Christian* Living? That "C" word seems to be a silver cross that blinds Oprah. Norman Vincent Peale never turned anyone away who was in need, regardless of their faith, or even lack thereof.

And, what about Dale Carnegie? His groundbreaking book *How to Stop Worrying and Start Living* has also been an ever present source of success with solid multi-million sales for over half a century. There is a Dale Carnegie course being taught in every state in America, every single day, and in over 60 countries around the world.

Why has the Dale Carnegie organization been ignored by Oprah? Could it be that Dale Carnegie encourages his readers to "Thank *God*" for what they have and what they can still achieve? And, that's God with a capital "G." It was Dale Carnegie who first said, "Count your blessings, not your troubles."

How about Reverend Franklin Graham who will explain "asking, believing and receiving" on Oprah's show free of charge. She might even want to contribute to Graham's global Samaritan's Purse and his African medical missions which provide free medical care to those in need. Of course, he's only able to provide that service when his World Medical Mission is not being bombed by militant African extremists because Graham is a CHRISTIAN, the same reason he's not welcome on Oprah's show.

The Watchman Fellowship, Inc. of Birmingham has followed Oprah Winfrey's career for over a decade and has noted that, "Oprah, in typical New Age fashion, has reduced God to human limitations, and dismisses objective absolutes, substituting emotions as the criteria of truth." They also note that Oprah is "clearly in the process of deconstructing Christianity and reframing it into a New Age perspective."

And, with Oprah's eye also focused on influencing candidates for president, look for a future where the currency reads, "In The Secret We Trust."

During a ten week period between March and May of 2008, Oprah was already on to another new wave of New Age promiscuity when she registered over 700,000 people to participate in a web seminar with her and Eckhart Tolle, author of *A New Earth*, a hybrid philosophy of Buddhism, Islam and many other "influences." Oprah called the book a "wake-up" call to the "higher self." Oprah said it was necessary for her to participate because people "need some help at first with the languaging of a new consciousness and things like that."

Oprah Winfrey started her show in the mid-1980s as the female Jerry Springer of the airwaves. According to lawyer and columnist Debbie Schussel, Winfrey now "acts as if her show has 'evolved,' but in fact, she still has the salacious sex and deviance stories, with a psychologist in the audience to make it seem highbrow and give it the kosher seal of approval. If this is the person whose morals we are putting on a pedestal, then America's moral compass is in much need of retuning."

* * *

The reason Crowley's New Age thinking became predominant in the entertainment industry throughout the last seventy years can largely be traced to his writings about spirit possession. This, combined with his open endorsement of drug abuse and sexual perversion, played well with the emerging secular Hollywood crowd that wanted nothing to do with "the establishment" or "rules."

Crowley's deep-rooted hatred of Christianity, of which he wrote frequently, also sat well with a rootless industry of atheistic drifters. Hollywood's particular penchant today for Christian-bashing can be traced directly to Crowley.

Second only to Crowley's *Book of the Law* in terms of influence among entertainers was his book *Magick in Theory and Practice* which specifically identified the "dramatic arts" as the best avenue for "inviting spirits" to infest your psyche and soul. In the book, Crowley wrote, "There are three main methods for invoking any deity . . . The third method is the dramatic, perhaps the most attractive of all. Certainly it is so to the artist's temperament, for it appeals to his imagination through his aesthetic sense."[23]

While many New Age religious offshoots and hybrids sprang from the Crowlean school of dementia, one Hollywood religion that was based directly on his teachings is Scientology. Founder L. Ron Hubbard was a close follower of Aleister Crowley's teachings and he was aware of Crowley's attraction to people in the entertainment industry.

According to James Hirsen, "Scientology's 8 million followers meet in some 3,200 churches in 159 countries, and the organization grosses an estimated $300 million a year."[24] Just another example of the very, very long arm of Mephistopheles.

SCIENTOLOGY, THE DEVIL AND THE DEEP BLUE SEA

Young girls with tight-fitting Capri pants, sailor-themed blouses and bright white smiles were standing next to the 39-year-old author of such books as *Sea Fangs, Carnival of Death,* and *Man Killers of the Air.* But, that's not why the herd of young girls was posing with the author who fashioned himself as a seafaring explorer with 22 medals from World War II for bravery and heroism above and beyond the call of duty. L Ron Hubbard appeared under the glowing sun as the superhuman man of the future with the world at his feet; a mental giant who was proclaiming a new era, a New Age of mental and physical clarity. The publicity photo was in celebration of Hubbard's best-selling book in 1950, *Dianetics, The Modern Science of Mental Health.*[25]

L. Ron Hubbard's bio painted the golden boy as a genius for the 1950s and beyond. But, perhaps the ancient Roman definition of "genius" was more fitting: either of two spirits, one good and one evil supposed to influence one's destiny.[26]

THE HOLLYWOOD CULTURE WAR

Truly evil was the best way to describe the man who would one day enslave 8 million people into one of the modern world's most elusive and destructive cults.

The problem began with the dashing bio attached to the staged photo. It was all a lie. And, it would be one of many lies over the next fifty years as his bio was updated, rearranged, revised, and edited as circumstance required. The circumstances were usually related to revelations of his fraud and deception as one of the world's most ruthless and manipulative cult leaders who first called his book a "philosophy" when it was released in 1950. But, even before the calendar year ended, cracks were already appearing in the Dianetic order of Hubbard's universe.

The major news weeklies began to question the "science" behind the philosophy Hubbard would soon call Scientology. By 1951, *Consumer Reports* even issued a warning that *Dianetics* was becoming "the basis for a new cult."[27] Before the end of that same year, questions about his 22 war medals were being raised as well as his role in certain suspect "break-ins" related to supposed espionage.

Book sales began to dwindle rapidly when details of his divorce in 1951 by second wife Sara revealed charges that Hubbard kidnapped their daughter and subjected her to "beatings, strangulation and torture experiments."[28] Furthermore, his drug addiction raised questions as to whether he was under the influence of massive opium intake while writing a book that chastised the medical industry for prescribing medication in cases of certain physical and especially mental illness. The only truth to his bio was that he did write horror and fantasy novels that in retrospect seemed heavily inspired by hallucinogenic drugs.

All these controversies were cleverly brushed off as an attempt to destroy Hubbard by those who opposed his brash new "science" of mental health. Hubbard officially changed Scientology from a philosophy to a religion in December of 1953, no doubt to avoid income taxes for his new church established in, where else, the movie capital of the world in Los Angeles.

More disturbing was the revelation that would come years later from Hubbard's son, L. Ron Hubbard, Jr. who identified his father's religion as another strand in the long dark thread that continues to run through the Hollywood entertainment industrial complex. In a biography of Hubbard, author Bent Corydon, wrote, "According to Ron Jr., his father considered himself to be the one who came after; that he was Crowley's successor; that he had taken on the mantle of the 'Great Beast.' He told [his son] that Scientology actually began on December 1, 1947. This was the day Aleister Crowley died."[29]

In fact, biographer Corydon noted that Crowley's *Book of the Law* was "perhaps the most important book in the life of L. Ron Hubbard."[30] Scientology's theology is based *directly* on Crowley's New Age self-absorbed perversity.

379

Hubbard was also cunning enough to start the church in Hollywood where perversity is a virtue.

L. Ron Hubbard, Jr., who is co-author with Corydon on *L. Ron Hubbard: Messiah or Madman,* explains that "the one super-secret sentence that Scientology is built on is 'Do what thou will. That is the whole of the law.' It also means that you are a law unto yourself, that you are above the law, that you create your own law. You are above any other human considerations."[31] This would become the core belief system for the "Beat" generation, the radical "hippie" counterculture and every New Age secular movement that has sprung up in various forms right up to the present day.

In 1946, Hubbard had become good friends with Jack Parsons, the head of Crowley's OTO Temple in California. Together, the two explored an eclectic blend of New Age pursuits. In letters recently discovered at Scientology's New York headquarters, notes were uncovered that were written by Parsons to Crowley in which Hubbard was mentioned on a number of occasions.

In the year before Crowley died, Parsons wrote to the wasted 71-year old founder of the New Age, "Concerning Hubbard, he is the most Thelemic person I have ever met and is in complete accord with our principles. He is also interested in establishing the New Aeon [New Age]."[32]

Literature and information about Scientology has been slowly leaked to the public over the years as former members speak out against the repressive, fraudulent operations and bogus philosophy behind the cult. Some of the most bizarre revelations surround L. Ron Hubbard's "science" about the origins of the universe.

No doubt influenced by his own opium-induced science fiction writings from the 1930's, Hubbard believed that alien beings in enormous spacecrafts came to earth long ago and dropped atom bombs into various volcanoes around the world which caused a deadly mist, or dust, that polluted the environment and basically caused all the ills mankind suffers today. (That's right; 8 million members.)

Scientology teaches that all people have inherited or incurred distorted states of existence known as "engrams" or psychological "loops" that make the individual's mind "insufficient and ill" and the mind must be cleared through an "auditor" who uses an "e-meter" to detect and help rid the individual of these engrams. Of course, some *very* expensive coursework is required also to help the new recruit become "clear." The early Scientology e-meters were reportedly made out of discarded V-8 juice cans. Perhaps that is the origin of the ad campaign, proclaiming, "Wow, I could have had a V-8!"

The "clear" individual is considered to have reached a god-like state that prepares them for even longer (and very, very expensive) journeys into upper levels of God-likeness known as "OTs" that vary in number from 0 to 20 with even higher levels available (for the right price).

Much of the inner workings of Scientology were discovered during a raid on Scientology headquarters by the FBI in addition to the revelations by former members, many of whom died after being physically and financially drained by the Hollywood super cult. Their stories are available on an insightful website "Scientology Kills" at www.scientologykills.org.[33] The web site won the Free Speech Online Blue Ribbon Campaign for not buckling under to threats from the Scientology goon squad which seeks out defectors or critics in order to deliver unknown forms of "punishment." Remember, according to L.R. Hubbard, Jr., Scientology believes that their members are not only above the law, they *are* the law. As Tom Cruise declared in a 2008 video, "Why ask permission? We *are* the authorities."

In one of the FBI raids on Scientology's main office, documents were obtained describing the OT-8 level which Hubbard explained as the level which reveals his "mission on earth." Hubbard's "mission" as described in the OT-8 document has achieved increasing public awareness as its contents continue to circulate widely.

Hubbard's goals were the same as Aleister Crowley; to destroy Christianity and everything it stands for. Hubbard felt it was his duty to fulfill the New Age destiny. Crowley, who Hubbard referred to as "my good friend," wrote in the self-published *The World's Tragedy*, "That religion they call Christianity: the devil they honor they call God . . . and it is their God and their religion that I hate and will destroy."[34]

Remember, it was Crowley who offered up his services to Communist Russia to help destroy any remnants of Christianity.[35] This obsessive hatred for Christians is one of the reasons L. Ron Hubbard referred to himself as the one who "came after" Crowley in order to finish what Crowley started, according to L. Ron Hubbard, Jr.

Hubbard's "mission statement" as described in the OT-8 documents reveals the cult leader's intention to literally reverse Bible prophecy. In the OT-8 document, Hubbard spoke about the Book of Revelation, writing that "During this period, there is a fleeting opportunity for the whole scenario to be effectively derailed . . ." and, by doing so, preventing the Second Coming of Christ.[36]

Most of Hollywood's celebrity Scientologists are at higher levels than OT-8. No wonder there is a rabid hatred of Christianity among the Hollywood entertainment machine. However, Hubbard didn't live long enough to see the Second Coming, having died in 1986, much to the chagrin of his followers who referred to him as "The Great Typewriter in the Sky."

So, we can only assume that the job of shooting Jesus Christ out of the sky with the super-secret Scientology laser gun has fallen on the shoulders of Tom Cruise, though John Travolta may have privately expressed interest in carrying out "the hit job."

Tom Cruise's fanatic promotion of Scientology was on full display during the theatrical release of *Mission Impossible III*.

In fact, his bizarre behavior during this period cost him, the theaters and the studios millions of dollars. The full potential of the audience was not reached when moviegoers decided not to spend their entertainment dollars on a possessed actor who might receive a percentage of the box-office take and then turn around and donate it to the Church of Scientology. *Mission Impossible III* fell far short of projections for the 2006 movie and DVD sales bombed.

Viacom-Paramount CEO Sumner Redstone promptly booted Cruise from his contract with Paramount. As Neil Cavuto said, "Cruise's behavior became 'unacceptable' by Paramount and they severed ties with the Scientologist actor. Pretty extreme for an industry that tolerates almost everything."[37]

As it turned out, Mrs. Summer Redstone was growing increasingly weary of Cruise's Scientology dribble and pulled on her husband's shirt sleeve. One can only imagine her command—*the weirdo has to go!*

Cruise and Paula Wagner were soon able to land a deal with United Artists which actually gives Cruise a stake in the studio production slate. Without any oversight on his egomaniacal astro-vision, any movie he produces is doomed to fail. But don't tell that to Merrill Lynch investors who gave United Artists $500 million in 2007 only to see his first movie, *Lions for Lambs,* bomb on impact. The same day the movie opened on November 1, 2007, Merrill Lynch CEO Stanley O'Neal was "let go" for his overall poor decision-making and "punished" with a $160 million dollar golden parachute. It is, after all, a *risky* business.

As for John Travolta, he is more subdued about his Scientology devotion, but admits he practices its teachings in every aspect of his life, including the raising of his children. Travolta also has a reputation as being among Hollywood's biggest politically correct hypocrites, which is a shared trait among Scientologists.

As one of Hollywood's major fear-mongering promoters of Global Warming, Travolta has no problem traveling to his Florida home with wife Kelly Preston and kids in tow on one of two jets he owns, including a massive 707 with dual globe warmers that he not only flies to Florida, but literally pulls the plane directly into his Sunshine State mansion's driveway.

Ironically, Travolta's first feature film was *Devil's Rain* in 1975 about the trials and tribulations of devil worshipers. The technical advisor on the film, who also shared a small part as the "High Priest," was none other than Anton LeVay. Perhaps Travolta picked up some pointers from LeVay about their mutual buddy downstairs.

One celebrity that Scientology refuses to recognize is Charles Manson, the convicted mastermind behind the Sharon Tate killings. The Church of Scientology undertook a massive operation to destroy Manson's Scientology records, but the FBI raid on their headquarters uncovered internal information about Manson's extensive involvement with the church. Apparently, Manson never reached the stage of "clear" or perhaps he was tested by the early V-8 e-meters that had already rusted.

HOLLYWOOD'S SCIENTOLOGY CELEBRITIES

Anne Archer	Juliette Lewis
Beck Hansen	Karen Nelson Bell
Billy Sheehan	Kaye Ceberano
Carina Ricco	Keith Code
Carl W. Röhrig	Kelly Preston
Catherine Bell	Kimberly Kates
Chick Corea	Kirstie Alley
Chris Masterson	Leah Remini
Corin Nemec	Lisa Marie Presley
Danny Masterson	Lynsey Bartilson
Edgar Winter	Marisol Nichols
Eduardo Palomo	Michael Fairman
Erika Christensen	Michael Roberts
Geoffrey Lewis	Michelle Stafford
Giovanni Ribisi	Nancy Cartwright
Haywood Nelson	Pablo Santos
Isaac Hayes	Priscilla Presley
Jason Beghe	Reverend Alfreddie Johnson, Jr.
Jason Lee	Sharon Case
Jeff Pomerantz	Sofia Milos
Jenna Elfman	Terry Jastrow
Jennifer Aspen	Tom Cruise
John Travolta	Xavier Deluc
Judy Norton	

Note: This is only a partial list as of 2008 of 47 celebrities who openly admitted membership into The Church of Scientology. Estimates range between 170 to 190 members in the movie industry, in front of and behind the camera, who are members. And, that is the most conservative estimate.

Elton John's response to "religion," Hollywood style or not, is "to ban religion completely around the world."[38] At the same time, Elton John called on the major religions around the world to convene a "conclave" to discuss "the fate of the world." Now, does Mr. John want the conclave held after religion is banned or just before the ban goes into effect?

What Elton John forgot, if he ever knew at all, is that banning religion had already been attempted on the world stage. It was called Communism, and a few countries still practice the obsolete ideology. With no salvation or redemption allowed under the likes of Stalin and Mao, the two leaders rendered their own sanctification called by various names such as firing squads, torture, hanging, electrocution, beatings and mass starvation.

Apparently, Elton John never learned any history while attending school as a young tyke in England. If he had, young Elton might have learned that 100 million people died in the 20th century under the official "ban" on religion.

In studying the roots of Hollywood radicalism, discussion of secular New Age philosophies and religions are sometimes a point of departure for these involved in the battle of the Culture War against Hollywood. The subject matter is either too frightening or simply mysterious beyond rational belief to engage in any kind of discussion.

In truth, these subjects are not as mysterious as you might think and are easily unraveled by the celebrity practioners themselves who constantly stumble and bumble over the "practice" of their fraudulent religions and New Age mystic beliefs. At the same time, thought and beliefs in Hollywood are often translated into words and actions, on screen and off. To deny yourself a working knowledge of this side of Hollywood only leaves you ill-equipped to fight all aspects of the Hollywood Culture War. In the study of Hollywood celebrity gods, the revelations are not much different than the entertainment industry's fascination with the failed ideology of Communism, which was basically a flirtation with the esoteric seduction of a godless utopia, a heaven on earth, whose "spiritual leaders" were promising orderly societies in return for the involuntary blood sacrifice of its citizens. As Chapter 10 demonstrated, the Communist allure in Hollywood was a time when dark values were given special attention and even rewarded as meritorious. Sterling Hayden was not far off the mark when he testified before Congress that Communism seduced him "by some occult power, to know what is best for people . . ."

The leap from Hollywood's embrace of political tyranny to the deep dark sea of New Age religious hypocrisy is as simple as leaping across a babbling brook. And that is why both Communism and the New Age have found fertile ground fed by a common stream in Hollywood where the seductive capacity to promote their personal evil as entertainment continues unabated. It is imperative to understand this new manifestation of the old Communist idea.

Engaging in these false religions and New Age philosophies of esoteric cult origins, without a complete turnaround in one's thinking and devotion can be dangerous in the least and deadly at worst. The entire history of mankind has been a struggle of good versus evil. The quest of mankind to understand the authority behind each, or the refusal to learn the origin of the two, guides the dialogue and debate behind the conversation and politics of everyday life.

The *true* powers behind the forces of good and evil are known best by those who have experienced the battles first hand either deeply in their personal lives or on a wider scale of nation against nation. Much can be learned about the real powers at work in this world because brave individuals called out the "powers and principalities" by name in times of trouble and triumph and the spiritual side of their stories are often neglected by a cynical and deeply secular press.

Consider two examples of two different people on opposite sides of the world who came face to face with evil and recognized their troubles and their victories.

After listening to a sermon, "The Love That Forgives," in the main sanctuary of the 16th Street Baptist Church in Birmingham, Alabama, four young girls were returning to their Sunday School class in the basement when a massive explosion near the descending stairwell killed all four girls and injured 22 others on September 15, 1963. Addie Mae Collins, Carole Robertson, Cynthia Wesley and Denise McNair were killed at 10:22 a.m., the clock frozen in time to this day.

Junie Collins, Addie Mae's sister, was asked to come to the morgue to identify her sister's body. What she saw shook Junie Collins to the core of her soul for decades afterwards. Nothing prepares a young girl to witness the result of ultimate evil and as a result, Junie Collins suffered the trauma of anxiety, nightmares and fear. At times, completing a simple sentence became a major challenge.

For many years, different people would try to console Junie Collins by telling her that God had a reason for taking her sister and that God did a lot of terrible things for good reason. This never did sit well with Junie who had always been taught that "God is a good God" and she refused to listen to the voices "kindly" blaming God.

After years of study, prayer and refusing to give up on God, a revelation came to Junie Collins, "It wasn't God that brought the bombing on . . . Just like there is a God of good, we have a god of evil, too. And it's no part of [my] God. And, when we realize that God has our best interests and He has a plan for each of us, a plan that's good and not for evil, then we can begin to come and receive healing."[39]

Junie Collins was not speaking figuratively or using allegory. She had confronted evil incarnate and called it out by name, the "god of evil," also known as the devil. She knew that the "God of good" did not kill her sister and recognized Him by undoubting devotion.

Junie Collins knew also that the devil's actions would backfire in the face of faith. And, as a result, the Civil Rights Act of 1964 was immediately signed into law. One person's undying faith in the power of good over evil, along with the faith of millions who *did not waiver*, also witnessed the liberation of her people that began one hundred years earlier.

The mainstream Hollywood media could never put those pieces together. To do so might imply a belief in the *true* God and their journalistic "integrity" would be called into question. Even worse, the invitations to the cocktail party circuit would stop instantly. The media *does* have its priorities.

The 20th century evangelist Rufus Mosely put true faith into perspective, "God is always trying to do the best for you and the devil is always trying to do the worst for you. Which way you vote will determine the election."

As President Shimon Perez told Larry King during the Iranian-backed Hezbollah 2006 attacks on Israel, "We shall never let the devil govern our destiny."[40]

The next three chapters will illustrate how warped individuals have dedicated themselves, very vocally and actively, to destroying the positive values of a cohesive society as they delve into mind-bending value manipulation while paving Hollywood's long road to perdition.

The long dark thread that runs through the industry continues and will even weave its way through a philosophical temple that is a fallacious parallel culture with Hollywood complete with its own God, theology, fashion, music and "way of thinking." It is the Bronx-born atrocity known as "The Temple of Hip-Hop."

CHAPTER 17

MIND BENDERS AND GENDER BENDERS

"Hollywood can stretch the truth and bend the mind."
—James Hirsen
Hollywood Nation

"We manipulate people like crazy in films . . . it's a tremendous release. I can make you feel any emotion I want you to feel at any time," boasted Eddie Manson, a popular composer for movie post-production (no relation to Charlie).[1] As we learned in Chapter 7, value manipulation is the entertainment industry's number one agenda as they market their own perverse and collective mind-bending vision of the world.

Again, we must ask what is the origin of these Hollywood deviant value systems which are increasingly dark, morose and bleak in their imagery and their message? At this point, we have learned that Hollywood is easily captivated by tyrannical politics, love affairs with drugs and alcohol and New age psycho-babble occult religions. This chapter will demonstrate how all of these obsessions come together in the mind of the filmmakers as they embark on their "art" to "entertain" (Translate: mentally assault) the audience.

These multiple influences are easily absorbed by already fragile psyches who believe it is their mission to change the world, and not for the better. But, these Hollywood creative types have to make a conscious decision to take these twisted influences and make them a part of their own belief system and act them out in the *real* world, with Oliver Stone being the most extreme example. And, as you will soon learn, there are many more where he came from actively working out their anger and nightmares on the canvas of the silver screen.

MICHAEL VINCENT BOYER

* * *

Movies, music, television, video games and other broadcast, downloaded or projected imagery and sounds described as "entertainment" do not appear out of a vacuum. Entertainment originates in the minds of their creators, shaped by the influences they personally value. These individuals could be authors, screenwriters, musicians, producers, directors or any individual who simply manifests an "idea."

While all ideas originate in the mind, they germinate deeper from the heart. There is much truth to the timeless proverb, "out of the heart flow the issues of life." This description of the heart is best defined in Webster's New World Dictionary, "a. innermost thoughts and feelings; consciousness or conscience, and, b. the *source of intellect.*"[2]

Some of the best, inspiring, thought-provoking and uplifting movies were written, produced and directed by men and women with basically good hearts. If their hearts were warped and darkened to a point of self-serving over-indulgence with the audience as victim instead of viewer, that is when the Production Code served it's purpose best, preventing mentally disturbed and drug-addicted filmmakers from leaving their blackened shadows on the screen.

Prior to 1968, Oliver Stone would have never been allowed to make a single one of his movies. And that would have been no loss to the nation, or the worldwide moviegoing audience. And, that applies to a majority of today's filmmakers as well.

When Jack Valenti, a man with his own darkened heart, took the moral quotient out of films officially in 1968, the preponderance of "dark" movies predominated the movie houses the very next year and continues in frequency and intensity to this day. Granted, many movies with dark themes were produced prior to 1968, but the Production Code provided a caveat of "moral compensating values" that prevented "evil" from being depicted as "good."

With a few outstanding exceptions each year, Hollywood is mainly focused on its mission to manipulate the better values of its audience while dragging them into the bottomless black pit of the filmmaker's mind. As author Neil Zawackie wrote, " . . . people generally prefer to cheer for the righteous protagonist, but they can be seduced into rooting for evil under the right circumstances."[3]

Jason Kovar, producer of the *Hollywood Unmasked* DVD series, has devoted years of extensive research into the individual minds and motives of Hollywood as it has evolved into its current moral swamp. He notes that "The entertainment industry is systematically hardening the hearts of the youth from following in the footsteps of what many contend to be appropriate. The belief systems of those who run Hollywood are for the most part opposite the mainstream views held by the vast majority of Americans."[4]

THE HOLLYWOOD CULTURE WAR

Kovar further states the point of the filmmaker's mindset, "Countering the popular belief, moviemakers do not make films to just entertain people. The stories on the screen are concepts that are deeply personal to them and they take them very seriously."[5]

Consider two seriously disturbing statements from two seriously disturbing filmmakers. Director David Cronenberg summed up his view of the world as translated to film, "[my] responsibility is not to care." And then there's the virtual mirror view with an added touch of profane anger from horror writer/creator Clive Barker who responded, "My responsibility is not to give a f____ about that. My responsibility is not to care."[6]

Barker, a deviated radical homosexual heterophobe, has spewed forth a series of blood-drenched B-flicks such as *Nightbreed* and *Hellraiser* which have developed a cult following among largely disaffected youth and gorefest worshippers. Barker and Cronenberg's movies are even more disturbing than the "fear as fun" films such as the *Scream* series by fellow radical heterophobe director Kevin Williamson.

As casting director Shirley Crumley once told me, "These new splatter movies by Rob Zombie and the rest are blood-and-guts 'for the fun of it,' which is sick enough in its own right. But, Barker, Cronenberg, Williamson and Oliver Stone are just plain evil to the bone. I worked with Oliver on *The Doors* and he was the inebriated walking dead with a chip on his shoulders and an axe to grind against *everybody*."[7]

Cronenberg used to hold the bragging rights for depicting the first exploding human head on film in the 1981 movie *Scanners*. A film critic friend told me that wasn't exactly true, trying to explain very technically and detached, "Actually, George Romero depicted the first exploding head two years earlier in *Dawn of the Dead*. However, the man's exploding head was induced by a shotgun blast as opposed to Cronenberg's use of spontaneous combustion through mind control."

The only rational response I could think of was, "Give me a break!" Film violence and television violence are literally wrecking severe emotional havoc on young people and will inevitably affect them well into adulthood. The Parent's Television Council (PTC) released findings of a study that showed the 2005 and 2006 television seasons as the most violent in TV history. As PTC spokeswoman Melissa Caldwell noted about the affect on children, "They become frightened at the very world they live in." Despite the debate about *influencing* violent behavior, violent media images can affect the way children view the world in ways that negatively impact their worldview, fomenting persistent fear at an early age. And we wonder why young people are becoming coarse and angry.

These filmmakers know this and, as they've stated, their responsibility is "not to give a f____" and "not to care." Tobe Hooper is another one of these filmmakers of gross negligence when his original *Texas Chainsaw Massacre* of 1974 set the foreboding tone for all the slice-and-dice splatter films to follow. Leonard Maltin called the low-budget flick "classic and *influential*."[8]

That would prove to be an understatement to 18-year-old Pete Roland who was convicted of brutally murdering his friend with a baseball bat while chanting satanic verses. University of Denver's Carl Raschke, an expert witness and leading authority on the occult, testified about Roland, explaining "He became obsessed with horror movies, of which his favorite was *The Texas Chainsaw Massacre*. At the end of the summer of 1987, Roland had assured himself that "killing is a way of life."[9]

Remember, these films are sanctioned and approved by the MPAA and the National Association of Theatre Owners as a result of Valenti replacing the Production Code with the Ratings Scheme. As a result of the MPAA's seal of approval granted to hundreds of these "blood and guts" movies over the last 40 years, an enormous body of evidence has been collected to demonstrate the detrimental and deleterious effects of the "I don't give a f____" brand of films churning out of Hollywood. And, with television ratings in place now for more than a decade, these splatter films come into the American home living room uncut.

Kovar points out that "The National Institute of Mental Health has over 1,000 studies confirming that TV violence and aggressive behavior are conjoined." Ironically, as Kovar notes "if the medical community released over 1,000 clear studies revealing that cancer was caused by milk, the dairy business would be out of business overnight."[10]

These 1,000 studies are only the ones conducted by the National Institute of Mental Health. Overall, there exist in excess of 3,000 studies about the influence of movies and music conducted by a wide variety of organizations and educational institutions around the world. Most of this research clearly links movie and television violence, drug use, promiscuity, social and sexual behavior to "real life" abusive behavior across the vast spectrum of society. In 1995, a survey by the Center on Addiction and Substance Abuse at Columbia University revealed that a vast majority of adults and teens believe that the movie, TV, and music industry of Hollywood—more than any other influence—aggressively encouraged illegal drug use among all age groups. National Drug Policy Director Lee Brown said the study should serve as a "wake-up call" for Hollywood. Jack Valenti and the MPAA refused comment. In 2000, the F.T.C. determined undeniably that Hollywood purposely and aggressively targets youth. Again, Valenti and the MPAA were conspicuously silent.

The American Academy of Pediatrics conducts studies on a regular basis to keep up with the ever changing technology of entertainment. In December of 2006, the institute released results from a study that researched the affects of violent video games. Psychiatry professor Brad Bushman from the University of Michigan pointed out the net effect, "In general, violent media increases aggressive thoughts [and] there's good reason to believe [participatory] violent video games have a stronger affect than violent TV programs or films."[11] These have come to be known as "FPS" games for First Person Shooter. The results were printed in a Newsweek article titled, "This Is Your Brain On Alien Killer Pimps of Nazi Doom."

The results of that study were "hotly disputed" by the Entertainment Software Association's Douglas Lowenstein who blamed "very sick troubled kids."[12] This was virtually the very same excuse used by Jack Valenti to explain the murder spree resulting from *Natural Born Killers*. Of course, neither Lowenstein nor Valenti ventured to say just how these children might have become "very sick troubled kids." If there's so many of these kids out there, why give them a trigger?

John Carpenter, director of the original *Halloween* in 1978, was quoted as saying "I think a lot of directors who make horror films . . . express through their movies very hateful and vengeful feelings."[13] Equally, filmmakers of ultra-left agendas also actively "use" entertainment to push their social/sexual/political agenda on unsuspecting audiences.

GOING DARK

During my 20 years of location scouting, I had the opportunity to converse with many of Hollywood's leading production executives, producers and directors. Over the years, I took note of a peculiar topic that popped up frequently known as "going dark."

The phrase referred to a particular director or, more frequently, an actor that had decided to shed their "nice-guy" or "nice-girl" image in order to play a "dark" role such as a prostitute, adulterer, thief, drug addict, rapist, murderer or child molester. Or, it might simply mean taking on a subject that would insult the moral sensibilities of "fly-over" country. "Let's see how *this* plays in Peoria," laughed one director who was describing his upcoming film.

"Going dark" was always discussed in the context of being a "positive move" for one's career. It dawned on me at this time that the only people who thought "going dark" was a positive career opportunity were those "dark ominous figures" riding in the same car with me.

On one location scout in the late 1980's, a group of production executives began to discuss potential opportunities for Lea Thompson and Kate Capshaw if they decided to "go dark." Many times, using this term in reference to actors was code for "going nude" or straight actors "playing gay." When the 2008 Golden Globe Award nominations were announced, *USA Today* printed the headline "The Dark Side of the Globes Takes Over." Movies no longer display redemption or closure and that is why they usually bomb at the box-office. Warning to investors: The trend to "go dark" is increasing every year as more angry, psychologically disturbed and drug-addled filmmakers are embraced by the studio conglomerates.

In an issue dedicated to the 2008 Academy Awards, *USA Today* declared "No Oscars for good guys; complex anti-heroes abound in nominated roles this year." Producer Tony Gilroy, reflecting Hollywood's deep-seated mental illness, added, "I don't know anyone who isn't confused and complicated, who is happy for more than 20 seconds." Almost every Oscar-winning film for 2008 bombed at the box-office.

Most often, the term refers to anyone in the film or music industry that is willing to engage in depressing, dysfunctional, bleak, hopeless and un-redemptive stories of perpetual gloom and societal deterioration. The following list outlines a small sample of entertainment productions and individuals who decided to "go dark."

- During the pre-publicity hype leading up to the May 2007 release of *Spiderman*, *USA Today* reported that the latest installment would be a "darker" version of the man-spider when "Alien infection *darkens* the duds, and mood, of our hero (Toby Maguire)." Director Sam Raimi said that a black organism called a symbiote bonds with Spiderman's suit and infects his psyche.
- On the debut of Norah Jones latest CD "Not Too Late," *USA Today* again spreads the word of a "darker tone" in the singer's newest recording. Jones herself is quoted as saying "it's a little darker" than her moody but uplifting 2002 "Come Away." Music critic, Elysa Gardner, described the "darker tone" as a sign that Jones has grown "older and more reflective."[14] Jones was 27 when the CD was released in 2007 and the play list includes a Bush-bashing song intended to at least get a Grammy nomination if not an award. It worked for Ludacris and The Dixie Chicks.
- In a review of the summer 2006 TV lineup, *Time* magazine noted the rapidly growing trend toward "villain protagonists" as "anti-heroes" like the world of Tony Soprano. Dark as this trend already is, *Time* reported "After *Heist* and *Thief* last spring, TV's new fixation on the criminal mind promises to get deeper-and *darker*."[15] The creator of *Thief* commented that the show is about "the moral choices of immoral men." That could be an equally fitting description of Hollywood filmmakers.
- Actor Jamie Foxx convinced former cocaine-crazed director Michael Mann into making a movie version of the 1980's TV hit *Miami Vice,* but Foxx didn't quite count on the movie being so "dark." Colin Farrell, who plays Foxx's partner in the film version said, "At the time, it was a really *dark*

THE HOLLYWOOD CULTURE WAR

subject matter." Writer Anthony Breznican noted that the trio of Mann, Foxx, and Farrell "brings a *darker*, grittier *Miami Vice* to the screen."[16] With a $135 million dollar budget, the "dark" movie went quickly into the "red."

- In the spring of 2006, producers of *Desperate Housewives* announced that comedian/actress Carol Burnett would join the cast as a "cold stepmother" named Eleanor Mason. The intent was to add a "darker" tone to episodes of the popular TV "sexcom." *USA Today* writer William Kleck noted that "Producer Cherry is writing Eleanor (Burnett) as an evil role to differentiate her from Burnett's characters on her 1967-1978 variety series."[17]

- As if the HBO series *The Sopranos* wasn't *dark* enough, the cable pay channel began running promos just as the last season of filming was announced in March 2006. The HBO clips depicted a *very dark* last season complete with shootings, beatings and blood. Lots of blood. Cast member Lorraine Bracco announced that the last season would be "even darker."

- When horror-fiction writer Joe Hill was identified as the real-life 34 year old son of Stephen King, critics began to compare his style to that of his father's *dark style*. Critic Bob Minzesheimer reviewed Hill's new book, *Heart Shaped Box,* and described it as "a supernatural thriller with an avenging ghost and a fifty something heavy-metal musician whose hits include 'Happy Little Lynch Mob' . . . *The New York Times* calls it a wild, mesmerizing, perversely witty tale of horror." Dark as dad and then some.

- During the build-up to the 2007 season of *Survivor*, the network began promoting the new episodes of cut-throat back stabbing reality TV as a *darker* journey for its new cast. As the creep-voiced announcer proclaimed on the promo, "It's so vicious it's delicious."

- Finally, David Duchovney spoke about his role in Showtime's first major porn series, "Californication," noting "It's not a *dark* show. It's the lighter side of self-destruction." Showtime mocks America by claiming the show is about "family values."

In George Lucas' *Star Wars* series, the evil Darth Vader tells young Luke Skywalker "Your choices will determine your destiny—choose wisely." It appeared that by 1999, Lucas' friend, Steven Spielberg, made the choice to crossover to "the dark side" after 25 years of insightful, exciting, funny and uplifting movies that left the viewer "feeling good."

"Feel good" movies might make you rich and popular, but they didn't allow entry into Hollywood's highest echelon of honor, "The Dark Boys Club," which helps ensure not only Oscar nominations, but Oscar winners as well. Teaming up with David Geffen, Bill Clinton's former Defense Secretary, Spielberg was told by his partner in DreamWorks SKG that he'd been a good boy far too long. Geffen had some close friends who wanted to make a "different" and "darker" American movie.

American Beauty was an original script by the brooding radical heterophobic screenwriter named Alan Ball. The short-lived television show *OK Grow Up* was created and written largely by Ball to introduce a homosexual roommate into the apartment of two bachelors. Ball had hoped to push the homosexual heterophobe envelope like his hero Ellen DeGeneres, whose show was canned by ABC only a year earlier. Ball's sitcom tanked even quicker than Ellen's show.

Determined to get his "message" out, Ball penned the *American Beauty* script about a dysfunctional suburban American family involved in adultery, sexual promiscuity, perversity and persistent drug use (never portrayed as *abuse*). The "subtle message" of the film was transmitted through the homosexual neighbors, two men named Jim and Jim.

As Ball described the inspiration for the gender-bending drama, "I just got in the zone and it seemed to have its own life and the characters seemed so real, and it was like channeling."[18] (Remember the theme music from *The Twilight Zone?*)

For some, it was not a surprise that Spielberg was jumping on the social/sexual/political bandwagon. Since teaming up with the hot-tempered "gay activist" Geffen to produce movies, Spielberg had resigned his board position with the Boy Scouts of America for their legally justified position prohibiting homosexual scoutmasters. Spielberg was being led by the hand into the deep, dark pit of heterophobia. The Boy Scouts said good riddance and Spielberg would soon direct the most depressing, downtrodden and disturbing propaganda film of the 1990s glorifying everything that deconstructs the cohesive nature of family, neighborhood, community and nation. *American Beauty* was also the first major film to promote heterophobia (fear and disdain toward heterosexuals.)

Months earlier, before Spielberg had signed on, Alan Ball had brought his dark script to the attention of two radical homosexual activist producers, Dan Jinks and Bruce Cohen. As the producers would recall, before selling the idea to Spielberg, they "had heard Steven talk on many occasions of his desire to make smaller movies, to make *darker* movies."[19]

Geffen helped engineer an aggressive marketing campaign among Oscar voters to help ensure the gender-bender message film cleaned up at the Academy Awards. At the time, nobody in Hollywood wanted to risk the wrath of a possible David Geffen conniption fit or become the target of a career ending gossip campaign. (Just eight years later, Geffen's fall from influential grace was evident at the 2007 Academy Awards when his over-hyped *DreamGirls* was largely snubbed by Oscar voters tired of being bullied.)

Producer Jinks affirmed the secret formula for Hollywood gender-bending adulation when he noted, "After screening the movie, people have said almost as an after thought, 'You know, I just realized that the only *normal* people in the movie are the gay couple.' That was one of the first things *we* noted when *we* read [the script]."[20]

Spielberg's "dark" journey is covered in more detail in Chapter 20, "The Velvet Mafia: Fact or Fiction?" The true intentions of Ball, Jinks, Cohen, Geffen and Spielberg are laid bare in sardonic detail in an article by Daniel Jeffreys of the *Daily Mail.*

Gender-bender films such as *American Beauty, Brokeback Mountain, Transamerica* and their television counterparts such as *Will and Grace, Ellen, Dirt,* and *Kings of South Beach,* to name only a few, have already affected their intended targets. On March 8, 2007, CNN Radio noted poll results about same-sex marriage, indicating that individuals born *after* 1970 were more accepting of "gay marriage" than those born *before* 1970. (Any proximity to 1968 is *not coincidental).*

As my good friend and veteran location manager Joe O'Har told me in 1992, "Steven's not the same guy we worked with on *Close Encounters.* He's really turned inward, gloomy and sometimes just plain *dark* and spooky. I think he's beginning to hang with a *darker* crowd." Digging deeper into the gutter, by 2008 Spielberg began production planning on a Showtime series that would be co-written by an internet porn blogger, stripper, and phone-sex matron named Diablo Cody. Former subscribers who have begun dropping Showtime are again reviving the old nickname, "Slut-Time."

As well as pushing his new found social/sexual/political agenda, Spielberg can also mold himself into the genre of horror picture directors who want the audience to feel their pain. When *Jaws* was released just before the summer of 1975, travel to American beaches dropped off dramatically throughout the entire summer of that year after viewers of the movie experienced anxiety and real fears of a bloody shark attack, which is exactly what Spielberg wanted to accomplish. Specifically, he wanted to inflict *real pain.*

Few people realize that Spielberg's movie about random shark attacks was not just another "fear as fun" summer flick. The young director's motives for making *Jaws* was a darkly perverse and premeditated plan to seek revenge for his own childhood of anxieties, phobias and the anger over his own parent's divorce.

"I had no way to subliminate or channel those fears until I began telling stories to my younger sisters. This removed the fear from my soul and transferred it right into theirs."[21] How would you like to have a big brother like that?

In a typical neurotic Hollywood diatribe, Spielberg explained, "I wanted to do *Jaws* for hostile reasons. I read it and felt that I had been attacked. It terrified me and I knew I wanted to strike back."[22] Soul transfers? Hostile? Attacked? Parents contemplating divorce for the "children's sake" may want to think twice before unleashing another "hostile" movie director onto the American scene.

In addition to New Age religions, philosophies and radical leftist politics, add "personal demon transfers" as another influence that motivates Hollywood filmmakers. As Spielberg's buddy George Lucas noted, "Emotionally involving the audience is easy. Anyone can do it blindfolded; get a little kitten and have some guy wring its neck."[23] WARNING: Do not take Lucas' advice on entertaining your friends and family. Just ask Michael Vick.

* * *

Many contemporary filmmakers speak very openly about their romance with the dark and demonic side of their psyches which, unfortunately, they feel obligated to splatter across the screen with the full support of the equally sick studio executives in Hollywood and the ratings administration at the MPAA. Yet another filmmaker in the genre of angry radical heterophobic directors, Gus Van Sant, verifies John Carpenter's view that many directors harbor "very hateful and vengeful feelings" that show up at the neighborhood multiplex.

Van Sant articulated his cultural orientation and mission in life, "I believe the properly manipulated image can provoke an audience to the Burroughsian limit of riot, rampant sex, instantaneous death . . . The primitive world of blood and sex is still with us."[24]

Van Sant's influence comes from Beat generation writer, drug addict and pedophile William S. Burroughs, one-third of the Beat forerunners including fellow pedophile promoter and part-time poet Allen Ginsberg and author Jack Kerouac of the Greenwich Village avant-garde of the 1950's. Their stories will be "fleshed-out" in the following chapter, "Hollywood's Road to Perdition."

For over 25 years, Hollywood filmmakers have even promoted their films through the industry's very own "voice of darkness," in the person of Don LaFontaine, also known as the voice of "that movie trailer guy." Lafontaine's deep, sinister and foreboding voice is even used to promote "upbeat" films with a "downbeat" tone, only because his voice has become so recognizable to the moviegoing audience.

Lafontaine often starts a movie trailer promo with a disturbing opening, "In a world where evil has met its match . . ." To most people, Lafontaine was a voice without a face until the Geico insurance company used him in the popular series of gimmick TV ads where he announces, with the full accompaniment of ominous bass string instruments, "In a world where both our cars were under water . . ."

Lafontaine's voice was even used in a Bird's Eye frozen vegetable commercial where he finishes by saying, grimly, "Perfect seasoning is in the bag." Somehow, the vegetables seem more frightening than inviting, a tone which is now permanently embedded in his voice. Don surely hopes the darkside trend in Hollywood continues, or he'll be forced to sell frozen food in a new way that will hopefully make your mouth water. Now *that* will be a challenge.

CHAPTER 18

HOLLYWOOD'S ROAD TO PERDITION: THE TWENTY YEAR BATTLE TO DESTROY THE CULTURE (1948-1968)

> *"Hollywood was taken over by a bunch of dope smoking hippies who are now grown up..."*
> —Ben Stein

"It's very obvious in what he writes that his dark fantasies happen to be sodomizing young boys as they're hanging. I can actually relate to that to quite an extent," director David Cronenberg explained calmly about his affection and admiration for William S. Burroughs, one of the three main perpetrators of the Beat Generation.[1] This is what director Gus Van Sant meant in the last chapter when describing the "Burroughsian limit" for which he also worshipped Burroughs as a demigod.

No more than a dozen individuals between 1948 and 1968 would propel themselves into the cultural scene in a way that would adversely affect the popular culture of America that reverberates even today. This group would initiate America's decline as an emerging international model of diverse societal cohesion, bedrock values and democratic prosperity as opposed to democratic deconstruction, moral depravity and perverse worldviews that have shattered the very life-blood of this nation. Burroughs was only one of the players in this demented group of culture-rot advocates who could not have solely propelled themselves onto the national scene without a little help from the post-war press and media elites.

These fastidious individuals—authors, poets, publishers, academics and filmmakers—were paraded by an aggressive news media looking to advance some radical, fresh "innovators" or "thinkers" that were going to shake-up the nation after World War II. The phrase "modern thinkers" would be applied to these motley anti-heroes by the Manhattan and Hollywood press in the same way they had described "modern architecture" or "modern furniture" through the 1930s and 1940s.

The press wanted so desperately to associate themselves with these "modern thinkers" in a mutually beneficial way and, in doing so, they downplayed or turned a blind eye to their common denominators such as drug addiction, alcoholism, sexual deviance and apocalyptical self-delusional politics of rage. In literary circles they were known as "same way thinkers" or in film circles as "like-minded" individuals. Author E. Michael Jones described them best as "Degenerate Moderns" in his book by the same name.

Most of the highlighted individuals in this chapter were basically philosophical fellow travelers of the Crowlean Church of God is Dead. The mainstream media then, as now, had developed a kinship with these New Age degenerate "thinkers" in order to maintain their prime position on the invitation list for the Bi-coastal Cocktail Party Circuit (BCPC).

The "like-minded" press of the 1950's *New York Times* and its imitators were the same ones who looked upon a severely damaged man named Jackson Pollock as he took buckets of paint and splashed them on enormous canvases in a Manhattan loft and proclaimed the dried dribble as masterpieces while swilling champagne at "art shows." Nobody dared dismiss this particular branch of "Expressionism" as trash and as a result, Pollock's dried paint now sells for millions of dollars per canvas. In 2007, David Geffen sold Pollock's splatter "Number 5" for *$140 million*. In the same year, a 710 year old copy of the original Magna Carta sold for a mere $21 million.

But, Pollock was just a sideshow among others who emerged during this twenty year period beginning mainly in 1948. The timeline will trace the people and events that culminated in 1968's Quiet Conspiracy by Jack Valenti that would officially "free" these "imprisoned" souls and their fellow travelers into the general population.

1948

In a dingy upstairs apartment in Upper Manhattan's Harlem district, a 21-year-old man with horn-rimmed glasses began to experience an "audible hallucination" which he believed was the voice of God reading poetry to him on this particular balmy evening. As the deep, domineering and determined voice continued, the young *Allen Ginsberg* realized, in his own mind, that the 19th century poet William Blake was the voice reciting to him such works as "The Sick Rose" and "Ah Sunflower."[2]

This late-night epiphany caused Ginsberg to awake and stare out the window at the tenement fire escape, in awe of its intricate iron detail and mechanism. He

THE HOLLYWOOD CULTURE WAR

then walked to the window, looking up at the night sky and realized that some "hand" or force had created everything, but he couldn't quite put a finger on it. Ginsberg certainly couldn't give God credit. That would take away his eternal yearning to find the source of the universe.

What Ginsberg did realize is that his favorite poet once wrote, "the eye altering alters all" from Blake's "The Mental Traveler." Eventually, Ginsberg's out-of-focus worldview would inevitably blur the vision and alter the eyes of millions. It is uncertain if Ginsberg realized that Blake was also a member of that curious school of English poets who believed the writer "is of the devil's domain" as Blake himself wrote.

What was certain is that Allen Ginsberg realized he was a young man alive and alone in the world, finally free from the clutches of his Communist paranoid schizophrenic mother. For Ginsberg, life began the night William Blake took leave from the grave to read poetry in the Harlem nights of 1948.

* * *

That same year, a 34-year old Harvard graduate heroin dealer in Greenwich Village named **William S. Burroughs** had recently released his common law wife Joan from the psychiatric ward of Bellevue Hospital after years of amphetamine use. Burroughs, the drifting no-count grandson of William S. Burroughs I, inventor of the Burroughs Adding Machine, decided to move to New Orleans in 1948 with their infant son Billy, and Joan's daughter from a previous marriage to start life fresh. His friends laughed at the time. New Orleans was definitely not the place to start life "fresh."

Burroughs wasn't motivated to work for a living considering the fact that his parents had decided to give him a monthly allowance of $200 upon his graduation from Harvard in 1938. Even though twelve years had passed, the checks arrived on time with precise regularity from his adoring parents.

In 1948, $200 was a hefty monthly sum to subsidize a wandering bohemian, his wife, her daughter and newborn son. Perhaps, Burroughs must have thought he could escape his addiction to heroin, his wife's addiction to speed and also leave behind his record of arrests and brushes with Gotham's finest. These included forging narcotics prescriptions and another incident in 1945 for failing to report a murder he witnessed along with his part-time roommate Jack Kerouac.

Burroughs and family didn't last long in the Big Easy after police raided his home and discovered a letter from his homosexual Manhattan friend Allen Ginsberg. Ginsberg was coordinating with Burroughs by mail for a shipment of marijuana.

To avoid facing a possible jail sentence in the dreaded Angola State Prison, Burroughs and family fled to Mexico and decided to wait out the five years needed before the statute of limitations expired. Burroughs decided that the free sweat of Mexico City was preferable to the forced sweat of hard labor at the notorious state prison, not to mention the ever present specter of forced homosexual rape, though a consensual rape might have been okay with Burroughs.

But, within a few years into his Mexican exile, the devil himself would come calling. Burroughs would later refer to this as the imminent presence of "The Ugly Spirit."[3]

* * *

While Ginsberg was hearing voices from the dead in New York and Burroughs was smoking dope and drinking heavily in Mexico City at the Bounty Bar, their fellow Greenwich Village buddy ***Jack Kerouac*** was "cruising" America in a dilapidated sedan in "search of his soul" and attempting to discover the "meaning of life." Kerouac would criss-cross the entire span of America on three separate occasions between 1947 and 1950.

To this day, Kerouac worshippers fail to mention that Kerouac didn't even know how to drive, though he was in his mid-twenties. To accomplish these cross-country journeys, Kerouac brought along fellow friend, "Village" homosexual and drug addict Neal Cassady.

Jack Kerouac and his part-time former roommate, William Burroughs, had already collaborated on a mystery novel in 1945 titled *And the Hippos Were Boiled in Their Tanks* based loosely on the real-life incident where the two had witnessed the murder of David Kammerer by his friend Lucien Carr.

Hippos turned out to be a pathetic attempt at writing by both Kerouac and Burroughs. It was obvious from reading excerpts that both men were either smoking dope or dropping pills. Kerouac was a relentless amphetamine freak and alcoholic. And, with a co-author whose blood bubbled with heroin, their attempt at writing became a futile journey into malfunction junction.

Kerouac maintained a rambling journal of his travels on the road and considered putting his collective thoughts into a book someday. He reveled in visiting honky-tonks and experiencing life on "the other side of the tracks."

Kerouac began to believe that blues and jazz music were as close to heaven as one could achieve. He made these observations while drinking late into the night as his liver sprouted another cyst and his brain swelled beneath the hard cap of his skull. Marijuana would lull him to sleep or, occasionally lead to a sexual encounter with a whore or various "drifters."

* * *

While the three stooges of bohemian drug addiction, sexual perversity and petty crimes were floundering around in their self-indulgent fantasies in 1948, a seemingly mild-mannered Indiana University professor named ***Alfred Kinsey*** had published a book that same year titled *Sexual Behavior In the Human Male*. This volume was an outgrowth of studies he had been conducting at the university and from travels around the Midwest between 1939 and 1947. It was in 1947 that Kinsey established The Institute for Research in Sex, Gender and Reproduction at Indiana University in Bloomington.

Prior to the establishment of the Kinsey Institute, Alfred Kinsey had spent the better part of two decades as an entomologist studying the mating habits of gall wasps. According to his own account, Kinsey "was asked" to be an instructor for a non-credit marriage course. This would allow him the "permission" to delve into the sex lives of his subjects for "scientific" purposes. Kinsey's account of being recruited as a marriage course instructor turned out later to be a total self-fabricated lie.[4]

Kinsey's 1948 book was controversial from the beginning as his "research" was considered by many to be flawed statistically and in its methodological errors. Kinsey had gathered most of his research from prison inmates, prostitutes and homosexuals. As author E. Michael Jones stated, "The fact remains that these groups were more likely to talk about their sex lives than the population in general."[5]

The general consensus from Kinsey's book was that a large percentage of the American population was homosexual. Furthermore, he "concluded" that *everyone* was bisexual along some fictional "continuum" that he termed "continuous variation" which he said "is the rule among men as well as insects."

Kinsey went on to push for sweeping change in American society under the guise of his insect studies and flawed human sexuality research. According to Kinsey biographer, Cornelia Christenson, "Our conceptions of right and wrong; normal and abnormal, are seriously challenged by the variation studies."[6] In other words, "Anything goes." Any resemblance to Aleister Crowley's philosophy is *not coincidental.*

Not only had Alfred Kinsey reduced man's behavior to that of a rare gall wasp, he was also expressing in murky and vague scientific terms the Crowlean motto of "Do What thou Will Shall be the Whole of the Law." It would soon be revealed that Kinsey was not only an admirer of Aleister Crowley, but had pursued his writings with much vigor and would eventually travel to Crowley's old stomping grounds in Europe.

Just as L. Ron Hubbard began Scientology on the date of Crowley's death in 1947, Kinsey picked this same year to begin his Institute in hopes of picking up where Crowley left off, albeit in a more "scientific" endeavor. However, as author Jones points out, "The scientist's lab coat became a more respectable version of the flasher's raincoat, and Kinsey could use science as the main club in bludgeoning the country's sexual morals into unconsciousness."[7]

MICHAEL VINCENT BOYER

* * *

In 1948, a young college student named **Hugh Hefner** was still being talked about on campus for his editorial in the school newspaper that expressed great enthusiasm and support for the Kinsey book on male sexuality. The following year, in 1949, Hefner would write his Northwestern University paper on sex laws in the United States, again, based on Kinsey's fraudulent and flawed studies of human sexuality.

Like all the other sexually obsessed rebels emerging in the late 1940s, Hefner would "blame" the comfort and prosperity of middle-class America for his urgent need to create a sexual revolution. In his usual condescending thankless style, Hefner reflected that his upbringing occurred "in a typically Midwestern Methodist repressed home." Of course, young Hugh never bothered to thank his parents for food, shelter, clothing and a quality education and who were not only loving, but financially supportive.

Poor Hugh Hefner was suffering from penis envy. He was so enthralled with his own genitalia he could not find enough activities to engage it or enough time to describe its endless possibilities. Hefner believed the time had arrived for all women to start showing their breasts as a form of "liberation" and that they should start showing their breasts (the bigger, the better) in a more "tasteful" manner than he was accustomed to from the cheap subway pornography he devoured throughout college.

Hugh Hefner wanted to separate pornography into "legitimate" and "illegitimate" forms and he would be the premiere spokesman for the "legitimate" variety, or "gentleman's" variety as he would describe it. Hefner loved Hollywood movies, but he would always complain that the sexuality in movies was being "repressed." Hefner wanted little or no clothing on women, not only in magazines, but in the movies, too. This was not for selfish reasons, of course, only for the sake of liberating "repressed" women. "Hef," as his friends would call him, wanted to take Alfred Kinsey's deceptive "science" on sex and turn the "anything goes" philosophy into a cultural campaign.

But, in 1948, all he could do is dream, visit the "grindhouse" adult movie theaters on the edge of town and masturbate, much to the chagrin of theater owners and ushers.

* * *

A book published two years earlier titled *Reveille for Radicals* was still selling well at book stores in 1948. The author was **Saul Alinsky** from Chicago, a bespectacled chain smoking, smooth-talking, behind the scenes political operative who would engineer the new post-war version of class warfare politics through the reprehensible tactics of pitting Americans against each other.

Though married into the Chicago mafia, Alinsky was beginning to receive enormous amounts of funding from guilt-ridden "socially conscious" liberal millionaire businessmen and from the Meyer family, owners of *The Washington Post*. Saul Alinsky believed in perpetrating conflict and controversy to achieve radical social change in America and would operate just under the radar screen of the press.

Alinsky would find the likes of Ginsberg and others useful in fomenting campus demonstrations in their early days, but would be later turned off as the hair grew longer and the music grew louder. Alinsky preferred to "penetrate" the middle-class through civic organizations and even "liberal-leaning" mainstream churches where he would gently whisper seeds of discord, all in the name of "community activism." He secretly planted the early seeds of the Evangelical left.

1953 to 1957

Allen Ginsberg, the young wannabe poet developed a regular circle of friends that hung out in the Greenwich Village section of lower Manhattan. He was, by now, so busy "hanging out" at basement jazz clubs and poetry readings in search of male sexual companionship that his writing was suffering. Further complicating his artful waste of time was Ginsberg's addiction to marijuana and other drugs. He would tell friends that his drug use was merely an attempt to recapture that night in Harlem when William Blake rose from the grave to read poetry.

Ginsberg's former dope supplier, William Burroughs, was not in an easy position to smuggle drugs back to the village from his hideout in Mexico. By 1953, Burroughs was in much deeper trouble than the 1948 "marijuana letter" between him and Ginsberg.

While waiting for the statute of limitations to expire so he could return to the U.S., Burroughs and his wife Joan spent many nights getting drunk and taking drugs that were as accessible as candy in Mexico City. In 1951, at a party on the second floor of the Bounty Bar, Burroughs and his wife were playing a perverse game of Russian Roulette known as William Tell. Burroughs took a revolver with one bullet in the chamber. After spinning the revolving cylinder, Burroughs took aim at Joan, pulled the trigger, and blew her brains out.

After 13 days in jail, Burroughs' brother came to Mexico City to "distribute funds" to various Mexican lawyers and bribe money to the police department.[8] While awaiting the continuously delayed trial, Burroughs managed to complete his first two novels appropriately titled *Queer* and *Junkie*. His village drug buddy Allen Ginsberg had encouraged Burroughs to write *Junkie* and was instrumental in getting it published in 1953.

Junkie was very similar to Aleister Crowley's *Diary of a Drug Fiend* from 1922. Burroughs had the makings of a new type Crowley for the post-war generation, but most of his life would be spent in heroin hazes, molesting children and dancing with "The Ugly Spirit." But, it was only 1953, and William Burroughs would be "hanging around" for another four decades.

After Burroughs's Mexican attorney suddenly fled the country over his own legal problems, Burroughs took the opportunity to skip back to the United States. He was convicted in abstentia of homicide and sentenced to a suspended two year sentence.[9] His two children were sent back to America to live with their respective grandparents.

Without a wife and children to "care for," Burroughs returned to New York in 1953 to pursue his passion for young boys and even made a sexual pass at Allen Ginsberg who refused Burroughs voracious homosexual appetite. By 1954, Burroughs would end up in Tangier where he would rent a room from a man who procured homosexual prostitutes for visiting American and English tourists.

In between heroin and molesting children, Burroughs would spend the next four years spewing out a major literary piece of cult garbage known as *Naked Lunch.* Just over 40 years old, Burroughs was *still* receiving an allowance from his parents.

Ginsberg would finally find his literary voice, such as it was, in a rambling piece of prose titled *Howl* which Ginsberg delivered publicly in a bohemian enclave in San Francisco in 1955. Ginsberg's diatribe of his angst-filled life was considered the beginning of the Beat Generation. In addition to applause, many members of the audience snapped their fingers in appreciation. Ginsberg had brought together the east coast and west coast Beat communities.

Ginsberg, who by this time was involved in a "full-time—sometime" relationship with Peter Orlovsky, was now feeling a sense of empowerment. He began to speak about a "New Vision" for American youth. Ginsberg began to push a radical social agenda that heavily promoted homosexuality, illegal drug use, and mystic eastern religions and philosophies.

Allen Ginsberg envisioned a "New Age" where "young people" would start demanding social change. Nobody was really sure what Ginsberg meant by "young people" since he was fast approaching that untrustworthy age of the 30 and over crowd. The poet, now free from his iambic pentameter, had come to the conclusion that Americans were too conforming, too middle-class, and too repressed. Like Hugh Hefner, Allen Ginsberg was going to "free" Americans from becoming "comfortable" as if that was some kind of sin of life's New Beat—the beat of a new generation—a generation of "beatniks."

Jack Kerouac, who was present at the 1955 reading of *Howl* had encouraged and influenced Ginsberg by promoting "spontaneous prose." In fact, Kerouac liked *Howl* so much, he would lead the chorus of Beat writers and poets to convince Ginsberg to publish *Howl,* and basement poets back in New York were snapping their fingers in approval.

At the same time, Kerouac was trying to convince William Burroughs to publish *Queer*, the story he wrote while rotting in a Mexican jail. Kerouac told Burroughs that the story would "appeal to east coast homosexual literary critics."[10] Like *Howl*, Burroughs book was a worthless piece of drug-induced paper chatter suitable for lining bird cages.

Kerouac himself had completed his own piece of rambling prose after compiling his road trip journals of 1947, 1949 and 1950. Between 1951 and 1954 Kerouac wrote a couple drafts of *The Beat Generation* which he renamed *On the Road*. He actually *did* compile the final draft together in fiction form onto a 120 foot scroll of paper during a 21 day period of non-stop "concentrated spontaneity" in 1955 while ingesting Benzedrine and Dexedrine, not "coffee" as revisionists claim. (In 2001, Indianapolis Colts owner James Irsay bought the "official scroll" at a Christie's Auction for $2.43 million.)

Ginsberg's *Howl* was published in 1956 by City Lights Press and Kerouac's *On The Road* was published by Viking Press in 1957. Apparently, the "east coast homosexual literacy critics" were not too impressed with *Queer*. But, with Burroughs already a published writer with 1953's *Junkie,* the three would become the founding fathers of the Beats.

Turtlenecks, tight pants, goatees and snapping fingers would rule for the rest of the 1950s for the "avant-garde" underground youth, even though most of America was quite comfortable in their much-deserved middle class serenity. This disturbed Ginsberg to no end who believed all Americans should become drug-addicted, homosexual Buddhist artists from outer space.

Because many Brooklynites had one or both parents as members of the communist party, as was the case with Ginsberg, the term "red-diaper baby" came into popular usage. In specific honor of Allen Ginsberg, radio talk-show host Michael Savage would coin the phrase, "Red-diaper *doper* baby."

During the mid-1950s, Ginsberg and Kerouac would delve deeper into various mystic eastern religions and philosophies, particularly offshoots of Buddhism such as the "anti-rational Indian sect" known as Zen. Ginsberg was also "turned on" to various surrealist artists and poets such as the deranged lunatic Anton Arnaud of France. Meanwhile, Burroughs was content searching for new drugs with telepathic powers south of the border. Burroughs' religion was devoted to molesting more young boys, something that greatly pleased "The Ugly Spirit."

These three men would inspire the counterculture hippie movement of the 1960s and the revival of the long-dead guru with the long-living arm of Mephistopheles, aka Aleister Crowley, embraced by the rock music industry.

* * *

Alfred Kinsey would not live long enough to see the Beat generation flourish, dying in 1956 of heart failure. However, in the years before he died, Kinsey voraciously continued his increasingly questionable "sex science" at Indiana University. In 1953, he published a companion study to 1948's *Sexual Behavior in the Human Male* with the title *Sexual Behavior is the Human Female.*

This equally flawed study earned Kinsey a cover story in *Time Magazine* in 1953. However, *Time* gave little attention, much less alarm, to his methodology and pseudo-science and some severely shocking results which would not be questioned for another 30 years.

Nevertheless, cracks were beginning to appear in Kinsey's highly suspect research. He was becoming more and more obsessed with homosexuals, prostitutes and inmates who made up the core of his research subjects. Even Kinsey's co-worker in the sex studies, Wardell Pomeroy, would later say, "One of the chief complaints was that he compiled too large a portion of homosexual histories."[11] It was becoming apparent to some, though not widely publicized for another two decades, that Kinsey was not constructing a scientific model of sexual behavior. Rather, he was creating and heavily promoting an ideology. As author E. Michael Jones described Kinsey's real agenda, " . . . Kinsey's contribution to modernity is homosexual entomology. It is an ideology—constructed with the help of Darwin—in which deviance is the engine that allows new things to happen. Because of Kinsey's fixation on deviance, as the engine of social and biological progress, the outcome of Kinsey's survey was pre-programmed form the beginning."[12]

The first group to speak up publicly after the 1953 issue of *Time* was the American Statistical Association (ASA). The group of statisticians claimed in 1954 that the sex research data was unclear and evidence was vague. Specifically, the ASA committee was concerned about the unknown number of homosexuals causing "bias in the sample."[13]

There would be far more horrific allegations to follow as the secrets of the Kinsey Institute would eventually become known around the world by a perceptive American psychologist named Judith Reisman who would challenge Kinsey's assertion that "loving sex" was possible between adults and children. More on her discovery at the end of this chapter under "Post Scripts and Post Mortems."

By 1955, Kinsey had filmed an enormous amount of sexual behavior at his institute including sexual activity involving students, faculty and even his own wife. Kinsey himself was fascinated with the seedy world of pornography in still photographs and "underground movies."

Alfred Kinsey developed a close intimate relationship with America's first "openly gay" filmmaker, Kenneth Anger. Both men were devout followers of Aleister Crowley and traveled together to inspect the ruins of Crowley's abandoned Abbey of Thelema in Italy in 1955. Kinsey and Anger had originally met in 1947 when Kinsey became the first customer to purchase Anger's sex film *Fireworks*.

Kenneth Anger would later help Kinsey build the Kinsey Institute Film Archive in Bloomington. With the addition of a growing collection of pornography provided by Anger and his sources, and with new material added everyday, the Kinsey Institute maintains the largest collection of porn in the *world*.[14] Kinsey compensated Anger by allowing the deviant filmmaker to masturbate in front of Kinsey's 16mm camera. All for the sake of research, of course.

As of this writing, Kenneth Anger, at age 80, is one of the last surviving original students of Aleister Crowley's New Age Thelema religion of sex magick, drug abuse and studies in bestiality. Anger would remain close to Kinsey right up until Kinsey's death.

Cornelia Christenson captured a piece of Kinsey's version of "Do What Thou Will" from a speech Kinsey gave to the Phi Beta Kappa society in which he declared, "individual [behavior] variations shape into a continuous curve on which there are no sharp divisions between normal and abnormal, between right and wrong." As Jones added in analyzing Kinsey's hypocrisy, "If there is no right and wrong, by what right does he claim the mandate to change the sex laws?[15]

All of this "scientific sex" research would "legitimatize" the Crowlean lifestyle which was being whole heartedly embraced by beatniks Ginsberg, Burroughs, and Kerouac. All three now felt "scientifically justified" in their self-indulgent drug addiction and self-obsessed penis envy. And, even before Kinsey's death in 1956, Hugh Hefner was commercializing his "New Morality" based directly on Kinsey's "New Sexuality."

The over-sexualization, or "hyper-sexualization," of American culture can be traced back to one sick man at Indiana University who called himself a researcher and whose findings basically said everybody in the world is either a homosexual or *at least* a bisexual. Worse, Kinsey created a "continuous curve" that "proved" there is no such reality as right or wrong.

Kinsey's flawed research would give birth to the radical "Gay Rights" movement, the "Feminist" movement and to the formation of NAMBLA (North American Many Boy Love Association). Kinsey would also be embraced, virtually without question, by the American public school system which insisted that sex education be taken out of the home and transferred to the classroom as early as elementary school.

As E. Michael Jones concluded, "In terms of external evidence, homosexuality is the piece that completes the jigsaw puzzle that is Kinsey's life and legacy. It explains, for example the 'heterophobia' that Edward Eichel, who received his degree in sex education from New York University, described as the hidden agenda in sex education."

As Eichel noted, "For Kinsey, blurring of sexual identity—bisexuality (as opposed to heterosexuality)—was an essential step in opening up an unlimited range of sexual opportunities. Kinsey supported an ideology that might be called *pan-sexuality*, 'anything goes' that might provide excitement and pleasure. But, in fact, it is an ideology that frowns upon monogamy and traditional concepts of normality, and considers intercourse between a man and a woman a limited form of sexual expression." (Pomeroy, in his article, "The Now of the Kinsey Findings" [1972] refers to heterosexual intercourse as an "addiction.")[16]

Alfred Kinsey would die in 1956 at the age of 62, reportedly due to complications from pneumonia and heart failure.

* * *

Hugh Hefner, the young Midwestern University student who wrote his 1949 term paper on sex laws in the United States based on Kinsey's bogus science, was now feeling fully mitigated and vindicated in his burning desire to promote a "New Morality" across America and around the world. Hefner decided that his first move would be to publish a "gentleman's" sex magazine.

In 1953, the same year Kinsey appeared in *Time* magazine, Hefner was busy in his home kitchen pasting up the layout for his first issue. Hefner would praise Kinsey in an article of this issue as justification for advocating a "New Morality" through an airbrushed, glossy façade of pornography.

However, nowhere in the laudatory article did Hefner question one single outcome of the biased and highly manipulated science. Nor did Hefner question the "supporting evidence" of "loving sex" between adults and children or how Kinsey came about "researching" that particular finding. To do so would have sunk his first issue before it ever left the kitchen on the way to the street corner newsstands. *Playboy* magazine was born out of a well-crafted lie that Hefner has maintained for six decades.

For his first issue, Hefner also undertook an unlicensed initiative to put a well-dressed Marilyn Monroe on the cover and an undressed Marilyn Monroe as the "centerfold." The nude photo was actually an old calendar shot of Monroe taken in the 1940's before her Hollywood career took off.

The first issue was also sprinkled with "intelligent" articles about politics, social issues, literature, cinema and men's style. A black and white photograph portrayed Hefner as a hard-working clean-cut gentleman clenching a pipe while typing away at an old typewriter. After the magazine hit the newsstands, Hefner counted sales exceeding 50,000 at 50 cents an issue. It was enough to pay back his small group of investors, including his mother; you know, the mother of his "typically Midwestern Methodist repressed upbringing?"

THE HOLLYWOOD CULTURE WAR

Hugh Hefner was going to take on the popular culture with all the bravado of a pervert in search of pre-pubescent looking girls who were, hopefully, old enough to pass consent laws. He had stumbled on a formula that remains in effect today; find a popular and attractive girl who is willing to take her clothes off for the magazine. Her birthdate would be given on the statistics page, much like a heifer on the "stat" page of a cattle auction. Included on this page would be her hometown, body measurements and "hobbies."

As the years passed into the middle and late 1950's Hefner would personally scout out the "right girl." His preference was to find "the girl next door" look as opposed to the obvious tight-sweater-and-shirt whores who appeared in his college porn collection.

However, as Hefner grew older, the girls in the magazine appeared younger. Finally, in 1958, Hefner was arrested for recruiting and photographing a 16-year old girl. The charge was "contributing to the delinquency of a minor." Hefner had received the full permission of the teen-ager's devoted mother who had lied about her daughter's age in the enthusiasm to see her child paraded nude in front of the whole world. Was she pimping her daughter for the money or for "Hef?" The charges were dropped against Hefner, but it would not be long before he was busted again by the authorities.

By the late 1950's Hefner had secured big name advertisers, mainly liquor companies and tobacco companies that added millions of dollars to his growing sex empire. Hefner would soon acquire the old Palmolive Building in downtown Chicago as his headquarters. The bleak but unique stone skyscraper was an appropriate early 20th century version of Babylonian Renaissance architecture in a city famous for its architectural innovations. Like the Beat generation and his idol Alfred Kinsey, Hefner was feeling "anointed" by some burning force to break America's social and sexual morals. Hefner and his Greenwich Village counterparts in New York were all under the false assumption that America was "repressed" during the 1950s and living in a world of "conformity." What Hefner and his "intellectual" followers didn't seem to understand is that most Americans were very content living in the post-war prosperity of their tidy suburban tree-lined neighborhoods where their children could play in green parks and neighbors gathered for backyard cook-outs on warm summer days.

This was much preferred to the alternative chaos of the Beat generation who shot heroin in their veins in dingy back rooms of subterranean jazz clubs and awaking at sunrise to puke in a littered alley after engaging in sex with strangers wearing rabbit masks and ending up with syphilis two weeks later.

Hefner and the emerging counterculture continuously confused "repressed" with "confident, mature self control." It was Hefner who was promoting *repression* by encouraging social and sexual *regression* in the name of "liberation" and "revolution." And, in Hefner's world and the world of the beatniks, children ceased to exist. Children were considered obstacles in the adult's pursuit of ultimate coitus.

And, like Kinsey, Hefner was determined to fake the science and social reality in order to fit his agenda. His growing deviance and perversity was the engine that pulled the train of morality down the hill of decency. The cumulative negative effects on the culture would not be felt for another decade as Hugh Hefner labored over a "Playboy Philosophy" that could somehow justify his "sophisticated" and "tasteful" version of the loutish teenager who never grew up, cruising the strip bars, drinking for the first time and shouting "Show Your Boobs!" without getting kicked out by the bouncer.

Basically, Hefner began emerging as a predatory sex capitalist junkie in order to fund his addiction and wield his radical social/sexual/political hammer. Most notably, Hefner began to believe that nudity should not be confined to the pages of a magazine.

In his early thirties, Hugh Hefner was planning a culture war of his own that would also liberate the movie screen, the repository of his favorite pastime, Hollywood films. It would be years later that Hefner would make friends with a man named Jack Valenti. And, Jack Valenti would become no stranger to the Playboy mansion.

Hugh Hefner also had his eyes on a woman more voluptuous than Marilyn Monroe who he desperately wanted on the cover of his magazine and in the buff of the centerfold. He, too, would even receive a little help from the devil himself in a bizarre series of events that would occur in the following decade of the 1960s. In the meantime, he was now happy in the 1950s to be counting his millions and planning the offense of his "New Morality" for the New Age of sexual liberation.

* * *

Also in Chicago, the elusive and slippery promoter of societal conflict and chaos, Saul Alinsky, was pulling in even larger donations from more socially guilty millionaires such as Marshall Field III, Sears's heir Adele Rosenwald Levy and other wealthy families. Soon, he would be pulling the same "sympathy shakedown" from the Wall Street power-house community.

Alinsky was orchestrating an "orderly revolution" that was increasing its secret infiltration and manipulation of the middle-class through unions, ethnic organizations, local political organizations and even more churches than he had penetrated before. Alinsky shamelessly pulled on heart strings and purse strings at the same time. Much of this money went into his organization called the Industrial Areas Foundation (IAF). Alinsky was recruiting "middle-class guerillas" to fund and promote his personal vision of social change through artificially induced class warfare.

Alinsky helped fill the void by Communism's demise in America, as Paul Jerricho noted, "there was not even enough people to sit down and figure out what we had done wrong."[17] As Howard Fast observed in the fading ranks of American Communists, "These people lusted for an Armageddon their mad dreams promised them."[18]

Saul Alinsky would teach other radicals how to steal money from corporations and government entities through protests and other disruptive means. There is little doubt that the "art" of his shakedown tactics were learned in part through his mobster in-laws. Alinsky adapted the same methods on a larger scale and called it "social justice," recruiting such students as Cesar Chavez in 1952.[19]

Alinsky's motto was "Pick the target, freeze it, personalize it and polarize it." He would soon infiltrate the Democratic Party and form the very early genesis of the radical left element which is dividing the Democrats today. George Soros would adopt the Alinsky model in the 1990s and transfer the tactics of guilt, smear, deception and attack to untold numbers of websites and non-profit organizations that he is using to advance a dangerous and malevolent agenda not only in America but around the world.

George Soros provides an interesting footnote to this intermediate period of the 1950s during the 20 year battle to destroy the culture on the road to perdition. Soros was a young portfolio manager for an old-money blue-chip investment company when he came to New York, settling in Greenwich Village. The Village was an unusual choice of residence for the Wall Street crowd.

But, Soros enjoyed cruising the late night jazz clubs, basement beatnik bars, and political coffee-houses with their social/sexual/political poetry and prose readings. The "Open Society" of Greenwich Village would almost certainly come to influence him later in life as he learned moral relativism as theology.

Though it is still nuclear whether Soros met the reigning members of the Beat generation during his Village years of the late 1950s, he would eventually become a very close intimate friend of Allen Ginsberg, who he met in the early 1980s. Ginsberg would become a frequent visitor to Soros' plush Fifth Avenue apartment and remained a lifelong friend to Soros even after Ginsberg became a lifetime card-carrying member of NAMBLA. This didn't bother Soros as he was planning his own open-sex society of the future complete with unlimited free drugs for all and no jail time for child molesters. He even named his foundation The Open Society Institute and openly admits to this day that Ginsberg influenced him, especially in advocating the legalization of dangerous drugs.

Again, another example of how one man's "audible hallucination" of a poetry reading from the dead came to empower the young Ginsberg into changing (read: destroying) the culture by captivating gullible fellow demons like Soros. But, Ginsberg was just the icing on the cake of influences that drove Soros into the megalomaniac he is today; the same man fully embraced by Hillary Clinton and Barack Obama.

Much of the "organized chaos" adopted by advocates of cultural decay can be laid at the doorstep of Saul Alinsky and his 1946 counterculture manifesto, *Reveille for Radicals*.

1963-1968

A curious and demented new freak would join the countercultural road circus in 1963. **Dr. Timothy Leary** was fired as a Harvard psychology professor after university administrators noted his perpetual failure to show up for his scheduled classes. But, there was *much more* to the story of the "Nutty Professor's" dismissal than perpetual tardiness.

Three years earlier, in a 1960 road trip to Mexico, a countercultural haven during the 1950s and 1960s, Leary sat down in a dilapidated village saloon and began shooting Tequila after a night of eating hallucinogenic mushrooms. The experience changed Leary's life forever, which is not hard to understand when your brain has been microwaved and soaked with Tequila.

That one night would also, by proxy, become the birth of "life-changing" experiences for millions to follow over the next five decades, though it was often a change from life to death or a *lifetime* of brain-fried psychosis and drug abuse that the nation continues battling today at an escalating pace.

After his "trip" to Mexico, Leary returned to Harvard and received permission to conduct experiments with the active hallucinogen compound LSD. Graduate students were recruited and their "experiences" recorded, many claiming the now famous line of "a deeply religious experience." However, when *undergraduate* students were being "actively recruited" by Leary, not unlike Hefner "actively recruiting" even younger girls, parents complained loudly to the Harvard Administration and Professor Leary was properly booted off campus.[20]

Leary, like all the Beats before him, was rebelling against his middle-class life in which he felt like a "robot" who drove home every evening in a line of automobile tail-lights only to sit-down, mix a martini and go to bed. Leary was already a raging alcoholic and a severely abusive personality. His wife had committed suicide in the late 1950s, leaving Leary with a son and daughter for whom he would become a monster of a role model. But, his role model to the college-aged baby-boomers would be more murderous in its true nature than any other single figure in the 1960s.

Leary fled to New York after his firing from Harvard. The heirs of the Mellon fortune began to give Leary money so that he could fund and further "experiment" with LSD at a sprawling mansion in upstate New York outside the small town of Millbrook. The subjects were little more than a large group of LSD junkies that zoned out and floated about the premises like zombies in *Night of the Living Dead*.

It would not be unusual for an occasional ambulance to show up on the property to take away the brain-dead. The mansion was frequently busted by a local assistant District Attorney named G. Gordon Liddy. Of this period at Millbrook, Leary was quoted as saying, "On this space colony, we were attempting to create a new paganism and a new dedication to life as art."

Meanwhile, back at Harvard, Leary's absence left a void among the students who had participated in his LSD studies and others who had wanted to experience the "trips" their fellow students had taken. An LSD black market sprang up on the edges of the campus at Harvard and would show up at other university campus towns across the country. Timothy Leary's "New Paganism" was not so new after all. In fact, the long arm of Mephistopheles would reach far and wide to wrap around the psychopathic acid-head professor. As Leary often bragged, "I've been an admirer of Aleister Crowley. I think I'm carrying on much of the work he started over a hundred years ago . . . He was in favor of finding yourself . . . I'm sorry he isn't around to appreciate the glories he started."[21]

Leary had joined the long list of Crowleans, always searching and never finding, which by now included Ginsberg, Burroughs, Kerouac, Kinsey, Hefner, Lennon, Jagger and other purveyors and promoters of cultural rot. And there would be many more to follow in their footsteps.

Leary was not above recruiting his own daughter for drug runs south of the border. The two were arrested leaving Mexico with a large haul of marijuana in 1965. "Father" Leary was kind enough to take the rap for his daughter.

For Dr. Timothy Leary, his sole purpose in life would be to wage a full-scale drug legalization campaign with the enthusiastic help of veteran doper and original beatnik Allen Ginsberg who was now serving as the "bridge" to transform the Beat generation into the hippie generation. Leary fought the Marijuana Tax Stamp Law and was cleared of his 1965 bust by the 1969 U.S. Supreme Court. However, he had been busted again the year before in 1968 and was sentenced to a ten year prison term.

In 1967, the Nutty Professor, who was now a walking vegetable, proclaimed before a crowd of approximately 30,000 hippies at Golden Gate Park that it was time to "turn on, tune in and drop out." The great unrealized potential for a significant portion of the peak baby-boomers had been snuffed out by a sociopathic drug addict who was now being labeled a "guru" by the likes of Ginsberg and John Lennon. The print media and television news treated Leary like a countercultural cult hero.

At the same time, the mainstream media completely ignored Leary's role, and their own complicity of free publicity, in starting the drug epidemic which has destroyed hundreds of thousands of lives and cost America billions of dollars to fight and rehabilitate addicts, not to mention the cumulative lost productivity from what could have been the brightest generation of the 20th century.

This is the very reason sadistic parasites like George Soros want drugs legalized; not to save the nation money, but to anesthetize the population into narcoleptic apathy which is much easier to control and whose pockets are much easier to pick.

What the press certainly ignored is the effect on Leary's own children, which may have given the country a periscope into the future effects of drug addiction at the family level up to the national consequence of an epidemic. Throughout Leary's theatrics, his children often cast their father as not only a hopeless drunk, but also as a demented drug fiend.

Leary's daughter, Susan, would eventually commit suicide, much like her mother had done two decades earlier. "Father" Leary would almost totally ignore his own son Jack for more than thirty years. To the increasingly secular liberal, leftist press, these details were not so significant. There was nothing "hip" or "sexy" about a couple of "troubled" children whose dad promised to be the great liberator of the American middle-class comfort level. Like the Beats and Hefner, children were a nuisance that impeded the adult's world of the perfect "high" or ultimate "orgasm."

* * *

While Leary was being bounced out of Harvard in 1963, Hugh Hefner was being hauled off to jail, again. With the death of Marilyn Monroe the year before, Hefner had set his sights on Jayne Mansfield, whose "statistics" far outsized Monroe's. And for Hefner the math was simple; bigger breasts insure bigger bucks.

But, Hefner wanted to "use" Jayne Mansfield as part of a larger campaign to "liberate" the motion picture industry from the Production Code and allow nudity at every opportunity. Hefner long believed that "adult" or "illegitimate" movie theaters should become "legitimized" by changing the rules of Hollywood production and distribution. The key component in his plan was Jayne Mansfield, who agreed to the publication of nude photos in a 1963 issue of *Playboy*.

Of course, Hefner's "bigger is better" marketing plan paid off handsomely when the Mansfield issue was released. Jayne Mansfield was the first mainstream actress to go from Hollywood films to grindhouse films where the main attraction was the "money shot" of nudity. Some in the industry and the public called Mansfield's move as a regression in her career. Hefner campaigned heavily that Mansfield's career was progressive, not regressive and certainly not repressive such as his own "typical Midwestern Methodist repressed upbringing" on which he harped constantly.

THE HOLLYWOOD CULTURE WAR

The grindhouse movies could not be shown in mainstream movie theaters because they did not receive the MPAA seal of approval under the guidelines of the Production Code. However, there were plenty of theaters around the country that showed "stag films" with the deceptive name of "Art House Cinemas." In small towns, the venue was the rogue drive-in theaters on the far outskirts of the county.

To help promote Mansfield's "brave move," which he had encouraged her to pursue, Hefner awarded Mansfield another 1963 photo layout titled "The Nudist Jayne Mansfield" with more provocative photos of Mansfield than previously published. As a result, Hugh Hefner was arrested in 1963 on obscenity charges.

Hefner was acquitted in a trial when the jury split 7 to 5 for acquittal. Hefner would deny that the jury was tampered with by "sympathetic" supporters or local Chicago "family" members. Hefner was unfazed and planned to continue his campaign to legitimize nudity and the swinger's life on every screen in America. In June of 2006, *Men's Fitness* magazine published a poll that determined 36% of men attend a movie just to watch the sex scene. In 1963, that figure would have translated into 100% of men going to "art house" cinemas for the very same reason.

Hefner knew that those "soft-porn" patrons would cross over to mainstream movies if the nudity was photographed "tastefully," which was a must in order to maintain the mainstream theater's core adults who didn't patronize the grindhouse circuit, but just might sit through a few seconds of Jayne Mansfield disrobing. Of course, in Hefner's scenario, there was no room or place for children who would only hinder the orgasmic fantasy of adults.

Hollywood had already tried to push the button of the Production Code with actress Marilyn Monroe's last film, *Something's Got To Give,* in which she was filmed partially nude emerging from a swimming pool. The director, George Cukor, knew the scene would be cut, but at least it allowed him voyeuristic artistic license to "experiment" with nudity in films, not unlike Alfred Kinsey asking Kenneth Anger to masturbate for the Kinsey Institute film archives.

In 1962, the year before Hefner's arrest, the budding porn publisher had begun fleshing out his *Playboy Philosophy* which would take four years to complete and encompass 150,000 words. With Kinsey becoming a distant memory to many Americans and to a whole new generation of the 1960s, Hefner was looking for a "legitimate justification" for his rapidly expanding campaign to take sexual relations away from the exclusive sanctity of one's private life and display them in motion pictures as nothing more than "entertainment" fodder for the price of movie ticket. Hugh Hefner was in the process of taking the theaters of the back street and moving them to Main Street.

Hefner's Playboy Philosophy was being published in a regular column as he worked religiously on his "thesis" between 1962 and 1966. Mansfield, a regular reader of *Playboy*, personally wrote Hefner a letter which started the whole process of stripping her down to nothing and eventually into oblivion, the fate of most women who pose nude for *Playboy*.

As Mansfield wrote "Hef" at this time, "I have just finished reading the October installment of the Playboy Philosophy . . . I strongly support you in your efforts . . . and in your championing each individual's right to make up their own mind."[22] This was just the kind of support Hefner was looking for in his "New Morality" philosophy that would tear the curtains down at the movie theater.

Between 1963 and 1967, Mansfield and Hefner would lead the campaign to "free the screen" from Puritanism; as Hefner referred to American values. In response to Mansfield's letter and her recent nude movie *Promises Promises* in 1963, Hefner wrote a column in Playboy that set the campaign in motion:

> "No capital in the world is more cunning at playing peek-a-boo with the human body than our film capital . . . The recent wave of 'nudie' movies, however, has injected a breath of fresh air upon the scene. Their unpretentious nakedness and their wide public acceptance have helped push bodices down and hemlines up (to where they virtually vanish) in otherwise 'straight' productions. It is therefore fitting and proper that the trail from 'nudie' [illegitimate] to 'straight' [legitimate] be blazed by none other than the undisputed of in-the-altogether brinksmanship, Miss Jayne Mansfield. Jayne now proudly heads the scant list of authentic Hollywood heroines whose feats of bearing do go beyond the call of duty."[23]

Notice Hefner's deceptive self-serving phrases like "wide public acceptance" (It was not) and "authentic Hollywood heroines," (she was not) and "It is therefore fitting and proper" (sounds a little Victorian?) Jayne Mansfield was slowly losing her grip on reality in the 1960s and Hefner was leading her down the path.

Hefner's Playboy philosophy was summed up in his term "in-the-altogether brinksmanship" and later phrases like "reinvent yourself." It was perhaps best summed up by the sign that still hangs on the door of the Playboy mansion, "If you don't swing, don't ring."

The Playboy Philosophy was Crowley and Kinsey couched together in the "hip" language of the sixties. Professor Benjamin DeMott of Amherst summarized Hefner's Playboy Philosophy better than any with eight simple words, "The whole man reduced to his private parts."[24]

In 1966 Hefner hired Robert Anton Wilson as his editor of the Playboy Forum section of the magazine and was given the task of "pushing" Hefner's New Morality philosophy across America and around the world through *Playboy's* international distribution network. What most people outside the *Playboy* publishing office did not know at the time was that Robert Anton Wilson was a deeply devout follower of Aleister Crowley's teachings from *The Book of the Law* and his Thelema New Age religion. Wilson shared his beliefs with the magazines "open minded" staff and with Hefner.

None of this was shocking or a problem to Hefner who was and remains a virulent Christian-basher. Wilson, who despised Jews and Christians, was particularly fond of Crowley's *Diary of a Drug Fiend* and the passage by Crowley which stated, "The true test of the perversity of pleasure is that it occupies a disproportionate amount of the attention." This was the true definition of Hugh Hefner himself.

Hefner also had no problem with Wilson's demon obsession considering his own familiarity with the subject as he watched Jayne Mansfield's descent into Satan worship through the guidance of San Francisco's Anton LeVay and his Church of Satan. As far as Hefner was concerned, if the devil empowered Mansfield to keep stripping, *What the Hell!* (No pun intended.)

By 1966, Mansfield was bragging openly about her "elevation" to High Priestess in the "Church" and wore the trademark black baphonet medallion at the 1966 San Francisco Film Festival. Also in 1966, there were very real signs on the horizon that the Motion Picture Association of America, under its new leader Jack Valenti, was planning to "open up" the movie industry. (We'll come back to the "climax" of Hefner, Mansfield, and Valenti as they truly defined the last stretch of Hollywood's Road to Perdition.)

* * *

Allen Ginsberg was refusing to fade away as the Beat generation was "maturing" by the early 1960s (translation: getting a real life). Ginsberg's "New Vision" for "youth empowerment" was now an obsession. Ginsberg would become the poster child for the emerging hippie movement of the early 1960's as he vigorously worked the east coast and west coast college circuit to keep alive his dream of an oversexed drug-induced generation that would cast off any attempt at materialistic conformity or middle-class dreams.

Ginsberg's new association with Timothy Leary in the 1960's would facilitate both of their goals to hook a new generation on LSD and other drugs. Not only did both men worship LSD, they both embraced the anti-rational offshoot of Indian Buddhism known as Zen. Ginsberg would help shepherd and influence Bob Dylan and Rod McKuen into new forms of song and prose that reflected some eternal flux and "searching" that Ginsberg wanted to maintain.

Ginsberg can be solely credited or blamed for creating the "aimless generation" and would do the same for each successive avant-garde countercultural movement that followed, right up until his death at age 70 when he was trying to "understand" the emerging "Temple of Hip Hop."

Ginsberg would be well-anointed as the father of "San Francisco values," a title also shared by "America's oldest hippie" and fellow NAMBLA member, Harry Hay. One thing Ginsberg always made sure of was epitomized by Bob Dylan, "The times, they are a changing."

Working together, Allen Ginsberg and Timothy Leary were America's biggest drug pushers. But Ginsberg managed to directly connect to the next tier of pushers, such as Jack Kerouac's "On the Road" driver Neal Cassady.

Though Ginsberg had a full-time "lover" in Peter Orlovsky, he maintained a homosexual relationship with Cassady while in California spreading the new hippie gospel with Leary. Cassady was the main character in Kerouac's Beat bible *On the Road* and was given the name Dean Moriarty. Page one began with Kerouac writing, "With the coming of Dean Moriarty began the part of my life you could call my life on the road." Beat "scholars" have tried to unravel the "true meaning" behind that one line.

Another up and coming hippie, Ken Kesey, would befriend Ginsberg in the early 1960s. Along with Leary, Cassady and a small group of others, this handful of people in 1963 and 1964 would wreck more havoc on America than seven years of the Beat generation. Up until that time, LSD was largely an east coast/west coast phenomenon, thanks to Ginsberg and Leary. And, the Beat druggies were mainly a big-city urban affair between 1955 and 1962.

Neal Cassady, Ken Kesey and a group of their followers bought a run-down school bus in 1963 and traveled the country with the banner of "The Merry Pranksters." The group stood out everywhere they traveled because of their long hair, unkempt appearance and brightly painted bus. Their travels were announced in college newspapers and by word of mouth.

When they arrived, young wanabe hippie groupies clamored to take the Electric Kool-Aid Acid Test, LSD-laced drinks that Cassady, Kesey and the others were more than happy to spread around. The national drug epidemic that continues today was largely started by this atrocious handful of hippies with the full guidance and enforcement of Ginsberg and Leary. By 1969, Woodstock and the documentary that followed would seal the image around the world of America as a country on the verge of a nervous breakdown.

One can only imagine the image of the greasy, bearded and disshelved Ginsberg sitting back at his dingy apartment blowing marijuana smoke into the nostrils of his kitty as the poor feline stumbled into the kitchen in disbelief. Even animals were not safe in the presence of this aging beatnik monster "poet."

But, Ginsberg was not satisfied with simple cultural disintegration. He also inserted himself squarely into the political arena by helping to engineer the first major anti-war rally along with SDS leader Tom Hayden at the Berkley-Oakland city limits in protest of America's war against Communism in Vietnam. This first major protest was a well-planned key strategy of the New Left's agenda to disrupt America's determination to stop the global expansion of Communism.

When Hell's Angel's leader Sandy Barger threatened to disrupt the protest of the long-haired "f____ing communist" demonstrators, Allen Ginsberg made a personal visit to Barger's home in Oakland and made a "peace offering" by distributing LSD to Barger and his top lieutenants. When the protests began the next day, the Hell's Angels were nowhere to be found.

* * *

While the hippies were spreading chaos across the country, the author of "orderly revolution," Saul Alinsky, was busy infiltrating the United States federal government by packing many of his "students" into the growing number of federal government agencies created by President Johnson's Great Society. These new programs included VISTA, Head Start, Job Corps and the Community Action Program (CAP) which fell under the Office of Economic Opportunity headed by Kennedy clan member Sergeant Shriver.

The collective effort by Presidents Kennedy and Johnson came to be known as the "War on Poverty." According to authors David Horowitz and Richard Poe, "The federal government spent more than $300 billion on War on Poverty programs. Much of this money went to street radicals like Alinsky."[25] Years later, questions would be raised about the true level of poverty in America which some academics placed as high as one-fourth of the U.S. population! Some of those academics were from the University of Chicago sociology department, many of whom just happened to be friends of Saul Alinsky.

In addition to conducting some of the greatest shakedowns of federal government bureaucracies in the history of America, Alinsky would continue his social activism in the private sector by engineering one of the first major "civil rights shakedowns" at the Eastman Kodak Company in 1967. He managed to receive major concessions, after his friend and U.S. Attorney General Robert F. Kennedy intervened behind the scenes. Jesse Jackson is now the 21st century incarnation of the civil rights shakedown, which is a mob-inspired tactic perfected by Alinsky and currently practiced by thousands of his followers across America.

Saul Alinsky was not happy with the garish tactics of the long-haired, drug-addicted hippies who were doing more harm to "the cause" by shocking the middle-class with their appearance and behavior. This is where Alinsky and Ginsberg shared *no* common ground.

In the late 1960's, shortly before his death, Alinsky began writing *Rules for Radicals* that stressed more subtle and stealth methods for disrupting the social order. One of his rules: Get a haircut! In his book, which was published in 1971,

Alinsky also bragged in a cavalier manner, "I feel confident that I could persuade a millionaire on a Friday to subsidize a revolution for Saturday out of which he would make a profit on Sunday even though he was certain to be executed on Monday."

Before the chain-smoking Alinsky died with a ravished heart of darkness, he would manage to recruit one last middle-class "guerilla" with whom he would share the secrets of his criminal mind. Young Hillary Rodham would even write her 1969 senior thesis on Saul Alinsky, a paper that would reveal the dark origins of Hillary Clinton's politics.

* * *

Jack Kerouac slowly dissolved into the seclusion of his parent's house, eventually moving to Orlando, Florida with his mother and third wife Stella. He spent much of the 1960's watching television and drinking beer while his famous Beat buddies were busy shaking up the "establishment" and the American culture at large. Kerouac didn't want any part of his beatnik past or to participate in the hippie future. Newspaper and magazine articles often were headlined "What Happened to Kerouac?"

When a reporter tracked down the elusive drifter in the late 1960s, he was asked to reflect about his years as beatnik. "I'm not a beatnik, I'm a Catholic." Kerouac pointed to a painting of Pope Paul VI and said, "Do you know who painted that? Me!" They were among the last recorded words that Jack Kerouac was known to have spoken.

Just like Syd Barrett of Pink Floyd and Kurt Cobain of Nirvana who followed in the same anti-establishment footsteps of Kerouac, all had come home to expire. It would turn out that "home" wasn't such a bad place, and being comfortable was not a sin.

The other one third and oddest bird of the former Beat trio, William Burroughs had left a life of opium and pedophilia in Tangier, Morocco to travel to Paris where his recently completed book *Naked Lunch* was being considered for publication. The book was a wickedly depraved nightmare vision of drug-induced hallucinations featuring giant genitals that vaguely resembled insects, or was it the other way around?

Unfortunately, *Life* magazine published a cover story about the book and the Beat generation and, in doing so, gave the whole grotesque movement free publicity that it could never have dreamed possible. Again, the ever-present Allen Ginsberg assisted Burroughs in editing the book and finding a publisher. Burroughs used the $3,000 advance from Grove Press and promptly re-supplied himself with drugs.[26]

This was a bold move for the predatory pedophile drug addict who had just received a suspended sentence in Paris for conspiring to import opiates into

THE HOLLYWOOD CULTURE WAR

France. While he could have faced a stiff sentence, the French judge had learned that Burroughs was a writer and, according to biographer Ted Morgan, a literary career was a "respected profession" in France. And, only in France could a lifelong drug trafficker and malignant child molester be set free to roam again another day (exceptions being Vermont and San Francisco).

The aging beatnik returned again to a life of opium, heroin, marijuana and young boys. *Naked Lunch* was becoming a cult classic among the college hippies of the 1960s with Allen Ginsberg giving it good mouth-to-mouth recessitation to keep the worthless piece of writing alive among the "Oh, hey wow, man" campus freaks.

Hugh Hefner, always a fan of sexual drug-addicted deviance, offered Burroughs a huge advance to write an article for *Playboy,* but Hefner demanded "style" revisions. Was Hefner possibly worried about the reputation of his magazine? It didn't bother "Hef" that he was already in bed with the High Priestess from the Church of Satan.

And, what about little Billy? The son of William Burroughs, who had been sent back to America after daddy shot mommy in a drunken stupor, was now a grown man and a full-fledged alcoholic who would eventually be arrested for prescription fraud in Florida, just like his father decades earlier.

After a stint in jail, Billy Burroughs would continue drinking so heavily that his liver literally disintegrated. The "father" managed to show up, and remarkably, was able to locate one of only two hospitals who performed liver transplants at the time. The "everywhere man" Allen Ginsberg showed up to give his "support" to the young Burroughs and his father during the long recovery period.

These pathetic men as adult and paternal role models were the very reason little Billy was lying in a hospital bed on life support. Billy Burroughs was among the first of millions of children who would be emotionally abandoned by one generation after another in search of selfish commitment to the ultimate "high" and the ultimate "orgasm."

Billy Burroughs, with only a 40% chance of survival, beat the odds and would later cut off all ties and contact with his father, even going so far as to publish an article in *Esquire* describing how his father had ruined his life. He also described an incident where he had been molested by a friend of his father's when only 14 years old.

Billy Burroughs would die four years after the liver transplant when he decided to quit taking the anti-rejection drugs. He joined the graveyard of the Beat generation's forgotten children who got in the way of their parent's pleasure.

* * *

Back at the Playboy mansion, Hugh Hefner was excited about the announcement of **Jack Valenti** as the new president of MPAA in 1966. Valenti had previously served as a chief aide to Vice President and later President Lyndon Johnson upon the assassination of John F. Kennedy on November 22, 1963. As a former ad agency huckster from Texas, Valenti helped Johnson shove huge tax hikes on the backs of every American to fund the largest bureaucracy in the world.

But, after three years, Valenti received a more lucrative offer from the Motion Picture Association of America and he quickly left the White House to take on the dirty laundry job as Hollywood's number one lobbyist in Washington. This was the beginning of Valenti's rabid mission to abolish the Production Code, or "Hays Code" as he preferred to call it. This made Hugh Hefner a very happy man as he expanded *Playboy* magazine's special section "Sex in Cinema." Years later, Valenti would brag endlessly about his role in destroying American culture. The current MPAA website, as of this writing, includes a page by Jack Valenti where he explained his actions in the summer of 1966 when "the national scene was marked by insurrection on the campus, riots in the streets, rise in women's liberation, protest of the young, doubts about the institute of marriage, abandonment of old guiding slogans and the crumbling of social traditions. It would have been foolish to believe that movies, that most creative of art forms, could have remained unaffected by the change and torment in our society"[27]

An interesting omission in Valenti's list of "reasons" for abolishing the Production Code was "churches losing authority" which was included in the list up until 2000. I personally had e-mailed Valenti and challenged his assertion that churches were "losing authority" at a time then, as now, when Christianity and evangelism was on the rise with more churches and more Christians in America than at anytime in history. By the fall of 2000, that line was struck from Valenti's web article titled, "How It All Began."

"Change" and "torment" in our society? "Protest of the young" and "crumbling of social traditions?" The "torment" that Valenti was referring to was caused by a small handful of perpetually malcontent people who were being promoted by an increasingly insular and sadistic media which gave free and *encouraging* publicity to every drug addict and sexual deviant mentioned in this chapter whose secondary occupations varied from poet, writer, professor and publisher.

Jack Valenti was altering the oversight of the most powerful medium in the world, motion pictures (and eventually television). And, his reason for doing so was the cumulative result of the previous twenty years of chaos that began with Allen Ginsberg, Jack Kerouac, William S. Burroughs, Alfred Kinsey, Hugh Hefner, Saul Alinsky, Timothy Leary, Ken Kesey, Neal Cassady and a host of others who wanted to "shake things up" by invoking the New Age so popularized by the lost generation's spiritual godfather of moral desecration, Aleister Crowley.

THE NEW AGE CONNECTION

- *New Vision* .... Allen Ginsberg
- *New Sexuality* .... Alfred Kinsey
- *New Morality* .... Hugh Hefner
- *New Paganism* .... Timothy Leary
- *New Kind of American Movie* .... Jack Valenti
- *New Radicalism* .... Saul Alinsky

* * *

Instead of stepping up to the plate to make a stand for even basic cultural decency, Valenti caved in to all the 1960's degenerates by declaring, "It would have been foolish to believe that movies could have remained unaffected." What Valenti was saying is that he totally agreed—unconditionally without protest—with everything espoused by less than a dozen beatniks, hippies, freaks, drug addicts, sexual miscreants and pedophiles that were *very easy to resist* if only someone with influence, like himself, would have stood up and said, "ENOUGH ALREADY; PULL UP YOUR ZIPPER!"

Valenti conveniently forgot that the very reason for the inception of the MPAA in 1922 was to counter the increasingly negative and destructive images and messages flowing out of Hollywood in front of and behind the camera, especially the drug and alcohol-fueled orgies, overdoses, deaths, adultery and even murder.

We didn't know Jack then, but we know Jack now. And we're going to learn more about the source of darkness that fell upon the deep.

* * *

Hugh Hefner took great notice and pleasure in 1966 of the promotional campaign for director Mike Nichol's production of *Who's Afraid of Virginia Woolf.* The movie, based on alcoholic writer Edward Albee's play, would be the first mainstream movie to carry a "Mature" theme warning. In other words, leave the children at home with the baby-sitter, there's no more room at the movie theater.

Except for the Gang of Four and a small group of industry insiders, the rest of America was being kept in the dark about Valenti's new plan to start segregating the American moviegoing audience into a sliding age scale of what is and what isn't "acceptable." He was replacing one production code with another, only Valenti's code more closely resembled the New Morality of Hugh Hefner's Playboy Philosophy. Valenti was granted "special treatment" at Hefner's mansion in Chicago and Los Angeles.

Hefner could see the writing on the wall. He would come to acquaint himself very intimately with Valenti and the "progress" being made at the MPAA. With children largely out of the way, Hefner could cross-promote movies in his magazine worldwide as long as they contained a New Morality money shot of nudity. And the new generation of "dope smoking hippie" producers and directors saw great potential in cross-marketing through Playboy. After all, they knew all about morality and the prerequisite lack thereof.

And, so did Jayne Mansfield. Hefner was positioning Mansfield to make a comeback to the "legitimate" theater in a very big and bare way. The 1960 version of an internet "hit counter" or "word search" was known as the printed "word count." Even in 1960, before she started stripping for Hefner and the low-rent movie theaters, Jayne Mansfield topped all press polls for more words about her in print than anyone else in the world. Even John Kennedy couldn't come close.

The world press would soon award Jayne Mansfield the title of "World's Number One Sex Symbol."[28] She would appear on over 500 magazine covers in her lifetime. Mansfield knew her day was coming when she could bare it all for America and the world and the MPAA would even award her a rating.

By 1967, Mansfield was already in production on her first "serious" role in which she would play a prostitute, a cripple and a pregnant mother. And there would be ample room for nudity. With "M" ratings abounding in 1967, the following year of 1968 would see Valenti establish the X-rating along with the other alphabet soup age restrictions. If the producers could hold out for another year, they could release the film in mainstream theaters uncut and Mansfield could thank Mr. Hefner and Mr. Valenti for "liberating" her—of her clothes.

Unfortunately for all the eager-beaver liberators, Mansfield was maintaining a curious side-show private life that would result in one of Hollywood's most often-told tragedies that would surpass even the strange case of the Black Dahlia.

A former carnival barker, hoodlum and "ghost hunter" for the San Francisco police department named Howard Stanton Levey was best known around town as the organist for the Lost Weekend cocktail lounge. On the side, he was also the self-proclaimed leader of the Order of the Trapezoid, a Satanic cult that drew interest from many in the Bay Area and Los Angeles in the early 1960s.

By 1966, the Lost Weekend organist shaved his head and became Anton LeVay, the self-proclaimed first "priest" of the Church of Satan which he established in a dilapidated three story house in San Francisco. Mansfield, already deeply involved in astrology and other occult pursuits, was eager to meet the new High Priest of Satan.

Jayne Mansfield jumped on board LeVay's bandwagon to hell without hesitation and joined the "church" as a full-fledged member. In fact, Anton LeVay, like Hugh Hefner, could credit Mansfield with the growth of his cult among the

THE HOLLYWOOD CULTURE WAR

Hollywood crowd. Only Sammy Davis, Jr. could rival Mansfield in their mutual zest of recruiting "converts for Satan."

Mansfield was eagerly anticipating her comeback to the big screen in a big way. But, she wanted to make sure the roles would keep coming. Mansfield feared becoming a one time "big bang" hit and then fading into oblivion. According to LeVay, Mansfield would plead with him for Satanic blessings and curses, calling him several times a day.[29]

She also sought out LeVay to help rid herself of an abusive boyfriend, Sam Brody. As Mansfield said of her meeting with LeVay, "Mr. LeVay called me into a back room! There he told me, the devil has placed a curse on Sam Brody . . . there is a heavy black cloud over him . . . He'll be killed in a car crash."[30]

Jayne Mansfield must have felt "on top of the world" in 1967. Hugh Hefner had reignited her career as poster girl for the New Morality. Jack Valenti was paving the way for the New Kind of American Movie, and Anton LeVay had granted her everything she wanted at his new Church of Satan—with a little help from the long arm of Mephistopheles—because he was, after all, a devout disciple of Mr. New Age himself, Aleister Crowley.

A few months after LeVay's last meeting with Mansfield, the blond bombshell was traveling with Brody on a stretch of Mississippi Gulf Coast highway near Biloxi when her car slammed into a tractor-trailer truck at a dark intersection in the road. Brody was killed instantly, as was Mansfield, whose career was cut short as her head lay in the back seat of the car, decapitated by the windshield according to her death certificate.[31]

Hugh Hefner was upset, truly. He was upset over all the possible future revenues he could have garnered from her future in the movie industry, especially since she embraced the Playboy philosophy, which basically was no different than LeVay's. In their worlds, rules did not exist. Anything goes. Even running a red light would be an act of honorable defiance. And, that's about all Jayne Mansfield is remembered for today when her name comes up in trivial pursuit.

*   *   *

By 1968, Hollywood's long road to perdition had rolled over the last bump in the road. Jack Valenti was preparing to announce a New Age in moviemaking as a "result" of the "torment" and "turbulence" of the 1960s. As he explained his reasoning to officially end the Golden Era of filmmaking, "The result of all was a 'new kind' of American movie—frank and open, and made by filmmakers subject to very few self-imposed restraints."[32]

What Jack Valenti and his philosophical fellow travelers didn't tell the public was that the New Age didn't necessarily mean a "better age," but was actually a blueprint for a new "dark age" which Valenti unleashed upon the world on

November 1, 1968, the first shot in the culture war between Hollywood and the global international cultural community.

The true results were immediate and sadly predictable. The movies that came out the following years were largely off limits to anyone under the age of 17 years old with titles such as *Midnight Cowboy, Easy Rider, Carnal Knowledge, and Five Easy Pieces.* Many of these and other films incorporated the New Age philosophy of "anything goes" with all the glamorization of drug use, obligatory sex, perversity, ultra-shock violence, hustling, profanity, adultery and the endless ad nauseum attack on the "establishment."

Even movies that were accessible to youth and families reflected the movie industry's pent up desire to destroy family life with such titles as 1968's *How To Save your Marriage (and Destroy Your Life)*. Dean Martin fans were sorely disappointed.

Only a high-paid huckster like Jack Valenti could rationalize this enormous broadside to the American culture by intentionally misinterpreting an April 1968 United States Supreme Court decision which basically upheld the constitutional power of towns, cities, and local governments to prevent the exposure of children to books and films that could not be denied to adults.[33]

In effect, the Supreme Court was saying that the Production Code was perfectly legal, appropriate and constitutional. In fact, the inception of the Production Code in 1922 had also been intended to stem the tide of thousands of separate city movie codes that made nationwide distribution of movies an exercise in futility.

Even though the 1968 Supreme Court ruling upheld a local government's right to go further in protecting children from the nightmarish drug-soaked fantasies of Hollywood adults, most felt that the Production Code was doing a fine job in the Golden Era of motion pictures which was drawing in 44 million people *per week* in 1965.

But, only a king of double-speak and moral ambidexterity like Jack Valenti could read the Supreme Court decision through a glass darkly and insert his own personal interpretation, shake it upside down and declare his version as precedent. After reading the court decision, Valenti declared, "It was plain that the old system of self-regulation began with the formation of the MPAA in 1922 had broken down."[34]

Nobody with their sharpest and most acute legal vision could find anything remotely related to a system "broken down" in the court's decision. Jack Valenti had invented this reinterpretation out of thin air and justified his version for secretly forming the Ratings Scheme which is still wrecking havoc on American and other world cultures to this day. A scheme based on a lie is still governing the production of movies coming out of Hollywood where lying, cheating and stealing are a way of life.

After dismantling the Production Code, Jack Valenti would boast that "the movie industry would no longer 'approve or disapprove' the content of a film."[35] Of course, that too was a lie and *remains* a lie. The Ratings Scheme is all about what content can or cannot be allowed on screen in order to receive a rating and the coveted MPAA seal. Valenti simply replaced one code with another. It's the same old Hollywood shell game. By 1968, Hollywood's road to perdition did not end. It became a superhighway wider than 1-75 north of Atlanta and faster than the autobahn through Nuremberg. The footprints of Valenti, Hefner, Ginsberg and all the New Age beatniks, hippies and radicals that preceded them can be seen in virtually every theater, on every television set, on every single magazine newsstand, every porn site on the internet and in the attitudes of the generation's children who drop F-bombs and reply "that sucks" as casually as "see ya mom." And, the hypersexual culture created by the New Agers have caused these very same children to become predatory victims of perverted adults who are most commonly their own school teachers. Joe Kovacs of *WorldNetDaily* referred to this as "the sexualization of America."

The first line of Allen Ginsberg's *Howl* is the most telling, even though it was written in 1955, "I saw the best minds of my generation destroyed by madness."

Could Jack Valenti not read between the lines of Ginsberg's angry *"Howl?"* What Ginsberg was really saying was, *"I saw to it that* the best minds of my generation *would be* destroyed by madness."

POST SCRIPTS AND POST MORTEMS

Allen Ginsberg—The original red-diaper-doper baby who heard William Blake reciting "Ah, Sunflower" in an "audible hallucination" in 1948 maintained a hand in every "movement" or "cause" of the New Age that flitted across the cultural scene for another 50 years. He was largely the force and the face behind the promotion of the Beat generation which he transitioned into the hippie movement, anti-war movement, pro-drug movement and the radicalization and politicalization of homosexuality.

In the 1980s, Ginsberg became a lifelong critic of tobacco, and cigarette smoking in particular and pushed for "smoke free" environments. However, he advocated that smoking marijuana was not only safe, but highly recommended. It was becoming clear by the early 1990s that years of smoking marijuana, taking LSD and countless other drugs were exacting their toll on the old beatnik's brain as he approached the age of 70.

Ginsberg's favorite and longest-lasting campaign was the promotion of sexual perversity. Even many of his closest friends in the homosexual community could not support Ginsberg's decision to join NAMBLA (North American Man Boy

Love Association). Ginsberg was long suspected of pedophilia as he grew older and his circle of boys grew younger.

Ginsberg denied any involvement with underage boys, but refused to define "underage." Like most aging Beats and hippies in the 1990s, he had fallen under the spell of Clintonian speech tactics such as the definition of "is." But, Ginsberg insisted he joined NAMBLA purely for reasons of supporting "free speech."[36]

Ginsberg waxed enthusiastic about unfettered free speech and association at the same time taking advantage of that "right" by describing his otherwise "general admiration" for young boys as a "celebration" of the "human form divine." Ginsberg's support of NAMBLA only grew stronger even as the ACLU stepped in to defend NAMBLA's effort to reduce the age of consent to 12 years of age. Ginsberg was 100% behind the ACLU's "pro bono" support of NAMBLA after one of its followers murdered a young boy with instructions from the NAMBLA "playbook" of seducing boys. Ginsberg was a long time friend of the ACLU's radical homosexual director, Anthony Romero.

Further, Ginsberg remained a close friend to fellow beatnik pederast Edward Burroughs whose later books advocated child molestation and child murder. Ginsberg always encouraged Burroughs to "push the limits" and in doing so gave immoral "empowerment" to all the sexual deviants of the second half of the 20th century and beyond.

George Soros remained a close intimate friend for the remainder of Ginsberg's life and "credited" Ginsberg for shaping his own "openness" about drugs and a more "open sexual society." Ginsberg remained a life-long drug addict and died in 1997 with his lover of 50 years, Peter Orlovsky by his side.

William Burroughs—By the mid 1970s, Burroughs was still entertaining the "Ugly Spirit" that had possessed him in Mexico 25 years earlier. A young Beat generation devotee named James Grauerholz came up with the idea of promoting Burroughs on "reading tours" much as he had done previously in promoting rock concerts. This would support Burroughs for the next two decades. Grauerholz even sunk so low as to navigate the murky underworld of each city on the traveling tour in order to buy drugs for Burroughs.

When *People* magazine began hitting the newsstands in 1974, celebrity worship took off with fervor and Burroughs began to hang around New York punks and acid-heads like Patti Smith, Andy Warhol and Dennis Hopper.

Burroughs' writing would "earn" him a place in the American Academy and Institute of Arts and Letters in 1983. It was Allen Ginsberg pulling the strings behind the scenes at the academy to make this possible. (Is this the example of literary acclaim to be achieved by new generations of young writers?)

Of his novel interest in having sex with young boys while strangling them to death, Burroughs, almost 70, remarked, "Certainly, who wouldn't? I can go as low as 15, perhaps 14 . . . I like boys."[37] Paul McCartney befriended Burroughs and became a fan of his perverted writing just as he had done a decade earlier in his worship of Aleister Crowley.

Director David Cronenberg, who said he could relate to Burroughs' pedophile strangulation fantasies, begged to direct the movie version of *Naked Lunch* which was released in 1991. The film of insect-type genitalia walking across tables and furniture was a big hit for movie critics and a big bomb for movie audiences except for the young brain-fried glue-sniffers and druggies who sat in the front row moaning, "Oh wow, man! Check that out!"

Cronenberg would use his "Burroughsian" style of filmmaking in the 1992 production of *Crash* about a young couple who become sexually aroused at the site of gruesome blood-soaked auto accidents. Another bomb, brought to the silver screen with the Jack Valenti seal of approval.

Burroughs delved deeper into the occult by 1993, joining a mystic organization called IOT that practiced a Crowley form of sex magick and perversion known as "chaos magic." His continuing descent into hell with his friend "The Ugly Spirit" made him a favorite among the rock music crowd. The group Steely Dan was named after a sex toy in *Naked Lunch.*

Burroughs' increasingly shameless decadence made him a special favorite of Bono and U-2 who were becoming famous for their concert performances of *The Fly, Mephisto* and *Sympathy for the Devil.* Bono and U-2 were such big fans of the 83-year old Burroughs, they even featured him in their 1997 music video "Last Night on Earth" which ended with a close-up of the walking skeleton's drug-drenched eyes. Burroughs would remain a major influence on Bono from that point on.

Three weeks after filming the music video for U-2, Burroughs was struck with a massive heart attack and died on August 2, 1997. Unfortunately, his sick collection of writings has gained a cult following among creative types mainly in the television industry, who often insert "inspired" scenes into various episodic television shows that are only noticed by hard-core Burroughs fans.

Jack Kerouac—The original Beat, whose novel *On the Road* was recently cited by *USA Today* as the "Beat generation's bible," had moved to Orlando in the mid-1960s with his mother and third wife Stella. By 1969, Kerouac was still watching daytime game shows and drinking alcohol from morning until night.

One afternoon, while watching television, Kerouac's mouth began to fill with blood as he wrenched in pain from his abdomen. Rushed to a hospital in St. Petersburg, he was diagnosed with esophageal bleeding that was indicative of advanced liver cirrhosis due to alcoholism. He was beyond help and died shortly after arriving, having bled to death. Jack Kerouac was only 47. His entire estate was valued at $91.00.

In January of 2007, Indianapolis Colts owner James Irsay announced that the 120 foot long "final scroll" for *On the Road* would be touring the U.S. in commemoration of its publication as a book in 1957. This is the same scroll Irsay purchased at Christies auction for $2.43 million. During the Christies auction, the scroll, a "spontaneous bop prosidy" as Ginsberg called it, was displayed, handled and guarded as if it were the sacred writings of Moses.

In 2007 Viking Press released the 50th anniversary edition of Kerouac's drunken and drug-induced nightmare including a reprint of Gilbert Millstein's' book review in *The New York Times* of September 5, 1957 which declared the book's publication as an "historic occasion." That, more than the worthless writing of *On the Road,* propelled the book's popularity. The re-release along with the publication of the "original scroll" by Viking reveals the deviated sexual psyche of the tormented writer from Ozone Park. Had he lived, Jack Kerouac may have been amazed to discover that a "large type" edition of *On the Road* was also set for release in 2007. He would have been 85 years old.

In 1999, original *Tonight Show* host and comedian Steve Allen said, "It is generally agreed on both the political right and left that our whole culture is sliding down a moral sewer." Allen may not have realized that one of the authors of American cultural rot was a guest on his show in 1957.

A sweating, shaking and pale addict named Jack Kerouac read portions of *On the Road* to a nationwide television audience. Those who tuned in that night sat in stunned silence as Kerouac rambled on in his spontaneous prose. Allen finally reached over and asked, "Are you nervous?" To which Kerouac replied, "Ah, naw."

Kerouac's *On the Road* driver, traveling buddy and part-time lover to Allen Ginsberg would precede Kerouac to the graveyard by one year. Neal Cassady, who later sang the praises of LSD for Timothy Leary, was in Mexico and hopped up on acid and alcohol as he walked between towns on railroad tracks after a wedding party. Sometime in the early morning hours, Cassady passed out and his bloated dead body was later found off to the side of the tracks. He was 41 and contributed absolutely nothing to society except the spread of drug addiction to American youth with the "Merry Pranksters" on a scale unprecedented up until that time.

Caleb Carr, best-selling author of *The Alienist,* said he remembered the Beat generation leaders best as a bunch of "loud drunks."

Alfred Kinsey—The author of the 1948 book *Sexual Behavior in the Human Male* was heralded by many in scientific circles, sociologists, "progressive" politicians and the media as a true "scientist" who legitimized the sexually deviant "urges" of humans even to the point of proclaiming that "loving sex" between adults and children was not only possible, but normal. This was obviously good news to Alien Ginsberg and William Burroughs.

And Kinsey's declaration that right and wrong were relative and basically impossible to define along a "continuous curve" of human behavior became the scientific atonement for the 1904 declaration of the New Age by Aleister Crowley. As author E. Michael Jones observed, Kinsey was "attempting to delegitimize the norm and substitute deviance in its place."[38]

Again, this was great news for the Beats who would pass their understanding of Kinsey on to the hippies and downward through the avant-garde countercultural generational slide. The reigning king of genitalia obsession, Hugh Hefner, would consider Kinsey's book as the bible for his lifelong "tasteful" molestation of girls and women. Kinsey was the true foundation of Hefner's Playboy Philosophy, also known as the "New Morality."

The American Psychiatric Association would quietly reference Kinsey's "research" as the reason for removing homosexuality from its list of mental disorders in 1973. Even homosexuals have sought out "better science" than Kinsey to explain homosexuality.

The problem with Kinsey was that almost all of his research was a sham and remains clouded in mystery to this day by the very institute founded in his name. The most shocking accusation was that most of the data on child sexuality was obtained by the largest *alleged* incident of mass child molestation in American history. Amazingly, though Kinsey died in 1956, his research went largely unchallenged until July 21, 1981 at the 5th World Congress of Sexology in Jerusalem.

An American researcher named Dr. Judith Reisman reflected on the reaction to her paper which questioned, finally, the actual specifics of Kinsey methodology. "I was confident my sexology colleagues would be as outraged as I was by these tables [tables 30-34] and the child data describing Kinsey's reliance on pedophiles as his child sex experimenters."[39]

Reisman also questioned pages 160 and 161 from Kinsey's 1948 book concerning children and infants as young as two months "enjoying" being sexually stimulated. How, she challenged the audience, did rape and molestation of children ever make the transition from criminal activity into research?[40]

Reisman's confidence was understandably shaken when most of the attendees at the conference condemned her paper, concluding in their post-Kinsey state of denial that children could, indeed, have "loving sex" with adults.[41] The child molesters at NAMBLA and their supporters at the ACLU are still celebrating.

Of course, all of these points were left out of the 2005 movie *Kinsey* starring Liam Neeson. Hollywood, like Hefner, wouldn't dare question Kinsey whose "research" provided a convenient mitigating standard for their own atrocious over-stimulated sexual misbehavior on screen and off. Kinsey gives Hollywood license to continue defining decency and deviance down in cooperation with the post-Valenti MPAA.

By the early 1990s, the National Institutes of Health were investigating the Kinsey Institutes grant records to determine how millions of dollars were spent by the institute, which apparently kept poor records of funds both coming and going. Also, hundreds of thousands of state tax dollars were granted to the Kinsey Institute each year with little or no meaningful public accountability.

Patrick Buchanan publicly reported the Reisman charges in July of 1983, writing "If Dr. Riesman's charges hold up in the storm that is coming, Kinsey will wind up on the same ethical and scientific shelf now reserved for the German doctors who conducted live experiments on Jewish children. And he will belong there."[42]

Timothy Leary—After being sent to prison for his 1968 drug charge, Leary eventually escaped with the help of radicals who many believed had ties to the New Left's ultra radical offshoot, the violent Weather Underground. Leary spent much of the early and mid 1970s on the run in Europe and even traveled as far as Afghanistan.

Timothy Leary eventually returned to the United Sates and was rumored to have cooperated with federal authorities about the actions and whereabouts of various radical groups, including the Weather Underground. Allen Ginsberg was said to be "furious" with Leary's "ratting out" members of "the movement" and was largely shunned by his former hippie friends. Governor Jerry "Moonbeam" Brown, himself an aging hippie, granted a release for Leary from prison in the late 1970s.

Timothy Leary, along with Ginsberg, Cassady, Kesey and a small handful of others were the key active perpetrators of drug addiction in America which the media overlooked as a lethal epidemic and instead crowned Leary as the LSD "guru" of the 20th century. From the 1980's on, Leary led a largely wasted life living in a hyper-space science fiction world of his own. He earned money on the lecture circuit but was eventually a lost cause that college students of the 1990s couldn't and wouldn't relate to.

Leary is noted for having established one of the first internet websites in 1990. As an accomplished computer programmer, Leary may have declared one last prophetic observation. He noted that the internet would be the "LSD of the 90's."

During this time, the 70 year old Leary began to hang around the techno-pop crowd and was spotted at many alternative rock clubs and concerts, including an embarrassing appearance at a Smashing Pumpkins concert. Eager to be "in" again, Leary began to drink heavily as he had in the late 1950s, and 1960s. He also developed an affinity for cigarettes as he remained in a stage of "arrested development."

By 1995, Dr. Timothy Leary was diagnosed with inoperable prostate cancer. Leary found this to be an exciting time. He was finally able to ingest illegal drugs

THE HOLLYWOOD CULTURE WAR

legally, preferring prescription pain killers and morphine, and he stepped up his favorite pastime of swilling martinis and smoking more cigarettes.

Leary had an opportunity to reconcile with his son Mark with whom he had rarely communicated in over thirty years. However, Leary was so busy chatting with a couple of his fellow ex-cons from Harvard days that he wouldn't even take the time to visit with his son, who finally left the circus environment that was always his father's life and home.

Dr. Timothy Leary believed that a pod-cast of his death would be both "educational" and "entertaining." In 1996 he spoke his last words, "Why not?" as he glanced at the video camera by his bed. The man who coined the phrase, "Turn on, tune in, drop out" had finally tuned out and dropped out forever. As someone muttered, "Now that's entertainment!"

In 1997 Timothy Leary's cremated remains were blasted into outer space along with the remains of "Star Trek" creator Gene Rodenberry and 24 others. It is uncertain whether the Pegasus rocket made it through earth's atmosphere or not before releasing all the dead body dust. But, reports of global warming began surfacing back on earth shortly thereafter.

Unfortunately, the man that the popular media proclaimed as a feel good "guru" has left a deadly legacy that continues today. On February 22, 2007, Lou Dobbs of CNN reported the results of a study that estimated more than 6.4 million Americans take drugs, legal and illegal, just for the sake of "getting high." Many of those Americans are already addicted, many will suffer lifetime pain and affliction, and many will die just for the sake of "getting high."

Hugh Hefner—With Jack Valenti's "free screen" movement of 1968, nudity and sex in mainstream movies finally became a reality, much as Hefner had anticipated. Hefner had been lobbying heavily for the move since 1963 when Jayne Mansfield stripped in "Promises, Promises" for the backstreet grindhouse theaters.

Under Hefner's Playboy philosophy of the "New Morality," the illegitimate became legitimate. Much like his idol and moral guide, Alfred Kinsey, Hefner believed in the "continuous curve" in which concepts of right and wrong were all relative. Hugh Hefner credited Alfred Kinsey's 1948 New Sexuality as the basis for his own New Morality which became "sanctified" for mass consumption by Jack Valenti's "New Kind of American Movie" in 1968.

What began as junk science at Indiana University in 1948 became the basis for a new movie rating scheme in 1968. And much of that 20 year road to perdition can be laid at the feet of Hugh Hefner.

In a George Washington University interview, Hefner spoke about witnessing the riots surrounding the 1968 Democratic National Convention, saying that it helped further "radicalize" him. When asked about the part he played in shaping and promoting the "Sexual Revolution" and the New Age of morality, Hefner gloated, "I take a great deal of pride in that."[43]

In the same interview, Hefner was asked "How do you think the American dream evolved?" Of course, for Hefner, the *true* answer would have been his admission as a malignant voyeur and infectious sex-addict clown scouring the country for teen-age girls to strip for his camera. But, Hefner passed the buck to the industry for which he worships above all else, "I think to some extent the reinforcement of it [the American dream] comes from Hollywood."[44]

The move of the Playboy mansion from Chicago to Hollywood was further evidence of where Hefner's heart and soul resided. Hollywood was Mecca and the mansion would be both home and temple. His own personal movie collection is nestled in a large room that directly adjoins his bedroom, and may well be the third largest collection of pornography in the world after the Kinsey Institute and the collection of North Korea's mentally ill leader, Kim Jong IL.

And, as a gesture of solidarity with the Timothy Leary school of "cool," Hugh Hefner never took a firm stand against drug use in his publication for fear of alienating his "hip" readers. And the glare of that neglect would shine brightly as Hefner and the Playboy mansion became the target of a major federal grand jury investigation in 1974 into cocaine trafficking at Hefner's home and the offices of Playboy Enterprises. This all culminated in Hefner's executive assistant, Bobbie Arnstein, being sentenced to 15 years for conspiracy involving a large cocaine sale.[45] Arnstein claimed Hefner had no knowledge of the cocaine trafficking and before she was to report to prison, Arnstein committed suicide.

By this time in the early 1970's, *Playboy* was selling 7 million issues a month. But the "pubic wars" began when *Penthouse* arrived on the scene and copied the *Playboy* format with one exception. The *Penthouse* women were "leg spreaders" who took away many of Hefner's "readers" who were getting bored just looking at "nude boobs."

This set off a flurry of even more copycats including the monster revolter of all time, Larry Flynt's *Hustler* magazine. It was all the natural progression of the Sexual Revolution which was actually a cultural regression. There are even student groups at Harvard, Columbia, Vassar and Boston University that publish their own porn magazines, some with the full support of the university administration.

Hefner maintained his cool, claiming that his magazine maintained "higher standards," meaning "soft core" porn. It was Hefner who largely popularized the phrases "soft core" and "hard core" as manipulative language to define decency down. Of course, Hefner's declaration of "higher standards" was just another lie in his very public pubic war with the competition. In reality, the Playboy empire was actually becoming one of the largest producers of hard core pornography in the world. This became official with the 2006 acquisition of Club Jenna, Inc.

In addition, Hefner acquired the deviant porn channel Spice Digital Network which is beamed by satellite into 72 countries around the world. Hefner was not satisfied with dragging down American culture, his plans are to take the whole world down with him, nation by nation.

Just as Hefner had no respect for American cultural standards, he maintains a hostile and aggressive marketing push into other countries such as Indonesia. With the world's largest Muslim population, Hefner opened a *Playboy* office in Indonesia in early 2006 and the building was stoned by over one hundred protestors. Hefner plans to keep the Indonesian office open even if it means the slaughter of its local staff by Islamic militants. But, for Hefner, they will have died spreading the mantra of the New Morality.

Hefner's former Forum editor Robert Anton Wilson continued supporting Hefner's sexual revolution right up until his death in January of 2007. As part of his last will and testament, the self-proclaimed devil worshipper requested that his ashes be blown into the faces of evangelical Christian leaders.

In 2005, Harper Collins published *Playground; A Childhood Lost Inside the Playboy Mansion* by Jennifer Saginor, the daughter of Hugh Hefner's close friend and doctor, Mark Saginor, or "Dr. Feelgood" as he was known by the mansion's bunnies, staff and guests.

After suffering and recovering from a stroke in 1985, Hefner invited Saginor to move into the mansion and extended the invitation to his very young daughter, Jennifer, who was given her own bedroom. Already known by Hollywood celebrities and sports figures as Dr. Q, for Quaalude, Dr. Saginor made sure everyone was accommodated for their physical and mental "prescription needs."

The ultimate victim was the young daughter Jennifer who was largely neglected by her father and was surrounded by role models who existed in the moral swamp of the Playboy mansion. As one reader said, "By the time she was 14, Jennifer was doing drugs and celebrities."

In a December 28, 2006 interview with Hollywood internet blogger Luke Ford, Jennifer Saginor reflected back on how Hefner's world had warped her perception of reality, saying "I thought everyone was on drugs. I thought everyone was bisexual. I thought everyone had neglectful parents." She added, "I do believe in God . . . if I didn't believe in something greater than myself, I probably would have committed suicide."

Again, this brings up the question: Where is the local and county police departments and drug investigative units? What about child social services? Is Hugh Hefner an accomplice to pedophilia at the mansion? After all, he does have an arrest record of contributing to the delinquency of a minor going back to the late 1950s. There is more than a fleeting allegiance to his idol Alfred Kinsey. When Anna Nicole Smith died of a drug overdose in February 2007, Hugh Hefner issued a brief statement that his "prayers" were with the family. What prayers? To what god? Hefner is a die-hard atheist.

Smith's death was a perfect example of Hefner's ongoing five decades old modus operandi: Take a "reasonably" attractive woman embroiled in controversy and convince her to pose nude for his magazine so that she can "liberate" herself. Afterwards, it's "good-bye" and "next?" After her death, Smith was only referred to as a former *Playboy* centerfold, playmate, model, bunny and stripper. Smith was everything the octogenarian pervert was seeking; a twisted hybrid of Marilyn Monroe and Jayne Mansfield on steroids, or in this case, methadone. Within five days of her death, a movie script was close to completion.

As of this writing, Hefner had celebrated his 82nd birthday and remains a sexual predator of international proportions and a de-facto drug abuse advocate by proxy. Dr. Victoria Zdrok, a psychologist and former visitor to the mansion, commented on Fox News about the drug problem, "At the mansion, it is widespread."[46] Hugh Hefner remains the last living original contributor to the cultural decline of America during the 20 year journey of Hollywood's Road to Perdition.

"Hef" provides almost weekly photo opportunities for the press of his current "crop" of three blond bimbo Barbie-doll look-a-like girlfriends, one of whom claims to be pregnant from time to time. If she ever does give birth, Los Angeles County authorities should demand the baby be tested for traces of drugs in its infant system.

In Hefner's world, children are irrelevant and good for nothing more than grooming as a future *Playboy* subscriber or *Playboy* bunny.

Saul Alinsky—The underground radical who weaved his web of deception just below the radar screen of the printed press and modern media would have one last book to write. In 1971, Alinsky published *Rules for Radicals* in which he chided the 1960s radicals whose increasingly freakish behavior and appearance probably did more to solidify the conservative base than any other social or countercultural movement in American history. From 1968 on, five out of seven presidents would be Republicans.

The dope-smoking, sex-in-the-streets, profanely vulgar hippies of the Abbie Hoffman and Allen Ginsberg school made Alinsky's goal of shaking down American government tax money and corporate business profits much more difficult. In *Rules for Radicals,* he taught activists how to blend in and work "within the system" in order to achieve socialistic radical redistribution of wealth and foment never-ending class warfare. And, for many, that meant tucking in shirt-tails.

It took awhile for the tucked-in shirts to catch on, but by 1980 most men and women no longer sported long hair or ragged shirts except tie-dyed in the wool die-hards who refused to assimilate, even if it meant destroying the hated "establishment" covertly. But, the majority that took Alinsky's advice became known as "Yuppies."

However they were still detectable to a keen eye who recognized the olive-drab "dress" clothing of women and collarless "dress" shirts for men who preferred a tiny black-onyx top button in lieu of a necktie which they were convinced was "the noose of the establishment." And a refusal to spank their kids for wrong doing was a dead give away, after all, in the New Age world there was no such thing as "doing wrong."

Alinsky's lasting and most destructive legacy was a seminal event in 1969 when the aging radical met a young Wellesley college student during a field trip planned by her liberal Methodist youth pastor, Don Jones. Jones had already been indoctrinated by Alinsky's church infiltration methods and often invited Jones to bring his youth group to the offices of his Industrial Areas Foundation. To Jones, this was as close as he could get to introducing his youth group to the Chicago underworld's version of Jesus Christ.

On this one particular field trip, Saul Alinsky made a big impression on Hillary Rodham, the Wellesley student who was also president of her student body. She even decided to write her senior thesis on Alinsky, which she titled, *There is Only the Fight . . . An Analysis of the Alinsky Model.*

Alinsky was impressed with the Wellesley senior, who was easy to impress, and he even let young Hillary read the pre-publication draft of *Rules for Radicals*. Alinsky, a world class liar and king of deceitful double-talking, obviously left his footprint on the woman who would later spread the "Alinsky model" to her future husband. Bill Clinton was elected and governed largely through a carefully crafted "centrist" Democratic image (read: lie) that he perpetrated on the electorate. And, wife Hillary Rodham Clinton, already accused of being a "congenital liar" by William Safire in 1996, would use the "Alinsky model" in her own bid for the 2008 presidential race.

If Saul Alinsky's life was any indication, assimilating even a portion of his "methods" would not be in the best interest of the American people who already had a taste of Alinsky-style corruption under Bill Clinton. As a typical New Age walking contradiction, Saul Alinsky was one step above a socialist and one step below a Communist, but every bit a "social justice' Chicago mobster. But, he was no Robin Hood. The smooth-talking Alinsky stole from the rich to enrich himself and his street level "community organizers" with a trickle reaching "the community" and "the people."

Not only is his footprint heavy on Hillary, the muddy footprints are all over Barack Obama who bares an amazing verbal likeness to the Alinsky "model" of smooth-talking deceiver. This would have only been natural for Obama to absorb in his work as a community and neighborhood "organizer" in Chicago before running for state senator in the Illinois legislature. Anyone working as a Chicago neighborhood organizer could not escape the legacy of Saul Alinsky's methods and tactics which linger throughout the entire "community action" bureaucracy in Chicago and other cities across the country.

Obama's "conversion" to Christianity in 1992 was a classic Alinsky ploy which he encouraged in order to "assimilate" and "infiltrate" larger social and political circles. And, Obama is stressing a "new evangelism" of "social justice" over "morality and ministry."

Scattered throughout Barack Obama's *Audacity of Hope* are seething hints of class warfare and disparity. Beneath his calls for national unity lies the true face of a simmering socialist and Neville Chamberlain appeaser. All of this and Obama's pledge to be all things to all people is classic textbook Alinsky.

As for old Saul Alinsky, he died in 1972 with lungs ravished by cigarettes, a soul darkened by deception and a heart-felt hatred for America. He and his present-day acolytes have come to represent the "blame America first" crowd, first identified by U.N. Ambassador Jeanne Kirkpatrick in 1984.

Jack Valenti—The Dark Prince of Hollywood died on April 26, 2007 at the age of 85 with barely a mention in the media he had dragged so easily into the gutter. President Bush commented that "Jack Valenti *transformed* the motion picture industry by establishing the Ratings System." Bush did not volunteer whether that "transformation" was a positive or negative on the country. The results are obvious. Valenti continued to boast, even in retirement, that he "saved" the motion picture industry in 1968 with the creation of the Movie Ratings Scheme.

In reality, Jack Valenti actually destroyed the integrity of the motion picture and television industries and pulled down a once optimistic American culture to the point it may never recover. Again, only a delusional former ad-agency hack from the 1950's like Jack Valenti could take the dismal truth and twist it in his favor.

In a November 1, 2005 Op-Ed for the *Los Angeles Times,* Valenti jokingly assessed his career at the MPAA as receiving a PG rating for "Pretty Good." He made the self-serving pat-on-the-back comments in the same article he used to smear Will Hays, the first president of the MPAA, as "one of those starched, high-on-the-neck, white collar orators, reeking of moral integrity."

That statement pretty much explains Jack Valenti, a man of absolutely *no* integrity who, with the stroke of a pen on November 1, 1968 planted a seed reeking of moral disintegration. And, almost everyone in America has been negatively affected in one way or another by Valenti's actions.

Not only did he establish a predatory segregational system to largely demoralize the nation's youth and family at the neighborhood cinema, he did the same for television in 1997, leaving very few safe havens of entertainment left. Once television fell under the Ratings Scheme, the Hollywood sleaze factor grew in due course.

As *USA Today* writer Robert Bianco noted in 2006, "Vulgarity has always been TV's stock in trade. But really, must the America that TV projects into our homes and around the world so often be stupid, whiny, greedy, crass and cruel? Is that all we are? Is that all we want to be?"

Jack Valenti's "New Kind of America Movie" was his personal label for the international campaign of cultural restructuring. His "Free Screen" movement would remove any barriers to entertainment content including those productions that may be deemed as culpable in actually influencing harmful behavior—even murder as was demonstrated by *Natural Born Killers*. Jack Valenti's New Age philosophy of motion pictures, in concert with friend Hugh Hefner's New Morality and their philosophical fellow travelers are largely to blame for the profane hyper-violent blood fests and over-sexualization of the culture including the destructive scourge of ever present internet porn.

Anybody attempting to put restraints on the rapidly growing sex industry on the internet including wide open portals for child sex predators are scolded as "enemies of the First Amendment" by porn defenders and patrons who inevitably invoke the name of Jack Valenti and his efforts to free the screen of any "self-imposed constraints." As Kim Kommando said it best, there exists on the internet "a sick underground world that disgusts me."[47]

Because drug glamorization is now allowed in movies and television, thanks to Jack Valenti, the former MPAA president was as complicit as Allen Ginsberg and Timothy Leary in spreading the plague of drug abuse and addiction. In perspective, he was more guilty than any of the other drug addict bohemians mentioned in this chapter because he held the keys to Pandora's box and the lock to keep the barbarians at the gate where mayhem was kept in check. But, by opening the box and unlocking the gate, Jack Valenti became the biggest promoter and exporter of drugs, violence, perversion, pornography and human malevolence in the history of the planet. That's how powerful the "unbridled" motion picture image has become.

To demonstrate the two faces of Jack Valenti, consider his comments in the same series of George Washington University interviews that included Hugh Hefner. When Valenti was asked about his feelings surrounding the popularity of illegal drug use beginning in the 1960's Valenti replied:

> "There was a kind of cult movement in the United States at that time; it was cool and it was okay, and this was the thing to do, to get stoned. Thank God that *receded* and my own young children at the time, somehow, miraculously, missed that era as it began to *diminish,* and so they grew up without the *menacing daily menace of drugs,* and all *these terrifying* things mean to you."

The emphasis was added to demonstrate how Valenti would manipulate speech in order to manipulate his audience, much like dialogue in a movie script. Valenti was thankful that the cult movement of drug abuse had "receded" and that his children "miraculously" missed that era as it began to "diminish," finally boasting how his children grew up without the "menacing daily menace of drugs."

First, drug abuse never "receded" and never "diminished." Valenti's children were well on their way to "growing up" when he abolished the Production code in 1968 which "officially" allowed the glamorization of drug use—which began immediately.

The epidemic became an avalanche and drug abuse continues to plague the nation. But, according to Uncle Jack, it "receded" and "diminished" a long time ago. There was a reason Jack Valenti was paid over a million dollars a year by the major motion picture studios. A professional skilled liar is an asset in a fantasy world where truth is irrelevant.

The irresponsible actions of Jack Valenti and the failure of the Ratings Scheme is the very reason so many media watchdog groups formed and continue to flourish since 1968 in order to provide individuals, parents, and families with the *true* information about entertainment content that the Ratings Scheme was designed to hide.

A cinematic analogy to describe Jack Valenti is a line by Cary Grant from Alfred Hitchcock's 1959 thriller *North by Northwest.* Grant, playing an ad agency hack from Madison Avenue, is leaving his office before embarking on a harrowing adventure. As he exits the elevator to leave the building, Grant turns to his partner and says, "You know the ad business. There's no such thing as lies, just expedient exaggeration."

That was the personal and public philosophy of the man who destroyed American culture.

* * *

The bottom line of this chapter is that words have meaning, meaning is translated into action, and actions have consequences. The consequences of the words and actions of these individuals who laid the asphalt for Hollywood's Road to Perdition are still reverberating and expanding in the popular culture today. Fighting their legacy and ongoing influence in the Culture War will take unwavering courage and conviction. As long as America remains a Hollywood nation, the chances of this country and its citizens reaching full potential as a productive, optimistic, positive and intelligent society will be greatly diminished. David Ben Gurion wisely noted, "The highest degree of intelligence is the moral code." Hollywood today has absolutely "no code."

The consequences of Hollywood's promotion of these degenerate perverts has drastically affected cultures around the world. This devastating impact has been extensively exposed in Diana West's book, *The Death of the Grown-Up: How America's Arrested Development Is Bringing Down Western Civilization*. West acutely recognized the 1950s as the genesis of a nation of eternal adolescents who can't say no, a politically correct population that cannot distinguish right from wrong.

The best synopsis of the legacy left by the New Age mind-benders of Hollywood is the complete quote by Ben Stein, "Hollywood was taken over by a bunch of dope-smoking hippies who are now grown up . . . but still very countercultural and they don't get what America is all about."

PROFANITY INSANITY: THE UNSUNG VILLAIN AND THE DEATH OF COMEDY

Sniffing glue in 1951 was not yet an established form of "getting high" among those prone to warp their brains "for the fun of it." Even George Carlin at age 14 had not discovered the "model-maker's curse." But some of his friends knew all too well. George preferred instead to make his classmates laugh and chuckle at Cardinal Hayes High School. And when they didn't laugh at his jokes or antics, he could always count on the "dirty words" to elicit giggles as a last resort.

Every classroom has one somewhere between sixth and seventh grade—a hood, misfit or insolent loner from a broken home—someone not only looking for attention, but demanding it, at any cost. The more foul the word, the louder the gasps—or, giggles. And that landed George Carlin in the principal's office more times than he could count.

Of course, that was another form of attention that Carlin perversely craved. The Brothers at Cardinal Hayes High School whacked again and again and Carlin came back begging for more. Carlin would later claim that the Brothers and the Priests enjoyed beating him. In reality, George enjoyed being beaten—tremendously—as he began his lifelong career as a self-destructive slow-motion suicide victim. Carlin would first blame God and later in life would specifically take out his petty vengeance on Jesus Christ. The love lost at home and school was the love lost for life, as he would later name a "comedy" routine "Life is Worth Losing."

At age 14 little George did discover alcohol. He loved to "get wasted." He would even enter the term into the common English lexicon. Carlin finally ran away from school and home at age 16 so he could indulge his drinking without interference. He thought this would be possible on the government dime by joining the United States Air Force. But, after his first DUI in 1957 and later his inability to physically control his bodily functions or even speak after a drinking binge, he was discharged. George Carlin would continue drinking uninterrupted for fifty more years.

By 1959, George Carlin was performing at Beat coffeehouses that were always located in building basements to give the occupants "underground" or "countercultural" credentials. For Carlin, it was the Cellar in Fort Worth, Texas. Later he would get "stoned" and hang out with Lenny Bruce before the Manhattan "comic" dropped dead from heroin in 1966.

This greatly inspired George who decided to take up LSD and peyote in addition to alcohol; anything to speed his arrival at the graveyard. Oh yeah, he also did stand-up comedy during this time when he wasn't laying down for weeks at a time overcoming non-stop hangovers. Even getting up to use the bathroom was too much of a "headache."

Carlin also started smoking marijuana. A lot of marijuana. He would smoke all day, every day, for the next thirty years. By 1972, George Carlin was still doing stand-up comedy and had taken on the "Dope Head" look complete with long hair, beard and tie-dyed shirts. Drugged-up, hung over, sleepless and seven weeks without a shower, Carlin appeared at Milwaukee's 1972 Summerfest. The laughs were not coming in as fast as he hoped, so George resorted to his old adolescent strategy. Soon, Carlin was sputtering a routine he had recorded earlier that year called "7 Words You Can't Say On Television."

It was like old times at high school all over again; the same format; the shock value; the giggles; but, mostly the gasps. Frustrated and "high," Carlin blurted out "I want to F____ all of you." And, like high school, the authorities came. This time he was arrested—just as he was hoping. After all, his record was not a best seller and he needed publicity.

One reporter at the police station asked Carlin if he was aware that children were in the audience. Carlin said he didn't care, telling the reporter that children "needed" to hear his profane rant so they wouldn't grow up "inhibited."

He was later released and used the incident for the much needed publicity to sell his "Class Clown" album to the "giggles" crowd who craved profanity in any form they could get it, much like porn addicts. Carlin became a grotesque Elmer Gantry confessing as if to Sister Falconer, "I tell dirty jokes to keep my buyers laughing."

The following year in 1973, Carlin recorded "Filthy Words" for his "Occupation Foole" release and WBAI-FM in New York played the album over the air uncut. A man complained to the FCC because his young son was in the car and heard the broadcast. Carlin was pleased that he had not only offended the young boy, but also his father. George would celebrate his anti-establishment crusade by increasing the drugs and alcohol.

The case against the radio station, owned by Pacifica, would weave its way up the ladder to the U.S. Supreme Court in 1978 which issued a ruling that the

FCC could assume the authority to prohibit such broadcast during the period of the day when children might be listening to the publicly licensed airwaves; 6:00 am to 10:00 pm in the case known as FCC vs. Pacifica Foundation, 438 U.S. 726 (1978). The WBAI-FM broadcast was ruled "indecent" and not "obscene." Obscenity is not protected by the First Amendment and Carlin would spend the rest of his life pushing that envelope, much like he goaded the teachers and the principal at Cardinal Hayes High School. (See Appendix IV).

Only the perversity of the New Hollywood could take the wasted trench-mouth addict and parade him as a First Amendment hero. To this day, almost every comedian from Pryor, to Murphy, to Rock and all the wannabes who appear on the Comedy Channel are basically cheap clown character imitations of Carlin.

But in 1978 when the ruling came down, George had been "partying" so hard since his 1973 "offense" that he was in no shape to capitalize on the newfound publicity he longed for. In 1976, at the age of 39, George Carlin suffered the first in a series of heart attacks. He appeared on television only spontaneously during the next five years. By the time of his third heart attack, Carlin was left with greatly diminished heart function and was unable to tour any longer. The decades of smoking pot and daily drinking had permanently destroyed much of his heart and lungs.

But, that didn't stop George. In addition to drinking and smoking even more pot after the heart attacks, Carlin added cocaine and painkillers to his diet. It was during this time that George ramped up his life-hatred philosophy. "I think we're already circling the drain as a species, and I'd like to see the circle get a little faster and a little shorter."

This was the kind of adult role model Hollywood loved to promote to the nation's youth and adults who suffered from arrested development. As a malignant narcissist, Carlin wanted to drag everyone down with him using comedy as a clever ruse. His multiple attempts at suicidal overdoses never quite hit the mark, though he kept trying with all his heart, or what was left of it. Carlin's appearances on Saturday Night Live were more a series of misses than hits. If no one laughed at his stand-up routines, he would either verbally insult the audience with slurs or simply walk off the stage. At other venues, he sometimes was written off as a no-show, depending on how much LSD, peyote, heroin, cocaine, codeine, hydrocodone, tramadol, dilaudid, qualudes, mushrooms and alcohol he had consumed the previous day.

In a low point for Carnegie Hall, Carlin was invited to appear and humor the Manhattanites by expanding his "Seven Dirty Words" into over 200 offensive words that he read from an oversized scroll as the "sophisticate" crowd giggled and guffawed at the burned-out comedian's endless diatribe that had begun thirty years earlier at Cardinal Hayes High School.

Perhaps Carlin was disappointed that no one came to arrest him, or at the very least, beat him severely. The audience had become mind-numbed to Carlin's filthy anti-establishment rants. As much as they liked him, they were getting bored. George added Christian-bashing to the routine and some perked up, but not for long. By now, Carlin was preaching to the choir of aging hippies who couldn't get enough First Amendment F-Bombs.

By December 2004, more than fifty years after his first drink, Carlin finally checked into rehab for alcohol and painkiller abuse. But, little George enjoyed substance abuse too much. It was his own masochistic way of enjoying the pain of slow death.

On February 1, 2006 Carlin appeared at a stand-up gig in a small town in California to pick up some spending money by promoting his depressing "Life Is Worth Losing" routine. Almost 70 years of age, the bitter free spirit looked like a ghost under the spotlight. His hair was snow-white and thin as his skin that revealed the blue veins barely moving blood through his virtually dead body. Carlin told the crowd that he had just been released from the hospital for heart failure and pneumonia—the first stages of the slow demise he craved for so long.

Carlin is still a drug-addict, only now the drugs are legal and prescribed. There's lasix to prevent fluid from building up in his lungs so he won't suffocate and coumadin to keep his blood viscous and thin so that it can reach his brain and maintain the sparks between the neurons. And there's a host of other bottled goodies that George swallows to keep his heart pumping, even though the pulmonary walls are the consistency of toilet paper.

Some people commit suicide quickly with a bullet to the head or a jump from the Empire State Building. Others, like Carlin, drag it out over decades in hopes the audience will follow his example and waste their lives much as he has wasted his own. In doing so, Carlin has been successful in at least coarsening the vocabulary of human discourse into a perverted verbal intercourse while sitting on a toilet seat that never completely flushes. Some examples of Carlin-influenced lingo:

COARSE AND COARSER

Pre-1968	**Post 1968**
That stinks	That sucks
I'm ticked off	I'm pissed off
I've been had	I've been ripped off
Don't mess with me	Don't F____ with me
Where's my stuff	Where's my S____
That's not exciting	That doesn't get me off

While Carlin recorded a few popular albums, they were never true best sellers. To this day, comedians such as Bob Newhart and Bill Cosby hold best-selling comedy record sales numbers. The reason for this was that comedians pre-1968 didn't believe in segregation—the division of the audience into multi-layer "age-appropriate groups." In 1960, Newhart bumped Elvis from the charts with his Grammy-winning "The Button-Down Mind of Bob Newhart." And, that was a time when the Grammy's still had credibility.

Carlin had scheduled a small number of appearances throughout 2008 and 2009, if he lives long enough. He has reserved these final appearances for special attacks on Jews and Christians and anybody who believes in "God." He may revert to his racist routine about fat businessmen and cigars. Rumors from tour managers are that he might imitate Bob Fosse's pretentious self-indulgent life retrospective from "All That Jazz." Carlin can be wheeled out in a hospital bed hooked up to IVs and an oxygen tank while scanty models dressed as nurses take turns popping pills into his mouth while the other holds a bottle of beer with a straw. In between barbs and insults to the audience he will take a pill, take a sip and keep on ticking until the heart explodes just under the sternum.

He's hoping the audience will laugh. He'll never know. It's just that he's run out of material and the morbidity has finally set in.

As it turned out, death came with no drama or fanfare. On June 22, 2008, Carlin walked into a Santa Monica hospital complaining of an "elephant on my chest." He was dead two hours later. His manager canceled the Broadway extravaganza and screenwriters began working overtime.

CHAPTER 19

WARNING! HIP-HOP AND RAP MUSIC CAN KILL YOU

> *"What we have here is a failure to communicate."*
> —Strother Martin

1959 Grammy Winner
Dinah Washington

"What A Difference a Day Makes"
What a difference a day a day makes,
Twenty-four little hours
Brought the sun and the flowers
Where there used to be rain
My yesterday was blue, dear
Today I'm part of you, dear
My lonely nights are through, dear
Since you said you were mine.

2006 Grammy Winner
Ludacris

"Slap"
I feel like slappin' a nigga today (slap-slap)
Slappin' a nigga today
Slappin' a nigga today
And I'm thinking bout killin' my boss today
Killin' my boss today
I'm thinking bout killin' my boss
Killin' my boss today.

Or, to paraphrase Dinah Washington, what a difference 47 years make. When a group of "professional" musicians and fellow Grammy members vote to award a Grammy to a profane "no-count" street thug who feels, "like slappin' a nigga" and is "thinking 'bout killin' my boss," it tells you just how far down the American culture has slid.

And, the Grammys have been granting awards to similar "artists" with even harsher and vulgar lyrics since the 1990s. In 2006, the Academy Awards membership gave the film category of Best Original Song Oscar for "It's Tough Out Here For A Pimp" by the crotch-grabbing slouch-masters known as Three 6 Mafia, formerly 666 Mafia. And the Academy Awards show producers wonder why viewership was among the lowest in 20 years.

Music in America largely died long before groups and individuals like these became the norm of today's youth and young adults, not just in America, but around the world. So profoundly has the hip-hop/rap phenomena accelerated the decay of contemporary society with its "mission," it was singled out in 1994 as one of the main polluters of the culture by Senator Bob Dole, former Secretary of Education William Bennett and C. Delores Tucker.

What stood out about this challenge was the first prominent voice of protest from the African-American community by Ms. Tucker, head of the National Political Congress of Black Women who joined Dole and Bennett in calling on Time-Warner to search their souls. Explaining the trio's cultural counterattack against hip-hop and rap to *Newsweek,* magazine, Tucker was defiant, "African-American women are getting tired of their children call them hos, bitches and sluts."[1]

Dole, Bennett and Tucker were trying to bring to the surface the frustration that had been boiling just below ground level for more than a decade.[2] *Time* described the onslaught against hip-hop and rap as "what appears to be a very real clamor on behalf of common sense and public sensibilities."[3]

At the time, Levin was trying to defend Warner's promotion of the debauched violent sex lyrics as "a legitimate expression of street culture, which deserves an outlet."[4] But Dole, Bennett and Tucker were making the very real and very timely point that in "promoting" this "street culture," Time-Warner was actually repackaging it by encouraging these hip-hop/rap groups to push the envelope in order to compete against other major Hollywood labels that were putting out even raunchier, violent, sexual, pornographic and profane lyrics. The recording industry had become players in rancid one-upmanship.

In fact, many in the black community as well as the white community were learning for the first time that the largely African-American hip-hop/rap music was being produced and "packaged" by mainly white record label executives at some of the largest music companies in the world who had cornered the hip-hop/rap market such as Time-Warner, Universal, Sony and Germany's Bertelsmann, among others.

Chief among these degenerate promoters and distributors of so-called "street culture" was Hollywood's preeminent Lying King of Entertainment, David Geffen who rushed to the industry's defense saying, "Artists make records, not record companies . . . No record companies tell them what to record."[5] Of course, that too, was a classic Geffen lie from the man who began his career at the William Morris Agency after lying about his education, experience and references.

Just before selling Geffen Records in 1990 to Universal, David Geffen was very actively promoting hip-hop/rap "artists" and some of the industry's most vicious, misogynistic and hateful lyrics were spilling out of Geffen Records. An insider at Warner Records, where Geffen Records was a division, confided that Geffen shared in the rapper's violent hatred of middle-class values and family life, partly because he was an outcast himself; very heterophobic and envied the rappers who were very openly more perverted than he was.

However, what Geffen didn't divulge in his defense of the record industry is that he once had to say "no" to one of his own favorite rap groups, the Geto Boys. The sexually violent group had presented Geffen with their masterpiece, complete with explicit lyrics depicting the bloody mutilation of women and then *having sex with their dead bodies.* Geffen had his limits—barely.

That was the late 1980s and the monster music only grew uglier and larger as record executives, studio executives and the presidents of MTV and BET ignored the public outcry. It was this group that had "created the demand" into a growing worldwide audience after carefully and patiently exploiting a group of "reformed" street musicians who sprang up in the Bronx in the early 1970's. The entertainment industry had spent billions of dollars promoting the hip-hop/rap message to the most easily influenced young people in the 12 to 18-year-old range through glossy magazines, music videos, TV and radio interviews. Especially key was the urban radio DJs who pumped up certain rappers through glowing accolades and 24 hour a day rotation on stations with taglines like "Non-Stop Hip-Hop." The original rappers, or "old schoolers," have long suspected that these DJs were paid off through classic record company bribery known as "payola."

And, what a difference a decade makes when it comes to political intolerance of "obscene" and "atrocious" lyrics as Vice President Al Gore described hip-hop/rap lyrics during the 1995 cultural counter attack. Gore added that he had no problem with Hollywood executives being shamed into reigning in their product. After all, wife Tipper had led a national campaign in the 1980s to add "explicit lyric" warning labels on albums and later CD's.

But as *former* Vice President Al Gore accepted his Oscar for Best Documentary propaganda titled *An Inconvenient Truth,* he had only kind words to say about Hollywood and gloated about always being a "big fan" of the movies. Now, Gore explained, he viewed Hollywood as a very important industry to "send a message."

Hollywood had effectively "shut up" both Al and Tipper by elevating the former Vice President to the status of Global Warming guru and the new religion he had created. The Gores had no comment about the Grammy Awards a few weeks earlier where Ludacris won for a CD about "slappin a nigga" and "killin' my boss." He must have decided that Ludacris just needed to "send a message." And Tipper had a zipper on her lips.

Meanwhile Hollywood is happy to continue business as usual even though the storm clouds are forming. As Allison Samuels noted in *Newsweek* magazine,

THE HOLLYWOOD CULTURE WAR

"Judging by sales and airplay, lots of rap listeners *still* aren't tired of songs celebrating grills (gold teeth), ice (diamonds) and big booties—especially when shaken by pole-dancing strippers for crystal-swilling playas." Hip-hop becomes strip-hop and pushes more sex, violence, drugs and crime than ever before. And, there just doesn't seem to be enough room on the human body for all the tattoos and body piercings that mark the slaves of hip-hop. The dope-smoking rap crowd flocks to the convenience store at midnight to pick out one of a hundred varieties of cigars which are used to "extend" marijuana highs.

And, body counts are increasing across America as the "culture" promotes night-club shoot-outs and parking lot stabbings. The whole hip-hop/rap industry foments not only violence against women and strangers but also against fellow hip-hoppers. Any subscriber of *XXL* or *The Source* magazines will read countless profiles of rappers whose hallmark is to bash, back-stab and curse their fellow rappers. The interviews are laced with such heavy doses of violent and vulgar profanity that the editors must resort to extensive censoring in order to secure shelf space at most retail magazine outlets and newsstands.

As the chart demonstrates, the rate of murder, sudden death, beatings, stabbings, shootings, indictments, arrests and jailed hip-hop/rap artists is staggering and represents a morbid phenomena never before seen in the history of any American music genre.

THE HIP-HOP "RAP SHEET"

DEAD RAPPERS

Aaliyah	Old Dirty Bastard	Mooseman
Baby Bleu	Mausbera	Mathew Roberts
Big Hawk	Mista C	Rapper Woodie
Big L	Scott LaRock	Damien Damme
Big Pun	Notorious B.I.G.	Deah Damm
Cool C	Seagram	Ricky Herd
Cowboy	Stretch	Karizma
Easy E	Tre' Stylez	Yaki Kadafi
Grym Reaper	Tupac Shakur	Rappin' Ron
Jay Dee	Prince Ital Joe	JoJo White
Jam Master J	Malcolm Howard	Dion Stewart
Israel Ramirez	MC Big L	Eric Carson
Freaky Tah	Mc Ant	Speedy Loc
Khadafi	Mr. Cee	Lil' Bob
MC Trouble	King Tubby	"Stak" Bundles
Poetic	Michael Menson	Freako

MICHAEL VINCENT BOYER

Philant Johnson	MC Rock	Holy Quran
Fat Pat	Trouble T-Roy	Jo Jay
"Papo"	Brandon Mitchell	Yusef Aflout Mohammed
Bugz	Charizma	Tonnie Shepherd
Proof	Bruce Mayfield	Coughut
Lisa "Left Eye" Lopez	"Mac"	Tactix
Amir Rashid Crump	Big Phil	Jughead Garard
D.J. Caravan	Buffy "The Human Beat Box"	

ARRESTED, JAILED, OR INDICTED

C-Bo	Don P	Dead Prez
Bennie Sigel	Jimmy Henchmen	Ja Rule
Black Rob	Cassidy	Sean "P. Diddy" Combs
Keith Murray	Steady B	Nas
MS-DL	Tony Yayo	Fabulous
C-Murder	Twisted Black	Cam'ron
Busta Rhymes	Killa C	Damon Dash
R. Kelly	Noreaga	Akon
Shyne	Deon Smith	"Don" Camron
Suge Knight	Justin Potts	Remy Ma
Supreme	Oriley Poindextor	Lil' Wayne
Snoop Dogg	Carl Morgan	Gucci
True	Young city	Plies
Lil' Kim	DMX	Jeezy
Chi Ali	Pimp C	J. Bone
Spiggy Nine	"T.I." Harris	Trick Daddy
Mysonne	99 Cent	Kafani
Slick Rick	Lil' Troy	Ronnie MC Koppok
Young Buck	Lil' Scrappy	"Mister" Till
Flesh N Bone	Brass Eagle	V.W. Keys
Lil' Shawn	Caliber .68	Ava Sectomie
Capone	Asher D	Mas D. Bates
Master P	M-I	Shawty Lo
Mos Def	D J Drama	R. Kelly

SHOT, BEATEN, STABBED OR ON THE RUN

Busta Rhymes	Obie Trice
Benzino	Dr. Dre
50 Cent	Tony Yayo

THE HOLLYWOOD CULTURE WAR

Irv and Chris Gotti
Poss Den
Curtis Jackson
D G Yola
Young Lay
C Murder
D.J. Sapho

Young Z
Hakim Green
Suge Knight
Cam'ron
Young Zee
Jay-zee

SEVERE IDENTITY CRISIS

Sean Combs, aka:

Sean "Puff Daddy" Combs
Sean "Puffy" Combs
Sean "P. Daddy" Combs
"Puffy" Combs
"Puff Daddy"
"Puffy"
Sean "Puff Diddy" Combs

"P. Diddy" Combs
"P. Diddy"
Sean "P. Diddy" Combs
"Diddy"
Sean "Diddy" John
Sean "P. Diddy" John, or finally:
Sean John

Note: These names represent only 60% of rapper crime statistics. The status of all rappers listed subject to change at time of publication. The only exception being "Dead Rappers." They're still dead.

But, these staggering figures may be part of the "The Plan" as described on a *Court TV* website that often covered the trials and tribulations of the hip-hop/rap industry. The ultimate conspiracy theory holds that certain record company executives who produce and promote rap actually conspire to kill targeted rappers because dead rappers—particularly rappers with legal problems—are better off dead, and a lot more profitable.

Ice Cube (O'Shea Jackson) certainly believes in "The Plan." He slams Interscope Records for continuing to profit off of Tupac Shakur ten years after his murder, chanting on one of his CDs "Keep your ass out of the casket—Interscope will spend your money." Then, Ice Cube, like one out of three musicians, also manages to slam President Bush for every problem in the world "since I was little." Actually, that would place him in the Jimmy Carter era.

The hip-hopper conspiracy theorists point to the fact that Tupac Shakur, a career criminal, is rising fast up the list of "Forbes's 15 Most Profitable Dead Celebrities." Tupac's rival in the East Coast/West Coast rap rivalry was Biggie Smalls who was shot to death in 1997 just six months after Tupac was riddled with bullets on the Las Vegas strip. Unfortunately for "Biggie," what happens in Vegas does not always stay in Vegas as his death was considered "payback" for

Tupac's murder. At least, that's the story the record companies and rap producers floated. When Biggie Small's unfinished CD was rushed to market before the flowers could wilt on his grave, it shot straight to the top of the charts.

Even today, producers for Tupac and Smalls continue to release remixes of the dead rapper's songs and they have always been best sellers. It's not always clear who has been shooting who in the vicious and nefarious world of hip-hop. Tupac's producer Suge Knight was driving the car the night Tupac was sitting in the passenger side as the car was showered with bullets worthy of Bonnie and Clyde's demise.

Amazingly, "producer/friend" Suge Knight walked away without even a scratch, even though he complained about a ringing in his ears from "all that gunfire." And, Knight continued to profit handsomely from Tupac even as Knight himself went to jail on an unrelated charge. As Louis Armstrong once sang, "What a wonderful world."

Those events transpired over a decade ago and hip-hop/rap has since grown exponentially around the world and is so pervasive that no one can escape its pernicious and turbid influence on the culture. Whether your car rattles at a stop light from the sub-woofer base beat thumping from another car or the spectacle of high-schoolers strutting down the shopping mall on a Saturday night while holding up their baggy pants with one hand and fondling a gold chain with the other, hip-hop is hard to avoid.

Hip-hop is used as background music on TV and radio to advertise everything from new cars to used furniture. The thug-look snarled lip on rappers such as Ice Cube and Sean Combs is used to promote scrappy clothing and men's cologne. Chrysler even put one foot in the sewer to promote their sedans by teaming together former Chrysler chairman Lee Iacocca with career criminal, pornographer and perpetual drug-addict Snoop-Dogg in a twisted strategy of trying to sell cars to our grandfathers and rappers at the same time. Does it take a business degree to predict why American auto makers are taking a dive?

Women are literally the real hounds in the hip-hop nation. In advertising and music videos, women are drug-faced props adorned in bikinis and stripper attire as they lounge around plush settings with their rear ends in the air like dogs waiting to be mated by a dread-locked flunkie shouting, "Bark, bitch, bark!!" Only in the world of hip-hop could the cleavage of a woman's chest be replaced with the cleavage of a woman's butt (that's "booty" in hip-hop lingo). According to author Akiba Solomon, this emphasis is a very real modern day vestige of slavery.

What is important to understand is that hip-hop is not the music. The music is only one "component" of the hip-hop "culture" which includes its own language, clothing, philosophy, "style" and attitude. Hip-hop culture is international and can be found in most countries, except largely Muslim nations. Hip-hop is actually taught as a cultural course for credit at many universities across the nation, including Stanford which maintains a vast hip-hop archive.

Hip-hop culture is also currently engaged in an all out campaign to influence and "change" the music of the Christian church in America, Latin America and Europe. This last "conquest" by the hip-hop culture is causing some of the fiercest battles in the Culture War that has been raging for almost ten years and is largely unreported in the mainstream press.

We'll introduce you to the major players in this turbulent daily battle being fought across the continents including an African-American pastor who is almost single-handedly exposing the malicious truth behind *all* of hip-hop, rap and its "components." So influential is his message, along with others who are literally fed up with the exploitation, a poll was taken in February 2007 which revealed fully 50% of African-Americans opposing the gangsta-style rap culture as promoted in the black community by the Hollywood entertainment machine.[6] That percentage is up significantly from the 1990s.

And, while C. Delores Tucker was one of the few voices among the black community to nationally denounce the destructive impact of the hip-hop/rap culture in 1995, she wouldn't be the last.

In March of 2007, Dr. Johnetta Betsch Cole, president of Bennett College for Women and president emeritus of Spellman College, came out strongly against the hip-hop culture and its promoters in Hollywood, asking, "what value can there be in descriptions of black girls and women as 'bitches,' 'hos,' 'skeezers,' 'freaks,' 'gold diggers,' 'chicken heads,' and 'pigeons?' What could possibly be the value to our communities to have rap music videos that are notorious for featuring half-clothed young black women gyrating obscenely and functioning as backdrops, props and objects of lust for rap artists who sometimes behave as predators?"[7]

The two most commonly asked questions are "How did this ferocious malignancy begin?" And, "Why is this hip-hop culture being so openly promoted in the most vulgar and increasingly inhumane manner?"

First, it is important to understand that "rapping" has been around for a long time among black and white musicians and was meant to convey a story, message or feeling not too dissimilar from whistling through a tune.

But one would hardly recognize that from the rap which was hijacked in the early 1970s when DJs began talking over music at house parties and dingy urban discos of the inner city. At the time, the original rappers referred to their "art" as "MCing" pronounced "emceeing." This referred to the "Master of Ceremonies" who was basically the DJ who made himself into the "star" of the party, which began as mass street corner gatherings in the Bronx. The MC would punctuate his message in an irregular monotone pentameter with a heavy instrumental bass beat background.

These were the early manifestations of rap and hip-hop confined to less than a dozen city blocks in the heart of the rapidly decaying lower Bronx. And, the "inspiration" that fed this movement is no less bizarre than the proclamation of the New Age by Aleister Crowley himself from the footsteps of the Egyptian pyramids in 1904. Hip-hop has its own Holy Prophet who, like so many before him, nurtured a morbid fascination and self-imposed infestation with ancient Egyptian gods that has literally captured the souls and imaginations of countless "spirit seekers" for centuries; individuals who believed the mysteries of ancient Egypt held the keys to "enlightenment."

This curious quest for ancient Egyptian esoteric knowledge and mysticism can be found in the work of medieval alchemists, fortune tellers, sorcery, mind-readers and the secretive "magical societies" such as the Rosicrucians, mystical variations of Freemasonry, Golden Dawn, Theosophy, Thule and Crowley's Thelema and Hubbard's Scientology.

Similarly, but with much broader impact, the quest for hip-hop began in the very early 1970s when a "reformed" Bronx gang leader who determined within himself to journey to Egypt and study the civilization of his "ancestors." In the process, he brought back a "New Understanding" of "Supreme Knowledge." The Egyptian journey would transpire into yet another strand in the long dark thread that runs through Hollywood to this day.

STRAIGHT TO THE SOURCE

No one is quite sure of Afrika Bambaataa's real name. Since the early 1970s he has always been known as Afrika or "Bam," a former gang leader and self-made street musician in the bombed-out remnants of the Bronx. After his trip to Egypt and the African continent sometime between 1970 and 1972, Bambaataa (pronounced:Bombâta) returned to the Bronx a changed man with a universal mission for "this planet-so-called Earth" as he referred to the global community.

In the Bronx, Bam began to hold large block parties with DJs spinning records including his own music that some called "electro fusion," "electro funk," "street funk" or Planet Rock music. Other fledgling musicians began to imitate his style of music and the parties often included elaborate "B-boy" demonstrations, better known as break-dancing and pop-locking that produced feats of human double-jointed gymnastic dexterity. It became more of a tribal ceremony and ritual than anything resembling "dance."

It was at this time that the DJs became known as MCs and began talking, or "rapping" with the music at the same time manually revolving vinyl disc records back and forth to create a scratching sound not too different from fingernails across a chalkboard. The 1984 movie *Breakin'* was an example of the record scratching break dancing style that had begun ten years earlier.

By 1973 "Bam" had set the foundation for these new urban cultural benchmarks as part of a wider culture he would personally call "hip-hop." And, he *made it clear* that the music, the dancing, the street lingo, clothing and rapping would all fall under the banner of "hip-hop expressions." Bam even told "aerosol artists" (graffiti vandals) that their "art" would also be known as hip-hop art.

In the same year, Bam established a hip-hop organization which he would call the Universal Zulu Nation and anointed himself as the "Amen-Ra of Universal Hip-Hop Culture," in effect, the "God of Hip-Hop." Bam was apparently quite taken with the ancient culture of the Egyptians, especially early Fifth Dynasty in which the Egyptian nation began referring to their leaders as gods. Amen Ra was one of the earliest Egyptian leaders to be worshipped as a god.

Bam thought that was all pretty "cool." Bam became the reincarnated Amen Ra of the "Amazulus." That's where the New Understanding and "Supreme Knowledge" of Bam's cultural odyssey into Egypt became somewhat fuzzy, but New Age nonetheless.

The Amazulus, or Zulus, are part of the greater Bantu people of Southeast Africa. The cultures of ancient North African Egypt and the Zulus of Southeast Africa had nothing in common. But, Bam was impressed with the Zulu's warring abilities in their fights against colonialism. And, as a cultural scavenger, Bam simply mixed and matched the cultural elements he admired, brought them back to the Bronx and created the Universal Zulu Nation with hip-hop as the "cultural marker."

The era of the ankh had arrived, the ancient Egyptian symbol for "soul life" and "man-woman as one." Soon, the ankh would be accompanied by a bevy of other gold chains bearing the likeness of dragons, dogs, snakes and skulls. The "attitude" became a scowl and the clothing became loose and baggy. Ebonics and "street talk" became the official hip-hop language. Any attempt to dress for success or conjugate verbs was considered taboo as an attempt to "be white."

Bam created a Supreme Council of the Universal Zulu Nation with many chapters in countries around the world. The purpose of the Supreme Council continues today as it was originally conceived; to enforce and "maintain the culture." In other words, ensure that hip-hoppers around the world, especially the younger generation, continue to maintain a perpetual downtrodden state of denial by speaking, looking and acting like cartoon characters out of a third-rate comic book.

This culture of decline was helped along by the mere presence of the flashy drug kingpens Nicky Barnes and Frank Lucas who wrestled control of the heroin trade from the white gangsters. These two men, along with their extensive network of dealers, exhibited their deadly image of success by outlandish dress, big cars and girlfriends who doubled as glamorous prostitutes. These were the earliest "role models" that many kids saw as Barnes and Lucas killed thousands of people, directly and indirectly, and hastened Harlem's downfall in the 1970s. Of course, Hollywood made a movie about Lucas in 2007 called "American Gangster" that fed on the hip-hop craving for "Gangsta" adoration.

What puts hip-hop in the same class as all the other New Age movements is the "self as god" dictate where the individual does not feel "constrained" by any social norms or conventions. To spare hip-hoppers from the hassle of leafing through a large dictionary, the Universal Zulu Nation website contains a section called the "Black Law Dictionary" so that converts can access the definitions of who they are and who they *should* be according to the Supreme Council.

Under the word "free," a follower of hip-hop is told that he or she is not a slave to anybody. It further defines "free" to mean "having power to follow dictates of one's own will.[8] Compare that to Aleister Crowley's New Age declaration, "Do What Thou Will Shall be the Whole of the Law."

Again, the hip-hop philosophy is the same rehash of anti-establishment rebellion and vacuous morality that can be traced back to the bohemians, beatniks, hippies, and the personal philosophies of Kinsey, Hefner, Ginsberg, Leary and Valenti. Or, as veteran acid-head Dennis Hopper once said, "There are no rules, man!"

The Universal Zulu Nation of Hip-Hop even has a fifteen point theology posted on its website complete with a computer generated parchment-style graphic scroll as a background. These are not considered "rules," but rather an "understanding."

The following three excerpts are from "The Wisdom and Understanding of the Fifteen Beliefs in the Universal Zulu Nation" as written by the Amen Ra, Afrika Bambaataa:

5. We believe in truth, whatever it is.
9. We believe in the mental resurrection of the dead.
11. We believe in the power of the mind, and that power is as infinite as God himself. [small *h*]

The preamble of hip-hop "Understanding" also expresses the belief that "God is you and me also." The "Wisdom" continues by exhorting the urgent need for the entire Bible to be *rewritten* and *reinterpreted,* presumably to reflect Universal Zulu hip-hop beliefs. The same document also demands the destruction of all history books around the world that do not reflect universal hip-hop "truth," and as Number 5 declares, " . . . whatever it is."

Bam's logo for the Universal Zulu Nation of Hip-Hop is the ever-present Egyptian pyramid topped with the "all-seeing eye." At the base of the pyramid is a motto engraved into the stones, "The Mind is A Weapon, Don't Refuse It," not to be confused with the United Negro College Fund motto "A Mind is A Terrible Thing to Waste."

While the Universal Zulu Nation of Hip-Hop does not promote education that could be used to better the individual, the Supreme Council does believe in the pursuit of "knowledge." The "knowledge" as demonstrated on the website is the quest for knowing all that is unknown. This is accomplished by pursuing New Age psychic phenomena such as mind-reading, time travel, molecular teleportation, astrology, parallel universes and the concept of "infinite Earth" (whatever that is).

The website also maintains a special section devoted to "UFOology" which encourages contact with alien space beings. The site contains links to just about every lunatic UFO organization in existence. Imagine the prospects of hip-hoppers putting all this "knowledge" down on a job resume. It's just too good to be true. They didn't even have to go to school to learn it . . . whatever *it* is. No wonder young people are flocking to hip-hop. Who needs school when you can get "knowledge" from outer space.

In order to truly promote hip-hop as "universal" throughout the "universe" the following message is posted by Bam on the International Worldwide Web, which certainly will be accessible by space aliens of ever greater supreme knowledge than our own:

MESSAGE TO THE PEOPLE BLACK, BROWN, YELLOW, RED, WHITE PEOPLE OF ALL HUMAN BEINGS AND ALIENS TO UNIVERSAL LIFE FORMS OF ALL FORMS:

"We, the Universal Zulu Nation are an organization and a universal nation for all people on this planet so-called Earth, as well as for alien life forms of people in the universe, whether your [his spelling] from Mars, Venus, Jupiter, Saturn, Pluto, Earth, etc. We the Zulus are not foolish people to believe that we are the only life in the Universe."

-Brother Afrika Bambaataa
The Amen Ra of Universal Hip-Hop Culture

Maybe Brother Bambaataa should contact Tom Cruise and John Travolta at Scientology headquarters. They can tell Bam everything he needs to know about space aliens.

A co-conspirator with Bam in pushing hip-hop as a cultural wasteland is a rapper named KRS-ONE, which stands for "Knowledge Reigns Supreme Over Nearly Everybody." KRS-ONE, aka Lawrence Parker, helped to promote the hip-hop practice of using slang for their name, which is a "gang thang." Before becoming KRS-ONE, Parker was also known as "The Blastmaster" and "The Teacha." Before that, the jowly future rapper was banging tambourines as a Hare-Krishna at Kennedy International Airport, another case of severe identity crisis.

KRS-ONE is the temperamental hot-head of the two founders of hip-hop and is known for spontaneously combustive loud defensive outbursts when hip-hop is under the microscope. One such verbal tirade happened at a Stanford University sponsored conference called "Know-The-Ledge" which was intended to "build bridges" between hip-hop "journalists" and hip-hop "scholars."

At the conference, KRS-ONE took off on a brief rant before settling down to the "bridge-building" conference. His loose-cannon tendencies became more widely known when he was quoted in a New Yorker magazine article concerning his response to the terrorist attacks of 9/11, "We cheered when 9/11 happened in New York and I say that proudly here . . . because it does not affect us . . . 9/11 happened to them . . ." referring to the corporate entertainment industry headquarters of the music industry such as Universal, Sony, Time-Warner and others including the New York radio stations that play "New School" hip-hop as opposed to his "old school" hip-hop. *The New York Daily News* wasted no time in calling KRS-ONE an "anarchist."

KRS-ONE claims to have successfully lobbied the United Nations to declare hip-hop as a "culture," though, at press time, I was unable to find anyone at the UN who was willing to talk about KRS-ONE's claim. What KRS-ONE did accomplish was the politicalization for hip-hop as a movement to be "consulted" by local New York politicians in need of the "Bronx Vote."

And, like Scientology's L. Ron Hubbard, KRS-ONE is now actively lobbying to declare hip-hop a religion. Many argue that it already is practiced as a religion, though BAM and KRS-ONE sure would like the tax break. KRS-ONE calls his sister organization "The Temple of Hip-Hop" which also functions to "maintain and promote the hip-hop culture."

"Scholars" of hip-hop like to point out that the first stage, or old school hip-hop, which lasted from 1973 to 1984, was fairly harmless "fun" music without the violence and vulgarity that followed. Almost anyone from that generation remembers "Rapper's Delight" from the Sugar Hill Gang in 1978.

But, the music was still part of the outer space religious lunacy of the Universal Zulu Nation and the dark side of Hollywood stepped in to add the deviant edge. Tinseltown exchanged one form of musical insanity with a capricious form of violent absurdity that is a hybrid of the producer's sick mind with that of emotionally lost youth in need of guidance.

The "New School" of hip-hop/rap began with the aptly titled album, "Raising Hell" by Run DMC just prior to 1985. Bam and KRS-ONE had kept the black man and woman imprisoned in a mental and cultural hell and Hollywood would step in to make sure they stayed there.

OLD SCHOOL VERSUS NEW SCHOOL

Even before Run DMC, Hollywood record companies were distributing hip-hop/rap music from the regional rap record producers and their independent companies. By the mid-80s, Hollywood was buying up all the "independent" labels as they quickly became divisions of the major record companies. With much of American youth already mind-numbed into the hip-hop beat, the rappers and their new producers turned up the heat by pushing the envelope of decency, a stage which has remained virtually unchanged for over two decades.

This is the New School of Hip Hop where the bass beat blares louder, the blood runs thicker, women are strippers and rappers are profanity-spitting junkie thugs. And, with the spread of the "culture" to saturation levels around the country, a power grab ensued between the Old School and New School to claim the hip-hop mantle of immoral authority.

Russell Simmons, New School founder of Def Jam Records and former producer of a large segment of hip-hop's most horrific and violent "music," sold his company to form an organization in 2001 called the Hip-Hop Summit Action Network (HSAN). The organization sponsors large gatherings in major urban areas to advance "the empowerment of youth." This is deja'vu Allen Ginsberg and the New Vision of "youth empowerment" from the 1950's all over again. Under Russell Simmons, the New School Hip-Hop Summit Action Network is one of the biggest manipulators of American youth on a mass scale since the hippie generation of the 1960s.

According to HSAN'S Mission Statement:

> "HSAN is dedicated to harnessing the cultural relevance of hip-hop music to serve as a catalyst for education advocacy and other societal concerns fundamental to the empowerment of youth. HSAN is a non-profit, non-partisan national coalition of Hip-Hop artists, entertainment industry leaders, education activists, civil rights proponents and youth leaders united in the belief that hip-hop is an enormously influential agent for social change . . . [9]

The last line might better be interpreted to read, "Hip-Hop is an enormously influential agent for further enslaving young urban youth in order to control and command at our will and to line our pockets and those of our close friends and Democratic politicians." In scanning the HSAN website, it becomes quickly apparent and glaringly obvious that HSAN is a phony front organization whose sole purpose is to register young urban youth between the ages of 18 and 30 to vote.

Once registered, the HSAN will directly, or indirectly, dictate to the young hip-hoppers who they *will* vote for in national and local elections. The prominent face of Jesse Jackson alongside Simmons and Ice Cube on the website is enough said about the "non-partisan" agenda of HSAN.

Further proof of "non-partisan youth empowerment" was evidenced in an ABC News article by Marcus Baram on January 20, 2007 where Russell Simmons was quoted, just prior to the next round of hip-hop summits, "'If you could take Barack Obama's image, add Hillary Clinton's money and John Edwards voice, that would be my candidate,' said Russell Simmons, who has yet to *endorse a candidate* . . ." When the press is anxiously awaiting the endorsement of the blood-spitting, misogynistic, hate-mongering "hip-hop choice" for president, this country certainly is in deep trouble.

Simmons is trying to distance himself from the UFO and alien outreach programs of the Old School founders Bam and KRS-ONE. At the kick-off of the 2007 seven-city tour of hip-hop summits (voting drives), Simmons stressed "taking charge" and "financial responsibility."

At the Houston kick-off in March, the theme for young hip-hoppers was "Get Your Money Right." To demonstrate how vacant and insincere the hip-hop summits are, consider this piece of financial wisdom from panelist/rapper "Bun B" who held up a chain hanging from his neck, encrusted with diamonds, "If you're gonna buy a chain for $30,000, be sure its not the only $30,000 you have." And the crowd went wild.

Or how about investment advice from Slim Thug who told the crowd of young star-struck hip-hoppers, "When you get your bread, you gotta keep your bread." Amazing! And we all thought Neil Cavuto, Lou Dobbs and Ben Stein had a sharp eye for finance and economics. Meanwhile, the "organizers" begin working the crowd to identify and register voters while they are on a hip-hop high.

Under the HSAN's website, a list of "accomplishments" under "Program Strategy" is a city by city run-down of voters registered at past summits and goals for registering new voters at current and future summits. Of course, voter registration for young people is highly encouraged, but Simmon's remarks about the ideal candidate for president and the participation of Jesse Jackson insure that this generation of voters will only be best served by voting on the strong "endorsements" of HSAN founder Simmons.

In other words, Simmons and Jackson have restored slavery to a large, easily impressionable group of young people. Pastor G. Craige Lewis criticizes the cultural practice of tattoos and body piercings by hip-hoppers because of its Egyptian origin "which was a sign of slavery—a sign that somebody owned you." And that's why Simmons and Jackson like the hip-hop slave trade. Their "property" is marked and easily identified.

By March 2007, Jackson had already endorsed Obama within days of the first Hip-Hop Summit Action Network gathering in Houston. Simmons was "expected" to "hold for Hillary" in a carefully coordinated manner of Jacksonian timing if Obama sank. However, by March 2008, Simmons was pressured into supporting Obama by his own inner Buddhist Karma which he stated was "in complete solidarity with the transformative consciousness" that emanates from the "hip-hop generation."

THE HOLLYWOOD CULTURE WAR

Jesse Jackson's mastery of the Saul Alinsky school of corporate shakedowns mixes well with Hollywood's own shakedown of its hip-hop musicians who in turn shake down the consumers into buying their well-polished trash—if they want to be "hip." One of the main sponsors of the HSAN is Anhueser-Busch, producer of Budweiser beer. Anhueser-Busch was "greatly encouraged" by Jesse Jackson to hire one of his sons in an executive job in order to avoid some vague "action" not to be confused with a boycott, you understand?

So, now the shakedown goes full circle; Jackson funds the Hip-Hop summit through his son's influence at Budweiser; the Hip-Hop summit stresses voter registration above all else; Jackson strongly "suggests" to Simmons who to endorse for the U.S. Congress and the presidency at strategically timed summits (there have been over 40 in just six years.) And, to cap it all off (not to be confused with tap a keg) Budweiser is helping to turn a new generation of hip-hoppers into alcoholics and life-long customers (even if their life isn't so long due to cirrhosis of the liver). This is all a theory, of course ... you understand?

The whole idea of "empowering" young people and "poor" people through the Hip-Hop Summits appears to some observers as a possible fraud of mammoth proportions intended to more greatly empower Simmons and Jackson politically, and ultimately financially, through lucrative paybacks by hip-hop endorsed elected officials. Harold Doley, Jr., one of America's top 100 African-American businessmen once believed in Jackson's fight for the disenfranchised in America until he encountered Jackson's shady dealings first hand. According to Marc Morano of CNS News in an October 22, 2001 report, Doley realized the "Jesse in fact stiffed the poor people of America."

Hip-hop organizers decided against a rap motto suggested for their future summits which proclaimed, "turn me up, turn me down ... shake, shake, shake, ... shake me down."

The HSAN is literally taking a page from Alabama Governor George Wallace's "block vote" strategy, which intentionally sounds like "black vote." Becoming a racial liberal after the 1972 assassination attempt on his life, Wallace could count on the "block vote" to elect him into office. This term neither offended his old time white supporters or his new-found forgiving black supporters. In his final run for governor in 1984 George Wallace won with an astounding 67% of the "block vote."

Jesse Jackson learned this first hand after befriending the Alabama governor in the 1970s. Jackson's involvement with Simmons and the HSAN is an attempt to corner the young "bloc" vote. (Jackson and others removed the "k" years ago to remove any hint of the highly ironic link to Wallace. Or, is that "linc?")

Notice how the HSAN mission statement mentioned "non-partisan" but says nothing about being multi-racial or multi-cultural. HSAN is a not-too-subtle racist attempt to tell mainly young African-American and Hispanic youth the "how to" and "who to" of bloc voting in local, state and national elections.

Curiously, the last two "accomplishments" of the HSAN listed on their website as of January 2008 were:

- Defended the hip-hop culture before members of the U.S. Congress and before Federal regulatory agencies such as the Federal Trade Commission and the Federal Communications Commission. (What were they in desperate need of defending?)
- Worked in alliance with the Recording Association of America (RIAA) in support of the Parental Advisory Label program that alerts parents to explicit lyrics in music.

The last "accomplishment" is placed at the bottom of the list for a reason. It is the most laughable and hypocritical considering Simmons past and present promotion of the most vulgar and violent music in American history. After mention of this "working alliance" with RIAA, a visitor to the HSAN website can readily connect to links such as "Hip Hop News." A click of the mouse simply sends you to the links for such sites as *XXL Magazine* online which is the most profanity-laced magazine of hip-hop interviews with up and coming and down and out rappers. It's also the number one source of tracking the latest hip-hop arrests, indictments, jailings and killings. Very uplifting. Advertisers include "booty" porn and cell phone sex.

The other hyperlink promoted by HSAN is to ALLHIPHOP.com, dubbed "The World's Most Dangerous Site," which is a toilet repository portal into everything bleak, dismal, misogynistic, violent and perverted in hip-hop culture.

Russell Simmons wins the award as "America's Worst New Role Model" for young adults, given the content he continues to promote and "artists" he defends. Some observers consider Simmons as a de-facto predator luring adolescents into a world of perpetual hatred, violence, pornography and crime committed by other "adults" who, of course, are not only absent of "maturity," but are deeply mentally disturbed and in need of therapy. Is Simmons, therefore a double-trouble predator, exploiting children and psychotic adults alike?

What Simmons has gained from his formal informal partnership with the Reverend Jesse Jackson is one; he can claim the hip-hop summits are supported by a major "religious" figure, even though Jackson has forgotten how to spell Jesus Christ—it's been so long. And, two; Simmons has learned from Jackson how to shakedown corporations for millions of dollars.

In 2003, Simmons coerced a "contribution" to HSAN from the Pepsi Corporation after the soft drink giant canceled a promotional contract with the foul-mouth rapper Ludacris for using music from his inspirational CD "Move

THE HOLLYWOOD CULTURE WAR

Bitch." Instead of telling Ludacris to "grow up," Simmons used the incident to shake Pepsi down for untold millions.

The HSAN refused to return my calls asking how the "contribution" was spent by the *non-profit* organization which also refused a financial disclosure request concerning the *tax-free* organization. Another lesson learned from Jesse Jackson who has also avoided accountability for his multiple non-profit organizations of cultural deception.

And, that's what New School hip-hop is all about; no accountability, no rules, and anything goes.

Meanwhile, back in the Bronx, the Old School of Bam and KRS-ONE has little regard for the crass commercialization of the mystic Egyptian culture they created four decades ago. So, not to be outdone, Bam established the Universal Federation for the Preservation of Hip-Hop Culture in 2003 for the purpose "to preserve hip-hop culture and provide instruction as to the manifestations, significance, social history and placement of hip-hop culture."

To help promote the new organization, Afrika Bambaataa, the original hip-hopper on the verge of Social Security, holds concerts in the Bronx on a regular basis. Bam appears in full King-Tut style head mask and Egyptian royal regalia as the living legend "who started it all."

One concert poster proclaimed "Old School Hip Hop Straight from the Boogie down Bronx" that was held on December 3, 2005. Sprinkled among the crowd were rich white northeast college students in Khaki attire holding camcorders, tape recorders and scribbling rapidly in notebooks. Like preppie anthropologists covering the last gasp of a dying tribe, Bam put on a show for them, no doubt requesting copies of their recordings for the Universal Federation "museum."

It is unknown whether any of the cultural anthropologists took note that King Bam was the man who became an Egyptian god after a visit to Africa and returned to spread more cultural rot to the national and international culture than any other musician in the history of song and dance. Hip-hop was and remains a sick triple-x vaudeville burlesque show that seemingly never ends. The only change is that the carnival barker on the street corner now dresses like a pastor and invites children in to watch and participate.

And, as the first decade of the 21st century draws to an end, hip-hop and rap continues to slide down the barometric scale of decency as hip-hop "artist" DMX demonstrated with his song "Bring Your Whole Crew."

> I got blood on my hands and there's no remorse. I got blood on my d____ cause I just f____ a corpse. I am a nasty nigga when u pass me nigga look me in the eyes. Tell me to my f____ face that you ready to die."

DMX likes to think of himself as a "minister of God." He has, on occasion, given money to financially strapped churches and suddenly assumed virtual sainthood by the congregation. Of course, they managed to overlook the lyrics of his songs, even though the color of money they received from DMX was red as blood, including dead dog blood.

This is just one incident within the larger mission by the hip-hop culture, and everything morose they stand for, to infiltrate Christian churches. In fact, the biggest battle within the larger Culture War is the current campaign by the hip-hop establishment to slowly and patiently insert itself into traditional black and new multi-racial mega-churches.

Unfortunately, this stealth campaign has become a two-way street in some of these battles to either keep hip-hop out or let hip-hop in to the sanctuary. While this battle is waged without much attention from the secular press, it has become a contentious issue in faith-based publications and threatens to divide congregations, which is exactly what the hip-hop entertainers want to accomplish.

But, the biggest shock, to both churches and rappers, came in 2006 when evangelist Creflo Dollar of World Changers Church in Atlanta appeared in a lurid music video called "Welcome to Atlanta" with thug rappers 50-Cent, Ludacris and Jermaine Dupri. The video contains all the usual profane rap and slithering strippers rubbing against the nearest stationary object.

For those of you who are not familiar with these rappers, they have produced some of the most contaminated and pornographic CDs and music videos in hip-hop history. 50-Cent alone has been arrested, jailed, shot and stabbed on numerous occasions as he slowly burns out in the hip-hop limelight.

Up until his appearance in this video, Creflo Dollar was the up-and-coming televangelist of the 21st century. His 23,500 member mega-church has 350 employees and maintains branches in half a dozen countries around the world. Pastor Dollar preaches prosperity and health, which is the message of the New Testament's "good news" for modern man and the key reason evangelism has experienced enormous growth in the last 40 years.

However, when Pastor Creflo Dollar began preaching incorrectly that God will not only meet your need, but also your greed, he made a wrong turn by showing off his brand new Rolls Royces. One is for him and one is for wife Taffi, with plans for more in the pipeline. His tailor-made pastoral suits have grown in flair and expense with each passing year and many began to see the once-promising pastor as the reincarnation of a new mega-monster Reverend Ike-like character.

All of this attracted the attention of hip-hoppers who worship money and gold in lieu of God. They were willing to "forgive" Pastor Dollar's belief in God because like the gangsters they are, the seedy rappers saw a huge market in the youth of the church who traditionally have been swayed against the hip-hop culture and music.

With his new creed of "God is Greed" instead of "God is Good," Creflo Dollar saw an opportunity for his Atlanta church to attract more young people if only his church could come off as "hip" as in hip-hop. This is the two-way street where nobody wins.

The hip-hoppers knew if they could get Pastor Creflo Dollar (who already has the perfect hip-hop name) to "cross over" many other churches would follow his lead. Traditional, classic gospel and regional music of the church would be shoved aside forever. Creflo Dollar reached out to the long arm of Mephistopheles and sold his soul in "Welcome to Atlanta." And, while he didn't lose many members of his Atlanta church congregation, he did lose a considerable cable and satellite TV audience, which he fully expects to replace with younger hip-hoppers and booty-dancers. As one former member told me, "He can get his soul back if he just quits sleeping with the devil." If not, the Elmer Gantry trap door is ready and waiting. It is widely believed that Creflo Dollar's pretentious behavior at this time led to the congressional inquiry into Dollar's finances by Senator Charles Grassley in November of 2007. This is the payback for Creflo Dollar's Faustian deal with the Temple of Hip Hop.

A rising voice in the escalating Culture War against hip-hop pointed specifically to Creflo Dollar's actions as a catalyst for an enormous negative impact on the church, noting "The message this sends out to these rappers is that the church is 'down' [hip] with what they are doing." G. Craige Lewis, a pastor from Ft. Worth, Texas has been gaining ground in his fight against the hip-hop culture as he was the first to publicly expose hip-hop's roots back to Afrika Bambaata and KRS-ONE. He is by far the most engaging, energetic, knowledgeable and informative individual on the hip-hop culture and the *truth* behind hip-hop.

ENTER THE MESSENGER:
THE TRUTH BEHIND HIP-HOP

Often referred to as "The Messenger" by his congregation and a rapidly growing worldwide following, Pastor G. Craige Lewis ventured beyond the question of *why* hip-hop came to exert such a vicious and oppressive influence on society and determined to find out *how* it started. By the late 1990's Lewis' teachings and revelations about Bambaataa, KRS-ONE and the origins of hip-hop began to attract attention beyond the sanctuary walls of his church in Fort Worth.

Asked to speak at a variety of other churches around the country, the young African-American pastor soon produced a DVD titled *The Truth Behind Hip-Hop* which sparked outrage from the hip-hop community and applause from hip-hop's critics who saw a man of exemplary energy and insight who decided to literally fight the good fight.

His message is considered extreme by the growing worldwide hip-hop culture because it is extreme—extremely true. Up until the time that G. Craige Lewis entered the battle, nobody could quite put a finger on how a mentally, physically and spiritually debilitating movement known as hip-hop came to be as influentially destructive to the culture as it has become.

As Lewis describes the nature of the culture, "Hip-hop is a sub-cultural movement, and cannot be considered an ethnographic or demographic culture. A sub-culture is defined as having distinctive characteristics within a larger culture."[10] Furthermore, Lewis explains that hip-hop, as a sub-culture, uses basic deconstruction of words and concepts that increases its visibility as it strives to be more visible in the society.

The rapid rise of Pastor G. Craige Lewis' message was helped by the establishment of his Ex-ministries, meaning; ex-criminal, ex-prostitute, ex-drug addict, and ex-hip-hoppers. And, the hip-hop entertainment machine was "none too happy" to watch the number of visitors to the Ex-Ministries website skyrocket into seven figures with no hint of slowing down. After several years on the internet, the site had drawn more than 1.2 million visitors to its website by March of 2006. One year later, the number of visitors had already doubled.

Many hip-hop "artists" were becoming worried that people had finally found a forceful critic who revealed the nasty beginnings and ongoing evolution of everything hip-hop from the clothing, the metal teeth grills, hairstyles, tattoos and music to the very words, attitudes and behavior of the suffocating sub-cultural movement. And, when Lewis' DVD *The Truth Behind Hip-Hop* began selling more copies than certain hip-hoppers were selling CDs, their worry turned into fury.

Even worse, as far as the hip-hoppers wee concerned, Lewis's DVD was being used as a ministry tool by churches and congregational gatherings around the world. This meant that the Ex-Ministry exposé of hip-hop was being seen by millions more who were learning for the first time about hip-hop's cumulative downward drag on individuals, families, neighborhoods, communities and entire national societies in America and abroad.

During the 2008 primaries, Barack Obama was even offering downloadable hip-hop ring tones from his website. Not unusual for a man who plans to *reform* American Christianity to *conform* to his personal worldview.

Further angering hip-hoppers around the world was Pastor Lewis' release of a follow-up DVD appropriately titled *Exodus Into Egypt* which explains the ever present New Age fascination with mystic ancient Egyptian gods and how the hip-hop culture was actually bringing people back into bondage. The backlash against Lewis would grow more intense as he released two more DVDs and published a book based on his original DVD exposé *The Truth Behind Hip-Hop*.

As Lewis explained in advance of his book's release in 2007, "hip-hop is a religion/culture or belief system that was birthed out of a desire to manifest one's self in a society that was deemed unfair to African-Americans in the 1970s. Because of the negative environments and social situations that plagued the black race at the time, Afrika Bambaataa and others created a way of temporarily overcoming these social obstacles by partying, making music and believing in one's self and one's own power.

"These parties were called 'Hip-Hop Parties' and they were viewed at the time as an opportunity to preach a newfound doctrine of self-worship and hate for the establishment—the white race. Hip-Hop targeted rap music and used music to preach a message that empowered the black race as 'true gods' and made Jesus Christ the 'white man's religion.' Hip-Hop taught the youth at the time, and still teaches indirectly that you can be who you want to be in the sense of not being what people want you to be."

Lewis further explains that this attitude "turns into rebellion against basic laws and truths that govern our society as a whole. Hip-Hop began to change the very appearance of its followers by creating a look, a way of governing yourself, and a language that should be spoken. What this created was a sub-culture of our American culture and it caused our youth to go against the basic pattern of society and manifest their own will regardless of what it cost them socially and spiritually."[11]

As for the trademark "gangsta" and "stripper" look, Lewis ascribes that tradition to hip-hop's roots in the Bronx where "Young boys began to emulate the look of thugs and gangsters because there was no real positive role models among them to emulate. Our young girls would begin dressing like whores or prostitutes they would see on a daily basis."[12] Add television and Hollywood to the mix, especially in the post 1968 "Free Screen" movement of Jack Valenti, and these detrimental and dysfunctional lifestyles were receiving increasing attention from the sleaze producers in the industry who were always "on the toilet" looking for something outrageous to fill the "entertainment" product line.

By the late 1980s and early 1990s, hip-hop and rap were becoming a staple of the video music industry which did more to spread the hip-hop culture rot than any other media. Promos still run on MTV and BET that proclaim, "Hip-hop is not music, it is a way of life."

If there was ever a justification for drug testing in the music, television and movie industry as discussed in Chapter 13, hip-hop is justification number one. What would happen to the "culture" if drugs and their abuse was detected and confirmed among the producers, directors, performers and distributors of hip-hop? What would hip-hop look like?

To hear Pastor G. Craige Lewis speak is an experience in divine revelation and a clarion call to long overdue action. Sacred cows of hip-hop have been explored and exploded with the simple admonition to go "straight to the source" when attempts are made to homogenize and mainstream hip-hop into society, just as Russell Simmons and Jesse Jackson are attempting to do with their Hip-Hop Summit Action Network.

As Lewis declares in *The Truth Behind Hip-Hop* while speaking to a packed house, "Hip-Hop glorifies everything that is bad; brothers walking with pants sagging down at the high school . . . and those tattoos and strange piercings, those were signs of slavery back in ancient Egypt—and that wasn't a good thing!"

The fascination among American youth with shaved heads, metal-punctured skin and tattoos are simply signs that they have signed on to the culture of Hollywood in general and hip-hop in particular as generational slaves to fashion and style. There are men and women now in their 30s and 40s who grew out of hip-hop, but concealed just beneath the fabric of their clothes are the barbed wire shackle tattoos around their arms and ankles. The "In-A-Gadda-Da-Vida" floral and butterfly designs on the small of women's backs are almost a rite of passage into the hip-hop cultural enslavement.

Lewis argues that these sub-cultural markers, fashion, behavior and hip-hop mentality follow youth into adulthood and robs them of their true personality and over time becomes harder for the individual to return to their true identity.[13] The promoters of hip-hop always target the youth, just as all New Age movements have done in the past, because young people are often the most impressionable and susceptible to the phony trappings and false seductions of Hollywood and so-called "progressive thinking," which is actually regressive by its own core philosophy. According to Lewis;

Hip-Hop Produces:

- Youth with no fear.
- Youth with no purpose.
- Youth with no respect for authority.
- Youth with no parental guidance.
- Youth with no regard for their bodies, appearance, self respect or future.

One of the major hip-hop predators of young people, in addition to Russell Simmons, is hip-hop entrepreneur Sean Combs, the "man" with the multi-polar name identity crisis who declared, "Rap is the music, but hip-hop is my life . . . as a matter of fact hip-hop is life!"[14] Combs is one of the major perpetrators of the new slave trade branching out into cologne, fashion, vodka and musical pornography. Purchasing his cologne or clothing line is tantamount to supporting and maintaining his plantation where souls and suckers are picked in lieu of cotton.

Russell Simmons and rapper Jay Z have also owned plantations in the past with the same marketing strategy that Michael Jordan used to sell $200 tennis shoes to poor urban youth.

The depressing, angry faces that glare from the covers of CDs, music videos and publicity posters is part of the convict thug look, or as Lewis explains, "looking like you just robbed a bank is the norm." Lewis also notes that the central theme that drives the hip-hop "attitude" and mindset is "Anything goes, as long as you are feeling it." Sound familiar? Straight from Hollywood, the long arm of Mephistopheles continues reaching out to the gullible, impressionable and rebellious.

HOLY HIP-HOP, GANGSTA GOSPEL AND CHRISTIAN RAP

Creflo Dollar's "Dance with the Devils" in 2006 brought to national attention a battle that has been percolating within the church for over a decade. The mainstream press has ignored the war that is raging within African-American and multi-racial congregations concerning the infiltration of hip-hop culture into the church, especially the youth ministries.

Not only is Pastor G. Craige Lewis leading the Culture War against the infestation of hip-hop into the general society, he is also fighting against the morbid influence of hip-hop into the Christian church, especially in the new era of mega-churches and the growing Evangelical Left movement. According to Lewis, this trend to embrace hip-hop is causing a "mass diluting of God's Word from the Bible" as some churches are desperate to prop up youth membership at any cost, which he calls, "Top-pop sermons of the new Pentecostal movement."[15]

Early tensions began back in 1997 when The Cross Movement began coinciding with the start up of Cross Movement Records, a recording company that produces mainly "Holy Hip-Hop" music by artists that have gained a following among some in the church who believe that these musicians are true Christian converts. They believe that these holy hip-hoppers are simply using the hip-hop "style" to become more accessible to the youth of the church in spreading the Christian gospel.

Lewis believes half of that strategy is true. Holy hip-hoppers are using the hip-hop style to become more accessible to youth, but not necessarily to spread the accuracy of the Bible. Instead, critics of holy hip-hop contend that the efforts of the Cross Movement and other hip-hoppers to tap into a fixed-market audience through the millions of mega-church evangelicals is another ploy to sell CDs. The record companies encourage the churches to establish "contemporary services" not too different from some "Christian Rock" movements.

But, as Lewis states adamantly, "Holy hip-hop is a joke." As Lewis points out, the whole creation of hip-hop and its "theology" was established as a direct perversion of the God of Abraham and specifically Christianity, considered by the Zulu Nation of Hip-Hop to be the "white man's god."

Furthermore, the holy hip-hoppers have maintained all the dreary cultural markers such as baggy pants to the knees, gang gestures, hooded jackets, the thug face and perpetuation of broken English.

According to Pastor Lewis, this movement by certain churches to embrace the hip-hop culture only drags the church down to the level of the hip-hop lifestyle and mindset instead of the church uplifting the hip-hoppers to a higher level of respect, dignity and freedom from the bondage of a corrupt culture.

"Wouldn't it be more effective to have a person that once dressed like a whore, gang member, or a prisoner to show the change that God made to *their* appearances?" Lewis points to the fact that the very terms "holy hip-hop" and "gangsta gospel" are oxymorons of hypocrisy that is becoming popular because "Youth pastors and churches do not effectively know how to reach out to the youth of their communities" and they are too eager to get young people in the church even if the Word of God is diluted to a handful of words in an otherwise "secular" hip-hop performance.

Lewis notes that these youth ministers "are so desperate for the attention of the youth that they will allow a Gospel Gangsta, a Holy Hoodlum or even a Prechin' Pimp to come and give their youth some tight beats and rhymes."[16]

As an example, Lewis explains how Saul of Tarsus, a Pharisee, was saved by God on the road to Damascus. He became a new man and no longer considered himself to be a Pharisee: he became a believer. He no longer dressed like a Pharisee, thought like a Pharisee or acted out the hatred of the Pharisees. He became the Apostle Paul.

As Lewis demonstrates, "If hip-hop is teaching rebellion and is a spiritual problem, then why join forces with it? I could not allow a person that is pierced all up, tattooed all over and dressed in black with dark make-up and a scary countenance to get up before my church and teach them anything . . . Many of our youth cannot get decent jobs or even finish school because they refuse to change their look for our society . . . and our kids can't get ahead looking like this."[17] Lewis adds, "What if the Goth movement came to the church with ministers dressed like Marilyn Manson? Is that supposed to edify God?"

Not surprisingly, Pastor G. Craige Lewis' ministry is coming under increasing attack by devotees of the secular and holy hip-hop movement because his growing influence is cutting into the hip-hop way of life and especially hip-hop profits. Lewis noted in postings on his website in July of 2007 that holy hip-hoppers were targeting him by disrupting his services at his home church in Fort Worth and also showing up at speaking engagements by Lewis at churches across America.

THE HOLLYWOOD CULTURE WAR

Bigger storms on the horizon are the open doors to the hard-core hip-hoppers made possible by Creflo Dollar. Even the aforementioned high-profile culture pimp and pornographer with 16 different names known currently, as of this printing, as Sean John is planning to release a special "gospel" CD under his Bad Boy Records label. Its just a temporary conversion from the tuxedo rapper whose "song" titled "Me and My Bitch" is the most profane in recording history complete with drugs, sex, violence, incest, crime and murder.

With more brave voices like G. Craige Lewis and others speaking out against the most corrosive and retrograde enemy in the Culture War, there is now a good chance we will all live long enough to watch the long slow fade of hip-hop into the same swampy sunset of other New Age dribble.

As Dr. Johnetta Betsch Cole surmised, "the power of words and the ideas they reflect cannot be ignored. For words, like images, can implant both negative and positive ideas and attitudes. The harsh and harmful gender talk in too much of rap music and hip-hop culture must be addressed by society conscious women and men who deplore violence and misogyny and understand the damage it does within our communities and around the world. For indeed, just as some words can and do teach, motivate and inspire, words that disrespect girls and women—and by extension boys and men as well—can and do hurt us."[18]

UNINTENDED CONSEQUENCES:
Don Imus Shakes Up Hip-Hop Nation

April 4, 2007 "Nappy-headed hos" turned out to be the three infamous words echoed around the world in April of 2007 after shock jock radio talk show host Don Imus used the term on-air along with producer Bernard McGuirk to describe the Rutgers University Scarlet Knights women's basketball team as they watched a televised game in the studio.

Late that evening, the Soros-funded speech police website known as Media Matters had sent transcripts of the broadcast to news organizations around the world. Instantly, America's two major Quadra-Pleaders (Paper Pastor Poverty Pimps) Jesse Jackson and Al Sharpton began demanding action from CBS Radio and MSNBC which simulcast the show.

All sides of the political/social spectrum felt that the remarks were inappropriate and cast a shadow on a shining moment of victory by the Rutgers Scarlet Knights. CBS decided to suspend Imus for two weeks, but the Quadra-Pleaders began to demand that Imus be fired immediately.

Two days later, Imus issued an apology and set himself up, unknowingly, by appearing on Sharpton's National Action Network (NAN) radio show and asking for forgiveness. Sharpton pounded Imus relentlessly as if he [Sharpton] was the model of moral authority. Some observers have described Al Sharpton as a walking de-facto co-conspirator in the deaths of nine people over the last twenty years.

April 6-10 A national debate begins about the Imus remarks, free speech, the First Amendment and "objectionable language." Television, radio, newspapers and internet sites begin to print the lyrics of the most popular rap music in the nation, to the shock of many who didn't realize that "ho, bitches, and niggas" was not only standard in hip-hop/rap music, it was pervasive everywhere in "the culture." Some began to suggest that as crude as they were, Imus' comments were beginning to reflect the cultural rot of hip-hop and its creeping prevalence in common every day conversation.

Immediately, the defenders of hip-hop culture began the futile attempt to explain that the language was okay for African-Americans but not for whites, especially a 66 year old white radio D.J. This was quickly tagged as the "hip-hop hypocrisy" and grew more intense as rap lyrics were being printed off the internet, including the week's "top hits" provided by Michelle Malkin.

Many of the vocal critics of the hip-hop hypocrisy began to be voiced from the wider African-American community, temporarily preventing Jackson and Sharpton from creating a black/white issue as they had hoped.

A book released in the previous month of March by African-American author Cora Daniels titled *Ghetto Nation* begins to pick up exposure and sales. Daniels' book is an insightful critique into America's embrace of a "ghetto personae" that is demeaning to women, devalues education among youth and "celebrates" the worst stereotype of African-Americans. As the introduction to Daniels' book explains, the volume is also an expose of "the central role of corporate America in exploiting 'ghettoness' as a hip cultural idiom to make money."[19]

A number of internet bloggers started to spill the "dirty little secret" that both BET and MTV have high level African-American women as executives for their raunch-laden music channels who are paid equally high level bucks by their corporate parents to serve as poverty pimp defenders of their fellow musical denigrators of dignity.

On April 11th with momentum building for Imus to be fired, senior BET producer Pamela Gentry said that the foul and vulgar gutter-filled videos shown on BET could not be compared to Imus because they [BET] serve a *different* audience! On the same day, Snoop Dogg chimed in and said the "niggas" and "hos" he raps about are *different* than the Rutgers basketball team. Of course, the perpetually stoned rapper made these "philosophical observations" on the same day he was being sentenced for drug and weapons convictions (a badge of honor for rappers.)

As a trifecta of dubious comments flowing simultaneously in one day, Senator Hillary Clinton joined the choir and condemned the Imus remarks, though she failed to mention that 12 days earlier she had attended a massive fundraiser hosted by producer-rapper Timbaland that brought in close to one million dollars. Timbaland is responsible for some of the most brazen, bloody, violent and racist lyrics in contemporary rap with no shortage of "hos, bitches, and niggas." Hillary did not return the blood-soaked money.

HIP-HOP FLIP-FLOP

April 12-15 CBS decides to cancel Imus' show on April 12th after Jesse Jackson and AL Sharpton met "privately" with CBS executives. It is doubtful that either one of the Quadra Pleaders threatened CBS with advertiser boycotts alone. Only they can confirm how much, if any, "contributions" were made by CBS to PUSH and NAN, not to be confused with "payoffs," if the two Paper Pastor Poverty Pimps would "shut-up and go away."

In the middle of this "April from Hell" controversy, a Virginia Tech student named Cho shot and killed 32 students and then shot himself at the Blacksburg, Virginia campus on April 16th. While law enforcement, psychologists and journalists tried to find a motive for America's deadliest college campus massacre, the hip-hop industry was shaking in its boots for fear that Cho's dorm room would reveal a plethora of hip-hop rap CDs. To this day, that information has still not been released.

With the hip-hop hypocrisy now taking on a larger and longer life than Don Imus and the usual 24 hour news cycle, defenders of debauchery and fence sitting hypocrites felt compelled to pump up the volume. While the rappers and the music industry executives quickly cut off any further comment, two "activists," Al Sharpton and hip-hop guru Russell Simmons made remarks that would come back to haunt then within a week.

- Al Sharpton—"Imus can say he wants to be forgiven . . . But we cannot afford a precedent established that the airwaves can commercialize sexism and racism."[20]
- Russell Simmons—"Comparing Don Imus' language with hip-hop artists poetic expression is misguided and inaccurate and feeds into a mindset that can be a catalyst for unwarranted, rampant censorship."[21]

A battle began to brew in Manhattan between Sharpton and Simmons to see who could gain the upper-hand on the low-road of hip-hop. Sharpton took the stand that his divine duty was to "take on" the big entertainment companies behind the hip-hop/rap labels.

April 17-19 As a way of "introducing" himself to the record company executives, Sharpton reportedly began selling additional table space at his April 18th opening conference of the National Action Network being held in New York. According to George Rush and Jeanne Rush of the *Daily News*, Sharpton began asking for $50,000 donations per table from the music companies based in Manhattan. [22] A spokesperson of NAN said the amount was "really" $15,000.

Aware of Sharpton's "contribution" scheme, Russell Simmons, director of the Hip-Hop Summit Action Network (HSAN) didn't want "his culture" co-opted by a Paper Pastor Poverty Pimp. On the 17th of April, the same day Sharpton is seeking tribute money for his conference, Simmons issues an urgent press release that he is convening a "private, closed door meeting" of executives of the music recording industry in the wake of controversy surrounding "hip-hop and the First Amendment." Hip-hop hypocrisy was now a bigger story than Don Imus and his "nappy-headed ho" comment, which consequently, however crude, was protected speech under the First Amendment.

In a new sub-categorical twist in the Culture War, the firing of Don Imus five days earlier opened the first national dialogue on the demoralizing hip-hop culture and the First Amendment to freedom of speech. But, of course, Simmons didn't want an "open door" discussion of the First Amendment since the record industry has always held a selective application of First Amendment freedoms.

Twenty-five major executives of the music industry decided to attend Simmons "private" conference on "free-speech" and rejected Sharpton's overture to attend the NAN opening day conference. After all, the tables were free at Simmon's gathering and the preacher would be preaching to the choir. Among the attendees slated for Simmons event was Antonio L.A. Reid, chairman of the Def Jam Record label under Universal. (Simmons had started Def Jam more than a decade earlier before selling the company.)

Ironically, L.A. Reid was scheduled to receive an "honorary" award the very next day on the 18th of April from Sharpton himself for his "accomplishments" to the music industry. Someone on Sharpton's staff with a few more cents of sense, pointed out to the Paper Pastor that Def Jam and L.A. Reid were responsible for some of the most violent misogynistic and profanely atrocious lyrics in contemporary rap music history with inspirational song titles that clearly indicated the content within such as "Move Bitch," "Ho", and "F___ You." These were obviously examples of the "poetry" of rap that Simmons had addressed in his April 13th press release.

"We don't want to be inconsistent," said Sharpton as he suddenly suspended the award to L.A. Reid. In protest, Universal Records rescinded their earlier offer to purchase a table at the NAN conference. Representative Charles Rangel of Harlem was so outraged by Universal's action that he offered to send Sharpton $15,000 "the next day" to compensate for Universal's intransigence.

The NAN conference was giving the spotlight to major Democratic presidential candidates and Barack Obama, not wanting to alienate the "hip-hop vote" that he had hoped Simmons would deliver, offered one of his usual double-entendre collective comments, "We're all complicit . . . let's not single out the rappers," noting that he had heard offensive language in many places other than hip-hop and rap songs.

Did that mean he was willing to include Hollywood movies and television programming in a campaign to curb indecent language? Doubtful, considering the fact that he was already bought and paid for by producer David Geffen and 700 Hollywood insiders at the time.

Sharpton also had to eat his words indicating "we cannot afford precedent established that the airways can commercialize sexism and racism." When asked why he had chosen to honor L.A. Reid in the first place, Sharpton was hard-pressed to find a coherent answer.

April 21-29 Ten days would pass before Simmons would issue a statement about his "private, closed-door meeting" with record executives. Events were charging so fast, the PR film handling HSAN press releases was furiously rewriting a statement with each passing day. During the week of April 21st, a series of news events and federal government press releases were also changing the climate daily concerning the national dialogue of speech, race and the violent "poetry" of hip-hop/rap music.

Word was rapidly spreading throughout the news community that correspondent Anderson Cooper was producing a special segment on the rap code of silence known as "Stop Snitchin" which is widely promoted in rap lyrics, emblazoned on T-shirts, ball caps, posters and other hip-hop paraphernalia. The hip-hop "street code" of silence mandates that if you witness a crime, you don't tell the cops because "snitches get stitches." The effects of such a lawless campaign promoted by musicians revealed a long list of mothers, family members, friends and onlookers who were threatened or murdered by rappers for testifying or informing on thugs who committed crimes. Furthermore, Anderson Cooper had been told, in confidence, by a major record company executive that record producers often encourage feuds between rappers because it makes "good" press and publicity that sells more records. As noted earlier in this chapter, any issue of *XXL* magazine is an example of the "strange fruit" that has resulted from the producer's blood marketing campaign.

Some have quietly questioned if this tactic by the major music corporations to foment violence is a federal criminal violation of RICO racketeering and conspiracy to commit violence for profit. Consider the fact that the ten year old murders of rivals Tupac Shakur and Notorious B.I.G. has yet to be resolved. More sinister is the fact that the record companies themselves produce the "Stop Snitchin" messages through lyrics in some of their rapper's songs, a double conspiracy to initiate feuds and promote "codes of silence" through slick advertising at the same time. In other words, inciting violence and obstruction of justice.

Anyone who has ever met a high-level record company executive knows that the sleaze factor is extremely high. Consider two record company executives from the 1970s and 1980s like David Geffen and Phil Spector. Character is not a quality among the people who make the music for you and your children.

In the Anderson Cooper investigations into the rapper's world of snitches and "street credibility," the straw that broke the hip-hop camel's back was an interview with rapper Cam'ron. When asked by Cooper if he would report that a mass murderer or serial killer lived next door to him, not unlike Cho of the Virginia Tech massacre, would Cam'ron alert the police? Cam'ron very calmly said no, he would not. Cam'ron did volunteer, for his own safety that he might "move from Apartment 4-0" but he wouldn't "snitch."

Anderson Cooper's interview almost didn't happen when he was turned down for interviews by almost every rapper he approached. The Cam'ron interview was fortunate in more ways than one. The more Cam'ron talked, the more he sputtered revelations about the shallow, empty and violently exploitative world of an "entertainment" industry gone morbidly awry. Cam'ron, who has been shot twice in both arms, said that the main reason, for him, in not "snitching" is because word of mouth would spread quickly that he was a tattle-tale and that would hurt his record sales! Never mind the fact that he could have put his attempted murderers behind bars before they managed to kill someone else. No, record sales first; justice last or not at all.

The Cam'ron comments sent chills down the back of everybody outside the hip-hop/rap industry. It was now clear that the violent subculture of hip-hop which once existed on no less than several city blocks of the devastated South Bronx in the early 1970s had been carefully nurtured, exploited and promoted as a culture of fashionable deviance by the masters of deviance in very white "liberal" Left Coast Hollywood.

April 23-25 In a fluke of timing amidst the hip-hop hypocrisy revelations flowing in daily during mid-April, the Federal Communications Commission (FCC) released a study on April 25th which had been commissioned almost a year earlier by Congress. The report stated that Congress had the authority to regulate violence on cable, satellite and broadcast television without violating the First Amendment. The report even cited Supreme Court precedent that stated what everybody knew, but refused to acknowledge, that the First Amendment freedom of speech is not unfettered. The report said that violence could be "relegated" to the late night hours.

The FCC already regulates network broadcast standards for television between 6:00 am and 10:00 pm. It currently has no regulatory authority over

THE HOLLYWOOD CULTURE WAR

cable, pay channels or satellite transmission. But, that could easily be changed by Congress which enjoys a rare bipartisan agreement on the danger of escalating hyper-violence and its very real effects on people's behavior. This could mean that all the rap video music channels that proliferate with violence in both lyrics and imagery could be shunted to the midnight and early morning hours. The report only made recommendations that Congress could legally pursue.

But, that was too close for comfort for Simmons who has become the de-facto defense attorney for the swamp called hip-hop. Finally, Simmons issued his press release follow-up of his "closed door, free speech" pow-wow with the recording industry executives. The press-release was much more subdued than his "poetry" of rap defense ten days earlier. Though his press release had been issued 2 days prior to the FCC report, Simmons had been informed of its very strict First Amendment clarifications.

In his press release, Simmons stated for the first time in his long hip-hop "anything goes" career that with freedom of expression comes "responsibility." Simmons, however made the ridiculous declaration of "partial" lyrical responsibility, recommending that "the recording and broadcast industries voluntarily remove/bleep/delete misogynistic words, *bitch* and *ho* and the racially offensive *nigger*."[23]

Simmons continued with his proclamation of hip-hop etiquette that these words "be considered with the same objection to obscenity as *extreme curse words*." But, he did not elaborate as to the other terms which are considered "extreme curse words."

Simmons' press release was purposely full of holes and left more questions than answers. As far as Simmons' definition was concerned, there was plenty of room for even greater levels of raunch. Even if the industry went along with Simmons' "three word ban," what about groups like DMX and "necrophilia" rap, "I've got blood on my d____, cause I just f____ a corpse." Russell Simmons wasn't concerned with "necrophilia" sex-with-dead-bodies-rap because, well, the dead aren't going to stand up for themselves and complain to the FCC.

Simmons also stated a recommendation for a Music Industry Coalition of Broadcast Standards. A recommendation was one thing; implementation was quite another issue for the perpetual "back burner" of hip-hop priorities.

Simmons ended his press release with the statement, "These issues are complex, but require voluntary actions exemplifying good corporate responsibility." Translation: Don't expect much. Its all window dressing until the storm blows over.

One insider in the music industry speculated privately that Simmons is trying to buy time until the 2008 presidential election when he hopes to swing his highly cultivated "hip-hop vote" to a candidate who will replace the political appointees at the FCC with liberal commissioners of low moral estate who will redefine decency back down again and overturn conservative Chairman Kevin Martin's recent report to Congress. And, there is a very real possibility that the Justice Department or Federal Trade Commission could investigate possible music industry collaboration in fomenting violence as a marketing strategy. The anti-racketeering RICO laws have been liberally applied in the last decade and a "Janet Reno style" attorney general could quell any investigation into the music industry's virtual creation of a criminal empire with the appropriate name "gangsta rap."

Both Barack Obama and Hillary Clinton had indirectly implied that they would turn a blind eye to the criminal culture growing out of hip-hop, in light of the enormous contributions and endorsements to both candidates from the hip-hop machine. I found Simmons' press release so full of contradictions and calls for vague cooperation among the "various players" that I called HSAN's public relations firm of JLM PR, Inc. to clarify a timeline for all these proposals, especially the Music Industry Coalition of Broadcast Standards.

Michael Falis, a spokesperson for HSAN's public relations firm told me that the April 23rd press release "pretty much summed everything up." There was no timeline, no agenda, no goals—just another elaborate hip-hop smoke screen from the "guru" of hip-hop, Russell Simmons. Falis assured me that Simmons had everything under control because, "as you know, Mr. Simmons' dedication to Yoga, astrology and spirituality gives him special insight into exercising karmic responsibility."

That answered everything I needed to know. Pastor G. Craige Lewis was right. The entire hip-hop culture is based on a secular New Age devotion to offshoot mystic eastern cultural paganism of moral relativism.

Geoffrey Canada, CEO of the Harlem Children's Zone is not fooled by the phony pronouncements of "restraint" coming out of the hip-hop community. Mr. Canada urges individuals and families to write the corporations behind the music labels. The upper echelons with the entertainment industry can exert control to stop the promotion of "base values of rap and hip-hop." Of course, that's assuming that the entertainment industry maintains moral values, which they obviously do not.

Simmons and Sharpton are a little late jumping on the social responsibility bandwagon—*20 years late.* As part of his "outrage" against hip-hop, on April 23rd, Sharpton promised to lead a "March of Decency" and "boycott" the corporate offices of Sony, Time-Warner and Universal in Manhattan. The question everyone asked, "What is he boycotting?" Did Sharpton plan to prevent employees from going to work? Stop the window-washers from doing their jobs? Prevent mail from being delivered?

Angela McGlowan, author of *Bamboozled,* is an African-American critic of the American Democratic Party's continued stranglehold and enslavement of the African-American community. As for Sharpton's sudden interest in cleaning up the rap industry, McGlowan noted that "Sharpton has conducted 'panels' for two years on 'gangsta rap.' He took out Don Imus in less than a week. If he really wanted to make a difference, he could."[24]

To show the effectiveness of Simmons' and Sharpton's moral crusade, Michelle Malkin exposed the antics of "R&B rapper" Akon less than two weeks after Russell Simmons' "final" press release on the need for "karmic responsibility." Posted on Malkin's website in early May was breaking news; a video showing the R&B rapper pulling a 15-year-old girl from the audience at a concert in Trinidad. For almost a full minute, the rapper known for his highly original song "I want to F____ You," proceeded to simulate sex with the girl as he tossed her around the stage and eventually slammed her to the floor where he continued his "act."

Neither Simmons or Sharpton made any comment about Akon's assault on the 15-year old-girl. I called both Simmons' and Sharpton's office, but neither one was "available" for comment. However, despite their short-lived moral awakening, Malkin's revelation led to Verizon dropping its sponsorship of Akon's concert tour and other corporate sponsors soon followed.

For those who didn't notice, Jesse Jackson tip-toed out of this whole debate early on so that Sharpton could catch the flack that showered down on his head. After all, Jackson is in bed with Simmons and the HSAN voting campaign to register and steer hip-hop youth into voting the "right way."

In the end of the "April from Hell" hip-hop hypocrisy, Al Sharpton maintained his buffoon status. The Paper Pastor Poverty Pimp demonstrated again that he knows very little about Christianity, but holds a hip-hop scholar's knowledge of the rapper's "spiritual" homeland of ancient Egypt. One of Sharpton's very famous history lessons goes down in the record books as the most hilarious outbursts of spontaneous combustion, "we built pyramids . . . white folks was in caves while we were building empires . . . We taught philosophy and astrology and mathematics before Socrates and those Greek homos ever got around to it."

In the perverted parallel universe of hip-hop/rap music, the "decision-makers" will forever exercise "selective moral outrage" and "selective moral enforcement."

On May 18, 2007, Bernard Goldberg told Sean Hannity that Americans should quit talking baby talk by using the politically correct phrase "the 'n' word." Goldberg, author of *Crazies to the Left of Me, Wimps to the Right* had the courage to say publicly what many people felt privately, "the rappers will continue to use the word 'nigger' as long as we speak like 3rd graders saying the 'n' word." Goldberg made the point that during the struggle for civil rights, when African-Americans were treated with far less than second-class status, they didn't complain about being called "the 'n' word," they complained about being called "nigger."

After that long bloody struggle, rappers now use the word for "entertainment value." As Goldberg noted, "We don't live in the United States of America; we live in the United States of Entertainment."

December 3, 2007 Don Imus returned to the airwaves at WABC in New York, eight months after he inadvertently turned the hip-hop nation upside down, telling the audience, "Hillary is still Satan."

GOOD NEWS! HIP-HOP IS DYING—FINALLY!

In June of 2007, Nielsen Sound Scan released sales figures that showed sales of hip-hop/rap CDs had dived a whopping 33% from the year before, which is twice the decline in overall music sales. Even better, hip-hop/rap sales have plunged almost 44% since 2000 and the trend continues to spiral downward. This is one of the largest and steepest digressions in a single musical genre in the last four decades. Downloadable rap sales are not faring much better.

As *USA Today* reported on June 15, 2007, American music buyers "are tiring of rapper's emphasis on 'gangsta attitudes', explicit lyrics and tales of street life and conspicuous consumption." Even KRS-ONE, the "anarchist" co-founder of hip-hop with Afrika Bambaataa told the paper that "The music is garbage." He added that "Rap music is being boycotted by the American public because of the images that we are putting forward." There may even be hope for KRS-ONE.

An interesting fact in the *USA Today* article summarizes the plight of hip-hop/rap as it fades into the sunset. The rap star Mims sold 634,000 downloads of his single "This Is Why I'm Hot," but the same song sold 1.9 million subscribers to the song's ring-tone version for cell phones. What was once considered the "hottest" music of the last 20 years has degenerated into nothing more than a novelty ring tone for a hand-held cell phone. In addition to rapidly plummeting CD sales for rappers, concert bookings for 2008 and 2009 are taking an equally deep plunge. Some hip-hoppers are hoping to transition to the silver screen. But atrocious singing translates to atrocious acting. As Scott Bowles noted in *USA Today*, "Indeed, much of the swagger that distinguishes hip-hop can fade fast on a movie set . . . Musicians turned actors are hardly sure bets." Omarian's *Feel the Noise* sputtered at $3.6 million. Big Boi's *Who's Your Caddy* bombed overnight.

Oh, and don't forget to pick up LL Cool J's new exercise at home book for a "hot" set of rock hard abs.

HIP-HOP HOLLYWOOD, SPORTS AND KILLING DOGS

One of my last location scouts in Atlanta involved finding sites for the Kim Basinger feature *The Real McCoy* in 1993. Scouting the downtown area with Universal Studios producer Lou Stroller, I asked why the movie *Scarface* had become the favorite movie for rappers, virtually turning Al Pacino into a demi-god.

THE HOLLYWOOD CULTURE WAR

Stroller, who produced the movie thirteen years earlier in 1980 was as surprised as the general public, "Who knew? It was a modern day gangster film with a very clear message. If you deal with drugs, you will die." Stroller, one of the very few decent, honorable and honest producers I had ever worked with, offered another possibility for the film's cult status among hip-hoppers, "It probably has more to do with Mario Van Peebles film *New Jack City* where this New York king-pen drug lord is hooked on *Scarface* and Pacino is his hero. Certainly, that was not our intention in making the movie. Pacino was clearly a villain—not a hero, not even an anti-hero."

In an interview with Bill O'Reilly of Fox News in 2007, columnist and sportswriter Jason Whitlock of the Kansas City Star would agree with that assessment. Not only was Pacino perversely turned into a demi-god with his "Money, Power, Respect" mantra, but Peebles also portrayed the drug-infested hip-hop crime past-time of dog fighting which only increased in popularity after *New Jack City* was released.

It also helped draw the line from a Hollywood movie's influence on the hip-hop culture all the way into professional sports where the hip-hop culture took over the family values of American sports and introduced talented athletes who dragged their bottomless pit criminal activities into the arena with them. The subject for O'Reilly and Whitlock was how a superstar quarterback for Atlanta named Michael Vick could squander a $130 million contract by engaging in pit-bull fights that often resulted in the electrocution, drowning, stabbing, shooting and beating to death of the losing dogs.

As Whitlock explained, "You have these young athletes immersed in this hip-hop culture and it just isn't a good partnership with professional sports. And you're now seeing what happened with Michael Vick is a symptom of this culture and the problems this culture creates."

Whitlock added that, "Hip-Hop culture has made normal [into] behavior that falls well outside the norm. And it is not healthy for people. We as African-Americans have to examine the culture that our youth are involved in—and some older people—we have to examine this and ask ourselves is the culture the problem, and not the skin color? Our youth culture, this hip-hop culture, we cannot deny is out of hand. It's harmful for our young people and look what's happened to Michael Vick—it's a prime example. If you can't make the transition into the mainstream and want to stay involved in this hip-hop culture, its going to lead to a coffin, a jail cell or a major embarrassment."

The day after Vick entered a plea in federal court, Arizona Sheriff Joe Arpaio of Maricopa County led a raid into the home of necrophilia rapper DMX and discovered an array of heavy weaponry, drugs and fighting pit-bulls.

Perhaps more bizarre is hip-hop's multiplier effect on society's priorities. A reporter for CNN told Nancy Grace that while domestic abuse and violence are problems in America, what Michael Vick did to those dogs *is far worse*, to which Nancy Grace replied, "Excuse me!?" Patrons of Manuels, Atlanta's oldest tavern, said that Vick's actions were far worse than what Atlanta wrestler Chris Benoit had committed a few weeks earlier such as killing his wife, young son and himself!

Vick was just the tip of the iceberg into the twenty-five year infestation of a criminal hip-hop element that is destroying professional sports. NFL commissioner Roger Goodell and predecessor Paul Tagliabeau have been forced to insert strong "personal conduct policies" into player contracts along with maintaining one of the toughest drug-testing programs in pro-sports (Another template for Hollywood?)

According to the San Diego Union Tribune, there have been 308 arrests and citations against NFL players for the years 2000 to 2007. Many have led to the immediate expulsion from the NFL. The arrests *do not* include minor traffic violations.

The following offenses are listed among the most frequent and repeat arrest warrants of NFL players and isolated lawbreaking:

Drug possession	Criminal trespass
Gun charges	Disorderly Conduct
DUI	Criminal mischief
Assault	Harrassment
Auto theft	Animal abuse
Hit and Run	Resisting arrest
Battery against police	Lewd conduct
Spousal abuse	Domestic violence
Prostitution rings	Child abuse
Drug dealing	Public intoxication
Sexual solicitation	Burglary
Terrorist threats	Reckless endangerment
Kidnapping	Rape
Theft	Bad checks
Outstanding warrants	Obstruction of Justice

Of the 308 citations and arrests to NFL players between 2000 and 2007, the Cincinnati Bengals and Minnesota Vikings accounted for 44 of these incidents. In addition to drug testing and a personal conduct policy, the NFL may want to institute a hip-hop culture identification quiz before a team is allowed to sign on a player.

CHAPTER 20

THE VELVET MAFIA: FACT OR FICTION

> *"Yeah, but money and fame doesn't mean anything when you're dead."*
> —David Geffen

On a hot spring day in 1998, I was scouting locations on second unit production sites for *Band of Brothers* near the Fort McClellan military base when Shirley Crumley called on my cell phone in a major huff that was extreme even for the veteran casting director and friend of over two decades. Shirley maintained her home in Birmingham to avoid the insanity of Hollywood, but often spent most of her time on location around the world.

As usual, Shirley only called me when she was upset or angry and needed to vent. "You're not going to believe this, but I interviewed for the assistant casting director job on a Spielberg—DreamWorks picture called *American Beauty*. When they interviewed me, the first question was concerning my sexual orientation."

"What?!" I had to admit this was one of the stranger curve balls Hollywood often threw during pre-production screening. "What did you say?"

"I told them the truth—I'm a heterosexual."

"And?"

"He said, 'sorry,' and then blathered on about how the producers wanted to be more 'inclusive' in the hiring for this particular movie, in other words; gays only. That's discrimination! That's heterophobia! You need to do something about this!"

Shirley always assumed I could take Hollywood to task just because I was a state film commissioner, which has absolutely no say over Hollywood other than finding locations.

"Shirley, I don't think President Clinton recognizes heterophobia as a legitimate form of discrimination, especially when you're dealing with a company run, in part, by his good buddy David Geffen."

"It's the Velvets again," she added, "they never play fair!"

It wasn't the first time I had heard the word "Velvets." Three years earlier, I ran across an article in the now-defunct *Spy* magazine that mentioned a group of men, mainly homosexual, that ran a hedonistic boy's club of power and pleasure. Geffen was pictured in the article with a group of others. The existence of a "Velvet Mafia" in Hollywood has never been disputed. The term, along with synonymous labels such as "Lavender Mob" or "Gay Mafia" refers to a group of influential homosexual *and* heterosexual power brokers in the entertainment industry who are purported to exert an inordinate amount of power in the hard-hitting deal-making atmosphere of movies and music.

While it is not disputed, finding members of the Hollywood entertainment community who will admit to its existence is tantamount to finding a needle in a haystack. In the intense and neurotic fear-driven atmosphere of Hollywood etiquette, the mere mention of the Velvet Mafia is akin to being labeled anti-Semitic, racist, or paranoid. Worse, any person in "the business" using the term may be labeled by the career-killing accusation of "homophobia," which is really a cover word for the accuser's own "heterophobia."

In an interview with the *San Francisco Chronicle,* Rick Leed of Wind Dancer Productions gave his thoughts on the subject, though diplomatically worded. According to the *Chronicle,* "On one level, 'Gay Mafia' pays homage to the supposed 'gay power' in Hollywood, but on the other it makes that power seem sinister. One of the unspoken implications of 'Gay Mafia' is that actors are sleeping their way to the top with gay executives. 'I don't know if it's to the top, but there are many who have slept their way to the middle,' Leed says."[1]

Certainly it was true for David Geffen who once secured a higher than middle-level position for his former boyfriend Bob Brassel after calling Warner Brothers president Mark Canton.[2] In the case of Geffen, the alleged de-facto leader of the Velvet Mafia, being a part of the "informal" cabal was not the "homage" of "gay power" as described in the *San Francisco Chronicle,* it was the "sinister" side that many whispered aloud. David Geffen was, and remains, the epicenter of Hollywood's darkest, evil underbelly.

As ultra-radical homosexual activist Michelangelo Signorile remarked, "Truth is, many gay men will tell you that there most certainly is a Hollywood/media gay mafia—using even that term or its synonym, the velvet mafia,—whether or not they are members themselves. It's made up of men such as DreamWorks co-chair David Geffen and *Rolling Stone* publisher Jann Wenner, plus many more well-known and lesser known individuals. They are men of a certain generation and status who travel together, throw swanky parties and introduce young beautiful things to one another. In other words, it's no different from the straight male mafia in Hollywood, where the casting couch for actresses is practically an institution."[3]

Straight male mafia? Sounds a little *heterophobic* to me.

According to Signorile, the Velvet Mafia " . . . can help you in your career, just as networking on other social scenes can, particularly if you're an actor who needs a break, or if you're an agent who needs five minutes with a certain producer or whatever"[4]

Five minutes? Or . . . whatever?

So, Michelangelo Signorile must be saying that the casting couch, homosexual and heterosexual is okay. What message does that send to aspiring young actors? And, the question this chapter raises, does homosexuality in high places lead to "pushing" heterophobia in entertainment product? Certainly, the heterophobic Signorile would claim the "straight male mafia" has been pushing heterosexuality long enough.

The first time the Velvet Mafia was "exposed" in any publication was the now infamous 1995 article in the May/June issue of *Spy* magazine. Written by Mark Ebner, the article was immediately attacked and demonized by Velvet fellow-travelers as "gay bashing" and "largely unsubstantiated." The central focus and enduring image of the article was the photograph of six Hollywood power brokers taken by celebrity photographer Steve Granitz of the Retna photo agency.

Pictured from right to left in a close-knit huddle were Barry Diller, David Geffen, Steve Tisch, Calvin Klein, an unidentified "tuxedo" and super-agent Sandy Gallin. Not all pictured were homosexual, but all were photographed at a controversial AIDS fundraiser at the Hollywood Bowl sponsored and organized in part by David Geffen. The young muscular male waiters at the swank event were dressed in ultra tight pants, shirtless, except for a flip collar and bow-tie; the "gay" version of the Playboy bunny.

Many criticized Geffen's orchestration of the event into a meat-market type of affair not unlike the other parties he attended which were "pre-stocked" with "young beautiful things." The inappropriate atmosphere for an AIDS fundraiser could clearly be seen in the face of Calvin Klein's stony gaze in the Granitz photo. Further, the financial accounting of the event and its fund's distributions have never been fully disclosed.

Had it not been for the blatant showmanship and mismanagement of the night's events and fundraising practices, Mark Ebner may have never written the article which exposed the tight-knit relationship among a group of Hollywood dealmakers. Not surprisingly, in true Mafioso style, part-time screenwriter Mark Ebner suddenly found himself without work for the next five years as he was summarily "blacklisted."

Ebner made a comeback as author along with Andrew Breitbart publishing *Hollywood Interrupted* in 2003 in which he asked, "Why do Hollywood stars, the most attractive, admired and highly compensated citizens in the world, have families more screwed up than even the notoriety-driven mongrels loitering around the green room of the Jerry Springer show?"[5]

Just as the memory of the *Spy* magazine article and all references to a Velvet Mafia began to fade, *Vanity Fair* magazine published an interview in 2002 with Michael Ovitz. At the height of his feud with Michael Eisner of Disney, the former super-agent claimed that an organized group in the entertainment industry, not too thinly veiled as a "Gay Mafia," was targeting him to make sure he would "never work in Hollywood again," which is considered one step harsher than "you'll never eat lunch in this town again."

Ovitz, a "straight" agent of legendary intimidation, threats and bullying in his own right, claimed that the ring leaders in this Velvet Mafia were David Geffen, former *New York Times* reporter Bernie Weintraub, various former employees of Ovitz at CAA such as Universal Studio president Ron Meyer and former Disney president Michael Eisner. Media mogul Barry Diller was also indirectly linked to the group.

The *Vanity Fair* article by Bryan Burroughs centered around the Disney stockholder lawsuit against Eisner for granting Ovitz a golden parachute approximating $100 million for less than one year of work as an executive at Disney. The suit would eventually cause Eisner to resign as head of Disney after 20 years as CEO. This ignited Eisner's defenders among the informal cabal of the Velvet Mafia.

As *The Los Angeles Times* reported in a July 2, 2002 article, "In a town where corporate brutality is suavely masked behind a smile, one time mogul Michael Ovitz has shattered protocol and stunned hard to shock Hollywood by lashing out at what he calls the industry's gay mafia."

Shattered protocol? Who set that protocol? Though Ovitz named many people in the *Vanity Fair* article, as the LA Times reported, "Most of the people Ovitz blames for his demise happen not to be gay." The conventional wisdom in Hollywood implied that Eisner's homosexual friends were coming to his rescue because of his long time promotion of sexual reorientation at Disney in both the work place and on the silver screen. This made Eisner a de-facto member of the Velvet Mafia despite the fact he was one of those heterosexuals that they could "work with." (Translation: threaten).

David Geffen didn't give the *Vanity Fair* article much attention since he had long ago become personally active in pushing homosexual themes on screen. As for Ovitz, Geffen had already been smearing and bad-mouthing the former super-agent for over a decade, just as he had done to so many other people who he relished in destroying as a perverse form of sport.

Others named in the *Vanity Fair* article took the "shock and awe-shucks" approach to the allegations "You're not serious," Barry Diller told *Vanity Fair* writer Bryan Burroughs. "Wow. He said that on the record? Wow . . . Wow. I'm stunned. I'm stunned." A very velvet-style denial.

Signorile said that "The shock and bewilderment among both journalists and Hollywood's liberals is pretty silly—not to mention a bit defensive and a tad dishonest."[6]

While the Velvet Mafia is not a Soprano or Corleone style of mafia where individuals gather in an ornate boardroom to plan criminal strategy, there exists in Hollywood a group of like-minded individuals, homosexuals and heterosexual, who agree that heterosexuality should be demonized when convenient—and hopefully at a profit.

This denigration strategy is carried out, in part, to satisfy the plethora of "gay rights" groups in Hollywood that began essentially, unionizing their sexuality in the early 1990s. The "like-minded" Velvet Mafia included heterosexuals like Eisner for his aggressive "inclusionary" hiring practices. The former Disney CEO bragged in May of 1995 that 40% of Disney's 63,000 employees were homosexual.

Eisner's sexual orientation employment practices deviated from "equal rights" to "special rights" which was the main factor in fellow Velvet mob members coming to his defense during the Ovitz lawsuit.

But, the heterophobia among power brokers in Hollywood transcended employment opportunities as the newly-empowered gender-benders sought to spread the "message" to the neighborhood movie theaters. As Daniel Jeffreys of the *Daily Mail* noted in April of 2000, "At some time in the past ten years, a new theory gained currency among gays, especially in the entertainment industry. This held that heterosexuality was a curse to be denigrated and mocked wherever possible, and that gays could never win the power they craved in society without undermining heterosexuals whenever possible.[7]

This would affirm the assessment made by Alfred Kinsey's fellow sex researcher W.B. Pomeroy who wrote an article in 1972 titled "The Now of the Kinsey Findings" in which he referred to heterosexual intercourse as an "addiction."

Of course, ultra-radical homosexual heterophobes like Signorile believe more can be done when he says "And still, many have little loyalty to the gay community—let alone are they garnering power on behalf of the rest of us."[8]

This perceived "lack of power" is the kind of sexual guilt trip that radicals like Signorile project onto the movie industry in order to push the heterophobia agenda. They cloak themselves in "gay rights" and "AIDS activism" but the true underlying cultural agenda is a hybrid of both terms to mean "gay activism," and activism with a vengeance.

While the Velvet Mafia may be a loose association of "like-minded" power brokers, the true designation of a "gay mafia" can apply to Signorile and his followers. In the late 1980s, Michelangelo Signorile became co-founding editor and columnist for the now defunct New York City radical homosexual heterophobe magazine *OutWeek*. He also became media director for the extremist group ACT-UP (AIDS Coalition to Unleash Power) which did more to harm AIDS outreach by staging brazen, loud lewd protests in public and private gatherings, disrupting speeches, conferences and even church gatherings.

Signorile's most controversial move was his personal campaign to publicly name celebrities that he claimed were homosexuals even if they did not want to be publicly or privately "outed" as his practice was dubbed by *Time* magazine. Signorile, himself a vapid heterophobe, felt that homosexual's private sex lives should be made available for worldwide public consumption. This was all to advance the cause of "AIDS awareness," of course, and by doing so exert financial contributions from the guilty confessors to be distributed to an array of "AIDS research" groups. Some would accuse Signorile of blatant blackmail, extortion and subterfuge. Signorile explained that he was merely exposing "hypocrisy."

One of his first outings was performed in a perverse post-mortem declaration after the death of multi-millionaire Malcolm Forbes. What infuriated Signorile the most was that Forbes was a conservative and Signorile felt "that the historical record also needed to show that he was homosexual."[9] Why? What purpose did that serve except to expose Michelangelo Signorile's hatred and disdain for anybody who did not share his sexual politics?

Signorile became a virtual mafiosa type who was consumed and obsessed with how he and other homosexuals should use their genitalia to affect social change. There is good reason that his magazine is described as "now defunct." His sexual preoccupation led him to write "*Queer In America: Sex, the Media and the Closets of Power.*" Of course, he is allowed to use the "Q" word whereas heterosexuals are not, lest it be construed as a slur. Signorile has been leading the language police of Orwellian conformity to declare from his New York bully-pulpit what words can and cannot be used in common conversation or journalistic articles. He berated the *New York Post* for referring to a "swishy source" which Signorile railed as "a retrograde code word for homosexual harkening back to J. Edgar Hoover's day!" Signorile then lashed out at the *Post* for calling former pop star George Michael a "washed-up pervert."[10] Signorile failed to mention that George Michael had been arrested in a Hollywood public bathroom soliciting sex. What term would Signorile prefer in his political correctness dictionary?

While the Post language has always been "unique" (If I'm allowed to say that), certainly Signorile is a believer in free speech. At the same time, his "outing" columns were the epitome of gross negligence and abuse of that First Amendment right.

Signorile's mafia-style theatrics would see their zenith in his crusade to "out" David Geffen through intimidation, forcing Geffen to declare his homosexuality to all the world; and by the way, could you write a check?

This sordid drama which played out between these two pariahs of American pop culture began in the late 1980s and early 1990s. First, it should be noted that Geffen was contributing an enormous amount of money by 1990 to AIDS causes, especially to AIDS Project Los Angeles (APLA).[11] And he was doing this without any public pronouncement of his sex life, which Signorile considered another case of hypocrisy.

While Geffen wasn't an exemplary role model of a human being, then or now, he did give a considerable amount of his time and money to AIDS research and awareness. But, that wasn't enough for Signorile. He wanted a public declaration of "gayness" as if that would somehow bring the AIDS issue closer to home and make it "personal" to the community. In reality, Geffen was the worst person anyone would want to associate with on a personal or professional level.

Signorile's venom resembled the consistency of a vicious envy. Geffen's biographer, Tom King, noted Signorile's behavior at the time, "In one column, he issued an ultimatum to 'closeted queers' in New York and Hollywood that seemed squarely aimed at Geffen and some of his friends: 'Either you join us or we will begin immediately tearing down every wall, exposing your hypocrisies . . . it's your decision which way you want to go. But don't think too long. Time is running out.'"[12]

Michelangelo Signorile's rants contained all the earmarks of a Mafioso-type threat. He also received support in his attack campaign from the repulsive Village Voice writer Michael Musto, a retro-style gossip columnist who reveled in writing about "closeted" homosexual celebrities who had sex on glass coffee tables high in the Hollywood hills.

Musto attacked Geffen by writing "David, the way to fight is to extinguish stupidity, not excuse it. Stop hiding behind checkbooks and hurt feelings . . . My friends are dying. We don't have time for this bull____!"[13]

Signorile followed up in his next column with his typical Act-Up angry homosexual rhetoric, "Geffen, you pig." Described by some as a malignant ingrate, Signorile then began to smear the Hollywood smear-master himself, shouting from the pen and ink of his column, "I don't care how much blood money you're giving to fight AIDS. You slit our throats with one hand and help deaden the pain with the other. You, David Geffen, are the most horrifying kind of nightmare."

A classic case, again, of the cat calling the kettle black. But, Signorile and Musto may have targeted Geffen for another reason. He had recently sold his Geffen Record label to Hollywood's last old school studio mogul monster, Lew Wasserman of Universal. This effectively put Geffen on the road toward billionaire status. Everybody wanted a larger share of the money, bloody or not.

Two years later, in 1992, Signorile's campaign paid off when Geffen, a taker by nature and giver by guilt, announced that he was "a gay man" at an APLA benefit honoring him for his service. The auditorium of 6,000 plus people cheered and whistled while giving Geffen a standing ovation. Though many in the audience were HIV positive or suffering from AIDS, the focus unfortunately shifted to the social/sexual/political agenda victory of Geffen's "outing" instead of the true progress and goals of stopping AIDS.

Biographer Tom King said the speech transformed Geffen into "a role model." Signorile had snagged his biggest fish and "anointed" Geffen as a hero while persuading *The Advocate* to name Geffen as "Man of the Year" along with a glowing cover photo. For some, it was the official crowning of Geffen as don of the Velvet Mafia, as the bickering "families" came to one accord of reconciliation.

Not surprisingly, the "outing" campaign of Signorile began to moderate with Geffen's announcement. It was obvious that he had wanted Geffen's admission more than anyone else because, more than money, Geffen was moving toward film production and the opportunities to push the Velvet agenda were limitless in a country fast becoming nothing more than a Hollywood nation.

In 1995, a year after Geffen, Steven Spielberg and Jeffrey Katzenberg announced the formation of DreamWorks SKG, Signorile developed a 14-step program called "Outing Yourself" which he described as "a guiding light for thousands in their struggle with coming out." In true Mafioso style, nowhere did Signorile offer a 14-step program for "Coming Out *OF* homosexuality," a legitimate concern for thousands more who seriously want out of the homosexual lifestyle. Signorile's "Outing Yourself" program would appear to suggest that he subscribes to the Kinsey Institute theory that 10% of the population is homosexual and the other 90% are bisexual, based on Kinsey's study of four million gall wasps, prison homosexuals, pedophiles and prostitutes. If that is the case, Signorile may just be fulfilling his "duty" to help the other 90% of the world "cross-over" to their "natural" inclination of homosexuality. Signorile's public service to create an atmosphere of heterophobia put him as a finalist for the New York Public Library Book Award for Excellence in Journalism.

David Geffen's "announcement" had the *expected* result of creating an even greater monster of chicanery and trademark vindictiveness. Now a partner in one of Hollywood's newest studios in half a century, Geffen would take the agenda of Hollywood value manipulation to the limit.

His new "role model" status sparked an inner anger of uncontrollable heterophobia which would increase in intensity with every passing year. In 1999, David Geffen found the dream project to channel his hatred through the DreamWorks studio. By doing so, David Geffen would attempt to turn the world of heterosexuality upside down by backing a movie that struck at America's heartland, a place for which he had no concept of other than bitter contempt.

DAVID GEFFEN AND HOLLYWOOD'S HETERPHOBIA

The following words and terms have been used to describe David Geffen from the time he was 18 and continuing even today as he fast approaches the age of 65:

"Irrational, screamer, contentious, manipulative, unfair, egomaniacal, predator, vindictive, deceptive, vitriolic, violent, untrustworthy, liar, thief, angry, vengeful, idiot, hateful, weasel, bully, nymphomaniac, dirty, backstabber, unconstrained, doper, impatient, hot-head, lurid, promiscuous, lunatic, ungrateful, indignant, bitter, ruthless, fake, savage, con-artist, depressed, cokehead, crude, irreverent, ghastly, phony . . . but, charming."

—Casting Director Shirley Crumley 1/30/05

By the time of Geffen's "open door" announcement in 1992, all of these words, and many more too foul to print, had already been ascribed to David Geffen, the role model. He wasn't alone. In many ways, these harsh terms had come, also, to be applied equally among other emerging power brokers in the New Hollywood that Jack Valenti created.

Throughout his record producing days in the 1970s and 1980s, Geffen would come to promote popular bands such as the Eagles and Crosby, Stills and Nash. He would also shamelessly promote, publicize and glamorize some of the most heinous and ghastly music to ever slither out of Hollywood such as heavy metal, the "grunge" of Kurt Cobain and rap's most profane, violent and vulgar recordings including the Geto Boys, who later came to popularize "necrophilia hip-hop" and "dead-booty sex."

When parents wonder how bands and "musicians" with atrocious lyrics creep their way across middle America, they need to look no further than the personal life of just one of the many like-minded promoters of culture clot that originates in Hollywood. David Geffen was, and is, a horrendously grotesque person in both his business life and private life. Because he admittedly has no conscience or even a concept of right and wrong, David Geffen likewise sees no problem in promoting these personal values to the youth of America.

People like Geffen use enormous entertainment promotion budgets that popularize otherwise worthless music by placing slick ads in music magazines, big-budget MTV videos, concert tours and radio station tie-ins. But, unknown to many outside the industry, one of the most influential ways of reaching young people is the larger-than-life music store posters of stylized photo shoots depicting musicians as nothing less than demi-gods.

Geffen's often-told story about how he lied on his resume to get a job at the William Morris Talent Agency would signify to many that he operated in a complete moral vacuum in which he alone would make the rules and break the rules. Author Tom King noted in his biography of Geffen, "in the surest sign yet that Geffen's moral compass was off kilter, he did not believe he had done anything wrong.[14]

David Geffen's step "out of the closet" in 1992 didn't change his behavior in any way, except make him angry at heterosexual America for "repressing" him throughout his life. Every problem David Geffen faced was *always* someone else's fault. And he would soon find a way, through the movie business, to forge the American audience into his list of enemies to rage against. His new company, DreamWorks SKG, formed in 1994 would be the vehicle to launch the attack.

Two years earlier, Geffen sat alone at home in August of 1992 and watched George H.W. Bush secure the nomination for the Republican party for re-election as president. In his heterophobic tunnel-vision, David Geffen could only see a political party that was Christian, heterosexual, and largely male. His double-edged hatred of Christianity and heterosexuality, all gathered under one big odious roof, steamed him to the boiling point. He wanted American "gay" and "atheist." And he wanted it now.

After jumping on the Clinton bandwagon in 1992, Geffen became very close to both Bill and Hillary Clinton. On the occasion of Bill Clinton's 48th birthday party in 1994 at the White House, Geffen met privately with President Clinton in the Oval Office and explained how best the president could "spin the press." (Translation: "lie to the press.") And who better to teach a liar how to lie than another liar.

Most Americans had no knowledge of this when the malignant back-stabber threw his support behind Barack Obama for president during a 2007 fundraiser. Geffen told columnist Maureen Dowd that the Clintons lied "with such ease it's troubling" and this is why he was supporting Obama!

The fact that David Geffen made the statement should have signaled to primary supporters of Barack Obama what kind of president he would be by whole-heartedly embracing Geffen's support and dirty money with open arms and no questions asked. So much for Obama's pledge to stop the undue influence of special interest money and power. How does "Velvet Mafia chieftain" look on the contributions report to the Federal Elections Committee? Obama will drop everything to take Geffen's phone calls.

New York Press columnist by the name Taki wrote an article in the March 3, 2000 issue stating that "Hollywood has never been a moral place, far from it, but until the 1960s and 1970s, it preached a hell of a moral lesson. God, the family, patriotism, even Mom were sacrosanct. Now, it's the exact opposite. Criminals are sympathetically portrayed, cops always negatively; people who think same-gender sex is wrong are fascists, businessmen are all crooks, while crooks are nice and quaint; drug takers are cool, drinkers are fascist bullies . . . What bothers me is not the bestiality of the Velvet Mafia. It's the message they send out through their movies. *American Beauty,* for example, is said to be a well-made film . . . but carries a subliminal message against the family."

It is *American Beauty* that radical heterophobe producers Dan Jinks and Bruce Cohen brought to Spielberg when the once family friendly director announced his intention to make "smaller, darker" films. But Spielberg was only one-third of the DreamWorks SKG production company that decided to finance the film and bring in Britain's Sam Mendes as director. Mr. "G" of SKG was quietly working much of the deal behind the scenes, in true Velvet Mafia "family" tradition.

As *Daily Mail* columnist Daniel Jeffrey's uncovered, *American Beauty* was the most radically subtle homosexual propaganda film from beginning to end. While many industry insiders and outsiders debated endlessly about *Brokeback Mountain* in 2005 and its overt homosexual "tone," few people remember and most people never even knew the secret agenda behind the making of *American Beauty* in 1999 which was promoted as "A Steven Spielberg Film."

Only Daniel Jeffreys was able to piece together the intricate web of players who came together to produce and exhibit the covert, cynically deceptive and deeply heterophic film to an unsuspecting heterosexual audience. Spielberg was more than ecstatic to participate. As a recent heterophobe convert, Spielberg had become a full-blown "useful idiot" to Geffen's sexual reorientation campaign against middle-class Americans. Spielberg was even developing an adoration for brutal Communist dictators like Fidel Castro. This would certainly guarantee Spielberg a membership into the "Dark Boys Club."

As Jeffreys' describes the process, ". . . Jinks and Cohen knew exactly where to take the *American Beauty* script to get it made—to fellow Out There sympathizer David Geffen, Spielberg's partner in DreamWorks."

Jeffreys further explains that producers Jinks and Cohen "got to know each other in 1995 when Cohen invited Jinks to be on the steering committee of Out There, an activist group of gay entertainment executives that he had co-founded. Sources say that one of Out There's key objectives is to promote the gay lifestyle within films and members talk openly among themselves about how best to mock heterosexuality.

"Members of Out There have been actively involved in films like *American Pie*, which makes adolescent heterosexuality seem like a monstrous affliction, and the U.S. TV series, *Will and Grace* where the leading gay men always seem to get the best lines, usually at the expense of a hapless heterosexual."[15]

With acute detail, Jeffrey's explains that *American Beauty* is heterophobia's propaganda masterpiece. "Its sweep of the Academy Award's top categories thrilled Hollywood's gay community, who have been trying to prove for a long time that heterosexuality is a sad form of sexual dysfunction." As I read the column, I came to understand my friend Shirley Crumley's exasperation at being denied employment on the film due to her heterosexuality, though she was equally ecstatic at having been turned down once she saw the finished film. "That's the Velvet Mafia at its best," she told me.

Daniel Jeffreys writes, in his own sardonic style, how the *American Beauty* filmmaker's creative thinking was shaped and developed from childhood into adulthood, warping all along the way.

> "The screenwriter, who won an Oscar for Best Screenplay, is Alan Ball. He grew up in the American South, in Georgia. Ball's family life was by his own admission, dysfunctional. He compares his childhood to American Beauty's Ricky, the son of Lester Burnham's mad neighbor and eventual nemesis. Ball's home included a father who was remote and distant, plus a mother who suffered severe depression after Ball's sister died in a car accident. Ball says he didn't even know he was homosexual until he went to university, but claims to have suffered enough persecution at the hands of heterosexuality to believe it is inherently evil.
>
> At school, he was weedy and bespectacled. He played in the school band and was bullied by members of the school football team, who always dated the prettiest girls. He recalled recently that it was a time when homosexuality was so taboo he could not even acknowledge to himself that he was gay.
>
> Once Ball arrived in Hollywood, he became successful writing scripts for TV comedies and it was here his contempt for heterosexuality hardened . . .
>
> He wrote *American Beauty* while working for Cybil Shepherd on her show *Cybil*. It was a relationship forged in hell. Shepherd, a vivacious blond, is an aggressive heterosexual . . . She is also the kind of girl who would have spent time with football players at school—the kind of guys who used to slap Ball around.
>
> Ball has made no secret of his hatred for Shepherd, and sources say much of the shrillness in Lester Burnham's wife—played by Annette Bening—is based on Ball's antipathy towards a woman who made no secret of her unalloyed enjoyment of the kind of macho hunk Ball has never been . . .
>
> In *American Beauty*, Ball's central characters, Lester and his wife, by focusing their drives on a teenage girl and a married man, are ciphers for the idea that heterosexuality must always mutate and become something damaging or perverse.
>
> The Fitts, who live next door to Lester, have different problems. Mr. Fitt is a violent ex-Marine who persecutes his wife—making the point that heterosexuality always tends to become abusive—and beats his son. Mr. Fitt's

problems, of course, stem from the fact that he is gay but cannot accept it. When Fitt mistakenly decides Lester Burnham is also gay, he makes a pass. Spurned, he shoots Burnham in the head.

The only battle Ball lost with his English director, Sam Mendes and star Spacey, as the script was filmed, tells much about Ball's motivations. In the final cut, Burnham stops just short of consummating his desires for his daughter's Lolita-like friend. Ball wanted the consummation to happen so that, according to sources, Burnham, the dark soul of heterosexuality revealed, could be seen as completely irredeemable.

But, Burnham is allowed to show a sudden emotional maturity, rejects this chance at a seedy seduction and dies gazing lovingly at a picture of his wife and child. The revised ending weakens Ball's attack on heterosexuality, but by then the main damage has been done.

Were Ball the only proselytizing gay character in this off-screen drama, the case against *American Beauty* could not be made, but that is far from the truth . . . [Geffen] rushed the script through the approval process—virtually unheard of for a screenplay by a writer with no previous hits—and maintained a close personal interest in casting. [Shirley Crumley's dilemma]

Geffen, Jinks, Cohen and Ball all attended half a dozen Oscar parties after the triumph of *American Beauty*. One producer who is close to Ball said they had good reason to be happy. After all, he said, they have created a film that is both a masterpiece and the most corrosive satire of heterosexual life that has ever made $100 million from the very people it vilifies.

And that is the hard truth about *American Beauty*. It exists and triumphed because, for some gays, it is not enough to win civil rights and equality of opportunity. They want more: a society in which heterosexuality is so condemned that homosexuals can win any increases in power they might choose."[16]

Producer Jinks affirmed the hoped-for results of their heterophobic attack when he noted, "After screening the movie, people have said almost as an after thought, you know, I just realized that the only *normal* people in the movie are the gay couple [Jim and Jim].' That was one of the first things we noted when we read the script."[17]

Geffen and Spielberg would not comment on Jeffreys' article in the *Daily Mail*, perhaps because Jeffreys unveiled one of the most accurate and in-depth exposés into the agenda driven filmmaking process in Hollywood and how the true heart and value system within the moviemaker's mind becomes a political crusade for moral dysfunction as entertainment.

As Jeffreys concluded about the Velvet Mafia's agenda behind *American Beauty*, it was only made because of "its heterophobia—the systematic denigration of heterosexual lifestyles that has become part of the Hollywood mainstream." DreamWorks SKG and David Geffen's deep hatred for the American middle-class suburbanites didn't stop with *American Beauty* which was set in the ideal suburban neighborhood. On April 13, 2007 Geffen and DreamWorks released a violent horror film titled *Disturbia* with the tag line, "How well do you know your neighbors?" The location, of course, is the idyllic middle-class American neighborhood where a slasher lives right next door to somebody like—you! Of course, the April 13th release date fell on a *Friday*. The film bombed quickly.

Geffen released this equally disturbing film despite years of psychoanalysis, constant mental therapy and his forays into controversial New Age self-help schemes like EST and Life Spring. Perhaps it was that mixed cocktail of Hollywood psychobabble that has left him mentally incapable of distinguishing right from wrong.

GEFFENS'S DARK LEGACY

According to Hollywood apologists and speech police, for anyone to write or speak of a Velvet Mafia, organized or not, is akin to conjuring up the worst stereotypes of Jews in Hollywood or African-Americans during the civil rights struggle in the South (never in the Northeast of Southwest). That kind of manipulative diversionary strategy just doesn't work.

In fact, most African-Americans are basically appalled that their struggle for civil rights has been hijacked and misappropriated by social/sexual/political groups looking to link racial/ethnic civil rights to issues of special rights based on sexual orientation, whether it be homosexual, bisexual, transsexual, pansexual, multi-sexual, quasi-sexual, auto-sexual, metro-sexual, or asexual.

If anything, David Geffen and his philosophical fellow travelers have been waging a two decade long campaign of value manipulation to change the way *you* think to the way *they* think. Geffen has to know that he and others like him in Hollywood perpetuated the worst stereotypes of African-Americans in their promotion of the most squalid forms of hip-hop and rap groups.

And, beyond music and feature films, the Velvet Mafia has spread its radical message of sexual reorientation to television, the most powerful form of media transmission in the world. It started in the early 1980's with pay cable, transitioned in the late 1980s to basic cable and finally to network television in the early 1990s with the lesbian kiss on *L.A. Law*, much to the shock of parents who were watching with their children in the pre-dawn era of television ratings. In fact, the heterophobic anti-heterosexual agenda helped speed up the initiation of ratings on television.

By 1995, researchers Stanley Rothman and Amy Black released research that showed, among Hollywood power brokers, 79% agreed that homosexuality is as "acceptable a lifestyle as heterosexuality" with 51% of that number stating that they "strongly agree."[18]

For the Velvet Mafia, it's as much about money as it is about promoting their sexually obsessive view of the world. According to Rebecca Hagelin of the Heritage Foundation, "Today's youth spend billions of dollars on trinkets and toys. And the way you get today's youth watching television is to be on the cutting edge and to promote provocative sexual images." Significantly, Hagelin notes, "Behind every media effort there is an agenda being pushed . . . sitcoms push a worldview where everything is up for grabs; where any kind of sexual behavior is up for grabs; where any kind of sexual behavior is harmless and should be something little boys and girls enjoy—and it's time for parents to stand in the gap."[19]

Hagelin also points out Hollywood's heterophobia when it comes to depicting men and boys on television "as dumb, stupid, and lazy." According to David Poland, this is understandable considering that "Gay men dominate the television business in Hollywood."[20]

Madonna explains how the whole process is executed in television, especially in sitcoms and music videos through the art of repetitious incrementalism inflicted on the audience. "They digest it on a lot of different levels. Some people will see it and be disgusted by it, but maybe they'll be unconsciously aroused by it. If people keep seeing it and seeing it and seeing it, eventually it's not going to be such a strange thing."[21]

Radical heterophobe writer Micah Mahjoubian then explains how this repetitious overload of sexual reorientation ends up changing the minds of viewers in ways that is not even realized, which is the *American Beauty* stealth method perfected by Velvet mobsters like Geffen, Jinks, Cohen, and Ball. "Most people aren't really paying attention to what's going on in Congress or the Supreme Court, but they do turn on the TV and they see people who are funny and make them laugh, who seem absolutely normal to them and yet they're gay. That I think, is much more powerful than anything going on in Washington D.C."

Mahjoubian probably didn't make any new friends in the homosexual community when he said that certain actors "*seem absolutely normal . . . and yet they're gay.*" So, is Mahjonbian saying that "gay" is not synonymous with "absolutely normal?"

As always, the target of Hollywood and its sub cultural Velvet Mafia are the young people of the worldwide audience who are exposed to the value manipulation agenda more than any other group, especially young people who watch the raunch and music video channels like VH-1, BET, and MTV which persistently portray aberrant and sub-human dysfunctional singers and actors 24 hours a day and broadcasts its erotopathic video signal around the world.

Bob Pittman, a founder of MTV said, "The strongest appeal you can make is emotionally. If you can get the emotions going, make them forget their logic, you've got them. At MTV, we don't shoot for the 14-year olds, we *own* them."[22] (There are laws governing the contribution to the delinquency of minors. Just ask Hugh Hefner.)

And the "lesbian chic" that began as an ambush scene on *L.A. Law* in the mid 1990s is now routine on television thanks to the Velvet strategy of mind-numbing redundancy. In April 2007, former male heart-throbs Courtney Cox and Jennifer Anniston locked lips at the request of *Dirt* television producers and directors. Similar scenes had already become common on *Grey Matters* and a number of other prime-time broadcasts and specials including the Grammy skit with lip-lockers Madonna and Britney Spears.

All of this lesbian chic on television runs parallel with the sleazy slick world of the print magazines aimed at young women. Many parents, and mothers in particular, have no clue that youth "fashion" magazines regularly print articles about "lesbian chic" and sexual techniques to "explore." Little do mothers know that the magazines they once read as teenagers are now largely "how to" guides for every kind of sexual behavior short of bestiality, and this "how to" trend has been a staple of "young adult" magazines such as *Cosmopolitan, Glamour,* and *Redbook* for more than two decades.

While Courtney Cox and Jennifer Anniston were locking lips, former short-term female heart throb Daniel Craig, the new James Bond in *Casino Royale* shocked not only his female fans, but producers, too, when he announced just three weeks into the theatrical opening that he wanted to do a vivid homosexual love scene in the next Bond installment. After three weeks on top of the domestic box-office chart, *Casino Royale* virtually disappeared off the radar screen the following weekend. Rushed to video in splashy center-isle displays at Wal-Mart, the DVDs gathered dust and sales were a bust.

Ironically, de-facto Velvet Mafia chieftain David Geffen purchased the home of Jack Warner upon the death of his widow. This is the same Jack Warner of the Quiet Conspiracy and Gang of Four who worked in secret with Jack Valenti to dismantle the Production Code, allowing future generations of erogenous degenerates like Geffen to use the medium of movies and music to promote heterophobic nightmares of deviancy to audiences across the world.

Geffen bought Warner's mansion intact from his heirs, down to the dead mogul's pens and pencils gathering dust in the study. In the not too distant future, Geffen will assume the Norma Desmond role from *Sunset Boulevard* roaming the grounds of his palatial estate when the pool boy will stop and say "You're David Geffen. You used to be somebody."

And if the hired help is lucky, he won't end up dead, floating face down in the swimming pool as the tabloid photographers converge on the scene, not unlike the swirl that surrounded Geffen's good friend Phil Spector whose habit of shoving guns into women's mouths would haunt him forever.

When Geffen biographer Tom King announced plans to write a book about the entertainment czar, David Geffen's brother, Mitchell, asked, "Why would you want to write a book about *him?* Why don't you write about somebody whose done some good for the world?"

The Velvet Mafia: Fact or Fiction?

CHAPTER 21

THE INCREDIBLE SHRINKING BOX OFFICE

"Hollywood celebrities are spoiled, discontented elitists who have no clue how the rest of America thinks."
—Glenn Beck

The first lesson to learn in reading the maze of movie statistics in your weekend newspaper entertainment section or listening to the "exciting" announcements from the infotainment broadcast industry is this: it's all show and very little substance. The entertainment media news seems all too eager to play along with the movie studio press releases that proclaim "highest weekend gross" or "highest holiday weekend gross" or the ever present "highest grossing film ever."

In reality, the motion picture industry has been largely successful in deceiving the public about the "growing popularity" of movies at your neighborhood cineplex. Nothing could be further from the truth.

ALWAYS REMEMBER: The "box-office gross" says absolutely nothing about the true attendance of the moviegoing public. A true indicator of a movie's popularity is the number of "tickets sold" or "box office admissions." When was the last time you read about the number of tickets sold for a big weekend opening? Did you say never?

To compare the gross receipts of a movie released in January to a movie released in December of the same year is just as misleading as comparing the gross receipts of a movie from the present year to the previous year. Why? Because the Hollywood PR departments and the Hollywood-hugging media never take into account the inflationary price of movie tickets which can rise as much as twenty cents a ticket in a single year.

THE HOLLYWOOD CULTURE WAR

Why all the tap dancing? The movie industry must not be seen as a loosing proposition regardless of the foul content it pumps out annually. Consider also the fact that some of the major entertainment news shows are also owned by movie studios. *Entertainment Tonight* is a production of Paramount. *Showbiz Tonight* on CNN is basically an approved production of its parent, Time-Warner.

The chart, U.S. Domestic Box Office, shows that one of the biggest ticket price increases took place between 1998 and 1999 when the average price rose 39 cents from $4.69 to $5.08 a ticket. To look at the *Total Gross* column of the chart, it would appear that movies are *slowly* gaining profitability almost every year. But, adjusted for inflation, the movie industry gross is virtually flat, and often declining.

Pull out your calculator and reference the chart for U.S. Domestic Box Office (1998-2006). Take the ticket price from 1998 (4.69) and multiply it by the number of tickets sold in *2006* (1,400). [The full number is in billions, so you don't need to add the extra zeroes].

Year	Ticket Price	Total Gross [1]	Tickets Sold [2]
2006	6.58	9,209.4	1,400.0
2005	6.40	8,840.4	1,381.3
2004	6.21	9,418.3	1,516.6
2003	6.03	9,185.9	1,523.3
2002	5.81	9,167.0	1,578.0
2001	5.66	8,412.5	1,487.3
2000	5.39	7,661.0	1,420.8
1999	5.08	7,448.0	1,465.2
1998	4.69	6,949.0	1,480.7

1—in millions
2—in millions

U.S. Domestic Box Office Chart

The point is that if ticket prices were the same in 2006 as in 1998, the total gross income would be $6.566 billion. That's even less than the total gross for 1998. Also, compare the *number* of tickets sold in 1998 to tickets sold in 2006. Individual ticket sales in 2006 were actually 80 million less than individual ticket sales in 1998. As for gross receipts adjusted for inflation, the movie industry actually made even less money in 2006 as compared to 1998.

In fact, a close look at the chart shows that individual ticket admissions in 2006 were lower than every year on the chart going back to 1998. The only exception was 2005 when even *less* tickets were sold.

More alarming, and rarely reported in the same breath as the "amazing movie grosses" of the week, is the record number of 606 movies released in 2006 as compared to 563 movie releases in 2005. The barely noticeable 1% increase in "tickets sold" between 2005 and 2006 is actually negative when the numbers are spread across the additional 43 movies added to Hollywood's output in 2006. The same scenario played out in 2007 when a new record of 630 movies were released throughout the year.

The first decade of the 21st century has not been a good time for motion picture attendance or gross receipts. Another catastrophic statistic is the number of consecutive weekend grosses, an indicator of audience attendance during weekends, which is the prime-time of the week when most people go out to see a movie. In 2004, the weekend box-office saw 18 consecutive losing weekends in a row. According to Patty Ruhle of *USA Today*, "That's the longest streak ever."[1]

As Richard Corliss of *Time* magazine notes, between 2003 and 2005, the domestic box office gross fell 13%.[2] As a percentage of the population and adjusted for inflation, that figure is even greater. As for the *worldwide* gross between 2004 and 2005, the industry experienced a "whopping" 7.9% dip according to Neil Cavuto.[3] While both national and international grosses have made slight rebounds, the industry figures continue on a roller-coaster track, largely downward.

When confronted with the *Time* statistics, industry insiders and apologists attempt to blame the advent of the DVD and home theatre. Experts in the field say otherwise as the executives in Tinseltown continue the famous Hollywood Shuffle. Not even video on demand, downloadable or shortened release windows can be blamed. There is something else suppressing movie attendance and the entertainment industry just can't bring itself to admit the obvious.

As DVD guru Dan Ramer of dvdfile.com notes, " . . . clearly a contributing factor is also the product, the films themselves."[4] And, when the Movie Advisory Board conducted a survey in March 2006 to determine why people are staying away from movie theaters in droves, the main number one reason was "Movies are not very good/did not meet expectations."[5] Number two and number three on the list were high ticket prices and expensive concessions.

The message is simple, "It's the content stupid!" Movies are increasingly the product of a deviated Hollywood philosophical mindset which desperately wants America to adopt as its own. Again, it's an ongoing campaign of value manipulation on Hollywood's terms, with film investors as the losers.

But, nothing could be plainer or crystal clear as the Movie Advisory Board survey suggests, "Movies are not very good." And you would never know it by watching *Entertainment Tonight or* other fluff entertainment reporters who get invited to the Hollywood Cocktail Party Circuit (HCPC).

Incredibly, there are still a few straight-forward executives in Hollywood who don't blame "new technology" for the movie's slide in popularity. In the observation of Clark Woods, president of distribution for MGM, "Let's be honest. We didn't exactly come out with the best products in the past few years."[6]

BLAME IT ON JACK

In his ground-breaking book *Hollywood vs. America,* author and movie critic Michael Medved revealed a cataclysmic statistical change in movie attendance between 1965 and 1969 that was so disastrous the movie industry, and the culture at large, has never full recovered from its impact. The numbers tell the effect of Jack Valenti's trial suspension of the Production Code in 1966 during the Quiet Conspiracy and the initiation of the MPAA's Ratings Scheme in 1968. Follow the dateline.

The year before Valenti arrived at the MPAA, the *weekly* movie attendance in 1965 averaged 44 million people. This weekly average had become a consistent level for more than a decade. Just four years later, in 1969, the weekly box-office attendance fell to a record low of 17.5 million.

As Medved noted "In the brief span of four years, some unanticipated and still unidentified hydrogen bomb exploded—wiping out more than 60% of the previously stable audience."[7] And, as Medved correctly predicted, "The impact of that explosion has proven permanent."[8]

In the forty years since Valenti dropped the bomb on Hollywood and the nation with his "New Kind of American Movie," the weekly audience attendance has never returned to the average 44 million weekly viewers. In the last four decades, weekly movie attendance has hovered between 20 million and 30 million viewers at its best.

But these numbers are even more dismal than they appear when U.S. population statistics are taken into consideration. Between 1970 and 2000, the United States population grew by an astounding 30%, exceeding 50 million people.[9] By March of 2007, the total United States population reached the 300 million mark. That's *100 million more people* than 1966 when Valenti began to dismantle Hollywood's Golden Era.

And still, weekly movie attendance could not return to 44 million weekly viewers? Not even 100 million additional people to the population could make an impact on the pre-Valenti weekly movie attendance. Relatively, the current level of weekly movie attendance is dramatically lower when measured as a percentage of the population. In other words, weekly movie attendance is shrinking—rapidly.

Again, the industry could not blame the VCR or cable television as these technologies and saturation levels across America arrived almost 20 years after the mass movie exodus. In fact, the decade following the box-office crash of 1969 should have proven to be one of Hollywood's best as the peak baby-boomers were entering the movie industry's prime movie attendance age range (15 to 25 years old). However, the fact that boomer children, by and large, joined their parents in leaving the theaters in droves indicated how deep the entertainment industry's failings manifested themselves and continue to this day.

I often talk to people who tell me, "I haven't been to a movie theater in ten years" or " . . . in twenty years" or even "I can't remember the last time I set foot in a movie theater." Most of these people have also admitted they don't watch "Made for TV" movies as they are just as abysmal. You won't hear about those people, who represent a very large segment of America, because the Hollywood media and TV entertainment shows ignore them completely.

But their impact is felt, not only in their absence at theaters, but in the rapidly declining ratings of network television. On Friday, September 21, 2007, the Emmy awards were taped for broadcast the following Sunday. An excerpt was played on cable stations Friday night showing "comedian" Kathy Griffin holding her Emmy high above her head as she cursed Jesus Christ and said, "this is my god now!" The following Sunday, Nielsen reported the lowest viewership in television Emmy history.

Most of this is intentional as discussed earlier in Chapter 9 "The Big Lie and Value Manipulation." The movie industry wants to create a new audience in its own image. The entertainment shows and magazine weeklies are preaching to the choir of regular moviegoers whose values they have already shaped to a greater or lesser degree.

The "missing moviegoers," as Medved refers to them are actually the growing demographic in the Culture War against Hollywood, much to the chagrin of the filmmakers who were hoping the "old audience" would literally "die off."

Medved identifies the blow Hollywood dealt to America, "The injury originated at the very heart of Hollywood—with the values of the people who produce the pictures and the messages in the movies they made . . . Between 1965 and 1969, the values of the entertainment industry changed and audiences fled from the theaters in horror and disgust. These disillusioned moviegoers have stayed away to this present day—and they will remain estranged until the industry returns to a more positive and populist approach to entertaining its audience."[10]

Matters have become so desperate that Valenti's successor, Dan Glickman, is considering an ad campaign to "get people excited about getting out of their homes to go to the movies."[11] Obviously, traditional word of mouth is doing more harm than good. In February of 2007, Glickman held a "summit" in Washington D.C. to highlight "the value of the American motion picture business and its contribution to the U.S. economy." Of course, the American motion picture industry's contribution to poor taste, vulgarity, hyper-violence, sexuality and profanity was not on the agenda.

Eventually, with international distribution, and returns on DVD and TV rights, the profit prospects for a theatrical release increase . . . sometimes. The true and few profit-makers are usually reserved for blockbusters and splatter films, with a rare gem wedged somewhere in between. But, the attendance levels at theaters have always been an indicator of the increasing lack of interest in new movie releases in recent decades. "The showcase debut" is a barometer of future success overseas and in ancillary markets such as DVD's, television and downloadable product.

CONDESCENDING CONTEMPT

In my twenty years in the movie industry as a location coordinator, I had the curiously simultaneous opportunity *and* misfortune to meet hundreds of individuals in the movie industry from studio moguls, producers, directors, actors and celebrities from all segments of the entertainment industry. During long hours and days on the road scouting locations, these industry insiders would open up about their values, politics, social philosophies, family life, personal problems and, most revealing, the innermost thoughts and nightmares that emanated from their hearts and minds.

Two overwhelming themes also remained consistent with most of these Hollywood insiders. The most disturbing was an unrelenting contempt for people who live outside of Los Angeles in general and Hollywood in particular. Secondly, the Hollywood insiders were gripped by a personal worldview that was hyper-cynical, dark—even evil—in their outlook on life. Most of them felt *very strongly* that it was their *duty* to get their dingy, gloomy, off-kilter messages on the screen.

While these themes have been covered extensively in the previous chapters, the movie industry's dismal theater profits and attendance levels as outlined here expose just how far the industry is willing to pursue and push their dark-hearted values and deep-seated contempt onto the American and worldwide audience.

Here we revisit how the demented values in Hollywood began the *contemporary* phase of their campaign of contempt for the very audience that buys the tickets at the box-office that pays the salaries of the same people who turn around and slap us in the face, unexpectedly, on the silver screen in a darkened movie theater.

If unabated, the valuable cohesiveness of a nation seduced by Hollywood will be at stake, and this country could very well be "destroyed from within" as historian Will Durant clearly discerned from other civilizations where entertainment became the rule rather than the exception.

The Hollywood insiders and decision-makers live in an isolated, hermetically sealed world with little knowledge or desire to know the heartbeat of the American audience. As George Clooney arrogantly boasted at the 2006 Academy Awards, "I'm proud to be out of touch."

One of the most blatant examples of condescending contempt I encountered in the movie industry occurred during a location scout for the Georgia Film Office in 1991 with the British Oscar-winning director John Schlesinger. During a break in our location scouting of Rome, Georgia, we stopped into a local diner on the town's broad, stately boulevard for a quick lunch.

The café was a popular spot among Rome's elderly and the downtown workforce who relished the noontime tradition to visit with neighbors, friends and fellow workers. It was a classic slice of Americana where no televisions were allowed to blare from every corner and where conversation remained an art form. Tommy Dorsey's "Song of India" played softly from one old mahogany speaker against the wall.

Then came the storm with no forewarning of dark clouds gathering above our table. "How pitiful! These wretched old people have lived their whole life in this dreadful, dull little town having done nothing but work 8 to 5 at jobs so mundane they're now stooped over and walking with canes. And this is their reward; a meat, two vegetables and cherry pie?"

"Well . . . ," I pondered, not wanting to offend the equally elderly director by telling him he was just an effete, cynical English snob with no respect for his hosts who were picking up his tab. Instead, I delivered my usual Aaron Copeland "Fanfare for the Common Man" defense speech as I had done so many times before with directors as arrogant or worse than Schlesinger.

"John, I see these people very differently. They've lived here their whole life because they've chosen to, for whatever reason, and at the very least they deserve to go downtown, have lunch, visit with old friends and feel content that they're connected to a community they helped build."

"Oh, go to hell, "Schlesinger exhaled. "These people have never contributed anything of lasting value. They probably couldn't distinguish a Matisse from a Monet." In Rome, Georgia, if that were true, it certainly isn't a vice and may well be a virtue.

Shifting moods, as he often did, Schlesinger wanted to press his own importance and "contributions" to the world community. "Did you know I still get royalties for my film *Midnight Cowboy* from the new video markets?"

I didn't know and at that point I didn't care. But it struck me that I was sitting at the same table with the man who received the first Oscar for an X-Rated movie in 1969. The film, starring Jon Voight and Dustin Hoffman, centered around homosexual hustlers wasting away in the seamiest section of New York City where dirt, grime, vice and rot are the consistent theme; probably second only to *Who's Afraid of Virginia Woolf?* (also an Oscar winner) as the most depressing movie in film history.

* * *

Hollywood's condescending contempt and darkside were emerging simultaneously in 1969 and Tinseltown began voting themselves awards for relentless pieces of trash since Valenti abolished the Code the year before. This is why 60% of the weekly movie audience fled the theaters, never to return. Just four years earlier, *The Sound of Music* had won the Oscar for Best Picture and 25 million *more* people went to the theaters weekly.

As Medved points out, "In practice, the day-to-day workings of the Hays Office [Valenti's predecessor] proved far more lenient than the written strictures of the Production Code might suggest; nevertheless for more than forty years, its operation executed a powerful influence that reached every corner of the popular culture."[12]

Likewise, the disappearance of the Production Code has resulted in the hyperkinetic culture of violence, sex and profanity that pervades not only the screen, but the personal lives of many who have become slaves to the lifestyle of the Hollywood nation. The very existence of the Code at least reminded filmmakers and entertainers of the "need to work within broadly adopted standards of decency and good taste."[13]

Of course, the philosophical fellow travelers within the movie industry will ask, "Who's going to determine *decency* and *good taste?*" Just take another look at the U.S. Domestic Box Office chart. Obviously, the shrinking audience has already made that determination. After reviewing the slipping box-office figures of recent years, Clark Woods of MGM notes, "I think we may have forgotten a little about Middle America . . . your success is going to be listening to what *all* the country wants to see."[14]

Rory Bruer, distribution chief for Sony Pictures, explains Hollywood's struggle to resist its own arrogant contempt for the American audience, "We try to be very cognizant that we live in Los Angeles and that you have to *reach out* to find things that entertain the whole country, not just the coasts."[15] Bruer's admission to a "coastal" state of mind shows just how far out of touch Hollywood is with reality.

Marketing executive Mark Joseph, a key promoter of films like *The Passion of the Christ, The Chronicles of Narnia* and *Facing the Giants* has faced the Hollywood "attitude" problem head-on in a number of high-profile marketing campaigns. With some major studios like Sony and others creating faith-based film production units after the enormous success of *Passion,* Joseph still has concerns as to whether Hollywood is pandering or if it is really trying to understand the market. In an interview with James Hirsen of *NewsMax,* Joseph said, "Their biggest mistake is a condescending attitude . . . They are servicing the 'crazy' people, those who they perceive as a small niche. This small niche is actually America."

It's even easier to catch Hollywood's ridicule of the American moviegoer when paging through the industry trade magazines. In a *Hollywood Reporter* business article, Adrian Howell, worldwide sales controller for Pearson Television

International, was boasting about selling episodes of *Homicide* to more than 56 countries through international buying agents around the world. "It's not an absolute ratings winner, but it appeals to the intellectual viewers. Thankfully, the buyers are more intellectual than most of the viewing public."[16]

Fred Barnes of the *Weekly Standard* once coined the phrase "Snob Populism." I can't think of a better term to describe Adrian Howell's contempt for "most of the viewing public." Does Howell have even a small clue as to where the money comes from to write his highly inflated paycheck?

Hollywood is increasingly producing entertainment for their own peers *within* the industry, not for the audience at large. In an industry of largely insecure, isolated, paranoid and extremely neurotic individuals, the old saying "You're only as good as your last film" continues to be the mantra and guiding force of fear that rules the entertainment business. Why risk losing an invitation to the BCPC by serving the entertainment tastes of that vast land seen only fleetingly through the tiny window of a jet airliner traveling between Los Angeles and New York?

Medved explains this deigning arrogance as part of a subtle evasion on behalf of filmmakers to reach only a certain *class* of moviegoers. "Feature films, by contrast, are connecting with a shrinking percentage of the American people. Sharply increased ticket prices and the controversial content of recent films have combined to make moviegoing a form of entertainment that appeals primarily to an elite audience."[17]

While there are plenty of examples of condescension from Hollywood that are causing Americans to find better ways to spend their entertainment dollar, the specter of "darkness" as a continuing theme of entertainment is worth revisiting here to explain how Hollywood turned "evil" into an "attraction."

Since the 1980s, Hollywood has developed a strong fascination with all things malicious, dark, mendacious, violent, perverse and deeply anti-social. Michael Medved, who has seen more bad movies than anyone would wish upon their worst enemy, has over thirty years of insight into these cinematic cultural trends.

As for motivation, Medved notes, "The most significant shapers of the entertainment industry, in their quest for artistic legitimacy, have adopted a view of the world that is surprisingly dark, even desperate, highlighting elements of chaos, cruelty, and random violence . . ."[18]

In his meticulous research of all aspects of the American culture, Medved came across a curious pronouncement in one of the hundreds of celebrity entertainment rags which attempt to take the temperature of "hip" in the nation's culture. The article announced what most people had suspected throughout the 1980s and 1990s.

Out of the June 1992 issue of *US* magazine, Medved observed, "In its annual summary of what's 'in' and what's 'out' in the American mainstream . . . the editors declared that 'Evil' is now officially 'In' and 'Good' is definitely 'Out' . . . Evil, not love, is what the movies are all about."

The article continued by noting that high-profile actors were coveting the opportunity to play "the devil incarnate," which led *US* to conclude that good guys and gals are a no-no because these "movie heroes don't generate the same kind of heat and simply don't exist, leading us to believe that there may be no God, but there certainly is a hell."[19]

Kevin Bacon is one of these actors who embraces evil as virtue, saying, "I'm more embarrassed by the nicey-nice movies I've made." That would be understandable since Bacon dabbles in the occult as we learned in the chapter on "Celebrity Gods."

Commenting on her new "dark" role in TNT's series *Saving Grace*, Holly Hunter said, "This character loves sex. She kicks (butt). She's generous as hell. She acts on her own desires. She's most at home in chaos. She's also mental. She does things people wish so badly they could do except it would wreck their lives. That's why I like her."[20]

Of course, that's not really out of character for Hunter who starred in the original 1996 *Crash* in which she played a pervert who could not reach sexual orgasm with her lover unless the two of them witnessed mangled, bloody bodies in the immediate aftermath of auto wrecks!

The singer/actress flavor-of-the-month sensation by the name "Fergie" told *Maxim* magazine in April 2007, "I tend to be attracted to dark, demented things. I love blood, guns and knives. I love to play with my dark side."

Even romantic comedies are not immune from the darkness. As Kate Kelly of *The Wall Street Journal* notes, "A far cry from the Katherine Hepburn-Spencer Tracy pictures of the 1940s and the feel-good Meg Ryan-Tom Hanks vehicles of the 1990s the modern romantic-comedy has moved past sexism, ambition and long-distance relationships. Now, romantic characters are dealing with phobias, infidelity and anger-management issues."[21]

Most of these "evil is good" projects are box-office losers or ratings failures. More perverse is that most studio execs know this in advance and expect to recoup their profits from one or two major blockbusters that will wipe off the red ink on the balance sheet at the end of the year.

And, it cannot be stressed too many times that all this "chaos" in "entertainment" began on November 1, 1968 with the abolishment of the Production Code and the sliding scale of age-based morality that is the Ratings Scheme. From that point on, as Medved noted, "The industry pursued its own decadent and self-destructive agenda."[22]

Whether the deviant minds of the creative community were raised in abusive or loveless childhood environments, or whether they "crossed over" as adults, the origin of their cynical perversions can often be traced to a "trigger event" in their childhood where adult role models were absent or highly dysfunctional. Those adults could be their own parents or adult role models viewed on television, movies or major figures in the news of celebrity culture worship.

Some of the cultural adult role models to movie industry insiders later became their cultural heroes and personal icons as adults. A review of Chapter 18, "Hollywood's Road to Perdition," is a condensed twenty year roadmap to the key players in America's cultural collapse who contributed heavily in defining decency down for Tinseltown's trendsetters.

And, many people who idolized these major figures of the counterculture are the ones who entered the movie business and ushered in the era of the incredible shrinking box-office with movie projects that most people ignored in large numbers and continue to do so today. "These projects reflect the shallow but unpleasant radicalism of an industry lost in its own curious time warp, its outlook permanently frozen in the worldview of the sour summer of '69, set in amber somewhere between the release of *Easy Rider* and the messianic mud fest of Woodstock," Medved reflected in *Hollywood vs. America*.[23]

As the aging hippie filmmakers push well into their late sixties with second and third face-lifts, the generation replacing them are surpassing technical expectations of production design, special effects and cinematography never thought possible. But, with their counter-cultural forefathers as mentors, the condescension and dark mindsets have only amplified weak and cynical storylines, producing enough bad scripts to fill any major urban landfill.

So, one generation of filmmakers with twisted, shared values replaces another and for this reason their bleak messages continue to make it to the big screen at the neighborhood cineplex and to the television screen in your living room. James Hirsen, author of *Hollywood Nation* and *Tales From the Left Coast* confirms that "there tends to be a group of like-minded people who occupy positions of power in Hollywood."[24] Radio talk-show host Larry Elder agrees, adding that "The people who green-light movies in Hollywood are overwhelmingly liberal or very inconsistent with how most Americans feel."[25] A poll taken in 2005 asked a cross sample of Americans, "Do Hollywood Filmmakers Share Your Values?" 13% answered "yes" and 70% answered "no."[26]

And, viewers are increasingly tuning out network television after the TV industry reported a precipitous drop in viewers and revenue during the network's annual "Up Front" gathering of TV producers and advertisers in New York in May of 2007. Kim Masters of National Public Radio noted that the networks were "in a panic."[27]

Apparently, the ghost-whispering, psychic-medium detectives from outer-space hell are formats that don't seem to connect to most Americans. And, as Martha Stewart would say, "That's a very good thing."

The fact that the Culture War rages on is a good sign that Americans have not become complacent about the damage being ravished upon society by dark-hearted, contemptuous and careless creators of contemporary culture; adults who do not see themselves as mature role models for future generations.

Instead, these adults exist in a vacuum of perpetual immaturity who cannot move beyond their personal fast times at Ridgemont High and exist only as opportunistic hedonists living the lush life of self-indulgent sexual-violent fantasies. In hip-hop mantra, "Everything is okay, as long as you are *feeling* it."

In Michael Medved's timeless observation, "The dark visions that Hollywood offers our present and our past not only influence the attitudes of children and adults in this country, but increasingly shape the image of America to the world at large."[28] Simply put, Hollywood is suffering "a true sickness in the soul."[29]

LESSONS FROM GRECO-ROMAN ENTERTAINMENT

Consider the fate of a mighty empire that did become complacent and suffered a collective sickness of the soul that has been etched into world history. During the short two year reign of Marcus Aurelius Claudius from 268 to 270 A.D., the emperor of Rome dragged the entertainment at the Coliseum to new lows. Nearing its 200th birthday, the Coliseum at that time was becoming more popular than anytime before as an escape for the never-ceasing pleasure-seeking Roman populace whose lives were increasingly centered around the great spectacles of the massive arena and other venues throughout Rome such as the Circus-Maximus for chariot races and numerous lavish amphitheaters for dramatic amusement.

These were the "movie theaters" and "rock concerts" of the ancient world and the Roman people simply could not get enough entertainment. The "producers" at the Coliseum, under the orders of Claudius, began scheduling shows starting early in the morning, continuing throughout the afternoon and well into the evening hours. Throughout the empire, Rome became a combination of Hollywood and Las Vegas offering every form of entertainment and vice, 24 hours a day, every day of the week. The insatiable demand and supply of "entertainment" to satisfy a bored, lazy and lascivious public continued unabated even as barbaric tribes from the north and the east were clearly chipping away at the empire's borders and its slipping supremacy.

Claudius was credited, among others, with encouraging the epic mega spectacles at the Coliseum. He was also one of the more prominent Roman emperors (read: studio moguls) who began demanding more blood and carnage. He instructed the Coliseum's producers to break all previous boundaries and spill blood morning, noon and night. These producers were the "Splat Pack" of 3rd Century Roman entertainment who provided "non-stop hip-hop."

A typical day at the Coliseum would begin in the morning with wild animal fights. Coliseum curators would bring in the wildest and most exotic animals from Africa and pit them against each other. The show would not end and until one or more animals were gored to death. After the animal fights, just before lunch, the drama would escalate with people being pitted against animals, sometimes with fanciful weapons and at other times with no weapons at all.

In earlier days, the gladiator versus animal shows wee often rigged in favor of the gladiator who triumphed against every imaginable animal known to mankind. But, under Claudius, the gladiator or some unfortunate enemy of the emperor was allowed to be eaten alive, much to the pleasure of the emperor who had insisted on these macabre gore fests.

During the lunch hour, the audience was feted to an unusually perverse spectacle of people killing one another for no other reason than to please Claudius with a show of infinite slaughter and bodily dismemberment. And if Claudius was pleased, equally satisfied was the audience—even at lunch time. The choreography of the entire day's entertainment was designed around an incremental increase in the intensity and deviancy of the "performances."

At these lunchtime "matinees" special "killers" would bring people out into the open arena to be whipped, beaten, stabbed, dismembered and beheaded. Some of these unfortunate souls were prisoners or even slaves who had outlived their usefulness.

Claudius and the audience took special delight in the butchering of Jews and Christians, a tradition that continues in contemporary Hollywood. And for these special attractions, slow death was often employed to extend their suffering, unlike the street urchins and vagrants rounded up the night before to fill in for any vacancies in the ranks of the Coliseum's living dead lineup.

But, after lunch is when the real competitions began. Highly trained gladiators arrived to compete in one-on-one fights. On other occasions, large numbers of gladiators were gathered together to recreate some glorious battle in Rome's past. These late afternoon spectacles attracted a large percentage of Roman women (read: groupies). A highly trained killer as a lover was a seductive fantasy for Roman women and the gladiators were promoted to attract that very specific "audience segment." Also, the "after lunch crowd" tended to draw more of the upper classes who felt that the morning and lunchtime entertainment of simple unskilled killing was nothing short of cheap, low-class vaudeville.

However, it was Claudius who helped introduce the gladiator era of fights to the death. For the most part, the previous two centuries had paraded gladiator fights in which one surrendered and was spared to fight another day. Claudius would set a new precedent that would remain largely unchanged until Constantine's reign in the following century.

THE HOLLYWOOD CULTURE WAR

* * *

There was an earlier time in Rome when the population and the entertainment audience was not so complacent about the amusements that were pushed on them by the emperor and his producer cohorts. In the 1st century AD, during the reign of Nero and before the Coliseum was even built, the emperor made it very clear to the citizens of Rome that he was more interested in Showbiz than he was in national leadership. Nero loved the stage more than anything the empire had to offer.

Nero would often inject himself into Roman stage plays at the city center's largest amphitheater. The audience found this more curious than entertaining. And many would soon find Nero's fascination with Roman Hollywood more than a little disturbing. Nero was particularly interested in playing the role of the killer in some contrived stage piece in which he would appear. He craved the "darker" roles.

The producers of these "specialty productions" would arrange for an actor, usually an unknown or little known player, to act out the part of murdered victim. But, there was no talent required. Nero's trademark performance was to stab the actor to death—literally.

This appalled the first century Roman audience who realized they had another lunatic as leader. But, the "last straw" occurred when Nero mounted the stage and allowed his homosexual lover to sexually ravish him before a shocked audience. The Roman audience did not care for an imperial version of *Brokeback Mountain* on their gilded stage.

Rome's most dreaded emperor would soon loose the support of the military and the Roman population after his "performance." This was a far different reaction than the complacent and debauched population of Claudius's 3rd Century Roman audiences during the "heyday" of the Coliseum more than two-hundred years later.[30] Moments before committing suicide, Nero moaned, "Oh, what an artist the world loses in me!"

Rome as a single entity nation endured for only 400 years. When this book you are reading was published, America was about to celebrate 232 years as a nation. The parallels between the Roman Coliseum and American entertainment have been debated endlessly in recent decades.

The American audience is now split between the Claudius era entertainment crowd that can't get enough blood, sex, violence, perversity, horror and vulgarity from Hollywood, so the industry ups the ante every year to levels not even seen in Roman times. On the other hand, increasing alienation of a large segment of the population is ongoing, much like the audiences Nero offended 2,000 years ago when the box office then, as now, began to shrink-incredibly.

As Medved observes," . . . the cynical sophisticates who run Hollywood not only separate themselves and their work from the domestic mainstream, but risk the alienation of serious and sympathetic people around the world."[31]

MTV, BET, VH1 and their copycat music video channels around the globe are expanding examples of mini-modern day Roman amphitheaters with their chronic mix of violently sexual imagery, "reality shows" and "music." As far back as 1991, Senator Robert Byrd (D-WV) delivered a speech on the floor of the U.S. Senate predicting the very decay of social cohesion occurring in 21st century America.

> "The central message of most of the music videos is clear: human happiness and fulfillment are experienced by becoming a sociopath and rejecting all responsibility . . . if we in this nation continue to sow the images of murder, violence, drug abuse, sadism, arrogance, irreverence, blasphemy, perversion, pornography and abomination before the eyes of millions of children, year after year and day after day, we should not be surprised if the foundation of our society rots away as if from leprosy." [32]

The very direct and now famous analogy of the Coliseum's reemergence was made by producer David Puttnam shortly before resigning as president of Columbia Pictures. Puttnam was among the last and very few producers in Hollywood whose name above the title virtually insured the audience would be treated to a quality movie.

After surveying the business climate of Hollywood, Puttnam stepped down and then assessed the state of entertainment in America. In an interview with Bill Moyers on PBS, Putnam made the historical correlation:

> "What we think of now as the excess of the Roman circuses, where in the end hundreds of thousands of people died, didn't start that way. They started legitimately as circuses, extremely mild entertainment. But, the audience demand for more and more resulted over a period of time of several hundred years in the form of entertainment becoming more bloody, more and more grotesque. What might have been a woman raped publicly by a centurion, a year later a woman raped publicly by an ass, and ten years later was ten women raped by a hundred asses . . . Someone has to say 'Enough' because this is disaster, we are destroying ourselves . . . We are untying the fabric of our society." [33]

When David Puttnam spoke those words in the early 1990s, people said, "That could never happen again, especially not in America." However, by the year 2007 Robert Redford and the Board of Judges at the Sundance Film Festival officially reopened the Roman Coliseum right here in America. Of 856 documentaries submitted to the festival for exhibition, only 16 were selected, including "Zoo."

The documentary by director Robinson Devor recounts the life of a Seattle man and Boeing executive named Kenneth Pinyon who died from a ruptured colon after having sex with his favorite Arabian stallion. Of course there was no gratuitous film footage as this is only stage one, the Opening Act in the display of "the last taboo."

Expect more in the future as this documentary exposed an "internet-based zoophile community" of people who trade tips on having sex with animals. Devor defended his film from possible complaints against *animal cruelty*, "I'm not in there wrestling with the legal or animal cruelty issues . . . I thought the marriage of this completely strange mind-set and the beauty of the natural world could be something interesting."[34] Interesting?!

The film was one of only five American films to be shown at the "prestigious" Director's Fortnight Sidebar at the 2007 Cannes Film Festival in France. This will allow the rest of the world to witness how low America has sunk. The film was not picked for "artistic" merit. The French chose the film so the international community could laugh with disgust at America.

Certainly we can thank Robert Redford for his "open mind" to allow this grand reopening of the Coliseum in America. If that's an example of an open mind, give me a little closure.

In the irony of all ironies, director Robinson Devor finally defended his film by quoting the *Roman* writer Terrence, "I consider nothing human alien to me."[35] How coincidental! The Roman emperors who presided over the Coliseum used to quote Terrence, too. It's a small world, after all.

CHAPTER 22

RIDING WITH THE DEVIL
(Christians & Jews Need Not Apply)

> *"In the ongoing war on traditional values, the assault on organized faith represents the front to which the entertainment industry has most clearly committed itself."*
> —Michael Medved

"Take Paul Newman, now he's a different story altogether. The problem with Newman is he won't f____ the girl." "He won't do what?" "F____the girl! F____ the girl!" "What girl?" I asked, finding myself caught in the up-tempo of Harry's Hollywoodspeak. "Any girl. A leading actress. If you have two main leads in a romance, drama or comedy, they're going to *have to* f____ if you want good box office."

Apparently, Newman had a policy about not "f____ing" his leading ladies and Harry saw that, somehow, as a flaw in the contemporary filmmaking process. His "f____ing" philosophy was not uncommon among talent agents-turned producers who litter the Hollywood landscape.

Producer Harry Ufland was ruminating about some of his experiences with actors as both a producer and talent agent. He had represented some of Hollywood's biggest name talent in the early 1980s. Ufland was affable, hurried and a "speed-talker," a common trait among former talent agents.

I had just picked up Harry Ufland at Atlanta's Hartsfield Airport only ten minutes earlier after dropping off director John Schlesinger from a grueling three day location scout. This was the spring of 1991 and Atlanta was booming as a site for making movies. The economic impact had just surpassed one billion

THE HOLLYWOOD CULTURE WAR

dollars and producers were calling Georgia "Hollywood South." Producers and directors were coming and going like a revolving door at the metro airport. The well-respected and veteran film commissioner Norm Bielowicz was controlling the inflow and outflow from his office in the Marquis Two Tower of Peachtree Center.

Ufland had arrived to scout locations for a Sally Field movie titled, *Not Without My Daughter*. Field was portraying the true-life story of Betty Mahmoody who managed a harrowing escape from Iran with her daughter after her abusive husband became inflamed with Ayatollah fervor shortly after the 1979 Iranian revolution. Ufland, producer of *Raging Bull*, was eager to squeeze out any remaining drops of sunshine for the day's scout. This was known as "Chasing the Sundown" in location scouting lingo. We were in the northern suburb of Dunwoody in a record fifteen minutes to look at the first site, a setting for Mahmoody's home in America.

It was time to change the subject of Ufland's "f____ing" actors recipe for successful filmmaking in Hollywood. "*Raging Bull* was quite an accomplishment," I interjected, changing the topic. The Martin Scorsese film followed the tragic personal and professional life of boxer Jake LaMotta.

"Yeah, yeah. Oh yeah, DeNiro was great as LaMotta. He stuffed his face for months so he could put on the weight," Ufland said, preoccupied with other thoughts as he grabbed my Motorola brick-phone to make a call to Hollywood.

"The 1980s must have been a busy decade for you after *Bull*?" I asked as he ended his call.

"Oh sure. Incredible. No doubt about that. *Last Temptation of Christ* was another biggie for me in '88. Marty [Scorsese] at his best—he got nominated for Best Director," Ufland gloated, waiting for some response from me.

I realized at that moment I was driving the devil around the northern corridor of the I-285 Perimeter Parkway. Certainly he wasn't the first Hollywood devil I had ever encountered, but certainly he was the boldest as no one had ever bragged so effortlessly about crucifying Christ twice.

Ufland, Universal Studios, and Martin Scorsese had undertaken the first large-scale, coordinated, intentionally offensive, blasphemous, profane and vulgar attack against people of both the Christian and Jewish faiths. *The Last Temptation of Christ* was produced in viciously spiteful high-heresy by depicting Jesus Christ in a purposely nefariously evil portrait promoted by a synchronized industry-wide agenda of lies to wickedly mock the man seen as the Son of God by more than two billion of the world's Christians.

"So, what did you think about it, Mike?" Ufland asked while fumbling through a map book of Atlanta. What I was thinking was how great a country America is by offering its citizens the freedom to elevate themselves to endless heights of achievement and the freedom to debase themselves to new lows in bottomless pits

517

of deviance. Ufland, like Scorsese, epitomized the Faustian dealmakers who had sold their souls by reaching out to embrace the Mephisphelean handshake.

Finally, shouting over the roar of eighteen-lane Atlanta metro traffic, I asked, "Harry, I never did hear the outcome, you know, the box-office? How did it turn out?"

"Incredible . . . oh, big time. It blew everything away. We're still making money off the film. Home video is taking off all over. We have a whole new window to make money." [Lie Number One]

"I didn't see the movie, but I read the book. I remember it caused quite a stir when it was released," I added.

"To say the least! There was a hundred thousand of those hard-core types who tried to censor the movie. They tried to stone the Black Tower (the aptly named corporate headquarters for Universal). Everybody inside was bolting the doors and grabbing anything they could use as a weapon to defend themselves." [Lie Number Two]

"Why do you suppose they were so upset, Harry?"

"Those crazies hadn't even seen the movie. Universal offered to screen the film for those religious types and they *refused*! That was the only real argument. How can you even discuss the movie, much less protest it, if you haven't even seen it? They should have seen it first and then made up their mind." [Lie Number Three]

The studio and Scorsese had played up the story that *Last Temptation* was simply based on the 1960 book of the same name by Nikos Kazantzakis. "Harry, I think a lot of people heard about the book, first, the one by Kazantzakis and how Christ was portrayed as having sex with Mary Magdalene and how he then weds Mary of Bethany and ends up having children by both of them. I could see how that would make a lot of people upset."

"The movie was different from the book," Ufland insisted and growing agitated continued, "Look, the studio hired a couple of Christian guys to bring together these religious leaders for a screening. But when Pollock [CEO Universal Productions] announced the screening date, they didn't show. Universal went out of their way for these small-minded people and they dropped the ball." [Lie Number Four]

"Marty himself said it was a faith-affirming film. Anyhow, the critics loved it and that's what really counts, you know?" Ufland smugged up. "Not to mention, Jack Valenti and the MPAA were behind us 100%. Can't beat that!"

No surprise there.

Ufland didn't realize that I had also read *The Last Temptation of Hollywood*, the book authored by one of those "Christian guys," Dr. Larry Poland. The book chronicled the well-organized campaign of deception to the Christian community and the worldwide audience at large by Universal Studios under the knowing leadership of the last old school mogul, Lew Wasserman.

THE HOLLYWOOD CULTURE WAR

The 1988 release of *The Last Temptation of Christ* would signal the beginning of the more vocal roots of the Culture War against Hollywood. Previously, the American audience had simply quit going to the theaters. Or, former moviegoers grumbled privately among themselves during the preceding twenty years as Valenti continued dancing the Hollywood Shuffle about how his Ratings Scheme provided "essential tools" for filmgoers.

But all that changed in 1988. Poland's book was a detailed look inside the mind, motivation and madness of Hollywood and how the industry is oiled by a continuum of never ending lies; a world where the fantasy does not begin or end on the screen. Dr. Poland has headed up a group of influential faith-based entertainment executives known as "The Key Group" and has published the *Mastermedia* newsletter.

In his book about *The Last Temptation of Christ* fiasco, Poland first used the term "Values War" in 1988, which soon translated into The Culture War by 1990.

More than any other religious faith in the world, Hollywood has increasingly pushed the button on Christians in a crude manner that the industry absolutely knows will offend them, even if it results in lost profits at the box-office as was the case with *Last Temptation*. Columnist and former presidential candidate Patrick Buchanan would be among the first writers to coin the phrase "Christian-Bashing" in a July 27, 1988, article titled, "Christian Bashing a Popular Indoor Sport in Hollywood." As Michael Medved observes, "Hollywood's persistent hostility to religious values is not just peculiar, it is positively pathological."[1]

The origin of this pathology comes from the filmmakers themselves. Christian-bashing is the central plank in Hollywood's escalating campaign of value manipulation. One of the reasons Jack Valenti sacked the Production Code is because it "reeked of moral integrity" as he openly and proudly boasted right up to his death in April of 2007.

Valenti also wanted to cover up very compelling language that pinpointed the true origin of a film's content and how it affected the population as a whole. Article II of the Motion Picture Production Code clearly stated:

> "The motion pictures, which are the most popular of modern arts for the masses, have their moral quality from the minds which produce them and from their effects on the moral lives and reactions of the audiences."
>
> —(Appendix III)

Article II of the Code also stated that "Art can be *morally good*, lifting men to higher levels" and also "Art can be *morally evil* in its effects." [2] This stated connection between good and evil and its "effects on the moral lives and reactions" from the audience was language Valenti wanted erased for all time. If the Production Code had been in effect in 1994, *Natural Born Killers* by Oliver Stone would have never been produced and many people who were murdered as a result of the film's "morally evil" effects would still be alive today. Valenti, as the movie industry's cheerleader, always insisted there was no connection between movies and people's behavior. The Production Code determined otherwise and had to be destroyed.

Likewise, if the Production Code was in effect in 1988, *Last Temptation* would have never been produced, sparing egregious and intentional insult on Christians and Jews. The movie originated from "the moral quality of the minds" that brought it to the screen, such as Martin Scorsese, Harry Ufland, Lew Wasserman and many more at Universal Pictures. And that "moral quality" was so low, it entered the domain of sheer evil and became another strand in the long dark thread that continues to run through Hollywood.

While there were a handful of other "softball" assaults on Jesus Christ before 1988, *Last Temptation* was the lifelong vengeful obsession that began with Martin Scorsese, a diplomatically bitter man who was known, then and now, as a "dark" director. He was one of a growing number of writers and directors that were intent on glamorizing "evil" as "cool." Scorsese himself had been influenced by the mentally ill director of 1950s grindhouse horror films, Val Lewton, described by *TCM* as a "tormented genius"—Hollywoodspeak for "lunatic."

And when Hollywood's biggest studio signed on with the full endorsement of Chairman Lew Wasserman, American Christians and Jews saw a vicious and diabolical side of the movie business that they couldn't possibly have imagined was simmering under the Hollywood Hills. Wasserman was also considered by many to be among the most corrupt of the old school moguls. And, the attendant presence of old mafia "suits" disappeared from the back lot when he died in 2002.

There have been an extraordinary amount of attacks on people of Christian and Jewish faith since *Last Temptation* in 1988 and we will chronicle some of them later in the chapter. And, since 1988, Hollywood's faith-based attacks have become more frequent, more vicious, and insidiously more sophisticated in an urgent attempt to lure more faith-based people into the theaters and then assaulting them in jabs, both blatant and subtle, that border on the truly sublime.

Strangely exempt from this religious persecution by Hollywood is extreme Muslim radicalism, particularly the brand of Islamic terrorism that wants America wiped off the map. This isn't all that unusual considering Hollywood's love affair with America's enemies, especially the thirty year love-fest with Soviet

THE HOLLYWOOD CULTURE WAR

Communism, which also wanted America wiped off the globe. A few recent examples:

- The 2005 film *Syriana* starred George Clooney who portrayed an American who is "run down" by the big, bad U.S. government and, in the end, the terrorists are given a pass and are even portrayed as "underdogs" to U.S. aggression.
- In the 2001 film production of Tom Clancey's *The Sum of All Fears*, the middle-eastern Islamic terrorists who were the center of the book are mysteriously missing as Hollywood replaced them with neo-Nazis as the "bad guys." (Clancey disassociated himself from the movie produced by Mace Neufeld.)
- In 2006, the Hollywood Foreign Press Association awarded the "Best Documentary" to *Paradise Now*, a sympathetic and not-too-subtle glorification of Islamic extremist suicide bombers. The terrorists were clearly portrayed as heroes in this film.
- Steven Spielberg released *Munich* in 2005 to a very disappointed box-office as it bombed on the vine. *Munich* was a semi-pseudo-quasi-fictional-factual account of the 1972 Olympic slaughter of Israeli athletes in Germany by Palestinian terrorists. Spielberg paints the terrorists with an ambivalent brush stroke, portraying them as ordinary "family men" no different than the Israeli secret squad on a mission to assassinate the guilty terrorists.
- In 2007 and 2008, Hollywood released a string of anti-American movies with a pro-Islamic terrorist slant such as *Lions for Lambs* by terrorist sympathizer director Robert Redford; *In the Valley of Ellah* by Communist fellow traveler director Paul Haggis; *Redacted* by anti-American activist director Brian DePalma and *Rendition* by Gavin Wood. *All four movies* turned into the biggest financial box-office disasters in the last ten years, money-losers for the studios and dumb-struck, star-struck investors.
- Only Paul Greengrass, director of *United 93* in 2006, portrayed Saudi Islamic terrorist highjackers as, well, Saudi Islamic terrorist highjackers. Greengrass remained as faithful as possible to the true story of the 9/11 highjacking of United Flight 93 in which the passengers became the first heroes in the current war on terrorism after overcoming their captors and crashing the plane into a field near Shanksville, Pennsylvania. Unlike the other films, *United 93* was ignored at the Academy Awards by the virulent members of the anti-American Academy of Motion Picture Arts and Sciences.

MICHAEL VINCENT BOYER

THE ABCs OF HOLLYWOOD JUDEO-CHRISTIAN BASHING

This section will identify and dissect the three main avenues of attack on faith-based people:

A. —The Confrontational Attack
B. —The Sophisticated Attack
C. —The Back Door Attack

Each section will focus on one movie that epitomizes each of these distinct avenues of attack on America's faithful.

A. THE CONFRONTATIONAL ATTACK
The Last Temptation of Christ

My drive through Atlanta with Harry Ufland would have been marked-up as yet another hilarious location scouting joyride with a typical left-coast Hollywood producer except for the sad fact that Ufland, Scorsese and the executive branch of Universal Studios embarked on the most blatantly bigoted campaign of lying and deception to smear its own audience's deepest and most sacred faith-based beliefs. This was no joyride.

Nobody *had* to go see the movie, but Universal was aggressively insisting that people *needed* to see the movie because, after all, the director Martin Scorsese himself said it was a "faith-affirming film." What most people in America found difficult to believe up until this film is that the tongue of Hollywood is almost always a double-edged sword, just like Ufland's inventive falsehoods in defense of the movie. (All of which will be picked apart in this chapter.)

Last Temptation was one of a handful of new films emerging from Hollywood in the mid to late 1980s with the intention of smearing Christians and Jews. But, *Last Temptation* was by far the most profane, vulgar and directly contaminated assault in the history of motion pictures against the oldest and most prolific of faiths in America. The movie was also one of the biggest box-office bombs in recent decades. Despite that, *Last Temptation* would spew a whole new slew of confrontational attack films throughout the 1990s with equally disastrous box-office results, suggesting that a deep-seated religious hatred in Hollywood was rising to the surface—the profits be damned.

Paramount dropped the idea of producing *Last Temptation* in 1983, but Martin Scorsese persisted—he was on a mission—but, this was no "mission from God,"

THE HOLLYWOOD CULTURE WAR

as the Blues Brothers would say. By the time production began with Universal in late 1987 and into 1988, Scorsese had spent fifteen years desperately trying to get the 1960 Nikos Kazantzakis novel to the big screen.

Both Kazantzakis and Scorsese had major chips on their shoulders that had to be filled in like so much bondo on antique autos. It is imperative to understand the motivations behind these men for taking actions so drastic it required putting their own neurotic demons on the screen. The hatred and petty jaundice of both these men ran so deep in their darkened hearts that they wanted everybody to not only *feel* their hate, but to embrace it fully.

As for the author, Nikos was a mentally disturbed and fanatically obsessed individual whose mindset fit like a hand in the glove with the Crowlean New Age secular thinking that had increasingly influenced authors, artists, musicians, actors and filmmakers beginning in the late 1920s. According to Helen Kazantzakis, Nikos' wife, the very real and true motivation for the author was his burning desire to create a new religion. This is what genuinely haunted and consumed him for decades.[3]

In a letter sent to his Swedish translator, Boris Knoss, Nikos wrote, "But while I was writing this book, I felt what Christ felt." [4] Even more bizarre was the observation of Nikos' work by friend Kimon Friar who translated Nikos' other New Age diatribe *The Savior of God: Spiritual Exercises*. Nikos tried to imbue this text as a new bible using chapters and verses in a fashion that resembled Aleister Crowley's New Age bible, *The Book of the Law*, which became the theology for virtually all New Age beliefs from 1904 to the present.

According to Friar, "God, for Nikos Kazantzakis, was not an already predetermined goal toward which men proceed, but a spirituality ceaselessly and progressively created by nature as it evolves toward greater and higher refinement."[5]

Keep in mind, these were people who considered themselves "Christians," just as Scorsese would later describe himself in a craftily written "PR" letter to help promote *Last Temptation*. This is classic *far-Left* New Age Christianity; basically, charlatan buffoonery. For Nikos, it all seemed so real. For Scorsese, it was a convenient lie.

* * *

The story behind the marketing of *Last Temptation* is as rife with drama as the perverse storyline of the movie itself. Universal Studios was engaging in one of the most comprehensive and premeditated attacks on Christianity by deceitfully using two popular figures in the Christian media community, Tim Penland and Dr. Larry Poland, to help promote the film to the Christian community.

Initially, Penland was brought on board with only a "concept" of the project. At first, Penland and Poland didn't realize the dishonesty, duplicity and cunning manipulation that Universal executives were capable of executing with false pretext and outright lies.

Tim Penland was gaining a reputation in Hollywood during the 1980s for helping to promote films such as *Chariots of Fire* and *The Mission* to the Christian moviegoing audience in America. Dr. Larry Poland founded the Christian advocacy group Mastermedia and his "Key Group" ministry included entertainment industry executives from Paramount, Disney, MGM and all the major television networks. The hatred and animosity toward Christians in the film business was, and remains, so pervasive that participants in Mastermedia's "Key Group" were a well-guarded secret to protect the careers of attending film executives, lest they be "found out" by Hollywood's emperor legions of die-hard atheists and New Age occultists who ruled in "high places."

Poland had helped Penland before by providing research for his marketing efforts on previous films. Penland approached his friend again after being "pitched" by four executives from Universal who wanted to retain his services for a film nearing completion by director Martin Scorsese. Those present from Universal for the initial meeting with Penland included Tom Pollack, Chairman of Production; Sean Daniel, head of Worldwide Production; Si Kornblatt, head of Marketing and Sally Van Slyke, head of Publicity. We say "head of" for the last three because their titles and responsibilities often changed as rapidly as the "truth" that they manufactured on a daily basis.

Tom Pollock explained to Penland that Universal needed help in "working with Christians" to promote a movie that "is going to be a faith-affirming film . . . It is not our desire to release a film defaming Christ."[6]

Penland told Poland of the meeting and the "assurances" made by Universal. Poland was quick to tell his friend that "if it is a faith-affirming film, it will surely bare little resemblance to the book." Word had already spread widely throughout Christian circles about Universal's desire to make the movie version of *Last Temptation*. Universal's Pollock had even told Penland at their first meeting that Universal was receiving an enormous amount of critical calls and letters. This should have signaled a red flag for Penland that he was being retained solely to play defense for a movie of offense.

In all likelihood, Don Wildmon of the American Family Association (AFA) had heard about plans to make the movie before production even began. Wildmon had mentioned Universal's intentions in a 1987 AFA newsletter. The AFA is one of the oldest and largest media watchdog organizations in the country, founded in 1977. Wildmon's devotion to family values and the basic tenants of positive morality has earned him the title of "The Most Hated Man in Hollywood," a title he wears with honor. And, within the vast secular labyrinth of Hollywood, a number of high-level sympathizers have kept a pipeline open to Wildmon to alert him when Hollywood is about to unleash another attack on Christians.

When Penland was hired in early January of 1988, Wildmon was already planning one of the largest mass mailings ever to the faith-based community across North America; more than one million direct mail appeals. But, after Penland called Wildmon, the AFA decided to hold off—temporarily. Wildmon had been burned before and he wasn't about to be burned again. He was willing to give Penland a chance to provide more details about Universal's "faith-affirming" movie.

The whole controversy of the "Christian consultants" centered around the curious timing of Penland's hiring and the anticipated release of *Last Temptation* in late October of 1988. Penland did suggest to Universal that screenings be set up as soon as possible. "Consider it done," Tom Pollack assured Penland.[7]

This would turn out to be the first of many back-handed deceptions and lies that Universal would issue over the ensuing months. Unfortunately, Penland was very naïve in the wily ways of Hollywood. He sincerely believed that a man's word was to be trusted. In Penland's mind, and according to assurances from Universal Studios, the movie would absolutely *not* resemble the book.

Penland liked to use the term "bridge-building," believing that this project would be an ideal opportunity to ensure biblical accuracy in the filming of Christ's life. For some reason unknown to Penland, Hollywood was taking a giant step in producing a film about Christ that would not even resemble the heretical book on which it was based.

At one of Larry Poland's "Key Group" fellowships, a high-profile producer of television and feature films warned Poland that Scorsese and Universal had no good intentions whatsoever. This was not to be the new *Ben-Hur*. As he explained to Poland, "Scorsese? A film on Christ from Scorsese? You're in trouble. Scorsese is a dark director . . . Martin isn't capable of producing anything with goodness and light. He's preoccupied with the sinister side, the occult side of life and characters."[8]

This warning came as a divine revelation for Poland who was unaware of Scorsese's deep preoccupation with occult themes. March had arrived and Penland was already securing commitments from a number of major Christian leaders to attend a screening. Good or bad, at least the screening would determine the true direction Universal was taking with *Last Temptation*. And, that's when the problem seemed to take on a diabolical life of its own.

Suddenly, Universal Studios couldn't agree on a date to screen the movie. Pollock, Kornblatt and Van Slyke told Penland that Scorsese wasn't finished with the film and even they had not been given an "opportunity" to see the footage themselves.

Don Wildmon was smelling a rat, again. In a godless industry, words and phrases like "assurance," "faith-affirming" and "no desire to defame Christ" all had double meanings and they were bubbling to the surface. In order to send out a mailing in advance of the film's October release, he would need 80 to 90 days to prepare and send over a million "Action Letters" to the faithful. Wildmon is an expert at timing and his clock began to run out.

March was spiraling to an end and still no news from Universal about a screening or even a script. Another one of the "Key Group" told Poland and Penland that they were being given the "party line." This particular member of Poland's inner circle of Christian executives had, himself, experienced numerous delays with Universal over the years. Universal, like many other production entities in Hollywood, was not known for straightforward honesty, integrity or character.

The executive told Penland, "You've been in the film business long enough to know that you usually watch 'dailies.' [Footage from the previous day.] You can't tell me that if Lew Wasserman or Sid Sheinberg wanted to see footage of this film there wouldn't be anything to see!"

Penland and Poland had no doubts now they were being used as window dressing while the clock ticked away. Curiously, just after their "Key Group" meeting, Universal's publicity chief, Sally Van Slyke, sent a script over to Penland and Poland for review. Whether she was authorized to do so has never been ascertained. Penland had always felt she was the only one at Universal who maintained a sincere knowledge and sensitivity to Judeo-Christian values. Within twenty-four hours of the script's arrival, a courier mysteriously arrived to retrieve the script.

During the brief window of opportunity, Penland and Poland's worst fears had come to light. Penland began reading to Poland the scene where Jesus is sitting with other "customers" of "prostitute" Mary Magdalene in the foyer of her "brothel." Mary is having sex with someone while Jesus is "patiently" waiting.

Penland then reads the homoerotic tongue-kissing scene between Jesus and John the Baptist when Jesus says, "His tongue is like a burning coal in my mouth." And then Mary, the mother of Jesus says, "Forgive my son! He's crazy . . . He's not well in the head." Then there was the sex scene between Jesus and Mary Magdalene . . . and Penland was barely into the script at this point.

Penland told Poland that he had marked offensive content on 80 of the script's 120 total pages. So much for consulting on historical accuracy and "bridge building." The two did not have time to copy the script before the mystery courier arrived and took the screenplay. Poland didn't think it was right to copy the screenplay that had been entrusted to them for that brief twenty-four hour window. It was, and remains, common practice in Hollywood to secretly code controversial scripts within the dialogue so that a studio can identify potential leakers if a script is made public.

Now the game of "touch" football with Universal had turned to "tackle." Tim Penland knew he was going to have to resign his "consulting" position with Universal. Poland was only advising Penland as a friend and was not required to resign from anything. And, Poland was not about to abandon his friend. This would actually mark that beginning of the next phase in Hollywood's entrenchment as one of the most famous episodes in the Culture War.

* * *

Twenty years after Valenti ushered in the tragedy of the Ratings Scheme, people would no longer remain silent about the culture rot he ushered in on such a grand scale.

"Tim," Poland suggested, "the most crucial element of this affair is the span of time between the screening and the release date of the film. If Universal is using us to hold off protests so they can profit from the controversy and if they do release a film over the protests of the Christian community, the Christian leaders need some time to mobilize protests."[9]

Wildmon had set mid-June as his non-negotiable deadline and he was prepared to pour a million dollars into the effort if Universal was "doing a number" on him. As events rapidly began to unfold, the script would become the turning point as much as the mythical screening for *Last Temptation*. Even before Penland reviewed his "twenty-four hour script" with Poland, someone at Universal had slipped an uncoded copy to Wildmon at his AFA headquarters.

Wildmon called Penland to let him know that AFA was sending two-hundred copies of the script to major religious leaders across the country. Universal had fired the first shot in its new hyper-stage attack on Judeo-Christian values in general and Christianity in particular. Wildmon would soon return fire in what would transpire as the first widely-covered battle of the contemporary Culture War.

Penland soon found that he had been viciously trapped in a snare which Universal executives had secretly planned from the beginning. Penland had already sent out invitations for a screening to be held on June 10, 1988. Van Slyke called in late May to say that a screening wasn't possible until August. His reputation among religious leaders would be tarnished forever—and Universal knew this. There was no way Christian leaders were going to wait until August to see a movie that was opening in October.

Penland dated his resignation for June 12. Before he could even deliver that letter, a small article appeared in the *Philadelphia Enquirer* on June 4, 1988, announcing that "Martin Scorsese clearly anticipates trouble when he releases his newest film, *The Last Temptation of Christ*, in the fall. In the spring, he signed on a Christian marketing expert to shepherd the movie past objections of religionists. Now comes word that he [Scorsese] has scheduled a series of secret New York screenings . . ."

This had all the obvious hallmarks of a Universal leak. The studio had learned Tim Penland was about to tender his resignation and they were beginning to set him up. This was all part of the studio plan to smear Christians on screen and off. When an angry Penland called Pollock at Universal about the article while simultaneously offering his resignation, Pollock began the classic Hollywood Shuffle, "You don't understand what we have here. This film will be a great work of art, even if it is somewhat controversial."[10]

Pollock was acting like a stuck pig in a puddle of his own mud. Surely, he thought, Penland would understand the *truly* higher purpose of the film—"art"—the Hollywood god, which trumped all other gods. Of course, Pollock was the man who said it *was not* Universal's *desire* to "defame Christ." Since "artists" create their own truth, he wasn't *really* lying.

Even though Pollock and Scorsese called *Last Temptation* a "faith-affirming" movie, Pollock had forgot to tell Penland it was a "faith-affirming" film about "art." Certainly, at this point, Pollock wanted to stand atop his desk and cry out, "Art for art's sake—heaven for God's sake!"

Soon after Pollock's pathetic blood-letting conversation with Penland, Universal would begin spinning the truth in a way that only the warped and skewed minds of Hollywood entertainment executives could accomplish. Despite Penland's departure, Universal tried desperately to convince the original group of Christian leaders to attend a special July 12 screening. But, there was no way the leaders would further allow themselves to be exploited, especially in light of Penland's resignation and the copies of the script in their hand thanks to Don Wildmon.

* * *

A friend of mine at Universal had told me long ago that Lew Wasserman was pulling the strings from his Chairman's loft, despite acting distant from the antics of his underlings. And, these very underlings at the end of the strings would begin spinning the line that was frequently used among the Hollywood-hugging press and movie critics alike, "Christian leaders protesting the film were invited to a screening by Universal which they refused to attend."[11]

As events rapidly unfolded, Tim Penland and Larry Poland eagerly joined the growing protests against the film as one of the most insensitive, vulgar and pornographically blasphemous films to ever come out of Hollywood. Aided by a "sympathetic insider" in the upper-level chain of command at Universal,

Penland was told that the film had already been screened for the distribution department, long before Penland resigned. Penland was astounded with the level of dark, duplicitous lies by virtually everybody involved in the marketing of *Last Temptation*.

The "sympathetic insider" was actually present at the screening and informed Penland that the movie was even *worse* than the book and even *worse* than the script. Apparently, Scorsese had let his inner demons loose on the set and was carried away by the screeching little voices screaming from deep inside his head. Even many inside the film industry felt Scorsese was "unstable."

In the Last Supper scene, the disciples drink wine only to have it turn to blood and drip from their mouths. Not only did Scorsese produce a sex scene between Jesus and Mary Magdalene, he directed it to resemble a bachelor-party porn film. One individual at the set remarked how Scorsese demanded numerous retakes of this scene, much to the delight of the on-location crew who rolled in laughter between takes.

The "sympathetic insider" also told Penland that the final print ran a whopping two hours and forty-eight minutes, and that was only after Universal forced Scorsese to cut out eight minutes of the self-indulgent sex scene between Jesus and Mary Magdalene. The only reason Universal forced the eight minutes cut is because they didn't want the film to be *too* controversial! Just *regular* controversial. (Scorsese would not return my calls to comment on stories that he shows the eight minute out-takes to friends at weekend parties at his home.)

Universal was waging a devious media war against the Christian community and against *anyone* who denounced the film. The media and the critics were almost unanimously *in the pocket* of Universal and Scorsese and did their part to scorch the Christian community from that point on.

Dr. James Dobson of Focus On The Family was able to accommodate Penland and Poland for an exclusive interview so that they could warn and inform the American audience of Universal's unusually brazen, even vindictive, assault on the Christian faith in America and internationally. Dobson's radio show was critical in getting the word out to as many people as possible. Dr. Dobson's radio program was and remains the most widely syndicated program in radio, secular or faith-based.

Wildmon sent out his "Action Alerts" in one of the biggest mass mailings in its history with details about the script's contents and urging people to register their concern with the studio. Sources from inside Universal said the letters arriving at the studio were being trashed as quickly as they arrived.

Universal quickly upped the release date to September instead of October. At this point, Wasserman, Sheinberg, Pollock and Scorsese were hoping, at the very least, to cash in on the controversy from the secular community. The marketing department at Universal felt that a certain demographic could be counted on to attend the movie for the sheer Christian-bashing joy that it would deliver.

At the same time, Universal, in all its manipulative duplicity, was not giving up on some supportive "Christian" comments that could be used in advertising. High-level executives from Universal actually flew to New York to "round up" some "religious leaders" for the July 12th screening in New York.

As Poland described their plan, "The Universal Pix crew headed for that hot-bed of religious Leftists in New York City at 475 Riverside Drive. The high-rise structure, also known as 'The God Box' or 'Heaven on the Hudson' houses headquarters for the World Council of Churches, the National Council of Churches and a host of other Left-leaning and not-so-Left leaning religious structures." Poland knew that "this address could be counted upon to cough up any number of clerics who would be most likely to tolerate or even support a film rewriting the narrative of the biblical Jesus."

In the meantime, word had spread through the worldwide Christian community about Scorsese and Universal's attack on their faith and values. The switchboard at Universal was choked for almost two weeks in early July. Calls were not coming in and calls were not going out. Much of the mail was arriving in batches of 100,000 pieces at a time.

Pastor Richard G. Lee of Atlanta's massive Rehobeth Baptist Church collected more than 135,000 signatures on a petition and attempted to personally deliver them to Universal. He was told at the gate, "Leave them with the guard, and we'll put them in the dump."[12]

Lew Wasserman had already been called by numerous old friends; Archbishop Mahoney, legislators from Sacramento and Washington, D.C. The chairmen of a number of large corporations had also called Wasserman asking him to show some sensitivity. Even Wasserman's chauffer turned in his driver's seat to face the bitter old mogul and said, "Mr. Wasserman, I wouldn't want to be in your shoes on judgment day."[13]

The storyline from the publicity department that Wasserman knew very little about the movie was just another in a long line of lies. Wasserman already had a reputation for bashing Christians and people of many faiths. He had no problem with the movie smearing Christians just as long as he didn't have to deal with all the problems surrounding the movie.

Wasserman kicked the responsibility down to Universal President Sid Sheinberg, a virulent anti-Christian zealot himself who was proud to have taken credit for the "Christian siege" battle cry. In addition to his hatred for Christians, he was also known within the industry as being one of the most coarse and verbally abusive executives in the industry, second only to the psychotic behavior of David Geffen.

As the July 12 screening date drew near, Sheinberg was demonstrating signs of losing control. During morning meetings, he would rant and curse Christians and his fellow subordinates at Universal with equal venom. At one point, Wasserman had heard enough and yelled at Sheinberg to "Shut-Up" and *handle* the crisis. This is known as the Pontius Pilate approach to crucifying Christ for the second time.

Before the press and Universal launched into a more coordinated counteroffensive against the Christian community, the Los Angeles Times did print a quote from Dr. James Dobson, "It would appear to be the most blasphemous, evil attack on the Church and the cause of Christ in the history of entertainment. Universal and Scorsese are not merely taking on evangelicals; they are taking on the King of the Universe."[14]

But, that would be the last time the press and mainstream media quoted anybody from the Christian community without twisting their words. The confrontational attack was rapidly moving in fast-forward mode. Universal desperately needed at least a dose of "religious" validation, which they found at the "God block" in New York. The "selected" Left-wing clergy attended the July 12th screening and by the 16th, the "de-briefed" group of "Christians" were making the talk-show circuit in full-force.

New York Episcopal Bishop Paul Moore would describe the film as "artistically excellent and theologically sound."[15] Andrew Cano of the U.S. office of the World Council of Churches had concluded that the film could be transferred to video for use in churches along with a *study guide*. Rev. David Pomeroy of the radical homosexual branch of the United Church of Christ and media representative for the National Council of Churches was quoted in the *Washington Times* as saying, "Yes, the film does depict Christ in a sexual relationship with Mary Magdalene, but it was tastefully done."[16] Only Hugh Hefner could have said it better.

It is necessary to point out those people are not really "Christian" spokesmen. These are well-paid bureaucrats from the "globalist" community better known as "charlatans." [Translation: quacks.] The World Council of Churches and the National Council of Churches are part of the "ecumenical" movement that gained momentum after World War II. Ecumenical is defined as the principle of promoting "cooperative" or better understanding among different religions.

In their attempts to find common ground among *extremely* diverse religious beliefs around the world, they end up finding very little in common and representing nobody. Their funding is questionable in a manner that would make Jesse Jackson green with envy. These council of churches are easily swayed to take up the cause of any group who *might*, and I emphasize *might*, be so kind as to leave a generous offering at the door. These council of churches take donations in the Bob Hope playbook, "Please . . . please don't . . . please don't stop!" The World and National Councils of Churches are a religion unto themselves.

As Larry Poland explains, "Pick a viewpoint, any viewpoint and, with a little time, I can roust out at least a handful of guys with backward collars to support it . . . A man of the cloth for homosexuality? Easy . . . A pro-communist pastor? No sweat . . . Pick a doctrinal aberration, any aberration, and you will surely find some Christian minister from the First United Church of Sheepclothing to espouse it."

With the New York charlatans out in force, other radical groups began to rally around Universal. The most notable among these groups was the inappropriately named People For The American Way (PFTAW), a Hollywood-funded group founded by guru Norman Lear to fight the conservative movement in America. PFTAW even pulled a "Reverend" out of its hat named *Rev.* Charles Bergstrom who said, "I was not offended in any way. Scripture was used and applied." Lear had left TV production in the early 1980's to persecute Christianity full time in his role as a "mumbo-jumbo" New Age guru.

The PFTAW would use its Christian-bashing defense of *Last Temptation* as a major fundraising tool for years to come. The group's alliance with Universal would propel it as a major player in the Culture War. (PFTAW now works very closely with George Soros and the pro-atheism campaigns of the OSI.)

The American Civil Liberties Union (ACLU) would also use its defense of Universal and *Last Temptation* as a major springboard into the national arena of the Culture War as a result of the publicity scramble surrounding the movie. The ACLU is also a largely atheist organization now headed by the radical homosexual heterophobe Anthony Romero who hates Christians *with a passion*.

The ACLU's rabid defense of Universal and Scorsese would mark its current foray into a long campaign against Christian and other faith-based groups that dates all the way back to the 1925 Scopes trial in Tennessee. It can be said that the contemporary incarnation of the ACLU began in August of 1988 at the height of the *Last Temptation* controversy. It is also important to remember that the glowing defenders of *Last Temptation* were all, largely, members of the Hollywood Cocktail Party Circuit (HCPC) and the Bi-Coastal Cocktail Party Circuit (BCPC). Any defense of the Christians in the arena could easily cause one's name to be dropped from the invitation list.

The studio and the press began to tout the First Amendment and their "freedom of speech" rights, something for which the Christian community was not eligible. The coordinated studio and media attacks also invoked two favorite phrases, "How can you pre-judge anything" or "How can you criticize the movie without seeing it?"

Of course, anyone who fell for that line, saw the movie, and said, "It's as bad as I thought" was no problem; because Universal was already adding the ticket price you paid to its overall gross. Refunds don't count because Hollywood doesn't participate in "cash back guarantees."

In rebuttal of the Hollywood line about not pre-judging anything without seeing it first, the Rev. Billy Graham said, "I do not have to see a rape in order to condemn rape . . . I do not need to see a murder in order to condemn murder. From what I have read, the film is sacrilegious."[17]

Billy Graham and millions of other moviegoers were exercising their First Amendment rights, exercising their "freedom of speech" by deciding that no person and no corporation could bully or threaten them into seeing a movie. This was Hollywood's lowest moment in its long history.

And, the clouds grew darker as Hollywood's own Dark Prince approached the podium of free speech with his angry arched eyebrows locked for battle as he bolstered the Universal and Hollywood position on *Last Temptation*. Twenty years after he abolished the very system which would have prevented the entire charade by an angry, bitter and vengeful movie director, Valenti had his first chance to deliver a direct attack on the faith-based and Christian communities which he deeply despised.

Valenti, born a Catholic, had long ago sold his soul and was no different than the charlatan leadership of the National Council of Churches. Valenti was bought and paid for and now was the time to deliver.

Representing Columbia, Disney, MGM/UA, Orion, Paramount and Warner Brothers, Valenti prepared to issue the definitive *confrontational attack* that would officially bring all the major studios at the time in line with Universal for a united front against Christianity, which Valenti would now redefine as a censorship issue.

In his statement, Valenti declared defiantly that "The key issue, the *only* issue, is whether or not self-appointed groups can prevent a film from being exhibited to the public . . . The major companies of the MPAA support MCA/Universal in its absolute right to offer the people whatever movie *it* chooses."[18]

His statement, in the midst of this controversy, was firmly intended to put the people of America on notice that the entertainment industry would no longer give the audience what *they* wanted to see, but would instead "offer to the people whatever movie *it* chooses." And the intent of that public announcement is at the heart of the first paragraph of this book.

As Michael Medved said, "This statement is not to insist that every possible release is equally defensible."[19] In other words, would Jack Valenti have called for the same united front if Salman Rushdie's *The Satanic Verses* was produced and released depicting a very different portrait of Mohammed? Doubtful.

* * *

On August 11, 1988, a planned demonstration of protestors gathered quietly outside Universal's Black Tower to protest the release of a film whose sole intention was now clearly stated to defame their God and their Savior. Police estimated about 25,000 people had gathered near the front of the building.

Earlier, Tim Penland and Larry Poland published a full-page ad in *The Hollywood Reporter* signed by a large number of sympathetic supporters in the film industry. The statement ended with, "Our Lord was crucified once on the cross. He doesn't deserve to be crucified a second time on celluloid."

Contrary to the spin Universal tried to inject, the police reported absolutely no incidents of violence or vandalism. The Universal publicity department was working overtime to fulfill the confrontational attack. And, they had plenty of friends in the media. Mike Duffy of the Detroit Free Press would describe the protestors as "the American ignoramus faction that is perpetually geeked up on self-righteous bile . . . And now the know-nothing wacky-pack has latched onto Martin Scorsese and *The Last Temptation of Christ*."[20]

Among the "whacky pack" that the condescending Duffy was referring to was Nobel Peace Prize winner Mother Teresa of Calcutta who called on all people of good will and faith to "use prayer as the ultimate weapon to fight their ultimate disgrace."

Also present at the protest were representatives of the National Council of Catholic Bishops, the National Catholic Conference, members of the 14 million congregants of the Southern Baptist Convention, the head of the Worldwide Anglican Church: The Archbishop of Canterbury and the Archbishop of Paris, Jane Chastain of Concerned Women of America (CWA), twenty members of the U.S. House of Representatives, members of Italy's largest political party: the Christian Democratic Party of Italy and Rabbi Chaim Asa, a Holocaust survivor and Reform temple Leader in Fullerton, California, who told the gathering, "Millions across the country are saying 'You are touching something very deep, very sensitive in my soul.' Please don't do it because this is not fair!"

Perhaps more perplexing than the bigotry and deviancy behind the movie industry and mainstream media's radical attacks on Judeo-Christian values was the subsequent barrage of praise heaped on the film by American movie critics after the release of *Last Temptation*.

Twenty years later, these reviews are an embarrassing enlightenment of the movie critic's deeply held prejudice and extreme bigotry:

- "Martin Scorsese, America's most gifted, most daring moviemaker, may have created his masterpiece."

    -Richard Corliss, *Time*

- "Anyone for whom the story of Christ . . . has any resonance at all is likely to find this an exquisitely powerful film."

    -Bill Cosford, *The Miami Herald*

- " . . . deeply felt and ultimately faith-affirming."
  -Joel Siegel, "Good Morning America"

- "It is without question one of the most serious, literate, complex and deeply religious films ever made, brilliantly directed by Martin Scorsese."
  -David Ehrenstein, *Los Angeles Herald Examiner*

- "Brilliant, thrilling, and profoundly spiritual."
  -Dennis Cunningham, *CBS*

- "Superbly crafted filmmaking."
  -Marshall Fine, *Gannett News Service*

- "It may well be one of the most doctrinaire visions of the life of Christ."
  -William Arnold, *The Seattle Post Intelligencier*

- "What I've tried to create is a Jesus who, in a sense, is just like any other guy in the street. In his struggle to reach God and find God, he reflects all our struggles. I thought it would give us all hope."
  -Martin Scorsese, *People*

* * *

And finally, a voice of *independent* thinking from a critic with an eye for quality cinema:

> "It is the height of irony that all this controversy should be generated by a film that turns out to be so breathtakingly bad, so unbearably boring. In my opinion, the controversy about the picture is a lot more interesting than the film itself."
>
> -Michael Medved

As Medved noted with accurate clarity in his timeless book, *Hollywood vs. America*, the saturation of sympathy among movie reviewers nationwide seemed suspect, "Critics invariably disagree about the quality of major movies, but the level and intensity of the disagreements on *The Last Temptation of Christ* went far beyond expected differences and seemed to suggest ideological agendas at work."[21]

Ultimately, what was the financial reward for Universal at the box office? The final tally was so pitiful, it actually earned a spot on the website of Box Office

Mojo's list of "Controversial Film Grosses." The grand total for domestic box office receipts barely exceeded $8 million.[22] International distribution flopped. After publicity and distribution costs, the film actually lost about $10 million. It would seem that Mother Teresa's prayer came true.

Compare the gross receipts of *Last Temptation* with those of the 2004 feature *Passion of the Christ* by Mel Gibson. The "consultants" on this film were four men with first hand knowledge by the names of Matthew, Mark, Luke and John. As of January 30, 2007, *Passion* had earned a worldwide gross approaching $700 million.[23]

Despite those staggering returns, even *Passion* brought out the Christian-bashers again; this time the assaults were stealth in nature, but no less blatant and *confrontational* in their intention. *Passion* was the first in a series of films whose ratings by the MPAA seemed to suggest the "ideological agenda" at work by the Ratings Board. As discussed in Chapter 7, "The Ratings Fiasco," the producers of Christian-themed movies were being singled out for more audience-restrictive ratings. Some producers speculate that the New Age mentality of the Ratings Board is now equating some films as "too overtly Christian" on the same par with violence and profanity.

In June of 2006, Rep. Roy Blunt (R-MO) called the MPAA for a special meeting with new MPAA president Dan Glickman, a former congressional colleague. Blunt wanted to know why a widely distributed Christian movie titled *Facing the Giants* by Destination Films was given a PG rating.

The producers at Destination Films were led to believe that the rating was given specifically because of Christian content, perhaps even "too overtly Christian." Blunt also questioned Glickman about the declining standards for the Ratings Scheme.

Glickman issued a statement to Blunt saying "Roy, I assure you that religion was not the reason the movie [*Facing the Giants*] got a PG rating. There are plenty of movies with religious themes that get all kinds of ratings from the MPAA, from *G* to *R*."

As Blunt replied in a television interview, "That's what I would say, too, if I were Dan Glickman . . . he actually didn't address the first part of my letter at all, which is the decline of the ratings."[24]

The Last Temptation of Christ did mark a new phase in the Culture War and, more than anything, revealed the long-simmering bigotry of Hollywood filmmakers. Don Wildmon, "The Most Hated Man In Hollywood," did take note of the broad spectrum of demonstrators outside the black tower on that August day in 1988 and declared, "Universal says they are releasing a movie. In fact, they are unleashing a movement."

Hollywood had unleashed a series of confrontational attack movies on Christianity before *Last Temptation*, but their plots were more subtle. However,

THE HOLLYWOOD CULTURE WAR

Last Temptation actually emboldened this particular brand of Hollywood Christian-bashing. Nobody doubted that Scorsese privately felt burned by the whole *Last Temptation* fiasco, especially in light of the fact that he had raised a third of the movie's production budget.

With an even bigger chip on his shoulder, Scorsese decided to lash out again at the Christian community in 1991 with his "personal" remake of the classic *Cape Fear* of 1962 in which Robert Mitchum played a paroled convict out to seek revenge against the prosecutor, Gregory Peck, who had convicted him. The irony of the plot would not be lost by those who had the misfortune of seeing the Scorsese remake, produced with the full backing again of Lew Wasserman's Universal Studios.

In the new version, Robert DeNiro plays the paroled convict. However, in the Scorsese version, DeNiro is portrayed as a member of the Pentecostal church and his body is emblazoned with tattoos of crosses and Biblical quotations as he carries a Bible tucked under his arm. In the film's climax, the blood-soaked DeNiro prepares to rape the female lead, played by Jessica Lange, and shouts, "Are you ready to be born again?"

As Medved noted in this obvious second-wave attack on Christians, "The emphasis on the religious dimension of the villain in *Cape Fear* might well be described as Scorsese's revenge on the born-again believer who had so passionately protested his previous picture. The fact that Universal Pictures, still licking its wounds from the *Last Temptation* fiasco, happened to be the company that financed and enthusiastically promoted *Cape Fear*, only strengthened the impression that DeNiro's characterization amounted to a deliberate slap at some old enemies."[25]

Even television has not escaped the confrontational attack on Christianity. Now that television has its own malfunctioning Ratings Scheme, the dark contents of Pandora's box can be unleashed in the family living room of almost every home in America, and you don't even have to subscribe to cable.

In the spring of 2006, NBC unveiled its prime-time drama, *The Book of Daniel*, television's most blatant and visceral attack on Christianity to date. The storyline for this inventive show centers around an Episcopal priest addicted to drugs who is married to a raging alcoholic. The couple's son is a homosexual who identifies himself as a Republican (two agendas in one character).

The couple's younger adopted son is involved in a nymphomaniac sexual affair with the local bishop's daughter. If this isn't enough Christian-bashing dysfunction, the drug-addicted priest's sister-in-law is having a lesbian affair with her husband's secretary. And, in a first for television, Jesus appears throughout the series talking to the priest like a Hollywood therapist.

When Donald Wildmon of the AFA told the crowd outside Universal's Black Tower that the studio had "unleashed a movement," he certainly wasn't kidding.

With almost 800,000 protest letters sent to advertisers and NBC, the show was quickly zapped due to lack of sponsors and rock-bottom ratings.

Just before the lights went out on *The Book of Daniel* only weeks after it debuted in 2006, the producers issued a statement, "AFA and bullies like them are hard at work to try and prevent you from seeing these beautiful shows." Did they say *beautiful*?! And, did I forget to mention that NBC and Universal are joined at the corporate hip, now celebrating 20 years of Hollywood Christian-bashing "entertainment?"

After years as one of Hollywood's most virulent Christian-bashers, Harvey Weinstein parted ways as Disney's X-Rated film division and the Weinstein Company was born. In 2007, Weinstein decided to make faith-based movies through his home video branch, Genius Productions. The division has developed films based on books by Joyce Meyer and Max Lucado. Weinstein is not expected to abandon his core audience of hard-core raunch-lovers through continued feature production from the parent company. Genius can prosper under this peculiar arrangement as long as Weinstein keeps his "creative nose" out of production decisions.

Lionsgate Films has partnered with Thomas Nelson Publishing, one of America's oldest and largest Christian booksellers, with plans to distribute films and DVDs through the Christian retail market. Lionsgate has acquired the rights to three works by Christian non-fiction author Lee Strobel. Unless Strobel has worked out an arrangement as technical advisor, his stories could end up looking much different on DVD than the messages that come across in his books. After all, Lionsgate has also agreed to distribute a major Christian-bashing diatribe by Bill Maher in 2008.

Twentieth Century Fox was one of the first major studios to start a faith-based film division, Fox Faith. The division has partnered with a growing number of independent faith-based film production companies including Namesake, among others. Fox Faith has discovered some of the pitfalls of making faith-based feature films that are reviewed by movie critics still under the spell of Jack Valenti. In March 2007, Fox Faith released *The Ultimate Gift* with Brian Dennehy and Drew Fuller. The film industry polling firm CinemaScore said 99% of viewers who saw the movie rated it an A or B.

But, the secular critics who crave porn, profanity and perversity used some old familiar language. Typical of *The New York Times* worldview, critic Jeanette Catsoulis said the film was "reeking of self-righteous and moral reprimand" and "is a hair-ball of good-for-you filmmaking." Producer Rick Eldridge saw that train coming and noted, "*The Ultimate Gift* is a people's film, not a critic's film." Most acutely, Eldridge points out "there is, increasingly, a big difference between those two things."[26] One needs only to re-read the reviews for *The Last Temptation of Christ*.

The problem for the viewer is that many movies are produced and released with titles that mask the director's agenda-driven Christian-bashing. Others have titles that are self explanatory, such as Harvey Weinstein's 1991 *The Pope Must Die*. With most of these faith-based attack movies still in circulation on DVD, it is wise to check with the Entertainment Resource Guide at the back of this book to research the actual content of movies that insert radical Hollywood lifestyle philosophies and agendas into the finished product. The Ratings Scheme does not address the hidden agenda.

A SMALL SAMPLING (1980 to Present)

The following list represents less than half of Hollywood titles that mock and bash Judeo-Christian values using the confrontational attack within the plot or sub-plot of the film; both subtle and blatant:

— *At Play in the Fields of the Lord*
— *Borat*
— *Chocolat*
— *The Closer You Get*
— *Crimes of Passion*
— *Edward Scissorhands*
— *Guilty as Charged*
— *Jungle Fever*
— *Last Rites*
— *The Magdalene Sisters*
— *Monsignor*
— *Nuns on the Run*
— *Orgazmo*
— *The Penitent*
— *Poltergeist II*
— *Quills*
— *The Rapture*
— *The Saint*
— *The Vision*
— *When Do We Eat?*
— *Boondock Saints*
— *Buddy Boy*
— *The Chosen*
— *Crimes and Misdemeanors*
— *Dangerous Beauty*
— *The Godfather III*
— *The Handmaid's Tale*
— *The King*
— *Light of Day*
— *Misery*
— *Naked Tango*
— *The Order*
— *Pass the Ammo*
— *Pleasantville*
— *Primeval Fever*
— *Radio Days*
— *The Reaping*
— *Salvation*
— *We're No Angels*

Needless to say, most of these films were box-office flops. As Michael Medved noted, Hollywood's anger towards religion runs "so deep and burns so intensely that they insist on expressing that hostility even at the risk of financial disaster."

It's also important to note that all of these films post-date 1968, the year Valenti arrived to "free the screen." The fact that many of these films bash Catholics may be a form of seething latent revenge given the fact that Catholic laymen and clergy helped draft the Production Code for the MPAA in 1930. The intention of the Production Code was to dampen the sick aberrations of the filmmaker's dark, over indulgent and dangerous nightmarish fantasies.

SLICING, DICING AND SPLATTERING THE FAITHFUL

The most grotesque form of the confrontational attack films on faith-based people arrive in the theaters or in the straight-to-DVD home video market as "splatter, slasher or slice-and-dice" films, which largely replaced the "horror" genre beginning in 1968. More than 10,000 of these gorefest films have been released since Valenti abolished the Production Code.

Lloyd Kaufman's Troma Films has distributed more than 1,000 of these types of films alone since the early 1970s. And more than 100 of these "blood-and-guts" productions are now released every year. Starz Home Entertainment releases as many as thirty titles in one year.

The vast majority of these films and DVDs have a decidedly anti-Christian bent as the contemporary common strand of the long dark thread that runs through Hollywood. Sometimes the bashing is subtle, maybe a word, phrase, dismissive laugh; or symbolic, such as the *abandoned* church where all the killing begins.

At the other end of these low-budget gorefests are very blatant attacks on all things Judeo-Christian involving bloody, dismembered demons quoting verses from the Bible. Unfortunately, because many of these films are made for the home video crowd, they are not subject to any kind of rating by the MPAA and sometimes slip by the numerous organizations that monitor movie content.

While the "big-box" retailers like Wal-Mart, Sears, Target and the others have point-of-purchase safeguards preventing unrated movies from being sold to minors, the titles are increasingly showing up at thousands of convenience stores across the country hanging from racks next to cherry cigars, rolling papers and condoms where the enforcement is often more lax, though their shelf placement couldn't be more appropriate.

In a 2004 column, Patrick Buchanan asked, "Who is in your face here? Who started this? Who is on the offensive? The answer is obvious. A radical Left aided by a cultural elite that detests Christianity and finds Christian moral tenets reactionary and repressive is hell-bent on pushing its amoral values on our nation. The unwisdom of what the Hollywood Left are about should be transparent to us all."[27]

And, as I learned during my three day "ride with the devil" through Atlanta in 1991, the producers of these anti-faith films will say anything to dismiss the harmful, hate-filled and violently bigoted messages these movies send out to children and adults alike.

Those who are potentially damaged the most are identified summarily by the Scottish Presbyterian pastor Dr. Lloyd John Ogilvie who declares that films like *Last Temptation* and others "disturb and destruct the life of Jesus for those who are thinking about Christianity, it will hurt those who have begun the Christian life and it will add to the moral decay of our time in history."

Ogilvie also recounted *Last Temptation* in one of the frequently used quotes by the media, "The most serious misuse of filmcraft in the history of moviemaking."[28]

B. THE SOPHISTICATED ATTACK
The Da Vinci Code

"Famed symbologist Robert Langdon is called to the Louvre museum in Paris where a curator has been murdered, leaving behind a mysterious trail of symbols and clues. Langdon, aided by cryptologist Sophie Nevin unveils a series of stunning secrets hidden in the works of Leonardo DaVinci, all leading to a covert society dedicated to guarding the ancient secret that has remained hidden for 2,000 years. The pair sets off through France, England and Scotland collecting clues as they attempt to crack the code and reveal secrets that will shake the very foundation of mankind."

This cunningly varnished description was one of the many "official" promos used to propagate author Dan Brown's revised Holy Bible titled *The DaVinci Code* and the 2006 movie by the same name under the direction of Ron Howard.

Cryptology, symbology, mythology, or simply follyology?

Like *Last Temptation*, the central offending theme of the Da Vinci Code is fully intended to bash Christianity. In this "high-concept" farce, the writer again returns to the "very real possibility" that Jesus married Mary Magdalene and their descendants are living among us today. (Remember that guy in college with the long hair and beard that you thought was just another hippie? Well, maybe . . . possibly . . . could it be?)

Unlike the comic book characterization of Jesus and Mary Magdalene mixed with the inner hatred and demons of Nikos Kazantzakis and Martin Scorsese, the devil now wears a turtle neck and sports a gentle smile in the publicity photos for the book and movie. And, unlike Scorsese's "confrontational attack" on Christians, Dan Brown and director Ron Howard carefully construct a whole new approach known as the "sophisticated attack."

Knowing that the Christian-bashing books and movies of the last thirty years have almost always bombed at the bookstores and the box-office, Brown wrapped his private bigotry against Christians in a tightly-wrapped thriller/mystery in which the protagonist, Robert Langdon (Tom Hanks), finally proclaims "Almost everything our fathers told us about Christ is a lie."

The word "sophisticated" originates from the word "sophistry," defined by Webster's New World Dictionary as "unsound, or misleading but clever, plausible, and subtle argument or reasoning."[29] The word "sophisticate" is even more precisely defined, and may cause many on the Hollywood Cocktail Party Circuit (HCPC) to think twice before stamping the label on their forehead, "to corrupt or mislead. To make impure by mixture or adulteration. To alter (a text, etc.) without authority; falsify."[30] To say that anyone in the literary or entertainment world is "sophisticated" is definitely not a compliment.

An example of a "sophisticated" person unknowingly complimenting small-town America came from Mitchell Goldman, president of marketing from New Line Cinema when asked by *USA Today* if the movie *Boogie Nights* would play well in middle-America. "It's possible that we are unable to sell this movie in a small *unsophisticated* town." [31] Thank you, Mitch—it's an honor.

* * *

In the film version of *The Da Vinci Code*, co-collaborators of the sophisticated attack include Sony Pictures producer Brian Grazer, director Ron Howard and Tom Hanks. (George Clooney had been chomping at the bit to play the Langdon role.) Sony severely limited press interviews with anyone on the crew of the movie during production and right up to the film's release.

And what few interviews were allowed were carefully controlled and scripted by studio publicists as to what questions could and couldn't be asked, specifically questions about the crew's own personal feelings about the story or about their own religious beliefs. The publicists knew that answers to such questions would speak volumes about their interest in a film that would bash Christians in a sophisticated manner and scale far wider than *Last Temptation* or any of the many lesser known faith-bashing films of the previous four decades.

By June 19, 2006, only one month after its release, *The Da Vinci Code* movie had been seen by over 35 million people worldwide and had grossed over $700 million internationally. Dan Brown's book was first published in 2003 and has sold more than 60 million copies in forty-four languages as of 2008.

What few sneering remarks offered up by the director and actors revealed was the not-so-subtle contempt for the audience and the negative impact they were hoping the movie would have in the worldwide market of believers and non-believers. The secular audience was in the palm of their hands, but the larger picture was to turn believers into skeptics. That's exactly why Howard and Hanks were hired. The Christian community could count on Opie and Forrest Gump to tell them the truth—right?

When director Ron Howard was asked about his reaction to letters from people concerned about the adverse effects of portraying Jesus Christ in high heterodoxy, the director snarled openly about not opening letters, "I'm not a caterer. I just have to stay with my creative convictions. At some point you have to just get past the special interest groups and do what you're there to do..."[32]

Howard's remarks sounded like talking points from Jack Valenti's fiery defense of *Last Temptation* eighteen years earlier by besmirching "self-appointed groups" who had valid concerns and questions that the industry whole-heartedly ignored. Tom Hanks, who had remained distant from the press so as not to reveal his core beliefs, laughed off a forbidden question during *The Da Vinci Code* premiere at the Cannes Film Festival.

When asked if he thought Mary Magdalene fathered a child by Jesus, Hanks answered, "Well... I wasn't around."[33] Ron Howard laughed hysterically while clapping his hands uncontrollably. The attending crowd and press corps at the coliseum laughed, too, champagne spilling from their plastic goblets.

All the faith-based community asked was that the producers please put a disclaimer at the beginning of the film because of the strong possibility, which has come to pass, that some viewers might take the film as literal truth. The request for a disclaimer was strongly supported by the Catholic League's president Bill Donahue.

Unlike *Last Temptation*, this movie would be rated PG-13, instead of R, which opened the door to many young and impressionable children. Marc Carroggio noted that "Any adult with a minimum of education can distinguish reality from fiction, but when history is manipulated, you cannot expect a child to make proper judgments."[34] Sony Pictures producer Brian Grazer and director Ron Howard adamantly refused the disclaimer request, not even at the very end of the credits when most people have left the theater. The Christian-taunting had begun.

Radical homosexual actor Ian McKellan, who co-starred in the film, answered the disclaimer question this way, "Well, I've thought the Bible should have a disclaimer in the front saying *this is fiction*."[35] And, he added, "When I read the book (*Da Vinci Code*), I believed it entirely... I'm very happy to believe that Jesus was married... this would be absolute proof that Jesus was not gay."

One of the over-riding reasons Christian leaders were asking for a disclaimer was a craftily written lie at the opening to Dan Brown's book which stated, "FACT: All descriptions of artwork, architecture, documents and secret rituals in the novel are accurate." Defenders of Brown claimed that his use of the word "novel" in the same sentence as "fact" trumped any claim of "truth."

543

But, Brown himself insisted that the four "descriptions" were "accurate" but refused to discuss the semantics of "accurate," "fact" and "truth," thus setting off a debate among theologians, authors, journalists and the public over definitions and synonyms. This was an intentional trap set by Dan Brown as part of the taunting and ridicule of Christianity. This was also one of the main reasons Hollywood optioned the book. The Christian-bashing agenda could continue, but this time it would be subtle and "sophisticated" without the circus antics of *Last Temptation*.

However, in *truth*, Brown's opening statement was a weak attempt to validate the storyline, which is basically a lie from beginning to end. As MovieGuide president and chairman of the Christian Family and Television Commission Dr. Ted Baehr commented, "but "90% of those facts are wrong."[36]

Unlike the "in your face" confrontational attack by *Last Temptation*, Sony devised a typical Hollywood Shuffle in sheep's clothing by forging a "sophisticated union" with certain Christian leaders to help promote *The Da Vinci Code*. Instead of hiring a Christian consultant in a failed attempt to sugarcoat blasphemy, Sony put forth an astounding $40 million promotional campaign to "establish a dialogue" with Christians.

But, the end-around Hollywood game message was the same: It's not fair to criticize the movie unless you have seen it first. And, in order for "all of us" to have a "dialogue," the movie has to be seen first. (Remember, no money-back guarantee at the theater.) Once you've lined the pockets of Sony and the talent, then everybody can sit around the campfire. Kumbaya.

First, Dan Brown's "claims" need to be broken down into real historical "facts." This is at the core of understanding why many readers of the book and viewers of the movie have actually changed their views on Christianity, often to the detriment of the Truth.

The author and the filmmakers absolutely knew this kind of Christian "rethinking" could and would happen. In order for Hollywood to establish a more secular society and justify their own New Age religions, they must continue to attack the faith in Jesus Christ which has dominated Western Civilization for 2,000 years.

One of the best analyses of the "DaVinci Claims" versus "Historical Facts" was compiled by James Hirsen, author of *Hollywood Nation* and *Tales from the Left Coast* and columnist for *NewsMax* magazine.

In the following chart, Hirsen lays out the fact and the fiction behind *The Da Vinci Code* according to biblical scholars and other experts in the field of Christian history.

DECODING DA VINCI'S FICTION[37]

Da Vinci Claims	Historical Facts
Opus Dei is a secretive society of monks.	Opus Dei has no monks. Opus Dei members, most of whom are lay members, do not seek to withdraw from society.
The Priory of Sion is a European secret society founded in 1099.	The Priory of Sion was created out of whole cloth in 1956 by the French fascist Pierre Plantard and others. Plantard served jail time for fraud and membership in an anti-Semitic group.
The Bible, as we know it today, was collated by the pagan emperor Constantine the Great.	Roman Emperor Constantine converted to Christianity in 310 A.D., four years after becoming Emperor. The four gospels, and 20 of the 27 books of the New Testament, had already been accepted by Christians as of the late first century. Constantine had no role in determining which books were included in the Bible.
Jesus married Mary Magdelene and the couple produced a child. One of Brown's characters cites a late third-century Gnostic writing called the Gospel of Philip, which he says states: "The companion of the Savior is Mary Magdelene. Christ loved her more than all the disciples and used to kiss her often on her mouth."	The so-called Gospel of Philip was not written by the Apostle Philip. It's actually not a gospel—it's a collection of writings. The text does not include the words "on her mouth." Kissing was—and still is—an accepted form of greeting in Middle Eastern cultures. The word "companion" in the Aramaic language did not imply "spouse."
	Finally, the Gospel of Philip is thought to have been written in the third century, long after the time of Christ. It is not considered an authoritative account.

Five million witches were murdered by the Church because of the Witches' Hammer Book, written by two Dominican priests in the 15th century.	Recent historians put the number at around 30,000.
The Dead Sea Scrolls contain messages about Jesus that the Church tried to suppress.	The Scrolls are Jewish writings that pre-date Christianity. They came from a Jewish sect that lived outside Jerusalem.
More than 80 gospels were considered for inclusion in the New Testament, yet only a few were chosen.	The real number of gospels thought to have existed has been estimated at from just 17 to several dozen, depending on one's definition of a gospel. And the four canonical gospels are the only ones dating from the first century.
Jesus' establishment as "the Son of God" was officially proposed and voted on by the Council of Nicaea in 325 A.D.	Jesus' divinity was part of Christian belief from very early on. The Apostle Paul embraced and wrote about Christ's divinity within years of the Crucifixion. And in the early second century, Roman historian Pliny the Younger wrote that Christians worshipped Jesus as the Son of God.
At the council of Nicaea, the doctrine of Christ's divinity passed by a "relatively close vote."	Only two of the bishops at the Council, variously estimated to have numbered from 250 to 318, refused to agree with the adoption of the Nicene Creed attesting to Christ's deity.

SOURCE: NewsMax

James Hirsen's piece, "The Da Vinci Con," in the June 2006 issue of *NewsMax* was one of many articles, books, websites and televised debates that appeared between the publication of the book and the premiere of the movie. Almost all of these counter-arguments provided comprehensive and penetrating examinations into the whole *Da Vinci Code* fraud and its detrimental effects on the faith-based community, especially on individuals who were young believers in the faith, only to have their beliefs shattered because of the book and the movie's persuasive arguments, though ultimately false. This effect was celebrated by the producers and Hollywood in general who felt that they had scored a major New Age victory in tarnishing Christianity in general and unhinging believers in particular. Unfortunately, there was some truth in their carefully crafted sophisticated attack.

Researcher George Barna stated on May 15, 2006, "Among the 45 million who have read *The Da Vinci Code,* only five percent—which represents about two million adults—said that they changed any of their beliefs or religious perspectives because of the book's contents."[38] Barna emphasized, however, that two million adults is still a significant number. Barna cautioned that younger people's beliefs may have been more adversely affected because, for many, it is a time when youth are in the process of developing their religious values.

Decima Research, Inc. found that *one in three* Canadians believe that descendants of Jesus are walking among the contemporary population today.[39] Even some nonbelievers had serious problems with Dan Brown's fictional book of facts. Tim O'Neil, a medieval scholar who describes himself as an atheist, conducted an extensive review of Dan Brown's sloppiness surrounding his historical "facts," especially in Brown's description of architecture, art portraits and ancient documents. O'Neil has placed his critique on *www.historyvsthedavincicode.com.*

A biblical scholar highly respected in the field of biblical truth as opposed to "fictional fact" is Amy Welborn of the Catholic Education Resource Center. After the publication of Brown's book, Welborn published a pamphlet titled *The Da Vinci Code: The Facts Behind the Fiction* in 2004 as a handy "fact-check guide." The guide was later made available on the internet just prior to the movie's release.

When Welborn wrote her question and answer style pamphlet in 2004, Brown's book had sold three million copies, already making it a Best Seller. Welborn saw early signs of the misleading and negative effect the book was having on its readers and wisely began to publish her educational tract for people who were experiencing confusion in their beliefs. Her early intervention was timely. Only two years later, the book had sold over 40 million copies.

Welborn's tract is still referenced as one of the essential guides to debunking Brown's "facts." Among the issues she exposes: The fraud of the Holy Grail as the "sacred feminine," portrayed as Mary Magdalene, not a cup or chalice; the myth of a hidden "code" in Leonardo Da Vinci's painting of The Last Supper; the fraud behind Brown's contention that Jesus intended for Mary Magdalene to be the head of the church; debunks the Jesus and Mary "wedding" and resulting children; dismissing the supremacy of the Gnostic Gospels and corrects Brown's fabrication as to when the books of the Bible came to constitute the official Christian canon.

Welborn's historical facts are more interesting and revealing than Dan Brown's novel and can be accessed on the web at *www.catholiceducation.*

org/articles/facts/fm0035.html. The introduction to Amy Welborn's tract is essential in understanding the core of the controversy behind the book and the movie. As Welborn explains:

> "In Brown's novel, the *Da Vinci Code* refers to cryptic messages supposedly incorporated by Leonardo Da Vinci into his artwork. According to the novel, Leonardo was a member of an ancient secret society called the "Priory of Sion" dedicated to preserving the "truths" that Jesus designated Mary Magdalene as His successor, that His message was about the celebration of the "sacred feminine," that Jesus and Mary Magdalene were married and had children and the Holy Grail of legend and lore is really Mary Magdalene, the "sacred feminine," the vessel who carried Jesus' children . . . Sounds like an intriguing bit of lost history. Is it? Long story short: No."[40]

If there was a bright side to *The Da Vinci Code* book and movie, the critics produced a wealth of valuable knowledge into the *true* history of the Bible's origin. For an excellent and comprehensive review into the *real* ancient documents that Brown perverted in his book, log onto *www.divineordavinci.com* and *www.thetruthaboutdavinci.com*. Also, to put the movie into context of the producers' private agenda, connect to *www.goodfight.org* for the book *Hollywood's War on God: Exposing Da Vinci's Code*.

One of the fascinating revelations in Welborn's work is her ability to unravel confusion over the "many Marys" referenced in the New Testament. This is factual information that has not only plagued readers and viewers of *The Da Vinci Code*, but has caused misunderstanding and bewilderment to centuries of Christian believers. There are *three* distinct women named "Mary" in the four Gospels and a fourth female referred only as the "penitent woman."

First, there is Mary Magdalene who was healed of demon possession by Jesus in Luke 8:2. Second, there is the mention of the "penitent woman" in Luke 7. (Nowhere is the "penitent woman" named as Mary Magdelene, nor is she referred to as a prostitute or adulteress; simply a "sinner.") Third, there is Mary, the sister of Martha and Lazarus (sometimes referred to as Mary of Bethany). Four, none are to be confused with Mary, the mother of Jesus.

Welborn notes that in the 6th century, Pope Gregory the Great conflated Mary Magdalene, Mary the sister of Martha and third, the "penitent woman" all into "one person." This has always been a disputed judgment from church fathers such as St. Ambrose and St. Thomas Aquinas. However, the Eastern Orthodox Church has always recognized the three as distinct individual women, which makes sense when reading the Four Gospels in context.

But, the centuries old dispute over these women was never pushed "underground" as Dan Brown tried to claim. It has always been a very open debate going back to the third century. Dan Brown took advantage of this theological debate and confounded it further to purposely confuse readers, specifically Christians young in the faith.

MR. AND MRS. DAN BROWN'S PRIVATE AGENDA

Dan Brown literally grew up on the campus of Phillips Exeter Academy where both of his parents were teachers at the boarding school. The social arrangement of Exeter was mostly Christian and Brown sang in the local church choir. In addition, Brown spent many summers as a youth at the church-sponsored summer camp.

Brown became an English instructor at Exeter in 1993 until he quit in 1996 to pursue his burning desire and obsession with writing a "blockbuster" novel, at any cost and by any means necessary. Many who followed Dan Brown's rise to fame questioned how an aspiring young Christian graduate of Exeter could sell out his faith and viciously and perversely denigrate the man he was taught as the Savior of the world, Jesus Christ.

Subsequently, by committing himself to this dark mission, he also proceeded to profane the entire Christian faith and its worldwide community of believers. The answer is easy; a Christian upbringing in youth does not translate easily into a Christian outpouring as an adult. There was a certain "deal" he made along the way. He wasn't the first and he won't be the last; the thread is long and the thread is dark.

Consider Martin Scorsese, raised a Catholic, attended mass regularly, and studied for the priesthood before being summarily and unceremoniously kicked out of the seminary. From that point on, Scorsese devoted his entire life to destroying Christianity and mocking Christ like a bad school boy who was spanked too hard. There was only one solution for Scorsese: Revenge on God. It is a theme that can be detected in *every one* of his movies.

And, yet, in the clamor to promote *Last Temptation*, Scorsese "politely" described himself as a Christian and his film as an "affirmation of faith." Dan Brown, like Martin Scorsese, fell easily into the category of Christian charlatans, much like the "Christians" who inhabit the National and World Council of Churches; people who will say and do anything to achieve overzealous earthbound ambitions, even if it takes crucifying Christ twice in diabolical and spurious heterodoxy.

Consider the parallel to Scorsese. Brown said that he was a Christian at the time of the controversy surrounding his book and the movie *The Da Vinci Code*. He considered the controversy a positive for *his* work because it would inspire "discussion and debate." Both Scorsese and Brown strategically introduced incomplete statements to promote their projects to the faith-based community—"affirmation of faith" and "discussion and debate."

Who's faith? Faith in what?

Discussion and debate; toward what end?

Scorsese's hypocrisy was blatantly evident in his movie, basically a porn film with Jesus as the star. It was easily dismissed after losing ten million at the box-office. In contrast, Dan Brown, an English instructor of suspect reputation, could twist the story of the Gospels with more subtle, seemingly intellectual and ultimately "sophisticated" rewording of historical truths into contemporary fictional conspiracy. The result was an international movie gross exceeding seven-hundred million, plus book sales.

Dan Brown knew the secret to one avenue of success and fame, a shortcut through a dark alley. As an English instructor, Brown was very familiar with a literary classic by Johann Wolfgang von Goethe known simply as *Faust*. The curious philosopher Dr. Faust wanted the key to all knowledge and wisdom in order to achieve fame and fortune. In exchange, Dr. Faust sold his soul in the great Mephistophelean deal with the devil. Goethe's work is a classic because history is riddled with individuals throughout the centuries who have made such a "bargain." Brown had no problem with such a deal because his claim of being a Christian was a clever ruse, just like Martin Scorsese.

But, it appeared that Dan Brown had a partner in crime, literally, his equally emulous wife, Blythe, who was revealed to be the source behind much of her husband's rise as a publishing powerhouse. And, this was only revealed after authors Richard Leigh and Michael Baigent sued Brown in February 2006 for copyright infringement over their 1982 book, *Holy Blood, Holy Grail*. The British Court, where the suit was filed, noted that Brown admitted to "re-writing" passages from *Holy Blood, Holy Grail*. Eventually, the judge ruled against Leigh and Baigent, even though the ruling noted that Brown may actually have lifted portions of the book, it did not amount to a "breach of copyright." The British Courts made the ruling final in March of 2007.

Apparently, Blythe had been "researching" a number of "high-heresy" books. Another author, Lewis Perdue of California, wrote a book in 2000, three years before *The Da Vinci Code*, titled *Daughter of God*. Perdue sued Random House claiming that Brown stole the actual plot for *The Da Vinci Code* from his book.

According to *Vanity Fair* writer Seth Mnookin, " . . . two respected experts agreed that Brown's book borrowed the plot from Perdue's book. The trail leads back to a series of e-mails from Brown's wife, Blythe. Blythe admitted only that it was her idea to inject the Jesus and Mary Magdalene bloodline."[41] Author Perdue has vowed to take his appeal all the way to the Supreme Court.

Both court cases have revealed much about Blythe's involvement and motivation in developing the plot and narrative, with Mr. Brown assuming the task of piecing together the heresy into novel form. Not much was known about Blythe Brown's influence until her forced testimony at the copyright infringement and plagiarism trials which revealed her overzealous pursuit of literary chicanery and "blockbuster" success—at any cost. Then again, Blythe is only fulfilling the pre-sale contractual obligations in the Mephisthophelean deal. As one observer noted, "The devil is in the details," and in this case, Blythe provides the details.

Also, there is little or no information about Blythe's religious upbringing, if any. But, Blythe Brown has certainly displayed a flagrant animosity for Christianity in general, and hatred of Catholicism in particular. Blythe Brown is the central source of the Christian-bashing agenda behind *The Da Vinci Code*.

As James Hirsen pointed out, "According to Brown's written and oral testimony at the trial, Blythe did much of his work for him. While Brown would write, Blythe would pore through volumes, conducting research for plot ideas and checking facts."[42] Obviously, Blythe is better at conjuring up blasphemy than checking facts. Dan Brown further stated that, "She is an enormous Da Vinci fanatic and really got me extremely interested in this topic."[43] Also, the idea of the "sacred feminine" theme that Mary Magdalene was intended to lead the church, since she was, after all, the mother of Jesus' children, was also conjured up by Blythe.

John Zmirak, writer for the popular website Godspy.com, wrote an article in June 2006 titled, "My Lunch With an Old Friend." Zmirak's friend knew Dan Brown from Exeter Academy school days and told Zmirak that Dan Brown is "not anti-Christian—he's not anti-anything—and he's probably not pro-anything."[44]

Therefore, Dan Brown is nothing more than the chalice for the Christian-bashing agenda of his conspiratorial ultra-feminist wife. She also knew that a "God-kicking" novel would surely guarantee them an option from Hollywood for movie rights. For people like Dan and Blythe Brown, a contract from Hollywood is the equivalent of a religious baptism. According to Zmirak, Brown started his career as a failed joke book author. The Brown's relentless quest to create the best-selling novel was given a boost when a friend gave Brown a book by Albert Zuckerman, *Writing the Blockbuster Novel*.[45]

Obviously, Dan Brown never advanced past his early publishing genre given that *The Da Vinci Code* is basically a bad joke told on a massive scale, in bad taste and intentionally offensive. Even when Dan Brown was writing bad joke books, his wife, again, provided the material with a radical feminist agenda such as the 1995 effort to publish *187 Men to Avoid: A Guide for the Romantically Frustrated Woman*. Given Dan Brown's new international popularity, his first book could be re-released with a new title, *187 Christian Men to Avoid: A Guide for the Romantically Frustrated Sacred Feminine Woman*.

MICHAEL VINCENT BOYER

ENTER THE HOLLYWOOD DEMONS: THE RON HOWARD YOU NEVER KNEW

The Da Vinci Code was tailor-made for a Hollywood feature film. The industry never showed much interest in Brown's earlier novels such as *Deception Point* and *Digital Fortress*. But, a book that so thoroughly torched Christianity with a Promethean touch of fact and fiction fell directly into the Hollywood agenda of value manipulation, and producer Brian Grazer snatched the film rights without hesitation.

Together with Sony Pictures and director Ron Howard, the filmmakers jumped eagerly at the opportunity to bash Christians in a more sophisticated manner than Scorsese's confrontational attack in 1988. (Ironically, two years after production of *The Da Vinci Code*, Sony would launch a Christian-based distribution label called Sony Provident, one of the companies that distributed the highly successful *Facing the Giants*.)

The mutual love affair between Sony and Ron Howard to turn *The Da Vinci Code* into a feature film contained an obvious marketing strategy. Sony Pictures, a monolithic studio that had no love lost on Christianity at the time, felt that Howard would be the best choice to direct the film version given his "nice guy" image and his solid twenty year history as an accomplished director. Howard's "publicized" credits include some of Hollywood's better films of the last decade such as *Apollo 13* and *Cinderella Man*.

The American public couldn't possibly imagine that lovable Ron Howard would direct a film that was intended to savage Christianity. After all, this was Opie from Mayberry, USA, and Richie from *Happy Days*. But, the American moviegoing public knew little or nothing about Howard's early and ongoing strategy to cast off the "Opie image" which he privately despised. Howard made "the deal."

Ron Howard knew that the first step to be considered as a "serious director" in Hollywood was to find a provocative project and "go dark." And, Howard had no problem crossing over to the dark side. Ron Howard's vehement desire to "do whatever it takes" rivaled that of Dan Brown himself.

For many people, the real Ron Howard did not emerge until the final days of production on Dan Brown's story when Howard blurted the "I'm no caterer" remark for his refusal to read letters from concerned Christians. And then came the *Newsweek* article where he proclaimed "no placating" and saying "It would be ludicrous to take on this subject and then try to take the edges off."[46] He wasn't just filming another movie; he was planning to *"take on the subject."*

Even Catholic League president Bill Donahue believed that Howard would at least place a disclaimer at the beginning of the film, saying "I'm trying to make

THE HOLLYWOOD CULTURE WAR

a distinction between the author, who is clearly an anti-Catholic fraud, and Ron Howard, who has a stellar reputation."[47] Donahue, a fierce and vocal defender of Christianity, never called for a boycott—just a simple request of courtesy for the world's two billion Christians.

Howard refused, as did Grazer and Sony. It was now clear that the filmmakers fully intended to create confusion and doubt in the Christian community and in the minds of those considering Christianity as their faith. But, what Donahue may have been unaware of was Ron Howard's own soul-selling decades earlier. In exchange: riches, fame and most importantly in Hollywood, "artistic respectability."

Ron Howard was instrumental in destroying the family-friendly reputation of Walt Disney Pictures in 1984. That same year, Michael Eisner had left Paramount to become CEO of Disney. Eisner's number one agenda was to rapidly dismantle the inclusive "all ages welcome" image of Disney. Walt Disney himself had been dead for almost twenty years and Eisner set out to banish every image of the studio's founder and Walt's philosophy of basic decency in providing entertainment to the public.

One of the first projects green-lighted by Eisner was the movie *Splash* starring Daryl Hannah. It would be one of the first Disney films not rated G. The movie escaped a possible R-rating after extensive editing. The director of the movie was a very ambitious Ron Howard.

Under Howard's direction, *Splash* would be the first Disney film to include profanity and heavy doses of sexual innuendo. (Howard was forced to leave the more extreme material on the cutting room floor.) Within five years, Eisner had created or acquired several shadow divisions, all under the Disney umbrella. His favorite among these was the studio's X-rated division known as Miramax.

But, Howard's official plunge to complete the sale of the soul came in 1991 with his film *Closetland* in which he is credited as co-executive producer. In Hollywood lingo, the film was labeled a "prestige film" which critic and author Michael Medved describes as "intended to impress critics and other insiders, rather than to please ordinary moviegoers. Not surprisingly, Hollywood shows its value system most unmistakably when it attempts to make serious statements."[48]

By no coincidence, *Closetland* was green-lighted by Hollywood's Number One Christian-bashing studio of *Last Temptation* and *Cape Fear* fame, Universal. Ron Howard's movie was not a pretty picture.

"The film used only two actors (Alan Richman and Madeline Stowe), and the action, such as it was, played out exclusively on one claustrophobic set, painted entirely in shades of silver and black. The filmmakers apparently intended some sort of searing parable about the universal oppression of women, and therefore showed the male 'interrogator' mercilessly and graphically torturing his female victim. He forces her to drink his urine, rips her toenails out with pliers, handcuffs her to a bed, spits a half-chewed clove of garlic into

553

her mouth, administers electric shock to her genitals, and penetrates her anus with a red-hot metal poker as she howls in agony."[49]

The film was a bomb and many were deeply offended. But, by Hollywood's criteria, it was a sign that Ron Howard had navigated the warped rites of passage into a "serious" filmmaker. His career skyrocketed after that point. Howard had preceded Spielberg as a member of "The Dark Boys Club." Even in the days of "Adults Only" theaters prior to 1968, a film like *Closetland* would have never been produced or exhibited by even the most ruthless of the old school grindhouse producers and theater owners.

This helps to explain why Howard had no problem taking on the job as director of *The Da Vinci Code*. A director who has no respect for basic morality certainly has no respect for values of the faith-based community. Christian-bashing in Hollywood is like an addictive drug where the addict needs to constantly up the ante in order to stay high—in Howard's case—high on the studio's A-list.

But, even more deceitful than the movie was the marketing plan to promote the film with Howard and producer Grazer in full agreement. The broader and more sinister marketing ploy was aimed to "engage" Christians in a "sophisticated invitation" to participate in the viewing of the movie. Howard, Grazer and Sony would take a "kinder and gentler" approach to encourage the Christian community to view the movie using a trick semantic variation of Martin Scorsese's confrontational approach; specifically, "one cannot criticize a film without seeing it first." The new gameplan called for actively marketing the catchphrase to Christians by encouraging the faith-based community to see *The Da Vinci Code* with a friend in order to "encourage dialogue."

Ron Howard wouldn't read *your* letters, but he certainly wanted you to see *his* movie. More people meant a larger percentage of the gross profits that he would receive from the total box-office.

It was the perfect Hollywood scam. The filmmakers would trick Christians into seeing the movie, kick the teeth out of their deeply held faith, and run to the bank with more money in their pockets.

CHRISTIAN COLLUSION

News of the "encouraging dialogue" approach by Sony began to emerge in early April of 2006, about a month before the movie's release. *USA Today* writer Scott Bowles quoted Sony Senior Vice-President Jim Kennedy, "We encourage everyone to visit sites like ours and join in a dialogue that can shed light on topics explored in *The Da Vinci Code*."[50]

"That's the hook," explained former nun Barbara Nicolosi to *NewsMax* magazine, "that you can't say anything about the movie if you haven't seen it—and everybody is falling for that line."[51] The approach became known as

THE HOLLYWOOD CULTURE WAR

"Scorsese light." Unfortunately, the crafty marketing approach only polarized existing divisions within the Christian community surrounding the book and the movie. Polarization is exactly what Howard, Grazer and Sony hoped would happen. Another example of Hollywood double-speak was demonstrated by Grazer when he appeared on *The Today Show* in March of 2006 and described *The Da Vinci Code* as "informed fiction."

The websites that Sony's VP Jim Kennedy was referring to were unclear because Sony created a number of them, some covertly. According to Bowles of *USA Today*, "Already, Sony Pictures is bracing for possible protests over *Da Vinci*. The studio has set up a website, *www.thedavincidialogue.com* that essentially distances Sony from the film's message by presenting counterarguments in the drama" and also "invites readers to chime in."[52]

Sony formed yet another website, *www.thedavincichallenge.com* as a "Christian roundtable discussion" to converse about the movie's merits and demerits. Curiously, the site contained many essays by Christian writers, many of them *encouraging* visitors to see the movie.

And then there was Sony's "official" website with the appropriately ominous name *www.SoDarkTheConOfMan.com* which was the glossy "must see" promo for the movie. All of this website euphoria and Christian co-opting by some in the faith-based community could be traced to Sony's massive $40 million plus marketing campaign, part of which was funneled to Grace Hill Media, a fairly new "Christian" marketing firm at the time created by former Warner Brothers publicity agent Jonathan Bock.

As James Hirsen explains, "To get their pastors to steer their flocks to the theater, Bock encourages the Christian press to meet the filmmakers, organize screenings and create Bible study guides" and Hirsen adds that "several Christian leaders have bought into Grace Hill's and the film marketer's agenda."[53]

Richard Mouw, president of the Fuller Theological Seminary, told *The New York Times* that *The Da Vinci Code* is going to be water cooler conversation, "so Christians need to take a deep breath, *buy the book and shell out the money for the movie* [emphasis added]. Then we need to educate Christians about what all this means."[54]

What "all this means" is that producer Brian Grazer and director Ron Howard were laughing around the water cooler at the Sony Studios executive offices. They laughed even harder when the producer and director listened to Robert Schuller of California's Crystal Cathedral remark publicly that he found the movie "entertaining."[55]

One parishioner noted that if every Christian who was encouraged to "buy the book and see the movie" had given that money to their own church, it would have benefited far more people in need than a very small handful of atheists who live in Beverly Hills and Malibu who deeply despise Christians. What was certain,

555

there were many more Christian leaders who were *not* buying into Grace Hill's and Sony's overt and covert marketing scheme. Dr. Ted Baehr of *Movieguide* magazine said, "I think that evangelicals telling people to see this movie is an insult to Catholics and Christians."

Some who bought into the Sony scheme said that Baehr was "unloving." But Baehr, a tireless crusader for bringing positive values back to Hollywood, recognized the true agenda behind Grazer, Howard and Sony. "Anyone who reads *The Da Vinci Code*, especially those who advocate reading it or seeing it and those who say it is okay for people to read or see *The Da Vinci Code*, are taking a stand against Jesus Christ and His gospel and it is they who are being unloving, not those who warn people about the dangers of such works as *The Da Vinci Code*. It is also they who will be encouraging the entertainment industry to make and market books, movies and videos viciously attacking Jesus Christ, His mission and the Bible."[56]

Amy Welborn, the author behind *The Da Vinci Code: The Facts Behind The Fiction* was one of the first to warn about the slippery slope of *The Da Vinci Code's* duplicitous message. Welborn believed all along that the "dialogue" approach was bogus, given the private agendas of the author and filmmakers, "I don't think you need to put money in these people's pockets in order to discuss this."[57]

Barbara Nicolosi agreed, claiming that Christians who recommend *The Da Vinci Code* are "going to go down on record as assisting probably the most patently offensive studio picture of all time. It's the first time a studio picture is really claiming that Jesus was a fraud."[58]

As for the film's success at the box office, after a big opening weekend in the U.S., it tanked quickly as word of mouth gave the movie less than stellar reviews. However, it thrived in the international market, especially in increasingly secular Europe where apathy and Christian-bashing go hand-in-hand.

* * *

Ironically, *Last Temptation* lost $10 million dollars and received overwhelmingly glowing reviews. Eighteen years later, *The Da Vinci Code* makes $700 million and received overwhelmingly bad reviews. A sampling:

" . . . it's not very good . . . long (2 hrs. 32 min) and most inert."
-Richard Corliss
Time

"Frankly, it's a stinker."
-Paul Arendt
BBC

THE HOLLYWOOD CULTURE WAR

"No, it's not as bad as you've heard, it's worse."

-Philadelphia Weekly

"You know a movie is a dud when even its self-flagellating albino killer monk isn't any fun."

-Memphis Commercial Appeal

"Feels far more like TV fodder than something worthy of the big screen."
-Ross Anthony
Hollywood Report Card

"The mystery of Hollywood: *Da Vinci* makes no secret of joyless acting, flat script."

-Joe Morgenstern
The Wall Street Journal

"There are moments when this film, like Tom Hanks hair, laid there like a limp noodle. Is this film, at times, pretentious, overlong and boring? God yes."
-Michelle Alexander

"A jumbled joyless affair that neither entertains nor enlightens."
-Shawn Adler
Filmforce

On the international scene, the farther east the film was shown, there emerged a mixed response from authoritative countries. In a rare move, some countries with *minority* Christian populations actually banned the movie while the western Europeans were eating it up as if it were Gospel. Even mainland Communist China limited *The Da Vinci Code's* release to a small handful of its coastal cities, an unusual move for a country that is officially atheist.

In other foreign countries where the film thrived, many audiences represented a variety of religious backgrounds and *The Da Vinci Code* was literally their first introduction to Christianity, and a very fraudulent introduction it was. This was the real danger in Sony's co-opting certain American "Christian" leaders into "encouraging dialogue." That is a virtual endorsement heard 'round the world where doubtless a foreign audience would leave the theater saying, "So, that's what Christianity is all about."

The Barna Research Group also noted in its study of the book and movie's impact, that young people could be more significantly and adversely impacted because their belief system is still in the process of development and as such are more susceptible to new teachings.[59] This was the similar conclusion made by Dr.

Lloyd John Ogilvie after *Last Temptation* when he said, "It will hurt and destroy those who have begun the Christian life," but added for emphasis, "it will add to the moral decay of our time in history."

Changing young minds to the Hollywood way of thinking was the main goal behind *The Da Vinci Code*. And it continues to be the goal long after the movie's release. As of 2008, the DVD is still being aggressively marketed at the retail level. Hollywood *desperately* wants to win back that huge audience segment that left the theaters in droves after 1968. But, Hollywood wants to bring the audience back on *Hollywood terms*, not middle-America's terms. This is the core battle in the Culture War against Hollywood.

This was demonstrated after the May 19, 2006 release weekend when the film grossed an initial $224 million. Sony resorted to its true colors, arrogantly boasting a much different tune, almost to the point of some mythical epiphany. Sony's Vice-Chairman Jeff Blake announced to *USA Today* "Whatever the controversy that surrounded the movie, the public has taken it over now, and they're embracing it." [60]

The subtle innuendo did not go unnoticed. Blake used Hollywood doublespeak implying "controversy" as Christian and "the public has taken it over" as implying a secular groundswell victory for, as Dr. Ted Baehr would say, "a massive blow to the understanding of Jesus."[61]

Besides, in Hollywood, you're not "hip" or "cool" unless you bash Jesus. As radio talk-show host Mark Belling observed, "The reason Dan Brown is pimping the story of Jesus is because there's a market for it. Brown came upon the idea because he knew it is cool to make fun of Christians."[62]

Perhaps author and columnist James Hirsen was one of the very few observers who recognized the even deeper core secret agenda being propagated by Dan Brown and Sony Pictures. "The book and film pound away on a primary theme about Christ and an antithetical theme concerning Mary Magdalene. After spending a great deal of time de-deifying Jesus and even claiming that early Christians did not believe that Jesus was divine, as it builds to its climax the story reveals that Mary Magdalene is the conduit of a divine, feminine energy: Mary Magdalene is a goddess.

"Brown and his Hollywood associates appear to be engaging in something more than the usual denigration of Jesus and the Christian faith. They are conjuring up a nouveau idol and in the process are creating a faux religion of their own."[63] Hollywood literally can't stand Jesus. But, a New Age goddess fits their belief system perfectly. Jane Fonda has already bought into this goddess worship along with a close circle of friends.

Dr. Ted Baehr summarized the Hollywood strategy of value manipulation through the sophisticated attack, stating that *The Da Vinci Code* is a "heretical indoctrination of pagan ideologies, which is perfectly propagated by the Hollywood media machine." Certainly *The Da Vinci Code* has awakened the community of believers that attacks on their faith are becoming more stealth, sophisticated and frequent. As Baehr added, "This is a Culture War that Christians dare not lose."

Sony is trying a repeat performance in late 2008 with the feature film release of Dan Brown's *Angels and Demons*, the prequel to *The Da Vinci Code*. The script was being tweaked in late 2007 to up the ante on the Christian-bashing aspect in the story line according to one member of the Writers Guild. Sony is also expected to repeat its "dialogue" sham marketing scam to once again trick Christians into buying tickets.

The studio may even exceed its previous $40 million marketing budget in order to "engage Christian pastors" to convince their congregations to "read the book and see the movie." There's an old Hollywood saying, "De-frock the flock." This is not to be confused with bribing pastors—you understand?

TWIST OF FAITH?

Just one year after The Da Vinci Code premiered in the spring of 2006, the movie industry began to show some interest in creating not only faith-based film divisions, but even in starting up "overtly Christian" movies. Yes, even Sony had joined in with its Provident Films as a Christian-based distribution unit. Sony's long-term motives are still suspect.

Lionsgate, Disney and Fox have developed "faith-film" units or partnered with independent Christian production companies which have been expanding exponentially. John Ware, founder of the 168 Hour Film Project said this development in Hollywood "is good and bad."[64] As Carmel Entertainment founder Larry Frenzel added, "There is a broad spectrum of people, different denominations, different theologies and different doctrinal beliefs. Faith-based refers to a very broad, diverse audience."

In order to get wide distribution, whether in theaters or in the direct-to-video retail market, the independents will inevitably be approached by the major studio faith-based units for "creative input." The concern is that compromises may be made in order to distribute film product.[65] As marketing executive Mark Joseph noted about the studio philosophy, "Their biggest mistake is a condescending attitude" toward Christian filmmakers. And the attitude is shared even more widely among the Hollywood talent who largely look down on "Christian" productions. As Joseph explains, "A-list talent will not sign up for a project they perceive will be marketed to Christians."[66] This is another example of how most Hollywood movie actors are deep-seated in their bigotry and hatred of Christians. Is it any wonder the planet may be getting "warmer?"

In the meantime, a number of faith-based Christian film production companies have been formed such as Big Idea, Cloud Ten, Codeblack

559

Entertainment, Goodnews Holdings, Namesake and "Five and Two Pictures" with brothers Rich and Dave Christiano. It does not matter to these producers if they cast well known talent or not. Christian movie audiences are more likely to attend a film for a good story with a positive message.

But, viewer, beware. Even before some new faith-based film companies shoot their first roll of film, Hollywood has already, and very intentionally, started blurring the lines between Christian films and "transformational" films; in other words, scatological New Age movies. Chief among the perpetrators is none other than Universal Pictures which steadfastly refuses to even acknowledge a Christian audience. After most of their string of Christian-bashing movies crashed and burned during the 1980s and 1990s, the monolithic studio has begun to embrace the phony and nefarious "spirituality" and "life changing" movies.

In early April of 2007, Universal re-released *Peaceful Warrior* based on Dan Millman's *Way of the Peaceful Warrior: A Book That Changes Lives.* Sounds "inspirational" and promises to be "transformational," but *Peaceful Warrior* is another New Age romp in the Shirley MacLaine variation of "I am god, you are god" man-made paganism with a sugar coating. John Raatz, founder and CEO of the New Age publicity firm Visioneering Group, said at the time of the movie's release, "This is a genre and movement that is absolutely coming of age."[67] Cami Winikoff, producer of *Peaceful Warrior* said, "It is one of the best-loved books in the mind/body/spirit genre."[68]

Adam Fogelson, Universal's president of marketing said, "People like Sting, Tony Robbins and Deepak Chopra are saying this is a movie that can help change people's lives."[69] What New Age promoters don't say is "how" it will change your life. And, if Sting, Robbins and Chopra can get together to endorse a movie, it's a sure sign for moviegoers to run as far and fast in the opposite direction as possible. Sting alone is a poor endorsement for any movie considering his fascination with, and devotion to, Aleister Crowley, "the Wickedest Man in the World."

Another travesty in this "transformational" genre of "mind/body/spirit" films was the movie adaptation of Neale Donald Walsch's series of books, *Conversations with God,* distributed by Samuel Goldwyn Films. Walsch claims to write down answers from "God" to questions he asks on a variety of subjects including politics, sociology and economics.

Again, a very "religious" sounding title to a story that Goldwyn president Meyer Gottlieb called "inspirational." The problem is Walsch doesn't believe in "God." He believes in god as in expressions such as *you are god, I am god; the moon is God; every little grain of sand in your backyard patio cement is god.* And, god is a little bit of Hindu, Buddha, Shinto and even Nietzsche, the German philosopher who said, "God is dead." Very inspirational.

Further complicating, or perhaps clarifying, the Hollywood approach to faith-based movies is the coverage given to the phenomena in the press. Just weeks before the release of *The Da Vinci Code*, *USA Today* unleashed an article titled "Hollywood Turns to Divine Revelation" on April 14, 2006. The subtitle of this amazing caption on the front page reads "Religion-based movies, once spurned, now have studios seeing the light."[70]

For a split second, the reader believes that Hollywood has made at least a partial about face by turning out more movies where plots declare victory over defeat, triumph over tragedy and miracles defeating hopelessness. It would appear that Hollywood's bigger budget fare are grasping some of the same values delegated to their smaller "faith-based" divisions. But, as usual, the devil is in the details.

The first paragraph leads the reader into the subtle deception behind the headlines. "In God, Hollywood is trusting it will find big profits. Inspired by *The Passion of the Christ* and *Chronicles of Narnia*, studios are not only casting an eye to religious-themed stories, but they're also marketing movies more aggressively to churchgoers." As it turns out, the initiatives of Hollywood are neither noble nor holy. As writer Scott Bowles continued, "The strategy has two aims: to use faith-based hits to help staunch a three year box-office slide [the longest continuous slide in four decades] and to convert those with little faith in Hollywood fare into permanent moviegoers. No fewer than a dozen films with religious themes are on tap through 2007."[71]

The article quickly and seamlessly turns into, first, a promotion piece for *The Da Vinci Code* which it terms as one of the "religious-themed movies." Second, writer Scott Bowles equates the release of *The Da Vinci Code* with that of an epic classic by declaring Sony's intention to "cash in on a demographic" that has been largely overlooked since Charlton Heston starred in *The Ten Commandments* a half-a-century earlier.[72] This is where writer Bowles and the entertainment industry just don't seem "to get it."

Not even cognizant of his own condescending remarks, Steve Feldstein of 20th Century Fox rambles about churches as the ultimate advertising venue where a thumbs-up from the pastor goes further than a film critic, adding, "For many families, church isn't just somewhere you go to pray, it's a social venue. There's an opportunity for discussion of things beyond just faith." Again, Feldstein said, "things beyond *just* faith." You know, important topics like Paris Hilton, Britney Spears and Lindsay Lohan.

That's right, Hollywood is again preparing to buy-off pastors of mega-churches with slick advertising campaigns and no one has put it past some Century City Hollywood executives to propose "love contributions" to churches for select movie releases. Pastors, beware.

Most ridiculous about the article is the list of "divinely inspired" movies that Hollywood planned to release during the 2007-2008 schedule. Hollywood didn't learn from its 2004 attempt to "cash in" on the faithful in light of the

Passion success. That same year Hollywood released a movie titled *Saved* starring Macaulay Culkin. Despite the intentionally deceptive title, the movie mocked Christianity in typical Hollywood fashion and the industry couldn't understand why this "religious" movie bombed.

The *USA Today* article ended with a list of the upcoming "religious" slate of "inspirational" movies in which Jews and Christians are slapped around in comic or demeaning style:

- *When Do We Eat?*—A comedy about a family Passover that turns upside down when the family patriarch unwittingly digests Ecstasy.
- *Evan Almighty*—In a sequel to the 2003 comedy Bruce Almighty, Steve Carrell finds himself with *heavenly* powers.
- *Peaceful Warrior*—Nick Nolte stars as the mysterious mentor "Socrates" who counsels a troubled gymnast.
- *The King*—William Hurt is a minister reunited with his troubled son. The results are less than inspiring.

On a positive note, C. S. Lewis' classic series, *The Chronicles of Narnia*, returns with the next entry, *Prince Caspian* in a classic allegorical tale of the virtue of good versus evil. And the diabolical nature of evil itself is explored in another Lewis classic, *The Screwtape Letters*.

Again, with Hollywood purposely blurring the lines and redefining words such as "religious," "inspirational," "spiritual," "transformational," "life-changing" and "divine," it would be wise to check in, again, with the Entertainment Resource Guide at the end of this book. The links will help you decide if there's really anything inspirational about a rabbi taking Ecstasy.

C. THE BACK DOOR ATTACK:

Harry Potter and *J. K. Rowling*

"I've never, to my knowledge, lied when posed a question about the books. To my knowledge . . . it's perfectly possible at some point I misspoke or I gave a misleading answer unintentionally, or I may have answered truthfully at the time and then changed my mind . . ."

And that is the dilemma, the intentionally concocted dilemma, of *Harry Potter* author J. K. Rowling in a July 2005 interview. This back door attack on God and Christianity would appear to be the most difficult to discern, especially considering the fact that she admits to having a problem telling the truth.

In *reality*, truth is not a problem for Rowling, because all truth is *relative*. J. K. Rowling is a believer in "Divine Dichotomy," meaning that two contradictory truths can exist, neither making the other untrue. This is the same New Age dribble perpetrated by Neale Donald Walsch and his fanciful fiction, *Conversations with God*. The "Divine Dichotomy" is also a colorful philosophical and distracting definition for "pathological lying."

In other words, "anything goes." Or to quote another famous British author, "Do what you will shall be the whole of the law." There is no right and wrong. Just follow the long dark thread of the New Age and everything ties together.

In one of the most comprehensive media snow-jobs in modern literary history, Rowling ruthlessly quashed even the slightest criticism of her story of Harry Potter. By 2002, the mainstream media had joined in lockstep to censor the critics of Rowling's epic story. At the release of book seven, *Harry Potter and the Deathly Hollows*, in July 2007, *USA Today* ran a massive two-page overview of the ten-year publishing history of Harry Potter. Criticism was condensed to only *two sentences* and even that was intended as a dismissive historical footnote slap in the face. According to columnist Carol Memmott, "Some Christian preachers denounced [Harry] from their pulpits for promoting witchcraft and the occult. They were mostly ignored." Boom. End of story.

Invoking the Divine Dichotomy to dismiss her critics, Rowling said, "I go to church myself. I don't take any responsibility for the lunatic fringes of my own religion." In other words, if you have even the most constructive of criticism toward Harry Potter, Rowling considers you a "lunatic." This is only one of the many "put-downs" Rowling has employed to squash her critics. For Christian believers in the true existence and origin of good and evil, being summarily dismissed by the secular culture is a centuries-old phenomenon. As John Zaffis declared, "To believers the evidence is clear. To non-believers, there will never be enough evidence."

After four years of research, we have cut through the multi-faceted layers of deception to reveal the true agenda of J.K. Rowling. Now we'll tell the whole story that the media refused to cover including the commentary, columns and writings of numerous authors censored by the mainstream media machine with the approval of Rowling's Wrecking Ball Express.

Only one mainstream columnist picked up Rowling's true intentions. In fact, he was even able to uncover the murder of a central figure in the books that flew right over the heads of the press. Just how the victim was disposed of so cleverly, and sadly, will be exposed in the following chapter.

The 2007 release of *Deathly Hollows* was the final book in the Harry Potter boy wizard series, which began ten years earlier with the release of *Harry Potter and the Sorcerer's Stone*. The same summer of 2007 saw Hollywood release the fifth movie based on book five, *Harry Potter and the Order of the Phoenix*.

The confrontational attack of *The Last Temptation of Christ* and the sophisticated attack of *The Da Vinci Code* shared a common denominator in that both stories portrayed a divine power over the universe. But, the authors and subsequent film directors twisted that divinity into a perverse revision of God reflected in the dark and fraudulent personal interpretations of their own private worldview.

Author J. K. Rowling introduced another attack that is so subtle, initially, in its assault on faith-based believers that Nikos Kazantzakis and Dan Brown would certainly blush in their relatively feeble attempts, by comparison, to deconstruct God through literature and ultimately movies. With her series of books about the boy wizard Harry Potter, author J. K. Rowling launched an assault on the Judeo-Christian worldview in a way no author had ever attempted, or even considered. Rowling managed to declare God as a non-entity in the world, refusing to even invoke the name of God in the thousands of pages that make up the seven book series. And, that was no accident.

Only after the release of book seven did Rowling admit that the entire Harry Potter series was driven by a personal agenda of her own making that takes a broad swipe at democratic Western Civilization, starting with her disdain of Great Britain. More on that later because chances are good that you didn't read or hear that news anywhere in the media.

Rowling's message brings full circle the Friedrich Nietzsche proclamation that "God is Dead" more than a century earlier, ushering in the secularization of Europe. J. K. Rowling had mastered a new assault on the faith-based community known as the "Back Door" attack. While much controversy surrounds the Harry Potter books from clergy and Christians across the country and around the world, the biggest victory among the secular community is Rowling's "ability" to render God irrelevant. As writer Mike LaVaque-Mantay wrote in the journal *Left2Right*, "Atheists and secularists love the books because religion plays no role. There are no churches, no other religious institutions, nobody prays or meditates and even funerals are non-religious affairs."[73] Sounds like the George Soros future vision of the world.

However "utopian" that may sound, quite the opposite is true. Rowling has managed to create a religion that is partly of her making and partly borrowed from centuries of counterfeit belief systems going back to medieval times. And, she has dipped into the fanciful New Age beliefs that have stirred the darker side of man's curiosity into the netherworld.

J. K. Rowling is, in fact, the emerging New Age queen for her ability to re-energize the "curious arts" back into popular culture in a phenomenal way of epic proportions. She declines publicly to accept such a title, much like Oprah blushes at similar comparisons. But Rowling knows that is exactly her new role in concocting a story, a way of life, a virtual religion that has roots in her early adolescent upbringing in the new, largely secularized England of the late 20th century.

THE HOLLYWOOD CULTURE WAR

The numbers tell the true story of how widespread her "Potterethics" have proliferated around the globe. At the beginning of 2008, eleven years after her first book was released, all seven books in the Harry Potter series have sold over 340 million copies and translated into more than sixty languages. The gross receipts of the five Harry Potter movies released so far have surpassed $4 billion. And, J. K. Rowling has become the first person in history to reach billionaire status solely on the merits of being a published author.

In addition, the Rowling empire includes "resource" books, tie-in books, DVD sales, video games, mass merchandising and numerous official web sites that further explore and promote Potterethics. With her final book released in July of 2007, Rowling was set to overtake the New Age divinity of Oprah Winfrey as *Fortune* magazine's richest woman in the entertainment industry. Rowling surpassed Queen Elizabeth in wealth halfway through her ten year literary spotlight.

Much of the media-suppressed controversy surrounding J. K. Rowling centers on allegations of promoting witchcraft, sorcery and other practices of magic which are considered highly antithetical to the religious values of the worldwide Judeo-Christian community. But, at the core of J. K. Rowling's creation and the core of her opponent's arguments reveal the classic eternal struggle of good versus evil. And this conflict says much about the present state of civilization and its future course. This particular conflict in the Culture War merits closer attention due to the enormity of its impact on individuals and the larger society.

Unfortunately, the press and the media's early coverage of this debate was largely superficial as the early books were released. And by 2007, with the release of the last title, the real life witchcraft and "dark arts" connection had been completely snuffed out by a Hollywood-seduced media machine that is almost exclusively secular in general and largely atheistic in particular. Besides, Rowling became a "media darling."

The press and pundits have no problem discussing the existence of good and evil, but when the conversation delves into the origin of each, everyone goes silent and the debate grinds to a halt, much to the pleasure of authors like Rowling who can redefine evil as "good" with media applause and praise. But, this controversy rages on within literary, religious, social and cultural circles. Unlike all previous debates about J. K. Rowling's effect on the culture, we have included a "Glossary of Occult Terminology" for the reader to reference. Writing and talking about magic and its counterparts in the very real world of witchcraft mean nothing if you don't have a clear understanding of the definition behind the terminology.

Words, written and spoken, in the world of fact or fiction have meaning. Thought gives birth to the word and the word gives birth to the deed. People who take action on these words, and the results they incur, can open themselves to either the life more abundant or the life of bondage to a world never thought possible to the average reader.

Acting on the spoken and written word invokes choices and choices have consequences. The world of Potterethics can *potentially* produce great misfortune in the belief system of its reader, young or old, because as Rowling openly admits, Harry Potter's world waxes "darker and darker" with every passing book.

Rowling and her defenders have casually dismissed any occult meaning behind her terminology, inferring "harmless storytelling." But that would negate the whole story of Harry Potter. If certain words have no real meaning, then there is no story even in fiction. In numerous interviews over the past ten years, Rowling has revealed herself as a master contrarian, like so many New Agers, very proficient in double-speak. Excerpts from many of those interviews are cited in this section.

The truth is J. K. Rowling is very skillfully adept in the English language and keen on the importance of meaning in words, past and present. She received the American equivalent of summa cum laude from Exeter University in England. Rowling's understanding of words and the definitions they convey is extremely sharp and employed earnestly in her story of Harry Potter. To selectively dismiss meanings behind certain words is a carefully calculated foil.

Rowling's books are a reflection of the influences she openly invited into her life from her earliest teens until shortly before her 30th birthday. To understand the younger J. K. Rowling is to understand the dark worldview she cultivated later in life through *Harry Potter*. Only here will you find the cultural connection that the press overlooked, ignored or refused to cover.

Rowling's intentions are cleverly masked in her unique and compelling style of storytelling. She is the classic literary epitome of author as wolf in sheep's clothing. J. K. Rowling's purpose in writing the Harry Potter series is a stealthy New Age revenge on a society and culture she despises, a holdover from her goth-punk-rock youth days that she never completely abandoned. Rowling's intentions are only malevolent and in no way benevolent.

Rowling's back door attack, masked in "magic" and "enchantment," is the most insidious of all because it deceptively feeds on the hunger of children and adults alike to be entertained and mesmerized simultaneously. Her writings also reach into the reader's inner psyche to, possibly, learn the secret of an invincible superpower liberating force. This is the embodiment of the Nietzsche theory of *Ubermensch* (superman), which Europeans have been dabbling in for over a century.

Sadly, the superb storytelling of Harry Potter is wrapped in a moral vacuum of endless ambiguity and cynically secret messages embedded in plot and character. In essence, moral relativity and the long, dark thread of the Crowlean theology emerge as the subtle guiding New Age message that is woven through all seven books and their companion Hollywood movies.

Not only is the Harry Potter series a back door attack on Christianity and "The Establishment," as Joe Schimmel of FightTheGoodFight.org explains, "It's a full blown open doorway into the occult."[74] Schimmel knows first hand, falling victim to other occult-based "attractions" of the popular culture of the 1970s.

Unlike some, Schimmel not only survived to tell his story, he has devoted his life to cautioning others of the very real dangers of pursuing obsessions into the esoteric world of the mystic arts. You won't read about Joe and others in the mainstream press because he will be either quoted out of context or ridiculed by the secular media whose loyalty and fascination is with the dark side of life.

For some readers, and by no means all, books like *Harry Potter* are but a small first step down a darker and deeper cellar that has the potential to make Rowling's Death Eaters look like candy-canes.

GLOSSARY OF OCCULT TERMINOLOGY

- MAGIC: *noun* (Old French; magique)—any mysterious, seemingly inexplicable, or extraordinary power or influence. a*djective*—producing extraordinary results as if by magic or supernatural means.

    Contemporary Synonyms
    - WITCHCRAFT & WIZARDRY—implies the possession of supernatural power by compact with evil spirits.
    - SORCERY—implies magic in which spells are cast . . . usually for a harmful or sinister purpose.
    - MAGIC—marvelous effects by supernatural or occult power.

- ADEPT: *adj.* (Latin; adeptus)—originally used by alchemists claiming to have arrived at the philosopher's stone; highly skilled.
- ALCHEMY: *noun* (Old French; alchimie)—the chemistry of the Middle Ages, the chief aim of which was to change the baser metals into gold and to discover the elixir of perpetual youth.
- ASTRAL: *adj.* (Latin; astralis)—in theosophy, designating or of an alleged supernatural substance. Often used with the word projection, meaning; to send forth in one's thoughts or imagination, as "project" yourself into the world of tomorrow.
- ASTROLOGY: *noun* (Middle English; astrologie)—a pseudoscience claiming to foretell the future by studying the supposed influence of the relative positions of the moon, sun and stars on human affairs.

- BEWITCH: *verb* (Anglo Saxon; wicca)—to use witchcraft or magic on; to cast a spell over.
- CHARM: *noun* (Old French; charme)—originally, a chanted word, phrase or verse assumed to have magic power to help or hurt.
- CURSE: *noun* (Old French; corocier)—a calling on God or the gods to send evil or injury down on some person or thing.
- DIVINATION: *noun* (Latin; divinatio)—the act or practice of trying to foretell the future or the unknown by occult means.
- ESOTERIC: *adj.* (Greek' esoterikos)—intended for or understood by only a chosen few; of or for only an inner group of disciples or initiatives.
- MEDIUM: *noun* (Latin; medius)—a person through whom communications are supposedly sent to the living from the dead.
- MYSTIC: adj. (Latin; mysticus)—of mysteries, or esoteric rites or doctrines. Of obscure or occult character or meaning.
- NECROMANCY: *noun* (Latin; necromantia)—the art claiming to foretell the future by alleged communication with the dead. Black magic.
- OCCULT: *adj.* (Latin; occultus)—hidden, concealed, secret, esoteric ... designation of certain mystical arts or studies, such as magic, alchemy, astrology, etc.
- SPELL: *noun* (Middle English; spel)—a word, formula, or form of words supposed to have some magic power.
- TRANSMUTATION: *noun* (Middle English; transmuten) also *verb transitive*—to change from one form, species, condition, nature or substance into another.

Source: *Webster's New World Dictionary: College Edition*[75]

By 2000, three years after the debut of her first book, Rowling finally admitted that she has been called a witch more times than she could remember.

"I'm neither a practicing witch nor do I believe in magic," author J. K. Rowling insisted adamantly in an interview with the Canadian Broadcasting Company seven days before Halloween of 2000. (Rowling considered seven as her "magic" number and Halloween as her favorite "holiday.") Rowling frequently scheduled interviews on days with "magic" numerical significance or on days that coincided with a magic event in history.

And, on this day, she wanted the world to know that she neither believed in magic nor was a *practicing* witch.[76] This interview would come back to "haunt" Rowling on a number of occasions over the years.

Nobody picked up on the fact that just four days earlier, Rowling had not only proclaimed her belief in magic, but elevated it as a "talent." In an online chat with children conducted by AOL, one child asked eagerly, "Does everyone have a little magic in them . . . And, if not, how did the magic start?" Rowling assured the young child, "I think we do . . . Magic is one of those odd talents that some people have and some don't."[77]

Rowling didn't bother to answer the second part of the online chat question. That was another question dogging Rowling every time she attended a book signing or gave an interview, especially with children. To answer such a question, honestly, would reveal much about her background and interests that she preferred to keep locked up in the "secret" chamber of her mind.

Rowling also knows that children are very inquisitive. Her books give plenty of references to dark mysticism that any curious child could conjure up on the internet in order to absorb more details. And, one link leads to another and another and eventually a child with burning desire can end up in a very dark room somewhere in the black hole of cyberspace.

The completion of the series in 2007 by no means signals an end to Harry Potter. Rowling's books and movies about the boy wizard and his mastery of magic, witchcraft, sorcery, curses and the entire spectrum of New Age occultism will impact children and adults for infinite generations. Of course, not all readers will be affected or infected to pursue the occult to the point of detrimental obsession with "familiar spirits." But, even one percent of hundreds of millions of readers and moviegoers over time is still a staggering number.

During her ten year journey from pauper to princess, Rowling has managed to corral a strange brew of supporters and apologists from both the secular and faith-based communities. She neither asked for nor sought out the odd combination of followers who display an obsessive and urgent desire to "rescue" her. This community of J.K. junkies stands ready to pounce on anybody who would dare criticize the British author, dubbed by the press as the "Shy Sorceress." Only half of that label is true.

Most peculiar among these disciples are certain segments of the mainstream and evangelical communities who appear awkwardly starstruck with Rowling and are equally awkward in their disparate and desperate writings to somehow attach Biblical significance to every word and phrase she writes and speaks.

And, it is this divide within the Christian community that has become the most pronounced and least covered in the media. In an eerie blue/red type divide, Rowling's defenders have come to fall largely in the category of the evangelical Left and her detractors stand largely on the evangelical Right; a religious/political phenomena that has ironically occurred during the same period as Rowling's back door debut in 1997.

Steven Greydanus of DecentFilms.com has written one of many insightful essays about this debate. Greydanus understands the nature of the divide given the complexity of the Harry Potter world created by Rowling, but he strongly argues for establishing some basic common ground on core faith and beliefs that some Christians are ceding to the New Age, "In principle, Christians on both sides of the Harry Potter debate ought to be able to agree on this much: According to Christian teaching, in the real world, it is wrong, potentially dangerous, and contrary to true religion to engage in any form of attempted magic (for example, the use of spells and charms, attempted astral projection, or the superstitious use of crystals), or to engage, summon, control, or otherwise interact with occult powers (as by consulting with mediums, astrologers, psychics, card readers, witch doctors, or any other kind of divination and fortunetelling). Historical Christian opposition to practices such as these is categorical and decisive."[78]

One of J. K. Rowling's Christian defenders is Terry Mattingly of Gospelcom. net who wrote, "The usual suspects will immediately say the usual things. Many Christians will quote Bible verses condemning magic. Academics will call the book a childish confection and analyze it as media myth and pop psychology."[79]

Mattingly's article was itself an apologetic introduction to an even bigger, and defiant, defender and promoter of Rowling's work. John Granger, author of *The Hidden Key to Harry Potter*, puts forth the theory that the Harry Potter series is a medieval Christian allegory replete with the universal theme of good versus evil. Mattingly begs the conclusion that "Anyone who cares about Pottermania must take Rowling more seriously."[80]

Writer Dave Kopel of *National Review Online* goes even further in glowing praise of Rowling by also promoting Granger's far-fetched "Hidden Keys" when he writes, "Granger demonstrates the absurdity of the claim that Harry Potter is anti-Christian . . . even if you've never worried about charges brought by *misguided* fundamentalists."[81] Rowling was surely laughing in her new Scottish castle home as difference of opinions within and among Christian denominations appeared poised to further divisions, speeding up a process which has been ongoing for centuries.

Just before Cardinal Joseph Ratzinger became Pope Benedict XVI, the obedient keeper of Catholic theology declared the Harry Potter books as "a subtle seduction which has deeply unnoticed and direct effects in undermining the soul of Christianity before it can grow properly." However, some of Rowling's "handlers" managed to find a Monsignor named Peter Fleetwood who "volunteered" that these remarks were "misinterpreted" and "likely" to have been written by some yet unnamed assistant of the former Cardinal turned Pope.

And then there is Rowling's American editor, Arthur Levine of publisher Scholastic, Inc., whose scorn for any hint of criticism is legendary. In an impudent tone of derision, Levine reduced Rowling's critics to fractionally insignificant "half-bloods" when he shouted that "the ratio of fans to protestors is maybe 10,000 to a half, so I can't be that concerned."[82]

But, the most vapid attack on Harry Potter critics came from J. K. Rowling herself. Rowling could not fathom why anybody would possibly criticize her books. Criticism is simply part of being a famous best-selling author, except for Rowling who hints, condescendingly, that *ignorance* must be at the root of her detractors.

In her CBC radio interview of 2000, the moderator asked Rowling about the concerns of "witchcraft and devil worship." Rowling responded sharply, "I get asked this a lot, as you can imagine. First of all, I would question whether those people have actually read the books, I really would question that."[83]

Ironically, exactly one year earlier in 1999, Rowling told *The Washington Times,* concerning her critics, "They don't have to read the book."[84] Doubtless, Rowling's agent, editor and publisher were shocked and instructions were carefully transmitted to Rowling to never say that people "don't have to read the book." It was hard enough to get Rowling to do book signings and wipe the goth-punk snarl off her face when greeting little children.

From that point on, as her CBC interview revealed, Rowling began the same savage campaign employed by Martin Scorsese-Universal and Dan Brown-Sony; "How can you possibly criticize the book if you haven't read it? How can you criticize the movie if you haven't seen it?" Rowling was *reminded* that there were others profiting from her success and she needed to pump up the volume.

As a result, Rowling joined the chorus of her editor Arthur Levine in berating their critics who were seriously impeding Rowling's race to become the first billionaire author in world literary history. Rowling now became obsessed with demonizing her critics and even took the giant leap of trying to hide behind the popularity of genuine classics from the past.

When the South Carolina School Board became the first among many states to advocate the limited use of the Harry Potter books in public schools, Rowling loftily and cleverly restructured the debate so she could address any questions or issues on *her terms only*, "My feeling about this is that if we are going to ban all books that mention witches ... we're going to be getting rid of a lot of classics."[85]

The only thing "classic" was her style of obfuscation and manipulation. Nobody mentioned "banning" her books or any books mentioning "witch." Educators and parents in South Carolina and certain other states simply wanted to put certain age and grade guidelines on the Harry Potter book's availability in public schools, because of the dark, ultraviolent nature of the books which contained, "a serious tone of death, hate, lack of respect and sheer evil."[86] The educators and parents knew full well that the books would be readily available at the local bookstore for those who wanted a copy. They were protesting Rowling's insistence that the books appear in *school libraries* which would add to the public education stamp of approval that Rowling craved.

The conditions being advocated by some school boards made Rowling furious, no doubt prodded on by her editor and publisher. The impatient imprint of Arthur

Levine was all over her "fractional" argument when she falsely invoked the "ban" word again and angrily proclaimed, "If you ban all books with witchcraft and supernatural, you'll ban three-fourths of children's literature."[87]

I called Levine's office at Scholastic to ask if he could compile a list of the "three-fourths" of children's literature that Rowling was referencing. But, after "seven" phone calls, no response from Rowling's editor. Apparently seven wasn't such a magic number after all.

J. K. Rowling has most of the mainstream media "snowed-under" to the point that anything written by the press or broadcast on the news is basically "puff-piece" journalism for the Harry Potter publicity machine. And the wordplay by journalists gives one pause for something more ominous than the repetitive window dressing accolades for Harry Potter and his creator.

As Malcolm Jones of *Newsweek* wrote, "Those of us under Harry Potter's magic spell are more reluctant to criticize Rowling's literary career."[88] Apparently, it was the first recorded episode of writer's block at *Newsweek* magazine due to a "magic spell." And then there are Rowling's more salty attacks that we won't print here, mainly leveled against certain publications of the British and Scottish press. Nevertheless, in any interview with the Harry Potter author where a question is asked concerning a downside to her darkside story, it is enough to set off the snob elitist Exeter intellectual in Rowling. "I vacillate between feeling faintly annoyed that I'm being so misrepresented, and finding the whole thing really quite funny . . . But there's always the rogue person who can't see what's right under their nose, and there you go."[89]

Again, anybody who criticizes Rowling's work is reduced to some moronic level of "rogue" personality. It is a constant condescending attitude that Rowling has carried over from her teen years. What *really* bothers J.K. Rowling is that so many people very accurately "represent" the intentions of her story, despite her best efforts to mask her "magical" agenda.

As author Gabriele Kuby noted in her book, *Harry Potter—Good or Evil?* "The ability of the reader to distinguish between good and evil is overridden by emotional manipulation and intellectual obfuscation." That "rogue person" who can't see what's right under their nose turns out to be J. K. Rowling herself . . . and there you go!

THE AMAZING ADVENTURES AND ALLURE OF HARRY POTTER

With glossary in hand and a small sampling of the author's dark personal worldview, it will help to give you a brief summary of the story that "dropped into my head" as J. K. Rowling describes first seeing Harry Potter in a "vision" during a four hour train delay in the early 1990s.

If you would like to delve into the story and world of Harry Potter, you can buy all seven books, see all the movies, purchase the tie-in books, the biographies, and remember to visit the many Harry Potter web sites everyday for updates and analysis. And, if you want J. K. Rowling to surpass Oprah as the New Age queen, spend as much as you can. Or, we'll break the story down for you simply over the next several pages.

The epic narrative of Harry Potter comprises seven volumes beginning with *Harry Potter and the Sorcerer's Stone*. The story begins on Halloween night in 1981 when the infant Harry is nestled quietly at the suburban home of his parents, James and Lily Potter. Though the Potters are living in the "Muggle" world (non-magical people) they are descendants of a long line of wizards and witches, "good" wizards and witches, that is. Their line of witchcraft is in dramatic opposition to that of the evil Lord Voldemort, leader and follower of "dark magic," who has been searching for Lily, James and their infant son, Harry.

Upon finding the Potters on Halloween night, Lord Voldemort violently kills James and Lily and when he turns his malevolent angry wand against Harry with a bolt of lightning, the burning curse boomerangs on Voldemort. The evil "Lord" is ripped from his body and forced into hiding. The failed attack leaves the faint image of a lightning bolt on young Harry's head.

The "magical community" is overjoyed by the events of that Halloween night and they refer to Harry as "the boy who lived." However, still an infant, and now orphaned, he is subsequently raised by his relatives, portrayed as the cruel and hateful Dursley family who keep the "unnatural" Harry locked up in the crawlspace under the central hall stairway. Harry's life takes a dramatic turn on his eleventh birthday when he is notified by special delivery that he is indeed a wizard and is invited to attend the Hogwarts school of Witchcraft and Wizardry.

Each of the seven books covers roughly one year in the life of Harry Potter during his schooling at Hogwarts. At the dark, isolated castle academy, Harry learns about the "magic craft" of wizardry, sorcery and witchcraft including the casting of spells, magic potions, divination, curses, charms, transmutation, conjuring spirits, telepathy and many other "arts," both "good" and "bad." The shifting boundaries between the two values are never clear and constantly in flux, but the practice of magic is central to all "power."

Harry's two closest friends at Hogwarts, Ron and Hermione, are central to the plot in each book and promote a portrayal of friendship and loyalty, though sometimes shifting, as they grow older. These "shifts" in their mutual friendship are depicted as the pains of adolescent youth. However, the strife intensifies with the increasingly darkening, ominous tone of each successive book.

The entire series focuses on Harry's mastering of sorcery at Hogwarts as he grows older and the magical journey and challenges he confronts on his road to manhood. Through the course of these explorations and adventures, the books delve into themes of friendship, ambition, choice, prejudice and love against a backdrop of the expansive magical world with its long and complex history, strangely perverse inhabitants, curious cultures and a "parallel society."

As for any semblance of "authority figures," Professor Albus Dumbledore is the seemingly wise sage opposite of the evil Lord Voldemort. Dumbledore is portrayed as Harry Potter's friend and trusted advisor in addition to serving as the headmaster of Hogwarts School of Witchcraft and Wizardry. His quote to Potter "It is our choices, Harry, that show what we truly are, far more than our abilities" appears to invoke a highly moral authority in the series.

However, because of his "status" in the "magical world," Dumbledore finds himself socially isolated and "vulnerable to reckless emotional mistakes" as one critic noted. One thing he certainly can't escape is the horrific and violent departure Rowling has cooked up for him and post-mortem sexual reorientation.

The trio also witnesses the violent and vicious death of one of their close schoolmates. Harry's friend Ron tries to "cast a spell" that backfires, causing a near death experience of choking on an endless stream of parasitic slimy black slugs. It becomes clear early in the series that Rowling seems to revel in a culture of death, more extreme than any other children's books written to date. And the movies are even more graphic.

As Harry grows older during his tenure at Hogwarts, Lord Voldemort's power increases, leading to a final showdown by the seventh book. By the fourth book, there is very little "fun" left in the series and the plot is one dark, diabolical turn after the other. This is also magnified in the movies. The fifth, *Harry Potter and the Order of the Phoenix*, resembles a big budget horror film distinctly darker than its predecessors. It's very easy to tell by reading the books and watching the movies as to when Rowling quit her two-pack-a-day smoking habit.

* * *

The Potter series also contains themes about racism, genocide, prejudice and a very heavy-handed dose of anti-establishment philosophy. Rowling admits that these themes are "deeply entrenched in the whole plot" but she prefers to let them "grow organically" rather than appear to sound "preachy." In fact, her "themes" are so deeply entrenched that only adults *may* pick up on them. And, because these "themes" are "entrenched" in a morally vacant world, they really have no meaning at all. The entire moral vacuum seems to be the *true* "entrenched" theme, which is a hallmark of New Age morality.

THE HOLLYWOOD CULTURE WAR

All of the themes that Rowling believes will "grow organically" seem to sprout from a soil of unknown origin. There is no moral "source," no "fertile ground" from which these vague themes arise and certainly no solutions are offered to overcome any assaults of evil except by use of magic. And, because magic is occult (secret) in nature, the plot is a series of confused ethics and endless behavioral ambiguity.

As Dr. Ted Baehr noted in his in-depth book, *Frodo and Harry*, this occult worldview by author Rowling "portrays the evil witches and warlocks as having tremendous power and says that the heroes can only succeed by participating in occult, and often secret, activity. There is no transcendent, sovereign person or principle controlling the use of this occult power. It is a power with no ultimate authority behind it."[90]

With all the contradictions and double standards, you may ask, "What is the big attraction that could sell more than 340 million books around the world to both children and adults?" As for storytelling ability alone, Rowling is a master of narrative and shrewd mystery. This makes Rowling's message easier to get across; a world of "anything goes" and a world where there are no rules because magic trumps everything.

Margaret Weir of *Salon* asked Rowling, "In this era of involved parenting, do you think that the notion of boarding school and the autonomy it offers might be an almost taboo allure for both kids and parents?" Rowling felt that Weir had hit the nail on the head. "I think that's definitely true . . . No child wants to lose their parents, yet the idea of being removed from the expectations of parents is alluring."

As one little boy boasted in a televised spot, "Harry's the greatest! He doesn't care what people tell him to do!" In another exchange, Rowling states that "A middle-class boarding school is a world where [children] are free of their parents."[91]

Rowling is actually perpetuating a personally radical worldview that she developed while growing up in the West Country of England. A deeper look, later in this chapter, at Rowling's "radical alternative" lifestyle in high school and through her university schooling will explain volumes behind the motivations of her subterranean themes.

Rowling's editor, Arthur Levine, also shed light on the allure of Harry Potter for children by focusing on "magic" as "the idea that a great power lives in each of us." Again, there's that "power" of the unknown—the dark esoterica. It's not a mystery to Shirley MacLaine, a big fan of Rowling's, who said "the power" is "I am god, you are god." For children, as Rowling manifests the "power" in her writing, the message is "run free, run wild." The Harry Potter author subscribes to the Dennis Hopper school of "F____ the rules. There are no rules, man!"

The resultant alluring message to children and adults alike may be the chipping away of moral character, especially epitomized by the seemingly benevolent, but fractured father figure Professor Dumbledore who rephrased the "right" and "wrong" debate into the "choice between what is right and what is easy."

More telling for the allure to children is a quote from Judith Krug of the American Library Association, "The storyline is wonderful . . . we have Harry Potter as an orphan. There's no one always telling him what to do, and what young person hasn't at one point said, 'Oh, if they'd only leave me alone' or 'I wish that I didn't have parents.' They don't mean this in a mean way. It's just that parents get in the way."[92]

This is the perfect example of the counterculture "wisdom" promoted in literature and movies that children know best and "stupid" parents might just learn something if they would shut-up and let children solve all the problems. The result is consecutive generations of hyperactive, bossy children with ADD. At least the pharmaceutical industry is grateful to Rowling and her supporters in the popular culture.

This is only part of the subtle social-political correctness that is a running theme throughout the Harry Potter books. But, as we'll see, the theme is much deeper and darker than sociology and politics, as Rowling admits, because Harry's story becomes "darker and darker" with every book.

Author Richard Abanes notes, "During a National Public Radio interview with Diane Rehm, J. K. Rowling explained that she did not write her books for children. She actually penned them as novels that she herself, as an adult, would enjoy reading."[93] Rowling herself has stated, "When I was quite young, my parents never said books were off limits . . . As a child, I read a lot of adult books. I don't think you should censor kid's reading material."[94] Does she mean *everything*, including the most vile and atrocious words and images of mayhem and perversion on the internet? She offered *no comment*.

The story of Harry Potter is the story of J. K. Rowling, and her Potterethics have ignited a much larger conversation about what is at stake in shaping the moral lives of children.

I ANTICIPATE A DEEPLY RELIGIOUS EXPERIENCE

While there has actually been some criticism of J.K. Rowling's writings from fellow authors in the literary world and the lofty halls of academia, the debate and criticism surrounding J.K. Rowling and her boy wizard continues to center around ethics, religion and faith-based values that are twisted and mocked by Rowling's tenuous manipulation of the written word.

Whether the supporters of Rowling welcome or dispute the criticism, the early objections by parents at the 1999 South Carolina School Board have grown exponentially across the country as theologians, educators, scholars and experts on occult studies have discovered that Rowling's pen is tainted with an even darker shade of ink. Again, those voices have been largely shut out of wider circulation by the mainstream media which, by the 2007 release of the final book, had become full-fledged mind-numbed converts.

In later interviews, mainly after Book Four, Rowling had largely refused to discuss her research into magic and the occult, realizing she may have been giving away too much information about "involvement" as opposed to "research." And, the subject of "occult research" is now "off the table" if journalists hang on to even a slim chance of an interview.

Rumors that Rowling and her first husband, Jorge Arantes, attended seances while she struggled as a teacher in Portugal cannot be confirmed as Arantes, who once talked openly about their relationship, is decisively mum, perhaps due to legal injunctions regarding visitation with their daughter Jessica. Furthermore, he has slipped in and out of substance abuse since the mid 1990s and his information would be suspect as to authenticity. Nevertheless, Rowling has never denied a strong interest in communicating with the dead, not unlike Oprah Winfrey who openly admits to lively conversations with dead people while preparing to tape her T.V. show. Necromancy is a deep stage in occult devotion.

And, Rowling's research into the occult is not only thorough, it comes across in her writing as exhaustive and enthusiastic with an intense tone of fascination, keen interest and a religiously zealous devotion. For J.K. Rowling and Harry Potter, the dark arts, also known as the "curious arts," hold the key to universal New Age understanding.

"I've *always* been interested in it, although I don't *really* believe in magic," Rowling acknowledged during a 1999 Barnes and Noble interview.[95] The first part of her statement is *very* true while the second part of her statement is *very* false. Self contradiction continues to be the hallmark of any J.K. Rowling interview or public statement.

It's important to understand that we're not talking about Houdini-style sleight-of-hand stage magic. Even Harry Houdini himself admitted that anyone could learn the "tricks" of his trade. And, he was an adamant opponent of mystical, esoteric magic. He even lobbied the U.S. Congress before World War I to make fortune-telling and palm-reading illegal. Unfortunately, precursor attorneys to the ACLU came to the defense of the "mind readers."

Rowling's defenders brand her form of witchcraft as "fantasy magic," and "totally harmless . . . in the *right hands*."[96] This is the common battle cry of Rowling fans and it is where Rowling's worldview is most frequently challenged.

Harry Houdini was not the only one warning of the *very real* danger of the *very real* world of witchcraft, sorcery and mystical magic. As scholars, students and experts in the occult will explain, association with the spirit world of orphic magic is little understood by the general public. Some of the most knowledgeable experts in the occult field were once victims themselves and hold first-hand knowledge of the unimaginable horrors that await people who dig too deep beneath the surface of worlds that some, like Rowling's supporters, try to sugarcoat as "fantasy witchcraft."

Rowling's apologists say there is a distinct theme of "good" versus "evil" in the Harry Potter series and this is what makes the entire story so captivating. But, the line in the sand is not so clear because the "good" guys utilize "white magic" and the "bad" guys practice "black magic" and the dark arts. In reality, there is no difference. This "white" versus "black" magic debate is old as mankind. Anyone who has driven down a rural roadway or walked down a busy city side-street has seen the ragged signs with the crudely painted hand "Palm Reader: God Based Fortune Telling" or "Psychic Reader: Jesus Loves."

The controversy between Christians and Potterites centers around the oldest written words that call out the names of magical practices as "abominations" against God. And the names are the same today as the words written around 1450 B.C., almost 3,500 years ago. Terry Mattingly, the Christian apologist for J.K. Rowling, desperately wants you to avoid reading any verses from the Bible that condemn magic. This is why he derided his fellow Christians as "the usual suspects" who might even resort to "quoting Bible verses."

We'll save you some time and quote the main verse that strikes fear in Mattingly like a silver cross in a vampire's face. As you've probably discovered by this point in the book, almost all New Age fascination with occult magic has its roots in ancient Egypt. Even Moses had to put up with this New Age dribble while captive in Egypt and during the 40 years of wondering in the wilderness after the exodus from Pharaoh's Nile delta empire in the fifteenth century B.C.

The land that God had prepared for Moses and his people was inhabited by tribes that preached all the very same forms of magic and witchcraft that exist to this day, including much of the magic and witchcraft used casually by Rowling in the *Harry Potter* series. The verse that Mattingly and the other Potterites wish you'd avoid is Deuteronomy 18: 10-14 where Moses warns the people before entering the new land: "There shall not be found among anyone . . . that uses divination, or an observer of times, or an enchanter, or a witch, or a charmer, or a consulter with familiar spirits, or a wizard, or a necromancer. For all that do these things are an abomination unto the Lord; and because of these abominations, the Lord thy God does drive them out before you. Then shall you be perfect with the Lord thy God. For those nations which you shall possess, harkened unto observers of times, and unto diviners; but as for you, the Lord thy God has not suffered you to do also."[97]

God was telling Moses that the practitioners of magic would be literally wiped off the face of the earth to make way for His people. This drives the Potterites and Rowling loyalists into a self-flagellating frenzy, "See, see . . . what kind of God is that? He kills *innocent* people, just wipes them off the face of the earth! Bad God! Bad God!"

God didn't say anything about wiping "innocent" people off the face of the earth. The example is pretty clear. You play with magic for too long and before you know it . . . POOF . . . BANG . . . BOOM! Or, as J.K. Rowling would say " . . . and there you go!"

When a visitor arrives at any of the hundreds of Harry Potter sites, official and unofficial, there is very little room to believe anything other than you have left the world of Harry Potter, the story, and entered Harry Potter: The New Age religion of the 21st century. As an example, under one of the *Harry Potter Lexicon* links to "Magic" is the "definition" that "Most magic is relatively neutral—it can be used for bad or good."[98]

Whether intentional or a convenient memory lapse, Rowling has a hard time discerning fact from fiction, especially when it comes to recollections of her younger days when the future author dwelled for many years among the black lipstick rainbow-hair-color crowd known as "Goths." Some say she never really left the lifestyle and its gruesomely dark philosophy. She simply changed the color of her lipstick . . . just like, "magic."

J.K. ROWLING: GOTHIC PUNK ROCKER FROM HELL

One point must be made clear from the very beginning in order to understand J.K. (Joanne) Rowling and her motivations from teenager to young adult to the present. Without a doubt, Rowling is a world-class fabricator of the truth in epic proportions. This talent is an asset in her professional life as an author, but a malignancy in personal and public agendas.

This pathology to lie is so ingrained that Rowling cannot even bring herself to admit where she was actually born. In a variety of interviews over the years, Rowling has offered a number of locations as her birthplace, most frequently Bristol, Tutshill, Forest of Dean, Kent, West Country and many others. The town she now most frequently cites as her birthplace is Chipping Sodbury. As biographer Connie Ann Kirk found out from another Rowling biographer, Sean Smith, Joanne "Jo" Rowling was actually born in Yate, a small non-descript British town near the border with Wales.[99] Smith was actually able to produce a birth certificate, though Rowling herself had no comment.

Kirk explains that Rowling decided on the town of Chipping Sodbury as her "birthplace" because the name has a *charming* ring. Kirk also explains that this choice may have more to do with status consciousness in a country where place of birth may have much to do with determining what "side of the tracks" one comes from.

Chipping Sodbury is more affluent than Yate and has an enchanting main street with old shops and antique stores. Ironically, as Rowling herself says, the theme of prejudice is "deeply entrenched" in her story of Harry Potter. However, in *real* life, Rowling has succumbed to the deception of her own birthplace in order to join the "elite," which is another sub-theme in her books that would appear to trump the "entrenched" theme in her stories. In Potter lingo, "magical" people possess "secret" knowledge that allows them "special privileges."

As biographer Kirk explains, " . . . information about (Rowling's) life remains sketchy and incomplete."[100] This is all by design, of course, lest anybody discover the *real* Joanne Rowling and the primal roots of her fascination with death, destruction and evil—later to be sugarcoated for consumption by children and squarely aimed at "eliminating" God.

But, fortunately, we have been able to uncover the "hidden keys" in Rowling's life, mainly between the ages of 15 and 25, years that would forever form her cynical dark view of the world which has followed her into adulthood. (Rowling's publishers, afraid that boys wouldn't read a story written by a woman, persuaded Joanne to use initials before her last name. In addition to *J,* Rowling took the *K* from her grandmother Kathleen as her middle initial.)

It was at the age of twenty-five that young Harry Potter appeared to Rowling "fully formed" as the "boy who appeared in my brain."[101] The image was so stark and sudden in its appearance; the vision has obsessed her daily since 1990. Biographer Kirk explains that Rowling's birth in Yate on July 31, 1965, occurred a couple of months after her parents married. "The woman behind the J.K. Rowling persona is, quite literally, a child of the 60s."[102] As Yate grew into a suburban sprawl of highways and shopping malls, the family, along with sister Diana, moved further into the country near the expansive 225 square mile Forest of Dean, an ancient forest still spotted with 2,000 year old Roman roads. This West Country area of England is known for its long mysterious history marked by legends and tales of haunting spirits, ghosts and witches.

The Little White House by Elizabeth Goudge would influence Rowling to a great degree in its similarities to Harry Potter's world. In the story, young Marie Merriwether is an orphan transplanted from a dull, drab life into a magical kingdom. Once inside, Marie discovers that she is the long lost princess of Moonacre Valley. The entire magical kingdom pampers her thoroughly and this image of a newfound famous princess was one Rowling saw as herself. She would carry this fantasy into secondary school and quickly gained a reputation for snobbishness.[103] As a result of the books she read and her elevated fantasy imagination, Rowling would tend to look down on all around her in a condescending contempt that would follow her into adulthood.

As an example of Hollywood's influence over its target teen audience, Rowling herself became totally mesmerized at the age of 13 with the "bad girl" character of Rizzo played by Stockard Channing in the 1978 movie *Grease*. Friends of Rowling recalled how she began to assume the Rizzo persona in full force, smoking cigarettes, wearing heavy eye make-up and sporting a trademark denim jacket. Her contempt for most of her fellow students only intensified. She became a spiteful loner; a rebel *looking* for a cause.

Rowling's parents didn't offer much resistance as this was marked up to a young teen phase that their daughter would soon outgrow. However, the teen phase would only grow darker and bleaker as the years progressed. Just one year earlier, Jo Rowling had written her first dark fantasy story titled, *The Seven Cursed Diamonds*. She was only 12.

* * *

Before going further, it is necessary to understand the culture of England at this time. Unlike the tourist posters and propaganda of picturesque cathedrals and quiet cottage churches, England was already a largely secular country when Rowling was a teen. The country had been sliding in that direction since the early 20th century and has slid even further after the dawn of the 21st century. The idea of Great Britain as a "Christian" country is largely a myth, as only a minority, less than 40%, describe themselves as such. Much of this can be traced to European philosophy that crossed the English Channel before and especially after World War I.

German philosopher Friedrich Nietzsche (1844-1900) had written in the late 19th century that "once the sin against God was the greatest sin; but God died." This was widely embraced by the bohemian culture between 1890 and 1910 and shortened to the famous statement "God is Dead."[104] Fellow dead-head French philosopher Jean-Paul Sartre would later state, "If God is dead, everything is permitted."

The British people, like many in Europe, began to find this very *liberating*, especially after World War I when the first fully mechanized war left hundreds of thousands of British soldiers dead or grotesquely disfigured. Many in the population began to blame God and started experimenting with the occult and the secret magical societies of which Aleister Crowley became the most prominent promoter.

By the time Jo Rowling was a teenager in the late 1970s, the prevailing allure of the "God is Dead" philosophy was already well-grounded in England and its "liberating allure" was just a fact of life for a godless home and country.

Rowling would display the undercurrents of this theme and nihilistic philosophy when she was quoted as saying that children love the *liberating* power in Harry Potter because "the idea of being removed (liberated) from the expectations of parents is alluring."

Rowling also expressed the central theme of this growing secularism in terms of "magical power" which fits like a hand in a glove with Nietzsche's writings on power for its own sake. As Rowling explained enthusiastically, "The idea that we could have a child who escapes from the confines of the adult world and goes somewhere where he has power both literally and metaphorically, really appealed to me."[105] Of course, Rowling recognizes no source of origin of this power. As author Richard Abanes stated, " . . . this leads to moral ambiguity and ethical confusion."[106]

In the increasingly godless Britain and Europe, Rowling's view of "power" as written into the character of Harry Potter is an outgrowth of Nietzshe's treatise where he wrote, "Suppose, finally, we succeed in explaining our entire instinctive life as the development and ramification of our basic form of the will—namely of the *will to power*, as my proposition has it . . . The world from inside . . . it would be 'will to power' and nothing else."

This sole paragraph was the guiding philosophy behind the formation of the Nazi party in the 1920s. It was also the guiding principle behind the Communist party of the Marxist-Lenin faction which took over Russia in 1917. The Marxist/Communist philosophy is also at the core of the modern day Socialist Party in Britain, of which Rowling is an avid admirer.

To show the extent of influence that these mega-atheist empires exerted, British Prime Minister Neville Chamberlain represented a very large segment of the British population when he sought a peaceful "alignment" with the Nazis and many English citizens had no problem siding with Hitler until Churchill stepped in.

This is only the background to the philosophical history that Rowling was born into, but which she also largely embraced. Rowling was further seduced into more than just radical fashion statements at school. She began to absorb the radical politics of books that she was exposed to by her parents and books given to her by friends.

The one book, more than any other, that helps explain J.K. Rowling's duplicitous worldview is *Hons and Rebels* by Communist activist Jessica Mitford. The book would deeply influence Rowling as a teenager and into adulthood and would coincide with Rowling's increasingly deeper walk into the darkside of life. Rowling was so taken with Mitford, she would devour everything ever written by her and would even incorporate some of Mitford's more radical Socialist-Communist themes into the Harry Potter story. To know Mitford is to know J.K. Rowling,

THE HOLLYWOOD CULTURE WAR

Jessica Lucy Freeman-Mitford was born in 1917, at the height of World War I to an eccentric upper-class family who described themselves as "nature socialists," a mystical-atheist-political New Age belief; basically, the fruit-loop fringe of British aristocracy that would later become the norm rather than the exception.

The family's bizarre secular theology would be passed down to Jessica (better known as "Decca") and her two sisters, Unity and Diana. They were among the first fully New Age families of the early 20th Century.

Sisters Unity and Diana grew up as young women staunchly supporting Adolph Hitler, believing that England should have joined with the Nazi leader to rule the entire world. But, this would not do for the young rebel Decca. She decided that the only course of action for the future salvation of the world was global Stalinist Communism with its atheist utopian heaven-on-earth vision of a perfect world; genocide, mass murder and all wrapped into one bloody package.

While the Nazis only hated and despised God, the Communists took it even further and made God "illegal." Young Jessica thought that concept was pretty "peachy-keen." Young Jo Rowling had no problem with that either.

Mitford brought her maniacal Communist love affair to America where she joined the Civil Rights Congress (CRC) as a secretary. The group fought against lynching laws in America during the 1940s by initiating legislation in Congress. The renegade Communist Brit couldn't understand why the CRC efforts were largely fruitless. Mitford knew that the CRC was a puppet front organization for the Communist Party USA, which took its marching orders directly from Moscow. How could that be a problem, she must have wondered?

Even after Stalin's death in 1953 and Khrushchev's revelation of Stalin's atrocities, which claimed roughly 50 million lives, Jessica Mitford continued her membership as a Communist for five more years until the Party literally fizzled in America.

Her attempts to fully engage in the Civil Rights Movement of the early 1960s also fizzled. By then, the movement was a largely Christian crusade led by a peace-loving believer in democracy and Southern Baptist minister named Martin Luther King, Jr. The movement wanted to distance itself from Communists and former Communists who, like Jessica Mitford, had hampered their cause in the past.

She faded away after a couple more books and died at age 78 from lung cancer as the leader of a kazoo band call "Decca and the Dectones."

Recalling Mitford's early foray into politics by fire after fighting with the Communists in the Spanish Civil War, J. K. Rowling told interviewer Lindsay Frazer in 2002 that she wished she "had the nerve" like Mitford to steal from her father to finance the purchase of a camera and "fight" in the Spanish Civil War.[107] (On the side of the Communists, of course.)

Rowling recalled that she greatly admired Mitford because "she was a self-taught socialist."[108] Rowling selectively forgot to mention she was a "self-taught Communist." The Marxist-Communist influence on Rowling by Mitford's writing is reflected in parts of the Harry Potter series, including Hermione's little club known as the S.P.E.W. which helps negotiate "fair pay" for "elves." The S.P.E.W. is an intentional allegorical salute to the secular-atheist Socialist Party of England and Wales. The Socialist Party in Britain is actually the Communist Party in disguise, even using Karl Marx as part of its logo. As Connie Ann Kirk noted, Jessica Mitford's *Hons and Rebels* made such a lasting impression on Rowling that she named her daughter "Jessica." Like many Socialist-Communists in Great Britain, the fall of the Berlin Wall and the end of Soviet Russia was not celebrated by the young author.

As her rebellious spirit grew during her mid-teens, Jo Rowling began to idolize the Beatles, even though the "Fab Four" had broken up almost a decade earlier in 1970.[109] Rowling was attracted to the latter-day, drug-addled, post Sgt. Pepper Beatles. It was the time when John Lennon openly boasted that the Beatles' "message" was based on the "anything goes" philosophy of New Age founder Aleister Crowley and that they were "more popular than Jesus Christ." Like Mitford, Rowling began to embrace the "God is dead" theology.

Biographer Kirk surmised that "If anyone ever wondered what effect Beatles music's driving beat and imagist lyrics may have had on a young child's life, certainly Jo Rowling's fertile imagination is one potential natural outgrowth," or as Rowling might term it, "organic" outgrowth.

But, this wasn't enough. Jo Rowling wanted to "go darker." Like Rowling's books, her teen life was plunging into the shadowy realm where rebellion was more religion than fashion. At the dawn of the 1980s, Rowling would dive deep and "turn toward alternative tastes" and away from any vestiges of her former amiable personality.[110] This is why she chose 1981 as the beginning of her novel.

Rowling began to adopt, wholeheartedly, the dreary frenetic look of the "punk" rockers, favoring musical groups like "The Clash" and "The Banshees" (The Banshees adopted their name from the spirit ghosts of Blarney, Ireland.) The Banshees were among Rowling's favorite and the young author-to-be began to imitate their heavy black eye make-up, black lipstick and black fingernails. The blacker, the bleaker, the better. The "punk" lifestyle was just the latest counterculture fad of disaffected youth whose common denominator was boredom. And Rowling was bored of small town life and the affliction in her home life was depressing her constantly. Rowling wanted bright lights—big city. Jo Rowling wanted self-gratification and *stimulation*.

Soon, the Banshees would "transmutate" into yet another self-absorbed angry youth subculture known as Goth, which attracted Rowling even more because of its fascination with darkness, despair and death. (This 3-D doctrine of Goth culture is the very same "triple-D" doctrine of hip-hop culture.) The Banshees would influence a new generation of sicko—Goth sub-derivatives, spawning such memorable groups as "Jane's Addiction," "Jesus and Mary Chain," "Garbage" and the ever popular favorite of West Country youth, "Jack Off Jill."

The Goth culture which Rowling was embracing well into college and beyond as her favorite lifestyle would be tagged with names such as "Gothic Rock," "Death Rock" or simply "Deathers." Any relation to Deatheaters is surely coincidental. And even more Goth music groups would spring up with names like "Sisters of Mercy" and "Christian Death."

Kirk notes that this ecliptic shadow graphic lifestyle became a prominent park of J.K. Rowling's life, "With home as a place to try to get away from, Jo took up smoking and dove deeply as she could into her alternative music, Gothic look."[111] Writer April Lynch termed this fascination with Goth culture as "Dancing on the Darkside."[112]

Yes, these are the same people you see at the shopping mall on Saturday night with the oversized black bell-bottoms collecting lint and dust as they drag the dirty floors; the jet-black hair and faux-silver chains hanging from neck to waist; the pale skin; the slumped shoulders; the black lipstick and eyeshadow; the pentagrams and black tee-shirts and, most noticeably, the oozing, infected lips, ears, and tongues from self-inflicted body-piercing and "body cuts." This makes the food-court a place to avoid no matter how hungry you are for a side-order of fries.

To understand Goth, like understanding the influence of Jessica "Decca" Mitford, is to complete the full picture of who J.K. Rowling used to be, and continues to be, in the very center of her "creative" heart that drives her gloomy imagination and writing. Goth culture has formed the contemporary worldview that encompasses the modern day persona of J.K. Rowling.

"Azhrarn," pronounced Azh-răn, is a self-described "Goth" who has chronicled the history and philosophy of the sub-cult. He also maintains one of the most popular sites on the web titled "Defining Goth." In a nutshell, Goth can be boiled down to a credo of "Live, let live, and leave a really good looking corpse."[113] An earlier slogan from the 1980s was, "I want to die, die, die." Like hip-hop and rap, there is "old school" and "new school" Goth.

And, the founders of this twisted incarnation of the Lost Generation give much credit to the alcoholic, drug-addicted perverts of the Beat generation such as Kerouac, Burroughs and Ginsberg. Another example of how the media elevated these Greenwich Village junkies to role-model status for untold future generations.

Azhrarn details the morbid self-made religion that Goth has become. "The central ideal that characterizes Goth is an almost compulsive drive towards creativity and self-expression that seeks to reach out and *ensnare* its audience using our current society's covert but deeply rooted fascination with all things *dark* and *frightening*. This act can be either *subtle* and *seducing* or *nightmarishly frightening*. The mediums of self-expression and creation can be anything from a mode of dress to *novels* or music."[114]

Basically, Harry Potter is the product of the Goth-cluttered mindset of its author complete with rebellion, fear, subtlety, frightening images, murky messages, and intentional moral ambiguity and a death culture fascination. There are really no *clear* messages that can be derived from the Harry Potter books and movies, and that's exactly what Rowling intended. What more would you expect from a Goth punk rocker . . . from hell?

Azhrarn continues to explain that Goth is an expression of frustration with their parents. Goths feel that they are "oppressed" by the adult generation (How many countercultures have we heard sing from that broken record?) But, the Goth historian does shed light on Rowling's consistent and dangerous view that children need to be "liberated" from their parents and released into an ethically voided world with an emphasis on ungrounded "organic growth" into adulthood. As Rowling herself said, children need to be set free to "do what they have to do."[115]

In other words, parents beware! When your child smears feces on the bedroom wall and tells the two of you to "F____ off" if you don't like it, just remember, the little tot is only doing "what they have to do." A pat on the head and a rambunctious "Good for you" will do the child good.

* * *

Rowling continued to maintain her Goth lifestyle for years to come. By age 17, Rowling had actually made friends with a boy named Sean who sported a "post-punk haircut" of the "New Romantic Spandau Ballet" sub-branch of Goth that descended from a "Punk" spin-off of the "New Wave" fusion movement. (Are you keeping up? Are you getting a better picture of J.K. Rowling?) Sean had a license and a car and that meant freedom from the fascist establishment oppression of small town life and home which was impeding the mental stimulation of her splendid fantasy nightmares.

Other than soaking up the darkside of nightlife, not much is known of Rowling's years at Secondary School and, again, questions to her about this time are off-limits to reporters. As for her earlier, primary school years, Rowling did slip up once and vent about her disdain of small town life and their "inhabitants."

During a radio interview to an audience of young children, Rowling volunteered about the trauma of moving from a big city to a small town and the pent-up hatred it engendered even into adulthood. "We moved from a school in Bristol, which is obviously a large city, and we moved to this tiny village school and I *hated* it. We had roll-top desks and I had a real dragon [bitch] of a teacher, who is now (dead), so I can speak freely."[116]

That kind of "punk" attitude from an adult cannot be lost on the impressionable minds of young children. While Rowling may be an adult, she is far from a mature adult and the manifestations of her adolescent Goth fascination is serving as a disastrous role model for children, in both her own public persona and in the "adult" characters in *Harry Potter*. J.K. Rowling is deconstructing the "parent" and "adult authority" in order for children to be the final arbiter of character and not mature adults. This is all part of the Goth "payback is hell" anti-establishment religion she practices.

J.K. Rowling continued her Goth lifestyle and death obsession throughout her university days at Exeter in the early 1980s during the heyday of "Dungeons and Dragons" and "Witches and Warlocks." The games were popular among university outcasts, upstarts and "lipsticks." It was a time when bored university students of the Goth variety experimented with the occult through "readings" at college bookstores and initiating impromptu séances and engaging in necromancy.

Rowling will not say whether or not she ever participated in the penumbra occult "adventures" of college life or communicated with practitioners of adept knowledge. The only statement she ever made, and never made again, was that, "I've always been interested in it." Of this time, biographer Kirk noted that Rowling liked "to think of herself as idealistic and radical."[117]

By 1990, the Goth punker Jo Rowling was twenty-five-years-old and still clinging to the fusion fashion fascination with darkness and death. Interviewing for a job in Oporto, Portugal as an English teacher, Rowling was sporting a "heavy black eye make-up that was showing an even more mournful look."[118] A small black tear-drop was painted under the left eye-lid. The headmaster was shocked that she would show up for an interview looking like the walking dead.

After a decade of dancing on the darkside, Jo Rowling was now in the total grip of full-time suicidal thoughts, rehearsing in her mind different scenarios that would leave her body bloody and breathless. "I really plummeted," she was quoted by the AP in early 2008. After nine months of intensive cognitive behavioral therapy, she returned to at least a basic semblance of sanity, though her grim attitude persisted.

Despite her frightening and depressingly bleak appearance, her high honors from Exeter were hard to ignore. Rowling was hired with the subtle understanding that she at least lighten her eye shadow, which she did during the school day, but quickly reapplied for the nightlife and weekends when she transformed into the "Queen of Moonacre Valley."

During this time, at the height of Rowling's Goth love affair, she began to see "visions" of a boy wizard during a delayed trip to Manchester. As Kirk described the event, "It was as if she had been put under a magical spell."[119]

By 1994, just short of her 30th birthday, the Goth make-up would start to disappear, but the roots of her Goth worldview would remain with her. Rowling's publishing success would arrive only three years later and spawn a media empire based on Harry Potter's seven books, movies, DVDs, video-games, mass-merchandising and a presence on the web that is second only to internet pornography.

Rowling has said in the past that religion plays a role in the Harry Potter stories, but she couldn't discuss it because readers might "figure out the plot." This was a very clever line because it was a very clever lie. It was necessary to make such a proclamation so as to sucker any of the world's religious followers into stumbling over themselves at the bookstore in hopes of finding a parallel to their beliefs.

Additionally, in 1999, Rowling said she couldn't reveal the "religious" component until the end of Book Seven. However, long after the book was released, I called again to Scholastic, Inc. publishers to find out what that component was, since she obviously forgot, again, to fulfill a promise. And, again, no phone calls were returned. And her agent, Christopher Little, was "unavailable."

J.K. Rowling's "membership" in the Church of Scotland was also a very well crafted ruse. Membership in the Church of Scotland would help spread the "image" of Rowling as a Christian, guaranteeing the earliest book sales in Scotland, Wales, Ireland and Great Britain. And, publishing success in the United Kingdom meant broader publishing success in America.

Any *genuine* member of the Church of Scotland would express a keen interest in the moral growth of their audience of readers, whether they be children or adults. Lev Grossman of *Time* magazine conducted an exclusive interview with Rowling, no strings attached, and wrote that the author "refuses to view herself as a moral educator to the millions of children who read her books."[120] Rowling explained that thinking in moral terms is "not healthy." And, God would serve no purpose in the new world of Harry Potter.

* * *

A Biblical scholar of Christianity and the occult, Dr. Wilbur Smith, best summarized the literary and entertainment industry's three phases of bashing the faithful; the "confrontational" attack, the "sophisticated" attack, and the "back-door" attack: "As the soul of man becomes increasingly depleted spiritually and the idea of God grows dimmer and dimmer in the souls of men, man's soul becomes, as it were, an undefended fortress into which these evil powers have easy access."[121]

This is why the Culture War has reached critical mass. These three forms of bashing the faithful can be found every year in the hundreds of feature films, television movies, sitcoms and episodic drama that flood the airwaves and movie screens. Recognize Hollywood value manipulation for what it is, an assault on your values—no matter how subtle or discreet.

The story of Harry Potter cannot be separated from the story of its author J.K. Rowling. The debate that now rages just beneath the radar screen has much more to reveal than the adroit harnessing of adept powers by wizards and witches. Rowling's story is an allegorical crusade of how she would like to see certain "world orders" dismantled into a New Age world of "liberating" values. Like her definition of magic, these liberating values are "neutral" and can be used for good or bad. In other words, moral relativity.

J.K. Rowling's world of Harry Potter is at once a history lesson and a roadmap to the decline of Western Civilization. Because the mainstream press and even many faith-based publications have stopped the discussion to avoid alienating or dividing their own readership, we will bring it out in the open, in depth, in the following chapter so you can decide for yourself about the future course of good and evil in the modern world.

Many of J.K. Rowling's followers have no belief system or are thinly grounded in a belief system that is easily expendable. As John Ratzenberger said, "If you grow up believing in nothing, you'll grow up believing in anything." These are the victims that have been ensnared by J.K. Rowling.

MORE BACK DOOR ATTACKS FROM HOLLYWOOD

While Harry Potter is the largest and most visible version of the back door attack against Christians and Jews, Hollywood has produced a number of other titles that glorify, glamorize and promote occult practices while taking a broad stroke against the faith-based community.

It is no coincidence that Time-Warner is the producer for all the Harry Potter movies. Of all the major entertainment conglomerates, only Time-Warner and Universal continue to be the most persistent and virulent in its attacks on Christians and Jews in all three of the categorical "attacks" covered in this chapter.

Time-Warner found time to release another "attack" film even during its busy schedule of filming the fifth installment of the Harry Potter series in 2006. In that same year, the company still nicknamed "Slime-Warner" for its consistent output of vulgar, low-estate entertainment, released another Christian-bashing, Jew-jabbing movie that was a combination of the *confrontational, sophisticated,* and *back-door* attacks.

According to Dr. Ted Baehr of *MovieGuide* magazine, "Time-Warner is continuing that policy by releasing *V for Vendetta*—a vile, pro-terrorist piece of neo-Marxist, left-wing propaganda filled with radical sexual politics and nasty attacks on religion and Christianity."[122] The movie, promoted as a "retro-gothic mythical mystery" turned out to be a grand plethora of Hollywood's and Time-Warner's social/sexual/political agenda messages weaved throughout the plot including a genuine sympathy for terrorism, bashing the world's democratic leaders who are fighting terrorism, promoting radical homosexual heterophobia and, as Dr. Baehr describes the audio overlay during the ending credits, " . . . actual recordings of radical feminist Gloria Steinem spewing her brand of male-hating, Christian-bashing, androgynous sexual politics."[123] The movie is also cleverly laced with anti-Semitic undertones throughout.

When *V for Vendetta* received a lukewarm reception at the box-office, Time-Warner waged one of their biggest marketing campaigns ever for a DVD release with enormous center-aisle display cases at the big-box retailers and video rental stores. The marketing campaign far surpassed what any other movie with a failing grade would receive at the retail level with a record *four* separate DVD jacket covers including one in 3-D!

Perhaps this movie was intended as the long-awaited counter-attack by Time-Warner against Sen. Bob Dole, William Bennett, C. Delores Tucker and the faith-based community who exposed Time-Warner's ultra-violent, hyper-sexual and profane entertainment agenda twenty years earlier. A more accurate title for the film that flopped might have been *V for Vengeance*.

MOVIE, TELEVISION, AND DVD "BACK DOOR" ATTACKS

With the rising popularity of DVD, Video-On-Demand and downloadable entertainment products, Hollywood has kept alive feature films and television shows that utilize the back door attack on faith-based people. Viewers who purchase these productions will not know anything about the content due to the deceptive labeling of the Ratings Scheme, which has no category for "Occult Content." So, we will list a few of the high-profile back door attack productions that have been released on DVD.

It's important to point out first that the Harry Potter series is available on DVD up to the fifth installment as of this writing and all seven are predicted to be available by 2011. As Rowling promised, the story gets darker with each installment and the MPAA finally had to put a "PG-13" on the fourth film, whereas the first three were rated PG. If the Ratings Scheme board at the MPAA had not been desensitized and "dumbed down" over the last 30 years, the fourth film would definitely have been rated "R" and the first three would have surely been rated "PG-13."

It is also very imperative to note that the first three DVDs offer much more material than the movie theater audience was treated to. These are called "challenges" on the DVD covers which include "lessons" on how to mix magic potions, perform transfigurations, casting spells and even "how to catch a snitch." The DVDs are far worse than the movies because they offer these "added features" that are not only presented in bad taste, but are indicative of J.K. Rowling's true agenda to "teach" her predatory New Age worldview.

- *The Golden Compass*—Based on a book in the children's "Dark Series" by lifetime atheist author Phillip Pullman, this story follows the "adventures" of a young girl (Dakota Blue Richards) who lives in a "parallel universe." Leave it to the veteran Christian-bashers at Warner Brothers to bring Pullman's "anti-God" hatred fantasy to the big screen. Unlike Rowling, Pullman does not hide his disdain of Jews and Christians. The movie was "toned-down" just enough to trick parents and children into seeing the movie during the 2007-2008 Christmas holiday season—a subtle slap at Christians. Due to extensive word-of-mouth and e-mail campaigns about Pullman's agenda, the $180 million movie bombed at the domestic box office. The third and final installment, *The Amber Spyglass*, scheduled for a 2010 release, planned to "let loose" with Pullman "killing God." Warner is having second thoughts.
- *Buffy the Vampire Slayer*—This TV series is best described by the season 3 DVD jacket cover, "A new slayer named Faith arrives in town, quickly winning over all of Buffy's friends . . . a few nights later she encounters Angel, who has somehow returned, feral and violent from the hellish demon dimension where Buffy had sent him." (Faith and Angel are curiously cast as the "bad guys".) This series eventually regresses into promoting radical homosexual heterophobia and actual occult practices.
- *Charmed*—Again, the best description is from the jacket cover itself from the complete first season. "The discovery that they are the descendants of a long line of witches finds three sisters battling demons and warlocks—and occasionally each other—they learn that each have a unique power"—(moving objects, freezing time, seeing into the future).
- *Tru Calling*—Seeing into the past of an individual is the same as seeing into the future by accessing the occult power known as psychic fortune-telling. This TV show, now on DVD, is a Hollywood hybrid of necromancy and New Age retro-psychic occultism. As the DVD cover summarizes, "What if you could change the future by reliving the past? A forensic scientist relives the previous day of the dead to try and save them."
- *Ghost Whisperer*—This contemporary TV show on CBS is summarized on the program's official website: "A young newlywed (Jennifer Love-Hewitt) endowed with the unique ability to communicate with spirits, has spent her entire life coping with this extraordinary gift, but who also

yearns to lead an ordinary life—if only the dead would stop talking." This show has a Hollywood psychic on staff as "technical advisor." Despite falling ratings, CBS renewed the show for another season in 2007. Considered CBS president Les Moonves' favorite TV show.
— ***Medium***—Another contemporary TV show with past episodes now appearing on DVD starring Patricia Arquette as Allyson Dubois, a "full-time" necromancer out to solve crime. "Everyday Allyson Dubois wonders if her psychic power is a blessing or a curse . . . despite the strain on family and danger . . . how can she refuse when the dead are calling out for justice?"
— ***Sabrina The Teenage Witch***—This TV show preceded and overlapped the Harry Potter series and helped to desensitize and "dumb down" children to the dangers of esoteric occult practices. The "cute young witch" casts spells and curses with the "intention" of doing good, though *good* is a morally relative value in the series just as it is in Harry Potter. The TV show, now on DVD, is a rehashing of the "good witch" and "bad witch" fallacy.
— ***The Craft***—This 1996 movie, transferred to DVD, began the Hollywood screenwriter's ongoing fascination with depicting *very young* girls as witches. As Leonard Maltin described the film in his *Movie and Video Guide*, "Four teenage girls, students at a private Los Angeles school, dabble in witchcraft. At first, they're gleeful about their powers, but eventually things get out of hand." The ending is a full-fledged occultic disaster.
— ***Bedazzled***—This feature film attempts to inject "sexy" humor into the depiction of the devil coming to wreak havoc on the life of a starstruck "dork." The front cover of the DVD contains a quote from *US Weekly*, "Hell-aciously funny." Elizabeth Hurley stars as the devil whom the studio describes in typical Hollywood-hokum promo-speak, "The devil has never been so *hot* or more hilarious."
— ***The Sixth Sense***—Buddhist director M. Night Shyamalin directed this feature-turned-DVD about a little boy who not only sees dead people, but carries on lively conversations with them. This child-necromancy glamorization was the product of a Disney collaboration, which embraced the anti-Christian undertones of Shyamalin (under the Michael Eisner regime). Fortunately, the director had a meltdown with Disney after directing his highly self-indulgent film, *Lady in the Water*, which was picked up by none other than the anti-God Warner Brothers in July 2006 and proceeded to bomb at the theaters and on DVD racks.

* * *

THE HOLLYWOOD CULTURE WAR

These are just a few of the more prevalent examples of Hollywood's back door attack on faith-based peoples. Increasingly, broadcast and cable television are creating and unveiling more of these kind of occult-based "entertainment" storylines.

In many cases, the attacks on God, Jews and Christians are transitioning more toward the *confrontational* attack. According to Darryn Simmons of *The Montgomery Advertiser*, "Shows such as *Family Guy, American Dad,* and *South Park* are constantly taking potshots at God and religion in general. Some portray Christ as a womanizer, others as clueless."[124] In one scene on *South Park*, Jesus is portrayed defecating on the American flag! Episodes like these are further justification for complete a' la carte cable choice by consumers, which will be discussed in detail later in the book.

The famous Yiddish writer Isaac B. Singer was well-known for his quote, "You write best what you know best." If Hollywood is any indication, then Tinseltown screenwriters and their counterparts in literary fiction, like J.K. Rowling, maintain a well-articulated and vast knowledge of the occult and the aphotic world of the demonic.

CHAPTER 23

J.K. ROWLING'S NEW WORLD DISORDER

*Nowadays, showbiz is
the religion of the masses.*
—Timothy Gray
Variety

"Death is the central theme of the books," J.K. Rowling declared to a Canadian radio audience in October of 2000. As the last chapter demonstrated, J.K. Rowling's world of Harry Potter is much more than a debate about the existence and exercise of witchcraft and the pernicious summons of dark powers for ambivalent crusades.

Rowling has been exposed for her bleak deconstructive worldview that she cultivated as a Goth teenager, once openly wearing her defiance as fashion, and then discarding the black lipstick for the black ink pen. The story of Harry Potter is the story of J.K. Rowling and her voluminous metaphor of moral relativity in politics, society, religion and culture.

As biographer Connie Ann Kirk noted, Rowling considered herself as an "idealist" and most notably as a "radical." She is still a radical who learned to keep quiet and subvert her message through the written word. And the message is an anti-establishment diatribe that is both a reflection and promoter of Western Civilization's decline and the decay of any cohesive society around the globe. There is a reason, cloaked in darkness, Rowling pushed for the book to reach into 100 countries in over 60 languages.

The "blackout" by the mainstream media, beginning in late 2002, was the most brazen move ever taken by the press to stifle even the most modest criticism of J.K. Rowling's writings. In fact, never before had a piece of fiction published in England and America been so "protected" and its critics so "demonized" than the publicity farce surrounding the Harry Potter books.

The whole story of Harry Potter is a magnifying glass of J.K. Rowling's condescending and misanthropic worldview through both her childhood and adult eyes. As a teenager, this allowed her to be "cool." As an adult, it allows her to be "famous." Rowling learned how to creatively harness mankind's base appeal to power for the sole sake of power alone.

But, her contempt is evident to the keen observer who recognizes the reality behind the "parallel cultures" that reside in the core of Harry Potter's world. There are the "magical" people, like Rowling, who live in the esoteric world of elitist, snobbish arrogance in which their secret knowledge of sublime powers trump the "other" culture of "muggles," simple-minded suburbanites, plain and middle-class, who she paints as petty little people who know not the "power of magic." Their simplicity is portrayed as a grinding bore where everybody is a Dursley, mean-spirited and just plain "normal."

Rowling prefers "disorder" because it is more "exciting," whether that disorder is a young child choking on slimy black slugs or the ever-present specter of sudden death befalling children and adult alike in Harry Potter's contorted world.

Rowling's ability to captivate children through morbid attractions of revolting visions reduces Rowling to the level of a literary mental molester of children's minds. True to her Goth mindset, the boy wizard author privately disdains even her public of devoted readers.

One of the quiet victories J.K. Rowling has enjoyed is the virtual disappearance of the earlier and wider public debate over her books and the movies adapted from them. Rowling and her editors at Scholastic have managed to mobilize an attack machine on anybody who would criticize the Harry Potter books or the author herself. Rowling has plenty of blind supporters in the print press and electronic media—secular and religious.

Much of the debate continues, thankfully, without the slanted mass media coverage as the dialogue now reaches a larger audience through the internet and alternative media. One factor that turns off the secular press and certain mainstream Christian publications is the recurrent references to the existence, or the lack thereof, concerning magic and the dark arts. They will not even enter the debate concerning these core issues.

Inevitably, Christian detractors of Rowling will, as they should, quote their book of authority by citing Bible verses. This appalls the secular media to such an extreme degree that some will resort to foaming at the mouth, falling on their face and crawling on their belly like a live reptile. And, so as to avoid a potentially ugly scene, the debate is squashed before it can begin. What few conversations about Rowling's books that do hit mainstream presses are predetermined editorials intended to misrepresent the debate by simply ignoring the wider implications of her "entrenched messages."

We have decided to bring the deeper details of the Harry Potter debate to this chapter in order to resurrect the voices shot down by Rowling and Scholastic Press. Whether you agree or disagree with any side of the debate is up to you. We made the conscious decision not to be intimidated by the J.K. Rowling Wrecking Ball Express.

ROWLING'S DEFENDERS

J.K. Rowling's defenders in the Harry Potter debate encompass the broad spectrum of American and global culture from the secular press, academia, the public library and public education system, a significant number of writers from the Christian press, clerics and entire church congregations desperate to find something—anything—that could be gleaned as "redeeming" in a book series that has sold 340 million copies worldwide. In the eyes of her defenders, Rowling must be doing something right if she became a billionaire in less than eight years after releasing her first book.

As for Rowling's supporters, most of their arguments, again, hover on sheer fascination and celebrity worship of the author as self-made pauper to princess *or* they eagerly attempt to draw strong allusions to Harry Potter as an allegory to some greater work, ranging from Milton's *Paradise Lost* to the Bible itself. Unfortunately, Rowling's defenders are extremely naïve as to the author's true intentions to spread a New Age secular agenda across the globe.

Rowling *is not* naïve in the least by this campaign of value manipulation. And, she certainly isn't going to dissuade her mutual admiration society because they represent a wide cross-section of philosophical, ideological and religious persuasions that help sell her books, even though most of them are clueless. Rowling's greatest tool is her silence.

This wasn't always the case. In the first couple of years after the 1997 debut of the first Harry Potter book, Rowling tended to be a little more open about her background and beliefs. By late 2001, she learned and was *instructed* by her "handlers" to very politely "Shut-Up."

As for the fascination factor alone, the following headlines will show just how much the secular press has engaged in celebrity worship unseen since the unanimous press accolades showered on Martin Scorsese in 1988 for *The Last Temptation of Christ*. In Rowling's case, the press has, in effect, become a voluntary subsidiary of the enormous Harry Potter publicity machine that has felt honored to be a participant and promoter of "Pottermania." As a result, by 2007 the media had virtually snuffed out any of the debate that surrounded the book's earlier releases. Some examples of the press fawning over Harry Potter:

THE HOLLYWOOD CULTURE WAR

"HARRY POTTER CHARMS A NATION"
-Telegraph—London 7/25/98

"SPELL OF BEST-SELLER MAGIC"
-The Scotsman 10/28/98

"MISCHIEF WITH A MAGICAL ALLURE"
-The Scotsman 6/27/98

"MAGICAL MYSTERY LURE OF A WIZARD WRITER"
-Birmingham Post 7/10/00

"CHARMED I'M SURE"
-Washington Post 10/20/99

"HARRY POTTER AND THE MAGIC KEY OF J.K. ROWLING"
-Associated Press 7/6/00

"MAGICIAN FOR MILLIONS"
-Newsweek 8/23/99

"ROWLING PROMISES SEX AND DEATH IN POTTER BOOKS"
-The Guardian Unlimited 12/28/01

"THE MAGIC OF POTTER"
-Time 12/25/00

"WIZARD WITH WORDS"
-Telegraph Magazine 7/3/99

"A WIZARD OF WORDS PUTS SPELL ON KIDS"
-The Newark Star Ledger 8/14/99

"HARRY POTTER AUTHOR WORKS HER MAGIC"
-Family Education 8/99

"HARRY POTTER CASTS SPELL OVER WASHINGTON"
-Reuters 8/19/99

"SPELL BINDER"
-People 7/12/99

MICHAEL VINCENT BOYER

"WILD ABOUT HARRY"

-*Time* 9/20/99

"BOY WIZARD FREES TRAPPED MOTHER"

-*London Sunday Times* 12/6/98

From the academic/religious community of J.K. Rowling promoters comes one of her most bizarre apologists, John Granger, who wrote a book titled *The Hidden Key to Harry Potter*. This book is especially popular among some Christians who are straining and stretching in their vain search for redemptive entertainment. Granger attempts to make the point that Harry Potter is not only an allegorical Christian tale; it is *profoundly* Christian.

If any writer came in second to Rowling in the field of wide-eyed fantasy storytelling, Granger would win by a landslide. First, like many supporters of Rowling—including the author herself—the defense begins with a blistering attack on anyone who would even dare to criticize J.K. Rowling or the story of Harry Potter.

Granger fires off plenty of pages attacking very bright, seasoned writers and authors such as William Safire and Harold Bloom, calling their reviews of Harry Potter "low-road criticism."[1] This allows Granger, a Greek and Latin teacher in Port Halock, Washington, to then elevate himself to "enlightened" scholar so he can proceed uninterrupted.

Columnist Dave Kopel attempts to describe Granger's grand "allusions" by explaining how "The phoenix (which saves Harry's life in *Chamber of Secrets*) rises to life from its own ashes, and is described by T.H. White as the 'resurrection bird.' This explains the title, *The Order of the Phoenix*—that is, the alliance of people who band together to fight for resurrection values.[2] *Order* also evokes the fighting Christian religious orders of the Middle Age, such as the Order of the Knights of Malta."[3]

Granger also makes the pale attempt to explain the *meaning* behind characters' names, going so far as to say that Harry Potter's father, James, is the same name as Jesus' brother and Harry's mother, Lily, must surely be a reference to the Easter Lily flower.

Can you say "stretch?" How about "BIG STRETCH?" In fact his stretches eventually cause foot-in-mouth syndrome.

As Granger enthusiastically explains, "In the climax of *Chamber of Secrets*, Harry descends to a deep underworld, is confronted by two satanic minions (Voldemort and a giant serpent), is saved from certain death by his faith in Dumbledore (the bearded God the Father/Ancient of Days), rescues the virgin (*Virgin*ia Weasley), and ascends in triumph. It's *Pilgrim's Progress* for a new audience."[4]

Pilgrim's Progress!? That would be an insult to Milton. And Dumbledore as God? Listen to J.K. Rowling herself when *Time* magazine writer Lev Grossman asked Rowling about her faith, a "no-no" which, of course, left Rowling "cagey." But, she did offer that " . . . obviously Dumbledore is not Jesus."[5]

Granger must have been dumbfounded, considering that Rowling made the comment three years after his book came out. On two more occasions, Rowling would completely contradict some of Granger's other far-fetched name-association metaphors. But, that didn't bother Rowling. Granger was just another voluntary dupe in her publicity train.

And, Granger was not deterred in his unwavering faith that Rowling was writing the ultimate allegorical masterpiece to the Bible. Granger even claimed to have discovered the *hidden key* to Harry Potter's name, according to Kopel, "Well, the name does *evoke* Harry Hotspur, the prince Hal of Shakespeare's histories. But, *if* you say it with a French or Cockney accent, it also reminds us of 'heir.' For 'Potter,' Granger tells us to look to the Bible's 'Potter verses' (Isaiah 64:8), in which God is described as the potter who shapes man out of clay."[6]

Granger left out the fact that, as a child, Rowling had neighbors named Mr. and Mrs. Potter. Nor did he mention that the same area where Rowling grew up, the West Country, was long known as the lifetime residence for the locally famous writer, Dennis Potter. Granger also neglected the fact that the Wicca witch religion has its own very specific definition for "Potter."

To again paraphrase Bob Hope, "Please . . . please don't . . . please don't stop laughing."

As for redemptive motifs and symbolism, Dr. Ted Baehr notes that "the phoenix and hippogriff that appear in the second and third Potter books have their origins in *Greek myth*, not Christian writings" and notes that Granger's "conclusions betray a lack of linguistic understanding."[7]

The Hidden Key to Harry Potter is filled with words like "evokes," "suggests," "reminds," "could be," and the game of charades popular retort "sounds like . . ." Dr. Baehr also reminds us that "Granger ignores the lying and deceit that occur in these books."[8] And that deception and crafty manipulation bares the distinct imprint of Rowling's warped mindset.

Kopel also falls victim to Rowling's lies by incorporating the central word of contention, *magic*, into his analysis and the perpetration of the "diagonal defense" theory, "The Potter books are a magical work aimed to *liberate* readers from materialism and to elevate their spirits. Harry leaves the temporal world by entering Diagon Alley—that is, by moving diagonally, not in the lines of the ordinary material world . . . a world which Rowling shows can be put aside if one can think and live *diagonally*."[9] What?!

In the United States, the public education system has been at the center of much debate over the proper place for Harry Potter in public-funded arenas.

After the books first arrived in America from Great Britain, the U.S. publisher, Scholastic, Inc., sent copies to practically every school library in America including most municipal and county-funded public libraries.

Since the 1999 American release of *Harry Potter and the Sorcerer's Stone*, more than thirteen states have put certain restrictions on reading Harry Potter in classrooms. As of 2008, school boards, local governments and states continue to debate the proper role of Harry Potter books in school libraries and especially as supplemental textbooks in the classroom.

Author Steven D. Greydanus of *DecentFilms.com* asks, "Is there, then, equally no danger of any young Harry Potter fans—particularly at-risk children whose spiritual development is not being properly cultivated by adequate parental advice—developing an unhealthy infatuation with the idea of magic, and in particular with the idea of studying and learning magic, of mastering magical forces?"[10]

A public school teacher, Ebony Thomas, of Cass Tech High School in Detroit is a "textbook" example of the multitude of Harry Potter promoters in the public school system. Cass Tech has a high proportion of at-risk children whom she teaches. As she explains, "Many of these kids have grown up without parents, but they still have to make moral choices in their lives. Before, these choices have been dictated by church, family, community; now you have to face that alone, and the choice lies within yourself. This is a generation that *really needs* Harry Potter." What's even more frightening is that Ebony Thomas is but one of countless thousands of teachers around the world who see no problem in replacing church and family with Rowling's New Age history book of a morally and ethically void world with a "boy wizard" as the teacher.

In addition to public educators, many of J.K. Rowling's strongest supporters come from the vast nefarious world known as the "witching community," a diverse group of New Age spiritualists known as Wiccans. The name was applied by occult author Gerald Gardner in the late 1940s in an attempt to "organize" the vast number of groups who practiced one form or another of witchcraft.

Among the many different critics of J.K. Rowling, the groups and individuals who practice witchcraft are not counted among the detractors. More specifically, Rowling refers to these followers as "*practicing* witches." In a radio interview, Rowling herself acknowledged, " . . . the two groups of people who seem to think in Britain that I'm wholeheartedly on their side are people who support the boarding school system and practicing witches."[11]

And, Rowling knows this "wholeheartedly" enthusiastic support from the witchcraft community is good for book sales and ultimately movie ticket sales. Rowling has also been very reverent in never criticizing Wiccans or any other form of witchcraft. Quite the opposite, Rowling has taken extraordinary steps to promote this New Age belief system in ways Gerald Gardner never thought possible, with special thanks to Hollywood and the worldwide web.

Dr. Ted Baehr noted in 2003 that, "The High Priest of British White Witches, Keven Carlyon, credited the popularity of the Harry Potter books with an increased level of paganism and witchcraft in Great Britain. Harry Potter has helped to create 'the fastest growing belief system in the world,' Carlyon told the Reuters news service."[12]

The overall New Age movement and its associated business enterprises have thrown their full weight of support behind Rowling. *The Wizard News* published an article in 2003 titled "Harry Potter Good for New Age Business." In the article, *Wizard News* interviewed Sterling Gallagher, owner of the Crystal Fox, "a thriving New Age store located in Laurel, Maryland, where an estimated 1,000 Wiccans live."

The article adds that "His store, a cornucopia of all things New Age, would fit seamlessly into the wizard world of Harry Potter books. Oils, herbs and incense; crystals and tarot cards; brightly painted dragon statues; Celtic and Egyptian goddesses; crystal balls and sphinxes; books on witchcraft, New Age and magic." And, store owner Sterling Gallagher offered, "More adults than children come in under the Harry Potter influence."[13]

The Wizard News article was posted on a web site called HPANA (Harry Potter Automated News Aggregator), one of the thousands of Harry Potter fan sites that litter the web, giving Potterites up-to-the-minute reports on anything relating to the world of Pottermania. These are the hard-core fan base of supporters that literally consider J.K. Rowling and Harry Potter as virtual New Age saviors in their multi-faceted world of ethereal spirituality.

Also, HPANA is a perfect example of how Pottermania is only one click away from the *very real* world of witchcraft and the dark arts. The web article by *Wizard News* mentioned here is peppered with blue-highlighted words that readers can click to hyper-link to "related" witchcraft sites. The Google promos on the same page advertise sponsors that can provide "Free Witchcraft Spells," "Solitary Witch Supplies," "Learn Psychic Reading" and "Death Cults." The site even provides a complete variety of "witch ringtones" for you and your children's cell phone.

Another witching world web site that caters to all things Harry and Rowling is *The Wren's Nest* with the main page banner announcing "The Latest in Witch/Pagan and Mainstream Religious News." The site covers Harry Potter News on a regular basis, catering to that twisted alliance of J.K. Rowling defenders such as phony Christians who also worship ancient Egyptian gods and practice witchcraft simultaneously. It is sites like these that cause Rowling to keep her mouth zipped. When I called for a comment from either her publisher or agent concerning these sites, my calls were *never* returned. This marketing strategy by Rowling and her handlers is known as STS (Support Through Silence).

Rowling does not want to upset the delicate balance of strange bedfellows such as "hybrid" Christian/Pagan/Secular "followers" who will buy the books and see the movies. This supports the assertion that Rowling is the most ruthlessly manipulative author currently shining darkly on the international literary scene. She is a powerful voice for freedom of speech and openness, as long as it doesn't require her to participate.

Rowling's *personal* brand of witchcraft is meant to purposely divide, deceive and conquer, especially among Judeo-Christian communities who are strongly divided between those who see Harry Potter as a "Jesus metaphor" and those who know better. Rowling exploits this division as *good publicity*.

THE CHURCH OF SCOTLAND DEFENSE

Not until the year 2003 did defenders of the J.K. Rowling empire begin to very timidly and quietly release news that J.K. Rowling is a member of the Church of Scotland. The debate does not come down to the sanctity of her faith, but rather, the deceptive motivation behind her affiliation.

One of Rowling's many unofficial, but no less adoring biographers, Connie Ann Kirk, ends her book, *J.K. Rowling: A Biography*, with just two sentences claiming some unnamed source as having *revealed* that Rowling admitted "to believing in God."[14] It sounded more like a coerced confession at the local police department. And, *which* God does Rowling admit to believing in, considering the fact that she is a supporter of the New Age Christian/Pagan Coalition. Could it be Electra, daughter of Agamemnon or possibly Pan, the god of joy?

In the three hundred plus articles, essays, books and interviews that were researched for this book, Rowling herself never talks about being a member of the Church of Scotland. She did admit to going to "church" more than "just weddings and christenings." In one interview with the CBC, Rowling did volunteer a belief in God, but she made it clear that it was fully intended to offend the "South Carolinians" who want her book's usage in public schools limited to certain grade levels. It's statements like these that reveal Rowling's "claim" of Christianity as just another ruse in her struggle to strangle her critics.

She certainly doesn't have to believe in God nor should it even be an issue except that this ambidextrous belief system is something she cultivates and is then reflected in the moral ambivalence of her story.

Time magazine columnist Lev Grossman was one of the few, if not the only journalist who requested, and was granted, an interview with no "pre-set" conditions in a one-on-one meeting with Rowling. As Grossman wrote later, "Interestingly, although Rowling is a member of the Church of Scotland, the books are free of references to God. On this point, Rowling is cagey."[15] [Translation: squirming in her seat.]

Also, despite comparisons to C.S. Lewis and his *Chronicles of Narnia*, Rowling is not the whole-hearted fan of Lewis that her apologists make her out to be. And, contradicting what you may have read or heard, Rowling herself has never finished the Narnia novels. As Grossman noted in his *Time* article, "There's something about Lewis' sentimentality that gets on her nerves . . . Her Hogwarts School is secular and sexual and multi-cultural . . ."[16] As one biographer noted, deep down, Rowling despises C.S. Lewis because of his positive moral messages.

As Rowling explains, "I don't think it's at all healthy for the work to think in [moral] terms. So, I don't."[17] In the 2005 interview with Rowling, Grossman noted that the author was again conspicuously dressed all in black, returning to her Goth-punk-rocker roots—sans the black lipstick, however. Rowling was even sporting the new retro "High-Goth" all-black leather boots complete with three-inch spiked metal heels.

In a 2003 speech, Rowling demonstrated that she is more interested in captivating her audience by sacrificing any moral lessons, " . . . children lose interest when the author is more focused in teaching morals than in captivating them with his or her tale."[18] Three years earlier, Rowling described her fluctuating focus concerning moral lessons in her writing, "I never sit down at the beginning of a novel and think, 'What is today's lesson?' Those lessons, they grow naturally out of the book. I *suppose* they come naturally from me."[19] This is what Rowling refers to as "organic outgrowth," which sounds intelligent, but means absolutely nothing. Sadly, these "lessons" that "come naturally" from Rowling are deeply rooted in her culture of death fascination which she has continuously embraced since her early teen years as the Goth-punk-rocker and its hideously cynical blood-lust philosophy.

The Church of Scotland defense by J.K. Rowling's defenders is a spurious claim. According to the Church of Scotland, "the basis of faith is the Word of God, which it views as being contained in the scriptures of the Old and New Testament."

Rowling's books about Harry Potter are a total contradiction of the Church of Scotland's "basis of faith." However, the Church of Scotland has a unique clause in its doctrine that allows for discussion of "issues other than those relating to basis of faith." If Rowling has chosen that "exemption," then she has taken a "leave of absence" from her faith to indulge in a total immersion of the dark arts and promoting it to the worldwide audience. Doubtful, that is what the Church of Scotland's founders intended by that "discretionary discussion" loophole.

Because Rowling refuses to discuss her faith or membership in the Church of Scotland, three theories have been floated as to her affiliation as a "believer."

1. *The Devout Believer*—Rowling's faithful would like to believe their favorite author falls into this category as one who keeps her belief in God close to her heart. But, her words and actions as an author and as a private citizen expressing her opinion strongly discount this.
2. *The Country Club Believer*—Many critics would agree this is at least partly true, as discussed in the last chapter. Being a "member" of the Church of Scotland gives the "impression" of "Christian credibility" which helps to win over readers of her book among the world's two billion Christians. She refuses to discuss when she made the "strategic" decision to join the church.
3. *The Ulterior Motive Believer*—Other critics make a salient point that she became a believer for ulterior motives that have everything to do with the underlying plot of her seven books. The "God is dead by omission" theory would imply she doesn't believe in *any* "Higher Power." The true affiliation of J.K. Rowling will be rendered obvious at the end of the chapter, again, where *one* observer cut through the murky penmanship and uncovered more than the Church of Scotland *defense* and uncovered the Church of Scotland *motivation*.

* * *

Rowling's supporters have no problem invoking the Church of Scotland defense because they know Rowling, ultimately, is a follower of the "Divine Dichotomy," again, the New Age philosophical pseudo-religious cant that two contradictory truths can exist, neither making the other untrue. This way, Rowling manipulates her readers and supporters and occasionally silences her critics through "contradiction overload."

Biographer Connie Ann Kirk is one of many writers and supporters who "invoke" Rowling's Church of Scotland membership as some "proof" that Rowling doesn't promote dark, malevolent New Age belief systems. Like Rowling, editor Arthur Levine and other defenders, Kirk first attacks the integrity of *anybody* who would dare criticize the Harry Potter author or her books.

Kirk goes so far as to call all criticisms of J.K. Rowling and her story of Harry Potter "mass hysteria."[20] Kirk continues by making a revealing charge that people who dislike Rowling's books are "afraid of witchcraft, the devil and cult behavior."[21] So, does that imply that Rowling *is not* afraid of "witchcraft, the devil and cult behavior" because she "works with it" on a regular basis?

And, although Kirk is not an "official" biographer, she states at the beginning of her book that she received full cooperation from Rowling's editor and Rowling's agent, Christopher Little. Kirk also states that her biography of Rowling was compiled "specifically for student use" and "in response to the high school and public library needs." [22] This is how Rowling spreads her New Age religion in the public and private schools and libraries around the world. If they won't allow Harry Potter books, they don't have a problem with an "unofficial" biography that is, in effect, fully endorsed by Rowling's publisher, editor and agent. In football parlance, it's called the "end-around," another example of Rowling's back-door assault.

* * *

In February of 2008, I tracked down a woman in Atlanta that used to work for a film and video production house in the early 1990's during my five year tenure at the Georgia Film Office. I discovered the former film editor, a self-proclaimed "Wiccan witch," now working for a major international cable news network in downtown Atlanta. During a brief 15-minute break in the lobby of the corporate office, she told me she was still a "practicing witch" and had been for twenty-one years.

I asked her opinion, as a practicing witch, what she thought about the predatory practices of Rowling, her publisher and her defenders to assault the integrity of any critics.

"I'd say that is classic modern day witchcraft, carefully coordinated and executed," she told me in simple matter-of-fact fashion. "[You people] are under the misconception, no doubt learned from reading grade-school story books, that witches are stooped-over, wretched ladies wearing black, wart on the bent nose, and stirring a black pot. Do I fit that description?"

She actually looked the part of the conservatively dressed 54-year old professional woman that she is; briefcase, designer glasses and jet-black Bettie Page bangs.

"They [Rowling and her handlers] operate the same way I do. Just yesterday I invoked witchcraft in order to boost the budget for a subordinate department that works under my direction."

"And how did you use 'witchcraft' to accomplish that?" I asked.

"The very same way, by *making* the CFO feel like a wimp if he didn't agree with me. He knows better than to criticize me, or I'll bring him down to size *again*. That's witchcraft. You don't have to wave a wand or say 'Abracadabra.' It's much more subtle and I suspect J.K. Rowling knows *exactly* what she's doing," the middle-aged witch volunteered with a smirk on her face.

"As for membership in the Church of Scotland," she added, "That means nothing. If I had the time, I could drive you past three churches here on Peachtree Street alone where witches are not only members, but sing in the choir and work administration. It's very popular in Midtown Atlanta to worship multiple gods. That's part of modern Wicca."

She left as quickly as she arrived, a busy Atlanta executive on her way to another meeting, perhaps to perform some witchcraft; perhaps not.

As for Kirk's biography of J.K. Rowling, it may be good that her book is circulating in school systems and libraries around the world. Its front cover is notable alone for displaying the only known publicly released photo of J.K. Rowling dressed as a sorceress-witch, complete with scarlet robe as she holds a crystal ball, staring blankly into the camera's lens with her classic expressionless face—the trademark look of the Goth-punk-rocker from hell.

COMPARISONS TO TOLKEIN AND LEWIS

During the first few years of the 21st century, the Harry Potter books and movies have been released simultaneously with reissued books and new movie versions of J.R.R. Tolkein's *Lord of the Rings* trilogy and C.S. Lewis' *The Chronicles of Narnia*. Inevitably, comparisons between all three series have sparked hundreds of articles, essays and books that argue the pros and cons of linking the three epic works as similar in their fantasy-mystical view of the world, as well as making major *distinctions* among the three as regarding a moral underlying theology or lack thereof. This debate frequently makes comparative similarities between Tolkein and Lewis but establishes a distinctive distance between them and Rowling.

Tolkein and Lewis were members of an Oxford literary group of authors known as "Inklings" who wrote fantasy fiction with at least an *inkling* of Christian faith woven into the plot, though never overtly mentioned. It was an attempt by these two famous authors to "baptize the imagination" of the reader by teaching moral lessons of right and wrong, good and evil. In fact, C.S. Lewis, a prolific Christian writer of the 20th century was an atheist until Tolkein converted him during one of their many marathon discussions on "the meaning of life."

J.K. Rowling, on the other hand, has no moral base other than her Goth-punk cultural lifestyle which left her with a morbidly warped, morose Western European secular worldview cultivated during the late 1980s and throughout the 1990s. Despite that, there are numerous Christian defenders who want desperately to like Harry Potter and, lacking knowledge, have made "wild-eyed" comparisons to the writings of Tolkein and Lewis. Rowling herself does not want to be compared to either.

Because this debate is so vast, it will be touched on only briefly here. Two excellent sources to read that thoroughly dissect this issue are *Frodo and Harry* by Dr. Ted Baehr and Tom Snyder and the essay *Harry Potter vs. Gandalf* by Steven D. Greydanus.

Greydanus' essay centers on "seven hedges" that can be used to differentiate between the three authors. According to Greydanus, "These seven hedges disprove the claim of some Harry Potter fans that parents cannot *consistently* disapprove of the magic in Harry Potter while approving of Tolkein and Lewis. There is no slippery slope here, but a substantial differentiation."[23]

As Greydanus writes, "for to write fiction at all is to imagine at least events, usually persons, and often places that have no real being in the world as God created it . . . Of course, our freedom to re-imagine the world, or to imagine other worlds, is not without limits: We cannot, for example, imagine a world in which love should be evil and hatred good. It's one thing to rewrite the order of creation in fiction (since God *could* have chosen to create the world other than how it is), but quite another to rewrite the nature of the Creator Himself (since God cannot be other than who and what He is)."[24]

Greydanus observed that, most of the time, Rowling's stories offer "no more potential risk to the reader than fantasies about traveling at warp speed like in *Star Trek*, or developing arachnoid super-powers like Spider-Man from the bite of a radioactive spider." He adds, however, that he's "never heard of a single child deliberately incurring a spider-bite, radioactive or otherwise, in an attempt to acquire spider powers . . . but I have heard of many children experimenting with the occult" and adds that "Rowling doesn't share Tolkein and Lewis' moral caution about attempted magic in the real world."[25]

Greydanus, an expert in the occult and its consequences, offers a critical warning about Rowling's aggressive approach in that "the imaginary situations she proposes involve a partial suspension, not only of real-world physics, but also of real-world morality, and that at least one element of the potential appeal of the books may tap into an impulse that ought to be resisted as a temptation, not indulged as a fantasy." Not only is J.K. Rowling's personal brand of witchcraft a taste to avoid in indulgence, Greydanus argues strongly that it "should not be gratified, even in imagination."[26]

POTTERETHICS

Perhaps one of the most decisive and in-depth examinations into the hypocrisy of J.K. Rowling and the Harry Potter series is author Richard Abanes' book *Harry Potter and the Bible*. Before delving into the very real world of witchcraft and its origins, Abanes also touches on the "moral ambiguity and ethical confusion" of the Harry Potter world as created by J.K. Rowling. Abanes calls Rowling's perversion of morality "Potterethics."

To demonstrate how Rowling has even managed to pull the wool over the eyes of the Christian community, Abanes cites a January 2000 article written for the Roman Catholic Journal *First Things*. In the article, Wheaton College literature professor Alan Jacobs gave rave kudos to the Harry Potter books, noting that Rowling's moral compass throughout the volumes "is sound—indeed, I would say, acute." Abanes also points to mainstream news articles that proclaim Harry Potter as the perfect role model to teach children lessons about endurance, kindness, wisdom and love. However, Abanes explains that breaking rules and lying by Harry Potter are almost routine and rarely punished. And, Abanes notes that "The adults in Book One hardly act any better. They not only break other people's rules, but also break their own rules."[27]

Greydanus has noted this also in his essay about Rowling's contorted ethical standards for Harry and his world, "Sometimes Harry is legitimately driven by necessity to break a rule; other times it's only because he feels like it. Harry and his friends are only ever really punished when they're caught by one of the *nasty* authority figures . . . when it's one of the benevolent authority figures, such as genial Dumbledore, or even stern Professor McGonagall, there are no real consequences for breaking any number of rules, because Harry's heart is in the right place, or because he is a boy of destiny, or something like that."[28]

Dr. Ted Baehr and Dr. Tom Snyder, authors of *Frodo and Harry*, also find a wayward moral compass in the life of Harry Potter perpetuated by his creator, Rowling. "Looking at the series as a whole, readers and viewers find Harry blackmailing his uncle, using trickery and deception, lying to get out of trouble and seeking revenge on his student enemies . . . Disobeying rules, practicing witchcraft, consulting the spirits of dead people and lying are all treated as praiseworthy, especially if they are successful."[29]

Columnist Michael O'Brien discovers the heart of Rowling's intentionally cynical manipulation of her readers which sets the entire foundation of her new world disorder. "While Rowling posits the 'good' use of occult powers against their misuse, thus importing to her sub-creation an apparent aura of morality, the cumulative effect is to shift our understanding of the battle lines between good and evil. The border is never defined."[30] Rowling has been reported as "livid" that some have unearthed the true agenda behind her writing about Harry Potter.

Furthermore, Baehr and Snyder describe the two-point nature of J.K. Rowling's back door attack on Judeo-Christian values that she feels have dominated Western Civilization for too long and are in need of deconstruction. As the authors explain, "Her defenders let her get away with it by (1.) creating superficial and even false descriptions of the pagan, occult world view that dominated the Harry Potter series, which tries to appeal to the masses by stealing some moral and redemptive elements from Christianity, and (2.) minimizing the negative impacts that such abhorrent, malignant worldviews, philosophies, theologies and ideologies can have on children, teenagers and adults."[31]

Gabriele Kuby explained the moral relativism cultivated by Rowling as meaning "there's no sure criteria for good and evil—and if that is sunk into the soul, it's dangerous." Kuby also notes that the Harry Potter series Rowling has authored is *truly* "a global long-term project to change the culture" by destroying children's inhibitions against cursing, magic and occult practices.[32]

Potterethics is the main reason Hollywood loves Pottermania. Changing the culture and value manipulation are now the driving motives behind Hollywood film and television production. If the industry can make this agenda "entertaining" at the same time, all the better in getting the message across. Abanes summarizes the dilemma, "These stories also contain material that is both unsuitable and harmful to children . . . and is just problematic."[33]

ROWLING'S DETRACTORS

With a better understanding of the true background and motivations of author J.K. Rowling, the debate inevitably surrounds ethics, morality and the voices of the faith-based community who feel, rightly so, that the Harry Potter books are a stealth attack on their core religious beliefs and the values they stand for. Rowling, her supporters, and the massive Harry Potter publicity machine have tried to "shame" any of their critics, especially the faith-based community, from even suggesting an occult agenda by Rowling. By doing so, Rowling has managed to split the Catholic and Protestant Christian communities and the Jewish faith into two camps—believers and non-believers—in Harry Potter magic, that is.

This divisive tactic worked especially well for *Da Vinci Code* author Dan Brown and Sony Pictures. They exploited the very gap they created by openly marketing a "dialogue campaign" among the faith-based community, spending over $40 million in their highly deceiving campaign where the end result was to create doubt about one's personal faith. J.K. Rowling managed to do the same without spending a single cent on "targeted" marketing.

The first major shock wave for Christians and a victory for J.K. Rowling was an editorial in *Christianity Today* that was published in January of 2000 titled "Why We Like Harry Potter." The article not only gave glowing reviews of the Harry Potter series, it encouraged children and adults alike to read Rowling's books, as if to suggest Harry Potter is "Witchcraft Lite" by telling readers, "We think you should read Harry Potter to our kids . . . The literary witchcraft of the Harry Potter series has *almost* no resemblance to the I-am-God mumbo jumbo of Wiccan circles."[34] Literary witchcraft? Wicca founder Gerald Gardner (1884-1964) started a magazine in the late 1940's with a familiar ring, *Witchcraft Today*, that began as *literary witchcraft* and quickly morphed into *real witchcraft*. It was Gardner who coined the term *Wicca* because it didn't carry the stigma of "witch," *which* no longer bares a stigma thanks to Harry Potter and a world where you can download "witch ringtones" to your cell phone.

While Rowling and her supporters have managed to split opinion in the Catholic church, one Catholic authority who knows better than most about the true menacing jeopardy behind Rowling's writings is Father Gabriele Amorth of the Vatican in Rome. Father Amorth is the Roman Catholic Church's highest authority on the occult and for over twenty years has served as the Vatican's chief exorcist. He has conducted over 3,000 exorcisms from individuals with maligned spirits. When Father Amorth began conducting exorcisms in 1986, Rowling was a 21-year old student still climbing the dark Goth-punk-rocker ladder of Exeter and in the streets and "private" taverns of Devonshire.

Father Amorth does not dance around the word "Devil" and "occult" like Rowling and her supporters are known to do, in addition to becoming "cagey" at the name of *God*. On February 28, 2006, Father Amorth stated very straightforwardly, "You start with Harry Potter, who comes across as a likable wizard, but you end up with the Devil. There is *no doubt* that the signature of the Prince of Darkness is clearly within these books. By reading Harry Potter, a young child will be drawn into magic and from there it is a simple step to Satanism and the Devil."

Father Amorth also reaffirmed the condemnation of the Harry Potter series by Pope Benedict XVI who said that the books were filled with "seductions which act unnoticed" and because of this subtle deception, young believers experience the destruction of "Christianity in the soul, before it can grow properly." Young people have no problem imagining the occult world of Harry Potter, but the same individuals cannot begin to fathom the *real* underworld and the horror it holds if they continue indulging their curiosity.

There are literally thousands of biblical scholars and experts on the occult, past and present, who have written extensively on the dangers involved in exploring the dark arts as entertainment and "leisurely journeys." For many years, studies and research on the occult have only been available in limited texts at certain seminary, theological or university libraries.

But, in the last twenty years, many works on the true nature of the occult have become available through mass printings of formerly out of print books and the immense growth of the mega-bookstores, Christian and faith-based bookstores.

A small sampling of the authors in the field include Derek Prince, Lester Sumrall, Karl Barth, Bishop K.C. Pillai, E. Stanley Jones, Marcia Montenegro, Rufus Mosley, Albert Cliff, Starr Dailey, Larry Huch, Glenn Clark, Thomas B. White, E. W. Bullinger, Caryl Matrisciana, Kenneth "Pop" Hagin, Dr. Jason Kovar, and Joe Schimmel. These are individuals that the mainstream media "conveniently" ignore in their role as "sympathetic journalists" to every word written and spoken by Rowling, suspending their integrity in adoration of the New Age author.

As leader of Fight The Good Fight Ministries, Joe Schimmel has noted that "Every biblical scholar on the occult has denounced the Harry Potter series."[35]

Steven Greydanus also notes that the secondary influences perpetuated by J.K. Rowling and the Harry Potter books are as dangerous as the primary source, which is the original seven books and movies, "What about children who go on to read 'tie in' books, that go into detail about what Rowling doesn't concerning real-life historical beliefs and superstitions concerning magic wands, astrology, hexes, basilisks and so forth . . . is it useful or helpful to read tea leaves, or how astrology works . . . Why are bookstores and libraries putting genuine occult works near the Harry Potter books?"[36]

To make a distinction, "genuine occult works" that find their way right next to the Harry Potter books are not to be confused with scholarly and expert books about the "dangers" of the occult. Books that "promote" the occult like Harry Potter and the "tie-in" books are easy to discern by the very wording and structure of the literature and cover.

As Michael O'Brien explains, "In Potter world the characters are engaged in activities which in real life corrupt us, weaken the will, darken the mind and pull the practitioner down in spiritual bondage. Rowling's characters go deeper and deeper into the world without displaying any negative side effects, only an increase in 'character.' This is a lie."[37]

Speaking of lies, the most-quoted line by Rowling and her defenders which always come back to "haunt" her was the October 23, 2000, interview with the Canadian Broadcasting Company in which she adamantly denied any belief in magic. It only took forty-eight hours for her to forget her "forceful" stand against magic. In an interview with the *Los Angeles Times*, Rowling was asked why "seven" was the number of books she needed to write in order to tell the full story of Harry Potter, to which Rowling replied that seven "is a *magical* number, a mystical number."[38]

One of Rowling's most infamous lies, often quoted by her supporters, comes from an interview in 1999 in which she stated emphatically, "I've met thousands of children now and I haven't met a single one who has told me that they've developed an interest in witchcraft because of my books."[39] She would also claim that no child ever asked her about casting spells. That, too, is untrue.

First, a child doesn't have to tell Rowling they've developed an interest in witchcraft or ask how to cast a spell because she has written the ultimate textbook on the subject, disguised as sugar-coated fiction. And, the tie-in books and web sites, especially the massive Harry Potter Lexicon, go into great detail in a very "authoritative" manner. The web sites are subjects she prefers not to discuss.

The author contradicted herself concerning the subject of children not asking her about casting spells. "It's a real joy," Rowling exclaimed in reference to a young boy who asked her to define the difference between transfiguration and charms. "He was really thinking about this very logically," and Rowling was happy to help.[40]

As for her assertion that not a single child has developed an interest in witchcraft as a result of her books, the web site of her publisher, Scholastic, Inc., maintains a "Discussion Chamber" for Harry Potter fans who write in from around the globe. Their comments are a disturbing testament to the dark desires children aspire to achieve after reading the Harry Potter books:

- "I dream about being a witch so I can get revenge on a few people."

  Rebecca—Age 12

- "I thought the story made you feel that you could be a witch or a wizard."

  Lilly—Age 11

- "Ever since I read Harry Potter it opened up a whole new world for me."

  Christian—Age 10

- "I think divination by numbers is quite interesting . . . I'm fascinated by potions."

  Zany—Age 12

- "I wish I could do magic. If I could do magic, I would be a necromancer."[41]

  Nicole—Age 13

In another Harry Potter "Discussion Chamber," children were asked, "If you were a member of a magical family, what magical items would be in your house?"

- "A closet that takes you where you want, and magical herbs and spices for spells."

  Candice—Age 13

- "We would have a tree that grows money, talking pictures, wands, and moving furniture."

  Natasha—Age 12

- "I would have wands that do a whole lot of spells . . ."

  DJS—Age 9

- "I would have a wand room. A library with spell books."

  Ben—Age 8

- "I'd have a dozen poltergeists around my house guarding it. Then I'd have curses guarding every door."[42]

  Camryn—Age 15

J.K. Rowling approves everything on her official web sites and on the Scholastic-Harry Potter site. This is the same J.K. Rowling who denies any child has ever "developed an interest in witchcraft because of my books." It's obvious to see where Harry Potter gets his "morally relative" view of the universe where the line between truth and lying is always shifting.

DIRE WARNINGS

Rowling knows she hasn't simply "made up" another story of fantasy fiction for children: she has created a whole new layer of dark arts according to scholars and experts in the occult. In a *USA Today* article, columnist Diedre Donahue observed that Rowling " . . . has worked out exactly the intricate laws governing Harry's magical universe in her head."[43] She later put her intricate laws into print for millions of readers to absorb as testified by the children's dark ambitions posted on the Scholastic web site.

Joe Schimmel, producer of *Harry Potter: A Spirit Conspiracy* by Adullam Films notes that there exists in the world numerous forms of occult practices that fall under the categories of witchcraft and sorcery. One form or another is practiced in almost every country of the world. In Haiti, for example, voodoo witchcraft has consumed the entire nation at all levels of government and even most of the major churches. And its effects are blatantly obvious to anyone who has visited the island nation.

As Schimmel notes, "There has never been a unified witchcraft system and Harry Potter is just another form that explores and encourages and seduces children in different forms of the occult that are condemned in the Word of God. And the Harry Potter series does deal with an enormous amount of *real-life* types of witchcraft."[44]

Caryl Mastrisciana of Jeremiah Films has also produced an in-depth video, *Harry Potter: Witchcraft Repackaged*, in which she agrees that "This *is* a *true* representation of witchcraft, and the black arts, and black magic. And yet we have people that say this is merely fantasy and harmless reading for our children. Actually, what makes this *more* dangerous is that it is couched in fantasy language, and children's literature, and made to be humorous and beautifully written and extremely provocative reading, and it just opens up children to want to have the next one. *This* is what is so harmful."[45]

Schimmel is quick to note that Rowling has projected a very real depiction of witchcraft, the kind that would almost require first-hand working knowledge and experience. This is a theme consistently noted by occult experts who are familiar with Rowling's writing.

As Mastrisciana also observed, "J.K. Rowling, the author of Harry Potter, has gone through an awful lot of research. She is very accurate (otherwise, we would have witches all over the country and the world saying 'this is not a true representation of our religion')."[46]

Marcia Montenegro, another expert on occult and New Age practices, agrees, noting carefully that Rowling "is *very* familiar with occult practices, using elements and philosophies behind pagan religions, celtic religions, druid religions, witchcraft and Satanism."[47]

Schimmel, Mastrisciana and Montenegro have unique insight into the occult because all three had fallen victim in their youth by dabbling deeper into horrifically dark worlds of "magical" seduction. Through personal perseverance and intervention by Christian intermediaries well-versed in occult bondage, they were able to escape the intense strongholds of their captivity and have dedicated their lives to helping prevent others from falling into the same snares of the dark arts.

These are the real-life victims and witnesses to the occult that Rowling finds "amusing" and whom the mainstream press totally ignore because they are the "usual Christian suspects." But, the media has no problem gloating over Rowling's nefarious and esoteric world.

Rowling's occult terminology of suspect origin has also not passed unnoticed by author Abanes who writes that "some of the information Rowling uses is not widely known by persons other than those who are *actively involved* in occultism."[48] Clara Sessions, manager of Living Waters Christian Books in Marion, Indiana, gave her frank assessment of Potterethics, "I don't think people fully realize what they're dealing with, and I think anyone who knows anything about spiritual warfare knows that these books can open the door to spiritual bondage. And I think it's worse that children are targeted."[49]

Greydanus agrees with these disturbing trends, noting, "This pattern might involve or lead to other potentially problematic materials such as the *Goosebumps* series and the anti-God fiction of Phillip Pullman (marketed specifically to young people as the children's *Dark Series*)."[50] Greydanus made this prediction in 2001. By late 2007, the same studio that produces the Potter movies, Warner Brothers, released the first installment of Pullman's trilogy about a little girl on a mission to "kill God." Pullman's books could be found on any bookstore bookshelf right next to the Harry Potter books, with no objection from Rowling.

According to a *Washington Post* article by Marguerite Kelly titled, "The Trouble With Harry," even many secular, agnostic, atheist and non-Christian parents have expressed deep concern with the release of all the Harry Potter books and movies. Parents have noticed an *intensely heightened fear* experienced by their children after reading Harry Potter books and watching the movies.[51]

Abanes has picked up on this fear factor by noting that the images Rowling paints by her words and transplanted to movies and DVDs consist of many incidents of "scenes involving gratuitous violence, gruesome images, cruelty and humor that often borders on perversity." These include a character whose head was not "completely" severed after a failed execution attempt with a blunt ax.

A scene strongly suggesting infanticide involves small "plant-creatures" called mandrakes, complete with faces and human features that are pulled screaming from their pots for teachers, wizards and students to kill for experimentation. Another frightening scene involves a student confronting the ghost of a fellow classmate in the Hogwarts school bathroom toilet. And the boomerang curse of Ron vomiting and choking on endless streams of squirming black slugs was a stopping point for many parents who began to question the character of the author herself, who we now know is the adult version of a delirious Goth-punk-rocker who dabbles in "literary witchcraft" for a living. It doesn't help parents that Rowling also boasts proudly that "Death is the central theme of the books."

And that assessment is no mere coincidence or creative flight of fancy. Rowling is fully consumed with the culture of death, and death as entertainment. The Harry Potter books and movies by Warner Brothers never rise above the author's morbid lifelong "death fascination."

Charles D. Chaput, Archbishop of Denver, has seen through the deception of J.K. Rowling and the larger picture that Harry Potter fits into, saying "I think any unusual focus on things like magic and witchcraft is a bad idea." The Archbishop recognizes that the Harry Potter controversy is part and parcel of "bigger and deeper battles going on all over the culture."[52]

J.K. Rowling's nihilistic philosophy and influence on multiple generations simultaneously over a ten year period certainly helped contribute to the bleak vision of a new world disorder as her New Age worldview helped to knock another chip off the foundation of Western civilization, as former British Prime Minister Tony Blair discovered.

WE KNOW HARRY, BUT WHO IS TONY BLAIR?

By 2006, 57% of Americans could identify Harry Potter, but only 50% could identify long-time Prime Minister Tony Blair of Great Britain, one of America's staunchest allies in the war on terror. His term coincided exactly with the ten year run of the Harry Potter books from 1997 to 2007.

And he had to struggle to convince his country and his own Labour Party that the war on terror was worth the sacrifice. Under Blair, numerous terrorist plots were uncovered, aimed at both the United States and Great Britain. And, yet, within Great Britain and the United States, there is an enormous segment of the population that believe this global assault by the Islamist radical terrorists will just go away if we just quit fighting back. If only we could just concentrate, meditate and summon the magical powers of Harry Potter, everything will be "peachy-keen" once again. By the free people of the world failing to fight back against the most radical evil to confront 21st century civilization these "free people pacifists" certainly do believe in magic.

The mainstream media must believe in magic, given their considerable de-facto support to extreme Islamist terror. On Tony Blair's last day in office, the female media-witch incarnation of Neville Chamberlain appeared on CNN to give her "professional" assessment of Blair's decade-long service to England.

In less than five minutes on the air on June 26, 2007, Christiane Amanpour could find very little in the way of accomplishments to attribute to the former Prime Minister. However, with her classic and subtle Amanpour snear, she proceeded to rip Blair apart, suggesting he would be *forever tarnished* and his credibility lost because he allowed his own "downfall" to begin by allying with President Bush in the war on terror. (It was Amanpour who was photographed smiling broadly with Iranian dictator Mahmoud Ahmadinejad in September of 2007.)

Less than one week later as London and Glasgow were targeted by Islamic terrorists, Amanpour conveniently failed to report that new British Prime Minister Gordon Brown banned his fellow government ministries from using the word "Muslim" in connection with "terrorism." He also declared the phrase "War On Terror" be dropped. After all, Gordon Brown was now in the pocket of George Soros, who doesn't believe such a war exists.

In the middle of all this New World Disorder, the French citizens elect Nicolas Sarkozy to replace Sadaam Hussein loyalist Jacques Chirac. And as Britain faded further into the sunset, Sarkozy made it clear that he had no problem defending Western Civilization. Meanwhile, Europe's last Christian country, Poland, refused to allow sexual reorientation textbooks (SRTs) into their classrooms despite angry rants from the European Union and their Ministry of Sexual Reorientation (MSR). This was all a relief to democratic countries who watched Britain's painful castration by the Potterite Party in Parliament.

Great Britain was becoming a *very* Harry Potterworld that July of 2007 as Rowling's final book, "magic" number seven, *Harry Potter and the Deathly Hollows* was being rolled out. At the same time, news was coming out from "old England" announcing bold new curriculums in the public school systems; Winston Churchill, Martin Luther King Jr. and Gandhi were being dropped in favor of global warming studies. English and Literature would place greater emphasis on the study of Harry Potter instead of the classics.

The government was even studying the possibility of replacing the Gross Domestic Product (GDP) index with the Happy Planet Index. Rowling, no doubt, was pleased to see the United Kingdom coming around to her fantasy vision of the world. That was the month the United Kingdom officially came to an end, and with it, the dominos of Western Civilization. The New Age, once the battle cry of the decrepit monster Aleister Crowley, was now official government and educational policy. J.K. Rowling couldn't have been more pleased to see the removal of Churchill as the icon of modern, "free" and democratic Britain. After all, Rowling's Communist idol, Jessica Mitford, surely considered him a capitalist pig who impeded the spread of Communism by declaring an Iron Curtain descending on Europe.

That same summer of 2007, as Britain lay bleeding in the shadow of Rowling's New World Disorder, Paul McCartney was across the Atlantic boasting to Larry King that "Winston Churchill's papers just get browner and crinklier, but our music just gets lighter and brighter." How fitting for one of Rowling's teenage idols to confirm the death of the leader of the free world, by name and country. Of course, old Winston saw it coming long ago. In 1946, only one year after he saved England and Western Europe, with help from the Yanks, he was ceremoniously booted out of office.

That's the kind of thanks you get from your own citizens when you have nothing to offer but blood, toil, sweat, tears and victory at all costs. The British people, deep down, knew that all of this toil could have been avoided if they had just embraced the New Age magic of Adolf Hitler as Chamberlain had suggested, with the magical endorsement of Ambassador Joseph Kennedy and aviation hero Charles Lindbergh.

* * *

J.K. Rowling's promotion of a strictly secular world took deeper root in Great Britain in 2006 as the country's Parliament, House of Lords and House of Commons passed the inaccurately titled law known as the Equality Act. Although Tony Blair was an ally in the War on Terror, he was also an ally with his successor Gordon Brown in supporting the law that has ushered in the most draconian persecution of the Christian Church in Great Britain in over 200 years.

The legislation, which is more properly titled the Sexual Reorientation Act, has empowered a whole new level of British government bureaucracy to take on the enormous task of assessing, organizing and managing the largest sexual reorientation of a nation's population ever attempted in the history of the world. George Orwell was right—he was just off by twenty-two years.

While the law is aimed at preventing discrimination on the basis of "sexual orientation" in the workplace, it is specifically aimed at the Christian Church and the British educational system, public and private. The Sex Act of 2006 comes complete with an extensive *government-mandated* list of SORs (Sexual Orientation Regulations).

Violators or conscientious objectors to the stringent socialist Sex Act can be hauled off to a special tribunal for severe punishment by the British government, as discovered by Reverend Anthony Priddis, Bishop of Hereford who was whisked away for judgment day.

Many Catholic Social Service organizations are deciding to close down or move to neighboring countries where they will not be told by the vast Harry Potter government of England who they can and cannot place children with for adoption. Heterophobic groups in Great Britain are calling for the government to dismember the Catholic Church first, starting with the closing down of the church's educational establishment. After 500 years of persecution, the British *may* have finally succeeded in getting rid of the Catholics, with generous help from the Stonewall Heterophobe Council special interest group.

Just before the law was to be voted on, a constituent wrote to Parliamentarian Alan Simpson asking that he oppose the SOR legislation. Simpson's aide, Paul May, sent back a nasty response with ink screaming from the paper, "You disgust me . . . Perhaps when we have managed to turn all our children gay, the problem of religious bigotry affecting our laws will no longer be an issue."[53] How's that for constituent relations in the New World Disorder?

J.K. Rowling has no problem with this anti-muggle legislation intended to muzzle the Christian church in the United Kingdom, incorrectly believing that the whole issue is about bigotry. As she once pontificated, "Bigotry is probably the thing I detest most . . . the whole idea of that which is different from me is necessarily evil." As usual, Rowling has manipulated and restructured the conversation, pulling out some vague quote without attribution from thin air, just like "magic."

In reality, J.K. Rowling's personal anti-democratic, anti-Christian agenda demonstrates that there is no greater *true* bigotry on the planet than her own private agenda of Potterethics.

Rowling has been a big supporter of the British Sex Act of 2006. On October 19, 2007, she appeared at Carnegie Hall for a reading of Book 7 to a group of very young children when she announced, by the way, "Dumbledore is gay." A former story editor for Warner Brothers has informed me that this theme will be "graphically depicted" as a "flashback scene" in the movie version of the final book set for release in 2010. But, a bigger shock for the audience will be the depiction of Harry in the Epilogue where "Harry will no longer be referred to as *he*, *him*, or even *Mr. Potter*." Apparently, Harry is coming out as a *trans*figured adult in the final cut.

As many British begin packing up and applying for U.S. citizenship to avoid any further religious persecution, they know in the back of their minds that the old trans-Atlantic motto of "What's good for the Brits is good for the Yanks" may prove a real issue of borrowed time in the New World. With that in mind, the new Brits coming to America will first avoid Massachusetts and San Francisco.

Perhaps San Francisco radio talk host Michael Savage had a point when he said Britain became a degenerate society once they took down the Union Jack and began puking on car fenders as a national sport. In the meantime, Gordon Brown, the Labour Party and the British Socialists are planning to replace the British education system with a new plan for learning based on the Hogwarts School of Wizardry and Witchcraft. And, so Muslim children won't be offended, *The Three Little Pigs* was officially changed to "The Three Little Puppies."

Either by design or neglect, the American media completely ignored an interview with J.K. Rowling conducted by Evan Solomon of Canada's CBC News World in which Rowling admitted that certain characters in her book that are portrayed as "bad" are intentional metaphorical references to contemporary politics in Great Britain. Solomon asked, "Is it fair to say that these are neo-conservatives and Thatcherites (Margaret Thatcher's Conservative Party)?" Rowling agreed, saying "I think in this book, too, you fully understand." Not only is Winston Churchill out of favor in Harry Potter's Britain, even the "Iron Lady" who forged an alliance with President Reagan and Pope Paul to bring an end to Communism is disparaged viciously by Rowling. Again, not unusual for an author with very deep, heartfelt sympathy for Communism, despite all the bloodlust it represented.

While Rowling was busy signing copies of her last book, publishers at Scholastic were busy in their new role as movie producers. The project they were co-funding with Warner's New Line Cinema was the overtly anti-God story *The Golden Compass* by world-class atheist Phillip Pullman who added a page to the Scholastic playbook of smears and jeers by calling Christian critics of his book "nitwits." Understandably, school systems around America are thinking twice about allowing *Scholastic Magazine* to maintain a presence in the classroom.

ROWLING'S *FINAL SOLUTION*: THE ULTIMATE DEATH

It is evident now that J.K. Rowling's affiliation with the Church of Scotland falls squarely into the "Ulterior Motive Believer." You cannot kill the Central Figure unless you first believe in the Ultimate Authority. When Rowling declared, basically, God is dead by omission, the author actually killed God by permission; granted and executed by her grand New Age Divine Dichotomy.

As Book Seven was being released, only one mainstream writer on the globe had figured this out. On July 12, 2007, *Time* magazine columnist Lev Grossman titled his article, "Who Dies In Harry Potter? God." While the world of Potterites gnashed their teeth over the possibility of Harry being snuffed out, Grossman provided the true spoiler, "If you want to know who dies in Harry Potter, the answer is easy: God. Harry Potter lives in a world free of any religion or spirituality of any kind. He lives surrounded by ghosts but has no one to pray to, even if he were so inclined, which he isn't. Rowling has more in common with celebrity atheists like Christopher Hitchens than she has with Tolkein and Lewis . . . In choosing Rowling as the reigning dreamer of our era, we have chosen a writer who dreams of a secular, bureaucratized all-too-human sorcery in which psychology and technology have superseded the sacred."

The fact that J.K. Rowling was born in 1965, the same year Winston Churchill died, is not a "magical" sign of a new beginning, but an ironic metaphor for the beginning of the end. With the release of the appropriately titled *Harry Potter and the Deathly Hollows*, 2007 will be remembered as the year England died. As Americans, we must decide to win the Culture War against Hollywood. As only Winston Churchill could say it, "Never give up . . . Never give up."

CHAPTER 24

FIGHTING BACK AGAINST HOLLYWOOD: TELEVISION Á LA CARTE

"During the 60's we unleashed some demons that needed to be called back."
—David Horowitz

Interested in watching people have sex? Or would you prefer watching a violent rape, especially one where the victim begins to enjoy the assault? Maybe you're interested in watching young teen sex, even a teen orgy? If that's just old hat to you by now, perhaps you'd prefer watching a father masturbate in front of his child? Or maybe you'd be much more interested in watching stories about incest, pedophilia and necrophilia, or maybe a combination of both? On the other hand, you may get your thrills by watching a hooker seduce a horse?

Don't have a computer? Not on the internet? No problem. Just turn on the television in your living room. Stories and themes exactly like the ones described above are already appearing on your home screen and are becoming more frequent every year on TV shows such as *Boston Legal, Medium, Nip-Tuck, Close to Home, South Park, Rescue Me, Keen Eddie, CSI, The Shield,* and *NCIS*, to name only a few.

And in many cases you don't have to subscribe to one of the movie channels like HBO or Showtime; you don't even have to subscribe to expanded basic cable. Much of this perversity enters your house free of charge courtesy of the public airwaves via the major networks. If you didn't know this, then you haven't been watching television and that's good. The fewer people who watch these shows result in lower ratings, and that results in shows that fizzle into the thin air.

Keep in mind that for every show that is broadcast on television, ten to fifteen "pilot" projects have already been filmed and are sitting in the can as producers try to sell the programming to interested networks and advertisers. A good friend of mine who has served as a production executive at Disney-ABC for over a decade explained a couple of projects he had the misfortune to screen along with other Disney executives. Another "emergency room" type drama unfolds its opening scene with a man shoving a rat and a baby squirrel into his rectum. Within minutes the man is calling 911 as blood shoots out of his mouth. Apparently, the little creatures got into a claustrophobic squabble as they shredded the man's intestines to pieces.

The network didn't reject this pilot or refuse to order additional episodes. Instead, program directors decided to put the pilot on hold by optioning the show for a *possible* January 2009 season premiere.

In truth, more of these perverse stories and plotlines are showing up in television every year because mentally disturbed screenwriters, producers and directors have absolutely no oversight over their self-indulgent fantasies. The network and cable executives share that mutual mental sickness and they eagerly want you to indulge in their nightmarish and drug-induced "revelations." Just another reason why mandatory random drug-testing in Hollywood could prevent mentally afflicted programming from spilling over from the screening room to the living room, and could increase ratings at the same time with better programs.

The seeds of this trouble began in 1982 when the National Association of Broadcasters (NAB) abolished their content code. Despite that, television remained fairly popular and stable until the early 1990s. The Federal Communications Commission (FCC) had been given authority by Congress to regulate and enforce indecent and obscene content, including profanity, going back to 1960.

Much of this regulation was unnecessary during the 1960s, 1970s, and 1980s because the industry was self-regulating. However, throughout the 1990s, television had degenerated to new lows of excessive abuses of decency, vulgarity, drug use, violence and sexual perversity on a grand scale. The administration of "Hollywood Bill" Clinton was no coincidence. The FCC commissioners are appointed by the president and under Clinton most complaints filed by consumers against programming content with indecency and profanity ended up gathering dust at the FCC.

Hollywood didn't contribute millions of dollars to President Clinton without expecting something in return. That "something" was lax or non-enforcement of *existing* laws. CBS president, Les Moonves, one of the biggest broadcast offenders, was a frequent golf-buddy of President Clinton and was hoping to see him return to the White House with Hillary. But, Obama also promised a blind eye and Les has a new "backup" friend.

THE HOLLYWOOD CULTURE WAR

The lack of response of the FCC to complaints under President Clinton caused Hollywood's twisted social/sexual/political agenda of insolent immorality to escalate so rapidly that by 1995, citizen groups and American consumers were flooding their congressional representatives with the complaints that the FCC failed to act on.

This resulted in the Clinton-Valenti brokered Ratings Scheme for television, discussed in detail in Chapter 7, "The Ratings Fiasco." The television Ratings Scheme was a Catch-22 opportunity for both Clinton and Valenti. For President Clinton, who didn't care at all about television content or the harm it incurred on children, the coming year of 1996 would be an election year. Clinton had to "act" responsible and interested because most voters in America did care about content and loss of those votes could have resulted in a lost re-election.

Once instituted in 1997, the television ratings proved a horrendous failure because it allowed the producers to push their increasingly edgy and grotesque imagery and language onto the television screen with no age-based stamp of approval. With the TV ratings in place, Jack Valenti walked away threatening to sue anybody who challenged his prescription for indecent television.

As for Bill Clinton, the "deeply concerned" president won his second term as president and *immediately* lost *all interest* in television content decency. And, his imminent lack of interest was handsomely rewarded through even more generous Hollywood campaign contributions than he received for his first campaign.

All of this would set the state for an even bigger war that may forever change the face of television content and how it is produced and distributed throughout the country. Brent Bozell, the tireless chairman of the Media Research Center (MRC), predicted the television Ratings Scheme failure after giving the plan an *F* at a 1999 news conference with Senators Joe Lieberman and Sam Brownback. According to Bozell, " . . . the system would backfire because some irresponsible members of the entertainment industry would see the opportunity to insert even edgier content into their shows."

Bozell, MRC and its affiliate organization, the Parents Television Council (PTC), would begin a campaign to expose the ruse of the television and cable industry's pricing scheme, basically an extortion of consumers to pay for egregiously offensive channels they never watch. Bozell would soon call for true a la carte television, or "Cable Choice," as it was commonly known.

Under this proposal, consumers and families would pick only the channels they want to watch and, in most cases, end up paying less on their cable bill. At the same time, consumers would be set free from subsidizing offensive programming.

According to James Poniewozik of *Time* magazine, "There's plenty out there to offend . . . In an episode of Fox's since-canceled *Keen Eddie*, three men enlist a hooker to arouse a horse to extract semen from the animal. The Parent's

623

Television Council recently protested an episode of NBC's *Medium* to find a suspect in bed—with a two-week-old corpse."

And their protests will not gather dust as they might have under the Clinton FCC: " . . . a reawakened Federal Communications Commission, prodded by values activists has rebuked or fined broadcast networks . . . . Now Congress is gearing up to give the FCC stronger weapons: for steeper fines and possibly the power to regulate decency on cable and satellite and radio."[1]

It was in March of 2005 that President Bush named Kevin Martin as the new FCC chairman. Martin continues talking tough and remains persistent. According to *Time*, "To emboldened decency monitors, this is a chance to tame an out-of-control pop culture in which *Real World* housemates have three-ways in hot tubs and shock jocks broadcast live sex acts on the air."[2]

As FCC Chairman Martin told the Senate's "Open Forum on Decency" shortly after taking office, "At the FCC, we used to receive indecency complaints in the hundreds; now they come in by the hundreds of thousands. Clearly consumers—and particularly parents—are concerned and frequently frustrated."

Even before Martin's arrival, the FCC was ramping up fines against broadcasters at a revolutionary pace due to the public outcry from an American audience that had been lied to for years from the broadcast and entertainment industries. Enforcement fines jumped from $440,000 in 2003 to $8 million in 2004. And that was before Congress and President Bush passed a ten-fold increase in fines from $32,500 to $325,000. In addition, the FCC can apply those fines "per incident" instead of "per program" and can fine the network affiliates as well as network-owned stations.

The "Broadcast Decency Enforcement Act" passed by one of the largest landslides and bipartisan efforts of Congress in the final version (S.193) by a margin of 379 to 35 in June 2006. Diane Watson (D-CA) voted against the bill because she felt the fines should have been set much higher.[3]

Even with a broad section of the American people speaking directly, and through their congressional representatives, the entertainment industry was preparing to fight back against the wishes of the people, confirming the fierce value manipulation campaign that the industry has been waging for decades. Their ongoing war against their own audience would also confirm the first paragraphs of this book; Hollywood will give you what *they* want you to watch and not what *you* prefer to watch. Rumblings about "Cable Choice" had already begun before an incident in 2004 that would significantly accelerate the Culture War with Hollywood.

THE BREAST SEEN 'ROUND THE WORLD

One of the largest network events of each year is the annual broadcast of the Super Bowl to millions of people across America and around the world. It was, until recently, one of the last venues where the entire family gathered around the same television set in the same room to watch the same program. If anything had become risqué about the Super Bowl over the last decade, it was isolated to the million dollar beer commercials that often featured buxom women in shredded clothes brawling in public fountains—the virtual wet t-shirt contest by proxy.

But, nothing prepared the American family and viewing audience for the half-time show at the 2004 Super Bowl that was staged by MTV. Exactly why the NFL contracted with MTV for a half-time show was initially a mystery. The cable channel is one of the most profane and patently vulgar outlets on television, spouting non-stop obscenities, racism, porn, drug use and orchestrated mayhem 24 hours a day. The true tie-in can be chalked up to cross-marketing—CBS and MTV are both owned by sleaze king Sumner Redstone of Viacom.

The half-time extravaganza featured a number of young pop stars to a backdrop of crushing sound volume and frenetic lighting effects, a Dante's *Inferno* of things to come. The show was off to a bad start when a persistent crotch-grabbing rapper strutted back and forth on the makeshift stage.

The climax of the poorly choreographed show featured Justin Timberlake and the nearly forgotten Janet Jackson who was attempting to revive her "sagging" career with a Super Bowl performance like no other. With a carefully planned sleight-of-hand, Timberlake pulled a section of Jackson's wardrobe that "suddenly" and "accidentally" revealed her breast.

After carefully counting down the seconds of her exhibitionist exposure, Jackson acted "surprised" at what she would later call a "wardrobe malfunction." Of course, it was all planned for shock value which is the only value MTV offers. Because the show was broadcast on CBS, it fell under the purview of the FCC which only has jurisdiction over broadcast or over-the-air stations like major networks that are free and do not require cable. (The FCC *is* pursuing the expansion of its regulation over cable and satellite TV.)

The FCC promptly fined CBS $550,000 and concluded that the incident was "crude," "lewd," and "sexually explicit." The FCC also fined other CBS programs for indecent programs. (For definitions of *obscenity*, *indecency* and *profanity*, see Appendix IV.)

While the fines were large, it wasn't the first and wouldn't be the last for the station once known as the "Tiffany Network." The FCC had already fined Viacom, the parent company of CBS, for a radio show broadcast by Opie and Anthony in which they aired a "Sex in St. Patrick's Cathedral" charade. The FCC then fined CBS for a TV episode of *Without a Trace* in which a teen orgy was graphically portrayed. That show alone garnered the highest fine in TV history at $3.6 million dollars. CBS tried to justify the graphic group sex because it "featured an important and socially relevant storyline warning parents to exercise greater supervision over their teenage children." The irony of that feeble excuse was not lost on anyone.[4]

Viacom entered into a Consent Decree as a settlement for the fines. Four years later, Viacom and CBS have yet to pay a single penny. The only exception was the fine for *Without a Trace*. In a move still shrouded in mystery, the FCC lowered the fine extensively in late 2007; a virtual slap on the wrist. CBS, like other fined broadcasters, have decided to go "judge shopping" and have filed numerous appeals in order to subvert the overwhelming wishes of Congress and the American people as ordered in the 2006 "Broadcast Decency Enforcement Act."

Most people have forgotten, and may have never known, that shortly after Janet Jackson's "wardrobe malfunction" and other network atrocities, entertainment executives were called before a congressional committee to testify about their personal and corporate commitment to the public airwaves. All gave token responses about the need for more oversight on their behalf.

They couldn't very well remind Congress about the "blocking technologies" available to parents given the "spontaneous" flash by Jackson. If anything, the network and affiliates completely failed to utilize their own five-second delay to prevent mass audience exposure to "wardrobe malfunction." Inevitably, the entertainment executives left Congress promising zero tolerance for indecency.

The executives left Washington, promising to "be good" as they laughed all the way back to Hollywood and New York. In an industry where lying, cheating and stealing is epidemic, the entertainment executives put on a decades-old dog and pony show of bait and switch.

In fact, since their appearance in 2004, television violence, gore, profanity and hyper-sexuality has increased exponentially, as if to purposely slap the Congress and the American audience in the face with an increasingly foul display of televised muscle-flexing that has left many people sick to their stomachs in the following four years.

It was after this wink-and-nod charade before Congress that American television paraded its most debauched shows and retrograde episodes in television history, including the child who watches his father masturbate, a mother-son-homosexual-incest murder triangle, graphic rapes, sexual predators and their perverted fetish fantasies.

Even in 2008, the television executives and producers from broadcast and cable were still broadcasting horrific scenes of grotesque images that one would be hard-pressed to find in the darkest crevices of the internet. Parents Television Council President Tim Winter testified to the U.S. Senate Committee on Commerce, Science and Transportation about the "ultra-violent" cascade that was unleashed in prime-time in front of millions of children.

In describing two episodes of the FX Channel's *The Shield*, now in syndication, one featured actor Michael Chiklis as a *heroic*, corrupt cop dragging a gang

THE HOLLYWOOD CULTURE WAR

member into a kitchen, turning on an electric stove burner, and pressing the gang member's face onto the burner at a camera angle where the audience could clearly see the man's face melting, dripping and charred against the coil.

Winter described another episode of *The Shield* to the committee, "A police captain is forced at gunpoint to perform oral sex on a gang member . . . the gang member asks him, 'You ever suck a d____ like a cell b____, cop man?' He threatens to kill the captain if he doesn't perform fellatio, and the officer is seen and heard gagging and whimpering until the gang member reaches orgasm."[5]

Apparently, the National Cable and Telecommunication Association (NCTA) has no problem with this. In fact, NCTA President Kyle McSlarrow seems to advocate this kind of programming. In truth, this episode is not about *indecency*; it's about *obscenity*, and obscenity is not protected by the First Amendment.

This is why expanded basic cable is rapidly becoming the red-light district of television and why the FCC oversight is urgently needed, especially considering that the shows are indirectly marketed to children. In 2008 the FX Channel only upped the ante by releasing a new sixty-second promo montage of ultra-violent imagery to a melancholy tune of blues music. Large black letters proclaimed, "THERE IS NO HERO . . . THERE IS NO VILLAIN . . . THERE IS NO KNIGHT IN SHINING ARMOR." And, yet, FX wonders why their ratings are facing a free-fall.

The "We're just giving people what they want" lie from the broadcasters proved that perverse private agendas are at work. Audiences and advertisers were losers when ratings from the fall 2007 season showed that most networks suffered *double-digit* losses, according to *USA Today*. Without flinching, network executives rolled out even raunchier circus sideshow programming in 2008.

But maybe you're still not convinced. Consider the new CBS show *NCIS* that airs during the once sacred last hour of television known as the "Family Hour." (Now extinct.) As PTC's Tim Winter explained to the Senate committee, the May 22, 2007 episode of *NCIS* depicted a dead drug smuggler who had been carrying packets of heroin in his digestive tract.

A group of drug dealers cut out the dead man's abdomen and pulled his blood soaked organs through the steaming cavity. When his intestines are sliced open, white powder spills over his bloody torso. A fight ensues and one character stabs the other drug dealer with a scalpel while another shoots him. Then the junkie sister buries her face into her dead brother's intestines and proceeds to snort the heroin residue from his guts.[6]

[If you're offended, we'll reserve this space to mourn the death of human civility—or if you need to rush to the toilet.]

It should be noted that CBS mislabeled the episode with a misleading rating, leaving the impression the episode was not as blatantly graphic as it turned out to be, much to the surprise of shocked viewers. This was no accident, just another example of how the television executives manipulate the ratings to throw off the V-chip and at the same time lure more viewers and advertising dollars into the Cabinet of Dr. Caligari.

Again, it could be argued from a simple technical standpoint that this scene from CBS's *NCIS* should be considered obscene in addition to indecent, even more so than the episode from *The Shield*. Because of this and the intentional application of a false rating, lawmakers may want to reconsider the enforcement provision to FCC law allowing for the arrest of network executives for virtual over-the-air predatory child molestation by proxy. Most states have laws with very plain language such as "Corrupting a minor," "Endangering the welfare of a child," and "Contributing to the delinquency of a minor." The entertainment executives will say the parents are the "gatekeepers," but Hollywood producers are the criminals who are breaking and entering the minds of children; no different than pedophiles.

The ultimate broadcast molestation of children by CBS began in early 2008 when the network picked up the weekly series *Dexter* from Showtime. The main character is a cop glamorized as a hero who suffers a minor flaw; he's a serial killer "on the side." As a result of the transfer from Showtime to CBS, the PTC unveiled results of ratings that show viewership of the series by children age 12 and under increased by 250 percent. TV critics, a perverse lot, have praised the show while ignoring public concerns about a series that very openly promotes mass murder as a virtue.

Viacom CEO Sumner Redstone and CBS President Les Moonves have repeatedly violated FCC rules and are refusing to pay government levied fines even as they continue to produce shows such as *NCIS* with people snorting heroin from the "excretory" organs of a dead man. Perhaps revoking their broadcast license and six months in a federal prison for Redstone and Moonves could send a clear message to the rest of the industry. Of course, that's only my opinion, not the FCC or the PTC.

TELEVISION IS NOW "A PUBLIC HEALTH CRISIS"

Tim Winter's testimony was intended to highlight the need for increased vigilance over a television industry that has lied to the American public for well over a decade. His comments come just two months after a report was released, at the request of Congress, by the FCC which stated that Congress could regulate violence on cable, satellite and broadcast television without violating the First Amendment.[7]

The report by the FCC outlined a very real correlation between bloodshed on television and violence in real life. As Chairman Martin stated, "Exposure to violent programming can be harmful to children."[8] Again demonstrating wide bipartisan support, fellow FCC Commissioner Michael Copps, a Democrat, concurred with the urgency and challenges to clean up the airwaves, " . . . given what amounts to a public health crisis at hand, I believe that it is a challenge that must be met."[9]

In the PTC's appeal to the Senate on June 26, 2007, Winter cited the entertainment industry's persistent and arrogant defiance of congressional and FCC law. Winter reminded the senators of the industry's *modus operandi*, "Rather than acknowledge the evidence manifested in over a thousand medical and clinical studies, they underwrite research and point to its differing conclusions" and Winter noted the industry's long history of "shifting the conversation."[10] That is a kind way of saying the industry is heavily populated with "shifty" characters.

While Winter was referring to one thousand of the more recent studies pertaining to televised violence, since 1933 over 3,000 studies on the negative effects of violent entertainment have been conducted beginning with the Motion Picture Research Council Study, also known as the Payne Studies.

In addition, the V-Chip, cable company blocking tools and satellite parental controls have all proven miserable failures, mainly because each television station, cable and satellite channels apply their own separate standards to rating programs for content, which renders the controls useless. After the much ballyhooed arrival of the V-Chip by President Clinton and Jack Valenti in 2000, less than 15% of television viewers utilize the technology because of the non-uniform Ratings Scheme developed by Valenti. The MRC's Brent Bozell predicted as much back in 1999 when he said the system would be "dead on arrival." Winter also revealed that instances of violence on television had increased 75% between 1998 and 2006. And, 2006 alone proved to be the most violent year on record for televised violence and gore.

In 2005 Chairman Martin addressed the U.S. Senate's "Open Forum On Decency" and confirmed Bozell's assessment that television ratings had failed and as evidence of the network's subverting the will of the American public, Martin noted that "the use of profanity during the 'Family Hour' increased 95% from 1998 to 2002. Another recent study (by the Kaiser Family Foundation in November of 2005) found that 70% of television shows in the 2004-2005 season had some sexual content, and the number of sexual scenes had nearly doubled since 1998."[11]

A Fox News Dynamic Opinion Poll conducted in February 2005 reported 70% of respondents who said entertainment content in movies and television *did not* reflect their values.[12] An AP/IPSOS Poll taken in 2007 found that 68% of Americans felt there was "too much violence" on TV and 66% said there was "too much sex" on the tube.

But the core finding of the poll supported a solution that had been promoted by a wide variety of advocacy groups and consumers including the MRC and

PTC and also the Consumers Union (CU), Concerned Women of America (CWA) and the American Family Association (AFA) among many others.

In the AP/IPSOS Poll, 78% of individuals responded that they would prefer to choose their own television station line-up.[13] Cable Choice would also become the main plank in FCC Chairman Kevin Martin's call for a major change in the way television programming would be offered to the public.

The CWA and CU had already conducted studies as early as 2002 showing the technological and cost benefits for consumers. The two main arguments for Cable Choice center around the fact that cable companies are increasing their cable fees at a rate four to five times the national rate of inflation.[14] Further, people who only watch a handful of channels are forced to buy a full "expanded basic package" that includes some of the most repulsive and expensive channels on television.

Of your cable bill, $9.60 goes to MTV per year, $9.00 per year for FX, and $7.20 per year for Comedy Central. ESPN charges the most in many areas of the country and can account for the largest portion of your cable bill. If you just want ESPN and a few other channels, you may not want to pay for MTV and the same scenario in reverse would apply. True Cable Choice means picking and choosing only the channels you want coming into your home and paying for those channels.

The response from the television industry was a flurry of lies for the five years following the 2002 reports advocating Cable Choice.[15]

A LITANY OF LIES

The entertainment industry's response is probably best summarized by a posting on the PTC's website titled, "America's Media Speaks Out for Cable Choice." the following is an excerpt from that posting:

- "A year ago we told you about the concept of 'Cable Choice,' being able to pick and pay for only the cable networks you wanted to allow in your home. A year ago, the cable industry said it was impossible. They said that technology prohibited such an option. We proved that the technology *did* exist.
- "Then the cable industry said that they would help customers to *block* networks they didn't like. We exposed the flaw that consumers would still be forced to *pay* for the unwanted networks that they chose to block.
- "Their next pathetic argument against Cable Choice was that it would force smaller, niche and minority-targeted networks into bankruptcy. Prominent consumer organizations exposed the fallacy of that argument showing evidence that such networks might actually *benefit* from Cable Choice.

- "Then the cable industry struck fear into the hearts of many by saying that Cable Choice would have the undesired effect of *increasing* the cost of a cable subscription while giving the customers *fewer* channels. We have exposed that, too, as a fallacy: and we pointed out that the cable industry already increases their fees at 4 to 5 times the national rate of inflation. And now the Federal Communications Commission is agreeing with us, saying that a recent analysis by their economists shows that costs would not increase with Cable Choice."[16]

The entertainment industry began feeling the heat more intensely than ever by 2005 as legislation was prepared in the Senate by Senators Kay Bailey Hutchison (R-TX) and Jay Rockefeller (D-WV) that would extend FCC indecency enforcement over cable and satellite providers.[17]

Immediately, the industry came up with an idea that they had previously said was impossible. The cable companies agreed to offer certain "tiers" of cable programming such as a "Sports Tier" or a "Family Tier" and a variety of other combinations. The problem with the tiers is that they offered a bizarre mix of programming that still reflected what "they" wanted you to see as opposed to what "you" want to see. The MRC's Brent Bozell appropriately called the offer a "red herring."

However, the Hutchison/Rockefeller bill was put on hold, in part to fast-track the indecency fine increase and in part to allow the cable companies to launch a multi-million dollar campaign to "inform" the public, again, about available blocking technologies for parents and consumers. However, the humorous PR blitz did nothing to address the fact that consumers still had to pay for the channels they blocked.[18]

The TVBoss.org is the umbrella group funded by the MPAA and NCTA to persuade families into using their cable and V-Chip blocking controls. The hypocrisy of this approach had already been challenged, but the industry was mainly interested in showing Congress that it has the "best interests" of the TV audience in mind in hopes of stalling further regulation. In one spot a delirious punk-rock drug addict is shown sprawled on the floor of a family's middle-class living room. The father walks in and sits down briefly to tell the junkie, "Your show's character is really great!" The drug addict is shown smiling, nodding his head until the father says, "But the drug content is too adult for the kids—so I'm going to have to block you—okay?" As he leaves the room, the junkie bobs his head around and says, "You're nice, Lee."

These intentionally deceptive ads by the MPAA and NCTA don't explain that you still have to pay for the drug addict to linger just around the corner of your TV set. A more appropriate ending to the spot would show the junkie laughing at the father as he leaves the room, shouting, "You can block me all you want, Lee, but you're still paying for my drug habit, you idiot moron!"

For this reason, among others, Chairman Martin is more focused now on promoting total Cable Choice, a position supported by Bozell and all of the other consumer advocacy groups. Any "tiered" compromise would have to offer an "opt out" choice by consumers to delete any channels they don't want and subsequently don't have to pay for. (Indecency fines will not apply to cable.)[19] Through all of this, the cable companies have been mum on the fact that Canada has been offering Cable Choice for over a decade.

Another initial stumbling block to Cable Choice came from televangelists like Paul Couch of TBN and Kenneth Copeland of KCM ministries and others who argued that the current system allowed for "channel surfers" to stop by and hear a pastoral message that may not be available through Cable Choice. However, the National Religious Broadcasters, a PTC ally, would not have any problem with Cable Choice as long as subscribers would still buy their local broadcast channels. In most cases TBN, a broadcast channel and not a cable channel, could still be made available under Cable Choice.

As for the cable companies, as Tim Winter noted, "Their backs are against the wall." Only an act of Congress is needed to allow consumers the freedom to set up their own cable line-ups. And the entertainment industry is livid to the point of hysteria.

Defenders of the current system of coerced raunch and rapid-fire price hikes call such a move "chilling." (The *chilling effect* is a worn-out phrase invented by Jack Valenti decades earlier.) Kyle McSlarrow of the NCTA said Cable Choice is "a very dangerous idea."

Perhaps the most "dangerous" and "chilling" comment to emerge out of this entire debate was made by none other than Time-Warner CEO Richard Parsons who appeared on a C-SPAN panel discussion on telecommunications on May 30, 2007. When asked what he thought about consumers' rights to exercise Cable Choice over the current system, Parsons resorted to the "Nazi persecution" talking points, indicating that anybody advocating Cable Choice as proposed in Congress should visit the Holocaust Museum in Washington to "see what happens" to people when government steps in to make decisions for them.

As Tim Winter pointed out in his testimony to the Senate on June 26, 2007, this tactic of restructuring the debate is a common tactic. However, most viewers of Parsons' comments were taken aback and many deeply offended, especially survivors of the Holocaust and their families. To use their eternal suffering and loss to make a cheap and blatantly false political point earned Parsons a cascade of demands for his resignation. Parsons' behavior fit a pattern of Jew-jabbing and Christian-bashing from Time-Warner.

Ironically, in an article totally unrelated to Parsons' comments, corporate compensation analyst Paul Hodges of the Corporate Library posted an article on MSN news on June 14, 2007, indicating that Parsons was one of the five most *overpaid* CEOs in America who should be "let go." Hodges made this recommendation in light of the fact that Parsons is constantly "rewarded" for the company's continued failing profits, with his most recent reward approaching $13 million. (Now you know why your cable bill is so high.)

Time-Warner stock lost 31% in the five years prior to December 2006. And despite that dismal performance, among the worst in the nation for any CEO, Parsons was granted generous raises almost every year. And he talks about a *holocaust* if Congress gives people Cable Choice? As Senator John McCain said at one Senate hearing, "It appears that the industry has been successful once again in distracting policy makers with a parade of horribles."

Four months later, *USA Today* announced that Parsons was stepping down as CEO. And, as punishment for five years of falling profits, the Time-Warner board elevated Parsons to Chairman of the Board with a multi-million dollar compensation package that is expected to increase annually until he dies. Of course, you have the right to adjust his compensation downward by thinking twice before buying a ticket to a Warner Brothers movie and cutting affiliate HBO from your cable bill. Remember, Time-Warner is fast surpassing Universal as the Number One Christian-bashing and Jew-jabbing entertainment conglomerate in the world.

Advocates of Cable Choice, spearheaded by Martin at the FCC and the million plus members of the PTC, are hoping for *genuine* support soon. The major telecommunication lobbyists have been spreading millions of dollars around Congress to sway legislators from voting on Cable Choice. The anti-democratic ACLU has also been circling like sharks. Their key concern is that porn channels and sexual agenda channels may no longer be forced on consumers through democratic Cable Choice.

In April of 2006, more than 800 individual stations issued a rare group statement that proclaimed their objection to "growing government control over what people should and shouldn't see on television." Of course, that is a lie multiplied by 800, no doubt coerced in part by the larger network conglomerates. It's not about *government control*; it's about *giving people choice*. That's called democracy.

It's not hard to determine who is "in the pocket" of the entertainment industry when it comes to something as simple as freedom for Americans to choose their own television viewing. It is also a sad statement when certain elected members of Congress look down on their own constituents with Hollywood-style condescending arrogance.

Consider the remarks made by Democratic Representative Gary Ackerman of New York as he "restructures the debate" in a purposely deceitful manner, "What is at stake here is freedom of speech and whether it will be nibbled to death by election-minded politicians and self-righteous pietists." If I want to pick and pay for my own choice of television channels, I guess I'm expressing piety. Well . . . okay.

One of the more petty acts of pandering for viewers of television came from the NCTA when they realized in 2005 that momentum was growing rapidly around the country at the grass roots level for Cable Choice. The NCTA, in addition to their meaningless "I'm gonna have to block you" ads promised to display television program ratings a little longer at the beginning of each show before dissolving and pop them up again after each commercial. (Something they should have been doing for the last ten years.) In addition, the NCTA and NAB promised to increase the size of the rating logo in the corner of the screen by 70%.

It seems that the television industry still "doesn't get it." This is a national debate where size doesn't matter. What the networks, cable companies and satellite program providers are doing is no different from what the movie industry attempted from the 1920s through the 1940s in a predatory attempt to circumvent the MPAA's own Production Code in a distribution system known as "block booking" or "blind booking."

Paramount founder Adolph Zukor is credited with devising the scheme and forcing blind booking on film theater exhibitors starting in the late 1920s. If a theater owner wanted the likes of Fairbanks, Pickford, Valentino or Swanson, they had to buy *everything* Paramount produced. This scheme would begin a long battle over the content of films, fully 80 years before the cable battles began.

As author Gregory Black described this subversive marketing and distribution plan by Hollywood, "Film reform groups maintained that these wholesaling practices adopted by the film companies forced small-town exhibitors to play 'immoral' films because they had to pay for them whether they wanted to show them or not. The *federal government* [emphasis added] also attacked this process of selling films as an unfair trade practice."[20]

The U.S. Courts even issued a cease-and-desist order in 1927, but the movie industry stalled the order through numerous appeals, much like the TV industry is doing today. But, by 1947 the federal government forced the studios to divest their vertical monopoly, a stranglehold from production to exhibition, and the industry was forced to stop block booking.

UNINTENDED CONSEQUENCES: NEW OPPORTUNITIES

By 2007, the push for Cable Choice was gathering increased momentum. Newspapers across the country were writing supportive editorials for Cable Choice and the ABC/IPSOS Poll showed close to 80% support among American viewers. The PTC, along with numerous other consumer advocacy groups,

THE HOLLYWOOD CULTURE WAR

were throwing their support behind the Cable Choice campaign. Perhaps more pervasive, intrusive, insulting and influential than Hollywood's self-absorption with sex and violence is the entertainment industry's obsession with profane vulgarity that has coarsened common conversation. The FCC's ten-fold profanity fines were hitting home.

Then a funny thing happened on the way to the courthouse. The major networks and their affiliates had been "judge shopping" since early spring of 2007 in order to find a "friendly court" that would overturn the indecent language and profanity fines that had been levied by the FCC.

On June 4, 2007, the 2nd U.S. Court of Appeals in New York ruled that the FCC's own rules and enforcement against broadcast TV profanity was "arbitrary and capricious" and was improperly applied against "fleeting vulgarities." The following day, Martin issued a statement in which he said, "I find it hard to believe that the New York court would tell American families that s____ and f____ are fine to say in broadcast television during the hours when children are most likely to be in the audience."[21]

It's not so hard to believe that the 2nd Court of Appeals in New York would rule 2 to 1 against even basic decency on television. The court is second only to the U.S. *Circus* Court of Appeals in San Francisco in legislating immorality from the bench. Of the many judges on the 2nd Circuit, nineteen were appointed by Bill Clinton and two by Jimmy Carter. Just another example of the long-term detrimental after-effects inflicted on American culture, not to mention national security, by the two ex-presidents.

The ruling does not affect the fines being appealed for Janet Jackson's "wardrobe malfunction" on CBS and a number of other "visual" indecency fines. Martin plans to appeal all the way to the U.S. Supreme Court if necessary in addition to pursuing legislation in Congress.

* * *

Judge shopping is a favorite pastime of the ACLU, which enjoys subverting legislation by the people. Earlier in 2007, the Child Online Protection Act (COPA) of 1998 was thrown out by U.S. District Judge Lowell Reed who said, "Perhaps we do the minors of this country harm if First Amendment protections, which they will with age inherit fully, are chipped away in the name of their protection."

Judge Reed's ruling contained the faint echo of *Variety*'s veteran child-hater columnist Timothy Gray who once wrote, "To hell with the little nippers. I want my adult entertainment and I want it now." Emily Sheketoff, Executive Director of the ultra-liberal American Library Association (ALA) called COPA and other acts to protect children, "stupid pieces of legislation."

Certainly the ACLU was pleased with the decision against protecting children. The organization has been a longtime ally of the porn industry and especially the pedophilia porn promoters and has forged a long-term relationship with the North American Man Boy Love Association (NAMBLA). Apparently, Judge Lowell Reed doesn't want to prevent children from visiting the NAMBLA website where they can learn how to become an unwitting victim of child molestation and even murder.

Another battle running concurrently with the televised profanity issue had its roots in the April 2007 FCC report that cleared Congress for exercising the constitutional authority to regulate violence on TV. Immediately, Senator Jay Rockefeller planned to introduce legislation that closely tracked his 2005 bill with Senator Hutchison.

Rockefeller is still considering the expansion of oversight by the FCC to cable and satellite. Rockefeller's intention, with the constitutional authority asserted by the FCC's legal department, is to push ultraviolent programming into the 10 p.m. to 6 a.m. time slot, a time period where the FCC does not regulate indecency. This eight-hour period of television programming has been dubbed with the ironic title of "Safe Harbor," meaning safe for sleaze merchants, cable porn and over-the-air carnival hucksters of perversity. (In December of 1988, President Reagan signed a bill banning indecent broadcasts 24 hours a day, including the "Safe Harbor." After suffering apoplectic fits of frenzy, Hugh Hefner and other late night pornographers found a D.C. Circuit court that overturned the law in 1990.)

Rockefeller is expecting a fight from the major entertainment conglomerates who want to continue the parade of televised stories of necrophilia, pedophilia, incest, bestiality, rape, head-chopping violence, teen orgies and, of course, infamous scenes such as junkies snorting heroin from the bloody sliced-open intestines of dead drug smugglers.

And, sure enough, the major trade associations such as the MPAA and NAB along with the four major networks and several cable companies have pooled their financial resources to retain Harvard Law Professor Lawrence Tribe to defend their right to expose children to the most disturbing images and dialogue ever displayed on television. As much as the industry leaders would prefer to molest your children in the privacy of their executive offices, they will opt, reluctantly, to assault them over the airwaves. Tribe is also a close friend and advisor to Barack Obama, a recipient of over 9.5 million dollars from the Hollywood entertainment industry.

But, Rockefeller's bill would have to pass first. And, if it follows closely to the language of his 2005 bill, there is an open-ended clause that could give FCC Chairman Martin the legal power to impose Cable Choice for television. As media analyst Adam Thierer said, "It's a very broad mandate."[22]

In addition to this anticipated legal action, the ACLU, under the direction of radical heterophobe provocateur Anthony Romero, will chime in to defend debauchery as he has done so many times before.

As for the 2nd U.S. Court of Appeals ruling in favor of 24-hour a day profanity and vulgarity, Chairman Martin sees this as justification for allowing television consumers to exercise Cable Choice. It is becoming increasingly clear that the entertainment industry is subverting the major mass appeal from the public for Cable Choice and resorting to judicial legislation from the bench in order to achieve undemocratic ends.

In the meantime, the television producers and executives have ramped up productions reflecting their personal social/sexual/political content onto prime-time audiences. NBC/Universal's new entertainment chief, Ben Silverman, has made no secret of his intention to wage value manipulation against the American people. He is known inside and outside of Hollywood circles as an ultra-liberal desiring to insert extreme left-wing messages and content into television programming as a challenge to the FCC. And as a slap to middle-America.

Silverman has made clear that he plans to *forcefully* "shift the tidal wave" of public opinion. Sex with dead people and mother-son incest will be child's play in contrast to the new horrors Silverman plans to shove on the American people, especially children. Expect the television ratings for NBC shows to be manipulated to the extreme in order to override the V-Chip. Silverman's resume includes a series of cable flops including "Queer as Folk," described by one internet cable guide as, "Five gay men come together for sex, drugs and adventure."

As the PTC's Tim Winter explained the nature of this major battle in the Culture War with Hollywood, "We face well-financed opponents who will spend literally hundreds of millions of dollars to turn public sentiment in their favor."[23] The hundreds of millions of dollars that Hollywood continues spending to stop the free-market economy of personal choice in television programming doesn't just go toward buying advertising time on television to promote the industry's highly rigged system of consumer price gouging. A large portion of that money goes toward "purchasing" influence in Washington, directly and indirectly.

* * *

I can attest to one of the more blatant examples of how this is accomplished by the biggest players from Hollywood and Washington. In 1995, Senator Howell Heflin stopped by my office at the Alabama Film Commission during one of his visits in Montgomery. He was planning to retire soon and wanted to remind me of the historic sites in north Alabama that would make good locations for movie companies.

I asked the senator if he ever had any dealings with MPAA President Jack Valenti. Heflin flashed a broad grin, noting he had met Valenti on a couple of occasions over the years and that the MPAA president was known as a "troller" who stalked the hallways of congressional office buildings, often with an assistant in tow.

Senator Heflin also explained that just six months earlier, Valenti had to be "politely ejected" from the senator's office and told "never to return." As the senator explained in his classic baritone north Alabama drawl, "Mr. Valenti had stopped by my office to talk, on the behalf of an industry friend, concerning some provision in the Communications Decency Act. After I thanked him for his kind input, Mr. Valenti remained seated and wanted to know how I might vote on certain future legislation. When I explained that I had not even seen the final draft, Mr Valenti told me that a vote in 'his' direction would be welcomed and *rewarded*."

"What do you suppose he meant?" I asked the senator.

"He was very straightforward about his intent. If I agreed with 'his way' of thinking, and promised my support right there—on the spot—he would leave my office and in five minutes his aide would come in and lay a tri-fold notepad holder, lined with 100 c-notes [$100 bills], on my desktop as a 'retirement gift' for being a 'good' Democrat."

"And . . ."

"And I assured him I am a good Democrat and that's why I was Chairman of the Senate Ethics Committee. And before I asked him to leave and never set foot in my office again, he was welcome to give me a list of all 'good Democrats' and 'good Republicans' he had been 'buying' for the last thirty years. He stood up, smiled briefly, and left just as quietly as he had slithered into my office like a snake in the Bankhead forest."

Clearly, not *all* members of the entertainment industry are quite that direct in subverting the votes of elected officials. But, the fact that Hollywood's Dark Prince was still operating in this fashion after thirty years on the job as the Number One official cheerleading lobbyist for all the major Hollywood studio conglomerates says much about the dark underbelly of the industry and, perhaps, explains why the overwhelming public voice is sometimes "conveniently ignored."

* * *

Fortunately, the Parents Television Council and the FCC's Chairman Kevin Martin are not giving up on Cable Choice for the American consumer. In June of 2007, the PTC issued a press release praising the efforts of Congressional Representatives Dan Lipinsky (D-IL) and Jeff Fortenberry (R-NE) for their introduction of legislation called the "Family and Consumer Choice Act of 2007." The bill is designed to provide individuals and families with the ability to choose and pay for *only* the cable networks they want. The FCC's Martin threw his full support behind the bill and joined with the PTC's Director of Corporate and Government Affairs, Dan Isett, to announce the bill at a joint press conference.

Isett was very clear about their adversaries in Hollywood, "Cable content is controlled by a handful of powerful media conglomerates who for years have extorted money from subscribers by creating new channels, adding them to expanded basic cable tiers, and forcing subscribers to pay for them—whether they wanted those new channels or not."[24] Isett concluded by noting that Congressmen Lipinski and Fortenberry were taking on "real political fortitude to side with families and stand up to the millions of dollars the entertainment industry spends to buy influence in Washington."[25]

A welcome boost to the Congressmen came in September 2007 when the United States anti-trust division filed a federal lawsuit that demands cable customers be given Cable Choice opportunities. The companies named in the suit are NBC Universal, Inc., The Walt Disney Co., Fox Entertainment Group, Time-Warner, Comcast, Cox Communications, The Direct TV Group, Echostar Satellite, Charter Communications and Cablevision Systems.

Antitrust lawyer Maxwell M. Blecher explained that the complicated web of contracts and arrangements among these companies amounted to a monolithic cartel that deprived consumers of choice, caused them to pay inflated prices and forced them to pay for cable channels they do not want. Ironically, the federal action was taken almost sixty years to the date since the federal government forced the movie industry to stop block-booking in 1947.

Many critics see a more ominous creature on the horizon. At best, the entertainment industry is appealing their fines and hoping to "buy time" to delay any changes until the next president is elected in November of 2008, whom they fully hope will be a Democrat.

When Clinton faltered, the entertainment industry felt equally comfortable with Barack Obama as President. Thanks to David Geffen's intervention and the financial contributions of more than 700 celebrities and industry insiders, Obama will deliver a hands off policy toward Hollywood's "fast-track" virtual media molestation of children at the movie house and your house. This policy caused much more money to flow into the Obama presidential campaign from Hollywood in addition to his assurance that he would strongly oppose drug testing in the Hollywood entertainment industry.

The FCC is on the front lines at the Culture War with events, issues and legal rulings changing rapidly. Both the Parents Television Council and the Media Research Center maintain excellent websites that not only allow you to track the news and legislation affecting television, they also give you resources to become involved in a meaningful pro-active plan for change. To stay updated, log onto *www.parentstv.org* and *www.mrc.org*.

CHAPTER 25

A GRASSROOTS VICTORY

> *Hollywood can make successful movies; they just don't want to.*
> —Mike Gallagher

Hollywood was fuming on April 27, 2005, as President Bush pulled out his pen and signed the Family Movie Act (FMA) into law. The victory was well deserved for Bill Aho, Chairman of ClearPlay. The Utah-based company was founded by brothers Matt and Lee Jarman in 1999 to develop proprietary consumer electronic software that literally "cleaned up" DVDs of their graphic violence, profanity and rapidly escalating scenes of pornographic sex.

Movies rated R, PG-13 and PG could now be viewed by individuals and families who had been divided into "age appropriate" rankings for forty years as a result of the Ratings Scheme. The Jarman brothers had created an inexpensive DVD player that is programmed with filtering technology that skips objectionable content in a movie, often with little notice by the viewer.

The ClearPlay DVD player can be customized to fourteen categories of objectionable content. The player will not automatically "correct" any DVD that is purchased for home viewing. Filtering software is already installed for a number of DVD releases when the unit is purchased. And, as new DVDs came into the market, consumers can easily download the new filters for that particular film directly from the internet. Another DVD player, MaxPlay—which uses ClearPlay technology—will allow new filters to be downloaded directly over the telephone.[1]

Oh, you didn't read about this in the newspaper or see anything on network news? You didn't know that the President of the United States of America had to sign a bill into law in order for this to be made available to you? No surprise

THE HOLLYWOOD CULTURE WAR

there. Now you have the downside of major movie studios owning the network news. This nifty technology is the last thing you needed to know. As far as the infotainment media is concerned, you really didn't need to know about this at all.

In September of 2002, eight major movie studios, the Directors Guild of America (DGA) and a host of directors, including sleaze king Martin Scorcese, filed a lawsuit against ClearPlay and a number of other movie editing companies that had arrived on the scene to provide family-friendly films such as CleanFlicks, CleanFilms, Play It Clean Video and Family Flix.[2] The very names of these new video companies clearly implied just how "dirty" movies had become in the last four decades.

Two companies, Trilogy Studios and Family Shield, went out of business fairly quickly, unable to mount the financial cost of defending their service. Ironically, Jack Valenti once cited Trilogy as an alternative to individuals and families who quit going to the theater and stopped renting DVDs because of the ever present debauchery of most movies.

In fact, these companies had discovered the "disappearing audience" that fled the theaters in horror along with their children in the late 1960s, seemingly never to return. And, just as some innovators found a way to bring them back, with no loss of profit to Hollywood—and actually an increased profit—the movie studios and directors protested, saying, in effect, "We want to stick our dysfunctional nightmares in your throat—down to the last foul word and severed head—like it or not!"

Director Martha Coolidge was the DGA president at the time of the suit and said consumer editing of movies is *just plain wrong*. Her successor, director Michael Apted, noted angrily, "Directors put their skill, craft and often years of hard work into the creation of a film . . . so we have great passion about protecting our work, which is our signature and brand identification.[3]

That signature brand identification is akin to tainted meat and is the main reason movie attendance is declining. Also, the argument between the directors and the studios fails miserably to mention that most movies debuting on network television are edited heavily. Furthermore, the "final cut" shown at theaters and most DVDs has already been extensively edited by movie producers and studio executives who disagreed with certain scenes or the length of the film by the director.

I have, as a location scout, heard more screaming matches between directors and producers over the final content of a film than I care to remember. The movie you see at the theater is rarely ever what the director initially wanted. There exists a love-hate relationship between producers and directors—but mostly hate.

* * *

The battle between the entertainment industry and the movie editing retailers came down to two important distinctions. The technology used by ClearPlay to clean up films was significantly different from the other companies. ClearPlay's technology does not physically alter the DVD. The software in ClearPlay simply deletes the offensive material that appears on the home screen.

The other companies offered a mail order service in which DVDs were delivered pre-edited, meaning the copy had been altered, much like the copies shown on airlines. But, the movie industry's lawsuit claimed that these physically altered discs were an infringement on their copyright. While legally accurate, these copyright holders give exemptions to television stations and to the airline industry, but not to retailers who are doing nothing different in removing the carefully constructed raunch.

By 2007, some airlines were accepting "less edited" versions of movies that still contained heavy doses of blood and gore. U S Airways, Continental and Virgin were among the biggest offenders. A spokesperson for Continental told *The New York Times* that parents who were offended should *turn their children's heads away* from the screen. Virgin Airlines founder, Richard Branson, does not "allow" edited movies on his planes. "With us carrying a lot of Hollywood VIPs and movie stars, we treat motion pictures with respect." Translation: We don't give a flip about your kids while our celebrities are swilling martinis and watching actors have sex in the passenger cabin.

Within four years of the entertainment industry's lawsuit, U.S. District Judge Richard Matsch ruled that CleanFlix, CleanFilms, Play It Clean Video and Family Flix must "cease and desist" production of any more family-friendly DVDs. The DGA and the studios really wanted to go after and destroy ClearPlay the most; Martha Coolidge had said as much when the lawsuit was filed in 2002.

Bill Aho, Chairman of ClearPlay, had spent almost one million dollars by 2005 in defense of his unique DVD home filtering player. The industry's desperate insistence on destroying ClearPlay made about as much sense as Jack Valenti's attempt to destroy the home VCR in the early 1980s. Sony, makers of the Betamax home VCRs eventually convinced Valenti and the narrow-minded studio executives that home video could open a whole new window for movie revenue, which is exactly what happened.

ClearPlay and the other companies were opening up new streams of revenue to the studios from people who had refused to watch "age-appropriate" movies. With most of the companies dissolved as a result of Judge Matsch's ruling, their former customers are not going to be coerced into buying DVDs with restrictive ratings. The market for that service potentially reached into the millions of customers domestically and abroad.

In 2005, Congress was preparing the Family Entertainment and Copyright Act (FECA) in order to institute stiffer penalties on individuals and groups that engaged in criminal and bootleg copying of films for international distribution on the black market. The bill also intended to restrict any future reincarnations of companies like CleanFlicks and CleanFilms.

However, ClearPlay, because of its distinct technology, was rescued at the eleventh hour by Senator Orrin Hatch (R-UT) and Representative Lamar Smith (R-TX) who drafted the Family Movie Act (FMA) and inserted it into the larger FECA bill. The FMA would exempt Aho's company and the proprietary technology from being considered as copyright infringement mechanisms. The movie industry and the Directors Guild were outraged. The meshing of the two bills together created a dilemma for the MPAA which had lobbied for two years to create FECA.

The movie industry was much more interested in stopping the expensive flow of bootleg products than fighting Congress to remove the "exempt conduct" language in the FMA, even if it resulted in "artistic rape," as the MPAA declared. Nevertheless, according to ClearPlay's Aho, the MPAA pulled out its most powerful lobbyists with pockets full of money in an attempt to surgically remove the Family Movie Act from the FECA bill.

For once, the entertainment industry could not bully or buy Congress as FECA was passed with the Family Movie Act intact. This was the bill signed by President Bush on April 27, 2005. Hollywood was fit to be tied. How dare the U.S. Congress give the American people something they have wanted for forty years.

Bill Aho called President Bush's signing of the bill "a victory for families" and said the legislation would benefit the growth and development of his company and others who wanted to ebb the flow of coarsening entertainment. Aho did not take advantage of this decision to monopolize the industry. Committed to the cause, ClearPlay is openly licensing its product and filtering technologies to consumer wholesalers and electronic retailers. Aho is passionate about sharing the technology because "moms and dads need all the help they can get to protect their children." ClearPlay founder Matt Jarman agreed, noting that this victory in the Culture War was an opportunity to pursue significant growth for parental control technology to filter scenes and dialogue that both individuals and families find offensive.

What the Ratings Scheme, V-Chip and blocking technologies could not accomplish because of their purposely oblique nature, ClearPlay accomplished with simple and basic consumer electronics. It was as if the venerable old Production Code had been resurrected and placed in a small box on top of the television. Pandora's Box was closed again almost four decades after Jack Valenti opened it.

Jack Valenti was only six months into retirement when the Family Movie Act was passed by Congress. Personally, the old Dark Prince was livid that some "do-gooders" from middle-America discovered a way to truly override his

Ratings Scheme of 1968, even if it was only in the home living room. The "Quiet Conspiracy" by the "Gang of Four" must have seemed like a distant memory to the old ringleader. Two years later, Jack Valenti suffered a stroke and died on April 26, 2007.

Though the MPAA could not stop the Family Movie Act, they made it clear that one of Washington's most powerful lobby, the entertainment industry, was not happy. The MPAA even hired lobbyist John Feehrey to appear before the House Subcommittee on Commerce, Trade and Consumer Protection for nothing more than a subtle, threatening finger-wagging speech.

It was here, at the nearly empty House Chamber meeting room that Feehrey made his patently misleading statement that, "I trust you would agree that all movies should not be geared to an audience of 5-year-olds." The few Congressmen present did not even try to hide their heavy eyelids as their chins fell slowly to their chests.

The true intention of Hollywood's lawsuit against the editing companies was best summarized by Kelly Boggs of BP News out of Alexandria, Louisiana, "The editing companies exposed the real motive of Hollywood. While the film industry has long maintained that it only reflects society, it is clear that it really wants to influence it. And, according to the movies that Tinseltown repeatedly produces, the culture Hollywood desires is overflowing with gratuitous sex, inane violence and prolific profanity."[4]

In the Culture War, Bill Aho and the Jarman brothers scored a genuine victory, adding, "It's a real grassroots story."

CHAPTER 26

THE ENTERTAINMENT RESOURCE GUIDE: WINNING THE CULTURE WAR

> *If you grow up believing in nothing, you'll grow up believing in anything.*
> —John Ratzenberger

Because of the wholesale failure of the Ratings Scheme for feature films, television programming, DVDs and video games, a large number of grassroots media watchdog groups have organized over the years to provide consumers with more extensive and detailed information about the vast array of entertainment product available in ever-increasing quantities. These sources allow individuals and families to make more informative decisions on how to spend their entertainment dollar.

These organizations represent a broad cross-section of viewpoints that identify themselves as faith-based, non-partisan, academic, secular, non-profit and for-profit. But, the common thread among all groups is that the one-size-fits all ratings provided by the movie, television and video game industries does not address key questions of content beyond simply, and sadly, segregating the audience into "age-appropriate" categories.

These groups also make an important point about the content of contemporary entertainment. Adults are not only educated and informed for the sake of their children, but for their own sake as not just "adult" role models, but "Mature Adult" role models. What does it say about mature adults who tell children *what not to watch* and then proceed to indulge in the same callous, coarse and profanely vulgar "entertainment?"

The grassroots media watchdogs in this section work tirelessly to list the titles to hundreds of thousands of entertainment venues including not only movies, television, DVDs and video games, but also the explosive growth in new music releases every day. A visitor to one site may find a detailed movie review that is completely different from another listed site offering a review of the same movie. But, whether viewed individually or together, visitors to the Entertainment Resource Guide will come away with a wealth of knowledge that will allow them to make up their own mind about what to watch and what to avoid when spending their entertainment dollar.

These sites do not give away spoilers as to the endings of each product, but they will alert you to the increasingly brutal imagery, dialogue and agendas that Hollywood inserts into almost all of their offerings. And, some sites offer advocacy into fighting against the cultural decay aggressively pushed by Hollywood.

By accessing this information, you can help rebuff one of Hollywood's biggest lies, "You can't judge a movie until you've seen it." You don't have to watch *anything* if you know in advance that an entertainment venue plans to assault your senses and attempt to crush your moral compass while picking your pocket.

Because the movie, television, video game and movie industries are among the very few that do not offer a money-back guarantee, being forewarned is being forearmed in what has developed into a very real Culture War. Winning will involve the determination to fight the good fight.

As Michael Medved concluded, "In short, the popular culture is now as unavoidable as any airborne pollutant. To say that if you don't like it, you should just tune it out makes as much sense as saying that if you don't like the smog, stop breathing . . . That is why the perspectives of the popular culture are the appropriate issue for all of us, not just for members of the entertainment industry."

There is the very real possibility you may not need to use the Entertainment Resource Guide. You may come to the point when you pass by the movie theater, shut off the television, unplug the video games, pull out the earplugs, stop instant-messaging, stop text messaging, shut down the internet and just take a deep breath. It may be a good time to call an old friend or family member and actually have a human conversation. You might even pull up a lawn chair on the patio with a neighbor.

Over twenty years ago, in 1985, author Neil Postman saw this day coming and declared, "We are amusing ourselves to death." But, should you decide to indulge in some entertainment, there is no better place to find the information you need than the Entertainment Resource Guide.

*   *   *

American Family Association (AFA)
    P.O. Drawer 2440
    Tupelo, MS 38803
    662-844-5036
    www.afa.net

Parents Television Council (PTC)
707 Wilshire Blvd. #7075
Los Angeles, CA 90017
213-669-9255
800-882-6868
www.parentstv.org

Plugged-In; Focus On The Family
Colorado Springs, CO 80995
1-800-A-Family (232-6459)
www.pluggedinonline.com

MovieGuide®
P.O. Box 190010
Atlanta, GA 31119
1-800-577-6684
www.MovieGuide.org

MediaWise®
National Institute on Media and the Family
606 24th Avenue South, Suite 606
Minneapolis, MN 55454
612-672-5437
www.mediafamily.org

Morality In Media (MIM)
475 Riverside Dr., Suite 239
New York, NY 10115
212-870-3222
www.moralityinmedia.org

Office for Film and Broadcasting
United States Conference of Catholic Bishops
1011 First Avenue, 13th Floor
New York, NY 10022
202-541-3000
www.uscb.org/movies

Crosswalk
4880 Santa Rosa Rd.
Camarillo, CA 93012
www.crosswalk.com

The Dove Foundation
535 E. Fulton, Suite 1A
Grand Rapids, MI 49503
616-454-5021
800-968-8437
www.dove.org

Fight The Good Fight Ministries
P.O. Box 2202
Simi Valley, CA 93065
805-522-7005
www.goodfight.org
www.goodfight.org/exposelist.html
www.goodfight.org/hollywoodunmasked.htm

EX Ministries
P.O. Box 24870
Ft. Worth, TX 76124
www.exministries.com
www.exministries.com/watch30.html

www.michaelmedved.com

www.decentfilms.com

Christian Spotlight On Entertainment
P.O. Box 200
Gilbert, AZ 85299
480-507-3621
www.christiananswers.net/spotlight

Common Sense Media
1550 Bryant St., Suite 555
San Francisco, CA 94103
415-863-0600
www.commonsensemedia.org

www.screenit.com

APPENDIX I

TV/MOVIES/MUSIC Top Contributors to Federal Candidates and Parties 2000

Rank	Organization	Amount	Dems	Rpbs
1	Time-Warner	$2,215,721	66%	34%
2	Saban Entertainment	$1,572,650	100%	0%
3	Viacom Inc.	$1,555,875	78%	22%
4	Walt Disney Company	$1,449,807	56%	44%
5	DreamWorks SKG	$1,101,865	100%	0%
6	Cablevision Systems	$1,026,104	67%	33%
7	Westwood One	$976,339	37%	63%
8	National Association of Broadcasters	$963,100	31%	62%
9	Vivendi Universal	$907,137	85%	15%
10	National Cable Television Association	$894,071	38%	62%
11	News Corp	$774,980	31%	64%
12	AT&T	$718,939	36%	64%
13	CSC Holdings	$705,000	57%	43%
14	Comcast Corp	$595,059	50%	50%
15	Chartwell Partners	$563,000	2%	98%
16	Post 391 Inc.	$529,000	100%	0%
17	AMFM Inc	$515,290	26%	73%
18	Falcon Cable TV	$469,000	100%	0%
19	Charter Communications	$467,350	28%	72%
20	Recording Industry Association of America	$464,243	50%	50%

TV/MOVIES/MUSIC Top Contributors to Federal Candidates and Parties 2004

Rank	Organization	Amount	Dems	Rpbs
1	Time-Warner	$2,612,039	76%	24%
2	Viacom Inc.	$1,399,621	81%	19%
3	Comcast Corp	$1,347,735	50%	50%
4	National Cable Television Association	$1,314,742	44%	56%
5	Walt Disney Co.	$980,957	71%	29%
6	Clear Channel Communicaitons	$884,046	34%	66%
7	National Association of Broadcasters	$697,778	38%	62%
8	News Corp	$607,056	74%	26%
9	General Electric	$581,986	75%	25%
10	Cablevision Systems	$579,400	68%	32%
11	Sony Corp of America	$559,499	65%	35%
12	EchoStar Communications	$453,200	54%	46%
13	DreamWorks SKG	$286,648	95%	5%
14	YES Network	$284,625	100%	0%
15	Salem Communications	$245,455	0%	100%
16	Chartwell Partners	$240,250	19%	81%
17	Univision	$232,600	30%	70%
18	Creative Artists Agency	$204,900	97%	3%
19	Saban Captial Group	$197,348	98%	2%
20	ASCAP	$192,900	66%	34%

Source: The Center for Responsive Politics

APPENDIX II

Individual Celebrity Contributions to Al Gore—2000 Presidential Race

Jane Alexander	Michael Douglas	Lisa Loeb
Steve Allen	Richard Dreyfuss	Rue McClanahan
Julie Araskog	Michael Eisner	Terrance McNally
Jon Avnet	Tovah Feldshuh	Dennis Miller
Billy Baldwin	Giselle Fernandez	Donna Mills
Paris Barclay	Harrison Ford	Thelonious Monk Jr.
Warren Beatty	Glenn Frey	Rob Morrow
Ed Begley Jr.	Lilian Garcia	Jack Nicholson
Peter Berg	James Garner	Gwyneth Paltrow
Candace Bergen	David Geffen	Jesse Peretz
Alan Bergman	Jami Gertz	Chynna Phillips
Gregory Bernstein	Robert Getchell	Lou Diamond Phillips
Stephen Bing	Peri Gilpin	Dean Pitchford
Edgar Bronfman	Jonathan Glickman	Brett Ratner
Roscoe Lee Brown	Berry Gordy	Sumner Redstone
Nicolas Cage	Matt Groening	Michele Singer Reiner
Frank Capra III	Steve Guttenberg	Rob Reiner
Kate Capshaw-Spielberg	Ronald Guttman	Daniella Rich
David Caruso	Larry Hagman	Denise Rich
Chevy Chase	John Hallum	David W. Rintels
Tina Chen	Herbie Hancock	Hilary Rosen
Bruce Cohen	Rita Wilson Hanks	Gary Ross
Michael S. Connolly	Tom Hanks	Carol Bayer Sager
Kevin Costner	Mariel Hemingway	R. Max Samson
Sheryl Crow	Don Henley	Cathy Sandrich
Lavinia Currier	Dan Jinks	Jay Sandrich

Beverly D'Angelo
Ted Danson
Ossie Davis
Robert DeNiro
Evans Donnell
Neal Doughty
Aaron Spelling
Mary Steenburgen
Nancy Stephens
Bunny Stivers
Oliver Stone
Sharon Stone
Barabara Streisand
Lily Tomlin

Robert L. Johnson
Quincy Jones
Tommy Lee Jones
Jeffrey Katzenberg
Sherry Lansing
Norman Lear
Jeane Trippelhorn
Jack Valenti
Bruce Vilanch
Ruth Warrick
Lew Wasserman
Eric Briant Wells
Tanya Wexler
Billy Dee Williams

Jerry Seinfeld
Cynthia Sikes
Nancy Sinatra
Jimmy Smits
Suzanne Somers
Steven Spielberg
Norm Woodel
Ahmet Zappa
Diva Zappa
Dweezil Zappa
Gail Zappa
Amy Zimmerman
Edward Zwick

Individual Celebrity Contributions to George Bush—2000 Presidential Race

Joe Bonsall
Pat Boone
Edgar Bronfman
James Burrows
Gary Chapman
Lionel Chetwynd
Gloria Carlin Chetwynd
Van Cliburn
Mike Curb
Joanna Heimbold Welliver
Warren Zide

Shera Danese
Michael Eisner
Bob Gale
Larry Gatlin
Morris Goldman
Eric Gustavson
Tom Joyner
Edward Kerr
Loretta Lynn
Donald Wrye

Joe McSpadden
Jim Nantz
Chuck Norris
Charles Perez
Russell "Red" Steagall
Craig Titley
Alessandro Uzielli
Jack Valenti
Kenneth Waissman

Source: The Center for Responsive Politics

APPENDIX III

THE PRODUCTION CODE
Motion Picture Association of America (MPAA)
(1930 to 1968)

Author's Note:
There does not exist an "original" or "extant" copy of the Production Code as formulated by Martin Quigley and Daniel Lord for the Motion Picture Producers and Distributors of America (MPPDA), the original name of the MPAA. Many versions were reprinted in journals, articles, books, and scholarly works over the years. There is good reason to believe Jack Valenti destroyed any originals that may have existed in his office. Nevertheless, the Production Code varied from version to version adding or deleting certain "working principles" over time. The version printed here is from one of the earliest known drafts of the Production Code. This copy covers the Reasons Supporting the General Principles that served as a basic guide for the committee at the MPAA when reviewing scripts.

The Code also contains a preamble that supports the justification for a production code by the movie industry. While the preamble is too long for this printing, it is worth noting certain provisions of principle that defined the distinction of movies and their impact as opposed to other forms of communication and art.

Under Section I of the preamble the code noted:
"Mankind has always recognized the importance of entertainment and its value in rebuilding the bodies and souls of human beings. But it has always recognized that entertainment can be of a character either HELPFUL or HARMFUL to the human race, and in consequences has clearly distinguished between:

    a.   Entertainment which tends to improve the human race, and
    b.   Entertainment which tends to degrade human beings.

HENCE the Moral Importance of entertainment is something which has been universally recognized. It enters intimately into the lives of men and women and affects them closely; it occupies their minds and affections during leisure hours, and ultimately touches the whole of their lives. A man may be judged by his standard of entertainment as easily as by the standard of his work.

So correct entertainment raises the whole standard of a nation. Wrong entertainment lowers the whole living conditions and moral ideals of the human race."

While many may think that part of the preamble to be quaint and outdated, a simple glance at today's culture and Hollywood's detrimental impact is evidence that the authors knew exactly the implications of their wording if not followed in at least basic principle.

Another insightful section of the preamble pinpoints the origin of a film's "moral quality," which does not spring out of thin air.

Under Section II of the preamble the Code noted:

"HENCE: The motion pictures, which are the most popular of modern arts for the masses, have their moral quality from the intention of the minds which produce them and from their effects on the moral lives and reactions of their audiences. This gives them a most important morality.

1. They *reproduce* the morality of the men who use the pictures as a medium for their ideas and ideals.
2. They *affect* the moral standards of those who through the screen take in these ideas and ideals.

In the case of motion pictures, this effect may be particularly emphasized because no art has so quick and so widespread an appeal to the masses. It has become in an incredibly short period the *art of the multitudes*."

Again, one need only tune into *Entertainment Tonight* or pick up any one of the hundreds of celebrity magazines to see the human train wrecks that make today's entertainment and the effect on the people who consume it. The abolishment of the Production Code dealt the single most devastating and destructive blow to American and worldwide culture by unleashing the unbridled nightmares of "creative" individuals and then celebrating their sickness as "art" to be embraced as lifestyle, religion, fashion, and "attitude." Martin Quigley and Daniel Lord were visionaries to the extent that they recognized film's power. As the father of value manipulation, Jack Valenti realized that power, too, and wanted to define decency down by destroying the Production Code.

THE HOLLYWOOD CULTURE WAR

The following is an abbreviated version of the Production Code.

THE MPAA PRODUCTION CODE
(Abolished: 1968)

REASONS SUPPORTING THE GENERAL PRINCIPLES

I. No picture shall be produced which will lower the moral standards of those who see it. Hence the sympathy of the audience should never be thrown to the side of crime, wrong-doing, evil, or sin.

   This is done:
   1. When *evil* is made to appear *attractive* or *alluring* and *good* is made to appear *unattractive*.
   2. When the *sympathy* of the audience is thrown on the side of crime, wrong-doing, evil, sin. The same thing is true of a film that would throw sympathy against goodness, honor, innocence, purity, or honesty.

Note: Sympathy with a person who sins is not the same as sympathy with the sin or crime of which he is guilty. We may feel sorry for the plight of the murderer or even understand the circumstances which led him to his crime. We may not feel sympathy with the wrong which he has done. The presentation of evil is often essential for art or fiction or drama. This in itself is not wrong provided:

   a. That evil is *not presented alluringly*. Even if later in the film the evil is condemned or punished, it must not be allowed to appear so attractive that the audience's emotions are drawn to desire or approve as strongly that later the condemnation is forgotten and only the apparent joy of the sin remembered.
   b. That throughout, the audience feels sure that *evil is wrong* and *good is right*.

II. Correct standards of life shall, as far as possible, be represented.

   A *wide knowledge of life and of living* is made possible through the film. When right standards are consistently presented, the motion picture exercises the most powerful influence. It builds character, develops right ideals, inculcates correct principles, and all this in the attractive story form.

   If motion pictures consistently *hold up for admiration high types of characters* and present stories that will affect lives for the better, they can become the most powerful natural force for the improvement of mankind.

III. Law, natural or human, shall not be ridiculed, nor shall sympathy be created for its violation. By *natural law* is understood the law which is written in the hearts of all mankind, the great underlying principles of right and justice dictated by conscience.

By *human law* is understood the law written by civilized nations.

1. The *presentation of crimes* against the law is *often necessary* for the carrying out of the plot. But the presentation must not throw sympathy with the crime as against the law nor with the criminal as against those who punish him.
2. The *courts of the land* should not be presented as unjust. This does not mean that a single court may not be represented as unjust, much less that a single court official must not be presented this way. But the court system of the country must not suffer as a result of this presentation.

REASONS UNDERLYING PARTICULAR APPLICATIONS

Preliminary:

I. Sin and evil enter into the story of human beings and hence in themselves are dramatic material.
II. In the use of this material, it must be distinguished between sin which repels by its very nature, and *sins which often attract*.

   a. In the first class come murder, most theft, many legal crimes, lying, hypocrisy, cruelty, etc.
   b. In the second class come sex sins, sins and crimes of apparent heroism, such as banditry, daring thefts, leadership in evil, organized crime, revenge, etc.

   The first class needs far less care in treatment, as sins and crimes of this class are naturally unattractive. The audience instinctively condemns and is repelled.

   Hence the important objective must be to avoid the hardening of the audience, especially of those who are young and impressionable, to the thought and fact of crime. People can become accustomed even to murder, cruelty, brutality, and repellent crimes, if these are sufficiently repeated.

   The second class needs real care in handling, as the response of human natures to their appeal is obvious. This is treated more fully below.

III. A careful distinction can be made between films intended for *general distribution* and films intended for use in theaters restricted to a *limited audience*. Themes and plots quite appropriate for the latter would be altogether out of place and dangerous in the former.

> Note: In general this practice of using a general theatre and limiting its patronage during the showing of a certain film to "Adults Only" is not completely satisfactory and is only partially effective.
>
> However, mature minds may easily understand and accept without harm subject matter in plots which do younger people positive harm.
> Hence: If there should be created a special type of theatre, catering exclusively to an adult audience, for plays of this character (plays with problem themes, difficult discussions and mature treatment) it would seem to afford an outlet, which does not now exist, for pictures unsuitable for general distribution but permissible for exhibition to a restricted audience.

I. CRIMES AGAINST THE LAW
   The *treatment of crimes* against the law must not:

   1. *Teach methods of* crime.
   2. *Inspire potential criminals* with a desire for imitation.
   3. *Make criminals seem heroic* and justified.

Revenge in modern times shall not be justified. In lands and ages of less developed civilization and moral principles, revenge may sometimes be presented. This would be the case especially in places where no law exists to cover the crime because of which revenge is committed.

Because of its evil consequences, the *drug traffic* should not be presented in any form. The existence of the trade should not be brought to the attention of audiences.

The use of liquor should never be excessively presented even in picturing countries where its use is illegal. In scenes from American life, the necessities of plot and proper characterization alone justify its use. And in this case, it should be shown with moderation.

II. SEX
   Out of regard for the sanctity of marriage and the home, the triangle, that is, love of a third party by one already married, needs careful handling. The treatment should not throw sympathy against marriage as an institution.

Scenes of passion must be treated with an honest acknowledgment of human mature and its normal reactions. Many scenes cannot be presented without arousing dangerous emotions on the part of the immature, the young, and the criminal classes.

Even within the limits of *pure love*, certain facts have been universally regarded by lawmakers as outside the limits of safe presentation.

In the case of *impure love*, the love which society has always regarded as wrong and which has been banned by divine law, the following are important:

1. Impure love must *not* be presented as *attractive and beautiful*.
2. It must *not* be the subject of *comedy or farce*, or treated as material for laughter.
3. It must *not* be presented in such a way as to *arouse passion* or morbid curiosity on the part of the audience.
4. It must not be made to seem *right and permissible*.
5. In general, it must *not* be *detailed* in methods and manner.

III. VULGARITY; IV. OBSCENITY; V. PROFANITY; hardly need further explanation than is contained in the Code.

VI. COSTUME

General Principles:

1. The effect of nudity or semi-nudity upon the normal man or woman and much more upon the young and immature person, has been honestly recognized by all lawmakers and moralists.
2. Hence the fact that the nude or semi-nude body may be beautiful does not make its use in the films moral. For, in addition to its beauty, the effect of the nude or semi-nude body on the normal individual must be taken into consideration.
3. Nudity or semi-nudity used simply to put a 'punch' into a picture comes under the head of immoral actions. It is immoral in its effect on the average audience.
4. Nudity can never be permitted as being *necessary for the plot*. Semi-nudity must not result in undue or indecent exposure.
5. Transparent or translucent materials and silhouette are frequently more suggestive than actual exposure.

VII. DANCES

Dancing in general is recognized as an *Art* and as a *beautiful* form of expressing human emotions.

But dances which suggest or represent sexual action, whether performed solo or with two or more, dances intended to excite the emotional reaction of an audience, dances with movement of the breasts, excessive body movements while the feet are stationary, violate decency and are wrong.

VIII. RELIGION

The reason why ministers of religion may not be comic characters or villains is simply because the attitude taken toward them may easily become the attitude taken toward religion in general. Religion is lowered in the minds of the audience because of the lowering of the audience's respect for a minister.

IX. LOCATIONS

Certain places are so closely and thoroughly associated with sexual life or with sexual sin that their use must be carefully limited.

X. NATIONAL FEELINGS

The just rights, history, and feelings of any nation are entitled to consideration and respectful treatment.

XI. TITLES

As the title of a picture is the brand on that particular type of goods, it must conform to the ethical practices of all such titling.

XII. REPELLENT SUBJECTS

Such subjects are occasionally necessary for the plot. Their treatment must never offend good taste nor injure the sensibilities of an audience.

Source: Gregory D. Black, *Hollywood Censored* (United Kingdom: Cambridge University Press, 1999).

APPENDIX IV

OBSCENE, INDECENT, AND PROFANE BROADCASTS—FCC Consumer Facts

IT'S AGAINST THE LAW

It is a violation of the federal law to air obscene programming at any time. It is also a violation of federal law to air indecent programming or profane language during certain hours.

Congress has given the Federal Communications Commission (FCC) the responsibility for administratively enforcing these laws. The FCC may revoke a station license, impose a monetary forfeiture, or issue a warning if a station airs obscene, indecent, or profane material.

OBSCENE BROADCASTS ARE PROHIBITED AT ALL TIMES

Obscene material is not protected by the First Amendment to the Constitution and cannot be broadcast at any time. The Supreme Court has established that, to be obscene, material must meet a three-pronged test.

- An average person, applying contemporary community standards, must find that the material, as a whole, appeals to the prurient interest;
- The material must depict or describe, in a patently offensive way, sexual conduct specifically defined by applicable law; and
- The material, taken as a whole, must lack serious literary, artistic, political, or scientific value.

INDECENT BROADCAST RESTRICTIONS

The FCC has defined broadcast indecency as "language or material that, in context, depicts or describes, in terms patently offensive as measured by contemporary community standards for the broadcast medium, sexual or excretory organs or activities." Indecent programming contains patently offensive sexual or excretory material that does not rise to the level of obscenity.

The courts have held that indecent material is protected by the First Amendment and cannot be banned entirely. It may, however, be restricted in order to avoid its broadcast during times of the day when there is a reasonable risk that children may be in the audience.

Consistent with a federal indecency statute and federal court decisions interpreting the statute, the Commission adopted a rule that broadcasts—both on television and radio—that fit within the indecency definition and that are aired between 6:00 a.m. and 10:00 p.m. are prohibited and subject to indecency enforcement action.

PROFANE BROADCAST RESTRICTIONS

The FCC has defined profanity as "including language so grossly offensive to members of the public who actually hear it as to amount to a nuisance." Like indecency, profane speech is prohibited on broadcast radio and television between the hours of 6:00 a.m. and 10:00 p.m.

ENFORCEMENT PROCEDURES AND FILING COMPLAINTS

Enforcement actions in this area are based on documented complaints received from the public about obscene, indecent, or profane material. FCC staff will review each complaint to determine whether it contains sufficient information to suggest that there has been a violation of the obscenity, indecency, or profanity laws. If it appears that a violation may have occurred, the staff will start an investigation, which may include a letter of inquiry to the broadcast station.

If the description of the material contained in the complaint is not sufficient to determine whether a violation of the statue of FCC rules regarding obscene, indecent, and profane material may have occurred, FCC staff will send the complainant a dismissal letter explaining the deficiencies in the complaint and how to have it reinstated. In such case, the complainant has the option of re-filing the complaint with additional information, filing either a petition for reconsideration, or, if the decision is a staff action, an application for review (appeal) to the full Commission.

If the facts and information contained in the complaint suggest that a violation of the statute or FCC rules regarding obscenity, indecency, and profanity did not occur, FCC staff will send the complainant a letter denying the complaint, or the FCC may deny the complaint by public order. In either situation, the complainant has the option of filing either a petition for reconsideration or, if the decision is a staff action, an application for review (appeal) to the full Commission.

If the FCC determines that the complained-of material was obscene, indecent, and/or profane, it may issue a Notice of Apparent Liability (NAL), which is a preliminary finding that the law or the FCC's rules have been violated. Subsequently, this preliminary finding may be confirmed, reduced, or rescinded when the FCC issues a Forfeiture Order.

For More Information:

Website:
www.fcc.gov/cgb/consumerfacts/obscene.html

Phone: 1-888-225-5322

APPENDIX V

THE TIMELINE OF NEW AGE PHILOSPHIES IN WESTERN CULTURE

The following New Age philosophies span a period of 125 years beginning with Friedrich Nietzsche and ending with George Soros. All of these individuals and movements share a common core belief that has promoted the deconstruction of healthy and cohesive societies around the world, but mainly in Western Civilization. While many others came before and can be traced back to ancient times, these philosophies are the ones that continue to reverberate today and are the root of the great divide in Western Culture.

1)
   - **MOVEMENT: Ubermensch (Superman) and (Nihilism)**
   - **PERPETRATOR: Friedrich Nietzsche (1844-1900)**
   - **OCCUPATION / PURSUITS: Philosopher / Drug Addict**
   - **GUIDING SLOGANS / CORE BELIEFS: "God is Dead"**
   - **TIME SPAN OF INFLUENCE: 1882 to Present.**

ELABORATION: Nietzsche's profound statement began the first major attack against the existence of morality and God in what is considered "modern times." It was the first ideological assault against Christians and Jews in Europe. Nietzsche promoted the concept of Ubermensch—Superman or Overman. This was the idea of power for its own sake, devoid of morals, values and especially religious faith. He called this "The will to power and nothing else." Nietzsche also believed democracy was useless. His occult philosophy of nihilism influenced Russian revolutionaries leading up to the Communist revolution of 1917. The

Nazis began to "officially" appropriate his philosophy in 1935. Mao said that this power emanated "from the barrel of a gun" which is the ultimate "will to power." Nietzsche influenced Sigmund Freud, Carl Jung, Jean-Paul Sartre and writers Albert Camus, Thomas Mann, William Butler Yeats, Aleister Crowley and hundreds more. Historical scholars have argued a distinction between Karl Marx and Nietzsche, but they both shared an unabashed disdain for the individual's opportunity and right to believe in a Divine power, especially as practiced in the Judeo-Christian norms of their day. The applied political philosophies of both have led to the deaths of over 100 million people since 1900, the year Nietzsche died after spending eleven years in a catatonic state as the result of a nervous breakdown in 1889. He became a favorite among the bohemian arts crowd, the first significant "counterculture," staring in the 1890's.

2)
- **MOVEMENT: The New Age**
- **PERPETRATOR: Aleister Crowley (1875-1947)**
- **OCCUPATION / PURSUITS: Occultist / Author / Drug Addict / New Age Founder**
- **GUIDING SLOGANS / CORE BELIEFS: "Do what thou will shall be the whole of the law."**
- **TIME SPAN OF INFLUENCE: 1904 to Present.**

***ELABORATION*:** Born in England, Crowley claimed he was "commanded" to bring in the "New Age" in 1904 by the spirit of the ancient Egyptian priest Aiwass, servant to the pagan god Horus. Organized the religion called Thelema to spread the word of "Do what thou will," later applied in popular culture as "Anything Goes." Crowley promoted every form of deviance known to mankind including demon worship, illegal drug use, casting evil spirits, sex with children and animals. Promoted homosexuality and pedophilia. Practiced a bizarre form of "Sex Magick" (his spelling) to cast spells and induce trances. Crowley would become the main inspiration behind most countercultural movements such as the beatniks, hippies and New Age beliefs. He received a renewed boost in the 1960s with devotees such as John Lennon, Paul McCartney, Mick Jagger and many more in the entertainment industry. Crowley was and remains an icon to many "Hard Rock" and Goth musicians such as Marilyn Manson. The British Press dubbed Crowley "The Wickedest Man In The World" in 1923.

3)
- **MOVEMENT: Existentialism**
- **PERPETRATOR: Jean-Paul Sartre ((1905-1980)**
- **OCCUPATION / PURSUITS: Philosopher / Drug Addict**

- **GUIDING SLOGANS / CORE BELIEFS:** "If God is dead, everything is possible."
- **TIME SPAN OF INFLUENCE:** Mid 1930s to Present.

ELABORATION: Sartre's guiding slogan was an addendum to Nietzsche's proclamation "God is Dead." Sartre's beliefs and writings reflected a cult of pessimism and nihilism (rejection of customary morality and religion) made popular in Europe after World War I and World War II. His signature book, *Being and Nothingness*, expressed his hatred of the Judeo-Christian ethic and helped accelerate the secularization of Europe begun by Nietzsche. Sartre coined the popular phrase "Bad Faith" and developed a philosophy around those two words. Sartre believed atheism was a form of personal power and he embraced Communism because of its official legal statutes against religion. Sartre's dark legacy was his encouragement of radical Islamic terrorism and he fully supported the return of the Ayatollah to Iran in 1979 in order to usher in the era of Islamo-Fascism that is now enveloping the entire world. Sartre was an occult writer of great contradictions equal to the writing and musings of Aleister Crowley. Former President Jimmy Carter was greatly influenced by Sartre.

4)
- **MOVEMENT: Church of Scientology**
- **PERPETRATOR: L. Ron Hubbard (1911-1986)**
- **OCCUPATION / PURSUITS: Drifter / Author / Drug Addict**
- **GUIDING SLOGANS / CORE BELIEFS: "Do as thou will. That is the whole of the law."—"Create your own law."**
- **TIME SPAN OF INFLUENCE: 1947 to Present.**

ELABORATION: According to L. Ron Hubbard, Jr., the senior Hubbard founded Scientology on the day Aleister Crowley died on December 1, 1947. Hubbard Sr. adopted the Crowley slogan virtually verbatim. L. Ron Hubbard claimed Crowley was a "good friend" and incorporated much of Crowley's occult teaching into Scientology. At one time the most mysterious of all occult New Age organizations, much has been revealed recently about the "church" from L. Ron Hubbard, Jr. and numerous ex-members. Hubbard, Jr. revealed that his father thought of himself as "one with Satan." Members reach "God-like" states varying in number from 0-20. Most Hollywood celebrities are OT-8 and above. OT-8 is most revealing about the basic mission of Scientology. According to this level of "clearness," Hubbard reveals that his main mission on earth was to derail specific events forecast in the Book of Revelation, such as the Second Coming of Christ. John Travolta states that he uses Scientology in all its premises "in my marriage and with my son." Hubbard was a world-class liar of epic proportions.

5)
- **MOVEMENT: Wicca**
- **PERPETRATOR: Gerald Gardner (1884-1964)**
- **OCCUPATION / PURSUITS : Occultist /Author / Wicca Founder**
- **GUIDING SLOGANS / CORE BELIEFS: "Do what you like so long as you harm no one."**
- **TIME SPAN OF INFLUENCE: 1940s to Present.**

ELABORATION: Gardner began publishing books about witchcraft in the 1940s and became more widely known by his publication of *Witchcraft Today* in 1954. Gardner attempted to organize the many varieties of witchcraft under one guiding organization, which he promoted under the name Wicca. He failed in this "Globalist Witchcraft" attempt due to the existence of thousands of forms of witchcraft around the world, most having little in common with one another. His major accomplishment was to promote pagan worship as compatible with Christian worship. Individuals could be both in Gardner's view of the world. It is far more pervasive in the Western World than most people realize. There are more than 1,000 "Wiccans" in the town of Laurel, Maryland alone as an example. Followers adopted Wicca because it sounded less intimidating than "witch." Gardner was a contemporary of Crowley's and was initiated into the same secret O.T.O. Society that Crowley had been a member.

6)
- **MOVEMENT: The Kinsey Institute**
- **PERPETRATOR: Alfred Kinsey (1894-1956)**
- **OCCUPATION / PURSUITS: Sex Researcher**
- **GUIDING SLOGANS / CORE BELIEFS: "The New Sexuality" "Anything Goes"**
- **TIME SPAN OF INFLUENCE: 1948 To Present.**

ELABORATION : An insect entomologist, Kinsey reduced the behavior of man to that of gall wasps, arguing the fraudulent science of "continuous variation" which he claimed was "the rule among men as well as among insects." Under this theory, "our conception of right and wrong, normal and abnormal, are seriously challenged by the variation studies," according to biographer Cornelia Christenson. While a professor at Indiana University, Kinsey transformed his "position" into a self-appointed "sex researcher" in which he created a Bell-Curve with no beginning and no end that he termed an endless "continuum" in which "there are no sharp distinctions between normal and abnormal." Kinsey's 1948 book, *Sexual Behavior In The Human Male,* was the skewed "scientific justification" for Crowley's "Do what you will" or

THE HOLLYWOOD CULTURE WAR

"Anything goes." Kinsey was an ardent admirer of Aleister Crowley, collecting his writings through close friend Kenneth Anger, one of Crowley's last students and America's first homosexual pornographer. Kinsey's major influence was on pornographer Hugh Hefner who created the "Playboy Philosophy" based largely on Kinsey's writings.

7)
- **MOVEMENT: The Beat Generation**
- **PERPETRATORS:** *Allen Ginsberg* (1926-1997)—Poet / Drug Addict / NAMBLA Member, *William Burroughs* (1914-1997)—Writer / Drug Addict / Pedophile, *Jack Kerouac* (1922-1969)—Writer / Drug Addict
- **GUIDING SLOGANS / CORE BELIEFS**—"The New Vision" "Hey man, it's all cool" Spiritual and Sexual Rebellion
- **TIME SPAN OF INFLUENCE: Early 1950s to Present.**

ELABORATION: A group of Greenwich Village homosexuals, writers, drug addicts and dropouts who felt the post WW II middle class was too "comfortable" and "conformist" came together to destroy certain facets of basic American values. The group promoted eastern mystic religions such as Tibetan Buddhism, Zen Buddhism (Hummmmm), existentialism and atheism. Promoted wide illegal drug use that spread from the ghettos to the middle-class via the nationwide network of artists and entertainers who no longer hid their drug addictions. The "Beat" generation promoted sex devoid of love and commitment as good and sexual perversion as the preferred avenue of personal relationships. Jazz was anointed as the "official music." Kerouac wrote the final draft of *On The Road* in the early 1950s in 21 days while "high" on amphetamines, not coffee, as revisionists insist. Ginsberg's rambling poem *Howl* became the Beat's anthem for rage. Burrough's *Naked Lunch* promoted the most grotesque forms of sexual perversion and drug abuse. "Beatniks" were devotees of Aleister Crowley's New Age writings. Ginsberg would also provide the bridge between the Beat religion and the hippie movement through Timothy Leary, Ken Kesy and Neal Cassady.

8)
- **MOVEMENT: The Playboy Philosophy**
- **PERPETRATOR: Hugh Hefner (1926-)**
- **OCCUPATION / PURSUITS: Publisher / Pornographer**
- **GUIDING SLOGANS / CORE BELIEFS: "The New Morality" "If It Feels Good, Do It"**
- **TIME SPAN OF INFLUENCE: 1953 To Present.**

667

ELABORATION: Publisher Hugh Hefner spent four years (1962-1966) and penned more than 150,000 words in an attempt to justify or "define" his Playboy Philosophy of hedonism and mainstreaming of pornography. Professor Benjamin DeMott said it best in 8 simple words, "The whole man reduced to his private parts." As Dr. Jason Kovar explained, "Hugh Hefner admitted that his Playboy philosophy was primarily based on the work of Alfred Kinsey's sexuality reports of the late 1940s and early 1950s. Kinsey's research was flawed with pre-determined methodology to advocate perverse sexual practices as normalcy. Hefner was attracted to Kinsey's "assertion" that there was no way to determine right from wrong, which Kinsey also appropriated from his study and admiration of Aleister Crowley. Actress Jayne Mansfield was Hefner's biggest promoter of the Playboy Philosophy. Her nude photo spreads helped bring pornography from the outhouse to the main house as she was the first mainstream actress to "cross-over" into porn. She was also a very boastful member of San Francisco's Church of Satan. Playboy Forum editor Anton Wilson, a prodigious drug addict, was also a formal member of Crowley's Thelema New Age religion.

9)
- **MOVEMENT: The Church of Satan**
- **PERPETRATOR: Anton LeVay (1930-1997)**
- **GUIDING SLOGANS / CORE BELIEFS: "You are your own god" Total devotion to Satan**
- **TIME SPAN OF INFLUENCE: 1953 To Present.**

ELABORATION: Originally founded as The Order of The Trapezoid in the early 1950s by Lost Weekend Lounge organist Anton LeVay, the name was officially changed to Church of Satan in 1966. Though almost comical in his appearance and demeanor, LeVay's allegiance was real and continues, even in death, to "buy souls" through the Satanic Bible which he authored in 1966 and is sold at most bookstores alongside books by J.K. Rowling and Phillip Pullman. While alive, LeVay was active in producing films and documentaries about the church, many filmed by radical homosexual porn producer Kenneth Anger. Anger was one of Aleister Crowley's last students and was also a close friend of Alfred Kinsey. Membership was more widespread than the press ever reported, including a Danish prince, grandson of a U.S. president, Sammy Davis, Jr. and Kim Novak. At the same time Jayne Mansfield was pushing Hefner's Playboy Philosophy, she was serving as a "High Priestess" for LeVay with Hefner's full support and encouragement. Shortly after pleading with LeVay to put a curse on her boyfriend, Mansfield lost her head, literally, in an auto accident not far from New Orleans, the spiritual witchcraft capital of America.

THE HOLLYWOOD CULTURE WAR

10)
- MOVEMENT: The Hippie Movement
- PERPETRATORS: Ken Kesey (1935-2001)—Writer / Drug Addict
- Rod McKuen (1933-)—Songwriter / Poet
- Bob Dylan (1941-)—Singer / Songwriter
- Timothy Leary (1920-1996)—Professor / Drug Addict
- Allen Ginsberg (1926-1997)—Poet / Drug Addict
- GUIDING SLOGANS / CORE BELIEFS: "Sex, Drugs and Rock-n-Roll"
- TIME SPAN OF INFLUENCE: 1963 To Present.

ELABORATION: In the early 1960s, Ken Kesey began holding "acid" parties in California that began the rapid spread of LSD and other drugs of abuse to other parts of the country. A favorite band at these parties was The Warlocks, later known as the acid rockers The Grateful Dead with Jerry Garcia. By 1964, Kesey took a brightly painted bus on a cross country tour from California to New York with an assorted group of drug addicts who became known as "hippies" because they were "hip" to drugs and justified this addiction because they were "dissatisfied" with the "establishment." Along the way, the group helped spread the abuse of drugs among young people who gathered around their bus at various stops. They freely handed out LSD and marijuana to many people, including adolescents. "Acid Rock" and "Hard Rock" music began during this period, fueled heavily by drug-addicted musicians which Hollywood and the news media promoted with a deceptively positive spin. Mick Jagger, John Lennon, Paul McCarney, Ozzy Ozbourne, David Bowie, Sting and many other musicians of the era gave open enthusiastic credit to Crowley as a key "influence" in their musical message and "hippie" philosophy. Musicians of the era also gave much credit to poet Rod McKuen and the "reluctant" Bob Dylan for igniting their "dissent." Allen Ginsberg and Timothy Leary acted as a bridge between the Beat generation and the hippies, insuring that drugs were the core of the movement. Anxiety, paranoia, confusion and massive drug abuse displayed by this generation would spread exponentially and continues today, afflicting all ages and socioeconomic classes around the world. Tomothy Leary, a disciple of Aleister Crowley, was quoted at this time as saying, "I think I'm carrying on much of the work that he started over 100 years ago, such as 'Do what thou will shall be the whole of the law' under love."

11)
- MOVEMENT: The MPAA Movie Ratings System
- PERPETRATOR: Jack Valenti (1921-2007)

- **OCCUPATION / PURSUITS: President—Motion Picture Association of America (MPAA)**
- **GUIDING SLOGAN / CORE BELIEF: "The 'New Kind' of American Movie"**
- **TIME SPAN OF INFLUENCE: 1968 To Present.**

ELABORATION: Valenti destroyed the Production Code of 1930 which had set broadly accepted standards of decency and taste in motion pictures, also known as the Golden Era of film production. This came to an end with Valenti's establishment of The Ratings System which introduced segregation into the moviegoing public based on age-appropriate "allowable" and "prohibited" audience groups, basically creating an industry standard of prolific immorality with a disastrous ripple effect on every form of media including television, video games, home video/DVD, music and print media. The Ratings Scheme set the foundation for the explosion of pornography and hyper-violence on the rapidly expanding formats of home video, downloadable content and the internet. The negative images & dialogue emanating from Valenti's "New Kind of American Movie"—free from even basic moral concepts—has adversely influenced the culture in almost every aspect from personal morality, values, religion, human behavior, sexuality, politics, education and accelerated the decay of American culture more than any other single act of the 20th century. Valenti's "Crumbling of Social Traditions" theory drew heavily on the philosophies of Kinsey, Hefner, the beatniks, hippies and other New Age "anti-establishment" movements.

12)
- **MOVEMENT: Hip-Hop / Rap**
- **PERPETRATOR: Afrika Bambaataa (?—)**
- **OCCUPATION / PURSUITS: Musician, Self-proclaimed "Amen-Ra" of Hip-Hop**
- **GUIDING SLOGANS / CORE BELIEFS: "You are your own god" Self-gratification. "The mind is a weapon—don't refuse it"**
- **TIME SPAN OF INFLUENCE: Mid 1970s To Present.**

ELABORATION: Pseudo-Religion based originally on a hybrid worship of ancient Egyptian gods and the Zulu tribes of Southern Africa. Bambaataa crowned himself "Amen Ra of the Universal Zulu Nation" based in The Bronx. Contrary to popular belief, hip-hop music is only a "component" of the larger hip-hop nation which promotes a self-destructive lifestyle culture of downward thinking and behaving. Bambaataa believes that the Bible is irrelevant and needs to be re-written at his direction. Fellow rapper, KRS-ONE, helped to add the violent-political bent to hip-hop/rap and created his own "Temple of Hip-Hop" to help further drag youth into a life with no respect, purpose, guidance or future. KRS-ONE is actively lobbying to have hip-hop declared a religion. Marijuana is the hip-hop drug of choice. Looking like a thug and going to jail is "good." Baggy pants, gold teeth overlays and a snarl is "the look." Violent, sexually explicit music are the main hallmarks of Hip-Hop/Rap.

13)
- **MOVEMENT: Goth / Punk**
- **PERPETRATORS: Banshees, The Clash, Sex Pistols, Christian Death,** (hundreds more)
- **OCCUPATION / PURSUITS: Music groups under three genres such as "Punk," "New Wave," and "Goth"**
- **GUIDING SLOGANS / CORE BELIEFS: "Live, let live, and leave a really good looking corpse." Death Fascination.**
- **TIME SPAN OF INFLUENCE: Late 1970s to Present.**

ELABORATION: Goth is the trash-heap leftover counterculture from the New Wave / Punk Rock era of the late 1970s and early 1980s. All three "movements" centered on self-gratification, rebellion against parents and "conventional" society—the same old sub-cultural mind-rot that says "I want to be left alone—but I want to be seen." Goth followers are the shopping mall rat people that dress in black with trench coats and silver studs, chains, jet-black hair and nails. Goths maintain a fascination with all things dark and self-destructive: drugs, alcohol, self-mutilation, the occult and suicide; or in Goth language, "Sudden Personal Spontaneous Combustion." The Goth historian, Azhrarn, describes the Goth philosophy as "a compulsive drive towards creativity and self-expression that seeks to reach out and ensnare its audience using our current society's covert and deeply rooted fascination with all things dark and frightening. This act can be either subtle or seducing or nightmarishly frightening. The medium of self-expression and creation can be anything from a mode of dress to novels or music." Goth is an otherwise throwaway philosophy which is mentioned here mainly as a history lesson to the dark bloodlust influence this "movement" has exerted on author J.K. Rowling, who in turn has influenced millions of readers with her books that introduce a Goth-inspired philosophy known as Potterethics. Early acolytes of Goth give credit to the Beat generation of drug-addicted authors such as Ginsberg, Burroughs and Kerouac. Researcher Jason Tamlin describes many

Goth web sites as "filled with desperation, depression, anger, hatred, despair and angst."

14)
- **MOVEMENT:** Potterethics
- **PERPETRATOR:** J.K. Rowling
- **OCCUPATION:** Author
- **GUIDING SLOGANS / CORE BELIEFS:** "Death Is The Central Theme," Moral Relativity. Children should "Do what they need to do."
- **TIME SPAN OF INFLUENCE:** 1997 To Present.

ELABORATION: Potterethics is crafted around the story of a boy wizard named Harry Potter as written by author J.K. Rowling in seven volumes. Rowling promotes the Divine Dichotomy which states that two contradictory truths can exist, neither making the other untrue. "Potterethics," as developed by Rowling in her story of Harry Potter, promotes moral relativism as the prevailing theme. The effect, as described by Gabriel Kuby, "The ability to distinguish between good and evil is overridden by emotional manipulation and intellectual obfuscation." After release of the final book in 2007, Rowling admitted that the story is partly a metaphor against the Conservative Party of Great Britain, especially the faction of Margaret Thatcher's rule in the 1980s. Many have also interpreted this, by extension, as an indictment of Western Civilization in general and Christianity in particular. Rowling, a sympathizer of Britain's radical Socialist and Labour party factions, employs the Crowlean and Kinsey philosophy that right and wrong cannot be defined so "anything goes" as long as it is successful; This includes lying, cheating, stealing and blackmail in a moral vacuum where children have no boundaries or rules and are encouraged "to do what they need to do," in Rowling's words. Rowling, heavily influenced in her teens and twenties by the Goth-Punk lifestyle, displays a strong fascination with the "culture of death" throughout her books. Rowling also promotes ancient, modern and "self-made" magic, witchcraft, sorcery and all forms of the Dark Arts. Because the books are targeted at children, the moral ambiguity and ethical confusion as "normal" behavior is considered to have created a detrimental New Age morality that children are emulating in their formative years. Many adults have also become followers of Potterethics with a substantial readership among this demographic. God is rendered dead by simple omission as "power for the sake of power" is promoted above all. This is the 21st century version of Friedrich Nietzsche's 19th century declaration of "God is dead."

15)
- **MOVEMENT:** The Open Society Institute (OSI)
- **PERPETRATOR:** George Soros
- **OCCUPATION / PURSUITS:** Chairman of Quantum Fund and Chairman of OSI. Promotes a global society where few rules exist.
- **GUIDING SLOGANS / CORE BELIEFS:** Legalization and deregulation of illegal drugs, prostitution, elimination of religion, elimination of traditional family, mandatory teaching of homosexuality in schools, elimination of prison terms for criminals.
- **TIME SPAN OF INFLUENCE:** 1980 To Present.

ELABORATION: A button-down version of Aleister Crowley, George Soros is one of the richest men in the world, but holds the title of "The Most Dangerous Man in the World." A die-hard atheist, Soros made his fortune in the secretive, unregulated world of financial hedge funds. Soros has been accused of destabilizing the currencies of entire nations and then profiting from the country's devalued currency in what is known as "risk investment." Soros first gained widespread attention as "The man who broke the Bank of England" in 1992. This left British citizens with greatly devalued currency, especially traumatic for the poor and retired on a pension. He is accused of manipulating many of the eastern European and Russian economies in the 1990s. Soros attempted a similar market manipulation in France and was convicted of securities fraud. Soros maintains a maniacal, megalomaniac "God Complex" in which he is attempting to create a global "Open Society" that is basically the fulfillment of the New Age in which few rules exist as he proposes the deconstruction of Western culture, family structures, elimination of religion (specifically Christianity and Judaism). Drug legalization is a top priority and he has funded the legalized drug initiatives in California and other states. Soros spent millions lobbying for the passage of California's Proposition 36 which has eliminated certain jail time for drug offenses, a key plank in his long-term goal of eliminating criminal penalties in addition to legalizing all drugs. Soros wants to create a new version of "The Brave New World" by Aldous Huxley in which the people are derived of their personalities and freedoms and were provided "holidays" via a hallucinogenic drug called Soma. Former U.S. Speaker of the House Dennis Hastert once "suggested" that much of Soros' money may come from the illegal drug trade, given the fact that Soros' OSI Funds are kept secured in an offshore bank in the self-governing island of the Netherland Antilles, an area the FBI describes as a major transhipment point for illegal drugs from South America into North America and Europe and a major money-laundering island for international banking. As a teenager in 1944,

Soros worked for the Nazi-backed Judenrat which passed out leaflets that tricked Hungarian Jews into one-way train rides to eastern European death camps. In 1945, he worked with an official of Hungary's puppet government charged with confiscating the estates and properties of Jews that had been sent to their deaths. In an interview with *60 Minutes* in 1998, Soros said he had no regret or guilt about his actions. Soros spent much of 2007 and 2008 raising money for Hillary Clinton and Barack Obama's presidential campaigns. As he did in 2004, Soros circumvents the McCain-Feingold Campaign Finance Reform Act by redirecting millions of dollars through "Section 527" groups that also double as "smear and slander" web sites that he uses to destroy his opponents.

ACKNOWLEDGEMENTS

I have to thank all my friends in the movie business who took the time to express their shared joy and frustration with an industry spiraling rapidly out of control despite its capacity to elevate the human spirit unlike any other man-made medium of communication. I also want to thank Ms. Louie Pace at Xlibris for her support and encouragement in my efforts to tackle the controversial issues now known collectively as The Culture War. Also, special thanks to Marjorie Josol and Lisa Fernandez.

Special thanks to Kathleen and Stephen Thompson for helping to collate the enormous amount of reference material and research I had collected during the last four years. Every day provides enough footnotes to write an entire new book on the constantly shifting tides in American and worldwide culture.

This book could not have been completed without the coordinated efforts and editorial direction of Coella Judkins who put in long hours, day and night, to pull together the chapters and charts that map the long and winding road of America's entertainment culture.

My thanks to everyone involved in this truly satirical parody into the people and events that compromise The Hollywood Culture War.

This book is dedicated to actor Carroll O'Connor (August 2, 1924-June 21, 2001) who told me in 1993, "The only way to clean up this industry is drug testing, across the board. The Olympics can do it, the NFL is going to do it. Why not Hollywood?" O'Connor's son, Hugh, died two years later, unable to kick a cocaine habit.

ENDNOTES

Introduction

1. Ben Stein, *Hollywood vs. America*, Fox News Special, Fox News Network, 20 February 2005.
2. Neil Cavuto interview with Mike Gallagher, *Your World with Neil Cavuto*, Fox News Network, 2 December 2005.
3. Patty Rhule, "Batman Hangs On as War 'Looms'," *USA Today*, 27 June 2005.
4. "Hollywood on Fire," *USA Today*, Section D, 29 November 2005.
5. Scott Bowles, "Hollywood Scans Horizon for More Passion," *USA Today*, 14 April 2005.
6. Ibid.
7. Published in *USA Today*, 20 June 2006. Source: March 2006 survey of 2,687 members of the Movie Advisory Board online moviegoing community.
8. David Ansen, "Is Anybody Making Movies We'll Actually Watch in 50 Years?" *Newsweek*, 11 July 2005.
9. David Horowitz, *Radical Son: A Generational Odyssey* (New York: Touchstone, 1997).

Chapter One: The War Escalates

1. "Viacom-CBS Merger to Erode Entertainment Content," editorial, *Goodbye Hollywood*, 2 December 1999.
2. Timothy M. Gray, "To Heck with Protecting Kids, What About Us?" *Variety*, 18 July 1997.

3. "Disney Financial Picture Continues Decline," *Goodbye Hollywood*, 5 December 1999.
4. Michael Medved, preface to *Hollywood vs. America* (New York: Harper Perennial, 1993), 23.
5. Ibid., xviii.
6. President George W. Bush, Acceptance Speech, Republican National Convention, 2 September 2004.
7. Ibid.
8. David Bossie, Citizens United, "Thank You Hollywood for George W. Bush's Election," http://www.citizensunited.org/oped-moore.html.
9. Interview with Sen. Zell Miller, *Hannity and Colmes*, Fox News Network, 22 April 2005.
10. Interview with Franklin Graham, *Hannity and Colmes*, Fox News Network, 5 April 2005.
11. Interview with Evan Maloney in *Fox News Special: Hollywood vs. America*, Fox News Network, 20 February 2005.
12. Interview with Newt Gingrich, *The O'Reilly Factor*, Fox News Network.
13. Linda Feldman, "A 'Moral Voter' Majority? The Culture Wars Are Back," *The Christian Science Monitor*, 8 November 2004. Information from a National Election Poll, Pew Research Center, 8 November 2004.
14. Linda Feldman, "How Lines of The Culture War Have Been Redrawn," *The Christian Science Monitor*, 9 November 2004.
15. Ibid.
16. Interview with James Dobson, *Scarborough Country*, MSNBC, 31 January 2004.
17. Michael Savage, *The Savage Nation*, radio promo, 8 December 2005.
18. Feldman, "A 'Moral Voter' Majority? The Culture Wars Are Back."
19. Interview with Paul Begalla, *Meet the Press with Tim Russert*, NBC, 22 January 2006.
20. *Webster's New World Dictionary of the American Language* (Cleveland/New York: The World Publishing Company, 1968).
21. Scott Bowles, "Brokeback Mountain: Milestone or Movie of the Moment?" *USA Today*, 21 February 2006.
22. Ibid.
23. Ibid.
24. Ibid.
25. Gray, "To Heck With Protecting Kids."
26. Bowles, "Brokeback Mountain: Milestone or Movie of the Moment?"
27. Ibid.

28. "Viacom-CBS Merger to Erode Entertainment Content," editorial, 2 December 1999.
29. Bill McCuddy, *Hollywood vs. America*, Fox News Special.
30. Gary Levin, "Oscar Ratings Fall," *USA Today*, 2 February 2006.
31. "Row Over Bush TV Assassination," BBC, 1 September 2006, http://news.cbbc.co.uk/l/hi/entertainment/5302598.
32. Ibid.
33. Ibid.
34. Ibid.
35. Ibid.
36. "Bush Approval Rating Up," CNN Radio News, 19 September 2006. Source: *USA Today*/Gallup Poll, "Bush Approval Rating," 15-17 September 2006.

Chapter Two: How the War Began

1. George D. Black, *Hollywood Censored* (United Kingdom: Cambridge University Press, 1994), 208.
2. Timothy M. Gray, "To Heck with Protecting Kids, What about Us?" *Variety*, 18 July 1997.
3. Ellen Goodman, "Movie Ratings Offer Lame Solution," *The Boston Globe*, 17 June 1999.
4. *The New Roget's Thesaurus in Dictionary Form* (New York: G. P. Putnam's Sons, 1961).
5. Michael Medved, *Hollywood vs. America* (New York: Harper Perennial, 1993), 277.
6. Jack Valenti, "How It All Began," MPAA, *http://www.mpaa.org/Ratings_HowItAll* Began.
7. Ibid.
8. Jack Valenti, "Rated PG (Pretty Good)," Op-Ed, *Los Angeles Times*, 1 November 2005.
9. Valenti, "How It All Began."
10. Ibid.
11. Jack Warner, preface to *Hollywood Be Thy Name* (Rocklin, CA: Prima Publishing, 1994), xii.
12. Valenti, "How It All Began."
13. Medved, *Hollywood vs. America*, 282.
14. Valenti, "How It All Began."
15. Valenti, "Rated PG (Pretty Good)."
16. "Jackie to the Rescue," *Newsweek*, 28 June 1999: 62.

17. Author in a phone interview with Father Patrick Callahan, 28 June 1996.
18. Medved, *Hollywood vs. America*, 283.
19. Jack Valenti, "The Birth of Ratings," http://www.mpaa.org/Ratings_BirthofRt.asp.
20. Valenti, "How It All Began."
21. Ibid.
22. Medved, *Hollywood vs. America*, 243.
23. Valenti, "Rated PG (Pretty Good)."
24. Valenti, "The Birth of Ratings."
25. Medved, preface to *Hollywood vs. America*, xxviii.
26. Ibid.
27. Ibid., 188.
28. Pastor Bill McNeese, "Father's Day," http://www.Harvestfamilychurch.com, 2004.
29. Black, *Hollywood Censored*, 11, 17.
30. Ibid., 2.
31. Medved, *Hollywood vs. America*, 283.
32. Valenti, "The Birth of Ratings."

Chapter Three: The War Heats Up: Hollywood and Washington

1. "Quayle: Ten Years after Murphy Brown," CNN.com, 10 May 2002, http://www.archives.cnn.com/2002.
2. Ibid.
3. Ibid.
4. The Center for Responsive Politics, http://www.opensecrets.org/clinton.
5. Richard Lacayo, "Violent Reaction," *Time*, 12 June 1995.
6. Larry Reibstein and Thomas Rosenstiel, "The Right Takes a Media Giant to Political Task," *Newsweek*, 12 June 1995.
7. Richard Zoglin, "A Company Under Fire," *Time*, 12 June 1995.
8. Ibid.
9. Reibstein and Rosenstiel, "The Right Takes a Media Giant to Political Task."
10. Lacayo, "Violent Reaction."
11. Reibstein and Rosenstiel, "The Right Takes a Media Giant to Political Task."
12. Zoglin, "A Company Under Fire."
13. Reibstein and Rosenstiel, "The Right Takes a Media Giant to Political Task."
14. Zoglin, "A Company Under Fire."

15. Morality in Media, http://www.moralityinmedia.org.
16. Lacayo, "Violent Reaction."
17. Ibid.
18. Ibid.
19. Ibid.
20. Ibid.
21. Ibid.
22. Samantha Power, The Atlantic Online, October 2001.
23. Ibid.
24. Statement from the Center for Security Policy, 10 August 1998.
25. Richard John Neuhaus, *First Things Magazine*, June-July 1999, 63-87.

Chapter Four: Hollywood Bill

1. Candace Roberts [pseud.] interview with author, 1987, 1988, 1994.
2. "Cardinal Mahoney Calls for Reform in Motion Pictures and Television Productions," press release, Catholic Archdiocese of Los Angeles, 1 February 1992.
3. Michael Medved, preface to *Hollywood vs. America* (New York: Harper Perennial, 1993), xxvii.
4. Ibid., xxviii.
5. The Progressive Review http://www.prorev.com/legacy.
6. David Limbaugh, "Clinton and the Flower Children," http://www.WorldNetDaily.com, 28 May 1999.
7. Harriet Rubin, "For Boomers, It's All About Them," *USA Today*, 11 November 2004, A15.
8. Ibid.
9. "Stay Tuned: TV Ratings, Coming Up," *Knight-Rider-Tribune*, syndicated, 1 March 1996.
10. Charles Case, "Banking on Hollywood," NewsMax, http://www.NewsMax.com, 6 October 2006.
11. Alan Bash, "TV Industry's Choice of Age Sets Off Debate," *USA Today*, 13 December 1996, A2.
12. Ibid.
13. "Stay Tuned: TV Ratings, Coming Up."
14. Bruce Sullivan, "Clinton Nips, But Can't Bite Hollywood Hand," CNS News Service, 18 May 1999.
15. Ibid.
16. *Spin*, August 1996, 34.
17. Johnny Lee Clary, http://www.johnnyleeclary.com/manson.

18. Jason Kovar, "Columbine Effect," http://www.goodfight.org/hwcolumbineeffect.html.
19. Ibid.
20. Ibid.
21. Ibid.
22. "FTC Youth Violence Report," as stated by FTC Chairman Robert Pitofsky, http://www.ftc.gov/us/2000/09/pitstatementviolence.
23. Ibid.
24. http://www.usdoj.gov/pardon/clintonpardon_grants.htm.
25. Ben Stein, "Hypocrisy Democrat Style," http://www.spectator.org, 2 October 2006.
26. Shelby Lynn, CNN Radio News, 8 September 2006.
27. Senator Thomas Kean, CNN Radio News, 8 September 2006.
28. Jessie McKinley, "Miniseries Is Criticized As Inaccurate and Biased," *The New York Times*, 6 September 2006.
29. Jeff Stein, "ABC Docudrama Sparks 9/11 Spat," *CQ Weekly*, 4 September 2006.
30. McKinley, "Miniseries Is Criticized As Inaccurate and Biased."
31. Ibid.
32. "Clinton Officials Protest ABC's 9/11 Miniseries," MSNBC Online, http://www.msnbc.msn.com, 7 September 2006.
33. Ibid.
34. Sean Hannity, *Hannity and Colmes*, Fox News Network, 7 September 2006.
35. Senator Thomas Kean, CNN Radio News, 8 September 2006.
36. Robert "Buzz" Patterson, *The Savage Nation*, 8 September 2006.
37. Ibid.
38. Ibid.
39. Dick Morris, interview with Sean Hannity, *Hannity and Colmes*, Fox News Network, 8 September 2006.
40. Ibid.
41. Max Blumenthal, "ABC '9/11 Docudrama Right Wing Roots," The Nation Online, http://www.thenation.com, 11 September 2006.
42. *Special Report with Brit Hume*, Fox News Network, 26 September 2006.
43. Interview with Bill Clinton, Fox News Special with Chris Wallace, Fox News Network, 24 September 2006.
44. *Special Report with Brit Hume*, 26 September 2006.
45. Ibid.
46. Lev Grossman, *Time*, 11 September 2006.
47. Interview with Michael Sheuer, *Chris Wallace*, Fox News Network, 2 October 2006.

Chapter Five: The Hollywood Media Defense

1. Christopher Hitchens, *No One Left to Lie To* (London, New York: Verso, 1999), 76-77.
2. "Senate to Hold Hearings on Clinton Clemency Offer," *USA Today*, 1 September 1999, 6A.
3. Jim Kouri, "Seven Years Ago This Week: Bill Clinton, Hillary Clinton, and the FALN," http://www. americanchronicle.com, 14 August 2006.
4. Ibid.
5. "Hillary Clinton: 'I'm Too Important to Testify'," press release, Judicial Watch, http://www.judicialwatch.org, 15 July 1999.
6. "Fighting Secrecy—Filegate (Alexander et. al. vs. FBI et. al.)" Judicial Watch, http://www.judicialwatch.org/filegate.
7. "Hillary Clinton: 'I'm Too Important to Testify'," Judicial Watch.
8. 2005, http://www.judicialwatch.org.
9. Candice E. Jackson, *Their Lives: The Women Targeted by the Clinton Machine* (Torrence, CA: World Ahead Publishing, 2005).
10. Hitchens, *No One Left to Lie To*, 15.
11. Ibid.
12. Ibid.
13. http://www.alamo-girl.com/0291.html.
14. Hitchens, *No One Left to Lie To*, 14-15.
15. Ibid., 87.
16. Ibid., 89.
17. "Chinese Spying Worse Than Expected," Conservative News Service, cnsnews.com, 29 April 1999.
18. John Barry, "Does the Administration Owe Lee an Apology?" SpeakOut.com, 9 January 2001.
19. Ann Coulter, *Godless* (New York: Crown Forum, 2006.), 99-100.

Chapter Six: The Rise and Fall of The Obama Nation

1. Tom Fitton, CBS News.com, 27 February 2007.
2. Joe Klein, "The Fresh Face," *Time*, 23 October 2006: 48.
3. Steve Sailer, "Obama's Identity Crisis," *The American Conservative*, 26 March 2007.
4. Andy Martin, "Barack Obama: Joshua Generation or 'just joshin'?'" Political Gateway, www.politicalgateway.com, 7 March 2007.
5. Klein, "The Fresh Face," 47.

6. E. Michael Jones, *Degenerate Moderns* (San Francisco: Ignatius Press, 1993), 122.
7. Sailer, "Obama's Identity Crisis."
8. Martin, "Barack Obama: Joshua Generation or 'just joshin'?'"
9. Tom King, *The Operator* (New York: Random House, 2000), 48.
10. Ibid., 515-16.
11. Ibid.
12. Jamaal Michaels, *http://.www.amazon.com/Shakedown-Exposing-Real-Jesse*-Jackson/dp/0895261650.
13. Rouses J. Rushdoony, *The Politics of Guilt and Pity* (Fairfax, VA: Thoburn Press, 1978), 9.
14. Michael T. Kaufman, *Soros: The Life and Times of a Messianic Billionaire* (New York: Vintage Books, Random House, 2002), 32.
15. David Horowitz and Richard Poe, *The Shadow Party* (Nashville: Nelson Current, 2006), 79.
16. Ibid.
17. Ibid.
18. Ibid., 80.
19. George Soros, Interview with Steve Croft, *60 Minutes*, 20 December 1998.
20. http://www.waynemadsenreport.com/diplomatic/foreign, 9 August 2005.
21. Richard Poe, "George Soros's Coup," NewsMax, http://www.NewsMax.com, May 2004.
22. Dirk Beveridge, "Soros: Attacks Will Speed Downturn," Associated Press, 19 September 2001.
23. Horowitz and Poe, *The Shadow Party*, 3.
24. Ibid., 21.
25. Ibid., 71.
26. Cliff Kincaid, "The Hidden Agenda," Accuracy In Media, http://www.aim.org/special_report2089, 27 October 2004.
27. Ibid.
28. Ibid.
29. Horowitz and Poe, preface to *The Shadow Party*, xi.
30. Ibid., 74.
31. Bill O'Reilly, *Culture Warrior* (New York: Broadway Books, 2006), 41.
32. Jill Stanek, "Why Jesus Would Not Vote for Barack Obama," WorldNetDaily, http://www.worldnetdaily.com, 17 July 2006.
33. Ibid.
34. Ibid.

35. Jill Stanek, "Obama's Constitutional Crisis," WorldNetDaily, 25 January 2007.
36. "Dutch Consider Legalizing Infanticide," NewsMax, http://www.NewsMax.com, 27 March 2006.
37. Ibid.
38. Diane Alden, "From Those Infirm Foundations," http://www.enterstageright.com/archive/articles/osoinfirmpart1.htm.
39. Stanek, "Why Jesus Would Not Vote for Barack Obama."
40. Barack Obama, The Audacity of Hope (New York: Crown, 2006), 211.
41. Ibid., 211-12.
42. Ibid., 210.
43. "World Growth at 19 Million a Year," *Christianity Today*, 16 November 1998.
44. BattlegroundPoll, http://www.intellectualconservative.com/2007/01/29/the battleground_poll_and_convervative_strength, 27 January 2007.
45. Ed Vitagliano, "Tugging Left," *American Family Association Journal*, February 2007: 18.
46. Barack Obama, Call to Renewal Keynote Address, 28 June 2006.
47. Ibid.
48. Ibid.
49. Vitagliano, "Tugging Left."
50. Ibid.
51. Ibid.
52. Barack Obama, Call to Renewal Keynote Address.
53. Erik Rush, "Obamination," http://www.reviewamerica.us/columns/rush, 21 February 2007.
54. Ibid.
55. Ibid.
56. Reverend Jesse Lee Peterson, interview, *Hannity and Colmes*, Fox News Network, 6 March 2007.
57. David Roozen, Hartford Institute for Religious Research FACT Study, 2001.
58. Barack Obama, preface to *Dreams from My Father* (New York: Three Rivers Press, 1995; 2004), xvii.
59. "The Hillary Spot," National Review Online, 27 March 2007.
60. Ibid.
61. Brian Fitzpatrick and Martin Fyfe, "To Protect Obama: A Journalist Excuses Lies," Culture and Media Institute, http:// www.cultureandmediainstitute.org, 29 March 2007.
62. Ibid.
63. Sailer, "Obama's Identity Crisis."
64. Martin, "Barack Obama: Joshua Generation or 'just joshin?'"
65. Mike Allen, "Rookie Mistakes Plague Obama," Politico.com, http://www.politico.com/news/stories/0307/3304.html, 27 March 2007.

66. Ibid.
67. Martin, "Barack Obama: Joshua Generation or 'just joshin?'"
68. Ibid.
69. Sailer, "Obama's Identity Crisis."
70. Allen, "Rookie Mistakes Plague Obama."
71. Ibid.
72. *The Companion Bible* (Grand Rapids, MI: Kregal Publications, 1990), 1770.
73. Oprah Winfrey, interview with Larry King, *Larry King Live*, CNN, May 2007.
74. "The Gospel According to Oprah," Watchman Fellowship, Inc., http://www.wfial.org/index.cfm?fuseaction:artNewAge.
75. Ibid.
76. Martin, "Barack Obama: Joshua Generation or 'just joshin'?'"

Chapter Seven: The Ratings Fiasco

1. Alan Bash, *USA Today*, 1 March 1996.
2. *Newsweek*, 12 June 1995.
3. Larry Reibstein and Thomas Rosenstiel, "The Right Takes a Media Giant to Political Task," *Newsweek*, 12 June 1995.
4. Alan Bash, "Critics Call PG Category Too Broad to Be Effective," *USA Today*, 13 December 1996.
5. Ibid.
6. Ibid.
7. *Broadcasting and Cable Magazine*, 26 May 1997.
8. www.mpaa.org/tv/content.html.
9. Timothy Gray, "To Heck with Protecting Kids, *Variety*, 18 July 1997.
10. Ellen Goodman, "Movie Ratings Offer Lame Solution," *The Boston Globe*, 17 June 1999.
11. Ibid.
12. Ibid.
13. "Parents Give Ratings Board High Marks," Press Release, MPAA 1 November 2006.
14. Frank Capra, *The Name Above the Title* (New York: Macmillan, 1971), 486.
15. www.ftc.org
16. "Parents Give Ratings Board High Marks," Press Release, MPAA.
17. Jack Valenti, "Rated PG (Pretty Good)," Op-Ed, *Los Angeles Times*, 1 November 2005.

Chapter Eight: The End of Television

1. Tim Brooks and Earle Marsh, *The Complete Directory to Prime Time Network and Cable TV Shows*, 6th edition, (New York: Ballantine Books, 1999), 33.
2. Sheldon Leonard, *And the Show Goes On* (New York: First Limelight Edition, 1995), 94.
3. FCC Chairman Newton Minnow, Speech to the National Association of Broadcasters (NAB), 9 May 1961.

Chapter Nine: The Big Lie and Value Manipulation

1. Gregory D. Black, *Hollywood Censored* (United Kingdom: Cambridge University Press, 994), 41.
2. Ibid.
3. Thomas Doherty, *Pre-Code Hollywood* (New York: Columbia University Press, 1999), 2.
4. Ibid.
5. Timothy Gray, "To Heck with Protecting Kids, *Variety*, 18 July 1997.
6. Interview with Richard Walter, *Scarborough Country*, MSNBC News Network, 14 March 2006.
7. Ellen Graham, "Changing Channels," *Wall Street Journal*, classroom edition, vol. 4, no. 3, 1997.
8. Ellen Goodman, "Movie Ratings Offer Lame Solution," *The Boston Globe*, 17 June 1999.
9. Jason Kovar, "Columbine Effect," http:// www.goodfight.org/hwcolumbineeffect.html.
10. "The Coarsening of Values," *Goodbye Hollywood*, 1, no. 2 (2000): 5.
11. Leonard Maltin, *Movie and Video Guide: 1997 Edition* (New York: Signet, 1996), 268.
12. Michael Medved, *Hollywood vs. America* (New York: Harper Perennial, 1993), 19.
13. Ibid.
14. "Editing Hollywood's Editors: Cleaning Flicks for Families," Press Release, statement by John Feehrey, House Subcommittee on Commerce, Trade, and Consumer Protection, 26 September 2006.
15. "Disney Financial Picture Continues to Decline," *Goodbye Hollywood*, 1, no. 1 (1999): 1, 5.
16. Ibid.
17. Ibid.

18. Michael Medved, *Hollywood vs. America*, 33.
19. Kovar, "Columbine Effect."
20. Lewis Grizzard, *The Atlanta Constitution*, 6 March 1992.
21. "'Sex and Violence' Hurt Our Image," NewsMax, December 2006, 28.
22. John Leo, "Notes of a Nonvictim," *U.S. News and World Report*, 6 October 1997.
23. Ibid.

Chapter Ten: Springtime for Stalin

1. http://www.fortunecity.com/skyscraper/lycos/1595/id278htm.
2. http://www.thebostonchannel/entertainment/1931445/detail.html.
3. Kenneth Lloyd Billingsley, *Hollywood Party* (Rocklin, CA: Forum, 1998), 11.
4. Ibid., 86.
5. "Source List and Detailed Death Tolls for the 20th Century," http://www.users.erols.com/mwhite28/warstat1.htm, 4, 7.
6. Ibid.
7. Billingsley, *Hollywood Party*, 241.
8. Ibid., 8.
9. Ibid., 273.
10. Ibid., 121.
11. Ibid., 45.
12. Ibid., 47.
13. *http://www.mediaresearch.org/BozellColumns/entertainment/column2003/col20031126.asp.*
14. U.S. House Committee on Un-American Activities, *Hearings Regarding the Communist Infiltration of the Motion Picture Industry*, 1947, 172.
15. Billingsley, *Hollywood Party*, 241.
16. Ibid., 57.
17. Ibid., 58.
18. U.S. House Committee on Un-American Activities, *Transcript of Executive Session*, Los Angeles, 23 November 1953, 45, 48.
19. Billingsley, *Hollywood Party*, 39.
20. Ibid., 157.
21. Ibid., 153.
22. U.S. House Committee on Un-American Activities, *Hearings Regarding the Communist Infiltration of the Motion Picture Industry*, 1947, 9, 10.
23. Billingsley, *Hollywood Party*, 186.
24. Ibid., 186-87.
25. Ibid.

26. Ibid., 184.
27. Sidney Hook, *Out of Step: An Unquiet Life in the Twentieth Century* (New York: Harper and Row, 1987), 493.
28. Billingsley, *Hollywood Party*, 201.
29. Ibid., 221.
30. http://www.moderntimes.com/palace/huac/htm.
31. Billingsley, *Hollywood Party*, 258.
32. Ibid., 222.
33. Ibid., 223.
34. Ronald Radosh and Allis Radosh, *Red Star Over Hollywood* (New York: Encounter Books, 2006), 238-39.
35. James Hirsen, "Nostalgic for Stalin," http://www.firstliberties.com, 4 April 2005.
36. Billingsley, *Hollywood Party*, 270.
37. Ibid., 256.
38. Ibid.
39. Ibid.
40. U.S. House Committee on Un-American Activities, *Hearings Regarding the Communist Infiltration of the Motion Picture Industry*, 1952, 2407-14.
41. Billingsley, *Hollywood Party*, 258.
42. Interview with Arthur Herman, *The Savage Nation*, 17 January 2006.
43. Billingsley, *Hollywood Party*, 97.
44. Ibid.
45. Ibid.
46. J. Barry O'Connell Jr., "Notes on Owen Lattimore," http://www.spongobongo.com/her9984.htm.
47. Adi Ignatius, "The Mao That Roared," *Time*, 31 October 2005, 82.
48. Ibid.
49. Twentieth Century Atlas-Death Tolls, http://www.users.erols.com/mwhite28/warstat1.
50. Interview with Arthur Herman, *The Savage Nation*.

Chapter Eleven: Jane Fonda

1. *The Wall Street Journal*, 3 August 1995, A8.
2. Stanislav Lunev, *Through the Eyes of the Enemy* (Washington, D.C.: Regenery, 1998), 78.
3. Michelle Malkin, "Hanoi Jane Rides Again," WorldNetDaily, http://www.worldnetdaily.org, 6 April 2005.
4. Ibid.
5. Ibid.

6. Ed Rampell, "Jane's Revolution," AlterNet, http://www.alternet.org/story/22131/, 4 June 2005
7. Ibid.
8. Ibid.
9. Ibid.
10. Kathleen Parker, "See Jane's Magical Mystery Tour," Independent Women's Forum, http://www.iwf.org/, 28 July 2005.
11. Ibid.
12. Malkin, "Hanoi Jane Rides Again."
13. "Traitor's Tour," http://www.DiscoverTheNet.org, 19 May 2006.
14. "Galloway: Blair's Assassination Justified," WorldNetDaily, http://www.worldnetdaily.org, 26 May 2006.
15. Jonah Goldberg, "If Fonda's Sorry, Let Her Say So," *Jewish World Review*, 23 June 2000.
16. Malkin, "Hanoi Jane Rides Again."
17. Ibid.
18. David Horowitz and Richard Poe, *Shadow Party* (Nashville: Nelson Current, 2006), 23.
19. Ibid., 25.
20. Ibid., preface, xiv.
21. *The Washington Times*, 7 July 2000.
22. Howard Fast, *The Naked God: The Writer and the Communist Party* (New York: Praeger, 1957), 29.
23. John D. Dennison, "Jane Fonda AKA Hanoi Jane," http://www.1stca?mediccom, 8.
24. Malkin, "Hanoi Jane Rides Again."
25. "Traitor's Tour," http://www.DiscoverTheNet.org.
26. Ibid., 5.
27. "Jane Fonda's Red Herrings," http://www.hannity.com/forum/showthread.php?t:3959.
28. "Traitor 1," http://www.geocities.com/dwnsmw56/Hanoi_Jane.
29. "Traitor's Tour," http://www.DiscoverTheNet.org.
30. Horowitz and Poe, *Shadow Party*, 26.
31. Ibid.
32. Fast, *The Naked God*, 35, 64-66.
33. "Traitor's Tour," http://www.DiscoverTheNet.org.
34. R. J. Rummell, "Statistics of Vietnamese Democide," http://www.hawaii.edu/powerkills/SOD.
35. "Death Tolls and Casualty Statistics Vietnam," *http://www.vietka.com/Death* Casualty.
36. Kenneth Lloyd Billingsley, *Hollywood Party* (Rocklin, CA: Forum, 1998), 273.

37. Jack Valenti, "How It All Began," MPAA, *http://www.mpaa.org/Ratings_HowItAll* Began.
38. Richard M. Nixon, *No More Vietnams* (New York: Arbor House Publishing, 1987).
39. Horowitz and Poe, *Shadow Party*, 15.
40. Author's phone interview with David Halberstam, 30 January 2004.
41. Jane Fonda, *My Life So Far* (New York: Random House, 2005), 567.
42. Don Wildmon, "Action Letter," American Family Association, *http://www.afa.net*, May 2006.
43. Goldberg, "If Fonda's Sorry, Let Her Say So."
44. *Webster's New World Dictionary: College Edition* (Cleveland/New York: The World Publishing Company, 1968).
45. E. W. Bullinger, ed., *The Companion Bible* (1886; reprint, Grand Rapids, MI: Kregel Publications, 1990), Appendix 123.
46. Fonda, *My Life So Far*, 567.
47. Robert Schlesin, *The Boston Globe*, 14 April 2002.
48. Fonda, *My Life So Far*, 568.
49. White House Press Release, "Vietnam Prime Minister Visits White House," 21 June 2005.
50. Ted Baehr and Tom Snyder, "Time-Warner Promotes Terrorism and Anti-Christian Bigotry in New Leftist Movie 'V for Vendetta'," MovieGuide, http://www.movieguide.org, 31 May 2006.

Chapter Twelve: Oliver Stone

1. Jason Kovar, "Oliver Stone," http://www.goodfight.org/hwstone.html, 1.
2. Jonathan Lemire, "Oliver Stone Drunk Driver; Police Say," Daily News, 29 May 2005.
3. Marc Cooper, "Oliver Stoned," http://www.marccooper.com/oliver-stone-d/
4. Kovar, "Oliver Stone."
5. Ibid., 2.
6. Ibid.
7. Ibid., 4.
8. Marc Cooper, "Oliver Stoned," 20.
9. Ibid., 20.
10. Ibid., 22.
11. Ibid., 24, 25.
12. Ibid., 33, 35.
13. Author interview with Joe O'Har, 6 June 1991.
14. Cooper, "Oliver Stoned," 37.
15. Ibid.

16. Ibid., 35.
17. Gregory D. Black, *Hollywood Censored* (United Kingdom: Cambridge University Press, 1994), 9.
18. Kovar, "Oliver Stone," 2.
19. Jason Kovar, "Columbine Effect," http://www.goodfight.org/hwcolumbineeffect.html, 7.
20. http://www.freedomforum.org/templates/document.asp?documentID:3962.
21. "Oliver Stone Loses Legal Appeals," *Goodbye Hollywood*, vol. 1, no. 1, December 1999, 4.
22. Ibid.
23. Ibid.
24. "Censorship of Motion Pictures," *Yale Law Journal* 49, November 1939.
25. Garth Jowett, *A Capacity for Evil: The 1915 Supreme Court Mutual Decision* (Historical Journal of Film, Radio and Television 10 [1990]),63.
26. "Oliver Stone Loses Legal Appeals," *Goodbye Hollywood*, 4.
27. Ibid.
28. "Statement of Robert Pitofsky on FTC Youth Violence Report," http://www.ftc.gov/05/2000/09/pitstatementviolence.
29. Ibid.
30. Jack Valenti, "How It All Began," MPAA, http://www.mpaa.org/Ratings_HowItAll Began.
31. Kovar, "Oliver Stone," 3.
32. Ibid.
33. Ibid.
34. Ibid.
35. Kovar, "Columbine Effect," 8.
36. "The Columbine Effect," *Time*, 19 March 2001.
37. Kovar, "Oliver Stone," 4.
38. http://www.nndb.com/lists/447/000085192
39. Emma Pivato, http://www.xarawe.trentu.ca/emma/belushi.html.
40. Bob Woodward, *Wired* (New York: Simon and Schuster, 1984), 24.
41. Ibid, 19.
42. Pivato, http://www.xarawe.trentu.ca/emma/belushi.html.
43. Ibid.
44. Woodward, *Wired*, 17.
45. Ibid., 15.
46. Ibid., 210.
47. Ibid, 398-99.

Chapter Thirteen: Stepping Up to the Plate

1. Gregory D. Black, *Hollywood Censored* (United Kingdom: Cambridge University Press, 1994), 31.
2. Jack Valenti, "Rated PG (Pretty Good)," Op-Ed, *Los Angeles Times*, 1 November 2005.
3. "Valenti Under Fire," *Goodbye Hollywood*, vol. 1, no. 1, December 1999: 3.
4. Zachary Coile, "Bill Seeks to Toughen Drug Testing in Pro Sports," *San Francisco Chronicle*, 24 April 2005.
5. Andy Nesbitt, "Why Barry Bonds Is Worth Cheering For," http://www.foxsports.com/mlb/story/5444456?print=tone.
6. Ibid.
7. Coile, "Bill Seeks to Toughen Drug Testing in Pro Sports."
8. Ibid.
9. Ibid.
10. Kathy Kiely, "MBL, Players Union Agree to Update Drug Policy," *USA Today*, 16 November 2005.
11. http://www.nfhs.org/scriptcontent/va_Custom/
12. "Pro Wrestling to Institute Random Drug Testing," Associated Press, 5 December 2005.
13. "USADA Announces Final Testing Numbers for 2005." Press Release, USADA, 8 February 2006.
14. http://www.theathlete.org/anti-doping-code.
15. http://www.atptennis.atponline.net/en/antidoping
16. Jason Kovar, "Jayne Mansfield," http://www.goodfight.org/hwjmansfield.html.
17. Jason Kovar, "Columbine Effect," http://www.goodfight.org/hwcolumbineeffect.html.
18. Edward Epstein, "Lawmakers from Rival Parties Team Up in Probe of Steroids," *San Francisco Chronicle*, 16 March 2005.
19. Ibid.
20. Kiely, "MLB, Players Union Agree to Update Drug Policy."
21. Robert H. Coombs, *Drug Testing: Issues and Options* (Oxford: Oxford University Press, 1991).
22. Michael Medved, *Hollywood vs. America* (New York: Harper Perennial, 1993), 155.
23. John Jurgensen, "Drinks, Drugs, Dysfunction Star on Summer Cable TV," *The Wall Street Journal*, 20 July 2007, B1.

Chapter Fourteen: Intermission

Chapter Fifteen: Dawn of the New Age

1. Aleister Crowley, http://www.illuminati-news.com/art-and-mc/rockmusic-and-crowley.htm.
2. Ibid.
3. Francis King, *The Magical World of Aleister Crowley* (New York: Coward, McCann and Geoghan, 1978), 5.
4. Lawrence Sutin, *Do What Thou Will: A Life of Aleister Crowley* (New York: St. Martin's Press, 2000), 38.
5. Ibid., 80, 90-91.
6. B. Gary Patterson, introduction to *Hellhounds On Their Trail* (Nashville, TN: Dowling Press, 1997).
7. Aleister Crowley, preface to *The World's Tragedy* (Tempe, AZ: New Falcon Publications, 1994), xxx.
8. Stephen Skinner, ed., *The Magical Diaries of Aleister Crowley* (Tunisia: 1923), 10.
9. Crowley, http://www.illuminati-news.com/art-and-mc/rockmusic-and-crowley.htm.
10. Ibid.
11. Ibid.
12. Steve Turner, *Hungry for Heaven* (Westmont, IL: Intervarsity Press, 1995), 97-98.
13. Patterson, *Hellhounds on Their Trail*, 56.
14. John Lennon, cited by David Sheff, *The Playboy Interviews with John Lennon and Yoko Ono*, 61.
15. Crowley, http://www.illuminati-news.com/art-and-mc/rockmusic-and-crowley.htm, 4.
16. *Circus Magazine*, 26 August 1980, 26.
17. Crowley, http://www.illuminati-news.com/art-and-mc/rockmusic-and-crowley.htm.
18. Ibid.
19. Ibid.
20. G. Craig Lewis, Exministries, http://www.exministries.com, 4.
21. Judy Rosen, "Pink Void," http://www.slate.com, 11 July 2006.
22. Steven Davis, *Hammer of the Gods* (New York: Ballantine Books, 1985), 237.
23. "Average Age of Death for Rock Stars," *World Almanac and Book of Facts* (New York: World Almanac Books, 1997), 973.

Chapter Sixteen: Celebrity Gods

1. "Madame Blavatsky," http://www.Kheper.net/topics/Theosophy/index.htm
2. *Hollywood Unmasked II*, produced by Jason Kovar, Fight the Good Fight Ministries, 2006, videocassette.
3. Jason Kovar, "Marilyn Monroe," http://www.goodfight.org/hwmmonroe.html.
4. Bob Rosio, *Hitler and the New Age* (Lafayette, LA: Huntington House, 1993), 137, 144.
5. *Hollywood Unmasked II*, Kovar.
6. Jason Kovar, "Oprah Winfrey," http://www.goodfight.org/hwowinfrey.html.
7. Interview with Goldie Hawn, *Larry King Live*, CNN News Network, 24 February 2006.
8. James Hirsen, "Kate Hudson Sees Dead People," NewsMax, September 2005, 16.
9. Ibid.
10. Kovar, *Hollywood Unmasked II*.
11. Ibid.
12. Ibid.
13. Jason Kovar, "Hollywood's Mission," http://www.goodfight.org/hwmission.html, 3.
14. Ibid.
15. Coral Amende, *Hollywood Confidential* (New York: Plume, Penguin, 1997), 160.
16. Ibid.
17. Ann Oldenburg, "The Divine Miss Winfrey?" *USA Today*, 11 May 2006, D 1.
18. Ibid.
19. Kovar, "Oprah Winfrey," 1.
20. Ibid., 2.
21. Ibid., 3.
22. Ibid.
23. Kovar, *Hollywood Unmasked II*.
24. James Hirsen, "Hollywood and Their New Age Faiths," NewsMax, September 2005, 17.
25. Bent Corydon and C. Ron Hubbard Jr., *L. Ron Hubbard: Messiah or Madman?* (Secaucus, NJ: Stuart, Inc., 1989).
26. *Webster's New World Dictionary of the American Language* (Cleveland/New York: The World Publishing Company, 1968).

27. "Dianetics Review," *Consumer Reports*, August 1951.
28. Don Lattin, "Scientology Founder's Life Far From What He Preached," *San Francisco Chronicle*, 12 February 2001.
29. Jason Kovar, "Tom Cruise," http://www.goodfight.org/hwtcruise.html, 2.
30. Ibid., 1
31. Ibid., 4.
32. Ibid., 1-2.
33. "Scientology Kills," http://www.scientology-kills.org/celebrity/celebrities.htm.
34. Aleister Crowley, preface to *The World's Tragedy* (Tempe, AZ: New Falcon Publications, 1994), xxx.
35. Aleister Crowley, *http://www.illuminati-news.com/art-and-mc/rockmusic-and*-crowley.htm.
36. Kovar, "Tom Cruise," 5.
37. Neil Cavuto, *Your World with Neil Cavuto*, 22 August 2006.
38. "Sir Elton: Ban Organized Religion," BBC News, 12 March 2006.
39. Interview with Junie Collins, *4 Little Girls*, HBO Documentary Films, 1997.
40. Interview with Shimon Perez, *Larry King Live*, CNN News Network, 16 July 2006.

Chapter Seventeen: Mind Benders and Gender Benders

1. Jason Kovar, "Columbine Effect," http://www.goodfight.org/hwcolumbineeffect.html, 3.
2. *Webster's New World Dictionary of the American Language* (Cleveland/New York: The World Publishing Company, 1968).
3. Anthony Breznican, *USA Today*, 12 March 2006.
4. Kovar, "Columbine Effect," 2, 3.
5. Jason Kovar, "David Cronenberg," http://www.goodfight.org/hwdcronenberg.html, 2.
6. Kovar, "Columbine Effect," 7.
7. Author's interview with Shirley Crumley, 30 January 2005.
8. Leonard Maltin, *Movie and Video Guide: 1997 Edition* (New York: Signet, 1996), 1336.
9. Kovar, "Columbine Effect," 6.
10. Ibid., 2.
11. Karen Springen, "This Is Your Brain on Alien Killer Pimps of Nazi Doom," *Newsweek*, 11 December 2006, 48.
12. Ibid.

13. Kovar, "David Cronenberg," 1.
14. Elysa Gardner, "Darker Tone: Reflective New CD Born of Maturity," *USA Today*, 30 January 2007, D6.
15. James Poniewozik, "The Rap Sheet," *Time*, 3 April 2006.
16. Anthony Breznican, "'Miami Vice': Just the Names Are the Same," *USA Today*, 27 July 2006, D1.
17. William Kleck, "Burnett Joins 'Desperate Housewives,'," *USA Today*, 2 March 2006.
18. Jason Kovar, "American Beauty," http://www.goodfight.org/hwamericanbeauty.html, 1.
19. Ibid.
20. Ibid.
21. Jason Kovar, "Steven Spielberg," http://www.goodfight.org/hwsspielberg.html.
22. Ibid.
23. Ibid.
24. Kovar, "Columbine Effect," 3.

Chapter Eighteen: Hollywood's Road to Perdition

1. Jason Kovar, "David Cronenberg," http://www.goodfight.org/hwdcronenberg.html, 3.
2. Author's phone interview with Allen Ginsberg, 30 June 1993.
3. William Burroughs, preface to *Queer* (New York: Penguin, 1985), xxiii.
4. E. Michael Jones, *Degenerate Moderns* (San Francisco: Ignatius Press, 1993), 95-96.
5. Ibid., 100.
6. Ibid., 97-98.
7. Ibid., 99.
8. James Grauerholz, "The Death of Joan Vollmer Burroughs: What Really Happened?" American Studies Department, University of Kansas, http://www.ku.edu.
9. Ted Morgan, *Literary Outlaw* (New York: Avon, 1988), 214.
10. Ann Charters, *Kerouac*: Straight Arrow, 1973,.
11. Wardell B. Pomeroy, *Dr. Kinsey and the Institute for Sex Research* (New York: Harper and Row, 1972), 397.
12. Jones, *Degenerate Moderns*, 99.
13. Ibid.
14. Ibid, 90.
15. Ibid., 98.

16. Ibid., 113.
17. Larry Ceplair and Steven England, *The Inquisition in Hollywood: Politics in the Film Community, 1930-1960* (New York: Doubleday, 1980), 408.
18. Howard Fast, *The Naked God: The Writer and the Communist Party* (New York: Praeger, 1957), 64-66.
19. David Horowitz and Richard Poe, *The Shadow Party* (Nashville: Nelson Current, 2006), 60.
20. Andrew S. Weil, "The Strange Case of the Harvard Drug Scandals," *Look*, 5 November 1963.
21. Aleister Crowley, http://www.illuminati-news.com/art-and-mc/rockmusic-and-crowley.htm, 4.
22. Jason Kovar, "Jayne Mansfield," http://www.goodfight.org/hwjmansfield.html, 4.
23. Ibid.
24. http://www.playboy.com/worldofplayboy/faq/philosophy.html#1.
25. Horowitz and Poe, *The Shadow Party*, 60.
26. Morgan, *Literary Outlaw*, 316-26.
27. Jack Valenti, "How It All Began," MPAA, http://www.mpaa.org/Ratings_How It All Began, 1.
28. Kovar, "Jayne Mansfield."
29. Ibid., 2.
30. Ibid., 7.
31. Ibid.
32. Jack Valenti, "How It All Began," 1.
33. Ibid.
34. Ibid.
35. Jack Valenti, "The Birth of Ratings," http://www.mpaa.org/Ratings_BirthofRt.asp.
36. Author's phone interview with Allen Ginsberg, 30 June 1993.
37. Kovar, "David Cronenberg," 3.
38. Jones, *Degenerate Moderns*, 99.
39. Jamie Jimenez, "Reconsidering Kinsey," *AFA Journal*, January 2005, 14.
40. Ibid.
41. Ibid.
42. Patrick Buchanan, "Kinsey: Medical Pioneer or Criminal Fraud," *Human Events*, 2 July 1983, 14.
43. Interview with Hugh Hefner, http://www.gwu.edu/~nsarchiv/coldwar/interview/episode13.
44. Ibid.

45. Bob Woodward, *Wired* (New York: Simon and Schuster, 1984), 317.
46. Interview with Dr. Victoria Zdrock, *Geraldo At Large*, Fox News Network, 24 February 2007.
47. Kim Komando, *The Kim Komando Show*, Westwood One Radio, 21 October 2006.

Chapter Nineteen: Warning: Hip-Hop and Rap Music Can Kill You

1. Larry Reibstein, with Thomas Rosenstiel, "The Right Takes a Media Giant to Task," *Newsweek*, 12 June 1995.
2. Ibid.
3. Richard Zoglin, "A Company Under Fire," *Time*, 12 June 1995.
4. Ibid.
5. Richard Lacayo, "Violent Reaction," *Time*, 12 June 1995.
6. Bill O'Reilly, *The O'Reilly Factor*, Fox News Network, 1 March 2007.
7. Johnnetta Betsch Cole, "What Hip-Hop Has Done to Black Women," *Ebony*, March 2007, 94.
8. "Black Law Dictionary," http://www.universalzulunation.com.
9. Hip-Hop Summit Action Network: Mission Statement, http://www.hsan.org/content/main.aspx?pageid=7.
10. G. Craige Lewis, http://www.exministries.com/charisma.html.
11. Lewis, "Why Hip-Hop?" http://www.exministries.com/whyhhh.html.
12. Ibid.
13. G. Craige Lewis, *The Truth Behind Hip-Hop*, Ex Ministries, 2006, DVD.
14. Lewis, "Why Hip-Hop?"
15. Lewis, http://www.exministries.com/charisma.html.
16. Lewis, "Why Hip-Hop?"
17. Ibid.
18. Cole, "What Hip-Hop Has Done to Black Women," 96.
19. Cora Daniels, http://www.coradaniels.com/ghettonation.html.
20. *Newsweek*, 23 April 2007, 35.
21. "Differentiating Don Imus from Hip-Hop," Press Release, HSAN, 13 April 2007.
22. George Rush and Jeanne Rush, Daily News, 17 April 2007.
23. "Recommendations to the Recording and Broadcast Industries," Press Release, HSAN, 23 April 2007.
24. Interview with Angela McGlowan, *The O'Reilly Factor*, Fox News Network, 30 April 2007.

Chapter Twenty: The Velvet Mafia: Fact or Fiction?

1. Rick Leed, as quoted in the *San Francisco Chronicle*, 28 January 1996.
2. Tom King, *The Operator* (New York: Random House, 2000), 414.
3. Michaelangelo Signorile, http://www.signorile.com/articles/nyp34.html, 2.
4. Ibid.
5. Mark Ebner and Andrew Breitbart, *Hollywood Interrupted* (Wiley, 2003), 3.
6. Michaelangelo Signorile, 1.
7. Daniel Jeffreys, "Hollywood's Heterophobia," Daily Mail, 1 April 2000.
8. Michaelangelo Signorile, 3.
9. Ibid., 4.
10. Ibid., 3.
11. King, *The Operator*, 486.
12. Ibid., 466-67.
13. Ibid., 467.
14. Ibid., 486.
15. Jeffreys, "Hollywood's Heterophobia."
16. Ibid.
17. Jason Kovar, "American Beauty," http://www.goodfight.org/hwamericanbeauty.htm.
18. http://www.mediaresearch.org/BozellColumns/entertainmentcolumn/2003/co/20031126.asp.
19. Interview with Rebecca Hagelin, *The O'Reilly Factor*, Fox News Network, 6 April 2007.
20. David Poland, http://www.hotbutton.com/today/hot.button/2002_thb.
21. *The Advocate*, 7 May 1991, 49.
22. "MTV Is Around the Clock," *Philadelphia Inquirer*, 8 November 1982.

Chapter Twenty-one: The Incredible Shrinking Box Office

1. Patty Ruhle, "'Batman' Hangs on as 'War' Looms," *USA Today*, 27 June 2005.
2. Richard Corliss, "Can This Man Save the Movies?" *Time*, 20 March 2006: 70.
3. Neil Cavuto, *Your World with Neil Cavuto*, Fox News Network, 10 March 2006 (per:Nielsen EDI).
4. Scott Bowles, "Hollywood Scans Horizon for More 'Passion'," *USA Today*, 14 April 2005, D1,

5. Mike Snider, "Hollywood Serves Movies Your Way," *USA Today*, 14 April 2005, D1.
6. Scott Bowles, "Box Office Sallies Forth," *USA Today*, 27 December 2006.
7. Michael Medved, *Hollywood vs. America* (New York: Harper Perennial, 1993), 277.
8. Ibid.
9. U. S. Bureau of the Census, Washington, D.C., National totals for 1970, 1980, 1990, 2000.
10. Medved, *Hollywood vs. America*, 278-79.
11. Scott Bowles, "Hollywood Considers Ad Campaign to Boost Attendance," *USA Today*, 15 March 2006, D3.
12. Medved, *Hollywood vs. America*, 281.
13. Ibid.
14. Bowles, "Box Office Sallies Forth."
15. "Talladega Keeps Hollywood on Track," *USA Today*, 7 August 2006.
16. *The Hollywood Reporter*, Special Issue, 8 April 1997.
17. Medved, *Hollywood vs. America*, 7.
18. Ibid., 27.
19. Ibid., 202-03.
20. "Holly Hunter Relishes Dark, Chaotic 'Grace' Role on TNT," *USA Today*, 23 March 2007.
21. Kate Kelly, "Hollywood's Romance Flicks Tackle Phobias, Anger Issues in Era of Reality Television," *Wall Street Journal*.
22. Medved, *Hollywood vs. America*, 259.
23. Ibid., 281.
24. James Hirsen, *Hollywood vs. America*, News Special, Fox News Network, 20 February 2005.
25. Larry Elder, *Hollywood vs. America*, Fox News Special.
26. *Hollywood vs. America*, Fox News Special.
27. Kim Masters, National Public Radio, 19 May 2007.
28. Medved, *Hollywood vs. America*, 232.
29. Ibid., 17.
30. "Roman Vice," The History Channel, 3 March 2006.
31. Medved, *Hollywood vs. America*, 235.
32. "Senator Robert Byrd's Speech on the State of Entertainment," *Electronic Media*, 30 September 1991.
33. Medved, *Hollywood vs. America*, 199.
34. Kenneth Turan, "Documentary on Beastiality Premieres at Sundance Film Festival," *Los Angeles Times*, 21 January 2007.
35. Ibid.

Chapter Twenty-two: Riding with the Devil

1. Michael Medved, *Hollywood vs. America* (New York: Harper Perennial, 1993), 71.
2. Gregory D. Black, Working Draft of the Lord-Quigley Code Proposal, *Hollywood Censored* (United Kingdom: Cambridge University Press, 1994), 303.
3. Helen Kazantzakis, *Nikos Kazantzakis: A Biography Based on His Letters* (New York: Simon and Schuster, 1968), 61.
4. Ibid., 515.
5. Nikos Kazantzakis, *The Saviors of God: Spiritual Exercises* (New York: Simon and Schuster, 1968), 20.
6. Larry Poland, *The Last Temptation of Hollywood* (Highland, CA: Mastermedia International, 1988), 18.
7. Ibid., 15.
8. Ibid., 43.
9. Ibid., 47.
10. Ibid., 10.
11. Ibid., 56.
12. Medved, *Hollywood vs. America*, 40.
13. Poland, *The Last Temptation of Hollywood*, 98.
14. Ibid., 85-86.
15. Ibid., 100.
16. Ibid.
17. Ibid., 153.
18. Ibid., 136.
19. Medved, *Hollywood vs. America*, 41.
20. Mike Duffy, "Yahoos Create Unholy Row Over Film About Christ," *Detroit Free Press*, 10 April 1988.
21. Medved, *Hollywood vs. America*, 48.
22. "Controversial Film Grosses," Box Office Mojo, http://www.boxofficemojo.com, 22 June 2006.
23. "Worldwide Film Grosses," Box Office Mojo, http://www.boxofficemojo.com, 30 January 2007.
24. *Your World with Neil Cavuto*, Fox News Network, 23 September 2006.
25. Medved, *Hollywood vs. America*, 87.
26. Kevin Jackson, "'Ultimate Gift' Producer Stunned by Bashing of 'Hidden Religious Content'," *Christian Post*, 17 March 2007.
27. Pat Buchanan, "The Aggressors in the Culture War," 8 March 2004.
28. Poland, *The Last Temptation of Hollywood*, 85.

29. *Webster's New World Dictionary of the American Language* (Cleveland/New York: The World Publishing Company, 1968).
30. Ibid., definitions 2, 3, and 4.
31. Andy Seiler, "Will 'Boogie Nights' Falter?" *USA Today*, 6 November 1997.
32. Scott Bowles, "Hollywood Turns to Divine Inspiration," *USA Today*, 19 April 2006.
33. Angela Noland, "Cannes Film Festival 2006," Associated Press, 17 May 2006.
34. James Hirsen, "The Da Vinci Con," NewsMax, June 2006, 21.
35. "Interview with Ian McKellan, *Today Show*, NBC Network, 17 May 2006.
36. Hirsen, "The Da Vinci Con."
37. Hirsen, "Decoding Da Vinci's Fiction," NewsMax, June 2006, 20.
38. Poll of Da Vinci Code readers, The Barna Group, http://www.barna.org, 15 May 2006.
39. Lee Strobel and Gary Poole, "Exploding the Da Vinci Code," 8.
40. http://www.catholiceducation.org/articles/facts/fm0035.html.
41. Seth Mnookin, *Vanity Fair*, July 2006.
42. Hirsen, "The Da Vinci Con," 28.
43. Ibid.
44. John Zmirak, "My Lunch with an Old Friend," http://www.Godspy.com, June 2006.
45. Ibid.
46. Hirsen, "The Da Vinci Con," 17.
47. Ibid.
48. Medved, *Hollywood vs. America*, 28.
49. Ibid.
50. Bowles, "Hollywood Turns to Divine Inspiration," 2.
51. Hirsen, "The Da Vinci Con," 24.
52. Bowles, "Hollywood Turns to Divine Inspiration," 2.
53. Hirsen, "The Da Vinci Con," 23-24.
54. Ibid., 24.
55. Interview with Robert Schuller, *The O'Reilly Factor*, Fox News Network, 19 May 2006.
56. Ted Baehr, "Salt and Light," http://www.movieguide.org, 25 May 2006. (archives)
57. Hirsen, "The Da Vinci Con," 27.
58. Ibid.
59. "*Da Vinci Code* Confirms Rather Than Changes People's Religious Views," The Barna Group, http://www.barna.org, 15 May 2006.
60. Scott Bowles, "Critics Can't Break 'Code'," *USA Today*, 22 May 2006.

61. Hirsen, "The Da Vinci Con," 27.
62. Mark Belling, "The Rush Limbaugh Show," 23 May 2006.
63. Hirsen, "The Da Vinci Con," 28.
64. James Hirsen, "Hollywood's Leap of Faith," http://www.NewsMax.com. (Archives)
65. Ibid.
66. Ibid.
67. "Movies Look to Aid Search for Greater Meaning," NewsMax, http://www.NewsMax.com, 4 April 2007.
68. Ibid.
69. Ibid.
70. Scott Bowles, "Hollywood Turns to Divine Revelations," *USA Today*, 14 April 2006.
71. Ibid.
72. Ibid.
73. Mike LaVaque-Mantay, "J. K. Rowling's Modern World," *Left 2 Right*, 19 July 2005.
74. Joe Schimmel, *Harry Potter: A Spirit Conspiracy*, Fight the Good Fight Ministries, Adullam Films, 2005.
75. *Webster's New World Dictionary of the American Language* (Cleveland/New York: The World Publishing Company, 1968).
76. Interview with J. K. Rowling, *This Morning, Sunday Edition*, CBC Network, 23 October 2000.
77. Online chat with J. K. Rowling, AOL Online, *http://www.mugglechat.com/aolchat1*, 10 October 2000.
78. Steven D. Greydanus, "Harry Potter vs. Gandalf," http://www.decentfilms.com/sections/articles/2567.
79. Terry Mattingly, "J. K. Rowling, Inkling?" http://www.tmatt.gospelcom.net/column/2003/06/18/.
80. Ibid.
81. Dave Kopel, "Deconstructing Rowling," National Review Online, http://www.nationalreview.com, 9 June 2003.
82. http://www.accio-quote.org/articles/list1999.html.
83. Interview with J. K. Rowling, *This Morning, Sunday Edition*.
84. Julia Duin, "Writer's Wizardry with Words Welcome," *The Washington Times*, 28 October 1999.
85. http://www.accio-quote.org/articles/list1999.html.
86. Ibid.
87. Weeks, "Charmed, I'm Sure," *The Washington Post*, 20 October 1999.
88. Malcolm Jones, "Her Magic Moment," *Newsweek*, 30 June 2003.

89. Interview with J. K. Rowling, *This Morning, Sunday Edition*.
90. Ted Baehr and Tom Snyder, *Frodo and Harry* (Wheaton, IL: Crossway Books, 2003), 29.
91. Schimmel, *Harry Potter: A Spirit Conspiracy*.
92. Richard Abanes, "Sorcery In a Stone: A Closer Look," http://www.adventistreview.org/2001-1547/story5.html.
93. Ibid.
94. Ibid.
95. Interview with J. K. Rowling, Barnes and Noble, 19 February 1999.
96. Online chat with J. K. Rowling, AOL Online.
97. *The Holy Bible: Good Shepherd Edition* (Great Britain: John C. Winston, 1946).
98. Magic "The Dark Arts," http://www.hp-lexicon.org/magic/dark.
99. Connie Ann Kirk, preface to *J. K. Rowling: A Biography* (Westport, CT: Greenwood Press, 2003), xii.
100. Ibid.
101. Interview with J. K. Rowling, *This Morning, Sunday Edition*.
102. Kirk, *J. K. Rowling: A Biography*, 9.
103. Ibid., 33.
104. Friederich Nietzsche, http://www.jacklaff.com/shebang6/nietzsche.
105. http://www.christiananswers.net/q-edem/harrypotter.html.
106. Abanes, "Sorcery In a Stone: A Closer Look."
107. Lindsay Frazer, "Harry Potter-Harry and Me," *The Scotsman*, November 2002.
108. Ibid.
109. Kirk, *J. K. Rowling: A Biography*, 10.
110. Ibid., 35.
111. Ibid., 40.
112. April Lynch, "Dancing on the Darkside," http://www.sfgate.com, 5 February 1999.
113. "Defining Goth," http://www.blood-dance.net/goth/origins/html.
114. Ibid.
115. Abanes, "Sorcery In a Stone: A Closer Look."
116. Interview with J. K. Rowling, *This Morning, Sunday Edition*.
117. Kirk, *J. K. Rowling: A Biography*, 45.
118. Ibid., 54.
119. Ibid., 66.
120. Lev Grossman, interview with J. K. Rowling, *Time*, 25 July 2005.
121. Wilbur Smith, *World Crisis and the Prophetic Scripture*, study of Ephesians 6:12 (Chicago: Moody Press, 1951).

122. Ted Baehr and Tom Snyder, "Time-Warner Promotes Terrorism and Anti-Christian Bigotry in New Left Movie 'V for Vendetta'," WorldNetDaily, http://www.worldnetdaily.com.
123. Ibid.
124. Darryn Simmons, "TV Takes on Religion," *Montgomery Advertiser*.

Chapter Twenty-three: J. K. Rowling's New World Disorder

1. John Granger, *The Hidden Key to Harry Potter* (Allentown, PA: Zossima Press, 2002).
2. Dave Kopel, "Deconstructing Rowling," National Review Online, http://www.nationalreview.com, 9 June 2003.
3. Ibid.
4. Ibid.
5. Lev Grossman, interview with J. K. Rowling, *Time*, 25 July 2005.
6. Kopel, "Deconstructing Rowling."
7. Ted Baehr and Tom Snyder, *Frodo and Harry* (Wheaton, IL: Crossway Books, 2003), 193-94.
8. Ibid.
9. Kopel, "Deconstructing Rowling."
10. Steven D. Greydanus, "Harry Potter vs. Gandalf," http://www.decentfilms.com/sections/articles/2567.
11. Interview with J. K. Rowling, *This Morning, Sunday Edition*, CBC Network, 23 October 2000.
12. Baehr and Snyder, *Frodo and Harry*, 195.
13. "'Harry Potter' Good for New Age Business," Wizard News, http://www.wizardnews.com, 2 October 2003.
14. Connie Ann Kirk, *J. K. Rowling: A Biography* (Westport, CT: Greenwood Press, 2003), 105.
15. Grossman, Interview with J. K. Rowling.
16. Ibid.
17. Ibid.
18. J. K. Rowling's acceptance speech, Principe de Asturias, 25 October 2003.
19. Interview with J. K. Rowling, *This Morning, Sunday Edition*.
20. Kirk, *J. K. Rowling: A Biography*, 104.
21. Ibid.
22. Ibid., Forward.
23. Greydanus, "Harry Potter vs. Gandalf," 14.
24. Ibid., 7.
25. Ibid., 17-18.

26. Ibid., 27-28.
27. Richard Abanes, "Sorcery In a Stone: A Closer Look," http://www.adventistreview.org/2001-1547/story5.html.
28. Greydanus, "Harry Potter vs. Gandalf," 4-5.
29. Baehr and Snyder, *Frodo and Harry*, 27.
30. Michael D. O'Brien, "Harry Potter and the Paganization of Children's Culture," *Catholic World Report*, 21 July 2001, 52-61.
31. Baehr and Snyder, *Frodo and Harry*, 38.
32. Jim Brown, "Harry Potter's 'Relativism' Dangerous for Youth, Says European Author," *Agape Press*, 13 December 2005.
33. Abanes, "Sorcery In a Stone: A Closer Look," 12-13.
34. "Why We Love Harry Potter," editorial, *Christianity Today*, 10 January 2000.
35. Joe Schimmel, *Harry Potter: A Spirit Conspiracy*, Fight the Good Fight Ministries, Adullam Films, 2005.
36. Greydanus, "Harry Potter vs. Gandalf," 42-43.
37. O'Brien, "Harry Potter and the Paganization of Children's Culture," 52-61.
38. Elizabeth Nehren, "Upward and Onward Toward Book Seven," *Los Angeles Times*, 25 October 2000.
39. http://www.accio-quote.org/articles/list1999.html.
40. Diedre Donahue, "Phenom Harry Potter Casts Spell Over Author, Too," *USA Today*, 9 September 1999.
41. Schimmel, *Harry Potter: A Spirit Conspiracy*.
42. http://www.scholastic.com/harrypotter/reading/magichouse.htm.
43. Donahue, "Phenom Harry Potter Casts Spell Over Author, Too."
44. Schimmel, *Harry Potter: A Spirit Conspiracy*.
45. Caryl Mastrisciana, *Harry Potter: Witchcraft Prepackaged*, Jeremiah Films, 2001.
46. Ibid.
47. Marcia Montenegro, http://www.christiananswers.net/q-eden/harrypotter.html.
48. Abanes, "Sorcery In a Stone: A Closer Look," 3.
49. "Latest 'Harry Potter' Books Meets Continuing Response from Christians," *Baptist Press*, 13 July 2000.
50. Greydanus, "Harry Potter vs. Gandalf," 41.
51. Marguerite Kelly, "The Trouble with Harry," *Washington Post*, 14 February 2001.
52. Nancy Gibbs, *Time*, 23 June 2003, 60.
53. Ed Vitagliano, "Road Map to Persecution?" *AFA Journal*, June 2007, 21.

Chapter Twenty-four: Fighting Back Against Hollywood

1. James Poniewosik, "The Decency Police," *Time*, 28 March 2005, 24.
2. Ibid.
3. John Eggerton, "FCC Indecency Fine Boost Passes," *Broadcasting and Cable,* 7 June 2006.
4. "FCC Upholds Super Bowl Decision: Proposes New Fines," *Baptist Press*, 8 June 2006.
5. "PTC Condemns Ultra-Violent TV Content and Calls on Industry to Shape Up," Parents' Television Council, Press Release, http://www.parentstv.org, 26 June 2007.
6. Ibid.
7. John Dunbar, "FCC: Government Could Regulate TV Violence," Associated Press, 25 April 2007.
8. Ibid.
9. Ibid.
10. "PTC Condemns Ultra-Violent TV Content and Calls on Industry to Shape Up," Parents' Television Council.
11. FCC Chairman Kevin J. Martin, statement before the Senate Committee on Commerce, Science, and Transportation, Open Forum on Decency, 29 November 2005.
12. *Fox News Special: Hollywood vs. America*, Fox News Dynamic Opinion Poll, Fox News Network, 20 February 2005.
13. AP/IPSOS Poll, 28 March 2007.
14. "America's Media Speaks Out for Cable Choice," Parents' Television Council, http://www.parentstv.org.
15. "Families Applaud Cable Choice Proposal," Press Release, *http://www.parentstv.org*, 14 June 2007.
16. "America's Media Speaks Out for Cable Choice," Parents' Television Council.
17. Stephen Labaton, Under New Chief, FCC Considers Widening It's Reach," *New York Times*, 28 March 2005.
18. Paul Davidson, "Report May Slow a' la carte Cable Push," *USA Today*, 22 November 2004.
19. Dave Eberhart, "Broadcasters Face 'Hefty Fines' for Indecency," NewsMax, http://www.NewsMax.com, August 2006.
20. Gregory D. Black, *Hollywood Censored* (United Kingdom: Cambridge University Press, 1994), 23.
21. Paul Davidson, "Court Weakens Broadcast Indecency Rules," *USA Today*, 5 June 2007, B1.

22. Ted Hearn, "Body Blow for Martin in Violence Bill," *Multichannel News*, 28 May 2007.
23. "Families Applaud Cable Choice Proposal," Parents' Television Council, http://www.parentstv.org.
24. Ibid.
25. Ibid.

Chapter Twenty-five: A Grassroots Victory

1. Michael Foust, "DVD-Editing Companies Close Instead of Appeal Ruling," *Baptist Press*, 17 August 2006.
2. Ibid.
3. Ibid.
4. Kelly Boggs, "First Person: What's Hollywood's Motive?" *Baptist Press*, 14 July 2006.

INDEX

50 Cent 450, 464
Aaliyah 449
Abanes, Richard 576, 582, 607
Abernathy, Ralph 139, 140
Ackerman, Gary 633
ACLU 148, 279, 336, 532, 635
Affleck, Ben 132
Ahmadinejad, Mahmoud 287, 616
Aho, Bill 640 - 644
Akon 450, 479
Albee, Edward 34
Albright, Madeleine 88, 90
Alda, Alan 366
Alden, Diane 685
Alinsky, Saul 140, 149, 279, 282, 402, 410, 419, 436
Allen, Fred 235
Allen, Mike 171
Allen, Steve 16, 430
Alley, Kirstie 383
Alter, Jonathan 22
al-Zawahiri, Aiman 101
Amende, Coral 695
Amorth, Gabrielle 610
Anderson, Louie 372
Anger, Kenneth 362, 406
Aniston, Jennifer 61, 498
Anstrom, Dexter 179
Apostle Paul 172, 290, 292

Arafat, Yasser 56
Arantes, Jorge 577
Arbuckle, Fatty 320, 321
Archer, Anne 383
Arendt, Paul 556
Armstrong, Louis 452
Arnaud, Anton 405
Arnold, Roseanne 70
Arnold, Tom 71
Arnstein, Bobbie 434
Arpaio, Joe 481
Arquette, Rosanna 70, 372
Asa, Chaim 534
Amanpour, Christiane 616
Asner, Ed 236, 241, 288, 372
Aspen, Jennifer 383
Azhrarn 585

Bacall, Lauren 257
Baehr, Ted 29, 296, 544, 556, 558, 575, 589, 599, 606, 609, 691, 703, 705, 706
Bambaataa, Afrika 363, 455, 457, 480, 670
Barna, George 547
Barnes, Fred 508
Barth, Karl 610
Basinger, Kim 70, 372, 480
Bauer, Gary 22
Baum, L. Frank 364
Baxter, Meridith 70

Beacham, Stephanie 372
Beatty, Warren 265
Beck, Glenn 92, 343, 500
Begala, Paul 23. 108
Begley, Ed 70
Belushi, John 315, 316-319, 328
Belling, Mark 558
Benge, Michael 282
Bening, Annette 70, 494
Bennett, Tony 71
Bennett, William 22, 49, 98, 178
Benoit, Chris 329
Ben-Veniste, Richard 86
Bereuter, Doug 177
Bergen, Candace 47
Berger, Sandy 84, 86, 88, 119
Bernall, Cassie 78
Bernstein, Carl 86, 107
Bernstein, Leonard 263
Bernsten, Gary 92, 124
Berenger, Tom 70
Berry, Halle 132, 371
Berry, Julie 113
Berry, Walter 249
Bertinelli, Valerie 372
Beveridge, Dirk 684
Bianco, Robert 201, 439
Bielowicz, Norm 517
Big Boi 480
Big Hawk 449
Billingsley, Kenneth Lloyd 243, 249, 251, 253, 256, 266, 288
bin Laden, Osama 80, 87, 91, 106, 113, 287
Black, Amy 246, 496
Black, Gregory D. 31, 44
Blair, Linda 372
Blair, Tony 276, 615, 616, 617
Blake, Jeff 558
Blake, William 398
Blavatsky, Madame 268, 368
Blitzer, Wolff 47, 82

Biggie Smalls 451
Bloom, Harold 598
Blumenthal, Max 92
Blunt, Roy 195, 196, 536
Bogart, Humphrey 245, 257
Bonds, Barry 325
Bono 429
Bork, Robert 146
Bowles, Scott 26, 554, 561
Boyer, Charles 257
Boyle, Peter 274
Bozell, Brent 69, 106, 182, 215, 220, 623, 629
Bracco, Lorraine 393
Branson, Richard 642
Brassel, Bob 484
Braun, Bennett 317
Brawley, Twana 142
Brecht, Bertolt 254, 256, 270, 278
Breen, Joseph 217
Breitbart, Andrew 485
Brewer, Roy 250, 252, 260
Breznican, Anthony 393
Brillstein, Bernie 317
Broaddrick, Juanita 110
Brody, Sam 425
Brokaw, Tom 45, 126
Bronfman, Jr., Edgar 74, 77
Brooks, Tim 203
Brown, Blythe 549 - 551
Brown, Gordon 616, 617, 619
Brown, Dan 541, 544, 549 - 551
Brown, Ron 118
Brown, Tia 343
Brown, William B. 233
Brownback, Sam 182, 623
Browning, Tod 216
Bruer, Rory 507
Buchanan, Patrick 20, 432, 519, 540
Buchwald, Art 207
Buckley, Jr., William F. 154, 155, 156
Buffy "The Human Beat Box" 450

Bullinger, E. W. 172, 610
Bullock, Sandra 372
Burnett, Carol 202, 393
Burns, Ken 125
Burroughs, Billy 421
Burroughs, Bryan 486
Burroughs, Joan Vollmer 399, 403
Burroughs, William 33, 364, 399, 403, 428
Burton, Bill 130
Burton, Richard 35, 38
Busey, Gary 315
Bush, George 19, 21, 22, 26, 122, 145, 164, 275, 279, 293, 297, 342, 624, 643
Bush, George H. W. 62, 492
Bushman, Brad 391
Byers, Patsy 298, 307
Byrd, Robert 514
Byrne, Rhonda 374

Caldwell, Melissa 389
Callahan, Patrick 680
Cam'ron 450, 476
Canada, Geoffrey 478
Canfield, Jack 375
Cano, Andrew 531
Canton, Mark 484
Capone, Al 255
Capote, Truman 25, 237
Capra, Frank 44, 194, 204
Capshaw, Kate 391
Carlin, George 441 - 445
Carlson, Tucker 126
Carlyon, Keven 601
Carmona, Richard 326
Carpenter, John 391
Carr, Caleb 430
Carr, Lucien 400
Carrell, Steve 562
Carson, Jay 87
Carter, Jimmy 106, 113, 126, 204, 208, 209, 451, 635

Carville, James 23, 108, 111
Case, Charles 46, 68
Case, Sharon 383
Cassady, Neal 400, 418, 430
Catsoulis, Jeanette 538
Caulfield, Holden 157
Cavuto, Neil 382, 460, 502
Ceplair, Larry 698
Chamberlain, Neville 582
Chang, Jung 269
Chaplin, Charlie 241, 321
Chaput, Charles D. 615
Charters, Ann 698
Chase, Chevy 21, 71, 271
Chavez, Cesar 318
Chavez, Linda 411
Cheney, Dick 103
Cheney, Lynne 103
Cher 53, 138, 372
Chiklis, Michael 626
Chopra, Deepak 560
Christensen, Erika 383
Christenson, Cornelia 401, 406
Christiano, Dave 560
Christiano, Rich 560
Churchill, Winston 242, 258, 267, 616, 617, 620
Clark, Larry 224
Clark, Mike 226
Clark, Ramsey 272
Clarke, Richard 85, 87, 90
Clary, Johnny Lee 78
Claudius 233, 511, 512
Cleaver, Emanuel 149
Clinton, Bill 29, 48, 52, 56, 60, 85, 99, 121, 622
Clinton, Hillary 53, 61, 62, 81, 97, 99, 105, 437
Clooney, George 25, 132, 219, 240, 250, 270, 505, 521, 542
Close, Glenn 70, 372

Cobain, Kurt 65, 138, 364, 420, 491
Cody, Diablo 395
Cohen, Bruce 394, 493
Cohen, Richard 168
Coile, Zachary 693
Colbert, Stephen 125
Cole, Johnnetta Betsch 453, 471
Coleman, John 295
Collins, Addie Mae 385
Collins, Junie 385
Colmes, Alan 678, 682, 685, 713
Colson, Charles 108
Combs, Sean "P. Diddy" 450, 451, 452, 468, 491
Connor, Joe 106
Constantine 512, 545
Cooper, Anderson 174, 475
Cooper, Marc 301
Copeland, Aaron 506
Copeland, Kenneth 631
Costner, Kevin 651
Copps, Michael 628
Corea, Chick 383
Corliss, Richard 502, 534, 556
Corydon, Bent 379
Cosby, Bill 174, 232, 444
Cotten, Joseph 257, 347 - 350
Couch, Paul 631
Coulter, Ann 125
Couric, Katie 220
Courtois, Stephanie 263
Cox, Courteney 498
Coyote, Peter 70
Crafts, Wilbur 191
Craven, Wes 79, 223
Cronenberg, David 389, 397, 429
Cronkite, Walter 42, 100, 283
Crosby, Bing 235, 254
Crosby, Stills, & Nash 138, 491
Crowe, Russell 335
Crowley, Aleister 148, 301, 354 - 364, 379

Cruise, Tom 70, 381, 383, 457
Crumley, Shirley 335, 483, 491
Crystal, Billy 53
Cukor, George 44, 415
Culkin, Macauley 562
Cunningham, David 84, 86, 92
Cunningham, Dennis 535
Currie, Laughlin 269

Da Vinci, Leonardo 541, 547, 548
Dailey, Starr 610
Dale, Peter 28
Daly, Tyne 70
Damon, Matt 132, 250
Daniel, Sean 524
Daniels, Cora 472
Danson, Ted 71, 306, 372
Darras, Ben 298, 306
Darwin 406
Daschale, Tom 74
Davies, Joseph 268
Davis, Bette 245, 347 - 349
Davis, Gail 163
Davis, Jr., Sammy 370, 425
Davis, Martin 52
Davis, Thomas 340
Davis, Steven 364, 694
DeCamp, Ira W. 153
DeGeneres, Ellen 24, 221, 394
Deluc, Xavier 383
Demme, Jonathan 373
DeMornay, Rebecca 70
DeMott, Benjamin 416
DeNiro, Robert 114, 265, 318, 537
Dennehy, Brian 538
Dennison, John D. 280
Depp, Johnny 230, 250, 371
Dern, Bruce 352, 353
Dern, Laura 70, 372
Devor, Robinson 515
DiCaprio, Leonardo 295, 371

Dickinson, Bruce 362
Dietrich, Marlene 369
Diller, Barry 65, 485, 486
Disney, Walt 221, 251, 254
Dixie Chicks 29, 392,
DMX 450, 463, 477
Dmytryk, Edward 248, 260
Dobson, James 22, 529, 531
Dogg, Snoop 50, 346, 450, 452, 472
Doherty, Thomas 216
Dole, Bob 48, 52, 55, 68
Doley, Jr., Harold 461
Dollar, Creflo 464, 469
Donahue, Bill 345, 543, 552
Donahue, Marlo Thomas 71,
Dorsey, Tommy 506
Douglas, Kirk 71, 261
Douglas, Michael 70, 71
Dowd, Maureen 131, 139, 492
Dowling, Robert 218
Doyle, Tim 20, 215, 222
Dreyfus, Richard 71
Driscoll, Jerry 282
Duchovney, David 393
Duffey, Patrick 71
Dunaway, Faye 70
Dunne, Phillip 247
Dupri, Jermaine 464
Durant, Will 505
Durbin, Dick 88

Ebner, Mark 485
Eckhart, Dietrich 369
Edmonson, Sarah 298, 306
Edwards, John 145, 300, 460
Eggerton, John 715
Egglseston, Neil 130
Ehrenstein, David 535
Eichel, Edward 407, 408
Eichman, Adolf 235
Eisner, Michael 67, 70, 220 - 230, 486

Electra 602
Elder, Larry 510
Eller, Jeff 130
Ellis, Bret Easton 52
Emmanuel, Rahm 126
England, Steven 698
Ensler, Eve 292
Epstein, Edward 693
Espy, Mike 129

Fabares, Shelly 70
Falis, Michael 478
Falk, Peter 71
Falwell, Jerry 158
Farah, Joseph 125
Farmer, Frances 255
Farnsworth, Richard 227
Farrakhan, Louis 163
Farrell, Colin 392
Fast, Howard 263, 280
Faust 365, 550
Fernandez, Giselle 651
Feldman, Linda 22, 23
Feldstein, Steve 561
Fennegan, William 134
Fergie 509
Field III, Marshall 410
Field, Sally 71, 517
Fine, Marshall 535
Fitzgerald, F. Scott 201, 214, 216
Fitzgerald, Zelda 201, 214
Fitzpatrick, Brian 685
Fitzsimmons, Brady 312
Fleetwood, Peter 570
Flowers, Gennifer 60, 64
Flynt, Larry 112, 434
Fogelson, Adam 560
Fogerty, John 53
Fonda, Henry 281
Fonda, Jane 71, 123, 141, 272 - 296
Forbes, Malcolm 488

Ford, Gerald 287
Ford, John 44, 351
Ford, Luke 435
Fortenberry, Jeff 638
Fossey, Dian 371
Foust, Michael 709
Foxx, Jamie 392
Frankenheimer, John 239
Freeh, Louie 103, 114
Frenzel, Larry 559
Frey, James 27
Fitton, Tom 131
Fosse, Bob 445
Fuchs, Klaus 259
Fuchs, Michael 50

Glover, Danny 271
Gable, Clark 245, 369
Gabler, Neal 230
Galanos, Mike 103
Gallagher, Mike 15
Gallagher, Sterling 716
Gallin, Sandy 132, 485
Galloway, George 276
Gandhi 616
Garbo, Greta 369
Garcia, Jerry 101, 306, 313
Gardner, Elysa 392
Gardner, Gerald 600, 609
Garfield, John 246, 257, 262, 263
Garibaldi, Rob 326
Garland, Judy 257
Garner, James 71
Garrett, Larry 179
Gilroy, Tony 392
Geffen, David 65, 66, 71, 113, 137 - 139, 373, 483 - 499
Gelernter, David 234, 235
Geller, Michelle 79
Gentry, Pamela 472
Gephardt, Dick 74

Gere, Richard 372
Geto Boys 51, 138, 448, 491
Giambi, Jason 138
Gibbons, Michael 75
Gibson, John 172
Gibson, Mel 536
Gingrich, Newt 22
Ginsberg, Allen 33, 398, 403, 417, 427
Giovanardi, Carlo 153
Gitlin, Todd 146
Giuliani, Rudy 83
Giuliano, Geoffrey 361
Gleason, Jackie 202, 209
Glickman, Dan 43, 196, 326, 327, 336, 340, 345, 504
Globus, Yoram 58
Goebbels, Joseph 79
Goethe 550
Golan, Menaham 58
Gold, Harold 259
Goldberg, Bernard 479
Goldberg, Jonah 277
Goldberg, Whoopi 20, 21, 74, 250
Goldblum, Jeff 71
Goldman, Albert 372
Goldman, Mitchell 542
Goldstein, Jeff 28
Goodell, Roger 338, 482
Goodman, Ellen 31, 185, 186, 191, 220, 353
Gorbachev, Mikhail 262
Gore, Al 24, 53, 81, 122, 127, 145, 295
Gossett, Jr., Louis 70, 334, 372
Gottlieb, Meyer 560
Grace, Nancy 482
Guttenberg, Steve 651
Graham, Billy 76, 126, 532, 533
Graham, Ellen 219
Graham, Franklin 22, 377
Granger, John 570, 598
Granitz, Steve 485
Grauerholz, James 428

Graves, Joan 191
Gray, Linda 372
Gray, Timothy 20, 27, 31, 218, 326, 594
Grazer, Brian 542, 552, 555
Green, Harold 206
Greenaway, Peter 200, 346
Greenblatt, Robert 346
Greengrass, Paul 521
Grenier, Richard 266
Greydanus, Steven D. 569, 600, 606
Griffin, Kathy 504
Griffith, Melanie 71
Grisham, John 308, 312
Grizzard, Lewis 231
Grossman, Cathy Lynn 165
Grossman, Lev 95, 588, 602, 619
Grudem, Wayne 165
Guerrero, Eddie 328
Guns N' Roses 138
Gyllenhal, Jake 26

Hack, Shelly 71
Hagelin, Rebecca 497
Haggis, Paul 270
Hagin, Kenneth "Pop" 610
Hagman, Larry 71
Halberstam, David 691
Hall, Gus 262
Halliday, Jon 269
Halperin, Morton 145
Hamilton, George 372
Hanks, Tom 71, 509, 543
Hannity, Sean 88, 103, 479
Hansen, Beck 383
Harrelson, Woody 71, 306
Harris, Eric 77
Harvey, Paul 291
Hasselhoff, David 315
Hawks, Howard 44
Hawn, Goldie 371
Hay, Harry 418

Hayakawa, S. I. 155
Hayden, Sterling 242, 257
Hayden, Tom 274, 280, 418
Hayes, Isaac 383
Hays, Will 30, 33, 44, 63, 217
Hecht, Adolph 246
Heflin, Howell 637
Hefner, Hugh 33, 39, 112, 301, 402, 408
 - 410, 414 - 417, 424, 433
Hellman, Lillian 261
Hendrix, Jimi 345
Henley, Don 71
Henning, Curt "Mr. Perfect" 329
Hepburn, Katherine 509
Herman, Arthur 25, 266, 271
Hicks, Esther 376
Hill, Joe 393
Hillary, Sir Edmund 170
Hills, Carla 51
Hilton, Paris 299, 315, 334, 561
Hirsen, James 75, 371, 378, 387, 507, 508,
 544, 555
Hiss, Alger 267, 287
Hitchcock, Alfred 44, 440
Hitchens, Christopher 104, 110, 114, 153,
 620
Hitler, Adolph 79, 238, 296, 323, 369, 617
Ho Chi Minh 275, 280
Hodges, Paul 633
Hoffman, Abbie 436
Hoffman, David 282
Hoffman, Dustin 506
Holden, William 257
Holton, Dwight 130
Holzer, Mark 272, 281
Hook, Sidney 689
Hooper, Tobe 223, 389
Hope, Bob 235, 274, 531
Hopkins, Harry 267, 577
Horowitz, David 16, 146, 148, 278, 283, 419,
 621

717

Houdini, Harry 577
Howard, Ron 541, 543, 552 - 554
Howard, Terrance 27
Howell, Adrian 507
Huang, John 117
Hubbard, Jr., L. Ron 379, 380
Hubbard, L. Ron 301, 378, 379, 380
Huch, Larry 610
Hudson, Kate 371
Hughes, Karen 232
Hunter, Holly 345, 509
Hurley, Elizabeth 592
Hurt, William 562
Hussein, Saddam 21, 275, 276, 616
Huston, Angelica 372
Huston, John 257
Hutchison, Kay Bailey 631
Hyde, Henry 112, 113, 114

Iacocca, Lee 452
Ice Cube 451
Ice T 51
Ickes, Harold 88, 108, 130, 148
Iger, Robert 87, 91, 95, 230
Ignatius, Adi 689
Imus, Don 142, 471 - 474, 480
Inge, Walter 274
Ingraham, Laura 29
Ireland, Patricia 111
Irsay, James 405
Irwin, Ben 165

Jackson, Candice E. 110
Jackson, Janet 23, 625
Jackson, Jesse 139 - 143, 459, 471
Jackson, Michael 23
Jacobs, Alan 607
Jaffe, Sherri 74
Jagger, Mick 26, 301, 362
Jarman, Lee 640
Jarman, Matt 640

Jeffreys, Daniel 487, 493
Jerome, V. J. 245, 247
Jesus Christ 162, 172, 173, 191, 198, 289, 290, 291, 293, 381, 437, 462, 467, 504, 517, 528, 544, 549, 556, 558, 599
Jinks, Dan 394, 493
John, Elton 384, 385
Johnson, Lyndon 36, 38, 100, 419
Johnson, Mitchell 72
Johnson, Van 245
Jolie, Angelina 186, 219
Jones, Deborah 163
Jones, Marion 328
Jones, E. Michael 135, 170, 398, 401, 406
Jones, E. Stanley 610
Jones, Emperor 140
Jones, Malcolm 572
Jones, Norah 392
Joseph, Mark 507, 559
Jurgensen, John 693

Kael, Pauline 250
Kamelson, Ben 36
Kammerer, David 400
Karenga, Ron 163
Kasich, John 194
Kates, Kimberly 383
Katz, Otto 247, 261
Katzenberg, Jeffrey 65, 71, 72, 138, 490
Kaufman, Lloyd 540
Kaufman, Michael T. 684
Kazan, Elia 237, 246, 260, 264
Kazantzakis, Nikos 518, 523
Kean, Thomas 29, 84, 89
Keegan, Rebecca Winter 200
Keith, David 70
Kelly, Gene 257
Kelly, Grace 372
Kelly, Kate 509
Kelly, Marguerite 614
Kennedy III, William 108

Kennedy, Bill 130
Kennedy, Bobby 191
Kennedy, Jackie 34, 37
Kennedy, Jim 554
Kennedy, John F. 34, 37, 174, 419
Kennedy, Patrick 116
Kerns, Joanna 71
Kerouac, Jack 33, 400, 420, 489
Kerry, John 20, 81, 145, 280, 360, 424
Kesey, Ken 418
Keyes, Alan 131, 154, 155, 156, 158
Kidman, Nicole 70
Kiely, Kathy 693
Kim Il Sung 275
Kim Jong Il 259, 275, 434
Kincaid, Cliff 148, 160, 162
King Tubby 449
King, Coretta Scott 140
King, Francis 694
King, Jr., Martin Luther 139, 583, 616
King, Larry 173, 371
King, Rodney 142, 156
King, Stephen 393
King, Tom 137, 138, 393, 489, 492, 499
Kingston, Kenny 369
Kinsey, Alfred 401, 409, 430, 433, 487, 668
Kirk, Connie Ann 579, 594
Klayman, Larry 108, 110
Klebold, Dylan 77
Kleck, William 393
Klein, Aaron 284
Klein, Calvin 65, 485
Klein, Joe 134, 136
Knight, Suge 51, 450, 452
Koestler, Arthur 258
Kohan, Jenji 346
Kommando, Kim 439
Kornblatt, Si 524
Kouri, Jim 106
Kovar, Jason 79, 230, 301, 307, 333, 336, 373, 610

Kozak, Jan 146, 279, 439
Krattenmaker, Tom 159
Krauthammer, Charles 94, 99
Kroft, Steve 64
KRS-One 363, 457, 480
Krug, Judith 576
Krushchev, Nikita 238, 287, 583
Kuby, Gabriel 572, 608

Lacayo, Richard 49, 52
Laemelle, Greg 320
LaFontaine, Don 396
Laine, Denny 361
LaMotta, Jake 517
Lancaster, Burt 257
Lord, Daniel 36, 216, 653, 654
Landis, Floyd 328
Landis, John 329
Lange, Jessica 255, 372
Lansing, Sherry 265
Lardner, Jr., Ring 249, 262
Lattimore, Owen 269
Lattin, Don 696
LaVaque-Mantay, Mike 564
Lawrence, Marc 249
Lear, Norman 71, 132, 203, 207, 373, 532
Leary, Timothy 33, 301, 412 - 414, 432
Led Zeppelin 362
Ledger, Heath 26, 335, 343
Lee, Ang 26
Lee, Harper 347 - 349
Lee, Jason 383, 530
Lee, Richard G. 530
Leed, Rick 484
Leigh, Richard 550
Lemire, Jonathan 691
Lemmon, Jack 70
Lenin, Vladimir 146, 240, 265
Lennon, John 285, 301, 362, 413, 584
Leno, Jay 125
Lenzer, Terry 108

Leo, John 49, 235
Leonard, Sheldon 204, 207
Letterman, David 125
LeVay, Anton 77, 382, 668
Levi, Eliphas 360
Levin, Gary 679
Levin, Gerald 50, 77
Levin, James H. 71
Levine, Arthur 570, 575
Levinson, Barry 114
Levy, Adele Rosenwald 410
Lewinsky, Monica 109, 114
Lewis, C. S. 603, 606
Lewis, G. Craige 363, 465 - 370, 478
Lewis, Geoffrey 383
Lewis, Jason 313
Lewis, John 149
Lewis, Juliette 383
Lewis, Peter 148
Libby, G. Gordon 413
Lieberman, Joe 69, 176, 182, 199, 623
Lil' Kim 450
Limbaugh, David 67
Limbaugh, Rush 102, 263
Lindbergh, Charles 617
Lindsey, Bruce 88, 161
Little, Thomas 36, 37
Livingstone, Craig 107
LL Cool J 480
Loeb, Phil 246
Lohan, Lindsay 299, 315, 561
Lopez, Jennifer 53
Lott, Trent 74
Louise, Tina 370
Love, Courtney 315
Lowenstein, Douglas 391
Lucado, Max 538
Lucas, George 393
Luce III, Henry 50, 51
Ludacris 392, 446, 463
Lunev, Stanislav 272, 280

Lyda, Morris 317
Lynch, April 585
Lynn, Shelby 83
Lyons, Jeffrey 20

MacLaine, Shirley 173, 367, 376, 575
Madigan, Amy 70, 265
Madonna 29, 134, 219, 284, 358, 497
Magdalene, Mary 518, 547, 548
Maher, Bill 125, 250, 538
Mahjoubian, Micah 497
Maloney, Evan 22, 530
Mahoney, Roger 62
Mailer, Norman 253
Malden, Karl 264, 265
Malkin, Michelle 276, 278, 479
Maltin, Leonard 390, 592
Maltz, Albert 254
Mann, Michael 392
Manoff, Arnold 262
Mansfield, Jayne 370, 414 - 417, 424
Manson, Charles 382
Manson, Eddie 387
Manson, Marilyn 76, 314, 362
Mao Tse Tung 267, 275
Maples, Marla 70
Marceca, Anthony 108
March, Frederick 257
Markey, Edward 177, 180
Marsh, Earle 203
Martel, "Marvelous" Sherry 329
Martin, Andy 135, 136, 174
Martin, Dean 426
Martin, Kevin 624, 628, 631, 635
Martin, Roland 345
Martin, Strother 446
Marx, Groucho 257
Mary of Bethany 518, 548
Mary, Mother of Jesus 548
Mason, Marsha 70
Masri, Abu al 126

Massoud, Ahmed Shah 84, 91
Masterson, Mary Stuart 71
Mathers, Samuel 356
Matrisciana, Caryl 610, 613
Mattingly, Terry 570, 578
Mature, Victor 198
Mayer, Louis B. 254
McCain, John 21, 150, 282, 324, 633, 674
McCarey, Leo 254
McCarthy, Jenny 71
McCarthy, Joseph 25, 243, 245, 258, 266, 267
McCartney, Paul 301, 361, 362, 429, 617
McClanahan, Rue 70
McCuddy, Bill 27
McGlowan, Angela 478
McGraw, Ali 71
McGwire, Mark 324, 329
McGuirk, Bernard 471
McKellan, Ian 543
McKinley, Jessie 682
McNeese, Bill 43
McLuhan, Marshall 209
McMahon, Vince 328
McNair, Denise 385
McNamara, Robert 284
McQueen, Steve 372
McSlarrow, Kyle 626, 632
McWhorter, John H. 141
Medved, Michael 20, 35, 43, 344, 353, 503, 507, 508, 511, 516, 535
Mellencamp, John Cougar 20
Mendes, Sam 493
Menjou, Adolphe 249
Mephistopholes 364, 365, 370, 378, 405, 465
Merideth, Burgess 372
Meyer, Joyce 538
Meyer, Ron 75, 486
Michaels, Jamaal 141
Michaels, Lorne 318
Miller, Arthur 253
Miller, John 84

Miller, Zell 22
Mills, Donna 70
Milton 596, 599
Miniter, Richard 86
Minnow, Newton 213
Mitchell, George 325, 342
Mitchell, Joni 138
Mitchum, Robert 334, 537
Mitford, Jessica 582
Mnookin, Seth 550
Monroe, Marilyn 76, 369, 372, 415
Montenegro, Marcia 610, 614
Montgomery, Robert 245, 254
Moonves, Les 20, 233, 592, 622, 628
Moore, Demi 132
Moore, Michael 21, 56
Morgan, Ted 421
Morgenstern, Joe 557
Morris, Dick 52, 90
Morrison, Jim 301, 363
Morrison, Robert 311
Morrison, Toni 373
Mosely, Rufus 386, 610
Moses 240, 578
Mother Teresa 534, 536
Mouw, Richard 555
Mulligan, Robert 31, 347 - 349
Mulzert, Todd 138
Munzenberg, Willi 247
Murrow, Edward R. 25
Musto, Michael 489
Myers, Lisa 111

Napolean 374
Neeson, Liam 431
Neir, Aryeh 145, 278
Nero 233, 513
Nesbitt, Andy 325
Neufeld, Mace 521
Neuhaus, Richard John 55
Newhart, Bob 444, 445

Newman, Joanne 70
Newman, Paul 70, 516
Ngor, Haing S. 286
Nichols, Lisa 376
Nichols, Mike 30, 34, 38
Nicholson, Jack 202, 271, 318, 329
Nielson, Brigitte 372
Nietzsche, Friedrich 241, 564, 581, 663
Nightengale, Bob 325
Nimoy, Leonard 70
Nirvana 138
Nixon, Richard 42, 112, 256, 279, 282, 283, 286, 302, 303
Nizer, Louis 36
Nolte, Nick 265, 315, 562
Norgay, Tenzing 170
Novak, Kim 370
Nowrasteh, Cyrus 84, 88, 92, 95
Nussbaum, Bernard 108

O'Brien, Michael 608, 611
O'Connell, Jr., J. Barry 269
O'Connor, Carol 70, 203, 335
O'Connor, Hugh 335
O'Connor, Jennifer 130
O'Donnell, Norah 88
O'Donnell, Rosie 219, 250
O'Donohue, Michael 318
O'Har, Joe 304, 395
O'Hara, Maureen 245
O'Reilly, Bill 23, 148, 288, 481
Obama, Barack 48, 82, 98, 126, 131 - 175, 412, 437, 438, 460, 466, 474, 478, 492, 622, 636, 639, 674
Obama, Michelle 153
Ogilvie, Lloyd John 541, 558
Oldenberg, Ann 373
Olivier, Laurence 369
Olsen, Mary-Kate 346
Omarion 480
Orlovsky, Peter 404, 418

Orwell, George 617
OSI 148, 360, 673
Osteen, Joel 160
Ovitz, Mike 67, 230, 317
Ozbourne, Ozzy 76, 362

Pacino, Al 480
Paige, Jimmy 362
Palmeiro, Rafael 325
Pariser, Eli 84
Parker, Alan 304
Parker, Eleanor Stacey 108
Parker, James 121
Parker, Kathleen 275
Parker, Mary Louise 346
Parker, Sarah Jessica 70
Parsons, Jack 380
Parsons, Richard 632, 633
Patterson, B. Gary 356
Patterson, Robert "Buzz" 89, 91
Peale, Norman Vincent 376
Peck, Gregory 70
Pelley, Debbie 72
Pelosi, Nancy 88, 279, 287, 342
Peltier, Leonard 132
Penland, Tim 523 - 534
Penn, Sean 21, 29, 250, 335
Perdue, Lewis 550
Perez, Shimon 386
Perkins, Elizabeth 346
Perry, Tyler 198
Paltrow, Gwyneth 651
Petersen, Jesse Lee 164
Petraeus, David 145
Petrie, Dorothea 209
Peyser, Peter 206
Pham Van Khai 293
Phan Xuan An 100
Pillman, Brian 329
Pink Floyd 285, 363, 420
Pryor, Richard 443

Pitofsky, Robert 79, 311
Pitt, Brad 185
Pittman, Bob 497
Pivato, Emma 316
Plato 374
Platt, Marc 84
Podesta, John 88, 130, 148
Poe, Richard 146, 148, 278, 283, 419
Poland, David 497
Poland, Larry 20, 518, 523 - 534
Pollock, Jackson 398
Pollock, Sydney 70
Pollock, Tom 518, 524
Polonsky, Abe 264
Pomeroy, David 531
Pomeroy, Wardell B. 406, 487
Poniewozik, James 623
Pontius Pilate 531
Pope Benedict XVI 570, 610
Pope Gregory 548
Postman, Neil 646
Pot, Pol 275, 285
Potter, Harry 562 - 579, 594 - 620
Pound, Richard 332
Power, Samantha 54
Pozner, Vladimir 237
Pran, Dith 286
Preminger, Otto 197, 261
Presley, Elvis 50, 369
Presley, Lisa Marie 383
Presley, Priscilla 383
Preston, Kelly 382, 383
Prince, Derek 610
Princess Diana 372
Prudhomme, Christian 328
Pullman, Phillip 591, 614, 619, 668
Puttnam, David 514

Quigley, Martin 36, 216

Raatz, John 560

Radosh, Allis 261
Radosh, Ronald 261
Raimi, Sam 392
Rambova, Natasha 368
Rampell, Ed 274
Randolph, Paschal Beverly 358
Rangel, Charles 175, 474
Raschke, Carl 390
Ratzenberger, John 589
Reagan, Ronald 55, 63, 208, 247, 252, 254, 260, 275, 619, 636
Red Hot Chili Peppers 29
Redford, Robert 70, 515, 521
Redgrave, Lynn 265
Redstone, Sumner 20, 234, 382, 625, 628
Reed, Lowel 635
Reeve, Christopher 366, 367
Reeves, Keanu 371
Rehm, Diane 576
Rehr, David K. 210
Reibstein, Larry 178, 686
Reid, Antonio L. A. 474
Reid, Harry 87, 88, 279, 287
Reid, Wallace 321
Reiner, Rob 70, 203
Reisman, Judith 406, 431, 432
Remini, Leah 383
Reno, Janet 106, 116, 478
Reuss, Theodor 356
Reynolds, Burt 680
Rhymes, Busta 450
Rice, Condoleezza 90
Rich, Mike 197
Richie, Nicole 299, 315
Robards, Jason 70
Rather, Dan 25, 372
Robbins, Tim 250
Robbins, Tony 560
Roberts, Candace 58, 82
Roberts, Tony 560
Robertson, Carole 385

Robertson, Pat 83
Robeson, Paul 260
Robinson, Edward G. 257
Rockefeller, Jay 631, 636
Rockefeller, Lawrence 153
Rodenberry, Gene 371
Roerich, Nicholas 268
Rogge, Jaques 331
Rolling Stones 362
Rollins, Howard 335
Romero, George 223, 389
Romney, Mitt 174
Roosevelt, Franklin 44, 267
Roozen, David 164
Rosen, Judy 363
Rosenberg, Ethel 123, 259
Rosenberg, Julius 123, 259
Rosenstiel, Thomas 680, 686, 699
Rosio, Bob 369
Rossen, Robert 249
Rothman, Stanley 246, 496
Rowling, J. K. 356, 562 - 589, 594 - 620
Rubin, Harriet 67
Ruddy, Christopher 125
Ruhle, Patty 16, 502
Rumell, R. J. 284
Rumsfeld, Donald 94
Run DMC 458
Rush, Erik 163, 164
Rush, George 474
Rush, Jeanne 474
Rushdoony, Rousas J. 134, 141
Russell, David O. 274
Russell, Rosalind 245
Russell, Theresa 372
Russert, Tim 111
Russo, Rene 71
Ryan, Meg 74
Ryder, Winona 371

Saban, Cheryl 71

Saban, Haim 71
Safir, Howard 106
Safire, William 127, 174, 437, 598
Saginor, Jennifer 435
Saginor, Mark 435
Sailer, Steve 134, 157, 168
Salant, Richard 101
Salt, Waldo 254
Sammartino, Brian 329
Samuels, Allison 448
Santorum, Rick 152
Sarandon, Susan 372
Sarkozy, Nicolas 616
Sartre, Jean-Paul 581
Savage, Michael 22, 89, 366, 405, 619
Savage, William 298, 312
Scarborough, Joe 219
Scarborough, Rowan 124
Scheider, Roy 372
Scheuer, Michael 85, 91
Schimmel, Joe 567, 610, 613
Schlesin, Robert 691
Schlesinger, John 506
Schrader, Paul 19
Schuemer, Chuck 88
Schulberg, B. P. 215
Schulberg, Budd 249
Schuller, Robert 535
Schwartzkopf, Norman 115
Schwarz, Bernard 117, 118
Scorcese, Martin 265, 304, 517, 520, 522 - 527, 549
Springer, Jerry 377, 486
Seidman, Ricki 130
Selig, Bud 327
Sellers, Peter 370
Sessions, Clara 614
Severin, Jay 126
Shakur, Tupac 50, 73, 449, 475
Shappert, Gretchen 147
Sharpton, Al 142, 471, 473, 479

THE HOLLYWOOD CULTURE WAR

Shaye, Robert 71, 314
Sheehan, Billy 383
Sheehan, Cindy 276, 287
Sheen, Charlie 286
Sheen, Martin 21
Sheff, David 694
Sheinbaum, Betty Warner 71
Sheinberg, Sid 526, 530
Sheketoff, Emily 635
Skelton, Red 202
Shepherd, Cybil 71, 372, 494
Shevardnadze, Eduard 145
Shyamalan, M. Night 370, 592
Siegel, Joel 535
Signorile, Michaelangelo 484, 485, 487, 490
Silverman, Fred 202
Simmons, Russell 143, 459, 462, 469, 473 - 479
Simms, Paul 71
Simon, Neil 34
Simpson, Alan 618
Simpson, Joe 307, 308
Sinatra, Frank 197, 257
Singer, Isaac B. 593
Singer, Peter 153
Sinise, Gary 288
Slim Thug 460
Smalls, Biggie 451
Smaltz, Donald 129
Smiley, Tavis 149
Smith, Cathy 318
Smith, Gary 223
Smith, Kevin 19, 200
Smith, Patti 428
Smith, Sean 579
Smith, Wilbur 588
Snyder, Tom 296, 606, 608
Socrates 479
Solomon, Akiba 452
Solomon, Evan 619
Soros, George 58, 69, 82, 110, 143 - 150, 279, 283, 295, 411

Soros, Tivadar 143, 296, 360
Sorrell, Herb 251, 252
Spears, Britney 284, 299, 334, 561
Spector, Phil 137, 476, 498
Spielberg, Steven 26, 65, 72, 113, 265, 393
Spiggy Nine 450
Springen, Karen 696
Springsteen, Bruce 29
St. Ambrose 548
St. Pierre, Allen 147
St. Thomas Aquinas 548
Stalin, Joseph 237, 238, 258
Stanek, Jill 151, 152, 153
Stanwyck, Barbara 245
Stapleton, Jean 203
Starr, Ken 108
Stearns, Cliff 327
Steel, Dawn 373
Steele, Shelby 135
Steely Dan 429
Steenburgen, Mary 71
Stein, Ben 15, 82, 397, 441, 460
Stein, Jeff 682
Steinham, Gloria 111
Stephanopoulos, George 108
Stern, Howard 27
Stewart, Jon 125
Stewart, Martha 508
Sting 363, 560
Stock, Barbara 57
Stone, Oliver 28, 50, 80, 132, 250, 271, 286, 297 - 315, 333, 389
Strasberg, Paula 369
Strauss, Gary 346
Streep, Meryl 265, 371
Streisand, Barbara 21, 71, 372
Stripling, Robert 254
Strobel, Lee 538
Stroller, Lou 366, 480
Struthers, Sally 203, 372
Sullivan, Bruce 73

Sullivan, Ed 181, 202
Sulzberger, Arthur 87, 288
Summers, John 205
Sumrall, Lester 610
Sutherland, Donald 274
Sutherland, Kiefer 315
Swayze, Patrick 371
Sweitzer, Peter 75
Sweitzer, Rochelle 75
Sylbert, Dick 237
Sylbert, Paul 237, 262

Tagliabue, Paul 338
Taki 492
Tarantino, Quentin 199, 200
Tarloff, Erik 112
Tauzin, Billy 180
Taylor, Elizabeth 35, 38, 372
Taylor, William Desmond 321
Tenet, George 84, 90
Tenny, Jack 245
Terrence 515
Thalberg, Irving 28, 215
The Banshees 584, 585
The Beatles 361, 362, 584
The Eagles 138, 149, 491
The Notorious B.I.G. 449
The Sugar Hill Gang 458
Thomas, John 164
Thomas, Parnell 255
Thomason, Harry 56
Thomason, Linda Bloodworth 56
Thomasson, Patsy 420
Thompson, Lea 391
Timbaland 473
Timmerman, Ken 141, 271
Tin, Bui 272, 281
Tisch, Steve 485
Tolkien, J. R. R. 606
Tracy, Spencer 509

Travolta, John 381, 382, 383
Trinh, Nguyen Duy 282
Tripp, Linda 109, 110
Trulock, Notra 122
Truman, Harry 258, 268
Tucker, C. Delores 50
Turner, Kathleen 71
Turner, Steve 360
Turner, Ted 97, 101, 276, 289

Ufland, Harry 516, 520

Valenti, Jack 16, 30, 32, 40, 68, 196, 278, 310, 421, 425, 438, 503, 533
Valentino, Rudolph 368, 634
Van Peebles, Mario 481
Van Praagh, James 371
Van Sant, Gus 396
Van Slyke, Sally 524
Van Susteren, Greta 310
Vick, Michael 481
Vincent, Fay 51
Vitagliano, Ed 160, 161
Voight, Jon 506

Wadleigh, Michael 344
Wagner, Paula 382
Wallace, Chris 92, 96
Wallace, George 461
Wallace, Henry 268
Wallis, Jim 157, 160
Walsch, Neale Donald 560
Walsh, David 195, 232
Walter, Richard 219
Ware, John 559
Warhol, Andy 428
Warner, Brian 75
Warren, Rick 160
Washington, Denzel 288, 371
Washington, Dinah 446

Washington, George 69
Wasserman, Edith 71, 72
Wasserman, Lew 65, 71, 77, 518, 520
Watson, Diane 624
Waxman, Henry 340, 342
Wayne, John 261
Weil, Andrew S. 698
Weinstein, Bob 224, 228
Weinstein, Harvey 71, 199, 224, 538, 539
Weintraub, Bernie 486
Weir, Margaret 575
Welborn, Amy 547
Welch, Raquel 372
Welles, Orson 44
Wen Ho Lee 119, 120, 121
Wenner, Jann 484
Wesley, Cynthia 385
West, Diana 441
West, Mae 369
White, Harry Dexter 268
White, Thomas B. 610
Whiting, Iris 263
Whitlock, Jason 481
Wickham, DeWayne 229
Wilder, Billy 44, 254
Wildmon, Don 228, 524, 526, 527, 528, 529, 536, 537
Will, George 231
Willey, Kathleen 110, 111
Williams, Brian 126

Williams, Robin 318, 371
Williams, Walter 24
Williamson, Anne 145
Williamson, Kevin 79, 222, 389
Williamson, Marianne 372
Wilson, Michael 266
Wilson, Robert Anton 416
Winfrey, Oprah 27, 173, 277, 292, 358, 373, 375, 377, 577
Winikoff, Cami 560
Winter, Edgar 383
Winter, Tim 626
Woods, Clark 503
Woodward, Bob 86, 107, 325
Wright, Jeremiah 141, 162, 169
Wurtzel, Sol 215

York, Michael 372
Yorkin, Peg 71
Young, Neil 29

Zaffis, John 563
Zawacki, Neil 388
Zdrok, Victoria 436
Zmirak, John 551
Zoglin, Richard 680, 699
Zombie, Rob 200, 233
Zuckerman, Albert 551
Zukor, Adolph 634

NOTABLE QUOTABLES

–That's when America was great, when the chrome was thick and the women were straight.
—Michael Savage

–I deny I ever said that actors are cattle. What I said was, actors should be treated like cattle.
—Alfred Hitchcock

–For three days after death, hair and fingernails continue to grow, but phone calls taper off.
—Johnny Carson

–Mark my words, when a society has to resort to the lavatory for its humor, the writing is on the wall.
—Alan Bennett

–If James Dean had lived, they'd have discovered he wasn't a genius.
—Humphrey Bogart

–Unfortunately, a lot of jerks make movies.
—Raoul Felder

–I don't know anyone who isn't confused and complicated, who is happy for more than 20 seconds.
—Producer Tony Gilroy

–We don't call it sin today, we call it self-expression
—Baroness Stocks

MICHAEL VINCENT BOYER

–Pictures are for entertainment; messages should be sent by Western Union
—*Samuel Goldwyn*

–Where do all these Hollywood actors and actresses get their crazy ideas?
—*Fred Barnes*

–I enjoy time at home, reading a good book . . . because otherwise you are reading scripts, which are most of the time the worst literature ever.
—*Javier Bardem*

–I don't want to be the last person to tell a joke about Britney Spears before she kills herself.
—*Dennis Miller*

–To educate a man in mind and not in morals is to educate a menace to society.
—*Theodore Roosevelt*

–Hollywood is simply geared to cheat you left, right and bloody center.
—*John Hurt*

–Abstract art? A product of the untalented, sold by the unprincipled to the utterly bewildered.
—*Al Capp*

–I don't see many men today. I see a lot of guys running around television with small waists, but I don't see many men.
—*Anthony Quinn*

–Hollywood is the only town where you can die of encouragement.
—*Pauline Kael*

–We're more popular than Jesus Christ now.
—*John Lennon*

–For what is a man profited, if he shall gain the world and lose his soul?
—*Jesus Christ*